PLANNING AND PROBLEM SOLVING
IN MARKETING

PLANNING AND PROBLEM SOLVING IN MARKETING

By **WROE ALDERSON**
Professor of Marketing and Chairman,
Management Science Center Advisory Board

And **PAUL E. GREEN**
Associate Professor of Marketing and
Deputy Director, Management Science Center

BOTH OF WHARTON SCHOOL OF FINANCE AND COMMERCE
UNIVERSITY OF PENNSYLVANIA

1964
RICHARD D. IRWIN, INC.
HOMEWOOD, ILLINOIS

Library of Congress Catalog Card No. 64–21029
PRINTED IN THE UNITED STATES OF AMERICA

PREFACE

This book is the product of collaboration between two authors who have a common interest in planning and problem solving. Their approaches are somewhat different, but it is hoped that they will prove complementary. Wroe Alderson is a veteran in marketing with many years experience in seeking solutions to the problems of industries and individual clients.

Paul Green, while not lacking industrial experience, was more recently and adequately trained in the newer statistics and quantitative methods. Today he is a persuasive exponent of the Bayesian approach to problem solving.

It was relatively easy to determine who should write the various chapters. Paul Green wrote all of Part II which deals with the more precise approach to problem solving within the framework of statistical decision theory. Wroe Alderson wrote Part I and Part III which deal with the management background and with the design aspect of planning problems.

There has been less progress in the application of quantitative techniques to these topics than to the evaluation or decision problems discussed in Part II. In addition to writing Part II, Paul Green contributed a section to Chapter 16 in Part III, dealing with exponential smoothing and related aspects of forecasting.

Both authors participated in the seminars on market planning held at the Massachusetts Institute of Technology over the five years 1959–1963. They wish to acknowledge the stimulation derived from the faculty of the seminars and the planners from business organizations who attended them. They also profited from the opportunity of conducting a joint course and presenting this material to graduate students over the past two years. They are particularly indebted to Michael D. Webber and Thomas Leggett, who were of great assistance in proofreading and the preparation of bibliography, to Richard Wendell who prepared the index, and to Miss Mollie Horowits who did much of the typing. Acknowledgment is also extended to the Marketing Science Institute which sponsored portions of the material appearing in Chapter 10.

WROE ALDERSON
PAUL E. GREEN

August, 1964

v

TABLE OF CONTENTS

Methods to Traditional Statistical Inference. Traditional Hypothesis
Testing. Use of Bayesian Procedures. The Relevance of Bayesian
Statistics to Market Planning.

INDEX

Part I

MANAGEMENT PERSPECTIVE

~~~~~~

This book is organized in three parts corresponding to the conceptual scheme of the general treatment. Part I is relatively short and undertakes to place the techniques of planning and problem solving in a management perspective. The three chapters making up Part I reflect a somewhat expanded version of the usual conception of the management functions as consisting of planning, direction, and control.

The first chapter stresses the view that planning and problem solving take place within an organized system of action and must conform to the system's needs for action. Leadership is the central force which enables a system to act as a unit. Effective leadership requires superior talents, but there is one factor which is even more vital than talent—the ability of the leader to identify completely with the system of which he is a part and to relate his personal success or failure directly to the success or failure of the system. Top executives are paid large salaries partly to assure identification with the organization.

The leader generally has a higher level of aspiration for the system than others who participate in it. He holds others up to a performance standard which exceeds that to which they might otherwise aspire. Those engaged in detailed activities of planning and problem solving may assume that he will push his general goals to the limits of feasibility although he may depend on interaction with his subordinates and staff assistants for the formulation of more specific goals.

The leader is broadly responsible for the choice of methods and techniques to be followed in pursuing company goals. By holding other participants to a high level of aspiration he focuses attention on possible methods of goal achievement. The demanding leader realizes that there is always some danger in pushing his subordinates beyond the limits of their capacity. He must understand the mechanics of power and his special place in the power system.

The struggle of individuals to advance within this system is described as positional behavior in contrast with operating behavior. This struggle can never be terminated, but a skilled leader can channel it in such a way as to keep the organization healthy and with a generally high level of morale. The concept of internal strategy refers to the continuous concern with maintaining the system in a healthy state, together with the facilities and form of organization which will promote ready adaptability to the requirements placed on the system. External strategy is concerned with the specific programs which the system is expected to generate. The chapter closes with some considerations concerning the grounds of business ethics and education for business.

Chapter 2 is organized as a kind of running debate between six alternative theories of system control. These alternatives range from the relatively permissive concept of management by improvisation to a condition in which there are taut lines of control administered under the concept of management as a negotiative process. Each approach in turn has something to recommend it, but most of them also have serious limitations. For example, some fundamental questions are raised about the concept of management by exception which has had considerable currency among business executives. This method will work well if top management has unerring judgment as to when to declare an exception.

The six management views are arranged in order from the most permissive, management by improvisation, to the most formal, management as a negotiative process. The method recommended goes still further toward formal and objective control. The focal point of negotiation is the acceptance of a fully structured plan of operation. Once a plan has been approved by the chief executive and accepted by his subordinates, it comes to be the central means for coordinating the separate activities of individuals and operating units. There is still room for skill and judgment and for the exercise of initiative within the framework of a plan. Problems arise because the operation is not proceeding according to plan. The responsibility devolves on the functional units affected to seek problem solutions so that the pattern of planned activity can be restored and continued.

The third chapter distinguishes between general marketing problems and planning problems. Every marketing problem requires evaluation. Planning problems are a subclass of marketing problems which also require design. To put it another way, every marketing problem involves an analytical effort for the choice of a solution among alternative solutions. A planning problem requires the design of patterned alternatives before the analyst can proceed to evaluate and select from these alternatives.

The two classes of problems are illustrated by two types of puzzles. In the first class the solver is presented with a set of elements and is asked to select the right one, usually subject to specified restrictions on procedure. This is an evaluation problem. In the second class of puzzles, the solver uses all of the elements and is asked to arrange or rearrange them in a manner that meets the goal conditions specified. This is a design problem. The main body of the book is divided into two parts of about equal length. Part II deals with problem solving or evaluation. Part III discusses the additional dimension of a planning problem which is the design dimension.

Chapter 1

SYSTEM AND LEADERSHIP

This book is a book about marketing management. It is written with the intention of making better managers of those who read it and complete its exercises. It is written in the hope that more marketing managers will reach the top in their companies. The executive who comes up through marketing has some special qualifications to serve as the chief executive officer. Whether the man at the top is a marketing man or not, he will soon discover that many of his most difficult decisions are in the marketing area.

This book is primarily a book about decision making and about the extension of decision making into the field of market planning. It is an attempt to systematize and formalize the art of planning, bringing it within hailing distance of the already well-developed science of decision theory. The techniques of planning and problem solving are not the whole substance of management, but they lie at the heart of it. Management also embraces direction and control and the elusive qualities which mark a man for leadership. Planning and problem solving are in some measure teachable. Skill in planning and problem solving provides the surest means of scaling the ladder of executive preferment.

The treatment of planning and problem solving in this book is essentially a normative treatment. That is to say, it deals with the way decisions ought to be made and not with descriptive statements about how decisions are actually made. The standard for a good decision is the way that people ought to behave in their rational self-interest. The executives directing a company, particularly those in the marketing area, are faced with many uncertainties. Obviously an effective means of dealing with major uncertainties is just what rational self-interest requires in problem situations.

While this book has a normative intent, the first three chapters are largely descriptive. Marketing systems afford certain possibilities for action. These introductory chapters tell what these possibilities are since the "ought" of a normative theory must be firmly rooted in what is possible. An action should be feasible to perform as well as having desirable results. The decision to take the action should be guided by a comprehensive view of what is desirable. At the highest reaches of executive power there is equal concern about objectives and the means of attaining them. There is always a choice of goals and some ordering of these goals on a scale of values. In the words of Chester Barnard[1] a primary qualification for executive status is the ability to bear the burden of moral complexity.

THE MARKETING CONCEPT

The marketing concept has been presented in recent years not only as a new departure in marketing but something approaching a new philosophy of general management. Only incidentally has the marketing concept meant an increased emphasis on marketing as one of the business functions. Correctly interpreted, the marketing concept has equal significance for finance, production, and research and development. The marketing concept underscores the importance of the market rather than exalting marketing. It says that the business as a whole, and hence each of the business functions, must take its marching orders from the market. There is no payoff for the scientist in his laboratory, for the production manager in the most modern plant, or for the wizard of finance except as the company's products find acceptance in the market.

Concern for the marketing concept reflected the change from a sellers' market to a buyers' market after World War II. In a longer perspective it meant the coming of an era of abundance, the end of an age in which all goods were scarce and consumers asked few questions. Once it was sufficient for the well-managed firm to focus attention on the end of the production line as the measure of its achievement. Capital and plant capacity rather than customers were the key problems. Now it becomes increasingly apparent that the producer must take responsibility for the smooth and continuous flow of products through the marketing system.

An early consequence of the new awakening was the emergence of the marketing director. For the first time all of the tools for dealing with marketing processes were made responsible to one man. His responsibility generally encompassed advertising, personal selling,

[1]Chester Barnard, *The Functions of the Executive* (Cambridge, Mass.: Harvard University Press, 1940).

sales promotion, and marketing research. In multiproduct companies a group of product managers was added under some such title as marchandising. Where a vice-president for sales had been the key figure on the marketing side, he now began to give way to a man of broader perspective who embraced the entire marketing function. The first five years of stress on the marketing concept was largely concerned with organizational changes such as the regrouping of actvities.

PLANNING AND PROBLEM SOLVING

The next phase in putting the marketing concept to work marked the growth of formal planning and systematic problem solving. In many companies a nucleus was already firmly established in the product manager group. A product manager, in the fullest sense of the word, was responsible for everything involved in marketing his product from the broadest strategy to the most detailed programs and schedules. He gave deliberate thought to how the product would be packaged, the price at which it would be sold, the way in which it would be promoted, and all aspects of its basic posture in the market. Market posture, taken as a whole, is what distinguishes a product from all others. It is the sum of its differential advantages, its reason for existence as a separate product, the combination of product features, price, promotion, and distribution policy which causes some people in the market to demand it above all others.

The product manager must "sell" his product to other groups in the company. He is competing for his share of the time of salesmen and for an advertising appropriation which he believes to be adequate. He looks to the marketing research department for sorely needed answers to marketing questions. He looks to the marketing director for overall policy guidance. He combines the attitudes of line and staff since he is not merely making recommendations but reaching final decisions concerning his product. He is, or ought to be, a salesman skilled in all of the arts of persuasion.

The two vigorous roots from which formal planning grew are the use of product managers and of marketing research. When the product manager had finished planning for the elements under his control, questions were bound to arise about other marketing elements outside his jurisdiction. How do consumers respond to the advertising of the product? What is the most effective way for salesmen to divide their time between large accounts and small accounts? between service to existing accounts and solicitation of new accounts? Should the sales force be larger or smaller in relation to the volume of advertising? What new products, not now assigned to any product manager, should the company be working on?

Marketing research usually addresses itself to specific issues rather than to marketing plans. Something is to be said for allowing marketing research to remain purely objective, rather than having to defend a plan as the product manager does. Marketing research is ideally concerned with designing surveys to get the facts on basic issues. A good research man lavishes much time on asking meaningful questions and trying to understand how the facts will be applied, whatever they turn out to be. Sometimes the product manager asks what could have gone wrong with the plans so carefully devised. The market research manager may be able to indicate the direction of change, but ordinarily the product manager would take the credit—or the blame—for what happened under the revised plan.

Marketing research is about to come into its own as a primary tool of planning. There is a place for the objective researcher to evaluate plans even though he may not be equipped to devise them. This type of evaluation requires that all of the principal variations be represented among the alternatives. Evaluation is only a screening process, and there is no way of uncovering the alternative which was not there in the first place. All of Part II of this book is concerned with the evaluation of plans or at least of the central strategy on which a plan is built. Serious technical difficulties are encountered in screening plans. Not the least of these is the problem of how to get reactions to plans without tipping off your competitors as to what you are thinking about. Some promising new answers to these technical questions will be discussed at length in another section.

Another avenue opened up by statistical decision theory is for the researcher to answer a whole sequence of questions put to him by the planner. The first question states broad alternatives, and the answers may pick alternative A out of alternatives A to D. The second question picks A_1 out of alternatives A_1 to A_5. Only time and cost set a limit to the extent to which this sequence can be followed. The task of the planner in this situation is to create a balanced design with all the parts appropriately fitted together.

THE CREATION OF A SYSTEM OF ACTION

The primary role of the executive, according to Oswald Knauth,[2] is to create a system of action and then to make it work. Dr. Knauth

---

[2]Oswald Knauth, *Managerial Enterprise* (New York: W. W. Norton & Co., Inc., 1948).

was speaking at that time as a former executive of the R. H. Macy Company, so he obviously had marketing systems in mind. He distinguished competitive enterprise from what he called "managerial enterprise." The difference lay in a planned system of action by a firm large enough to make its plans effective. He argued that managerial enterprise was a relatively new thing. It did not respond to competition by day-to-day adjustment of price and quantity sold but by rounding out and perfecting its plans for moving vast quantities of goods. Managerial enterprise starts with the marketing concept, with a preconceived idea of service to the market, and works backward toward a plan of action with every link in the sequence filling its proper place.

To build a marketing system means looking backward to the firm's suppliers and forward to its customers or beyond. The firm is a station on the road to market. If there are shorter, lower cost routes, someone will find them and use them. It could be the supplier who no longer requires the firm as an outlet. Sometimes it is the customers of the firm who find that they can dispense with its services. Many firms who are in the main stream of modern marketing, whether manufacturers, wholesalers, or retailers, would be out of business in five to ten years if they stuck to a rigid product line. As the product line changes, the firm must change so that it will still lie on the shortest route to market for its current product line.

A system which has survived for any considerable period has a core idea which gives it stability in the market. In fact, a growing system might be reduced to its core idea and its strategy for expansion. The three essential elements are faith in the core idea, strategic use of growth opportunities, and sufficient elapsed time for growth to occur. This formula does not always work, but its violation at any point usually looks toward failure.

The boundaries of the system cannot always be strictly defined, and, indeed, the boundaries may change according to the light in which the system is viewed. For a bulk commodity sold to large buyers, the marketing system may extend no further than the first change in ownership. In other cases the marketing system properly includes the retailers and wholesalers who purchase the product for resale. The question of whether to include a level of distribution within the system depends on whether the firm is able to exert any significant influence at that level. It is customary in studies of industrial dynamics to take all levels, including the consumer, into the system. Even when the firm cannot exert significant influence directly on consumers the consumer level might be included in the system because perturbations arising in the consumer market can influence the seller in odd and unexpected ways. Store panel reports by the A. C. Nielsen Company have been helpful for food manufacturers. They learned, for example, that a new campaign might be moving goods off the grocer's shelves even though wholesalers were not reordering at the normal rate but supplying retailers mainly out of inventory.

The structure of a market is made up of options which can be exercised either positively or negatively. That is to say, the firm counts on the fact that some customers probably will not buy its products and others probably will. To say a buyer is a customer is to imply that it is customary for him to buy from a given source. Similarly, a firm is linked to its suppliers by custom and by the presumption that it will be given service equal to that of any other customer. The marketing system, defined as a set of interacting variables, usually remains fairly stable over substantial periods of time.

Periods of rationing provide evidence of whether a customer is truly in the system or on the fringes. The supplier obviously tends to favor customers who have been most dependable in normal times. An apparent slight when goods were scarce is not easily forgotten. During World War II some companies were very concerned to maintain the health of their marketing systems and helped their dealers to build income from services or to discover items which could be offered for sale and were not strictly rationed. Some companies have been notably lax in their development of foreign trade, welcoming foreign customers when business fell off, but acknowledging no responsibility for continuing service in good times. The decision as to who is really in the system is fundamental. In normal times the success of a system of action depends on the acceptance of plans formulated by the leader in the channel. The marketing executive is obliged to make judgments as to whom he can count on in a pinch, which is equivalent to counting them in or out of the system.

AUTHORITY AND RESPONSIBILITIES OF LEADERSHIP

The trend among college graduates today is toward working for large corporations. Some seek leadership and some do not. Some men are eager to be among the few who can rise to the top, and probably an even greater number experience some frustration through losing out. The great majority, perhaps, find niches which are comfortably within their range and which will not distract them too much from their other interests. But while there is not always room at the very top, there is substantial room in responsible and well-paying positions. Each man of executive rank carries the authority and responsibilities of leadership with respect to his own subordinates. Even at very modest levels in the executive hierarchy there is satisfaction to be gained from a better understanding of the system and from the continued growth which is likely to arise from better understanding.

Firms can be roughly divided into those under authoritarian and democratic leadership. More accurately, the dividing line reflects the aspirations and temperament of the chief executive since neither extreme is strictly possible. There are too many checks on autocratic power for real abuses to develop except in rare instances. Men must be persuaded in most large organizations. Valuable subordinates have alternatives, and the autocrat may end up talking to himself. At the other extreme there is no place in the large organization for democracy in the town meeting sense. Time is too short for balloting, but everyone entitled to an opinion should be heard. A man wins this title, incidentally, by depth of knowledge in his area of functional specialization or by acknowledged wisdom in the field of human values.

There is a difference only in degree among the larger firms. Men must be persuaded, but some chief executives are more abrupt and impatient than others. Some are more perceptive than others, particularly in their appraisal of subordinates and what can be expected of them. The application of political terms to business does not precisely fit, although every great center of power is in the ultimate sense political. What emerges might be called functional democracy. Every major functional area should be heard from on matters of great moment if all are to act in unison when the issue is joined. If this sounds too much like a military model, let it be remembered that in a free country everyone has the option of seeking employment elsewhere or of accepting the policy line after stating his objections.

The leader has all the resources of the company at his command, subject only to constraints imposed by the board of directors and the stockholders. Often he initiates policy, but in other cases he speaks for the office of the president, as the executant of policies rather than the policy maker. In either case, whether he initiates policy or executes it, his seat at the center of the power structure is unique for his organization.

First of all, he is head of the status system in the company and is the source of status for most of those below him. He can confer status or withhold it even by a casual conversation but more typically by continued reliance on a trusted advisor. He can rely on the formal structure of the company for sources of counsel and information, or he may turn to someone of lower rank. In a very large company differences in rank and informal status should be corrected as quickly as possible. Conditions are unhealthy if the gap should become too great.

Formal status is a primary reward for good performance. It is one of the chief executive's primary tools. Policies of promotion from inside are commonly followed when there is a clear line of succession among subordinates. One reason for going outside is that the choice between two equally likely candidates on the inside may leave one of them permanently disaffected. A continuous program of evaluation is one solution. The installation of such a system can lead subordinates to engage in more realistic self-appraisal. Periodic review with each individual provides a balance sheet of skills attained and weaknesses overcome.

The leader's own personality may be regarded as one of the tools of his trade. He may have charisma, that magnetic quality which enables a leader to instill enthusiasm in masses of people and unswerving loyalty in an inner circle. Most business leaders lack charisma but come to the top post with assured self-confidence. It is a long road and a steep ascent in all large companies, and the successful candidate has had an opportunity to take the measure of his chief competitors on the way up. A common characteristic is that he wants more than other men and is willing to give more to achieve his objectives. He wants money, power, distinction, and, if his executive talent is of the highest order, the privilege of holding himself to a stricter account than he holds anyone else.

THE MECHANICS OF POWER

The chief executive is expected to identify with his company and to find it difficult to separate his destiny from that of the firm. Presidents and chairmen are paid large salaries not on ability alone but to assure identification insofar as possible. To fall from a place as head of a large company is a precipitate drop. The type of man who wants to sit at the head of the table will give everything he has to avoid this drop. He is tactful or blunt, forceful or insinuating, patient or short-tempered, but nearly always demanding. His role is never to be satisfied, never to believe that outstanding performance was quite good enough. His place in the hive is as strictly determined

as that of the queen bee who is fattened on special foods to perform
a special mission. Not all presidents are effective, but the way in
which they attempt to perform their roles is basically similar.

The able chief executive sets the highest standards his subordinates can bear and watches for opportunities to jack them up still
further. He works for profits, for growth and diversification, for
morale and the health of the organization, but always for progress.
He is not obviously unhappy but only single-minded. He is rational
in a high degree, but he also has an obsession. What he wants is
what is good for the firm since it follows that what is good for the
firm is also good for him. He is capable of coping with opposition,
often to the extent of selecting remote and hazardous goals. Quite
often he dies in harness but not infrequently with a larger-than-
average measure of fulfillment.

The men who serve under such a chief are challenged to perform
beyond their native level. He is the spokesman for their aspirations—not so much what they want as what they would like to want
if fully aroused. The aspiration level of the group is a factor in
market dynamics. Men with greater than average expectations have
an incentive to perform with greater than average effectiveness. If
these men are marketing men their job in turn is to awaken the
expectations of others. The market is stimulated at both levels by
the demands of the executive group and of the general public.

MAINTAINING A HEALTHY ORGANIZATION

The executive undertakes to maintain a healthy organization and
hence the capacity of the organization to act. He fights against
inertia and apathy, the tendency to drift downward from an established standard or to drift back into established ruts. Maintaining a
healthy organization is partly a matter of avoidance. As with the
human body, an organization stays healthy by avoiding illness. A
large organization can even avoid old age by maintaining a judicious
mixture of veterans and newcomers.

Of special importance is the effort to avoid the downward spiral
which may be called the extinction mode. The extinction mode
means that a downward trend resembling a terminal illness has set
in and that the firm will almost certainly fail to survive. In the extinction mode one factor in the situation brings about an adverse
trend in another which, in turn, reacts upon the first. The specific
factors may differ, but the common principle in the extinction mode
is the tendency to get locked into a self-perpetuating downward
trend.

Only heroic measures have a chance of working when the downward spiral has been established. Assets are being used up faster than they can be created, and the end appears to be in sight. Since the extinction mode is nearly always fatal when it strikes, it is the part of wisdom to avoid it. The act of avoidance means maintaining flexibility and the resilience to stage a comeback after a bad break. It means acting in such a way as to promote the power to act. There is nothing mysterious about this principle (the power principle). It says that, given a choice, it is wise to conserve assets, that it is not wise to bet all one's chips on a risky venture, and that the constant aim should be to broaden freedom of choice rather than allowing it to become foreclosed.

A hypothetical example may serve as a further illustration of the extinction mode. Suppose a manufacturer of hard surface floor covering is beginning to slip but is still showing black figures. Suppose he invents a process for repairing his product but which calls attention to the fact that it is temporary rather than permanent. If he does nothing he will probably continue to slip. If he builds an advertising theme on the repair process, he may slip even faster. This is a case in which a market survey might show that there was still room for escape by presenting the new process as refinishing rather than repair. A number of examples are presented in the recently published second edition of *Theory in Marketing*."[3]

ASPIRATIONS AND TECHNOLOGY

The executive or the power center through which he operates must make two crucial decisions in relation to the environment surrounding the system. One of these, it has already been said, is to set the level of aspirations at or near the limit. These aspirations represent the ideal goals to which people can be expected to respond and not necessarily the goals which people actively entertain. The executive should be responsive to the goals of the whole body of employees. He is looking for the motive power which can harness all of their energies. He cannot afford to neglect any aspect of the bundle of aspirations, whether conscious or yet to be awakened.

The employee, either salaried or wage earner, expects to have more dollars in his pocket as the result of increased productivity. This means more good things for his family, including the fringe benefits which will continue their incomes into the future. There is

---

[3]Wroe Alderson, "A Normative Theory of Marketing Systems," in Cox, Alderson, and Shapiro (eds.), *Theory in Marketing*, 2d Series (Homewood, Ill., Richard D. Irwin, Inc., 1964.)

more development in store for the individual who takes on greater responsibilities under stimulus. He is a better man because he has been obliged to earn more and because he too has been confronted with some of the ethical questions which face all ranks of executives.

The second major task of the executive is to choose a technology which is equal to the task of satisfying aspirations. Technologies are either modified incrementally or through drastic and sudden change. Economies of scale are not automatic. It requires deliberate action to take advantage of scale opportunities. Each forward step removes another bottleneck, enabling the system to operate more smoothly than before. Changes such as automation are of a different order, resulting in economies of a spectacular nature. The system as a whole moves forward because of the liberation of manpower for tasks which only human beings can perform.

Marketing technology plays a crucial role in the movement of goods as production technology plays a crucial role in the transformation of goods. Information enters in new ways into the matching of goods and people. Information handling by electronic means is amply illustrated in a recent book, *Marking and the Computer.*[4] The road to market grows shorter through the new types of stores, new developments in advertising, and comparable developments in marketing research.

A steady stream of new products is emerging from the laboratory and is offered on the market. Product design is closely linked to marketing technology since all of these new products are seeking a place in the sun. A product is scarcely offered before ways are found to improve it resulting in a sequence of product innovations. New products serve an expanding consumer technology which carries part of the load of continuous adaptation to the environment. Industrial marketing is one or more stages back of the producers of consumer goods, with every industrial supplier competing to provide his latest ideas in materials or components.

THE GREATEST AREAS OF UNCERTAINTY

The uncertainties of the market place outweigh those of the production line or the research laboratory. Many products are offered, but it is still true that only a minor fraction succeed. The uncertainties of marketing infect the other functional areas such as finance

---

[4]Wroe Alderson and Stanley J. Shapiro (eds.), *Marketing and the Computer* (Englewood Cliffs, N.J.: Prentice-Hall, Inc., 1963).

and production with uncertainty. Decision making under uncertainty finds its greatest application in marketing. Progress has been made in financial and production planning, but this is planning in a vacuum unless marketing can be planned also.

Competition in sales and promotional channels, no less than new product introduction, accounts for a large area of uncertainty in marketing systems. Something is being learned about consumer response to advertising, but it is still but a feeble beginning. There are great unresolved questions of media selection, copy appeals, and the optimal amounts to be spent for advertising. Similarly, there is much to learn concerning the interaction of items in retail and wholesale assortments. Channels are being reshaped and sometimes steps in the channel eliminated to find a shorter road to market. The creation of marketing systems through market planning is only in the crude initial stages of development.

MEASURING SURVIVAL POTENTIAL

The objective of keeping a system viable and healthy is a worthy rival for the goals of growth and profit. There is some technical difficulty in quantifying survival potential, but a beginning can be made. In a sense survival has only two values, which can be represented by one or zero. A man or a firm is either alive or dead—there being no halfway stations. The concept of survival potential provides a partial answer to quantification. The first question to be asked is, "How likely is a firm to survive?" The question can be answered at least in relative terms if not by an absolute measure.

The size of assets is directly related to survival potential although the correlation is obviously not perfect. To increase assets is a good thing if it is desirable for a firm to survive. Assets have a very different weight for survival in various industries. For example, the situation is quite different in meat packing and aviation. Within a given field the emphasis should be on changes over time rather than assets at a given time. A simplified example will show how survival potential might be calculated.

Suppose a company makes one strategic decision a year over the next five years. Five years is taken to be the strategic horizon within which the company can foresee the major competitive issues. This does not mean, of course, that it can foresee the actual choices competition will make but only the alternatives which are offered for choice. The outcome of the five successive choices can be evaluated on the basis of prior probabilities within the framework of Bayesian decision theory.

Suppose the first choice seems likely to increase assets by 10 percent or more. Suppose, further, that there is a probability ratio of .7 that this will happen. The new level of assets would be multiplied by the conditional probability ratio to determine the expected value of assets at the end of the first year. The calculation would proceed in precisely the same way for the second year on through the fifth. The size of assets under one set of assumptions as to strategies would be different from the size of assets under another set of assumptions. Theoretically there would be a best value for the value of assets at the end of the period, although nothing more elegant than trial and error would be available for identifying it.

Several possibilities are to be considered in choosing the measure of survival potential. One is to set the dividing line between a low expectation of increase in assets and a high expectation. Intuitively it would seem reasonable to set the breaking point low enough so that there would be at least a 50 percent probability that assets would increase by this or some higher value. In addition, there is the highly arbitrary assumption that just one strategic choice was to be made each year. It would doubtless be a simple matter to generalize this formula for a varying number of choices spread over the interval in any given manner.

A further refinement would be to set up mortality tables for firms in various fields and to try to estimate the probable longevity of a firm. A substantial increase in assets over the period would argue for the firm being around for quite a while. A decrease in assets could indicate that it would disappear from the scene in the near future. All estimates of longevity would be subject to unforeseen developments such as mergers or the introduction of radically new products. The development of mortality tables might at least serve as a sobering corrective when compared to the bland assumption in nearly every firm that its own immortality can be taken for granted.

INTERNAL AND EXTERNAL STRATEGY

Formal planning is one way in which a firm can be made ready for action. A plan is a specific program for taking the initiative or meeting competitive counterattacks. But the state of being ready for action is somehow broader than planning as a military example will serve to illustrate. Suppose a commander has been informed that he will be attacked by superior forces. He begins at once to prepare for the emergency by digging in at a strong position. The attack may hold off until he has completed his preparations, or it may catch him only partially prepared. It would be possible to express his state of readiness as "nearly ready," "not quite ready," "poorly prepared," or even to plot his state of readiness on a percentage scale. This is somewhat different from having selected a plan or strategy from a set of alternatives and being prepared to move in one direction or another.

A useful distinction can be drawn at this point between internal and external strategy. Internal strategy is wholly concerned with the forces over which direct command is exercised. Given a limited period for action the commander is perhaps obliged to do some things and leave other things undone. He can be imagined as setting up a rank order of what needs doing and giving first attention to the step which will add the greatest incremental strength to his position. A chess amateur is faced with a similar problem in deciding when to castle. He may have his own plan of attack and be tempted to delay too long in castling.

There is a superficial parallel between internal and external strategy and defensive and offensive strategy. There is a difference since internal strategy refers to what can be done to prepare a state of readiness before the battle is joined. Opportunities for offense as well as defense may be presented in the course of battle. Hannibal at Cannae took up what appeared to be a carefully prepared defense position but only after determining the precise point in the melee to throw in his reserves and destroy the Roman army.

It is a commonplace of game theory that the field of battle is determined by the joint choice of both parties to the encounter and not one alone. The essential point is that the presence of an opponent who is free to choose introduces an element of radical uncertainty into the situation. Timing is crucial in external strategy which now becomes a question of how much time our competitor will allow us before he makes his move. In fact, the two aspects of strategy are linked together in such a way as to bring a contingent uncertainty into the area of internal strategy. The strategist must decide whether he is free to continue with a methodical preparation of his own position or must be ready with a positive plan of action whenever the competitor strikes.

The state of readiness is of prime importance in business planning. On the whole too much time is spent worrying about what competitors are going to do and not enough about being prepared for any contingency. Direct competitive threat cannot, of course, be discounted completely since it can be highly disruptive if it occurs. In most fields there is some cushioning of the blow since markets are generally organized on the basis of differential advantage. Ordinarily there is a definite limit to the losses which any one competitior will sustain as a result of new entries into the field. The crash program for new product introduction has introduced a new range of uncertainties into marketing. A major example was the successful introduction of Gleem and Crest toothpastes by Procter & Gamble backed by a multimillion dollar initial campaign.

Hereafter the term *internal strategy* will be replaced by the term *state of readiness*. It seemed advisable in the beginning to draw a sharp contrast between the two aspects of strategy since they are so closely linked together. In a strict sense the term strategy is equivalent to external strategy since it always implies the presence of an opponent. The state of readiness will be limited to preparations which stop short of the formulation of specific programs or campaigns.

INFORMATION SYSTEMS IN MARKETING

The idea of a negative feedback system was introduced by Norbert Wiener in his book *Cybernetics*.[5] Negative feedback refers to corrective action which tells the operator what he should not do. It is negative feedback which guides one eventually to the correct solution when fumbling for a keyhole in the dark. Cybernetics got its start from the theory of electric circuits or servomechanisms. Information on the state of a system, whether electrical or behavioral, must be transmitted through closed loops if it is to affect the state of the system. A description of marketing systems would not be complete without some reference to feedback circuits. These ideas will be developed further in the chapter on "Direction and Control."

The most comprehensive treatment of marketing systems in terms of electric circuits is by Jay Forrester. His book *Industrial Dynamics*[6] is notable for simplicity and clarity. His model of a marketing system recognizes five or six basic flows such as money, materials, customer orders, and flows of information connecting various points inside the system. There is much to be learned from this model about the way that a marketing system responds to its environment. The logic of the analysis is based on delays in the system and the amplification of these delayed responses in a way that frequently distorts the true meaning of the signal from the market place. The author shows how small changes in the rate at which customer or-

---

[5]Norbert Wiener, *Cybernetics: or, Control and Communication in the Animal and the Machine* (Cambridge, Mass.: Technology Press, 1948).

[6]Jay W. Forrester, *Industrial Dynamics* (New York: John Wiley & Sons, 1960).

ders are received can be built up into the wide fluctuations of a self-generated cycle.

The fact that marketing systems do not always behave as badly as Dr. Forrester implies is no disproof of his fundamental thesis. In some cases there are special offsetting factors. In the grocery industry many manufacturers bought the A. C. Nielsen service to provide reports on how goods were moving at various points in the system. In other cases the inertia of the system seems to moderate the overresponse to the market signals which Dr. Forrester predicates. Often a marketing system is not a good enough system to get into as much trouble as Dr. Forrester's charts would indicate. Nevertheless there are some extreme examples of the tendencies he describes. One illustration is the fantastic buildup in retail inventories which occurred some years ago in the television industry before they took the precaution of creating their own Nielsen type service.

ACCOUNTING INFORMATION AND MARKETING MANAGEMENT

The Forrester approach leads inevitably to the doctrine that only a model of the total system can yield correct conclusions about industrial dynamics. Anything less will almost certainly come up with the wrong answer. Working from a decidely different perspective, C. West Churchman reaches a similar conclusion in his *Prediction and Optimal Decision*.[7] He raises questions concerning managerial accounting and arrives at pessimistic answers. A key issue for management is the separability of a system into its component parts. So-called profit centers are usually artificial entities involving joint costs to such an extent as to block all efforts to consider the parts independently. Churchman suggests that subsystems cannot be separated unless an equally clear separation can be made among the information flows which are essential to the viability of the subsystems.

In 1963 the president of the American Marketing Association brought together a group of financial and marketing executives. His purpose was to explore common problems, in particular the problems of what could be done to improve the quality of marketing information emanating from the comptroller's office. Comptrollers complained about wide variations from budgets in the marketing department. Marketing executives complained about the paucity of

---

[7]C. West Churchman, *Prediction and Optimal Decision* (Englewood Cliffs, N.J.: Prentice-Hall, Inc., 1961).

information or the need for complete recasting of information before it could be used for marketing purposes.

Marketing management is caught in a dilemma. Churchman and Forrester say that you cannot understand the system except as a total system. Yet the total system is beyond the grasp of most people in the company since they have spent years specializing in some component subsystem. The answer doubtless lies in new ways of studying total systems. One way is to match inputs with outputs, probably with the use of computers to work out all the possible combinations. Another way is to look at marketing campaigns or programs as identifiable outputs. The ability to mount a program is an index of marketing capacity. It may be that the constraints affecting these programs can only be discovered by simulating the programs themselves.

If marketing programs are the primary output of marketing systems, then marketing management should be chiefly concerned with the management of these programs. Market planning comes to be defined as the planning of systems, the planning of programs, and the planning of facilities and organization structure required for mounting the programs. Problem solving in marketing tends to be concerned with difficulties encountered in the mounting of programs and with suspected flaws in the underlying marketing system or in the facilities and organization structure which it utilizes.

Marketing programs can be divided into short range and middle range. Short-range programs should be restricted to programs which are fully committed so that the only point at issue is effective performances. Sometimes a deal offered to the consumer or the trade is determining and a change of front is not practical, at least while the deal is on. Other organizations tolerate some deviation from plan, at least among broad regions of the country. The most rigorous enforcement of plans as specified is found in some of the ethical drug companies. A product manager lays out the precise course to be followed at each level and only minor departures are permitted.

Longer-range programs attempt to look ahead as far as the basic marketing issues are predictable. This limit on projection into the future is aptly called the planning horizon, meaning as far into the future as we can see. The planning horizon may be only a year or two ahead, and it is seldom more than five. This phase of planning will be designated here as strategic planning. It might be regarded as the prototype of all planning in marketing. If the purpose of market planning is to mount programs, then strategic planning is the most comprehensive version with short-range campaigns constituting successive segments of the strategic programs. All other types of planning, including the revision of the marketing system itself, are incidental to the main issue of mounting marketing campaigns or programs.

POSITIONAL BEHAVIOR

Much of the information moving through channels in an organization has nothing to do with the operation for which the channel was created. The term positional behavior is applied to this aspect of group behavior and implies that much that goes on is intended to improve the position of the individual and is only indirectly related, if at all, to the operating goals of the firm. The chief executive has the job of reacting rationally to this aspect of life in the firm, minimizing its impact, if possible, and perhaps putting it to constructive use.

There is no way to put an end to the struggle for status within the firm. Everyone who is trying to get ahead in the firm competes in one way or another. It is only when the conversations concerned with positional behavior begin to interfere with operating signals that the man at the top is necessarily involved. The distortion of reports on performance, the fixing of blame on someone further down the line, or open bickering about responsibility for failures are things he should not tolerate.

This type of discussion will be at a minimum if the chief executive drives his team with a taut rein. If he has a clear conception of what he requires of individuals and departments, if the lines of force radiate outward from the executive chair, there will be less room for the type of behavior which cuts across these lines of power. Holding an executive responsible for whatever happens in his department is harsh but effective. If the subordinate has delegated with the same skill that his superior expects of himself and if he has been perceptive in filling key positions below him, he will not find any injustice in this arrangement.

Reference has been made to the power principle which says that rational man will act in such a way as to promote the power to act. A similar principle, although not quite so clear cut, can be formulated for communication. The chief executive is engaged in an eternal quest for talent. He must know his people to know where talent is to be found. From his viewpoint the communication principle might be stated as follows: "The leader of an organization should encourage the type of communication which will disclose the talents of his subordinates."

The precept is not an easy one to follow. Men with unsuspected talents may be found in routine positions. Men fail to be recommended for promotion because they are too valuable in their present niches. Other men are not given proper credit because they have aroused the jealousy of their immediate superiors. Taking account of the varying rates at which men develop and of the impact of a promotion on the seniority structure lies close to the heart of management.

ECOLOGICAL SANCTIONS

Ecology is the field which studies the relation of a population to its environment. An ecological sanction is a pressure on the individual to conform to high standards, the pressure constituting a threat to survival in one way or another. An individual may fail to survive in a position of power at the head of his company, the company through which he exercises power may fail to survive, or the larger community of which his company is a part may suffer a decline in its ability to support life. Ecological sanctions are beginning to be understood by people at the top. As understanding increases, these sanctions will exert a profound influence in the lives of responsible executives.

Legal sanctions are backed by the penalties of the law. Moral sanctions are generally observed in matters of personal honesty and keeping promises. Ecological sanctions embody the laws of nature which cannot be ignored with impunity. Strong pressures exist to enforce identification of the executive with his company. Ecological sanctions provide the link between identity and survival to enforce further constraints upon the rational man. Behind these limited sanctions stands the threat of annihilation which in the Atomic Age is part of the inner life of every rational individual.

The concept of habitability provides a test of fit between a society and its environment. Decline in habitability over any considerable portion of the earth's surface is a sure sign of maladjustment. A map of the United States, showing the location of stranded populations, provides a mirror image of mined-out, farmed-out, and cutover land. In many areas of the world habitability is steadily declining whereas excessive population pressure results in less efficient agricultural methods and hence in greater population pressure than before. The conservation of natural resources comes to be recognized as one of the first laws of nature. Incidentally, there is no built-in doctrine of conservation under pure and perfect competition. The bias in the use of resources has been toward full exploitation.

Exceptions include agreements reached under some difficulty to limit wasteful exploitation of petroleum in the Southwest. Tree farms, it is said, have now succeeded in turning the trend about so that more timber is being grown than is consumed annually.

Ecological sanctions are presented to some in a form that goes beyond physical resources to touch the basic values of the culture in which we live. Marketing men especially can ask themselves whether they are prepared to live in the kind of world their efforts may help to produce. Is it to be a raucous and contentious world, a feverish and overstimulated world with gnawing frustrations just below the surface? Habitability surely means not only that life can be supported but also that life is tolerable. One wonders whether some intellectuals who deal in such concepts as "overkill" have stopped to consider whether life is worth living in the world of their imagining.

TRAINING FOR BUSINESS

Business conducted at a truly professional level is certainly a noble calling. It is as broad and varied as the entire range of goods and services which are produced and marketed. It is as deep as the roots of value to be found in our common humanity. Training young men for business at the highest level or for some lesser role is an exacting and difficult task. Every business student should be immersed in some form of apprenticeship, as close to reality as his imagination and good teaching can take him. He should acquire confidence in his own ability to make decisions, and he should come to realize that the responsibility for decision will presently rest on his shoulders.

His monitored, risk-limited experience in making decisions should not reproduce the experience of yesterday. It should be as modern as day after tomorow at least in its conceptions of planning and of problem solving. The exercises in this book are designed to provide some familiarity with current techniques and to encourage the student to cast his problems in these more precise and analytical frameworks.

The well-rounded executive needs more than classroom experience. Before he is too long out of school he would be fortunate if he could arrange for time off to see our culture in a new perspective and preferably from the outside. There are opportunities of this sort in odd corners of the world. He may be able afterward to place the world he knows in ecological perspective.

The rewards of business are substantial, not only in money, but in opportunities for growth. There are ethical problems which the young executive will discover for himself in the business setting and which he is not likely to encounter anywhere else. He will learn that leadership is valuable for its own sake and for the sake of those who will follow the leader. He will gain increasing understanding of the kind of man he would like to become and the pitfalls he will meet on the way.

THE DRIVE FOR EXCELLENCE

Dr. John Gardner, president of the Carnegie Foundation, has had a lot to say within the covers of a small book called *Excellence*.[8] He regards the drive for excellence as a fundamental attribute of every educated man. The drive for excellence enjoys some of its greatest rewards in the business setting. The challenge in marketing management or in general management is on a par with that in other professional fields.

Dr. Gardner speaks of three ethical viewpoints which are part of the American tradition. He has little to say about the aristocratic conception of life although it derives from such honored sources as Washington and Hamilton. He develops more fully two other conceptions, one associated with the frontier and the other with the urban centers of the East. The frontiersman is the spokesman for equality, and much of the frontier spirit is alive today. The flaw in the equalitarian view is the tendency to level downward rather than upward.

The drive for excellence is associated with professional specialization as realized through university education. It tends to become narrow and exclusive unless it is touched with the fundamental humanity of the equalitarian spirit. Dr. Gardner pictures the uneasy balance between equalitarianism and the drive for excellence as the central fact of ethical striving in the United States today.

The aristocratic ideal should not be neglected in a comprehensive vision of ethical progress. The noblesse oblige of the aristocrat is certainly present at the highest levels in business and in other areas. Too many generations of self-centered people have given aristocracy a bad name. Aristocracy at its best blends readily with the drive for excellence. Its own special flavor is the call to use superior talents simply because they exist. The genuine aristocrat can also accept common humanity at its own evaluation. The aristocracy considered

---

[8]John W. Gardner, *Excellence* (New York: Harper & Bros., 1961).

here is obviously not one of hereditary privilege but an open aristocracy of talent with a sense of inborn obligation for service.

West Churchman has embarked on what may turn out to be the most critical task of our generation: laying foundations for a science of values. This book recommends the more conservative aim of providing guide lines for executive leadership securely anchored to the concept of rational self-interest. Even this more limited proposal lies in the area where the rules run out and the executive must make his own rules under the pressure of ecological sanctions. But after Churchman one must grant that any book about decision making is a book about values as well. In the long run individuals are obliged to revise their expectations upward because of increased power over the environment. They are compelled to do better because they are able to do better.

Selected References

CLARK, JOHN MAURICE. *Alternative to Serfdom.* New York: Alfred A. Knopf, Inc., 1950.

The late great economist speculates on the future of business enterprise and the need for progress toward responsible executives in responsible organizations.

CYERT, R. AND MARCH, J. G. *A Behavioral Theory of the Firm.* Englewood Cliffs, N. J.: Prentice-Hall, Inc., 1963.

A conception of the business firm as a system of organized activity with multiple objectives which cannot be reduced to simple profit maximization for the firm.

KNAUTH, OSWALD W. *Managerial Enterprise.* New York: W. W. Norton & Co., Inc., 1948.

A small but important book which describes the process of creating a system of action and stresses executive responsibility in that connection.

WHITEHEAD, T. N. *Leadership in a Free Society.* Cambridge, Mass.: Harvard University Press, 1950.

Discusses the responsibilities of leadership with respect to the diverse objectives and conflicting interests of those he is called upon to lead.

Problems

1. Define and discuss the marketing concept.

2. Discuss marketing research and the use of product managers as the "roots of formal planning."

3. What did Oswald Knauth mean by the executive responsibility for creating a system of action?

4. What are the two crucial decisions to be taken by the executive or the power system through which he operates?

5. Contrast internal and external strategy.

6. Discuss ecological sanctions as constraints on executive action and relate them to business ethics.

Chapter 2

DIRECTION AND CONTROL

The arts of management are commonly discussed under the headings of planning, direction, and control. Planning comes first in this familiar phrase but not because everyone is convinced of its vital importance. The total systems approach and the responsibilities of leadership are regarded here as keys to the study of management. Planning and problem solving give effect to the total systems approach which will be discussed in the next chapter. The day-by-day managing of the business is bracketed under direction and control.

There are six or seven general views of how to manage a business. This chapter is organized around these various viewpoints which are arranged from the most permissive to the most formal and completely structured. At one end are methods which are almost equivalent to letting the business run itself. At the other end are methods which leave nothing to chance and at least try to define the issues even when the outcomes are uncertain.

The first proposal as to how to manage is to keep the business so well tuned up that it can run itself. The chief executive is cast in the role of friend and counselor who would hardly ever take the initiative himself. He would wait until a subordinate came to him for help and would concentrate his attention on problems of morale.

The second view relies on improvisation by resourceful executives. Improvising is in the American tradition and most large businesses have been built in this way. Each executive is given plenty of leeway in his functional area without any strings except that he is promptly replaced if he does not measure up.

The third view is called management by exception. The chief executive exercises close surveillance but does not interfere when things are going well. Most of the time he acts as though the business could run itself but is expected to be a good improviser when he steps in and takes over.

The other approaches all visualize a more closely coordinated system with initiative from the top. The fourth approach is management by decision rule which is associated with the new techniques of management science. The place of the analyst looms large under this perspective. Management's function is to evaluate decision rules and put them into effect if they appear sound.

The fifth view is management through conflict. It assigns a more active role to middle and top management, both as contestants and as umpires in the dispute. Management through conflict is open-ended both as to ends and means for securing these ends.

The sixth view is management as a negotiative process. It assumes that internal conditions are constantly changing and that adaptive adjustment must be a continuous process. This view is not inconsistent with the exercise of a strong hand by the chief executive.

Finally there is the viewpoint of formal planning, the view which is advocated in this book. The planning viewpoint is already becoming standard in large organizations. Others will move toward formal planning as they grow and find themselves in competition with larger companies fully committed to planning. Under formal planning, management takes on some of the features of management by decision rule, management through conflict, and management as a negotiative process. The need for formal planning and the means of accomplishing it through such devices as electronic computers seem to have matured at about the same time.

TUNING UP A BUSINESS TO RUN ITSELF

The notion that a business can run itself under the watchful eye of the chief executive is certainly appealing. Chester Barnard was generally very perceptive in his observations about management. In this instance he must have been relying heavily on the monopoly position of the business he headed which was the Telephone Company of New Jersey. A well-structured enterprise with a program for gradual extension of its services could afford to take this view, but even the telephone company has recently experienced swift changes calling for a strong guiding hand, as in the rapid adoption of nationwide direct dialling and the project that put Telstar I and Telstar II into space to create improved links in the worldwide network of communication.

The permissive view of management has the virtue of highlighting the importance of morale. Barnard was preoccupied with this central theme which continues to be a fundamental topic for management consideration. He gained wide attention in management

circles by saying that the chief executive should be well equipped
to deal with moral complexity and that one of his primary functions
was to project a morality that men might live by. Moral complexity
is made up of the numerous claims, often conflicting, which the man
at the top must take into account. He is a member of numerous
groups including his profession, the people who make up his company, his church, his political party, and his community. His attempt
to balance out these claims is still less complex than that of today's
executive who is conscious of ecological sanctions. Projecting a morality that men may live by also has a parallel in the executive's function of setting the level of aspirations for the members of his firm.
In either case the main distinction lies in the effort to find firmer
foundations for these values than what would be required of him
purely in his rational self-interest.

Poor morale can usually be traced to disturbances in the power
structure or disturbances in the communication structure. A disruption of the power structure can mean either that the executive is no
longer concerned to represent all of his people in their strivings or
they have lost faith in his ability to find the means for realizing these
objectives. Absolute power corrupts only when the personal desires
of the executive becomes absolute. It is sad to see the kind of meg-
alomania developing in which an imperious and overriding requirement replaces the sense of sharing. Last to go is the belief that
our leader will somehow pull us through. This faith can be under-
mined either by the feeling that he has lost touch with the environment or is no longer sincerely interested in the welfare of his group.

A disruption of communications creates additional uncertainty as
to the intentions of management. Communications can deteriorate
when the business is prosperous and the central power group is no
longer sensitive to the aspirations of subordinates. A failure of communications can also occur when the business is under pressure and
all of the news begins to seem like bad news. The inner group may
find that it is talking only to itself and that the group enjoying the
full confidence of the chief executive tends to shrink still further.
Pushed to its limit over a long period of time, a group can become
listless and apathetic. A decline in morale can also be the product
of fear when one person after another is being let out and no one
quite knows where the axe will fall next.

Keeping a system tuned up to run itself implies very limited control and practically nothing in the way of positive direction. There
are very few instances in which large organizations are actually so
permissive. It sounds almost as if the organization has some ma-

chinery, independent of the chief executive, for agreeing on its objectives and choosing an appropriate means for achieving them. The question might well be raised as to whether executives at the next lower level would be equally permissive. One concludes with some regret that this viewpoint, with its concern for morale for its own sake, is not a workable theory of management. The pace of change today demands that the chief executive take the initiative in setting the general direction which the firm is to follow.

EXPERIENCES IN MANAGEMENT

Before a more detailed description of other management philosophy is given, some simple but fundamental issues which rest heavily on the conscience of the responsible manager should be considered. There are the everyday problems of anyone who has ever managed a business of his own. He soon learns that his conduct as head of his own enterprise requires some new rules of behavior which are not easy to reconcile with ethical conduct as he formerly viewed it.

Suppose he is in the early stages of building a business and has encountered some hard sledding—a very frequent occurrence—in getting the business off the ground. Can he afford to be pessimistic during this period? If not, how does he reconcile himself to a double standard of candor and honesty? He would prefer to be frank, and yet he cannot afford to say anything which will be harmful for the future of his business at this crucial stage.

He is on even more doubtful ground when he represents what he only hopes for in the development of his business to be an accomplished fact. Is he entitled to convey the impression that certain facilities can be assumed when he is actually taking a gamble that he can provide the facilities or talent which is needed? He would not be much of an enterpriser if he was not willing to take a reasonable chance, and yet there is a lingering danger that his plans will not work out and his operation will be discredited.

At a later stage he will be trying to recruit ambitious young men because he needs them to realize his own growth objectives. How far can he reasonably go in trading on their expectations for the future? The applicant's future expectations provide the motive power for loyal and effective service. Yet exploiting these expectations unfairly by painting too rosy a picture may lead to disillusion and recrimination.

There is never enough room at the top to satisfy all of the expectations of the members of the company. Examples are readily found of promising too much. The top man may have caused several of his associates to believe that each is the heir apparent. Perhaps no outright pledge was ever given, but each man puts the most favorable construction on an encouraging word here and there. When a man who has given such half-promises retires, there may be a rude awakening and a decline in morale for all but one fortunate candidate.

All communications affecting the status of a subordinate must be handled with care. The subordinate can build a hope for promotion on very slender evidence. Whatever bears on a man's position should be made explicit or related to specific future performance. It is not enough to maintain a discreet silence when the subject is brought up, for only a definite statement of what management is prepared to do can prevent misunderstanding later. An objective evaluation in writing once or twice a year is good management practice.

At a later stage in his career the executive may feel called upon to share the profits of an enterprise with the men who have helped to build it. In purely business terms the loyalty of the group may be worth more to him than optimizing short-run profits. He may be shocked to learn that his associates take a narrow view of profit sharing and often hold out for restricting the plan to a very limited group at the top. Successful plans have often taken years to develop, adding one feature at a time and gradually evolving a balanced program.

Another problem of moral obligation which is now assuming considerable proportions lies in the subsequent period of service following an educational growth opportunity offered an employee. Postgraduate work of up to a year's duration is paid for by the employer in some cases of men with special promise. The employee need not pledge himself to work for the company permanently, but rough justice requires that the period of service to follow should at least be long enough to realize the new level of efficiency toward which the special training was directed. The trend for the future is toward more and more arrangements of this type. In the future it is conceivable that employees with the greatest aptitude for learning will be taken out of the line every four or five years and sent back to school.

Another type of human problem is the individual who takes up far more than his share of administrative attention and relies on the boss to deal with all of his personal difficulties. For some individuals this is a way of seeking notice from their superior. It can be quite insidious with the executive becoming thoroughly enmeshed in the subordinate's problems before he quite realizes what has happened. Too often this game is not worth the candle, but in rare instances there is a satisfying sense of achievement when the employee is finally able to stand on his own feet.

Much of this book will be a plea for formal procedures in planning and problem solving and other aspects of management. There is a human and ethical side of management also which has a vital bearing on the general philosophy of management presented here. The experiences recounted here should serve as a reminder in the face of the more technical and objective material to be presented later. The manager is never quite a selfless automaton but a human being who can sympathize and understand and yet strive to keep business relations objective for the benefit of the organization as a whole.

MANAGEMENT BY IMPROVISATION

To speak of management by improvisation is a bit of a paradox. Improvising solutions to problems day by day scarcely seems like management at all. Yet most businesses which exist today have depended solely on this type of management. For centuries the skills of production rested on traditional arts so that it was scarcely to be expected that general management would suddenly achieve a scientific approach to total systems. The concept of a total system is slow to develop for the very reason that the heads of business are immersed in the details of daily affairs and lack a vantage point from which they can see the system in perspective.

For a long time there was little cumulative advance in management since each executive learned to manage as he learned to walk— step by step. The universities, as sources of organized knowledge, did not take business seriously enough for intensive study until toward the end of the nineteenth century. There was some carry-over of management skills from one generation to another and some inevitable pioneering as businesses came to be larger. In marketing the era of improvisation was to hang on for some years longer. The great sales stories of the past feature anecdotes of imaginative approaches thought up in a moment or overnight. Often the sales manager was the star salesman set on a pedestal for emulation by his fellows.

Management by improvisation makes the assumption that the manager is equal to all possible emergencies. He places confidence in his mental resourcefulness which has seldom let him down. He takes responsibility for decisions because his knowledge of the

market is at least as great as any other man's. Sometimes his resourcefulness is largely manifested in explaining why things did not
work out exactly as planned. His decisions are validated by his place
at the top of the pecking order, and his place is secured through
an extensive and detailed, albeit somewhat fragmented and incomplete, knowledge of the market.

Management by improvisation is not restricted to small and stable
companies but is followed in many large and rapidly growing companies. The underlying factors when they are successful are the
momentum of growth and the quality of experience. The other
requirements are energy, somewhat better-than-average intelligence,
and a strong belief in the correctness of one's own opinions.

The momentum of growth is the central influence in any industry
in which some firms, for whatever reason, are rapidly outstripping
their competitors. The more successful firms may have better or bet-
ter-known products or may have discovered a shorter road to market.
While they are gaining position in the market, they are like an army
in pursuit which does not need to be too well organized to overrun
an opponent. Momentum is a substitute for a coordinating plan so
long as the rout continues.

Each day is sufficient unto itself under these circumstances since
every day inevitably leaves many things undone. Typically such a
business is always running shorthanded. There is little time for
training subordinates when each man feels that he can perform any
task more effectively himself. The direction is sharply upward; the
opportunity is now; and the application of effort to opportunity is
direct and scarcely debatable.

Each man on the team in these circumstances gravitates toward
the role in which he feels most comfortable. He tends to be given
his head in this functional area and to exercise an effective veto
power concerning proposals affecting his specialty. There is some
overlapping of responsibilities since they are not clearly defined.
Coordination is probably made more effective by overlapping jurisdiction, and friction is minimal because overlapping is at the fringe.
The total system view is implicit only, but a view of the whole collection of functional areas is necessary for complete understanding
of the business.

THE NATURE OF EXPERIENCE

Management through improvisation places a premium on experienced executives. Experience is often treated as though it could
not be analyzed. You either have it or you don't have it. Experience

certainly means more than the passing of years. Some men surely learn more from experience than others. Experience is qualified by such terms as "intensive" experience, "long" experience, "broad" experience, and "high level" experience. "Narrow" experience would not be used as an honorific term, but it is often implied in stating the qualifications for a position.

A question frequently asked a business consultant is whether he has ever worked for a firm exactly like the one engaging him. He may be tempted to reply that it is a good thing he has not because a firm exactly like this would doubtless have fallen into the same kind of trouble. On one occasion a manager in the textile field seemed about to sign a contract for a substantial project. At that point he asked whether there was a good needle engineer in the organization. Subsequent inquiry disclosed that possibly a half dozen men in the United States were sufficiently specialized to be known as needle engineers.

West Churchman in a recent essay[1] has classified market managers as particularists or generalists. The particularist is described as an opportunist who does not follow definite policies but is able to seize on the main chance as it occurs. The generalist observes a pattern in nature and believes that there are some basic principles governing its operation. The distinction is useful, but it may not do full justice to the manager who is called a particularist. Generalization is a kind of shorthand which most men need to cope with reality. Others may grasp the phenomena presented to them with much more of the rich color and detail of events. For some types of activity their single-minded concentration on the world as they see it may represent a superior talent.

The factors in business success are varied, but they certainly include some element of luck or chance. It has been pointed out that if a group of 256 men make 8 successive decisions at least one of them may be right every time purely on a chance basis. Suppose that all are making a simple either-or decision, being right or wrong each time with no doubtful scores in between. Each time a decision is made, if it is a close one, the chances are that about 50 percent of the group will be right. The number 256 is the eighth power of 2. After the eighth decision is made, assuming equal probabilities, the chances are that only one man will have been right on all 8 decisions. Should this fact become known to his fellows, he is very likely to

[1]C. West Churchman, "Marketing Theory as Marketing Management," in Cox, Alderson, and Shapiro (eds.), *Theory in Marketing*, 2d Series (Homewood, Ill., Richard D. Irwin, Inc., 1964).

gain a reputation as a towering genius whose judgment is sought on all types of issues thereafter.

Dr. Charles Ramond, of the Advertising Research Foundation, raises a very disturbing question about the reasons for business success. He calls attention to the factor of random reinforcement as it is utilized in animal experiments in the laboratory. Suppose that a pigeon pecks at a red dot and is sometimes rewarded with food. But suppose further that reinforcement of his pecking behavior is on a purely random basis. No one knows, including the pigeon, whether he will be rewarded or not on a given occasion. The pigeon may have happened to whirl about just before he achieves success, or he may have approached from the left rather than the right. Thereafter Dr. Ramond tells us, he will always whirl about or always approach from the left. The preliminary flourish has been stamped in as part of the successful pattern of behavior.

Dr. Ramond's applications to the behavior of business men is somewhat devastating. How is the business man to know what makes a really successful marketing campaign? How can he tell whether a given marketing policy has a positive effect or a negative effect? The campaign or the policy seemed to be quite successful the first time, but perhaps this was only coincidental and very different factors are really associated with success or failure. This line of reasoning resembles the other illustration in which 256 men make 8 successive choices and one of them is very likely to be right.

Actually business men appear to do a good deal better than these considerations imply even when they are only improvising. A. C. Nielsen, in one of his company's promotional brochures, is responsible for the statement that in the absence of market information business men are right 58 percent of the time. He goes on to say that this is really a remarkable score since there are usually more than two alternatives facing the executive. We apparently need an explanation of why he does so much better in improvising answers to his problems from day to day.

The answer lies in the nature of executive experience and subsequent reflection upon experience. He has in his mind a large inventory of models of what is likely to work or to fail in many different situations. He may never use the word model, and he may not even be clear as to the meaning of the word. Some of these models are very simple but very powerful since he knows that certain arrangements hardly ever work and can tell you why. In other instances his models approach the sophistication of elegant mathematical models even though he cannot be articulate about the model in mathematical terms.

Rationality in any field is demonstrated more by ability to learn than by the correctness of unaided judgment in the first instance. In marketing there are many interested parties to point out one's mistakes at least from the viewpoint of the speaker. Any reflective person comes to the end of a particular marketing campaign with some ideas about how it could be improved if he were doing it again. There is an enforced rationality in some areas of marketing because a consensus has gradually emerged as to the best or easiest way of accomplishing a result. The pricing of products to intermediary sellers, for example, usually takes account of the principal cost variables in the marketing of any given product.

A talent often found in leading executives is that of seeing things simply and directly. A third road to truth besides inductive logic and deductive logic is the ability to see significant structure in a situation. Gestalt psychologists say that this ability to see into the heart of a problem is a form of perception as is suggested by the etymology of the word insight. Admittedly the intuitive grasp of behavior patterns in a complex situation is only a guess as to the way that the variables interact. Forming these guesses or hypotheses is the more difficult part of the process of knowing. The improviser is a man who in some of the outstanding cases may be justified in trusting his intuitive flashes and his urge to act, more fully than he would trust anything so ponderous as to be called a plan.

Management by improvisation has brought many businesses into the multimillion dollar class with the momentum of growth as the principal coordinating factor. The test comes when growth slows down, and no one is confident that he has a sure formula for success. Businesses may be in trouble for various reasons, but a common one is that they are no longer experiencing the rapid increases which cover up many mistakes and inefficiencies. Executives are working just as hard with less to show for it. Improvisation will no longer serve. Some kind of plan must be in evidence as a backdrop for showing that everything possible is being done to set the firm back on the road to progress.

MANAGEMENT BY EXCEPTION

The concept of management by exception has been very fashionable in recent years. The implicit thesis is a plausible one, namely, that he manages best who manages least. It really combines the two ideas of keeping a business tuned up to run itself and leaving subordinates free to improvise so long as they are doing well. The manager who follows this concept is preoccupied with morale on the one hand and the need to make judicious appointments of resourceful executives on the other.

Management by exception implies that the firm is working smoothly most of the time and needs only an occasional nudge to keep it moving in the right direction. There may be a plan of action in the background, but the phrase itself has the ring of antiplanning about it. It says only that any case that warrants intervention is an exception. It does not say what it is an exception from. It must mean also that a business is in pretty healthy shape. If the business is in a constant struggle for solvency, the exceptions calling for intervention are likely to be pretty frequent.

One conception of management by exception is presented in a small book by Robert Kirk Mueller.[2] Here the phrase is given rather precise meaning by relating it to the Shewhart charts often used in quality control. The charts can be applied to any statistical series as, for example, company sales. Forecasts of sales are prepared showing the range of deviation from the forecasts which can reasonably be expected. So long as the figures fall within the confidence limits (the amount of permissible variation on either side), no remedial action is required. If the figures drift downward out of this band, some action will need to be taken to pick up the lagging sales trend.

Interestingly enough, Mueller's view is that the system is running out of control if the sales figures continue to be too high no less than if they are too low. If the actual figures are persistently higher than the forecasts, it may mean that the target has been set too low and the sales department is not having to exert itself to the full to produce the forecast results. Sales expectations are usually fitted to the indicated trend with a calculation of the confidence limits above and below. Variation up and down provides no cause for concern, but a definite trend in one direction or another does.

It can readily be seen that this approach gives some definite content to the phrase management by exception. Action is taken when the figures fall outside the confidence limits and not until then. The method can be applied to net profits as well as to sales. It is clear that some remedy is called for but not what action should be taken. Remedial action might take the form of a complex program to be initiated when the actual figures drift away from the forecast.

---

[2]See References at end of chapter.

The precise nature of the remedial action is another matter. Suppose net profits vary from expectations on a class of products. Should prices be lowered, taking advantage of an elastic demand? Is there a wide margin after distribution costs, suggesting that the product will stand greater marketing costs? Or is the situation one that calls for strict control of marketing costs for more efficient distribution? Management by exception is a somewhat empty phrase in these circumstances since the crucial decisions are those that occur after the exception is made.

It is difficult to find a perfectly objective decision maker who could derive satisfactory guide lines from the principle of management by exception. He would be likely to be strongly biased in favor of interfering or not interfering with the business. Leaning toward the side of tolerance and forbearance, he might wait for a substantial deviation from expectations before he took a hand. The executive who was biased toward interference might be constantly waiting in the wings, eager to dash out onto the stage. A characteristic danger would be that of overcorrection for moderate deviations. As Forrester[3] has shown, such a man might send the operation into needless and hazardous oscillations. Positive planning rather than episodic intervention would appear to be indicated in these cases.

At the other extreme a considerable lapse of time might occur while the executive was deliberating whether to take action or not. Each day would mean fresh hope that the trend figures would be restored to normal. For the executive who is reluctant to take positive action there is always an upswing just around the corner. The tendency to procrastinate would be encouraged by the fact that management by exception gives no clear indication of the remedial action to take. This philosophy says only that there is a critical problem and something ought to be done about it. It does not say for sure whether prices should be raised or lowered, whether marketing expenditures should go up or down, and if they go up, what should be the nature of the expanded program. In short, the doctrine of management by exception throws too much weight on the capacity of the executive to improvise and may leave too little time for him to improvise successfully.

The military services have had some experience with management by exception which turns out to be subject to the flaws which have been indicated. Among the questions which have never been resolved is how far down in the organization this principle should be

---

[3]Jay W. Forrester, *Industrial Dynamics* (N.Y.: John Wiley & Sons, 1960).

carried. Is it only the man at the top who should remain passive until remedial action is called for? If those immediately below him are expected to maintain a more active stance, how can he be sure that his apparent inertia will not be catching? Suppose, on the other hand, that the man at the second level is also applying management by exception. If this executive delays too long in declaring that an exception exists, should his superior make an overriding decision and step in while there is still some hope of improvising a satisfactory solution?

On the favorable side some justification exists for the view that the business operates under broad policies and deals with special problems within this framework. It is hardly an apt description to call this approach management by exception. It is more in line with a kind of sequential decision making in which an effort is made to gather more facts when the time for a difficult decision is near at hand. Seen in this light the so-called management by exception is related to the planning and problem-solving approach. Some of these strictures would no longer apply because an effort to deal promptly and systematically with successive problems arising within the framework of policy would be consistent with this approach.

There is some reason to ponder the meaning of information under this management philosophy. If the guide figures can be reduced to a few simple statistical series, and experience has shown that remedial action is like turning a valve on or off, this point of view may serve as well as any. It is quite a different situation if possible problems need to be anticipated well in advance to give some assurance that they can be dealt with in time. Management by exception is somewhat more sophisticated than the other methods described so far but in its pure form should be reserved for relatively simple situations.

MANAGEMENT BY DECISION RULE

The decision rule approach is consistent with the concept of flows in a total system. A decision rule determines the rate of flow at various points in the system. The chief business of management under this view is to determine these rates of flow. In the Forrester[4] view it is essential to know the whole system and adjust all the flow rates accordingly. Others favor the view that some progress can be made on a piecemeal basis, a view which seems to be justified by experience in some industries. Corrective action, with respect to inventories, is a case in point.

---

[4]*Ibid.*

All inventory models boil down to the adjustment of a single flow rate. That is, the rate at which inventories are replenished. Rules of thumb are frequently employed, such as the rule of maintaining a month's supply on each product. This rule is a very poor one when it is applied product by product. Slow-moving products require a larger back-up stock proportionately than those with rapid turnover. A simple rule is that the inventory needed goes up, not in proportion to the volume of sales, but in proportion to its square root.

Quite large sums of money have been saved on inventory by developing new decision rules for inventory replacement. Sometimes relatively simple variables are weighed against each other such as the cost of reordering versus the cost of storage and interest on larger inventories. Sometimes the inventory problem can become quite complex because of the number of variables which must be specified to describe the situation completely. One case that is fairly easy to deal with is the one that assumes that precisely the same level of service will be maintained and the problem is to determine inventory levels accordingly. The more difficult case is the one in which it is proposed to improve the level of service and the marketing department is called on to put a value on a lost sale. It should be clear that it is never possible to give perfect service to customers. The cost of holding enough inventory so as never to be out of stock would be prohibitive. It may be possible to calculate under a given decision rule that orders could be filled 99 percent of the time. To eliminate the 1 percent of failure remaining is where most of the added costs would lie.

The inventory problem is cited here mainly as an example of operating under decision rules. There are other examples of the decision rule approach. Among these are various allocation models such as the choice of levels of advertising or the choice among media. In one study for a leading brewer it was discovered that there was little relationship between advertising and sales if the company spent less than 10 percent of the total advertising dollars in a market. Above 10 percent advertising and sales generally rose together. A fairly obvious decision rule was that the company should spend at least 10 percent of the advertising dollars in a market or else stay out of the market altogether.

In general, decision rules for the choice of advertising media can be generated by studying threshold and saturation levels as they vary among media. Newspapers may show some results even for a very small amount of advertising. Magazines may require a fairly substantial advertising program to obtain any results at all. Television is likely to have a fairly high threshhold, meaning that no sig-

nificant results are attained below this level. The saturation level
for television may be very high. A problem is posed as to the optimal way of allocating expenditures among these media. Suppose
that all of these response functions are plotted on a chart, with
advertising expenditure on the horizontal axis and sales on the vertical. As the total expenditures increase it is possible to determine
the best allocation by inspection. The decision rule can be very simply stated. At any given point, as the total budget increases, the
executive making the allocation should be using that segment of a
response function which has the steepest slope.

Decision rules have two primary sources. One of these is a general model purporting to show how the system operates. The principal variables have been specified as in the inventory models
described above. This procedure would be the chief reliance if all
flow rates in the system could be fully specified.

Another way of deriving a decision rule is by constructing a model
of the decision process for an ideal decision maker. This procedure
has been followed in various studies of decision makers including
department store buyers and managers of investment funds. The
ideal decision maker should be completely objective with no bias
for or against risk taking as such. The advertising agency which
apparently has made the greatest progress toward setting up a
media allocation model has followed the approach of studying the
behavior of media buyers. Actually there is no one media buyer who
approaches this ideal. The ideal is a synthetic ideal put together on
the basis of the judgments which the buyer makes on a purely
objective basis.

A third line of investigation which is relatively new is to investigate the validity of various rules of thumb. Dr. William J. Baumol
and Dr. Richard Quandt[5] are responsible for this approach. Their
first effort was to look at rules of thumb in pricing. This is a realistic
approach because it can be assumed that pricing often has no logical
foundation other than rule of thumb. Also, as the authors point out,
the more refined the decision-making process the more expensive
it is likely to be.

In these studies hypothetical demand functions were generated
by the use of random numbers. A calculation was then made as to
how the seller would make out under these circumstances. Some
rules of thumb consistently came up with better results than others.

---

[5]W. J. Baumol and Richard Quandt, memorandum report to the National Science
Foundation, 1963.

In one case the seller was asssumed to set a fixed price near the middle of the established price range. This price policy worked out remarkably well without responding to any information about cost and demand functions. A rule which also worked very well was one where the entrepreneur was assumed to calculate his optimal price under the assumption that both the demand function and the cost function could be represented by straight lines. There were many arbitrary assumptions in this set of experiments, but they are highly suggestive as to what might be learned by fairly simple means.

Management by decision rule is an advance over some of the previous approaches, but it also has limitations. A question arises as to when the set of decision rules is complete. In a large company several thousand rules might be required, assuming that this number of people would be making genuine decisions. By the time such a large number of rules had been determined for every decision maker, significant changes would already be showing up in some parts of the system.

Decision making becomes unduly fragmented by an extreme application of the decision rule approach. It assumes a standard package of highly routine functions and the repetition of the same decision process many times over. It makes little provision for gathering and processing information in the unique instance. Data would be collected to implement the decision rules which had been established, but strategic decisions might be relatively neglected.

Finally there would be a tendency to put greatest stress on decisions at lower levels of the decision-making hierarchy. The system would fit the case of the minor executive making many decisions every day. It would not be so suitable for middle management which might be making a decision every week or so or for top management where real decisions may be made only a few times a year. On one side are relatively simple decisions occurring very frequently and readily amenable to decision rules. On the other side are decisions which are based on a large amount of data subjected to close analysis. No decision rule could possibly be stated for the latter situation except for very general rules about logical inference from qualitative or quantitative data. The decision rule approach has the merit of being in the direction of scientific management. While the operations of top management might not be amenable to this view, they can be fitted into a consistent picture of the entire decision-making process. Decision rules at the bottom of the ladder would surely reveal some paradoxes if rigidly applied. One purpose for the several layers of authority in the company is to reconcile these working rules with each other. Ideally they are brought together for final resolution in the mind of the chief executive.

The large corporation is equipped with a board of directors and executive committee and other rule-making bodies. Some rules or rulings are made for the special situation which may never occur again but which needs to be reconciled with policy. Others call for revisions or clarifications of policy and serve as guides to action thereafter.

MANAGEMENT THROUGH CONFLICT

A fifth approach to a management philosophy is management through conflict. Under this view there is a preoccupation with major objectives and a reconciliation among them. Some political scientists hold that conflict is an essential step in reaching a real consensus. Without conflict some members of the group may only be giving lip service to the stated objectives. Seymour Lipset[6] reviews the political history of the United States in the light of this idea and shows that the consensus of democracy emerges only after there has been an alignment of opposing forces and a full debate of the issues.

Business is usually not conducted as a democracy, but still it rests on the assent of the participants. To move effectively all departments of the business must move together. This movement will not be vigorous or effective if some members of the group are only half convinced. At some point the executive will be obliged to call a halt to discussion and lay down the policy line in spite of opposition. When this is done he will have a better chance of carrying the dissenters along with him than if debate had been suppressed.

Attitudes of management toward conflict vary considerably. Some actually stir up conflict in an organization as a way of crystalizing issues and reaching a final decision. A manager must have a deft technique to follow this course. The debate has to be kept moving ahead in terms of the main issues. It cannot be allowed to degenerate into irrelevant comment or the exchange of personal gibes. Others deal with conflict more gingerly, using it to get a sense of direction and not allowing it to stir up the really deepseated animosities which are sometimes just below the surface. The production and marketing functions, for example, will have to go on living with others despite differences in viewpoint which may never be resolved. A debate should have a point of termination, and the group should move from debate to action on the given date. Ideally

---

[6]Seymour Lipset, *Political Man* (Garden City, N.Y.: Doubleday & Co., 1960).

there should be a steady progress from point to point, leaving a narrow and well-defined area of contention to be resolved by authoritative decision.

At this point it may be agreed that the action to be taken should be to gather further information. The group should agree in advance on the kind of evidence which will be taken as determining. Suppose, for example, that a study is to be made of the market acceptance of a new product. The group could agree in advance that they would introduce the new product if 40 percent of the market sentiment was favorable and that they would take no action if the figure was less than 40 percent. Where no decision rule has been established in advance, both sides are likely to interpret the evidence as favoring their side of the case. Nothing has been accomplished toward resolving the issue, and the new information simply adds fuel to the flames. The decision to seek further information as the basis for resolving an issue is consistent with the approach of statistical decision theory.

One hypothesis about conflict is that it exists at various levels and the problem is not to resolve conflict but to raise the level of conflict. The charter of a business enterprise makes some basic assumptions as to the kind of business the company expects to conduct. Fundamental policies are gradually established concerning the way in which that business is to be conducted. Programs and procedures are adopted for carrying out the policies. Sometimes only a single issue creates a division among participants who are otherwise committed to the same program. One measure of morale in a business under pressure is how long it can maintain the level of conflict on the customary plane despite adverse circumstances. The tempo of the debate increases as the outlook gets worse. Concern for personal position in the company is aroused by the threat that the joint opportunity generated by the operation will no longer support so large a group.

Suspicion and recrimination enter as people wonder what went wrong and who has failed to do his part. Cabals form in an effort to be numbered among the survivors and are directed against the leader of one faction or the other. Some of those who try to stay clear of the conflict or who are dazed by the general confusion can be disposed of rather quickly when the time arrives that heads must fall. As the conflict becomes more intense, nearly everyone is obliged to line up on one side or the other. At this point no quarter is given, and the battle rages until one side is victorious or the organization disintegrates completely.

What is most interesting about this phenomenon is the gradual decline in the level of conflict, dropping down from one level to the next. As the last level of sheer animal antagonism comes closer one constraint after another drops away until literally anything goes. This last stage is only approached in times of riot and civil warfare and almost never in organized systems. One reason is that the system will almost surely break apart before this final stage. Nevertheless observation of organizations under stress show an unmistakable trend toward step-by-step lowering of the level of conflict.

To summarize, there are various outcomes for conflict when carried to the ultimate conclusion. The organization may be liquidated or forced into bankruptcy. One side may win and leaders of the other side be so far out of sympathy with the victors that they are obliged to resign. If the organization continues to be in trouble, new factions may develop within the victorious party with another round in the battle ensuing. A few dissenters may stay on if they have managed to stay clear of bitterness even though making their position clear. If the wounds begin to heal and the organization is once more on the way up, the dissenters may serve as a kind of loyal opposition, performing their duties faithfully but with some remaining reservations as to basic policy. Finally, if the official policy line fails, the dissenters may come to the top and take over with a new policy line. The deliberate use of a loyal opposition might be a useful experiment, but it might have to be carried out at the level of the board of directors. A roughly equal split between two factions would scarcely be tolerable in a corporation.

It should be possible to draw a clear line of distinction between constructive conflict and destructive conflict. A debate over means can often be held to the technical level. A debate over objectives readily overflows these boundaries and may start the decline in level of conflict. The debate over objectives can usually be limited to a more select group so long as it remains a discussion of company objectives. When the objectives or benefits to a broader group are in question, such as members of a labor union, the issues can scarcely be resolved without their representatives being present. One good reason for purely formal statements of objectives such as the maximization of profits is to avoid bringing the private and confidential objectives of individuals into the open for debate. An instance in which this would scarcely be constructive is a case in which a company executive with a large amount of company stock is trying to liquidate that stock. He could take a very short-run view of all marketing programs in the hope of increasing stock values during the period.

Management through conflict is a fairly apt description of what is going on in a number of leading companies. Companies which have basic policy questions to settle would tend to be in this category. In some companies these issues are especially complex and dynamic. When the issues might appear about to be settled, one may find only that the center of debate has shifted to another area. Individuals have their own personal leanings toward conservative or more radical viewpoints, some wanting to risk very little and others ready to venture all.

Conflicting proposals are often self-serving because the individuals sponsoring them hope thereby to win preferment. A production-oriented plan is likely to be sponsored by a production man, and a marketing-oriented plan by a marketing man. The bias is understandable and is quite possibly constructive from an organization point of view. This is certainly one way in which alternative proposals are originated for consideration by top management.

Management through conflict is in sharp contrast with management by decision rule. In one case the assumption is that the system is open-ended, is extremely dynamic, and involves ends as well as means. In the other case it is assumed that the system can be regarded as a closed system directed toward clear-cut objectives and changing primarily in the way that objectives are implemented. The two philosophies are contradictory at the extremes but tend to be reconciled in more moderate situations. There could be a spirited debate at the technical level over what the decision rule governing a type of situation ought to be. There is also room for debate about the exact nature of the system and what decision rules should next be formulated even though the system is regarded as a closed system.

As between these two views, it is realistic to assume that more businesses are governed through conflict than through decision rule. That is to say, the element of conflict is always present while the practice of setting up formal decision rules is only in its infancy. Conflict is inherent in the internal competition between strong-minded individuals. There is never enough room at the top to satisfy the ambitions of all concerned. Men compete for the symbols of status as well as for the substance of power. Management by decision rule reflects the natural bias of the staff analyst who would prefer to see a system operating more or less automatically under analytical decision rules. If business would only settle down and firms adhere to simple, clearly-stated objectives, it would be possible to approximate this vision.

The total systems approach is embraced in this book because it is evidently an excellent analytical perspective. In practice no human behavior system is ever entirely closed. It is an ecological system with the special property of possessing the capacity for replacing its own parts—the individuals who made it up. So long as this can happen the system will never be entirely closed. That is to say, the system would have to be closed in terms of the objectives for which it is operated. Whenever a system absorbs new members into itself it brings along with them some nuance with respect to objectives or style of behavior which makes it in some degree a new system. The vitality of ecological systems lies in their capacity to modify both ends and means as occasioned by continuous adaptation to the environment.

MANAGEMENT AS A NEGOTIATIVE PROCESS

A sixth and final concept of management views the interchange between levels of responsibility as a continuous negotiative process. Often the process of negotiation is implicit, and the conditions of the bargain are not formally stated. The negotiative view has no implications as to democratic or autocratic management. It can work in either type of structure and can be formalized in considerable degree or left informal. The essence of the negotiative view is that the top executive strikes a series of bargains with his principal subordinates.

A bargain must provide adequate incentives or considerations on either side. It must have an identifiable point in time when the bargain is struck, and it should have a reporting period when an accounting will be rendered. There must be two-way commitment, with the top executive offering support and incentive and the subordinate pledging himself to performance. Executives differ greatly in their methods of obtaining pledges of performance, but it is this function more than any other which determines whether a man is of executive caliber.

The top executive has some advantages on his side in these negotiations. He usually has the ultimate authority to terminate a man's tenure with the firm. He has a range of freedom with respect to the incentives offered in the form of promotion or other benefits. It is he who stands as spokesman for the aspirations of the group. Even if these aspirations are higher than the man would set for himself, there is a psychological pressure in wanting to live up to the opinion which the executive entertains of him. The executive is the final authority on the techniques to be employed and should have as clear a view as anybody concerning the position of the firm in its market.

The subordinate has some notable advantages on his side of the bargain. He knows that his superior cannot perform the given task himself but must delegate this task to the subordinate. Having confidence in his special skills, he will ask for the support he needs to complete the job successfully. Sometimes he will try to hedge his commitment by asking for a large amount of support. Reminded that resources are scarce, he may scale down his stated requirements. His request may include the names of people whom he can rely on in turn as well as the dollars he needs for advertising and personal selling.

Negotiation can be quite informal in the relations between superior and subordinate. There is seldom time for protracted discussion, but the elements of negotiation are there just the same. Better techniques of negotiation are worthy of study. Many of the two-way commitments are purely verbal although it would be a good idea to make a brief memorandum of the most important matters. The superior might ask the subordinate to put down on one page the essence of what had been said. The superior would review these memoranda and initial them if they were in accordance with his understanding. If not, a further meeting might be required.

The executive is committing the resources of his company in the effort to obtain certain objectives, and it is worth taking some pains to be sure of a precise understanding. The executive needs to have a good memory of what transpired if it was not committed to writing. There should be nothing casual or vague in the way he talks about performance and the commitment of resources. These matters are of the essence of management. They are part of what it means to hold a taut rein in managing a company.

Large companies generally have procedures which reduce some of these aspects of negotiation to formal agreements. Division managers are required to submit budgets and, more recently, marketing plans, in support of a budget. The occasion for budget review enables management to observe whether the plan is well conceived and whether it is sufficiently precise and detailed. Plans are sent back for reconsideration if they will cost too much money or if the results promised are not a sufficient return for the expenditure. In some very large companies control is chiefly on an incremental basis. Here again production and marketing plans are submitted in the effort to demonstrate that the proposed program constitutes a good investment opportunity.

A negotiated decision is a joint decision arrived at through agreement between a superior and a subordinate. There is a kind of equality in a joint decision since results will not be attained unless both sides stick by their promises. Sometimes the joint decision is a qualified agreement in which the superior asks the subordinate to proceed along a stated line with a subsequent review to determine how he is making out. The agreement may be finally confirmed or invalidated at the review period. A joint decision can be set up so as to offer either side an escape. The subordinate may come back to the superior to cite the difficulties and to state either that it cannot be done or that it will take more money. Together they may settle for a more moderate goal, or the superior may suggest new strategies by which the goal may be attained after all. The superior may have to back down on the ground that the money may not be available or another target has been identified with overriding urgency. In either case the new deal should be a matter of formal record between them.

The negotiative framework makes it almost essential that the superior provide a clear statement of his objectives at least for the limited situation. It will scarcely serve to present the problem only in terms of uncertainty as to the means to be employed. Knowing the problem, the subordinate may know better ways of doing it. On the other hand, the executive may warn him against pitfalls which developed when the program was last tried, or he may be aware that the subordinate favors certain habitual methods of approach and that this may be the time to try something new. The subordinate cannot put his imagination to work in an untrammeled way unless he knows just what is to be accomplished.

Some issues should be regarded as not negotiable either in general or in the context of the given problem. Underlying policies are still to be taken for granted, but where needful these limitations should be made explicit. Matters of compensation ordinarily should not be part of a task discussion. Naturally, if the subordinate feels that morale is sagging in his division as a result of long overdue raises and that these changes are essential to getting the job done, he should incorporate them in his budget.

Negotiation is the means of keeping the internal structure of the company vigorous and healthy. When two people sit down to negotiate they are deciding to get organized for a particular purpose. Negotiation is sometimes discussed as if it were an external matter, but it plays an equally vital role inside. Negotiation can be traced through similar stages from testing each other out to a simple reconfirmation of an existing arrangement. Men get to know each other better, but the superior can never afford to relax the tension he seeks to maintain. The basic bargain should be with the boss, and to the extent that this is true, it will leave less room for any side deals or coalitions.

Management as a negotiative process is the view that is favored here. It incorporates some of the elements of all the other perspectives but is more flexible in adaptation while preserving the leadership role in expressing aspirations and electing technologies. It involves a disclosure of objectives which sound relationships with subordinates would appear to require. It lays the groundwork for direct, personal accountability for performance. It builds on the principle of two-way commitment in asserting that both sides should honor their commitments. Since a negotiated decision is a joint decision, it should also be a dated decision—carrying the date that it was made and the date by when it is expected to be completed. It recognizes that objectives as well as methods can change. It is adapted to the spirit of the times both in its dynamic aspect and in the insistence that decision processes should be made more formal and explicit.

The negotiative perspective is practically identical with the approach from the standpoint of planning and problem solving. Plans are programs for getting jobs done which are accepted or rejected through negotiation. Problems arising within the framework of a plan lead to plan revisions on the basis of later and more current information. The next chapter will develop further the concept of management as a negotiative process and management through planning and problem solving.

Selected References

BARNARD, CHESTER, I. *The Functions of the Executive.* Cambridge, Mass.: Harvard University Press, 1940.
 A classic treatment of the organization and control of business. The passing references in the text are to one view propounded by Barnard and possibly not the most important one.

KUSIK, J. E. "Financial Planning and Control", *The Controller,* June 1953.
 Describes a comprehensive mechanism for the control of business activities and the coordination planning of marketing, production, and finance.

Management Planning and Control, H. J. Heinz, Approach Series 2, Report #6. New York: Controllership Foundation, 1957.
 A study in management planning, emphasizing the techniques of control for keeping the operation in balance.

MUELLER, ROBERT KIRK. *Effective Management through Probability Controls.* New York: Funk & Wagnalls Co., Inc., 1950.
 A quantitative approach to management by exception, modeled on procedures for quality control.

Problems

1. Name the six alternative views of the nature of direction and control. Can you think of any others?

2. What is the meaning and value of experience in management?

3. Discuss the advantages and disadvantages of management by improvisation.

4. Discuss the advantages and disadvantages of management by exception.

5. If management through planning and problem solving should be set up as a seventh alternative view, how would you relate it to the other six?

Chapter 3

PLANNING AND PROBLEM SOLVING

Marketing problems, as seen by management, are very simple in essence. The firm wants to expand its volume of sales, or it wants to handle the volume it has more efficiently. Nearly all of the problems encountered in a long career as a marketing consultant could be boiled down to market expansion or marketing efficiency. The complications arise in looking for answers to these simple questions. There is no phase of human culture which cannot enter into a marketing problem and perhaps turn out to be the crucial factor in its solution.

MARKET EXPANSION STUDIES

For new products, one means of achieving market expansion, the task is to define market opportunity. Is there a distinct and separate place for the product in the market? Will some consumers prefer it to any other? What is the estimated number of these consumers, and how strong is their relative preference for the product expected to become?

These questions can be answered when we have determined whether the product will solve a problem for any of the users it hopes to attract. Consumers come into the market to solve problems and for no other reason. Sometimes these problems have urgent technical significance as when the product has an essential use and represents a much better way of serving that use than was ever achieved before. Sometimes the problem seems trivial to the technician or is involved with secondary issues such as status and self-esteem. The best policy is to give the consumer a voice in deciding what he wants and then provide it if it is not positively harmful to his person or his pocketbook.

Some other questions must be answered before risking the investment in a new product. There may be a market for it eventually, but is this the right time for it? A product can establish a market for itself quickly if it is a little ahead in technical advances, but usually it cannot afford to be too far ahead. Sometimes the slow start of a new product means that demand is gradually catching up with it. The resources of the original sponsor may have been dissipated; meanwhile a luckier management has taken over in its stead. Consumers have some problems that are acute and urgent and others of which they are scarcely conscious until the time arrives when they feel that they can do something about them.

The single-product firm is a diminishing factor in our economy. Large companies talk of product lines rather than products. Firms continue to expand into adjacent fields, duplicating products sponsored by others. The product line is the new base line for plotting marketing strategies. Theoretically products can now be added or dropped without substantial risk to the core position of the firm. The same principle still holds that each product must solve a problem and be preferred by some group of customers even if it solves it in only a slightly different way.

The freedom to add or subtract products is not always true in practice because of organizational problems arising in the company. Someone who has a personal stake in a product will plead for it to be continued even in the face of an indifferent performance. Similarly, new products do not always get a fair chance because of entrenched resistance. In principle a multiple-product line promotes adjustment to changing markets by limiting the risks involved in particular expansion programs compared to the company's total market. The company can make incremental additions to its marketing programs on successful products and withdraw bit by bit from those with declining markets.

Internal growth in a company must come either from the introduction of new products or from growth of old products. The third source of growth is from mergers and acquisitions. Firms conduct active campaigns directed toward finding suitable mergers. It is by no means the easiest road to growth because of the problems encountered in absorbing a new company. Many of the larger companies have reached the end of the acquisition road with a tacit understanding that the Antitrust Division will take vigorous enforcement action the next time they try it. Mergers exhibit some of the features of game theory since a merger refused may mean that the chance to combine will be snapped up by another company offering stronger competition in the field. An exhaustive study at Harvard a few years ago[1] showed that mergers tended to be disappointing to all concerned. It is not very likely on the whole that some other group has put together an operation which will make a perfect fit when merged into your company's operation. Nevertheless there are companies which have been brilliantly successful through a series of mergers and acquisitions.

What might be recognized as a fourth route to growth is the joint venture. Two companies can combine in a joint venture where each possesses basic skills at different levels. The Chemstrand Corporation as a joint venture of Monsanto and American Viscose was a case in point although the company later became a wholly owned subsidiary of Monsanto. At first Monsanto was skilled in making nylon and acrilan staple and American Viscose, in spinning and weaving, the proportionate investment in Chemstrand resulting in the equal sharing of profits.

Marketing research does not enter equally into the solution of all these problems. Its demonstrated value is roughly the reverse of the order stated. It is true that a substantial amount of problem-solving research is concerned with both joint ventures and acquisitions. The limiting factor is that these combinations tend to represent unique opportunities, and the issue is often decided as a matter of high policy with little opportunity for a comprehensive evaluation. Multiproduct companies are second best as markets for research services. At one time they seemed to feel that they could afford to give every product a full market test and that enough of them would be successful to turn in a good profit showing for the company. Today the multiproduct line is getting a larger share of the analytical attention it deserves because of the increasing cost of attempting to introduce a product only to have it fail in a majority of cases. An interesting case represents the request of a client for a post mortem. He is to provide the full record on a product which failed to make the grade, and the consultant is to give his best judgment as to what went wrong.

Companies with relatively narrow product lines were among the first to use problem-solving research. More is at stake relatively for the single-product company. There is greater urgency in being right both in the initial introduction and in subsequent marketing programs. Entering an entirely new field with distinctive channels and promotional methods is, of course, more hazardous even for the established company. It is difficult to get started without experience

[1] J. Fred Weston, *The Role of Mergers in the Growth of Large Firms* (Berkeley, Cal.: University of California Press, 1953).

with the customary channels. Research is relied on for filling in the missing facets of the picture but may still have little influence on the choice of marketing strategy.

↓ Marketing studies designed to evaluate marketing opportunity are conducted under conditions of great uncertainty. Future reactions of consumers to the product cannot be known but only estimated. Competition is equally unpredictable. A competitor may have a similar product ready to come out at the same time. He may be stirred into action by a new product introduction or rumors of it. The field is regarded as a vital one for him to occupy and in which he will tolerate no invasion if he can prevent it. The rapid growth of a new market attracts new investors and thus limits the future prospects of those who are already entrenched in it.

Uncertainty is compounded by the fact that the firm is actually interested in future markets as forecast over some period ahead. Starting from today some time will elapse before a marketing program could get under way. Many market surveys are either directly aimed at forecasting or confirm forecasts made in other ways. For example, a study of a new chemical product starts out with some knowledge of the amounts of various chemicals devoted to the particular use. A market study enables the analyst to estimate how fast the new product can be substituted for the older ones under various assumptions as to price and the amount of promotional expenditure.

Strictly speaking, markets always have a time dimension. A forecast states that a given volume of sales will occur over the next five years or the next ten years. Sometimes it is worth predicting when the product will go out of style or become obsolete. Many products are built for an expectation of a short life but with the hope of maximizing sales while they last. It is often said that the chemical industry, for example, obtains most of its sales from products which did not even exist ten years ago.

MARKETING EFFICIENCY STUDIES

Marketing efficiency studies are largely made inside the companies and under conditions of uncertainty which are not quite so serious. These studies deal with the established flows in an ongoing business, and the margin for error is in one sense restricted. All the facts are available or potentially available for a solution of the problem of efficiency. Knowing what to do with the facts is another issue. The joint-cost problem, where several products make use of the same facilities, has never been satisfactorily solved. There are a variety of theories about how to solve it, ranging from the extremely naive but feasible to the very sophisticated methods with no hope of obtaining the relevant data. This kind of uncertainty might be called analytical uncertainty as compared with informational uncertainty.

The solution of a problem of marketing efficiency is usually stated in relative terms as compared to a study which says that a market does or does not exist. One product is to get more advertising and another less. One product is to be given priority because of expectations of future returns, and another which may be doing equally well at present is labeled as being on its way out. In other words, these are problems in the allocation of scarce resources, having in mind the principle of diminishing returns as it affects each product. This is the area of economics as applied to marketing although it is sometimes dealing with novel subjects such as the cost of information. The economics of information is a vital aspect of the whole marketing process.

In traditional economics the manager can reduce his price and try to maintain his volume, or he can keep his price fixed and accept whatever sacrifice is required in volume. In marketing economics there are additional variables. The firm may increase or decrease its advertisting expenditure. It can change its marketing mix as between advertising and personal selling. It can put more effort into getting more stores to handle a product as compared to trying to get the stores who handle it to put active effort behind it. It can attempt to reorganize the methods for distributing the product as compared to accepting existing methods. It can assume that it has no further responsibility when the product is sold to customers at the next level. The firm, on the other hand, can serve as a channel captain and prevail on others in the channel to accept an elaborate plan for moving the product to the ultimate consumer.

Marketing efficiency information is organized in various ways to suit various problem solvers. Marketing cost analysis is organized by outputs—sales by product classes or customers grouped by territories. This form of analysis is ideally suited to wholesalers who are relatively free to drop unprofitable lines or add new lines in profitable categories. It takes present methods of doing business as given and moves toward an optimal profit by manipulating its outputs.

Other problem-solving techniques are geared to a study of inputs. A simple example is the use of queuing theory in the study of check-out counters in the supermarket. How many check-out counters and check-out clerks should it have to result in maximizing profits, assuming that the product mix remains constant? For this study the store either actually or theoretically varies the number of check-out counters which is a single input into the retailing system. Similarly, an experimental or statistical study might be made of the amount of space in the store to determine the point at which the space produced only enough additional sales to cover the additional revenue.

Linear programming is a flexible analytical method which can work in either direction. It can point the way toward maximizing profits by coming up with an indicated schedule of outputs. It can be used to solve for a minimal cost solution which specifies the inputs under the stated technology. There is a relative lack of methods directed toward improving the technology itself, partly, perhaps, because more marketing men have been trained as economists than as engineers. A crucial question in problem solving, and indeed in market planning, is just when particular improvement in methods should take place, considering the current and projected sales of the company. Problems in physical distribution and delivery have largely been taken over by analysts with engineering background. A principal reliance for such studies is cost-benefit analysis with some experimentation with possible departures from standard procedures. In the better practice there has been some formalization of the underlying theory which gives guidance to practice.

The rapprochement between economics and engineering in these vital areas may lie in the concept of economies of scale or diseconomies of scale. As a company grows it has opportunity for scale economies which may not have been realized. Management should always be alive to these opportunities, but there can be a lag in recognizing them. Opposition or inertia within the staff can be a serious obstacle. To achieve the potential economies may require investment in new equipment which is not easily adapted to the particular situation. The experience with the installation of computers has shown how complex and uncertain the return from economies of scale may be. The problem of internal economies or diseconomies is sometimes acute in the relations among divisions within a company. Strangely enough, when divisions are buying from each other, they do not always serve the internal customer as well as the external. The price is likely to be set as the market price, and yet quality and uniformity and priority ratings in service are not equal to that given outside customers. This topic will be discussed further in dealing later with the design of marketing systems.

THE PROBLEM-SOLVING PROCESS

Skill in problem solving should be teachable to intelligent students. Students will vary in their native aptitudes and in their in-

terest in a given type of problem. Yet it should be possible to inculcate some degree of expertness in all students of marketing management. The process of problem solving—of looking for answers
in a problem situation—has some universal elements which should
carry over from one setting to another. It is more than knowing any
one general formula. Some of the best minds in history have taken
time to be reflective about the problem-solving process.

Descartes in the seventeenth century wrote a short but luminous
work called *Discourse on Method*.[2] He tried to reduce the art of
problem solving to four basic principles. The first of these four principles is obviously the hardest.

1. Put all preconceptions out of your mind.
2. Break the problem up into its parts.
3. Solve the easy parts first.
4. Recheck to make sure you have not left anything out.

Francis Bacon also spoke of banishing all preconceptions, and
both men were forerunners of modern science. The reason for getting rid of your prejudices is that you are otherwise likely to get the
wrong answer. This was an especially odd statement to come from
a pure mathematician like Descartes. He was referring to intellectual
bias or habits of thought. A simple example will illustrate the reason
for this admonition. There is a classic puzzle in which three canni-
bals and three missionaries are traveling together and are stopped
by a river. There is a boat, but it will carry only two people. The
missionaries want to arrange things so that they will never be out-
numbered on either side of the river and subject to possible attack.
Hidden bias is the only obstacle to solving this problem. There is a
point in the comings and goings across the river where two men
must bring the boat back. No one has said that this is against the
rules, but many people get no further with the puzzle because they
assume that one man should be enough.

Descartes' second principle is the key to the process as he sees it.
By breaking the problem up into parts the solver is able to make an
intensive examination of each part. For some of these parts he may
see the answer immediately once the problem has been partitioned.
That is the logic of solving the easy parts first. The gain in certainty
is greatest if the solver proceeds in this way. As he goes from the
easy parts to the hard parts he will experience increasing confidence
that he has the right answer. Simple cryptograms are usually solved
in this way. The solver may make a guess at the word "the" or "and"

---

[2]René Descartes, *Discourse on Method* (Chicago: Henry Regnery for the Great
Books Foundation, 1949).

because of its position in the puzzle. If this guess is right, it often leads to the deciphering of more difficult words.

The final step of rechecking is also important in practical affairs. Descartes, as a mathematician, wanted to be sure that the student had left no gaps in his logic. A marketing answer has to be checked and rechecked for the same reason. Marketing is people, and people are more complicated than numbers.

John Dewey,[3] the eminent exponent of pragmatism, saw life in terms of the problems of men. He said some important things about putting the problem first and then drawing on whatever techniques the solver has for finding a solution. Northrup[4] went further than Dewey in talking about a thorough analysis of the problem as an essential to a solution. Advertising agencies typically begin the study of an advertising problem with what is called a situation analysis. This is an attempt to be aware of all facets of the problem and its relations with underlying factors which could possibly determine the answer.

A contemporary mathematician, G. Polya, has devoted intensive study to problem solving. He has written a small book about it called *How to Solve It.*[5] He has in mind mathematical problems primarily, but his suggestions are applicable in other fields. He also enumerates four problem-solving principles, but they are rather different from those of Descartes. He summarizes what he has to say under the headings of understanding the problem, devising a plan, carrying out the plan, and looking back.

He means something quite specific with respect to understanding the problem. He asks: What is the unkown? What are the data? What is the condition? The unknown in a marketing problem is usually the answer to a basic question of policy or strategy. The data are the evidence that the policy is valid or the strategy will work. The condition is the limitations inherent in the statement of the problem. Can I set up a department store in Wilmington, Delaware, in 50,000 feet of selling space? No, because the volume of trade generated there by a full-line department store would greatly exceed that area. Will there be sufficient market for a new chemical product to justify the building of a plant? Yes, under stated assumptions as to price and promotion.

Polya has a number of things to say about devising a plan of solution. One arresting suggestion is that you try to solve first some

[3]John Dewey, *Logic: Theory of Inquiry* (N.Y.: Henry Holt & Co., 1938).
[4]F. C. S. Northrup, *The Logic of the Sciences and the Humanities* (N.Y.: Macmillan Co., 1947).
[5]G. Polya, *How to Solve It* (Princeton, N.J.: Princeton University Press, 1948).

related problem if you cannot solve the proposed problem. Sometimes looking at an individual market is a similar approach to trying to solve a national marketing problem. The conditions and relationships in the individual market are likely to seem more concrete even though the national market is only a collection of such local markets. The key to the Polya procedure is in understanding the problem and devising a plan to match.

One cannot push the analogy too far since the mathematician wants precise answers and is not interested in what is only probably true. Probable truth, on the other hand, is the only kind available to the marketing specialist. Polya suggests that there are two kinds of mathematical answers. The first is to find an arithmetical answer; the second is to find a proof of a logical or mathematical proposition. The market analyst can find answers and state the amount of confidence he is entitled to place in them. To obtain proof in the Polya sense is a luxury which the marketing man hardly ever enjoys.

THE MEANING OF A SOLUTION

Problem solving is an activity conducted for the purpose of producing answers to questions. It is useful, therefore, to consider what one means by a solution. Obviously there are several rather different meanings, including those especially applicable to problems of action. From an operational standpoint a solution is what you get when you carry out specified operations successfully. In solving a mathematical puzzle you may reach the point of being confident that you have the right answer and yet be mistaken. The writer was once briefly under the happy illusion that he had solved the Goldbach conjecture for which no general answer is known to exist. In fact, a momentary oversight may indicate that a solver has solved the Koenigsberg bridge problem although it can be proven very simply in this case that no answer is possible.

The structure of mathematics sometimes determines the type of answer we are prepared to accept. The calculus is so constructed as to yield a maximum or minimum figure as the answer to many problems. In marketing it can serve us well, at least in theory, if we accept the premise that the manager seeks to maximize net profits. The answer to many marketing problems is then identified as the level of operations which will enable him to reach this net profit objective. Actually it is seldom possible to make such a calculation even approximately, and marketing answers turn out usually to be more modest in scope and more in the nature of a step-by-step approach to better results.

All marketing answers are approximations, and only rough approximations are required for planning or problem solving. "Is it a lot or is it a little?" is sometimes all the marketing executive wants to know, but he wants to know this much with a pretty high level of reliability. He cannot afford to be caught on the wrong side of this issue as, for example, treating the market as if it were only a little market when it turns out to be a lot. The consultant learns that what he needs to tell his client is often very simple almost to the point of embarrassment. "Do this." "Don't do that." "Double your effort if you propose to develop this market." The marketing organization which the executive controls does not respond to precise refinements. Once the actual effort is under way he gets a more sensitive feeling for market response. Sometimes the consultant lavishes much care and thought on precision in his research to be as sure as he humanly can be that he is right. Yet his recommendations may be sweeping and unqualified because he doubts whether anything less ambiguous can trigger action.

An answer to a marketing question reduces uncertainty to tolerable limits. It cannot eliminate uncertainty since what we want to know about markets lies largely in the future. The executive would be told, in an ideal relationship with his consultant, that the chances were, say, three out of four, that a recommended strategy would prevail. He might choose to gather more information on the factors of risk in the plan and perhaps be ready to adopt it when revisions in the plan raised its chances of success to nine out of ten. We are not as yet able to rate a strategy quite so accurately or to determine what more we ought to know to choose strategies with higher ratings. But something like this is what we should mean when we ask an executive to choose among strategies.

Generating solutions or answers to policy questions usually implies that there is a recognized set of alternatives from which to choose. There are several steps to be specified to make the recommendation more definite. The first step may only point the direction in which action is to take place. The next step tells the executive how much money would be involved in a successful program and some further indication of how much it would be worth to him. Finally he needs to be told how long in the judgment of the analyst this effort should persist. He does not want to give up too easily on a program which holds promise, but neither does he want to go on indefinitely fighting against hopeless obstacles.

Sometimes a recommendation tells the executive to avoid a course of action, perhaps permanently. The market prospect is fair, but the consequences of a move might prove disastrous on some other front. Similarly, a recommendation might place a temporary stay on an action. A prospective market is there, but the time is not ripe for exploiting it.

In summary, marketing solutions are probabilistic, the facts not being sufficient to determine the answer completely. Marketing solutions ordinarily deal with future markets and expectations concerning them. Marketing recommendations are often couched in bold and sweeping form because an organization cannot always respond to more precise and subtle answers.

INSIGHT—THE SEARCH FOR SIGNIFICANT STRUCTURE

When problem solving is viewed as an aspiration, it seems to consist of three parts or aspects. These are insight, trial and error, and systematic calculation. Insight, as the word suggests, means seeing into or through a subject. Insight can be trained to some extent because the student can be taught to look for the right things. The key to insight is the search for significant structure. Bertrand Russell[6] once said that there were three ways to advance knowledge, the first two being the two basic forms of logic—induction and deduction. There is a third method, according to Russell, which deserves separate recognition, namely, the search for significant structure.

This third method is the domain of insight. It provides the hypotheses which in a fully developed science are subsequently tested by a combination of induction and deduction. The process starts with a guess about the nature of things and the reason why they appear to work as they do. The next step is deductive and says that if this hypothesis is correct the consequence B should follow from the hypothesis A. The third step is inductive, consisting of gathering evidence to confirm or refute the hypothesis.

The search for significant structure may usually be regarded as the search for a predictive model. This means putting together the controlling variables in a situation to find a pattern of action which will work. The interaction of these variables is by no means obvious else there would be no marketing problem. Some variables are operating in ways that are not well understood, and the aim of the study is to contribute to understanding. Variables are sometimes divided by controllable variables, uncontrollable variables, and target variables. The target variable is the end result to be achieved. The controllable variables are those which can be changed or modi-

---

[6]Bertrand Russell, *My Philosophical Development* (N. Y.: Simon and Schuster, 1959).

fied in the effort to achieve these results. The uncontrollable variables are those which are part of the situation but presumably beyond control which may become active obstacles in the path of the marketer.

Closely related to the idea of a predictive model is the idea of a productive plan. The predictive model takes the situation as given and states the expected outcome. The productive plan says that if we will intervene in a prescribed way the situation will yield a different and more productive result. The question then is whether we have the resources which will enable us to intervene and whether intervention in the direction of alterantive *A* would be as productive as intervention in the direction of alternative *B*.

Psychologists of the Gestalt school contend that insight is literally a form of seeing. Some say that the first glance at a problem is likely to provide the clue which then may need to be worked out more laboriously. Wertheimer is a member of the Gestalt school who pursues this view pretty far in his book *Productive Thinking.*[7] This group of psychologists illustrate their points with optical illusions and other visible objects. It is not so clear that the same principles hold when the situation is not visible at all but is presented in the abstract to the imagination. That is the case of marketing problems when we talk about such things as channels and marketing campaigns but we cannot see them.

It is not too difficult to make the transition to a picture which is seen only in the imagination. The problem is that this type of seeing is less vivid, less constant, and lacking some of the helpful clues provided by direct observation. There are, of course, visual aids such as tables and charts which help us in recalling what the main contours of the marketing situation appear to be. There is the further complication of uncertainty or incomplete knowledge. Some of the most important factors often lie in this region of the unknown. It is something like the game of concealing the lower half of a photograph. We are called on to guess at significant structure, and this includes guessing at the contours of that part of the face which is concealed.

There are two classes of puzzles which will repay study in considering the search for significant structure. These two classes of puzzles embrace most of the logical or mathematical puzzles which are not based on a mere verbal trick. These two classes of puzzles are roughly parallel to problem solving on the one hand and plan-

---

[7] Max Wertheimer, *Productive Thinking* (N.Y.: Harper & Bros., 1959).

ning on the other. In the first class of puzzles the solver starts with a set of elements and is asked to select an item from the set which meets specified conditions. Usually there is some stated restriction on the methods to be used in reaching the solution. The classical coin-weighing problem is of this type. The solver is told that there are twelve coins, eleven of them perfect and one defective. The problem is to find the defective coin, tell whether it is lighter or heavier than the others, and to accomplish this result in three weighings on the balance scale.

The second type of puzzles are those in which the solver is asked to arrange a set of items in a sequence of steps or a specified order. There is some overlapping between these two types of puzzles, but the emphasis in the second class is on the state of affairs at the end of the solution and the condition which should be attained at that time. An example is the single corner problem set upon a checkerboard. The single corner diagonal has eight squares. Four black checkers are placed at one end and three white checkers at the other, with an open space between. The solver is to move in such a way as to reverse the positions of the white men and the black men. He can move a man or jump a man, always moving forward toward the opposite corner and not removing any pieces from the board.

This type of puzzle resembles the special class of marketing problems called planning problems. The end-result is the rearrangement of the seven checkers in a new form under stated restrictions as to how they can be moved. What makes the puzzle interesting is the fact that the sequence of steps must abide by the restrictions but the solver is not told what steps to take. There is a simple principle to be followed in a successful solution, and this is usually true in most puzzles of this type. The single corner problem illustrates the power principle. At each step along the way the move which seems most natural is quickly seen to cut off all further progress. It turns out that the result in the single corner problem is accomplished mainly through jumping rather than moving. The process must obviously start with a move because in the beginning no piece is in position for a jump. After that, always make the move which contributes most directly to an alternation of black and white checkers. This is the design principle which controls the whole process. It is the design principle controlling the sequence in a reordering of the elements which makes this problem comparable to a planning problem.

It is worth setting up another example to make this point quite clear. This has been called the red cap problem and involves a set of eight black checkers and seven red ones. The black checkers are arranged in a square. The solver is told to place a red cap on seven of them, obeying stated restrictions. He caps the first checker by touching three successive checkers and putting a cap on the fourth. He continues in the same way throughout. A checker which already has a cap on it can be counted as his second or third but he cannot count it as his first. Again the moves which seem most natural are violations of the power principle. A simple design principle should control the sequence. The principle states that after the first move the starting point for each move should be taken as the end point or target for the next move.

There is a place for aesthetic principles in planning which may be a way of acknowledging that planning is still an art. However, there is a place for aesthetics in science as well. A beautiful formula often turns out to be a "good" formula. Aesthetic principles include those of relative simplicity, balance, symmetry, and dominant theme. Quite often it turns out that the attempt to force a symmetrical pattern on reality leads to trouble. A very powerful working tool of the mind is the simple dichotomy in which things are judged to fall in either one of two classes, white or black, good or bad, users who prefer red widgets and users who prefer blue widgets. The tool can be used as a quick and easy way of moving into a situation, but it should be remembered that some of the cells which are set up in this fashion may turn out to be empty. In planning it often happens that events repeat themselves but not quite in the same fashion. It is the small departure from symmetry which may turn out to be most significant.

Additional principles involved in the search for significant structure are derived from Gestalt psychology. The most important and all-prevading principle is the principle of closure. We are told that the eye tends to see forms as organized wholes and that we respond to the elements which make up a pattern only at a secondary or more analytical level. The Gestalt group has made hundreds of experiments to establish this fundamental principle concerning the nature of perception. The principle of closure is consistent with this theory of vision. It says that if we recognize a familiar form such as a circle and it is not quite complete, the eye will automatically fill in the missing part. If the gap is large we find it slightly upsetting, but we will still tend to see the figure as a circle. Closure applies to many other figures which are more or less familiar to the observer. The circle is perhaps the simplest of all geometrical figures. It is said to have been regarded as the ideal form by the ancient Greeks.

Closure applies equally to such a form as the figure 4 which is not a closed loop. The eye will still see a figure 4 if the horizontal bar is partially missing but probably not if it is missing altogether. Sometimes the eye will isolate and identify the figure 4 even when it appears in a mass of otherwise confused and meaningless scribbles. In particular, the figure 4 and other numerals will be discovered quickly if the observer is instructed to look for them. Numerals become the significant thing to look for if the solver is told that he will get a reward for finding a stated number of them in five minutes.

Returning to marketing problems, the solver is no longer looking at a display but seeing a set of factors at work in his mind's eye or using visual devices to help his imagination. The search for structure, for what seems to hang together, is now conducted at a more difficult and abstract level. The solver is looking for causal relationships, linking one factor to another. He makes judgments as to what may be the probable cause of a result and further judgments as to whether the cause could be regarded as a sufficient cause. He also takes account of obstacles which work in a counter direction in order to explain why the magnitude of the effect is just what it is and not higher or lower.

FOREGROUND AND BACKGROUND

Another basic principle of Gestalt distinguishes between foreground and background in a visual display and attempts to apply this distinction to problem situations in general. Very often when we look at a visual display, one set of elements tends to hang together to form the foreground, and another set of elements hangs together to form the background. The foreground elements are dominant but are thrown into relief in being seen against the background. The parallel in a marketing problem is between the set of elements which enter actively into the model and those which are apparently neutral and exert no material effect on the outcome. Some optical illusions are so delicately balanced that background momentarily moves into the foreground and vice versa. A problem situation can be ambiguous in much the same way. At one moment the solver guesses that one constellation of factors has produced an outcome, and at another time he is inclined toward quite a different set of factors as the underlying cause.

Sometimes the solver starts out being interested in factors which turn out to have little bearing on the outcome. These features of the problem situation are the most conspicuous and attract more attention at first than the real underlying causes. The puzzle fan is quite often misled by features which really have no bearing on the problem. In the red cap puzzle solvers often pay attention to the corners of the square as if they had some special significance. Actually the layout is nothing more than a closed loop for the purposes of this puzzle and the corners mean nothing. In searching for significant structure in a marketing problem the solver should ask himself what is significant about it. This is another way of raising the question of just how the given factor function is bringing about a result. Working backward from the final outcome is often a good way of linking up the causal sequence.

TRIAL AND ERROR

In many problem situations a considerable amount of trial and error manipulation of the variables may prove fruitful. This is true for a number of simple puzzles such as the cryptogram or the problem in long division worked out in code letters. The initial manipulation serves to limit the possibilities and to help the solver in concentrating on the possibilities which remain. Thus in the long division problem a digit in the quotient is obviously one if the partial product it produces is the same as the divisor. The first inspection and manipulation recalls Descartes' dictum of solving the easy parts first. Trial and error is a very easy method when the possibilities are quite limited. It becomes tedious and laborious if there are many possibilities.

In arranging the successive steps in a sequence to form a plan, the number of possibilities equals N factorial. Suppose there are only 3 steps in the sequence and we assume for the moment that we have no way of knowing which comes first. There are 6 possible arrangements for the symbols ABC. At this level the simplest way of choosing among them may be to try all 6. The number of possibilities rises very rapidly thereafter and soon surpasses all hope of selection through trial and error. For 4 steps in the sequence there are 24 possible arrangements, and for 6 steps there are 720. By the time the number of steps has risen to 10, the number of possible combinations already stands at 3,628,800.

Experiments were conducted at the University of Michigan[8] which threw a good deal of light on the use of trial and error in problem solving. A machine was devised which made it possible to pose the same logical problem to hundreds of subjects. This machine, known as the PSI machine, was equipped with a round dial

---

[8]"An Investigation into, and Speculation about, the Formal Nature of a Problem-Solving Process," *Behavioral Science*, Vol. 5 (1960), pp. 39–59.

on a horizontal surface. There were eight light bulbs around the circumference of the dial and one in the center. The problem was to press three buttons, one associated with each of the light bulbs on the circumference, and thereby cause the center light to light.

Lines were drawn on the face of the dial to indicate that two bulbs were logically related to each other. These lines did not indicate the nature of the relationship which could be one of three kinds. Both buttons might have to be pressed to cause a certain bulb to light up. One bulb might inhibit the action of another and prevent the designated bulb from lighting up. Again it might happen that one or the other of the buttons had to be pressed but not both.

These experiments reflected no great credit on the problem-solving prowess of those who participated. On the average there was far greater use of trial and error than the situation called for. That is to say, the average solver went well beyond what was required to familiarize himself with every relationship shown on the dial of the PSI machine. He not only tried out all of the connections but tried a number of them over and over. Only in a few cases did the solver test out each relationship systematically and then proceed directly to a solution.

The concept of selective exploration says that trial and error should not be completely random but should proceed in an order which permits some successive clarification of the problem situation. Thus, on the face of the PSI machine only two or three lights show connecting lines to the center bulb, indicating a logical relationship. Selective exploration would work backward from these partially specified relationships to try to find the right combination. The coin weighing problem mentioned earlier provides a good example of selective exploration or intelligent trial and error. Limited to three weighings the solver has to stop and think about how to use them effectively. Suppose he makes a naive move such as picking two coins out of the group of twelve. The chances are one out of six that one of these is the defective coin. If so, then it will take another weighing against a third to determine whether the defective coin is light or heavy. If neither coin was the defective coin, the solver would draw another pair until the supply was exhausted. It would take from two to seven weighings to find the solution. The average number of weighings would be four and a half as compared to the three stated in the problem. Thus, giving thought in advance to the plan of exploration can reduce substantially the amount of pure trial and error involved. Rational thought is a great economizer. It even has a variety of ways of economizing itself.

To anticipate some of the things to follow, what are called design principles for planning are largely of this character. In the area of planning it is essential to try to formulate such principles. This need becomes obvious in comparing the number 10 with 10 factorial, which is 3,628,800. As long as we are dealing with single issues at the level of problem solving, it would be possible to frame ten separate hypotheses about the elements thought to be present in the problem situation. At the planning level the parallel procedure would be clearly out of the question. With present techniques it would be very wasteful to list over three million arrangements as the alternatives calling for decision.

SYSTEMATIC CALCULATION

The great promise for problem solving in the future rests in the steady improvement in methods of systematic calculation. New ways of looking at problems emerge, such as the Markov processes and linear programming discussed in Part II. These methods may be regarded as providing very general models of the problem situation. Variables react in a still more complex way in the actual situation. Indeed it is beyond the capacity of the analyst to construct a model which will mirror reality in all of its rich detail. Usually the model builder stops far short of this goal, and in many cases he can solve the problem using only very general models.

At this point the way in which insight, trial and error, and systematic calculation work together to make a balanced operation of problem solving can be summarized. First of all, the problem situation is presented by the client or executive endeavoring not to leave out anything significant. From the first the consultant is trying to get an insight into the problem. He asks questions as the exposition proceeds and he tries to relate the factors in the situation. He pays close attention at this time since he brings a fresh viewpoint to the situation as yet uncolored by the details of the problem. If the Gestalt psychologists are right, this is his opportunity to exercise a flash of intuition which may set him on the path to a solution. He then begins to manipulate the variables in his imagination, considering briefly what would happen if one or another factor should be increased or decreased. This means mentally considering changes in the product, its pricing, its promotion, and its distribution channels. The analyst may expose himself at this stage to factual information shown in chart or tabular form. If figures are not available, he may go out into the market and observe what is going on in retail stores. He normally moves in this way from his first exposure to factual data to the formulation of an initial hypothesis.

The first hunch as to what the problem is may be a good one, but it should never be accepted by the analyst as the only hypothesis. There is an all too human tendency to be moderately vain about arriving at an answer so soon and to devote the research so-called to piling up evidence to support this answer. At the very least the analyst should consider the alternative proposition that the factor which is suspected of being the principal cause of the problem has little or no bearing on the case. The search for alternative hypotheses can be put in reasonably systematic form by means of check lists, either of general character or prepared for the special occasion. These check lists would rank the major variables in order of their presumed importance. After considering each one, a preliminary judgment would be made as to what remained to be explained after each factor was considered. There is always an easy way out of saying that the problem arose from a combination of factors. The question then is to assign some tentative weights to the several factors entering into the combination. Research can then be directed toward testing these factor weights. Several alternatives should usually be set up, making sure that they are sufficiently distinct so that the results can be conclusive as favoring one hypothesis or the other.

The third element, systematic calculation, consists of a more or less elegant analytical machine for producing answers for the problem as formulated. Sometimes this analytical program is designed simply to discriminate among the various alternative hypotheses and determine where the weight of the evidence lies. The program can be extremely simple at this point as, for example, the analysis of a sampling survey on consumer preference. The answers to questions in the survey may point to an increase in demand or a decrease in demand, to a further differentiation of products to serve the various segments of demand or a tendency toward the acceptance of a standard product as adequate. All that is involved in an evaluation of this type is choice among the several hypotheses which may mean a decision to move in one direction or another in the marketing of the product. Behind each of the alternatives there may be a model of the way the market works. This type of evaluation, therefore, is not a test of a model but involves a choice among models.

The simple elements of a marketing model would describe in graphic or mathematical terms the process of moving goods from producer to consumer. It would assume a rate of consumer response to advertising and other forms of product selling. It would also assume a rate of response by dealers and others in the marketing channels to the inducements offered by the supplier to stock and push the product. A model may go considerably further toward showing the various stages through which consumers may pass on their way to repurchase of the product. A tire consumer, for example, may go from a position of having a new car and no tire requirement to a period two or three years later when his tires are showing considerable wear, to an awareness of tire advertising, to a visit to a tire store, and finally to his reaction to the arguments offered by the tire dealer.

The analyst now has before him one or more models of the way a market works. To test a particular model to see how well it fits the market is quite a different thing from making a decision on a single issue even though each of the possible answers to the issue has a model embedded in it.

These two kinds of evaluation, which result from systematic calculation, correspond roughly to the two subjects embraced by this book. That is to say, the evaluation of a single decision issue is in the realm of problem solving while the evaluation of a model of how the system works lies mostly in the area of planning. The first stage of evaluation may not tell us very much about the models of the market which are implied by deciding an issue one way or the other. By contrast, any one model of how the system works tells us very little about other possible models.

Reference has already been made to the somewhat broader sense in which mathematical models are discussed and applied. Here the analyst might decide that the problem situation looked like a linear programming problem and proceed accordingly. By this he would mean that the essential problem appeared to be a problem of allocation of scarce resources and that the allocation was to be made within certain fixed limits. These limits might represent the productive capacities of certain pieces of equipment. Sometimes it is possible to specify limits on marketing capacity and turn this problem into a linear programming problem. The point is that the analyst has not attempted here to construct a model of the market. Instead he has considered the tools he has available and concluded that linear programming will serve in this case. If he is a skilled and creative applied mathematician, he may make some refinements in the course of this application. Essentially, however, he has used a very general model because he happened to be familiar with it, and without regard to the particular subject matter.

The use of Markov processes in marketing is an illustration of another very general model which might be applied in many other situations completely foreign to marketing. Markov models can be interpreted as the rates of switching among brands, the net effect of which may be growth for one product and decline for another. All of these models, which are quite empty in the sense that they have no implications with respect to particular content or subject matter, represent forms of systematic calculation. There is a sort of a leap here between the trial and error which is an aid in formulating hyoptheses and the form of systematic calculation adopted. In effect this leap avoids the construction of a specially prepared problem-solving mechanism by saying that a technique can be selected from among those which are ready made.

The adoption of an approach to systematic calculation can be expressed in another way. Suppose that a problem occurred over and over so that it might be worth building a special analog computer for solving it. Tide levels at ports all over the world are calculated by such an analog device located at the Coast and Geodetic Survey in Washington. To solve a unique and nonrecurring problem, the analyst might be pictured as drawing up the blue prints for an analog device and developing the equations which will control its operations. He would probably refrain from building the device, however, since he does not expect to use it again. He has carried through the thought processes required in the act of designing it. At this point he may decide to use one of these general models on the ground that it represents a close enough approximation to what is going on in the market. He may move another stage toward simplification and decide not to apply the general model as a method of calculation but simply to use the logical structure of the general model and to draw some conclusions as to the way the variables interact. Much of general economics follows this course in drawing conclusions about the nature of economic systems without using quantitative data at all. One purpose of this book is to equip the student with enough knowledge of the general models so that he can judge when they apply and when they do not apply.

The prognosis for business is that such massive calculation will generally be needed in marketing that computers will be required for any but the simplest approach to systematic calculation. More and more companies will build models of their markets as they conceive them and will make test runs showing the expected outputs in relation to specified inputs. The computer comes into play in three major areas so far as marketing problems are concerned. At the first level marketing executives have data needs which cannot always be satisfied by other means. They need more data, or they need them faster. At the second level greater analytical power is needed. The data, it may be assumed, are available, but new methods for systematic calculation are required. Finally, marketing executives and analysts require prediction. The relevant markets are in the future, and computers are required to forecast how the markets will develop under alternative assumptions as to marketing plans.

MANAGEMENT UNDER PLANNING AND PROBLEM SOLVING

In Chapter 2 it was stated that there is a basic similarity between the view of management as a negotiative process and management through planning and problem solving. It is now in order to amplify this statement somewhat further. The negotiative process in business suggests continuous interaction between line executives. The planning and problem-solving approach suggests a somewhat different emphasis, with the primary interaction taking place between the chief executive and a staff group. Actually both views are true and can be readily reconciled.

Staff analysts and planners should regard themselves as working for both the chief executive and for executives at lower levels. They should avoid being relegated to the sidelines as may occur if they appear to be working for the chief executive alone. The strategy embodied in a plan originates with the top marketing executive or has the benefit of his approval. The details embodying the strategy come from the planner or from executives at subordinate levels. The planner is in the stream of negotiation because he is working toward a plan that will be fully acceptable, both in strategy and tactics. There is a continuous process from the choice of strategy to the outlines of a plan to the fully deveolped plan, the adoption of the plan, and finally its installation. By installation is meant the process of getting the plan fully understood and implemented with the knowledge that manpower is available and has been fully instructed in the part that it is to play.

Operating within the planning and problem-solving framework means extending the predicted course of the business as far into the future as seems prudent, but being constantly alert to changing markets and competitive conditions as they affect continuous adjustment under the plan.

A plan is an agreement between the top executive and his principal subordinates. As such it should have the force of a contract over its term. It should not be revised except by mutual consent, either as to the stated target or the expenditure deemed necessary to meet the target. Some flexibility may be permitted as to the means of accomplishing objectives but even the means tend to become frozen in the short run. Advertising contracts have been placed and manpower has been recruited and assigned. The negotiation of agreements which are regarded as binding in both directions is implemented through the planning approach.

A plan may also be regarded as the principal means of coordinating group effort. The chief executive has accepted the assurances of his subordinates that certain goals can be reached and has provided the budget which they believe to be essential for that purpose. It is up to the members of the division or other organizational unit to deliver against the promise stated in the plan. Ideally this means coordination to the point of minimizing waste and lost motion under the assumption that the whole division will receive commendation for making its target. Morale should be high when everyone is working toward a well-understood short-term objective and can note progress made month by month.

Working within the framework of a plan should mean that fewer unexpected problems arise as the year proceeds. A minor disturbance occurring while the plan is in force is no longer a problem if the reaction of consumers or the trade has been discounted in advance. Too often in the past no attempt has been made to foresee or measure adverse reactions, and, as a result, they may cause a state of temporary alarm. The exercise of foresight is not infallible, of course, and adverse reactions which greatly exceed expectations can constitute a problem for study and adjustment. Sometimes there is an unexplained gap between budget figures and those actually realized. To deal with these within the framework of a plan means to make a study of the apparent causes and then take remedial action to bring the figures back into line.

To operate without a plan means to operate without setting up standards of performance in advance. The planless organization does not really know whether it is doing well or poorly. Living only from day to day, it does not know except very informally what it will be doing the day after tomorrow. The organization that looks ahead decides that it can reasonably aspire to certain goals. If results do not measure up at the end of the period, the basis exists for asking questions. These can be very specific questions as to just where mistakes were made and how to improve performance in the future.

The extent to which planning is carried varies considerably even among organizations which have adopted planning as a way of life. In some cases the emphasis is primarily on budgeting rather than on the schedule of activities by which it is proposed to meet the budget figures. In some cases there are elaborate procedures for capital budgeting but with relative neglect of the detailing of marketing programs. Some companies take a strong policy stance and generally abide by these policies. Yet if marketing programs are not made precise and specific, policies largely remain a negative restraint without the full backing of positive marketing activity.

As staff planning becomes better established, companies will do a better job of organizing for planning. They will also understand how to lay out the planning year so that planning becomes a continuous full-time activity. It has been said in the past that a position as planning director should be reserved for those who wish to live dangerously. Actually there is no more basis for this comment than if it were leveled at the now well-established function of marketing research.

One difficulty in talking about planning is the great variety of planning tasks. Every enterprise engages in planning at one or more levels, and sometimes planning is considerably further advanced in other aspects of the business than it is in marketing. It has been said before that one justification of market planning is to complete the circle. If it becomes possible to plan the marketing side of the business with any degree of precision, then the whole enterprise can be managed in a more systematic and scientific fashion.

Finally, the several tasks of planning may be enumerated to conclude this chapter, although they will be taken up again in Part III. The first thing to be planned is marketing programs or campaigns. In a sense these are the principal outputs of a marketing organization. Secondly, marketing facilities are planned or replanned from time to time. This includes retail stores and warehouses. In a sense the sales force stationed at strategic points across the country with territorial assignments is a marketing facility. At this point the concept of facility merges into the concept of organization as the structure of supervision to assure sales performance. Marketing organization is periodically planned or replanned. Marketing organization is a more dynamic factor than marketing facilities. In the case of facilities, they inevitably become outdated and must be enlarged. In the case of organization, change within the structure is continuous so that it begins to be outmoded from the day that a reorganization is completed. Finally there is the planning or replanning of a whole marketing system. This is a major task, but it must be undertaken from time to time as marketing technology evolves. In particular, there should be a periodic review in many large organizations to be sure they are taking advantage of economies of scale in the marketing area.

APPENDIX

Two puzzles were used in the text of the chapter to provide primitive models for evaluation and design as aspects of problem solving. It will be remembered that evaluation was regarded as the act of picking one out of a set of possibilities. Design, on the other hand, consists of arranging and rearranging elements in a set in accordance with specific criteria. The twelve coin problem provides a model for evaluation and the single corner problem for design.

The solutions are included here to make a further point with respect to the value of a formal notation, both in working out a problem which has inherent logical complexity and in recording and communicating the solution to others.

The Twelve Coin Problem

In a collection of 12 apparently identical coins it is known that one is defective but it is not known whether it is light $(-)$ or heavy $(+)$. With just three weighings on a balance scale, find the defective coin and tell whether it is light or heavy. There are 24 possible answers (2×12). Designate the coins by letters and group them as follows:

$$x \qquad\qquad y \qquad\qquad z$$
$$(a\ b\ c\ d) \qquad (e\ f\ g\ h) \qquad i\ j\ k\ l$$

The parentheses around the first two groups indicate that they are to be weighed against each other.

1st Weighing—x against y

$x > y$—the defective coin is $a+, b+, c+, d+, e-, f-, g-, h-$ (8 possibilities)

$x < y$—the defective coin is $a-, b-, c-, d-, e+, f+, g+, h+$ (8 possibilities)

$x = y$—the defective coin is $i+, i-, j+, j-, k+, k-, l+, l-$ (8 possibilities)

2nd Weighing (if $x > y$ on first weighing)

	x $(a\ e\ f)$	y $(g\ h\ i)$	
$x > y$	$a+, g-, h-$	*3rd weighing*	$(g)\ (h)$
$x < y$	$e-, f-$		$(e)\ (f)$
$x = y$	$b+, c+, d+$		$(b)\ (c)$

Results of third weighing

		$x > y$	$x < y$	$x = y$
(g)	(h)	$h-$	$g-$	$a+$
(e)	(f)	$f-$	$e-$	
(b)	(c)	$b+$	$c+$	$d+$

2nd Weighing (If $x < y$ on first weighing)

	x	y	
	$(a\ e\ f)$	$(g\ h\ i)$	
$x > y$	$e+, f+$	$3rd\ weighing$	$(e)\ (f)$
$x < y$	$a-, g+, h+$		$(g)\ (h)$
$x = y$	$b-, c-, d-$		$(b)\ (c)$

Results of third weighing

	$x > y$	$x < y$	$x = y$
$(e)\ (f)$	$e+$	$f+$	
$(g)\ (h)$	$g+$	$h+$	$a-$
$(b)\ (c)$	$b-$	$c-$	$d-$

2nd Weighing (if $x = y$ on first weighing)

	x	y	
	$(h\ i)$	$(j\ k)$	
$x > y$	$i+, j-, k-$	$3rd\ weighing$	$(j)\ (k)$
$x < y$	$i-, j+, k+$		$(j)\ (k)$
$x = y$	$l-, l+$		$(h)\ (l)$

Results of third weighing

If 2nd Weighing is		$x > y$	$x < y$	$x = y$
$(x > y)$	$(j)\ (k)$	$k-$	$j-$	$i+$
$(x < y)$	$(j)\ (k)$	$j+$	$k+$	$i-$
$(x = y)$	$(h)\ (l)$	$l-$	$l+$	

The Single Corner Problem

Seven checkers are arranged on a checkerboard along the single corner row in the manner shown in Chart I. The problem is to transfer the four black checkers to the lower left hand corner and the three white checkers to the upper right hand corner, as shown in Chart II. This is to be done by moving and jumping as in a checker game. A checker is *not* removed from the board after it is jumped. It is not necessary for black and white to take turns as in checkers. It is necessary, however, for black to advance steadily toward its position in the lower left hand corner without retreats and for white to advance steadily in the other direction.

The accompanying exhibits display the initial position; the final position; a standard checker notation; and the solution stated in this notation.

CHART I
INITIAL POSITION

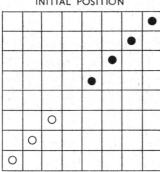

CHART II
FINAL POSITION

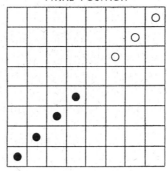

NOTATION

	1		2		3		4
5		6		7		8	
	9		10		11		12
13		14		15		16	
	17		18		19		20
21		22		23		24	
	25		26		27		28
29		30		31		32	

SOLUTION

15 – 18	18 – 25
22 – 15	11 – 18
25 – 22	4 – 11
18 – 25	8 – 4
11 – 18	15 – 8
8 – 11	22 – 15
15 – 8	18 – 22
22 – 15	11 – 18
29 – 22	15 – 11
25 – 29	

Selected References

Bowman, Mary Jean (ed.). *Expectations, Uncertainty and Business Behavior.* New York: Social Science Research Council, 1958.
    Problem solving as reduction of uncertainty with respect to the expectation of the firm.

Polya, G. *How to Solve It.* Princeton, N. J.: Princeton University Press, 1948.
    A noted mathematician discusses some general rules for problem solving which have application beyond the range of mathematics.

Simon, H. A. *The New Science of Management Decision.* New York: Harper & Bros., 1960.
    A discussion of decision making and problem solving from one of the leaders in the development of heuristic methods to provide a systematic problem-solving procedure.

Spencer, Milton H. and Siegelman, Louis. *Managerial Economics: Decision Making and Forward Planning.* Rev. ed. Homewood, Ill.: Richard D. Irwin, 1964.
    Decision problems and the special problems of planning are treated in terms of creating conceptual structures which lend themselves readily to quantification.

Problems

1. What are the principal routes of growth available to the business firm?

2. Describe some of the techniques which have been applied in marketing efficiency studies.

3. List the steps in the problem-solving process as discussed by Descartes.

4. Discuss the search for significant structure as an aspect of problem solving.

5. What are the characteristic differences between problem solving and planning as illustrated by the two types of puzzles?

Part II

EVALUATION PROBLEMS

In Part II of this book the process of plans evaluation is considered. The evaluation of marketing plans involves choice among alternative courses of action and, hence, is included in the general domain of decision making. It is concerned with both (*a*) techniques for choosing among alternative plans and (*b*) the major functional areas of marketing planning in which these procedures may be used.

In recent years several analytical techniques have emerged from the fields of applied mathematics, statistics, management science, economics, and other disciplines, for formally dealing with decision making. To show the contribution of these procedures to marketing problems, the point of view of how decisions *ought* to be made is adopted in this section. In stressing a normative approach it must be borne in mind that the word *ought* reflects what the planner knows (or thinks he knows) how to do at present. As progress in decision theory continues, interpretation of how decisions should be made will likewise change.

The foundations of decision theory and associated techniques go well beyond the level of mathematical sophistication which is assumed here. The approach used here will emphasize the intuitive aspects of decision theory rather than its mathematical elegance. The pragmatic features of the theory in terms of illustrative problems will be stressed. Many of the examples used will be drawn from real business situations, suitably modified, and condensed for expository purposes. A critical review of the limitations as well as the advantages of decision techniques accompanies the discussion.

So much for point of view. In terms of what is to be described in Part II, a dual approach will be employed, covering both methodological considerations and the major functional areas in marketing planning in which these techniques can be—and, in some cases, have been—used.

Chapters 4, 5, and 6, are primarily methodological and set the stage for application of the techniques. In these three chapters the major concepts and tools used in later chapters of Part II are developed. More specifically, the nature of model building, alternative theories of decision making, Bayesian decision theory (possibly the most useful of these techniques), and value theory are discussed. The role of sensitivity analysis and computer simulation in augmenting the operability of decision theory is also discussed.

In the remaining chapters of Part II, decision theory and some other selected techniques from the management sciences are applied to a variety of problems arising in the major decision areas of marketing. To illustrate, Markov processes and their use in predicting shifts in brand share are introduced in Chapter 7. The application of multiple-factor break-even analysis in evaluating the impact of alternative marketing efforts is also covered in that chapter. In Chapters 8 and 9 Bayesian decision theory is applied to problems arising in the areas of new product development and pricing. The reader is also introduced to some applications of the marginal analysis, capital budgeting, and sequential decision making as they relate to the concept of the planning horizon.

Chapter 10 discusses the use of allocation models (the calculus, dynamic programming), decision theory, and experimentation in measuring the effectiveness of advertising while Chapter 11 discusses decision making and mathematical programming in the context of distribution channels. Finally, in Chapter 12 a methodological point of view is again adopted and the use of decision theory in the control of marketing programs discussed. Such concepts as statistical stability and the cost of control are covered.

In essence, then, Part II is first structured along methodological lines, in Chapters 4, 5, and 6. Chapter 7 provides a bridge between methodological and substantive topics. Chapters 8, 9, 10, and 11 focus on substantive applications of the various techniques, and Chapter 12 comes back to methodological issues. Technical appendices are included to discuss some of the underlying mathematics. They may be treated as optional sections for the reader whose mathematical background or interest is not sufficient to warrant his review of somewhat more technical areas.

It is also relevant to point out the limited nature—both intensive and extensive—of the coverage in this book of formal decision-making techniques. First, it does not delve deeply into any of the techniques which are discussed. This book is directed to marketing planning and problem solving, not management science per se. Second, such limited coverage precludes description of many interesting techniques, such as waiting line theory, production control theory, replacement analysis, symbolic logic, and so forth, whose pertinence to marketing planning is less direct than the techniques selected for inclusion. In order to remedy this situation, at least partially, a set of selected references to some of the management science literature is appended at the end of each chapter in Part II for the reader whose interest and background provides the spur and capacity for more extensive reading in this area.

Finally, our espousal of some of the formal techniques described in this part of the book is not without an accompanying prudence. Decision theory and related management science techniques provide a provocative and useful subject for the planner to study. Like any tool, these procedures can be abused as well as used. The reader who wishes to employ them in his work will be well advised to study the procedures carefully from the standpoint of both relevance and operability to his particular problem assignments.

Chapter 4

UNCERTAINTY AND DECISION MAKING
IN MARKET PLANNING

∽ᵒ∽

This chapter is concerned with the role which uncertainty plays in market planning and the major types of formal procedures which have been developed to aid the planner in making rational choices under conditions of uncertainty. In line with the central theme of this book, the activity of planning can be viewed as designing and evaluating purposeful behavior sequences for the firm. These activities include (a) problem recognition, (b) the developmental and search activity associated with the design of alternative plans, (c) plans evaluation or choice among alternative plans, and (d) implementation and control of the selected plan. The concern in this part of the book is largely with the evaluation stage.

First, the characteristics of marketing planning problems will be outlined. Next, the model-building process, both in general and more specifically as it relates to problem situations, is discussed. Finally, the role of formal analysis in decision making is introduced by means of a discussion of the main types of procedures which have been proposed for dealing with decision making under uncertainty. Amplification of one of these approaches—Bayesian decision theory—is considered in the following chapter.

CHARACTERISTICS OF THE MARKETING ENVIRONMENT

The design and evaluation of marketing plans obviously arises out of problems. It is relevant, then, to consider the particular characteristics of marketing problems which dictate, to a large extent, the nature of the techniques required in solution. It is recognized that some of these characteristics are shared by problems arising in the areas of production, research, and finance, and that differences are largely a matter of degree. However, as the marketing executive knows only too well, several characteristics of the marketing environment frequently militate against the use of a more highly structured and analytical approach which has frequently been found useful in dealing, for example, with many types of production and financial problems.

These (interrelated) features are (*a*) high degree of uncertainty involved in marketing problems, (*b*) complexity of structure, (*c*) lack of containment (that is, emphasis on the firm's relationship to the outside world of customers and competitors) coupled with the role which cooperation and conflict play in this broadened sphere, (*d*) emphasis on change and the time dimension, and (*e*) paucity of relevant information for reducing uncertainty. Each of these characteristics wil be discussed briefly, in turn.

Unlike the characteristics of many production line, quality control, and inventory problems where reasonably stable processes exist over the short run, the problem of making accurate and reliable forecasts in the marketing sphere is almost bewildering in its complexity. *Uncertainty of outcomes,* given alternative marketing actions, is a key feature. This uncertainty arises from the fact that the marketing executive is usually dealing with unique situations, for example, changing a packaging design or launching a new type of promotional campaign. Unlike the quality control engineer who frequently can utilize the past history of some production process to make, at least, probability estimates concerning the occurrence of some variable of interest, the marketing executive must usually resort to very imprecise analogues of the events in question. The variability of possible events associated with marketing actions is due, in part, to the decision maker's relative lack of control over outcomes. For example, the quality control analyst, when making machine adjustments in order to achieve a certain average quality level, can reasonably assume that the machine will not counter attack. Contrast this situation to the uncertainty surrounding the introduction of a new package design where the firm's sales can be affected not only by the attributes of the design itself but by the retaliatory actions of competitors as well.

Closely related to the high degree of uncertainty associated with the outcomes of marketing decisions is the *complexity* of structure noted in these problems. In inventory control problems, it is apparent that an explicit structure can be logically developed by balancing the costs of carrying inventory (costs which will increase with increases in the average inventory level carried) against the costs of procurement (costs which, for a given sales level, will decrease with increases in the average level carried). In contrast, the functional relationships in marketing problems quite frequently defy precise mathematical expression. Price increases in some products at some stage in their life cycles can lead to increases in sales; in other stages, sales decreases will probably result, or, given similar price increases by competitors and a market with no close product substitutes, sales might not appreciably change at all.

As would be surmised, the fact that marketing problems usually involve the firm's relationship to its external environment contributes to the difficulty of predicting outcomes, adds to the problem of choice among alternative actions, and leads to difficulty in plans control once a choice is made and the plan is implemented. Consider a marketing manager faced with a choice between two promotional campaigns. Campaign A might lead to higher sales than campaign B if competitors do not retaliate. A competitor's retaliation may, however, be costly for him (the competitor) to implement. The marketing manager is thus forced to try to evaluate the net impact of each course of action on a variety of goals, including the value attached to a weakening of a competitor's position even if his own firm's short-run sales may be weakened.

Moreover, in an oligopolistic market setting, where each firm must consider the actions of rival firms, a given firm's courses of action have to be considered in the light of their impact on both total industry sales and the firm's share of the market. In terms of the example above, a marketing manager might wish to pursue an alternative which involves a high chance of retaliation if total industry sales are stimulated thereby, even if no change in the firm's share of the total were effected.

The relationship of the firm to its outside environment of customers, customers' customers, competitors, and regulatory bodies, that is, the problem's *lack of containment*, may evoke a role of both cooperation and conflict among firms. In some instances tacit acceptance of a price set by an industry leader is a reflection of the need for cooperation. Lack of cooperation may result in a series of price reductions which are injurious to all firms. In other instances, some firms may exercise more daring options if they feel that the capabilities and/or intentions of competitive retaliation present little danger. Emphasis on the tactics of nonprice competition, for example, product differentiation, promotion, and customer service, may frequently be interpreted as the pursuance of a conflict role which carries less risk of "snowballing" to the detriment of all firms concerned than does overt price competition.

The marketing manager also lives in a world of *change* and the associated influence of the time dimension on the formulation, choice, and execution of his plans. In the marketing of new products, for example, a primary question could involve the relative speed with which one course of action, such as bypassing market pretests, might result in earlier market penetration than a slower, but perhaps less risky, course of action involving advance testing of the product's appeal to prospective customers. Costs of decision delay are frequently important in the marketing area and reflect the characteristics of a race between the firm and its competitors.

The changing nature of the firm's marketing environment is also reflected in the *paucity of relevant information* on which the firm can base decisions. This may sound strange in view of most companies' increasing use of marketing research and similar information-gathering activities, but the fact remains that survey findings are frequently subject to systematic error (statistical bias) as well as sampling error. The time interval between, say, market pretesting and commercial introduction of a new product may be fraught with changing conditions as manifested by competitors' activities, changes in consumer interest, and changes in the firm's courses of action as well. The marketing manager must take these (and other) factors into account as he evaluates the results of marketing research activity. Data rarely "speak for themselves" in a clear, unambiguous voice. Nor should the manager necessarily strive to attain minimal uncertainty with respect to the outcomes of marketing plans. Uncertainty reduction is seldom, if ever, without cost.

THE ROLE OF MODELS IN MARKETING PROBLEM SOLVING

The word model has several notations in ordinary discourse. Sometimes the word is used to refer to a replica of an object—a model airplane or boat. In this case the model captures on a reduced scale, some, but not all, of the relevant characteristics of the real thing. In other cases the word is used to refer to an ideal—a model city or model mother. In this instance the real thing captures some, but not all, of the characteristics of our idealization. In other contexts the word may be used to signify a demonstration—to model a dress or new suit of clothes. In this case a characteristic purpose of a model—to display the properties of an object—is emphasized.

Models of marketing situations are all these things and more. In every real marketing problem the possible action–event sequences are myriad. A marketing manager who attempted to study the consequences of all possible levels of his firm's advertising would soon throw up his hands at the enormity of the task. The word "model" has been frequently used to characterize a simplified representation of reality. That is, the model builder attempts to abstract the salient elements of a complex situation with a representation of the real world which is simple enough to be comprehended and manipulated yet realistic enough to mirror the *essentials* of a situation. The specific conceptual model developed will reflect the purposes of the model builder; that is, more than one model exists for any given real-world situation.

While explicit models will be stressed in this book, it is recognized that the "representations" of businessmen, while frequently not explicated, are no less a model for their being implicit in the businessman's decision. For example, business economists frequently "explain" the rationale underlying their forecasts of next year's sales by making a list of "favorable" and "unfavorable" factors in a credit and debit manner not unlike the accountant would use. The economist may then predict a ten percent increase in his company's sales and assert that the favorable factors underlying this increase are increased personal disposable income, government spending, and the introduction of a new product, and that the unfavorable factors are an expected sales decrease on older products, an anticipated competitor's advertising campaign, and so forth. But it usually is not at all clear how the economist deduced his forecast from the factor listing. Are some factors weighted more than others? Are all factors relevant to the conclusion? Is the effect of each factor additive?

In other words, the economist's model in this case is still largely implicit. It is questionable whether his deduction is reproducible and how his deduction would change if the level of some factor(s) changed or if factors were added to or subtracted from his original list.

In this book an argument will be made for the use of more *explicit* models. Not that explicit models are necessarily better than implicit models or are always worth the cost of construction. This preference for explicit models is more pragmatic; these are models which can be more easily communicated and, hence, subject to interpersonal testing and (perhaps) control.

Models can be classified on several bases in terms of structural and/or functional properties. Models may be static or time-dependent, deterministic or probabilistic, quantitative or qualitative, particular or general, descriptive or normative, explanatory or predictive, and so on. In this brief introduction to the subject, interest will be focused on a proper subset of models—*symbolic* models of problem situations. The purpose for stressing the symbolic model, or equation, is that symbolic models are generally easier to manipulate and provide a wider range of application to prediction and control. For example, the formula, which relates the area of a circle

$$A = \pi\, r^{2}$$

to its radius, can be used to predict the area of *any* circle, given its radius. On the other hand, a lot plan for a particular property in suburban Philadelphia, while useful to the owner of the property, would find little applicability to a home owner in Moline.

PROBLEM SITUATION MODELS

A special class of models with which much of this book will be concerned consists of problem situation models. The evaluation of marketing plans involves choosing a plan from among alternatives under conditions of uncertainty. The various theories of making choices under uncertainty can all be related to the following general model of a problem situation:

$$V = f\,(A_i,\, S_j)$$

where

V = a measure of the value to the decision maker of the action which is chosen

A_i = the factors which are subject to some control by the decision maker, that is, alternative courses of action

S_j = the factors which affect the outcomes and hence, the decision maker's value but which are not under the control of the decision maker

$f(\cdot)$ = the functional relationship between the factors, $A_i,\, S_j$ and the dependent variable V

Choices available to the decision maker may, of course, be discrete, for example, a choice among several labels which could be used to identify a new product. In this case the model would consist of a set of equations, one for each option, that expresses the value to the decision maker as a function of each particular course of action and the uncontrollable factors. This particular form of the problem model will be used quite frequently in later discsusions.

The above model arises, in very general form, from a consideration of what a problem is. Since both decisions and models of problems obviously arise out of problems themselves, the principal components of a problem, marketing or otherwise, can be summarized.

A problem consists of

1. A *decision maker*. This is the person who presumably has the problem and will make the final choice. For expository purposes it will usually be assumed that the decision maker is a single entity, although this simplification is hardly deemed realistic.

2. A *problem context*. Problems frequently arise in an environmental context of competitors, customers, governmental bodies, and so forth, and accordingly, must be solved subject to the influence of factors outside the decision maker's control. In terms of the problem model these variables represent the S_j's and will frequently be referred to as "states of nature".

3. A set of at least two *courses of action*. Another necessary condition for the existence of a problem is that more than one distinct option must be available for choice. These options are the A_i's of the problem model and may include, of course, the option of maintaining *status quo*, that is, the currently pursued course of action.

4. An *outcome-value* relationship. Given the implementation of particular courses of action, it is assumed that the decision maker can determine the functional relationship between the value of each choice and the combination of A_i's and S_j's which lead to the value.

5. A *state of doubt*. In order to have a problem, some question must exist in the mind of the decision maker as to which course of action is "best."

CRITERION OF CHOICE MODELS

Choosing the best option, however, may well involve a second model, namely, a *criterion of choice* model. This model is particularly germane when the decision maker is faced with choices under uncertainty, unfortunately the usual case in dealing with marketing problems. The relationship of choice models with problem models can be tied in by means of the following simple illustration.

Suppose a marketing manager is faced with the problem of changing over to a new package design or retaining the old design for a particular product in his line. Heroically assume that all of the relevant information can be summarized in Table 4–1.

Table 4–1.

PACKAGE DESIGN PROBLEM

Courses of Action	S_1: New Design Is Superior to Old	S_2: New Design Is Not Superior to Old
A_1: Adopt new.	$V_{11} = f(A_1, S_1) = 10$	$V_{12} = f(A_1, S_2) = -5$
A_2: Keep old.	$V_{21} = f(A_2, S_1) = -1$	$V_{22} = f(A_2, S_2) = 2$

The reader will observe that Table 4–1 illustrates application of the problem model but one is still faced with a criterion model for choosing between acts A_1 and A_2. The study of choice criteria is in the province of *decision theory,* the focal point of interest for the remainder of this chapter and the succeeding chapter as well. Decision problems can be partitioned into three classes,—choices under (*a*) certainty (*b*) risk and (*c*) uncertainty.

Decisions under certainty involve the simplest procedure of choice. Suppose that the decision maker *knew* that state of nature S_1 was bound to occur. In value units, taking act A_1 leads to 10 units while A_2 results in -1 unit. The decision maker would, of course, select A_1. Decisions under certainty may involve extreme difficulty in determining (*a*) the functional relationship linking the decision maker's value index with the A_i and S_j factors, (*b*) the relevant variables to be included, and (*c*) the proper values of the variables included. Once formulated, however, the *choice* criterion is simple —merely choose that course of action which leads to the largest value index, V.

Decisions under risk assume that the decision maker knows the true probabilities attached to the occurrence of each state of nature. To illustrate, suppose the decision maker *knew* that a 60-40 chance existed for the occurrence of S_1 and S_2. (The philosophical question of when, if ever, the *true* probabilities of actual problem events are really known will not be examined.) The prevailing criterion for choice in this situation is to choose that act which maximizes expected value, a weighted average of conditional payoffs. In symbols, the decision maker would choose

$$\underset{A_i}{\text{Max}} \left[\sum_j P_j \, V \, (A_i, S_j) \right]$$

In terms of the problem, act A_1 would be chosen since

$$0.6 \, (10) + 0.4 \, (-5) = 4.0,$$

which is greater than

$$0.6 \, (-1) + 0.4 \, (2) = 0.2,$$

the expected payoff associated with A_2. Notice that decisions under certainty are a special case of decisions under risk in which the probability is unity under one state of nature and zero for all the rest.

Decisions under uncertainty constitute the most important class of real problem situations and lead to the most difficult task of specifying criteria of choice. In problems under uncertainty the decision maker is not assumed to know the true probabilities underlying the occurrence of each state of nature. In some formulations of decisions under uncertainty, it is assumed that the assignment of any probabilities is not even meaningful. Many of the problems of the market planner would seem to fit the category of decisions under uncertainty, and, indeed, it is to this third category that the remainder of this chapter is devoted. The objective will be to discuss the various criteria of rationality which have been proposed and to offer supporting arguments for the particular criterion which appears to be most fruitful for the market planner.

THE MAXIMIN CRITERION

The maximin criterion was first formulated by Abraham Wald. This criterion of rationality assumes that the decision maker's ignorance about the probabilities attached to alternative states of nature is of a type in which the assignment of probabilities is meaningless. Instead, proponents of this criterion suggest that the decision maker focus his attention on the *worst* possible state of nature for each course of action. He should then choose that act for which the minimum payoff is maximum; that is, he should choose that act which maximizes his minimum payoff.

Application of this criterion to the preceding package design problem is illustrated in Table 4–2.

Table 4–2

APPLICATION OF MAXIMIM CRITERION—PACKAGE DESIGN PROBLEM

| Courses of Action | New vs. Old Design | | Minimum Payoff |
	S_1: New Design Superior to Old	S_2: New Design Not Superior to Old	
A_1: Adopt new.........	10	-5	-5
A_2: Keep old..........	-1	2	-1 (Max)

Notice that the worst payoff under act A_1 is -5 units (associated with S_2) while the worst payoff under act A_2 is only -1 unit (associated with S_1). According to the maximin criterion the decision maker should choose

$$\underset{A_i}{\text{Max}} \quad \underset{S_j}{\text{Min}} \quad \left[V(A_i, S_j) \right]$$

That is, he should choose the act leading to the maximum of the minimum payoffs.

This criterion is so pessimistic as to neglect all of the decision maker's information about any other state of nature associated with a particular course of action. For example, if $V(A_1, S_1)$ were 1,000 instead of 10 units and $V (A_1, S_2)$ were -1.1 instead of -5 units, the decision maker would still choose A_2. Critics of this criterion of rationality would insist that to use this procedure one would have to assume that nature is a conscious and calculating adversary, a rather odd interpretation of the natural world, at the very least.

MINIMAX REGRET

The minimax regret criterion, formulated by L. J. Savage,[1] is related to the maximin criterion. Minimax regret also assumes that the assignment of probabilities over states of nature is not meaningful when dealing with problems under uncertainty. But, minimax regret takes the view of hindsight. Suppose each possible state of nature did occur. Then, under each possible state of nature the act which would have produced the largest payoff could be determined. Arbitrarily, call this payoff zero. If the decision maker then took some course of action *other* than the best, the criterion assumes that a "regret," equal to the difference between the best payoff and each inferior payoff, would be suffered. The decision maker should list the set of maximum regrets under each act and then select the act carrying the least regret of the set of maximum regrets. Table 4–3 shows the regret matrix derived from our package design problem.

Table 4–3

APPLICATION OF MINIMAX REGRET CRITERION—PACKAGE DESIGN PROBLEM

	New *vs.* Old Design		
Courses of Action	S_1: New Design Superior to Old	S_2: New Design Not Superior to Old	Maximum Regret
A_1: Adopt new.........	0	7	7 (Min)
A_2: Keep old..........	11	0	11

Table 4–3 lists the various regrets derived from the original data of Table 4–2. For example, if S_1 actually occurred, it is clear that act A_1 would have led to the highest payoff of 10 value units. If this entry is replaced by 0 in the $V (A_1, S_1)$ cell and then the -1 payoff entry, noted in the $V (A_2, S_1)$ cell of Table 4–2, is subtracted, there are 11 "regret" units, as shown in Table 4–3. Similar calculations apply to S_2, where, of course, A_2 is the higher payoff act under this state of nature.

---

[1] L. J. Savage, "The Theory of Statistical Decision," *Journal of the American Statistical Association*, No. 46, 1951, pp. 55–67.

In symbols this operation can be expressed as

$$\underset{A_i}{\text{Min}} \quad \underset{S_j}{\text{Max}} \quad \left[V\ (A_i^*,\ S_j)\ -\ V\ (A_i,\ S_j) \right]$$

Where A_i^* represents the highest payoff in original value units under each specific state of nature. Notice that in this case, application of minimax regret would result in the selection of act A_1, a reversal of the choice made under the maximin payoff principle. As can be noted, the original payoff of 10 units in the (A_1, S_1) cell plays a prominent role in the derived figure of cell (A_2, S_1) in the regret matrix of Table 4–3.

Like the maximin payoff criterion, the minimax regret rule also implies a malevolent nature, but now in terms of the regret matrix. This criterion also assumes a conservative decision maker.

THE LAPLACE CRITERION

The two preceding criteria of choice assumed that under complete ignorance it is meaningless to consider the assignment of probabilities over the states of nature admitted as possible events. The Laplace criterion, however, does employ probabilities but of a rather special sort. The Laplace criterion is based on the so-called *principle of insufficient reason* which states that if there is no reason leading one to think that one event from a partition (a mutually exclusive and collectively exhaustive set) of possible events is more likely to occur than another, then the events are to be treated as equally likely to occur. Application of this criterion is shown in Table 4–4.

Table 4–4

APPLICATION OF THE LAPLACE CRITERION—PACKAGE DESIGN PROBLEM

		New vs. Old Design			
Courses of Action	$P\ (S_1)$	S_1: New Design Superior to Old	$P\ (S_2)$	S_2: New Design Not Superior to Old	Expected Value
A_1: Adopt new...	0.5	10	0.5	−5	2.5 (Max)
A_2: Keep old.....	0.5	−1	0.5	2	0.5

As noted in Table 4–4, an equiprobable assignment over the states of nature, S_1 and S_2, would involve assigning the probability, $P = 0.5$, to each event. The expected value of 2.5 value units under act A_1 is then found by taking a weighted average $[2.5 = 0.5\ (10) + 0.5\ (-5)]$ of the value units assigned to each state of nature;

similar remarks pertain to act A_2. The course of action leading to the highest expected value is chosen under this criterion. In symbols,

$$\underset{A_i}{\text{Max}} \left[\underset{j}{\Sigma} P_j \, V \, (A_i, \, S_j) \right]$$

where $P_1 = P_2$, etc., and $\underset{j}{\Sigma} P_j = 1$

One of the problems which occur in attempting to use the Laplace criterion is that *many* possible listings of states of nature arise in real problems which can lead to different expected values if the equiprobable measures is assigned indiscriminantly. For example, the decision maker might change the S_1 *versus* S_2 assignment of our package design illustration to something like the following: S_1—new design is "highly superior to old"; S_2—new design is "moderately superior to old"; S_3—new design is "slightly superior to old"; S_4—new design is "not superior to old". If the decision maker blithely assigned an equiprobable measure over these four states of nature, the state "new design is not superior to old" would be assigned a weight of only 0.25 in contrast to the 0.5 assignment under the original partition of states of nature. Other criticisms of the Laplace criterion will be covered in a later section of this chapter.

PARTIAL IGNORANCE—THE BAYESIAN APPROACH

In all three preceding criteria—maximin payoff, minimax regret, and Laplace—"complete" ignorance about the true state of nature was assumed. In real problem situations, however, the decision maker usually possesses *some* information about states of nature. Indeed, the fact that states of nature are admitted to the problem implies that the decision maker has assigned at least a nonzero probability to their occurrence.

The case of partial ignorance (which is usually still classified under the "uncertainty" category) introduces the notion of personalistic probability, a concept which reflects the contributions of B. de Finetti, L. J. Savage, R. Schlaifer, H. Raiffa, and others. The use of prior probability distributions (personalistic, objective, or combinations of so-called objective and personalistic) is known as the Bayesian approach to decisions under uncertainty. The Bayesian approach also uses the rationality criterion of expected value which has already been noted with respect to decision making under risk and application of the Laplace criterion. The distinguishing feature among these three concepts concerns the nature of what is assumed about the *probability distributions,* not the criterion itself.

To illustrate the Bayesian approach, suppose that the decision

maker, faced with the problem of whether to change his package
design, believed, on the basis of past experience with perhaps
broadly analogous situations, that the chances favoring the occurrence of S_1 substantially exceeded the probability of S_2 occurring.
Suppose his judgmental probabilities were 0.7 and 0.3 for the occurrence of S_1 and S_2, respectively. Table 4–5 shows the application of
these judgmental (also referred to as personalistic or subjective)
probabilities.

Table 4–5

APPLICATION OF THE BAYESIAN APPROACH—PACKAGE DESIGN PROBLEM

		New *vs*. Old Design			
Courses of Action	$P(S_1)$	S_1: New Design Superior to Old	$P(S_2)$	S_2: New Design Not Superior to Old	Expected Value
A_1: Adopt new.	0.7	10	0.3	−5	5.5 (Max)
A_2: Keep old...	0.7	−1	0.3	2	−0.1

As shown in Table 4–5 the decision maker would select act A_1
with its expected payoff of 5.5 value units. Notice that the calculations are identical in format with those carried out under the Laplace criterion. The subjective probabilities—the $P(S_j's)$—are expressed so as to obey the postulates of probability theory. However,
they can be viewed as merely numerical weights falling in the interval of $0 \leq P(S_j) \leq 1$ which are assigned to a set of mutually
exclusive and collectively exhaustive states of nature. The weights
add to unity. In symbols, under the Bayesian approach, the decision
maker chooses the act which leads to

$$\text{Max}_{A_i} \left[\sum_j P_j \, V(A_i, S_j) \right]$$

but, while $\sum_j P_j = 1$, the individual probabilities, P_j, P_k, and so on,
need not be equal.

WHAT DO WE MEAN BY RATIONALITY?

As has just been seen, the terms "rational" and "uncertainty"
hardly mean the same thing to all students of decision theory. Consideration in this book of the various approaches from the viewpoint
of evaluating marketing plans obviously stops far short of any exhaustive analysis of these procedures. As has been noted, however,
the concept of rationality is imbedded in the various models of
choice making, that is, in the assumptions underlying each criterion.

No attempt has been made by the proponents of the various choice criteria to say that decision makers really act this way. Rather, the arguments are "if the assumptions are granted, then such and such follows." The models prescribe rather than describe behavior and "rationality" merely means behavior consistent with the assumptions underlying each particular criterion.

The maximin payoff and minimax regret criteria both assumed that *any* assignment of probabilities over states of nature was meaningless in problems under uncertainty. The decision maker should focus upon the worst of circumstances. (A "gambling-type" decision maker, however, might wish to pursue a "maximax" payoff strategy, that is, to focus his selection on the best rather than worst payoff under each act.)

The Laplace and Bayesian approaches both employed the notion of probabilities attached to alternative states of nature and assumed that the decision maker wished to maximize expected value. This criterion also applied to the category of decisions under risk. The nature of the probabilities used in the three approaches was the distinguishing feature. In decisions under risk the probabilities were assumed known. Under the Bayesian approach the probabilities could be either subjective, objective (based on relative frequencies), or a combination of the two. Under the Laplace criterion equal probabilities were assigned, purportedly reflecting total ignorance.

Some of the logical difficulties which stem from consideration of the Laplace criterion have already been discussed. The question now concerns the fruitfulness of limiting this purview to objective probabilities. Without consideration of the philosophical questions which still surround the concept of probability as "the limiting value of a relative frequency," it is clear that marketing problems do not typically possess the characteristics of stability and reproducibility which are associated with the usual situations in which the concept of objective probability has been found to be useful.

The marketing planner is usually dealing with more or less unique events. Unlike many production-type problems which deal with a repetitive phenomenon whose characteristics are reasonably stable over time, the marketing man must rely on less precise analogies of his current situation.

This is not to say that he should not try to use whatever partial information he may have at his disposal. It is to say, however, that marketing situations in which the decision maker knows the probabilities to be attached to alternative states of nature are rare situations. If the decision maker chooses to act as though the probabilities *were* known, it is clear that no further information is needed; he would be dealing with a situation under risk. More realistically, if the decision maker chooses to act as though the prior probabilities are subject to change through incorporation of additional information, then we are dealing with the Bayesian approach to decisions under uncertainty. Of course, sometimes the cost of information gathering may outweigh the value of increased reliability. (This and other aspects of the Bayesian approach will be considered in the next chapter.)

Probably the most realistic position with respect to the degree of uncertainty which surrounds real problem situations would appear to lie between the cases of complete ignorance and full knowledge of the probabilities attached to alternative states of nature. This viewpoint stresses the role of *learning* in decision making. That is, while a decision maker may possess, or assume he possesses, partial information about the relevant probabilities, he may wish to elect a strategy of collecting more information—provided its value is worth the cost—before making a final choice among alternatives. In any event, he will be receptive to *changing* the probabilities attached to alternative states of nature as he accumulates more knowledge about his environment.

In summary, support of the Bayesian approach is bolstered by the need to consider subjective as well as objective probabilities in the solution of marketing problems. In this class of problems the decision maker's knowledge about the occurrence of alternative states of nature usually precludes the assignment of objective probabilities. Relative frequency notions are seldom applicable to the situations with which the marketer deals. Not only may courses of action be defined in any number of ways, but *who* implements the course of action can affect the probabilities associated with alternative outcomes. The Bayesian approach considers both objective probabilities (where applicable) and personalistic probabilities. Moreover, in many actual decision problems these probabilities do *not* need to be known precisely in order to make good decisions.

DOMINANT STRATEGIES AND INDIFFERENCE PROBABILITIES

In many real problem situations choice of the best course of action may not be highly sensitive to the probabilities attached to alternative states of nature. In the extreme case one strategy may dominate another as illustrated, via our package design problem, in Table 4-6.

Table 4–6

ILLUSTRATION OF DOMINANT STRATEGY—PACKAGE DESIGN PROBLEM

Courses of Action	S_1: New Design Superior to Old	S_2: New Design Not Superior to Old
A_1: Adopt new................	10	2 (Dominant Strategy)
A_2: Keep old.................	−1	2

Notice in Table 4–6 that the payoff $V(A_1, S_2)$ has been changed from our original value of −5 units to 2 units. This has the effect of making A_1 a dominant course of action. It is clear that regardless of whether S_1 or S_2 prevailed, A_1 would lead to at least as high a payoff (under S_2) and a higher payoff under at least one state of nature (S_1).

This notion may be formalized by stating that a *dominant strategy* (or course of action) is a choice which leads to at least as high a payoff as a dominated strategy under *all* states of nature and a higher payoff under at least one state of nature. In this case the decision maker does not have to worry about the probability assignment over S_1 and S_2. All that is assumed is that their probabilities are positive, and this is implied whenever a state of nature is deemed admissible to the problem.

The implications of this simple illustration are important to note. Perhaps much of the creative talent that goes into the task of designing marketing plans is associated with attempts to construct dominant strategies or at least strategies whose payoffs are relatively insensitive to adverse events. This notion, to an extent, lies in back of those plans which are designed to be flexible, that is, where the decision maker is able to shift his course of action relatively quickly and painlessly should future events warrant it. And, the cost of providing flexibility may well be justified by the additional protection provided.

As an illustration, building a plant to produce a new product could involve the initial construction of some ultimate capacity or a stepwise approach to ultimate capacity. In the latter case the decision maker is balancing the costs associated with an increased risk of short-run supply difficulties and perhaps increased total construction costs against the costs associated with increased risk of underutilization of capacity and process and/or product obsolescence. The latter costs may be so great as to warrant a sequential approach to capacity expansion. This alternative would avoid unneeded future construction outlays should high sales fail to occur.

While neither strategy is clearly dominant, a flexible course of action (the stepwise approach to capacity expansion) can materially reduce the costs of wrong decisions without necessarily incurring high costs for this insurance.

In most instances a dominant strategy will be difficult—if possible at all—to design. Still the decision maker may not need to possess precise probability estimates in choosing among acts where no dominant act exists. In fact, he may use the payoff entries themselves to *impute* the probability ranges which are relevant to choice. This technique of solving for indifference probabilities is illustrated in Table 4–7.

Table 4–7

ILLUSTRATION OF IMPUTED PROBABILITIES—PACKAGE DESIGN PROBLEM

Courses of Action	$P(S_1)$	S_1: New Design Superior to Old	$1 - P(S_1)$	S_2: New Design Not Superior to Old	Expected Value
A_1: Adopt new..	$\frac{7}{18}$	10	$\frac{11}{18}$	-5	$\frac{15}{18}$
A_2: Keep old....	$\frac{7}{18}$	-1	$\frac{11}{18}$	2	$\frac{15}{18}$

Indifference Probability Calculations:
$$10\,[P\,(S_1)] - 5\,[1 - P\,(S_1)] = -1\,[P\,(S_1)] + 2\,[1 - P\,(S_1)]$$
$$18\,[P\,(S_1)] = 7$$
$$P\,(S_1) = \tfrac{7}{18}$$
$$1 - P\,(S_1) = \tfrac{11}{18}$$

As noted in Table 4–7, the calculation of indifference probabilities involves solving for the particular $P(S_1)$ and $1 - P(S_1)$ which equate the expected values of acts A_1 and A_2. The relevant probabilities in this illustration are $\frac{7}{18}$ and $\frac{11}{18}$ for $P(S_1)$ and $1 - P(S_1)$, respectively. If the decision maker's prior probabiilty for the occurrence of S_1 exceeds $\frac{7}{18}$ he should take act A_1. If this probability is less than $\frac{7}{18}$ he should take act A_2. Notice that the decision maker does not require a precise estimate of $P(S_1)$; he needs only to know whether this value either exceeds or is less than $\frac{7}{18}$. Should it exactly equal $\frac{7}{18}$ (the indifference probability), the decision maker could choose either course of action.

This illustration points out another essential feature of plans evaluation, the asymmetry of payoffs. In marketing problems the costs of wrong decisions may *not* necessarily be, and frequently are not, equal. Recognition of, and dealing explicitly with, this phenomenon is an essential feature of Bayesian decision theory which will be elaborated upon in future chapters.

ANCILLARY TECHNIQUES IN DECISION THEORY

The foregoing discussion of decision theory has centered around an introductory and nonrealistic illustration, the package design problem. This selection has been made deliberately in order to describe the various concepts, unencumbered by technical detail, which actual marketing problems possess. It is now time to introduce a few of the *computational* difficulties which are attendant with the solution of realistic marketing problems.

First, the considerations of (*a*) length of planning horizon, (*b*) opportunity cost of capital, and (*c*) calculation of the payoffs themselves have been temporarily neglected. Consideration of these problems suggests the need for employing various ancillary techniques which can extend the operability of decision theory. While mention of some of these techniques will be made here, detailed elaboration on the applicability of these and other techniques to real problems will be deferred until future chapters.

In actual planning situations the effects of most courses of action are anticipated to extend over quite a long period into the future. For example, a decision to construct a facility for producing a new product entails a series of nearer term outlays which, hopefully, will be recouped in subsequent years. It is clear that the wisdom of making the present investment rests upon estimates of future revenues and costs. In decision problems under uncertainty it is also true that many possible revenue and cost streams can be imagined as related to a consideration of alternative states of nature.

Calculation of alternative financial flows in a realistic decision model is frequently a tedious and time-consuming task. Fortunately, the growing availability of computers provides an efficient resource for calculating the payoffs of large-scale planning problems. The label *simulation* has been used to describe a process in which the system is run on paper (or in a computer) under a variety of assumptions about the environmental variables. The effect of alternative states of nature on the plan's financial flows can be readily calculated once the program is set up. Moreover, values of the variables in the model can be changed after the basic payoff is derived in order to examine the impact of changed assumptions on the relevant payoffs.

Emphasis on the planning horizon and financial flows raises the question of incorporating a time value for money, that is, discount function, under the assumption that plans in which the financial flows occur earlier along the time dimension should be credited with the opportunity to reinvest the funds so generated. This is to say that payoff tables should reflect, at least partially, the concept of opportunity costs with respect to time. In planning problems involving a reasonably lengthy time horizon all payoffs can be discounted to present value, using an interest rate which reflects the anticipated earning power of investment funds in alternative uses. Here, again, the determination of an appropriate discount rate may constitute a difficult problem, and the planner may wish to assume several possible numerical values for this function. The simulator can easily be programmed to incorporate a series of possible discount functions.

Simulation also provides a flexible means to conduct *sensitivity* analyses of the values of the states of nature used and the effect on payoffs associated with structuring the environmental variables in different ways. As will be shown in subsequent chapters, sensitivity analysis represents a procedure for examining the effect on the payoff function associated with some best course of action as payoff values and/or probabilities associated with the underlying states of nature are changed.

Finally, decision theory provides a means to combine various *analytical* techniques with subjective probability estimates. It may turn out, for example, that a portion of a planning problem may be amenable to standard calculus techniques for finding maxima or minima. If so, this part of the problem is solved analytically while other parts of the problem are handled by simulation or various procedures involving numerical approximation.

SUMMARY

In this chapter the characteristics of marketing problems (high uncertainty associated with outcomes, lack of control, time-dependent nature, paucity of information) have been emphasized as these characteristics dictate, to a large extent, the types of procedures which are required to evaluate alternative marketing plans.

Attention then was directed to a consideration of mathematical models—particularly problem models and choice models—as a tool for assisting the planner in choosing among alternative courses of action. Various models (maximin, minimax regret, Laplace, and Bayes) for making decisions under uncertainty were discussed. While it is clear that no universally best model is yet available for handling these problems, some supporting arguments were offered for the Bayesian model.

Finally, the usefulness of various ancillary techniques, such as computer simulation and sensitivity analysis, in increasing the operability of decision models was briefly described.

Selected References

ACKOFF, RUSSELL L. *Scientific Method*. New York: John Wiley & Sons, Inc., 1962.

Presents a lucid and extended treatment of problem models and decision criteria and explicates many of the philosophical issues underlying these concepts.

BURSK, EDWARD C. *Text and Cases in Marketing*. Englewood Cliffs, N. J.: Prentice-Hall, Inc., 1962.

Discusses some of the characteristics of marketing problems which have militated against the fruitful application of many of the techniques of management science and operations research.

CHURCHMAN, C. WEST. *Prediction and Optimal Decision*. Englewood Cliffs, N. J.: Prentice-Hall, Inc., 1961.

Provides a penetrating discussion of objective and subjective probability, concluding that both concepts can be useful. Points out the necessity of studying judgmental probabilities if one is to cope with many important problems of decision making.

LUCE, R. DUNCAN, AND RAIFFA, HOWARD. *Games and Decisions*. New York: John Wiley & Sons, Inc., 1957.

Presents a detailed listing and critique of models developed for decision making under uncertainty as well as models of conflict situations.

Problems

1. The president of a small publishing house is considering publishing a new marketing research text. At the present time the president *must* make a choice between the following acts:

1) Publish the new book (A_1).

2) Do not publish the new book (A_2).

The president believes that if the new text is published and is successful the company can expect a cash flow of $10 million over the next five years. If, however, the text is published and is not successful the company can expect a cash outflow of $5 million. If the text is not published the company can expect a cash flow of $0.

a) Evaluate the acts available, given that the president assumes that the "true" probability of the text being successful is 0.7. Select the act that satisfies the following:

$$\operatorname*{Max}_{A_i} \left[\sum_j P_j \, V \, (A_i, S_j) \right]$$

b) Using the maximin criterion, evaluate the available acts and choose the act that would satisfy this criterion.

c) Using the minimax regret criterion, evaluate the available acts and choose the act that would satisfy this criterion.

d) Using the Laplace criterion, evaluate the available acts and choose the act that would satisfy this criterion.

2. The Dodd Company is at present a small manufacturer and distributor of proprietary drugs. The company has a limited line of products and is very dependent upon one product. The patent on this particular product will expire within the next five years. The marketing manager of the Dodd Company believes that it is economically necessary that the company begin to diversify its product line. The alternative actions that are presently being considered by the marketing manager are

1) Introduce another proprietary drug that would complement and fill out the present line of proprietaries (A_1).
2) Introduce an antiseptic mouthwash that is similar to several products that are presently on the market (A_2).
3) Introduce a revolutionary new cream that will eliminate shaving of the face for at least 3 days. The cream has been thoroughly tested by the Dodd Company and has been demonstrated to be effective from 3 to 7 days. The cream is easy to apply and apparently has no irritating effects on the skin (A_3).

Given the above three alternative acts the marketing manager of the Dodd Company postulated three possible demands for the product: low sales (S_1), moderate sales (S_2), and high sales (S_3). Also he was able to calculate conditional payoffs given each possible act and state of nature combination. The results of his investigation are summarized below.

Courses of Action	Possible Demands (Millions of Dollars)		
	S_1	S_2	S_3
A_1.................	0	1	3
A_2.................	-3	2	5
A_3.................	-7	3	15

a) Is there a dominant strategy for the manager? Why or why not?

b) Evaluate the acts available to the Dodd Company given that the marketing manager assumes that the "true" probability of high sales occurring is 0.6; of moderate sales occurring is 0.3; and of low sales occurring 0.1. Select the act that satisfies the following:

$$\underset{A_i}{\text{Max}} \left[\sum_j P_j \, V \, (A_i, S_j) \right]$$

c) Using the maximin criterion evaluate the available acts and choose the act that satisfies this criterion.

d) Using the minimax regret criterion evaluate the available acts and choose the act that satisfies this criterion.

e) Given that the marketing manager of the Dodd Company postulates the following subjective probabilities:

$$P(S_1) = 0.70$$
$$P(S_2) = 0.25$$
$$P(S_3) = 0.05$$

evaluate, by the Bayesian method, the possible acts. Select the act which leads to

$$\text{Max}_{A_i} \left[\sum_j P_j V(A_i, S_j) \right]$$

3. *a*) Discuss the relative advantages and disadvantages of the maximin and minimax regret criteria. What are the logical and practical inconsistencies of the two criteria?

b) Briefly describe the type of businessman that would be most prone to use either the maximin or minimax regret criterion.

c. What are the logical difficulties that arise when employing the Laplace criterion?

d. Discuss the basic underlying assumptions of the Bayesian approach. What are the drawbacks to the use of the Bayesian approach?

e. Explain what is meant by a dominant course of action.

4. Illustrate two marketing problems whose characteristics argue against the use of a highly structured, quantitative type of approach to solution.

5. Discuss at least one nonmathematical model that might be used by a marketing manager. Explain in detail

a) The characteristics of the model.

b) The application of the model.

c) The difficulties associated with trying to quantify the relationships of the model.

6. What role can simulation play in the development of Bayesian decision theory?

Chapter 5

THE FUNDAMENTALS OF BAYESIAN
DECISION THEORY

In the preceding chapter it was noted that Bayesian decision theory represented only one of several procedures for making decisions under uncertainty. Arguments were presented in support of this particular procedure's usefulness to the marketing planner, but no attempt was made to elaborate upon the fundamentals of the theory.

In this chapter the basic framework of Bayesian decision theory within a marketing context is explained. The notions of prior analysis, posterior analysis (through the use of Bayes' theorem), pre-posterior analysis, and sequential decision making are developed and illustrated by simple numerical problems.

Since the reader is assumed to be already familiar with the rudiments of classical statistics, Bayesian procedures are next related to the traditional approach to hypothesis testing, and Bayesian analysis is shown to provide a fruitful bridge between statistics and microeconomics.

The concluding section of the chapter is devoted to an overview of marketing plans evaluation within the methodological framework of Bayesian decision theory. In it are discussed such concepts as (a) the essentiality of managerial judgment in planning, (b) the asymmetry of opportunity loss functions, (c) the sequential commitment of resources, and (d) the costs of overplanning and under-planning.

Throughout this chapter it is assumed that the planner is trying to maximize the expected value of some *monetary* payoff, for example, cash flow or return on investment. Chapter 6 describes quantitative procedures for dealing with the decision maker's attitudes toward risky outcomes and the role which value theory plays in decision making under uncertainty.

Finally, the application of Bayesian techniques to full-scale marketing planning problems is left to subsequent chapters.

PROBABILITY THEORY AND THE MAXIMIZATION OF EXPECTED VALUE

Probability can be studied from many viewpoints depending upon the purposes and predilections of the researcher. A mathematician may view probability theory as an abstract structure composed of a few basic axioms from which a set of theorems can be derived. His purpose may be to see how large a system of theorems can be deduced from a given set of axioms, and the mathematician may or may not be interested in whether the system corresponds with the real world.

An amateur (or, more likely, professional) gambler may wish to learn the rudiments of probability as a guide to placing bets in various card or dice games. His interest may be very pragmatic but limited to the somewhat artificial world of games of chance. On the other hand, the insurance actuary or quality control analyst may study probability from the standpoint of real-world phenomena involving man–machine systems. The actuary is required to estimate probabilities by compiling large masses of data on, say, the proportion of deaths in a specified age and sex category to the estimated total population in that category which is alive at the beginning of some reference period.

The man on the street, however, may employ a much different notion about probability, a notion which does not convey the impression of relative frequency in some long series of repetitive trials like coin tossing. Rather, the layman may use the term to express his *degree of belief* in the occurrence of some more or less unique event. Many of us have used phrases such as, "I'd give you odds that the Joneses will be back together within six months," or, "I probably won't be able to take a vacation this year." Degrees of belief may be stated numerically in this kind of context but more often than not words like "probable," "possible," "certain," or "improbable" are used.

The problems which market planners (and businessmen generally) face often deal with more or less unique events. "Will demand for the new product be sufficient to make it worthwhile to expand our production facilities?" "What are our chances for keeping Smith's business next year if we increase our transportation charges by 10 percent?" If the planner is to deal with questions like these, it is clear that probability theory may have to serve many purposes, or, perhaps more accurately, several interpretations of probability may have to be studied.

The axioms of probability theory can be stated in nonrigorous language as follows:

1. A probability is a real number between 0 and 1 (including the end points) which is assigned to an event.
2. The probability of an event which is made up of a set of mutually exclusive events is the sum of the probabilities of these subevents.
3. The sum of the probabilities assigned to a set of mutually exclusive and collectively exhaustive events is equal to 1.

Probabilities, then, are merely numerical weights of a rather special sort which are assigned to events. According to the Bayesian viewpoint, the decision maker is not limited to making probability statements for which the notion of relative frequency is applicable. (If this were not the case, most of the strategic problems of business would not be amenable to statistical methods.) Many problems will arise in which the planner must rely on his experience and judgment regarding the assignment of weights to those possible states of nature which could represent the underlying "facts of life," given the implementation of a particular course of action. Consequently, the decision maker will need to augment the relative frequentist view of probability with a more personalistic appraisal of the possible events which can occur and the weights which he wishes to assign to their occurrence. According to this viewpoint the "true" state of the world, *relative to the decision maker's knowledge*, may be regarded as a chance event.

The philosophical foundations of probability are not to be explored here, but it should be mentioned that all probability notions which are relevant to real-world phenomena involve at least some aspects of judgment and that the more recently explicated theory of personalistic probability should not be regarded lightly, though at first it may give the impression of being arbitrary and unscientific. (Some of these philosophical issues are covered in the references cited at the end of this chapter.)

RANDOM VARIABLES

The concept of *random variable* plays an important role in Bayesian analysis and, for that matter, in statistics, generally. The mathematician would define a random variable as "a function on a sample space." For our purposes a random variable can be considered as a rule which assigns a numerical value to each possible chance event. The quantity so assigned to the event is called the value of the random variable.

As illustrations, consider the throw of 3 true coins and visualize the total number of heads which may turn up. The numerical values so assigned are 0, 1, 2, 3 heads. Similarly, the market planner may consider the possible levels of unit sales in the first year after the introduction of a new product. The values assigned to each possible event may be 0, 1, 2, 3, . . ., 10,000 (assuming that he can conceive of no first-year sales level beyond 10,000 units, the annual capacity of the new plant).

Random variables are of particular importance to Bayesian analysis because they permit the calculation of useful summary measures like the expected value of a random variable. As noted in the preceding chapter, the expected value of a random variable is merely the average of the variable. If X is a random variable whose possible values are $X_1, X_2, \ldots, X_n$, then

$$E(X) = \sum_{i=1}^{n} X_i f(X_i)$$

where $f(X_i)$ represents the probability of occurrence of each X_i. In the coin tossing illustration, the expected value of X is

$$E(X) = \tfrac{1}{8}(0) + \tfrac{3}{8}(1) + \tfrac{3}{8}(2) + \tfrac{1}{8}(3) = 1.5 \text{ heads}$$

That is, *on the average,* each trial (consisting of tossing three coins) will result in the appearance of 1.5 heads. Notice that this is a calculated, rather than observed, value. Inasmuch as the decision maker is usually concerned with numerical measures like profits, sales, and number of customers, the concept of a random variable fits in quite naturally with business problems.

THE COMPONENTS OF BAYESIAN DECISION THEORY

Bayesian theory deals with the following aspects of decision making under uncertainty.

1. *Prior Analysis.* Frequently in marketing planning problems the decision maker must rely on his business judgment alone; that is, the nature of the problem (for example, a proposed price change) or the length of the planning horizon may preclude the opportunity to secure additional information bearing on the problem before a commitment must be made. In this case the decision maker must decide solely on the basis of past experience. This segment of Bayesian theory is known as prior analysis.

2. *Posterior Analysis.* Business experience is, of course, always changing as the decision maker secures feedback data from past courses of

action. The revision of his prior judgments by incorporating new information is handled in a rather special way by Bayesian theory. This segment of the theory is known as posterior analysis.

3. *Preposterior Analysis.* Sometimes the decision maker will have the option of delaying his decision pending the receipt of more information bearing on the problem. But, the decision maker will typically incur costs in obtaining the information and may also incur costs in delaying his original choice. Seldom will the additional information be perfectly reliable. He must, then, evaluate the wisdom of delaying his final choice (which will be called a *terminal decision*) and using this delay period to buy additional information regarding the unknown states of nature, against taking action without the additional information. This segment of Bayesian decision theory is called preposterior analysis.

4. *Sequential Decision Making.* Decisions may, and frequently do, involve a sequence of actions (including information collection and analysis) to be taken over time. That is, many actions, such as additions to production capacity, may be taken sequentially, and some current courses of action may permit greater flexibility for making more informed choices in the future. A special segment of Bayesian theory which applies preposterior analysis to multistage decision processes is known as sequential decision making under uncertainty.

Each of these aspects will be covered in turn, by way of illustrative planning cases.

BAYESIAN ANALYSIS

Consider the following hypothetical planning problem. Suppose a marketing executive is concerned with whether he should open a new sales territory for a product now being sold on a regional basis. As he thinks through the problem he notes that opening a new territory would involve establishing a regional sales office, a warehouse, and the employment of several new salesmen. If potential sales turn out to be high, his additional outlays will be more than justified. If sales turn out to be low, however, and the territory were opened, a substantial out-of-pocket loss would be involved.

At this point the problem is just beginning. What is meant by "high" and "low" sales? What is the appropriate length of planning horizon to use? Do the appropriate cash flows reflect the impact of competitive activity? Do they reflect the opportunity to dispose of the office and warehouse and relocate salesmen, if the product turns out to be unsuccessful? Might the decision be delayed pending the receipt of additional information?

It is clear that any real decision problem involves a host of assumptions about which variables to include, the values of those variables, and the functional relationship which links the decision maker's payoff with the controlled and uncontrolled variables. Suppose the decision maker feels that all variables except potential sales can be treated as "known." That is, the financial outlays for office, warehouse, and salesmen are assumed to be known without error, and, furthermore, the decision maker "knows" what is meant by "high" and "low" sales. (Later chapters will show what happens as many of these assumptions are relaxed.)

The decision maker possesses two options if he wishes to make a terminal decision now: that is, to open the new sales region or not. But, suppose that the decision maker could delay his terminal choice and elect to have a marketing research firm conduct a survey of potential sales in the new territory. The survey firm has a sliding fee scale which reflects the cost of achieving greater or lesser reliability in its findings. For example, a 100 percent reliable census of the territory would cost much more than a survey which would sometimes (say, 20 percent of the time) indicate high sales potential when low sales would really be the underlying state of nature, and vice versa. It is clear that the opportunity to gather additional information about the problem provides another course of action, namely, to purchase some type of survey first and *then* decide whether to open the new sales region. Each problem is considered in turn.

PRIOR ANALYSIS

Suppose the marketing executive, after examination of the relevant financial outlays and suitable quantification of what he means by high and low sales, prepares a table of conditional payoffs as shown in Table 5-1.

Table 5–1

CONDITIONAL PAYOFF MATRIX—SALES REGION PROBLEM
(CASH FLOWS IN MILLIONS OF DOLLARS)

	Potential Sales Levels	
Courses of Action	S_1: High	S_2: Low
A_1: Open region..................	5	−2
A_2: Do not open region............	0	0

The reader will note the similarity between Table 5-1 and the conditional payoff tables of the preceding chapter. The relevant events are S_1 and S_2. The payoffs, 5 and − 2, associated with A_1, represent values of a random variable, that is, a numerically-valued function on the possible events S_1 and S_2 which are assumed to be mutually exclusive and collectively exhaustive of the possible events which can occur. The values, 0 and 0, associated with A_2, refer to the fact that if the new region is not opened, no *additional* cash flows (positive or negative) would be involved. Relevant to this particular problem situation, the decision maker need not consider the fact that *existing* territories might produce sizeable cash flows during the planning period. Usually he would be interested only in those cash flows which would be expected to *change* as a consequence of the plans being evaluated.

Suppose now that the marketing executive, based on his business judgment and personal knowledge of the new region, feels that the chances assigned to the occurrence of state of nature S_1 against S_2 are 0.4 and 0.6 respectively. While his probability judgments might be considered to fall on the pessimistic side, it is of interest to note that the conditional payoffs, given act A_1, are asymmetrical. That is, the firm can gain a possible \$5 million while it stands to lose only a possible \$2 million if A_1 is selected.

If, for some reason, the decision maker had to choose *now* between terminal acts, he would calculate the expected monetary value for each course of action and choose that act leading to the largest expected or weighted average payoff. Clearly, the expected value of act A_2 is zero. The expected value of act A_1 is

$$0.4 \ (5) + 0.6 \ (-2) = \$0.8 \ \text{million}$$

hence act A_1 would be chosen.

Notice further that the payoffs of Table 5–1 can be transformed to opportunity losses similar to the regret matrix of Table 4–3 of the preceding chapter. In terms of the present problem the opportunity losses are shown in Table 5–2.

Table 5–2

OPPORTUNITY LOSS MATRIX—SALES REGION PROBLEM
(CASH FLOWS IN MILLIONS OF DOLLARS)

Courses of Action	Potential Sales Levels				Expected Opportunity Loss
	$P \ (S_1)$	S_1: High	$P \ (S_2)$	S_2: Low	
A_1: Open region..........	0.4	0	0.6	2	1.2
A_2: Do not open region....	0.4	5	0.6	0	2.0

One can solve for expected opportunity loss under each course of action by similar application of the prior probabilities

$$P(S_1) = 0.4 \text{ and } P(S_2) = 0.6.$$

The last column shows that the *lowest* expected opportunity loss, $1.2 million, is associated with act A_1. In terms of this transformed table, the decision maker would like to minimize expected loss; hence act A_1 is again optimal. Notice that the *difference* between expected opportunity losses

$$2.0 - 1.2 = 0.8,$$

agrees with the difference between the expected payoffs of acts A_1 and A_2

$$0.8 - 0.0 = 0.8,$$

in the original statement of payoffs.[1] This is a necessary consequence of the procedure used to derive opportunity losses and can be easily shown in Table 5–3.

Table 5–3

COMPARISON OF MONETARY DIFFERENCES BETWEEN ACTS DERIVED FROM EXPECTED PAYOFF AND EXPECTED OPPORTUNITY LOSS CALCULATIONS

Courses of Action	Original Matrix		Opportunity Loss Matrix	
	S_1	S_2	S_1	S_2
A_1.......	$P(5)$	$(1-P)(-2)$	$P(5+a)$	$(1-P)(-2+b)$
A_2.......	$P(0)$	$(1-P)(\ 0)$	$P(0+a)$	$(1-P)(\ 0+b)$
	$EP(A_1) - EP(A_2)$		$EOL(A_1) - EOL(A_2)$	
	$[5P+(1-P)(-2)]-[0]$		$[P(5+a)+(1-P)(-2+b)]$	
	$= 7P-2;$ let $P = 0.4$		$-[P(0+a)+(1-P)(0+b)]$	
	$= \$0.8$ million		$= [5P+aP-2+2P+b-bP]-$	
			$[aP+b-bP]$	
			$= 7P-2;$ let $P = 0.4$	
			$= \$0.8$ million	

As noted in Table 5–3 arbitrary constants can be added to each column of the payoff table. Still, each method yields the same numerical difference of $0.8 million when $P = 0.4$ (the prior probability of this problem) is substituted into the general formulation.

At this juncture it may seem superfluous to have two schemata (expected payoff and expected opportunity loss) for expressing the value of outcomes related to decisions under uncertainty. As will

---

[1] In this case concern is with absolute (without regard to algebraic sign) differences.

be seen later on, however, some definite computational and conceptual advantages are associated with this dual approach.

REVISION OF PRIOR JUDGMENTS—BAYES' THEOREM AND POSTERIOR ANALYSIS

As stated earlier, in many problem situations the decision maker may elect to delay a terminal decision pending the receipt and analysis of new information. Concern in this section is with the statistical procedures used to modify the decision maker's prior probabilities. In order to develop the necessary apparatus for performing these calculations some of the basic theorems of introductory probability will first be reviewed.

Consider the following marketing research problem. A survey has been conducted on the readership habits of a particular population. The survey results are shown in Table 5–4.

Table 5–4
READERSHIP AND PURCHASING HABITS OF SURVEY RESPONDENTS

Purchasing Habits of Respondents	Number of Respondents Reading Magazine Bj			
	B_1	B_2	B_3	Total
A_1: Purchase product............	10	5	10	25
A_2: Do not purchase product.......	50	25	0	75
	60	30	10	100

The data of Table 5–4 can be used to estimate some probabilities of readership and/or purchasing for the population of interest. For example, the estimated probability that a person reads magazine B_3 is 10/100 or 0.1. The estimated probability that a person reads magazine B_2 *and* purchases the product, A_1, is 5/100 or 0.05.

THE ADDITION THEOREM

In its simplest form the addition theorem of elementary probability applies to mutually exclusive events. (Two events are said to be mutually exclusive if they cannot both occur on a single trial.) The theorem states

If E_1 and E_2 are any two mutually exclusive events, the probability that either E_1 or E_2 occurs is

$$P\ (E_1 \text{ or } E_2) = P\ (E_1) + P\ (E_2).$$

In terms of the readership-purchase problem it can be noted that the events A_1 (purchase) and A_2 (not purchase) are mutually exclusive. Hence, the probability that a person purchases or does not purchase the product is

$$P (A_1 \text{ or } A_2) = P (A_1) + P (A_2)$$
$$= 0.25 + 0.75$$
$$= 1.00$$

Similar comments would pertain to the (assumed) mutually exclusive events, B_1, B_2, and B_3.

In more general terms, however, the addition theorem does not require that events be mutually exclusive. In terms of two events the theorem states

If E_1 and E_2 are two outcomes (not necessarily mutually exclusive), the probability that either E_1 and/or E_2 occurs is

$$P (E_1 \text{ and/or } E_2) = P (E_1) + P (E_2) - P (E_1 \text{ and } E_2).$$

In terms of the survey data suppose one wished to estimate the probability that a person reads magazine B_1 and/or purchases the product, A_1. In terms of the formula

$$P (B_1 \text{ and/or } A_1) = P (B_1) + P (A_1) - P (B_1 \text{ and } A_1)$$
$$= 0.60 + 0.25 - 0.10$$
$$= 0.75$$

Notice that the probability of the *joint* occurrence of these two events, $P (B_1 \text{ and } A_1)$ is subtracted inasmuch as this probability has already been added in twice—once under $P (B_1)$ and once under $P (A_1)$—and should not be counted double. Notice further that if the events are mutually exclusive then $P (E_1 \text{ and } E_2)$, the joint probability, is zero. Hence, the more general formula can handle the special version which deals with mutually exclusive events.

Extending the more general version to deal with more than two events becomes somewhat cumbersome. In the case of three events

$$P (E_1 \text{ and/or } E_2 \text{ and/or } E_3) = P (E_1) + P (E_2) + P (E_3) - P (E_1 \text{ and } E_2)$$
$$- P (E_1 \text{ and } E_3) - P (E_2 \text{ and } E_3) + P (E_1 \text{ and } E_2 \text{ and } E_3).$$

If the events are mutually exclusive, however, the formula for k events is simply

$$P (E_1 \text{ or } E_2 \text{ or } \ldots \text{ or } E_k) = P (E_1) + P (E_2) + \ldots + P (E_k).$$

THE MULTIPLICATION THEOREM

In the special case of independent events, the multiplication theorem states (for the case of two events)

If E_1 and E_2 are two independent events, then the probability of their joint occurrence is

$$P \ (E_1 \text{ and } E_2) = P \ (E_1) \ \cdot \ P \ (E_2)$$

The simplest illustration of this theorem occurs in coin flipping. For example, the probability of throwing two heads in a row is simply

$$\tfrac{1}{2} \ \cdot \ \tfrac{1}{2} = \tfrac{1}{4} = 0.25$$

If one looks at the data in Table 5–4, however, the probability that a person *both* purchases the product, A_1, and reads, say, magazine B_2 is

$$P \ (A_1 \text{ and } B_2) = 0.05$$

which is *not* equal to the product of their individual probabilities,

$$0.05 \neq 0.25 \ \cdot \ 0.30$$

In this case the two events are *not* independent and the more general formulation of the multiplication theorem must be used. That is, if it is *known* that a person purchases the product, A_1, then the probability that he reads magazine B_2 is changed by this information. Before knowing that the person is a purchaser, the probability assigned to reading magazine B_2 is

$$P \ (B_2) = 0.30$$

But if it is known that he is a purchaser, then only the A_1 row of entries is relevant. The *conditional* probability $P \ (B_2 \mid A_1$ is thus

$$0.05/0.25 = 0.20$$

The multiplication theorem can be generalized to deal with two events (not necessarily independent) as follows:

If E_1 and E_2 are two events (not necessarily independent), then the probability of their joint occurrence is

$$P \ (E_1 \text{ and } E_2) = P \ (E_1 \mid E_2) \ \cdot \ P \ (E_2) = P \ (E_2 \mid E_1) \ \cdot \ P \ (E_1).$$

In the case of independent events

$$P \ (E_1 \mid E_2) = P \ (E_1)$$

and

$$P \ (E_2 \mid E_1) = P \ (E_2)$$

where $P \ (E_1)$ and $P \ (E_2)$ are each greater than zero. Hence for independent events

$$P \ (E_1 \text{ and } E_2) = P \ (E_1) \ \cdot \ P \ (E_2)$$

Returning to the data of Table 5-4, suppose one wishes to find the probability that a person does not purchase the product, A_2, and does read magazine B_1.

$$P (A_2 \text{ and } B_1) = P (A_2 \mid B_1) \cdot P (B_1)$$
$$= \frac{5}{6} \cdot \frac{6}{10}$$
$$= 0.50$$
$$= P (B_1 \mid A_2) \cdot P (A_2)$$
$$= \frac{50}{75} \cdot \frac{75}{100}$$
$$= 0.50$$

The notation $P (E_1 \text{ and } E_2)$ will be used throughout this chapter to refer to the probability of the *joint* occurrence of E_1 and E_2. The notation $P (E_1 \mid E_2)$ will be used to refer to the conditional probability of E_1, given the occurrence of E_2. Finally, the notation $P (E_1)$ will frequently be used to refer to the *marginal* (or unconditional) probability of E_1.

The multiplication theorem can be generalized to deal with the joint occurrence of k events as follows:

If k is any integer $(k > 2)$ and $E_1, E_2, \ldots, E_k$ are any k events for which $P (E_1 \text{ and } E_2 \text{ and } \ldots \text{ and } E_{k-1}) > 0$, then

$$P (E_1 \text{ and } E_2 \text{ and } \ldots \text{ and } E_k) = P (E_1) \cdot P (E_2 \mid E_1).$$
$$P (E_3 \mid E_1 \text{ and } E_2) \ldots \cdot P (E_k \mid E_1 \text{ and } E_2 \text{ and } \ldots \text{ and } E_{k-1}) \cdot$$

PARTITIONING A SET

In using Bayesian procedures frequent reference is made to a set of mutually exclusive and collectively exhaustive states of nature. Set partitions have already been encountered in the data of Table 5-4. The A_i's (purchase vs. nonpurchase) and the B_j's (magazine readership of B_1, B_2, and B_3) already formed partitions over the total set of interest, frequently called the universal set. The formal properties of a set partition are as follows:

A partition of a set E is a set $\{E_1, E_2, \ldots, E_n\}$ with the following properties:

(a) $E_j \subseteq E \ (j = 1, 2, \ldots, n)$. Each event E_j is a subset of the universal set E.

(b) $E_j \text{ and } E_k = \phi \ (j = 1, 2, \ldots, n; k = 1, 2, \ldots, n;$ any events $j \neq k)$. E_j and $E_k \ (j \neq k)$ have no events in common, that is, ϕ stands for the "empty set" containing no events.

(c) E_1 and/or E_2 and/or $\ldots$ and/or $E_n = E$
The events $E_1, E_2, \ldots, E_n$ exhaust the set of all possible events.

In terms of the data of Table 5-4 all respondents can be classified by readership of the three magazines, B_1, B_2 and B_3. Any reader of, say, magazine B_1 is not a reader of magazine B_2 or B_3, and vice versa. Finally, the three magazines, B_1, B_2, and B_3, exhaust the possible readership classes. Thus each respondent reads one and only one of the three magazines. As has already been noted, a set may be partitioned in more than one way, for example, by readership or by purchase of the product in the data of Table 5-4.

BAYES' THEOREM

In order to describe Bayes' theorem, which is central to later discussion, return to the multiplication theorem, now stated in terms of conditional probability.

$$P (E_1 \mid E_2) = \frac{P (E_1 \text{ and } E_2)}{P (E_2)} \qquad P (E_2) \neq 0$$

In terms of the data of Table 5-4, the probability that a respondent purchases the product and reads magazine B_3 is

$$P (A_1 \text{ and } B_3) = P (A_1 \mid B_3) \cdot P (B_3)$$
$$= 1.0 \ (0.10)$$
$$= 0.10$$

Also, the probability that a respondent reads magazine B_3 and purchases the product is

$$P (B_3 \text{ and } A_1) = P (B_3 \mid A_1) \cdot P (A_1)$$
$$= 0.40 \ (0.25)$$
$$= 0.10$$

Thus, in general notation

$$P (E_1 \text{ and } E_2) = P (E_2 \text{ and } E_1) = P (E_1 \mid E_2) \cdot P (E_2)$$
$$= P (E_2 \mid E_1) \cdot P (E_1).$$

But from the last relationship

$$P (E_1 \mid E_2) = \frac{P (E_2 \mid E_1) \cdot P (E_1)}{P (E_2)}$$

In more general terms, Bayes' theorem is written as follows:

Let $[E_1, E_2, \ldots, E_n]$ form a partition and for all E_j, $P (E_j) > 0$. Let R stand for any event for which $P (R) > 0$. Then for each integer i,

$$P (E_i \mid R) = \frac{P (R \mid E_i) \cdot P (E_i)}{\sum_{j=1}^{n} P (R \mid E_j) \cdot P (E_j)}$$

Bayes' theorem can also be illustrated in terms of the data of Table 5-4. Suppose that before the type of magazine a respondent reads is known, a *prior probability* (marginal probability) of 0.25 that the respondent purchases the product and a probability of 0.75 that the respondent is a nonpurchaser are assigned. Now suppose it is observed that the respondent reads magazine B_1. Given this new information, how would the prior probabilities regarding purchase and nonpurchase of the product be revised?

Let the event B_1 stand for the event R in the general formulation of Bayes' theorem. Solve first for the revised probability that the respondent purchases the product based on the information that he reads magazine B_1.

$$P(A_1 \mid B_1) = \frac{P(B_1 \mid A_1) \cdot P(A_1)}{P(B_1 \mid A_1) \cdot P(A_1) + P(B_1 \mid A_2) \cdot P(A_2)}$$

$$= \frac{0.40 \cdot 0.25}{(0.40 \cdot 0.25) + (0.67 \cdot 0.75)}$$

$$= 0.17$$

In other words, before receiving the new information regarding the fact that the respondent reads magazine B_1, a 0.25 probability that he was a purchaser would have been assigned. Now that it is known that he reads magazine B_1, the probability that he is a purchaser decreases to 0.17.

Now solve for the posterior probability of nonpurchase, given that the respondent reads magazine B_1.

$$P(A_2 \mid B_1) = \frac{P(B_1 \mid A_2) \cdot P(A_2)}{P(B_1 \mid A_2) \cdot P(A_2) + P(B_1 \mid A_1) \cdot P(A_1)}$$

$$= \frac{0.67 \cdot 0.75}{(0.67 \cdot 0.75) + (0.40 \cdot 0.25)}$$

$$= 0.83$$

Close examination of Table 5-4 shows why the additional information on readership of magazine B_1 increases the probability that the respondent is a nonpurchaser. Notice that 5/6 or 0.83 of the total probability under B_1 is assigned to the event A_2. It is clear that Bayes' theorem is just another way of expressing conditional probability. This notion will be expanded in the following section.

THE VALUE OF PERFECT INFORMATION— PREPOSTERIOR ANALYSIS

After this digression, whose purpose was to review some elementary probability theorems, the problem confronting the marketing manager on whether to open a new sales territory can be further examined. Suppose first that the marketing manager could delay his terminal decision pending the purchase of a perfect market survey which would tell him without error which state of nature, S_1 or S_2, represents the real facts. How much could the manager afford to spend for such a survey?

Assume that the survey can yield only two results, Z_1 and Z_2, where Z_1 indicates that S_1 (high sales) is the correct state and Z_2 indicates that S_2 (low sales) is the correct state. According to the ground rules of the problem

$$P\ (Z_1\mid S_1) = 1.0$$
$$P\ (Z_2\mid S_2) = 1.0$$
$$P\ (Z_1\mid S_2) = 0$$
$$P\ (Z_2\mid S_1) = 0$$

It will be recalled that the marketing manager has assigned prior probabilities of 0.4 and 0.6 respectively to S_1 and S_2. Also note that S_1 and S_2 form a partition over the set of possible states of nature. Suppose a table of joint and marginal probabilities is now set up as shown in Table 5–5.

Table 5–5
JOINT AND MARGINAL PROBABILITIES—SALES REGION PROBLEM

	S_1	S_2	Marginal Probabilities	Posterior Probabilities $P\ (S_1\mid Z_i)$	$P\ (S_2\mid Z_i)$
Z_1....................	0.40	0.00	0.40	1.0	0.0
Z_2....................	0.00	0.60	0.60	0.0	1.0
Marginal Probabilities....	0.40	0.60	1.00		

The joint probabilities of Table 5–5 are found by application of the multiplication theorem. For example, in the first cell of the table

$$0.40 = 1.0\ \cdot\ 0.40$$

and so on. Notice that the revised or posterior probabilities reflect the application of Bayes' theorem in this rather trivial case. For example, if Z_1 is observed, then the revised probability of S_1, given Z_1, is clearly 1.0. If Z_2 is observed the revised probability of S_1, given Z_2, is zero.

Now calculate the expected value of acting under certainty with regard to S_1 and S_2. If Z_1 were to occur, the marketing manager knows that S_1 is the true state of nature; he would accordingly take act A_1 with its conditional payoff of $5 million. If Z_2 were to occur, the marketing manager knows that S_2 is the true state of nature; he would accordingly take act A_2 with its conditional payoff of $0 million.

Before the decision is made to purchase the perfect survey, however, the manager must still apply the appropriate marginal probabilities, $P(Z_1)$ and $P(Z_2)$, as to which survey result will occur. That is, he must "pay his money" before getting the results of the surveys. In the special case when the conditional probabilities $P(Z_1 \mid S_1)$ and $P(Z_2 \mid S_2)$ equal 1.0, it is clear that the marginal probabilities assigned to Z_1 and Z_2, respectively, will equal the marketing manager's prior probabilities of 0.4 and 0.6 assigned to S_1 and S_2, respectively. His expected payoff under certainty is shown in Table 5–6.

Table 5–6

EXPECTED PAYOFF UNDER CERTAINTY—SALES REGION PROBLEM

	$P(S_1)$	S_1	$P(S_2)$	S_2	Expected Payoff
A_1	0.4	5	0.6	–	2.0
A_2	0.4	–	0.6	0	0.0
					2.0

As shown in Table 5–6 the expected payoff under perfect information conditions is $2 million and is interpreted as a strategy which would select A_1 if Z_1 were observed and A_2 if Z_2 were observed. Without bothering to purchase the perfect survey it is already known that the expected payoff associated with taking the better act A_1, in the face of current uncertainties, is $0.8 million. The difference between these two payoffs

$$2.0 - 0.8 = \$1.2 \text{ million}$$

represents the *expected value of perfect information* and, hence, the cost of uncertainty attached to taking act A_1 without the perfect information.

If the decision maker had to pay *more* than $1.2 million for the perfect survey it would not be worth while, that is, the cost of the perfect information and optimal terminal action would exceed its expected value. The difference between $1.2 million and the cost of the survey, if positive, would represent the *net gain* of purchasing perfect information.

Notice further that the $1.2 million agrees with the *expected opportunity loss* (Table 5–2) associated with taking the better act A_1 in the light of current uncertainties. This is no accident, and one can reason why this is so by reflecting on the results of the perfect survey. For example, if Z_1 (indicating S_1) were to occur the decision maker would *not* have changed his course of action A_1 which he would select in the absence of the new information. Hence, no opportunity loss would be suffered. If, however, the survey were to result in Z_2 (indicating S_2) the manager would suffer an opportunity loss if the act were not changed from A_1 to A_2. That is, if S_2 were the correct state of nature, the decision maker who selected A_1 would incur a loss of $2 million when, if he had selected A_2, he would have incurred a payoff of $0 million.

In terms of the problem, 40 percent of the time a zero opportunity loss would be incurred, and 60 percent of the time a $2 million opportunity loss would be incurred. The *expected opportunity loss* is thus

$$0.4 \ (0) + 0.6 \ (2) = \$1.2 \text{ million}$$

which is again the value of perfect information. Table 5–7 shows the relationships among expected payoff, expected opportunity loss, and the expected payoff under certainty.

Table 5–7

EXPECTED PAYOFF AND EXPECTED OPPORTUNITY LOSS—
SALES REGION PROBLEM

	Expected Payoff	Expected Opportunity Loss	Total
A_1.............	0.8	1.2	2.0
A_2.............	0.0	2.0	2.0

As noted in Table 5–7, the expected opportunity loss of the *better* act A_1, at $1.2 million, represents the expected value of perfect information, that is, the difference between the expected payoff under certainty, $2 million, and the expected payoff of the better act A_1 (at $0.8 million) in the absence of perfect information.

In summary, one always compares the expected value of further information to the expected payoff of the *best* act in the absence of the new information. The expected value of perfect information will equal the expected opportunity loss associated with the best course of action taken in the absence of the new information. As has been seen, this figure also equals the difference between the expected payoff of the best strategy under certainty and the expected payoff of the best act in the absence of the new information. Finally, decision making under certainty will result in an expected opportunity loss of zero since the best act is always assumed to be taken under these rather artificial conditions.

IMPERFECT INFORMATION—PREPOSTERIOR ANALYSIS

Rarely, if ever, do surveys (or experiments generally) yield perfect information at any cost. More realistically, the decision maker must cope with sampling error and/or systematic error in his sample findings. In the preceding two sections both posterior analysis (revision of prior probabilities on the basis of sample evidence) and preposterior analysis (ascertaining the advisability of gathering more information) in the special case of perfectly reliable surveys were discussed.

Now, consider the more general case in which survey results are *not* 100 percent reliable. No radically new principles will be involved, but it should be shown how the analysis would proceed in this more usual case. Assume that the marketing manager can purchase a survey which is only 80 percent reliable. That is, the survey can result in two findings, Z_1 or Z_2, but the relevant conditional probabilities for this case are

$$P\ (Z_1\ |\ S_1) = 0.8$$
$$P\ (Z_2\ |\ S_2) = 0.8$$
$$P\ (Z_1\ |\ S_2) = 0.2$$
$$P\ (Z_2\ |\ S_1) = 0.2$$

Again, the question arises as to how much the decision maker should pay for this imperfect survey. The same general procedure as before is followed by setting up the table of joint and marginal probabilities shown in Table 5–8.

Table 5–8

JOINT AND MARGINAL PROBABILITIES—SALES REGION PROBLEM
(80 PERCENT RELIABLE SURVEY)

	S_1	S_2	Marginal Probabilities	Posterior Probabilities $P\ (S_1\ |\ Z_i)$	$P\ (S_2\ |\ Z_i)$
Z_1.	0.32	0.12	0.44	0.73	0.27
Z_2.	0.08	0.48	0.56	0.14	0.86
Marginal Probabilities. . . .	0.40	0.60	1.00		

The joint and marginal probabilities are calculated similarly to the computations described in Table 5–5. The posterior probabilities $P(S_1\ |\ Z_i)$ and $P\ (S_2\ |\ Z_i)$ are found by application of Bayes' theorem. For example, suppose Z_1, a result suggesting S_1 as the underlying state of nature, is observed. To find $P\ (S_1\mid Z_1)$ and $P\ (S_2\mid Z_1)$ simply divide each joint probability assigned to Z_1 by its marginal probability, that is

$$P\ (S_1\mid Z_1) = 0.32/0.44 = 0.73$$

and

$$P\ (S_2\mid Z_1) = 0.12/0.44 = 0.27.$$

In terms of Bayes' theorem

$$P\ (S_1\mid Z_1) = \frac{P\ (Z_1\mid S_1)\ \cdot\ P\ (S_1)}{P\ (Z_1\mid S_1)\ \cdot\ P\ (S_1) + P\ (Z_1\mid S_2)\ \cdot\ P\ (S_2)}$$

$$= \frac{0.8\ \cdot\ 0.4}{(0.8\ \cdot\ 0.4) + (0.2\ \cdot\ 0.6)}$$

$$= \frac{0.32}{0.32 + 0.12}$$

$$= 0.73$$

Similar procedures apply to the calculation of $P\ (S_2\mid Z_1)$, $P\ (S_1\mid Z_2)$, and $P\ (S_2\mid Z_2)$.

Now that the posterior probabilities have been obtained, how much the marketing manager can afford to spend for a survey which is only 80 percent reliable must be determined.

To follow through these calculations, a *decision tree* which represents a diagram of this problem is introduced. This tree diagram is shown in Figure 5–1. The decision tree of Figure 5–1 provides a convenient way to trace through the implications of this problem. The main branches refer to the two options under evaluation—"do not purchase survey" (make terminal choice now) and "purchase survey" before making terminal choice.

The upper main branch refers to the original problem where only the marketing manager's *prior* probabilities were relevant. As is already known, in this situation the better act is A_1, which leads to an expected payoff of $0.8 million. In terms of the tree diagram, the probabilities are branch weights which are assigned to the conditional payoffs appearing at the terminal nodes. Note that the A_2 branch is blocked off with a double slash since, given that he does not purchase the survey, the decision maker would take act A_1.

The lower branch of the tree diagram refers to the strategy "purchase survey" and *then* take optimal terminal action. If he elects this option it is clear that the survey can result in Z_1 or Z_2 with associated marginal probabilities obtained from Table 5–8. Given each sample outcome he can take either A_1 or A_2. Note, however,

Figure 5–1

DECISION TREE—SALES REGION PROBLEM
80 PERCENT RELIABLE SURVEY
(PAYOFFS IN MILLIONS OF DOLLARS)

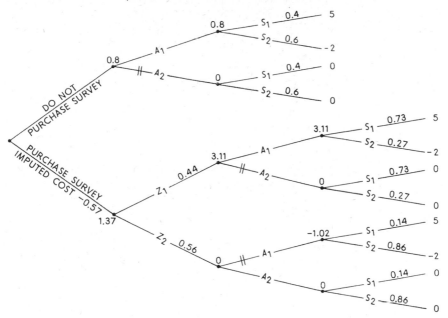

that the branch weights assigned to S_1 and S_2 are now *posterior* probabilities also derived from Table 5–8. If he observes Z_1 his better act is A_1, leading to an expected payoff of $3.11 million, clearly higher than the zero payoff associated with act A_2; hence A_2 is blocked off. *Before the fact*, however, he can observe Z_1 or Z_2, with associated marginal probabilities of 0.44 and 0.56, respectively, as shown in Table 5–8. He must then apply these probabilities to the expected payoffs found by taking the *higher* payoff act, given each survey outcome.

The expected payoff of this whole strategy is $1.37 million, clearly higher than the $0.8 million associated with foregoing the survey and taking terminal action immediately; that is, the *expected value of the survey information* (including optimal terminal action) is

$$\$1.37 - 0.8 = \$0.57 \text{ million}$$

He can afford to spend up to $0.57 million for this type of survey. Any cost under $0.57 million would result in a net gain. Any cost exceeding $0.57 million would be uneconomical; the cost of the information would exceed its expected value.

SEQUENTIAL INFORMATION COLLECTION—
PREPOSTERIOR ANALYSIS

Up to this point it has been assumed that just *one* survey could be taken, after which the decision maker would have to choose between termnial acts. Suppose now that the marketing manager can take *two* surveys (if he so desires) before choosing between terminal acts.

In order to recapitulate earlier results, assume that the marketing manager is faced with four options.

1. Experiment e_0: Do not take any survey; make terminal choice now.
2. Experiment e_1: Purchase a perfect survey; cost of this service equals $1.0 million.
3. Experiment e_2: Purchase a survey which is 80 percent reliable; cost of this service equals $0.5 million.
4. Experiment e_3: Purchase a survey which is only 70 percent reliable in the first stage but which is 80 percent reliable if a second stage is undertaken. Cost of the first stage equals $0.2 million while cost of the second stage, if justified, is $0.4 million. (Since some setup costs need not be duplicated, the second stage, 80 percent reliability survey, can be performed more cheaply if preceded by a first stage survey than if conducted alone.)

From earlier analyses it is already known how to handle experiments e_0, e_1, and e_2. However, a table of joint and marginal proba-

Table 5–9

JOINT AND MARGINAL PROBABILITIES—SALES REGION PROBLEM
TWO STAGE SURVEY

	S_1	S_2	Marginal Probabilities	$P(S_1 \mid Z_i)$	$P(S_2 \mid Z_i)$
First Stage					
Z_1............	0.28	0.18	0.46	0.61	0.39
Z_2............	0.12	0.42	0.54	0.22	0.78
	0.40	0.60	1.00		
Second Stage					
Z_1, Z_1........	0.49	0.08	0.57	0.86	0.14
Z_2, Z_1........	0.12	0.31	0.43	0.28	0.72
	0.61	0.39	1.00		
Z_1, Z_2........	0.18	0.16	0.34	0.53	0.47
Z_2, Z_2........	0.04	0.62	0.66	0.06	0.94
	0.22	0.78	1.00		

bilities which refer to the e_3 experiment is now required. These probabilities are shown in Table 5-9.

No really new principles are involved in the calculations underlying Table 5-9. What is required is to compute joint, marginal, and posterior probabilities for *two* stages. For example, the joint probability, 0.28, entered in the first cell of the upper table is merely the probability of observing Z_1 with S_1 as the underlying state of nature. This joint probability equals

$$P(Z_1 \mid S_1) \cdot P(S_1) = 0.70 \cdot 0.40 = 0.28$$

If a second *survey* is undertaken, it is clear that, given Z_1 on the first stage, another Z_1 response or a Z_2 response can be observed; similarly, given Z_2 on the first stage, Z_1 or Z_2 can be observed on the second stage. The posterior probabilities computed for S_1 and S_2 *after* the first stage is completed become the *prior* probabilities for the second stage. To illustrate, the entry, 0.49, in the first cell of the second stage problem represents the joint probability of observing a second Z_1 under state S_1, given that the first-survey outcome was Z_1. This joint probability equals

$$0.8 \cdot 0.61 = 0.49$$

In effect each piece of data can be combined sequentially. The reader might wish to convince himself that this procedure yields the same second-stage posterior probabilities as would be obtained by treating the sample outcomes as pairs, given each state of nature.

Now that the appropriate joint, marginal, and posterior probabilities have been computed for pertinent experiments, the expected payoffs of each strategy in Figures 5-2 and 5-3 can be summarized. Figure 5-2 summarizes the data of Figure 5-1 and also adds the e_1 experiment and relevant survey costs for experiments e_1 and e_2. Experiment e_0 (a dummy experiment) involves no survey cost. By solving the decision tree backwards expected values of \$0.8 million, \$1 million, and \$0.87 million for experiments e_0, e_1, and e_2 respectively are reached. Of these *three* experiments, strategy e_1 (purchasing a perfect survey) leads to the highest payoff; hence the main paths of e_0 and e_2 are blocked off. Still, however, e_3, the sequential experiment, must be evaluated.

Figure 5-3 summarizes experiment e_3. As before, this strategy is traced through by starting at the right of the chart and working backwards. First, note that the posterior and marginal probabilities of Table 5-9 have been affixed to the appropriate three branches. Note also that branches labeled "stop" and "go" have been inserted;

these branches reflect the decision maker's option to forego a second survey if the expected payoff of the second stage does not justify its cost.

Illustratively, trace through the upper main branch of the chart. Note that, given "go", if Z_1, Z_1 (e_3) is observed, the decision maker's better choice is act A_1, leading to an expected payoff of

Figure 5–2

DECISION TREE—SALES REGION PROBLEM
(PAYOFFS IN MILLIONS OF DOLLARS)

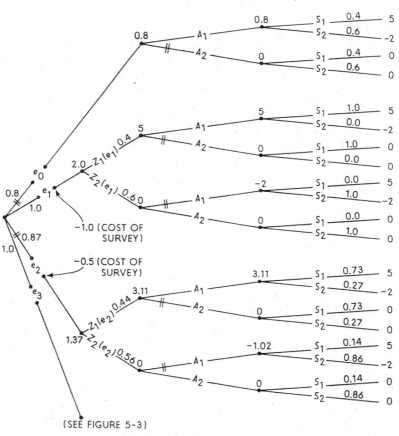

(SEE FIGURE 5-3)

$4 million; hence act A_2 with an expected value of $0 million is blocked off. If Z_2, Z_1 (e_3) is observed, act A_2 at $0 million is preferable; hence act A_1 with an expected payoff of $—0.04 million is blocked off. Since *either* Z_1, Z_1 (e_3) or Z_2, Z_1 (e_3) can be observed, their respective probabilities must be applied to the expected payoffs associated with taking optimal action from that point forward.

Expecting over these average payoffs leads to an expected payoff of $2.3 million before deducting the $0.4 million cost associated with the second survey.

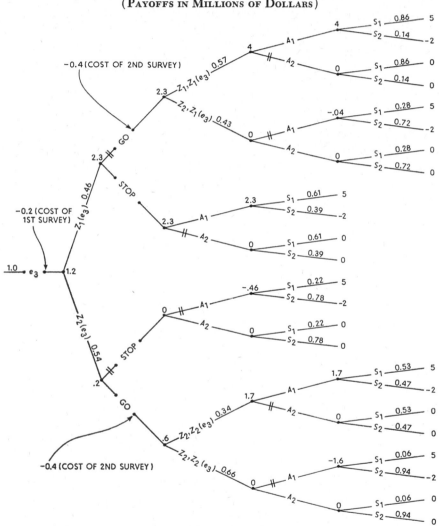

Figure 5–3

DECISION TREE—SALES REGION PROBLEM
(PAYOFFS IN MILLIONS OF DOLLARS)

Suppose, however, the decision maker elects to stop after the first survey and take optimal terminal action. As can be noted, if $Z_1 (e_3)$ is observed and "stop" action is taken, the expected payoff is also $2.3 million. That is, if $Z_1 (e_3)$ is observed, the expected value of "stop" will clearly exceed that of "go" after the cost of a second survey, given "go," is deducted. Hence, the "go" option is blocked off. Similar reasoning applies to the lower main branch of the tree diagram. In the case where Z_2 (e_3) is observed, however, it pays the decision maker to "go," that is, to undertake a second survey.

After all calculations are performed it is noted that strategy e_3 also leads to an expected payoff of $1 million. Thus the decision maker, other things being equal, possesses two strategies, e_1 and e_3 yielding the same expected payoff; he could select either one. (In realistic problems, of course, it would be rare that two different strategies would yield exactly the same expected payoff.)

The reader should observe that at each stage of the tree the decision maker is interested only in which strategy is best *from that point forward*. "Sunk" costs are truly sunk. They become relevant as the problem is solved recursively by moving back a step at a time toward the beginning of the tree diagram. Note that the decision maker's complete strategy is laid out in advance. In e_3, for example, if Z_1 (e_3) is observed, the marketing manager selects terminal act A_1 and foregoes a second survey. If Z_2 (e_3) is observed, his decision is to delay terminal action and take another survey. If the second survey indicates Z_1, Z_2 (e_3) he selects act A_1. If the survey indicates Z_2, Z_2 (e_3) he selects act A_2.

In summary, it has been shown, albeit by an oversimplified, expository case, how the decision maker can evaluate alternative data-collecting procedures before undertaking them. As has been noted, his strategy will be to compare the expected payoff of the best course of action, given no additional information, with the expected payoff which involves information collection (one or several stages) and terminal action. In general, he will balance the cost of additional information against its expected payoff in reducing the costs of uncertainty.

It should be added that best strategies will not necessarily involve the collection of additional information, even perfect information; the costs of securing the information may exceed its value. On the one hand, information may be so unreliable as not to be worth even a modest cost of collection. On the other hand, the decision maker's costs of uncertainty under his *present* state of knowledge may be so low as to preclude the expenditure for additional information even if the data are highly reliable.

THE RELATIONSHIP OF BAYESIAN METHODS TO TRADITIONAL STATISTICAL INFERENCE

The market planner trained in traditional statistical methods may well wonder if Bayesian procedures really provide anything new insofar as statistical inference is concerned. While it is not the purpose of this chapter to provide any exhaustive review of traditional statistical inference, perhaps one illustration can serve to point out the relationship between the two sets of techniques. The sales region example of preceding sections can be modified to demonstrate the essentials of each procedure.

First, our marketing manager is endowed with somewhat more detailed information about his payoff functions and their relationship to consumer preferences for his product than was assumed earlier. As before, however, the data are oversimplified and hypothetical.

Continue to assume that the decision maker is faced with the choice of whether or not to enter a new sales territory. But this time assume that the manager has been able to relate the desirability of entering the market to the *proportion of total customers* in the new territory who would prefer his product were it available for sale. Figure 5-4 portrays the conditional payoffs and opportunity losses associated with A_1 and A_2 as a function of the unknown parameter p, the proportion of total customers in the new region who would prefer his product to competitive products, were it available.

Figure 5-4 (A) indicates that, if act A_1 were taken and if no customer in the territory preferred the product, the manager's firm would suffer a $3 million loss associated with withdrawing his product from the new territory. In fact, act A_2 remains the better act until the true proportion of customers who would favor the product reaches 0.3 or 30 percent. If the true proportion exceeds 30 percent, it can be seen from the chart that the decision maker gains $0.1 million for each percentage point change until a conditional payoff of $7 million is reached when the true proportion is 1.0 or 100 percent. The right hand portion (B) of Figure 5-4 shows the conditional opportunity losses associated with each act as a function of the true proportion, p. As can again be noted, act A_2 (do not enter the territory) is preferable if the true proportion is less than 0.3, and act A_1 is preferable if the true proportion is greater than 0.3. If the true proportion is exactly 0.3 assume that act A_2 (*status quo*) would be taken, although at this specific value it makes no difference which act is selected.

Now suppose the manager is presented the results of a market survey of fifty randomly chosen potential customers in the new territory. (In this introductory illustration, the interesting questions of whether fifty was the correct size sample, whether any survey at all should have been taken, or whether the answers of survey respondents truly reflect what they would do if the product were

actually available have been neglected.) Of the fifty total respondents, sixteen indicated a preference for the manager's product when
it was compared to other products already being sold in the new

Figure 5–4

CONDITIONAL PAYOFFS AND OPPORTUNITY LOSSES—SALES REGION PROBLEM

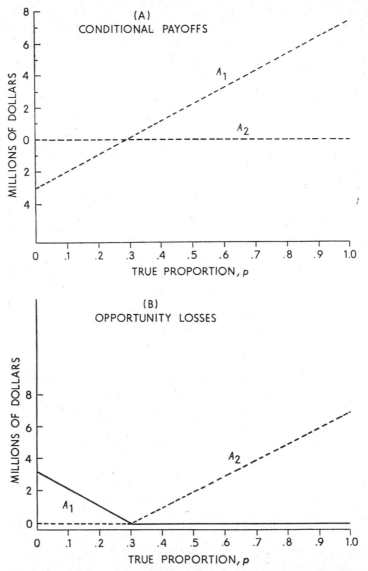

sales region. The manager assumes no bias in response; for example,
he assumes that what the respondents say during the pretest reflects
the attitudes which they would possess during full-scale introduc-

tion. His task now is to examine how this sample evidence might be treated, in turn, by traditional and Bayesian statistical procedures.

TRADITIONAL HYPOTHESIS TESTING

The traditional statistician might set up the following hypotheses:

$$H_0: p \leqslant 0.3$$
$$H_1: p > 0.3$$

The hypothesis H_0 is typically called the null hypothesis, that is, the hypothesis of no change, thus implying the choice of act A_2. The hypothesis H_1 is typically called the alternative hypothesis. As the reader may recall from elementary statistics, a type I error, or error of the first kind, consists of rejecting H_0 when it is true. Similarly, a type II error, or error of the second kind, consists of accepting H_0 when it is false. The probability that the statistician assigns to making a type I error is called the alpha risk; the probability that he assigns to making a type II error is called the beta risk.

In traditional statistical practice the analyst usually sets some kind of fixed limit on the alpha risk (say alpha = 0.05) when p exactly equals 0.3 and then examines the various beta risks associated with making a type II error since the size of this error will depend upon the true parameter, p. In this particular problem (one-sided test) he may also examine the alpha risk as a function of the true parameter, p, for values of p less than 0.3. In the illustration, if the alpha risk is set at approximately 0.05 (actually 0.0478) for $p = 0.3$, the decision maker would not reject the null hypothesis unless the number in the sample of fifty respondents who expressed a preference for the manager's product exceeded twenty. Examine the consequences of this rule by examining Figure 5–5.

Figure 5–5 is known as an error characteristic curve which shows the alpha and beta risks associated with the decision rule "accept H_0 if the number of respondents, r, favoring the manager's product (out of a total of fifty respondents) is less than or equal to twenty; otherwise reject H_0." As explained above, the consequences of this rule which is based on an alpha level of .05 when the true parameter, $p = 0.3$ are being examined. That is, if the true proportion of respondents favoring the product is exactly 0.3, then about five times out of one hundred the analyst who employs the above rule will reject the null hypothesis when it is true. In other words, if the random sampling process were repeated a large number of times (and drawn from a universe whose $p = 0.3$), only about 5 percent of the samples of fifty each would show $r > 20$, hence leading to a rejection of H_0, when H_0 was really true.

Notice, however, that a decision rule so stringent as rarely to reject H_0 leads to an extremely high probability of accepting H_0 when it is false. That is, even if the true proportion favoring the product were, say, 0.5, H_0 would be accepted about 10 percent of the time when, of course, it should have been rejected. It is clear that the preceding alpha risk level of 0.05 leads to a rather stringent

Figure 5-5°

ERROR CHARACTERISTIC CURVE—SALES REGION PROBLEM

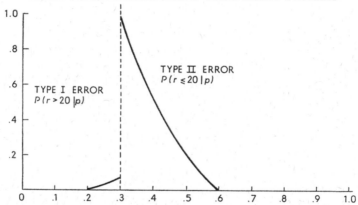

°The reader will recognize the error characteristic curve of Figure 5–5 as a composite curve from elementary statistics. The curve to the left of the vertical dotted line is a portion of the "power curve" of elementary statistics which shows the probability of rejecting the null hypothesis as a function of the true value of p. The curve to the right of the dotted line is a portion of the familiar "operating characteristic" curve which shows the probability of accepting the null hypothesis as a function of the true value of p. The reader will also observe that the probabilities making up these curves are derived from standard tables of the binomial distribution. It is assumed that the sample is a random one drawn from some appropriate Bernoulli process.

decision rule in favor of accepting H_0. Obviously, other decision rules can be examined, but first consider what would happen to these curves if the opportunity losses associated with wrong decisions are introduced.

To calculate conditional expected opportunity losses Table 5–10 is next prepared.

Table 5–10 was constructed in the following way. First, some discrete values for p, the true proportion of our population, namely, 0.25, 0.35, 0.40, and 0.50, were selected. Then the expected opportunity losses associated with taking terminal action on the basis of the *decision rule* were calculated. These losses are still *conditional*, however, on what the unknown parameter p turns out to be. These conditional expected losses are plotted in Figure 5–6, and a curve is faired in between the points.

Table 5–10

CALCULATION OF CONDITIONAL EXPECTED OPPORTUNITY LOSSES—
SALES REGION PROBLEM

| Sample Outcome | Decision | Probability | Opportunity Loss | |
			Conditional	Expected
$p = 0.25$				
$r \leq 20$..........	A_2	.9937	0	0
$r > 20$..........	A_1	.0063	0.5	.0032
				.0032
$p = 0.35$				
$r \leq 20$..........	A_2	.8139	0.5	.4070
$r > 20$..........	A_1	.1861	0	0
				.4070
$p = 0.40$				
$r \leq 20$..........	A_2	.5610	1.0	.5610
$r > 20$..........	A_1	.4390	0	0
				.5610
$p = 0.50$				
$r \leq 20$..........	A_2	.1013	2.0	.2026
$r > 20$..........	A_1	.8987	0	0
				.2026

When the plot of Figure 5–6 is observed, a rather startling result is noticed. While the decision rule

Accept H_0 if $r \leqslant 20$
Reject H_0 if $r > 20$

leads to very low opportunity losses if the true proportion is less than (or equal to) the breakeven $p = 0.3$, the opportunity losses associated with the true proportion exceeding $p = 0.3$ are very high.

Figure 5–6

CONDITIONAL EXPECTED OPPORTUNITY LOSSES—
SALES REGION PROBLEM

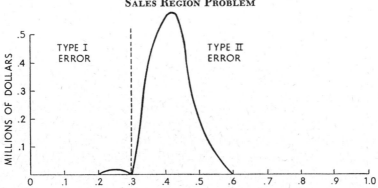

Other *decision* rules which could lead to a more balanced loss function could, of course, be evaluated, but observe that *only* if the decision maker attached an extremely high prior probability to the population proportion p being less than 0.3 would he wish to give this particular rule very much attention.

To return to the problem of analyzing the sixteen out of fifty respondents from our *particular* sample who showed a preference for the decision maker's product, according to the traditional decision rule which has just been set up (based on an alpha risk approximately equal to 0.05 when $p = 0.3$), the decision maker would accept H_0 if and only if the number of respondents favoring the product, r, is less than or equal to 20. Inasmuch as $r = 16 < 20$, he accepts H_0; that is, he takes act A_2 and does *not* enter the new sales region.

USE OF BAYESIAN PROCEDURES

Now that traditional hypothesis testing has been touched upon, apply Bayesian procedures to the same problem. Assume that the *same* sample evidence has been collected and that the decision maker wishes to handle the problem by Bayesian techniques. Assume that his *prior* probability assignment to states of nature $S_i = p_i$ (before viewing the sample findings) is shown in Table 5–11. The appropriate posterior analysis for this specific sample is also shown in the table.

Table 5–11

POSTERIOR ANALYSIS—SALES REGION PROBLEM

States of Nature $S_i = p_i$	Prior Probabilities $P(S_i)$	Conditional Probabilities $P(r = 16 \mid p; n = 50)$	Joint Probabilities $P(S_i) \cdot P(r = 16 \mid p; n = 50)$	Posterior Probabilities $P(S_i \mid r = 16; n = 50)$
.10	.10	.0000	.00000	.000
.20	.20	.0164	.00328	.059
.30	.40	.1147	.04588	.824
.40	.10	.0606	.00606	.109
.50	.10	.0044	.00044	.008
.60	.10	.0000	.00000	.000
			.05566	1.000

The entries of Table 5–11 show (a) the states of nature, $S_i = p_i$, or true proportions which the marketing manager is willing to admit as possibilities; (b) his prior probability assignment over these states; (c) the conditional probabilities (derived from standard binomial tables) of observing $r = 16$ in a sample of 50 respondents, given each state of nature $S_i = p_i$; (d) the joint probabilities; and (e) the posterior probabilities, $P(S_i \mid r = 16; n = 50)$. Notice that incorporaton of the sample evidence leads to a high posterior probability associated with the breakeven probability of 0.3. When the posterior probabilities are applied to the conditional payoffs of Figure 5–4 (A), the result is

Expected Payoff of $A_1 = 0.059 (-1.0) + 0.824 (0) + 0.109 (1.0) + 0.008$
$$(2.0)$$
$$= \$\ 0.066 \text{ Million (Max EP)}$$
Expected Payoff of $A_2 = \$0$ million

If the data are analyzed in terms of opportunity losses, the result is

Expected Opportunity Loss of $A_1 = 0.059 (1.0) + 0.941 (0.0)$
$= \$0.059$ million (Min E.O.L.)
Expected Opportunity Loss of $A_2 = 0.883 (0.0) + 0.109 (1.0)$
$+ 0.008 (2.0) = \$0.125$ million

as derived from the conditional opportunity losses of Figure 5–4. (B).

Hence, act A_1 is selected under either procedure. Had a familiar 0.05 level of significance (a level so frequently used in traditional statistical practice) been used, A_2 would have been selected. But, as has been seen in this illustration, application of so pat a rule would have led to rather absurd treatment of the conditional expected loss function, at least in this illustration.

THE RELEVANCE OF BAYESIAN STATISTICS TO MARKET PLANNING

While an elementary introduction to the subject of Bayesian procedures has been presented, later chapters will develop the subject in sufficient depth to deal with the characteristics of real problem situations. At this juncture, however, some of the features of Bayesian decision theory can be related to the structure of marketing planning problems.

The Essentiality of Managerial Judgment

A key feature of Bayesian statistics is that the decision maker's judgment becomes a part of the decision model. In marketing planning problems it cannot be overemphasized that management judgment is an essential part of planning. The planner is always dealing with the futurity of present decisions and/or the immediacy of future decisions. That is, the decision maker is often acting so as to *promote the power to act.* This means that he is pursuing present courses of action which in some sense increase his capacity for making better future decisions as his information state changes. This notion will be encountered again when multistage decisions are more extensively dealt with.

From the planner's standpoint the essentiality of managerial judgment in Bayesian statistics also provides the opportunity, even necessity, for managers to become *directly involved* in the planning process. This involvement should increase the chances for plans to be implemented. The staff planner who uses these procedures cannot be isolated in some cubicle drafting plans (which may never materialize). Rather, he must actively seek and secure the necessary prior probabilities from those in the organization best equipped to supply these judgments.

Also, Bayesian procedures provide a mechanism for modifying original judgments on the basis of new information. A type of learning function is introduced. A preponderance of objective data will tend to swamp initial judgments which are vague or assign a large variance to the possible states of nature.

The Asymmetry of Opportunity Lossses

It has also been seen that Bayesian procedures provide a way to introduce the economist's principle of opportunity losses right into the decision model. It will not infrequently be the case that these losses will be asymmetrical. That is, if the decision maker makes a wrong decision, the costs of a wrong decision might vary greatly with the particular act chosen. By being cognizant of this asymmetry the decision maker can devise his strategy accordingly.

For example, if commercializing a new product too soon can lead to a sizable loss in terms of corporate prestige and profits while commercializing a new product too late can lead only to a deferral of profits (assuming no important competitive inroads in the relevant time span), the decision maker may wish to be deliberately conservative in his estimate of future sales. This bias may be well taken, in view of the asymmetry of decision error, and could suggest a test marketing procedure which "errs on the safe side." Thus, some marketing plans may be formulated with explicit bias in mind; the best estimate of future conditions might not, nor, in some cases, should not, be the one most likely to occur.

The Sequential Commitment of Resources

Another feature of Bayesian statistics is that this model provides a way to deal with sequential decisions which include the changes in the decision maker's state of knowledge over the future. As was seen in the sales region illustration, a sequential information plan could be devised in which the decision choices at some stage may be to take terminal action or collect more information. This concept can be extended to deal with a sequence of "terminal" actions (and information states) as well.

For example, a decision maker need not make all "final" commitments of resources. Plants may be expanded in sections, product lines may be extended sequentially, promotional campaigns can be formulated in stages, contingent upon earlier outcomes. Bayesian procedures provide a way to view a sequence of actions so that present courses of action are taken which reflect the interaction of present alternatives and the states resulting therefrom with future options.

The Costs of Overplanning and Underplanning

The Bayesian model also gives insight into the always present problems of how much and how far ahead to plan. Obviously there are costs incurred in too much planning as well as too little planning. For example, a firm which proceeded to plan a detailed advertising media budget before the new product is out of the laboratory stage could well encounter needless costs in the sense that the probability that the product will even be commercialized may still be low or, even given its eventual commercialization, the media plan may well be obsolete by the time the product is ready for this stage.

The planner must keep in mind the costs of planning as well as the benefits. The fact that additional information may be highly unreliable as well as expensive should temper one's enthusiasm to "always be right no matter what the costs." Bayesian procedures provide the means to balance the costs of decision delay and information collection against the costs of making decisions on too little information and thus represent a framework in which the costs of overplanning and underplanning can be reasonably handled.

SUMMARY

This chapter has introduced the reader to the use of Bayesian procedures in plans evaluation by way of illustrative, hypothetical examples. It started with a discussion of some alternative interpretations of probability theory and proceeded to a discussion of random variables and a statement of the addition and multiplication theorems of probability.

The Bayesian notions of prior and posterior analysis were discussed and the mechanics and rationale of Bayes' theorem which underlies posterior analysis were reviewed.

Next a powerful concept of Bayesian statistics, was described—preposterior analysis in which the decision maker evaluates the wisdom of collecting additional information *before* making a terminal choice. This led to such measures as the costs of uncertainty, the expected value of perfect information, the expected value of sample information, and the net gain from new information. It was shown how both fixed stage and sequential stages could be solved by backward (recursive) averaging techniques, always taking the best course of action at any given stage and using the marginal probabilities to expect over "nature's" moves.

The relationship between traditional statistical techniques with their emphasis on type I and type II errors and Bayesian procedures which use conditional expected loss functions was then briefly discussed. Illustration of how the use of some arbitrary alpha risk like 0.05 can lead to a poor decision rule was made.

This chapter concluded with a description of those features of Bayesian analysis which appear particularly applicable to the characteristics of plans evaluation. The importance of managerial judgment, asymmetry of loss functions, the sequential commitment of resources, and the costs of overplanning and underplanning all represent notions which are compatible with Bayesian analysis and highly germane to a reasoned approach to marketing planning.

Selected References

CHERNOFF, HERMAN, AND MOSES, LINCOLN E. *Elementary Decision Theory.* New York: John Wiley & Sons, Inc., 1959.

    A good elementary book in decision theory which covers maximin, minimax regret as well as Bayesian decision rules. Also develops the theory in both "normal" and "extensive" form.

GOLDBERG, SAMUEL. *Probability.* Englewood Cliffs, N. J.: Prentice-Hall, Inc., 1960.

    An elementary yet rigorous presentation of probability for finite sample spaces. The treatment is exceptionally clear and complete for this branch of probability theory. Requires no calculus background.

GREEN, PAUL E. "The Computer's Place in Business Planning: A Bayesian Approach," *Marketing and the Computer* (ed. WROE ALDERSON AND STANLEY J. SHAPIRO). Englewood Cliffs, N. J.: Prentice-Hall, Inc., 1963.

    Discusses in some detail the relationship of Bayesian techniques and the computer to the characteristics of marketing and business planning problems.

RAIFFA, HOWARD, AND SCHLAIFER, ROBERT. *Applied Statistical Decision Theory.* Cambridge, Mass.: Harvard Business School Press, 1961.

    This monograph presents Bayesian theory at a sophisticated level. Not recommended to readers who have not covered the elementary books first and who do not have a good command of the calculus and matrix theory.

SCHLAIFER, ROBERT. *Probability and Statistics for Business Decisions.* New York: McGraw-Hill Book Co., Inc., 1959.

SCHLAIFER, ROBERT. *Introduction to Statistics for Business Decisions.* New York: McGraw-Hill Book Co., Inc., 1961.

Schlaifer's two books constitute definitive works on Bayesian statistics at a level understandable by the nonmathematician. These books are necessary reading for anyone wishing to explore Bayesian decision theory in any depth. The 1959 book is the more comprehensive of the two and includes interesting chapters on related operation research techniques. The 1961 book discusses the traditional statistical approach and its relationship to Bayesian concepts.

Problems

1. The sales manager of a small division of the March Corporation is considering the addition of a new man to the sales force. Given that the sales manager must make a terminal decision now, the following acts are assumed to be available to him:

1) Hire the additional salesman now under consideration, (A_1).

2) Do not hire the additional salesman now under consideration, (A_2). The sales manager believes that the new salesman could possibly produce three levels of sales during the coming year—high, medium, and low—and is also able to postulate the following prior probabilities of the new salesman attaining the various levels of sales and the resultant conditional payoffs given act A_1:

Sales	Prior Probability	Conditional Payoff
High................	0.2	$10,000
Medium.............	0.5	3,000
Low................	0.3	−12,000

Given act A_2, the conditional payoff is $0.

a) Evaluate the two acts using expected monetary value as the criterion of choice.

b) Evaluate the two acts using expected opportunity loss as the criterion of choice.

c) Will the two criteria listed above result in the same choice?

d) Explain in simple language the reasons underlying your answer to part *c*.

2. The Old Label Company, a national beer manufacturer, is deeply concerned about the recent developments in the beer container industry. To date, many companies have introduced a number of revolutionary beer containers. Among them are the easy-open aluminum-top cans, the self-opening aluminum-top cans that need no opener, and the wide-mouthed glass mugs that require no opener and allow the consumer to drink the beer from the container in much the same manner that he would drink from a mug. The marketing manager of the Old Label Company believes the time is ripe for the company to switch its canned beer distribution from the cans presently employed to one of the new types of cans or mugs. Given the above information the marketing manager believes that the following choices are available:

1) Adopt the easy-open aluminum-top cans, (A_1).
2) Adopt the self-opening aluminum-top cans that need no opener, (A_2).
3) Adopt the widemouthed glass mugs that require no opener, (A_3).
4) Keep the old-style beer cans, (A_4).
5) Delay a decision and conduct a marketing research study, (e_1). This study would be 70 percent reliable; that is, if the market study results indicate d_1 (namely that forecast D_1 will occur), there is a 15 percent chance that this information could have been assembled if the true underlying demand was D_2 and also a 15 percent chance that this information could have been assembled if the true underlying demand was D_3. The study would cost $.2 million.
6) Delay a decision and conduct two marketing research studies, (e_2). The first study would be 60 percent reliable (that is, $P(d_1 \mid D_1) = 0.60; P(d_1 \mid D_2) = 0.20; P(d_1 \mid D_3) = 0.20$) and would cost $0.1 million; the second survey would be 90 percent reliable (that is, $P(d_1 \mid D_1) = 0.90; P(d_1 \mid D_2) = 0.05; P(d_1 \mid D_3) = 0.05$. Cost of second survey is $0.15 million.

The marketing manager is able to postulate the following information:

CONDITIONAL PAYOFF MATRIX—THREE POSSIBLE DEMAND SITUATIONS (PAYOFFS IN MILLIONS OF DOLLARS)

	Demand 1	Demand 2	Demand 3
A_1..........	4	1	-4
A_2..........	-1	3	10
A_3..........	-2	2	8
A_4..........	5	1	-3

Prior probabilities for the occurrence of each demand situation are

$$\text{Demand } 1 = 0.5$$
$$\text{Demand } 2 = 0.3$$
$$\text{Demand } 3 = 0.2$$

a) Evaluate acts A_1, A_2, A_3, and A_4 using expected monetary value as the criterion of choice. What do you notice about the outcomes associated with acts A_1 and A_3?

b) Evaluate acts A_1, A_2, A_3, and A_4 using expected opportunity loss as the criterion of choice. What do you notice about the outcomes associated with acts A_1 and A_3?

c) What is the expected value of perfect information associated with acts A_2 and A_4?

d) Assuming that the marketing manager has eliminated acts A_1 and A_3 from the list of possible acts, evaluate strategies e_1 and e_2 using expected monetary value as the criterion of choice. Briefly interpret the results.

e) Using expected monetary value as the criterion of choice, construct a decision tree for terminal acts A_2 and A_4. (One branch of the tree should show the no-study option (e_0); one branch should show the one-study option; and one branch should show the two-study option.)

3. Explain the following terms: (*a*) random variable, (*b*) marginal probability, (*c*) conditional probability, (*d*) conditional payoff, (*e*) posterior probability, (*f*) sequential decision making, and (*g*) expected opportunity loss.

4. When using Bayesian decision theory and decision trees to make decisions, why should the decision maker (at any stage of the tree) be interested only in which strategy is best from that point forward?

5. *a*) What are the disadvantages inherent in the use of traditional hypothesis testing?

b) How does the Bayesian approach to problem solving promote a decision maker's power to act? (Alderson's power principle.)

Chapter 6

VALUE THEORY AND ITS RELATIONSHIP TO DECISION MAKING

The value measures used in the illustrative problems of the preceding chapter were referred to as payoffs, which were rather vaguely defined as cash flows. It is the purpose of this chapter to explore some of the ramifications of the process of specifying value measures. It will be seen that value theory goes hand in hand with decision theory; in fact it has already been noted that a necessary condition for a problem to exist is that the decision maker is assumed to want something, either gaining an objective or retaining what he has.

The discussion begins with a description of the meaning of the term objective and the attendant problems of specifying objectives and defining suitable measures of effectiveness (this measure being dependent upon both the relative importance of the objectives and their probability of attainment, given each course of action). The general problem of weighting multiple objectives, the meaning of scales, and some of the models, namely the Churchman-Ackoff measure and the von Neumann-Morgenstern utility function, which have been proposed for scaling multiple objectives are examined.

Since the planner, by necessity, will frequently use some monetary measure such as profits or cash flow as an approximate measure of effectiveness, the meaning of "profit planning over the horizon" is next discussed. Some of the desirable characteristics which financial measures should embody in market planning are described and illustrated by a discussion of discounted cash flow procedures.

Finally, some research done in an attempt to measure businessmen's attitudes toward risk taking and some of the difficulties associated with trying to use von Neumann-Morgenstern utility measures on a routine basis in market planning are reported.

THE DIFFICULTY OF MEASURING OBJECTIVES

An objective can be defined as a valued outcome. Objectives can be qualitative or quantitative. For example, a firm desirous of being "first in the market" with a new product possesses a qualitative objective. The firm either obtains that goal or not; various degrees of attainment are not considered. On the other hand, a quantitative objective can be obtained in various degrees. Most people desire more rather than less income, and the amount of value placed upon varying amounts of income can be differentiated, in principle, by gradations along some scale.

Market planning objectives may be myriad and involve both qualitative and quantitative properties. The firm's goals may include such considerations as market position, product quality, growth, financial stability, community service, and so on. These objectives may change over time and, obviously, are tempered by the firm's resources. Moreover, a *particular* decision maker's objectives may reflect the firm's goals, his department's goals, and his individual goals as well. The marketing planner will rarely, if ever, be cognizant of the objectives of *all* decision makers concerned with the choice and implementation of marketing plans. The practice of trying to choose some best plan in the light of less than full knowledge of objectives is a particular case of the general problem known as *incomplete optimization.*

In addition to the difficulty of specifying planning objectives, the planner may have to deal with the problem of conflicting goals as well. The term *suboptimization* has been used to describe decisions made to achieve a limited set of goals at some organizational level other than the highest. The achievement of some lower set of objectives, however, may not be consistent with higher-level goals.

Decision makers' attitudes toward risk taking also vary. That is, even if the manager agrees to adopt some monetary measure of effectiveness like return on investment, he may prefer an investment option with a lower average return to one which, on the average, is expected to lead to a higher return, if the return of the latter option is much more variable. Operational procedures for formally dealing with risk attitudes (utility functions, for example) have been developed and will be considered later on in this discussion.

THE STRUCTURE OF OBJECTIVES AND
MEASURES OF EFFECTIVENESS

Before some of the procedures which management scientists have proposed for weighting multiple objectives are considered, the expected value (payoff) criterion which constituted the measure of effectiveness in earlier chapters will be reviewed briefly. As noted in the two preceding chapters, a set of courses of action A_1, A_2, . . . , A_i, . . ., A_m and states of nature S_1, S_2, . . ., S_j, . . ., S_n leading to a set of outcomes was postulated. A set of values $V (A_i, S_j)$ was postulated as a function of the conjunction of each act with each state of nature, probabilities were assigned to the occurrence of each S_j, the conditional payoffs were averaged and then the act leading to the highest expected payoff was chosen. In the examples used, the value measure was monetary—cash flow. The expected value criterion should now be expanded upon so as to deal with a set of multiple objectives—market share, return on investment, and so forth.

Suppose O_{ij} stands for the outcome of taking act A_i under state of nature S_j and $V_1 (O_{ij})$ represents the value of outcome O_{ij} with respect to objective 1. Similarly $V_2 (O_{ij})$ could stand for the value of outcome O_{ij} with respect to objective 2, and so on. In the case of multiple objectives $V (O_{ij})$ could then, in principle stand for a functional value measure which reflects the relative importance of outcome O_{ij} to each of the objectives 1, 2, . . ., k.

$$V (O_{ij}) = \text{f} [V_1 (O_{ij}), V_2 (O_{ij}), . . . , V_k (O_{ij})]$$

While the above function may be easy to state, the task of determining a weighting function is far from easy.

However, a simple illustration might make clear the nature of the problem if not its solution. Suppose there are two objectives to be attained by two courses of action, one of which leads to a higher expected payoff for objective 1 and the other to a higher expected payoff for objective 2. This situation is shown in Table 6–1.

Table 6–1
EXPECTED PAYOFFS INVOLVING TWO OBJECTIVES

	Objective 1					Objective 2				
	$P (S_1)$	S_1	$P (S_2)$	S_2	EP	$P (S_1)$	S_1	$P (S_2)$	S_2	EP
A_1	0.6	5	0.4	−1	2.6	0.5	3	0.5	1	2.0
A_2	0.6	2	0.4	0	1.2	0.5	6	0.5	0	3.0

As can be inferred from Table 6–1, the decision maker's choice will depend on his evaluation of the relative importance of objective 1 and objective 2. Assume that the decision maker believes that the "value weights" to assign to the expected payoffs associated with objective 1 and objective 2 are 0.7 and 0.3 respectively. The payoffs could be combined as follows:

$$WEP\ (A_1) = 0.7\ (2.6) + 0.3\ (2.0)$$

$$= 2.42\ (\text{maximum})$$

$$WEP\ (A_2) = 0.7\ (1.2) + 0.3\ (3.0)$$

$$= 1.74$$

where WEP represents a "weighted" expected payoff.

In dealing with so simple a scheme as the above it is clear that one can merely take weighted averages of expected values. In practice, however, the problem of determining composite measures of effectiveness will be much more complex than illustrated here and will involve both substantive and methodological considerations.

In practice the planner may try to obtain a list of corporate objectives and their relative weights by a variety of means. He may merely ask the relevant decision makers to specify objectives and weights; he may suggest various objectives and weights and see if the ones selected are appropriate; or he may study the values which appear to be imputed by past decisions.

For purposes of discussing formal techniques for *combining* objectives (finding the appropriate weighting function) it will be assumed that the planner does possess a complete list of relevant objectives. That is, it is assumed that the planner has culled redundant objectives and those goals which would be unaffected by the plans under evaluation. For the reader actively engaged in market planning the oversimplicity of this assumption is obvious. A discussion of what is meant by "scaling" objectives precedes discussion of some formal procedures which have been developed to perform this function.

THE NATURE OF SCALES

The problem of combining multiple objectives into some overall measure of effectiveness by which alternative courses of action can be compared gives rise to a consideration of what is meant by "scales", generally. In the preceding chapter a dollar scale, cash flow, was used. Although the term "cash flow" requires definition (which will be undertaken later on in this chapter), nevertheless a dollar scale possesses some important attributes. One can intuitively grasp (*a*) the concept of zero dollars as a "natural" zero and (*b*) the concept of four being "twice as much" as two dollars. Not all scales possess these desirable properties of an absolute zero and constant unit of measurement.

The purpose of measurements is to convey information of general applicability about real-world observations on objects, events, or properties. Most frequently, numbers are used to convey this information. In using numerical measurements the market planner must be on his guard against imputing the properties which numbers possess to the observations themselves; he must be careful in the choice of a scale to represent the real phenomenon. The three major classes of scales are (*a*) nominal, (*b*) ordinal, and (*c*) cardinal.

A *nominal* scale is simply a measure which uses a number to name an entity and/or property of an entity. For example, in "party bridge," team players are assigned numbers for the series of rounds. It is clear that any number can be assigned to any player so long as each player has a unique number. It makes no sense to perform arithmetical operations on these numbers, and very little information is conveyed by the use of these numbers other than as means of identification.

An *ordinal* scale is a ranking measure which tells which of any two items is higher, lower, or the same on the scale. For example, one may wish to rank the series of bridge scores at the end of the evening's play. While a wide choice of numbers is available with which to do this, care must be taken that the numbers *preserve the ordering relationship*. If the decision is made to associate high numbers with high ranks, than a higher ranking person must be assigned a higher number than a lower ranking person. Ordinal scales are, of course, also nominal. That is, two persons with the same rank would receive the same number. However, one must be careful not to infer that the *numerical difference* between rank numbers measures how much better the higher-ranking person performed, or that rank differences can be subjected to standard arithmetical operations. For example, if the top ranking bridge player is assigned the number 16, it cannot be said (on this basis alone) that he performed four times as well as the person who received rank 4.

Cardinal scales permit the use of numbers to make predictions about items in combination. The two major subclasses of cardinal measures are *interval* scales and *ratio* scales. An interval scale has an arbitrary zero point and a constant unit of measure while a ratio scale has both an absolute zero point and a constant unit of measurement.

The centigrade and Fahrenheit scales are illustrations of interval measures while inches, pounds and dollars are examples of ratio scales. In the case of interval scales *differences* between scale values can be expressed as multiples of each other, but in general, individual values cannot. For example, it is not correct to say that 100° F is twice as hot as 50° F. On the Centigrade scale the equivalent temperatures, 37.8° C and 10° C are not in the ratio 2:1. However, we *can* say that the *differences* between 100° F and 0° F and between 50° F and 0° F are in the ratio 2:1. On the centigrade scale these differences would correspond to

$$[37.8 - (-17.8)] = 55.6° \text{ C and } [10.0 - (-17.8)] = 27.8° \text{ C}$$

which are in the same ratio, 2:1. This notion is formalized by saying that interval scales are unique up to a positive *linear transformation*. That is,

$$y = a + bx; \; b > 0$$

Notice that a centigrade scale can be derived by making a linear transformation of a Fahrenheit scale, namely, the familiar

$$T(C) = \tfrac{5}{9} [T(F) - 32]$$

where

$$b = \tfrac{5}{9} \text{ and } a = -\tfrac{5}{9} \times 32 = -17\tfrac{7}{9}$$

in the given algebraic expression.

In the case of ratio scales, however, it *does* make sense to talk about values on one scale being multiples of values on another. For example, 1 yard is equal to 3 feet and 1 foot is equal to 1/3 of a yard. In scales of this type an absolute zero (zero length) is available. Scales of this type are unique up to a proportionate transformation

$$y = cx; \; c > 0$$

and the arithmetic operations typically associated with numbers can be performed.

It should be reiterated that in the preceding hierarchy of scales, higher-order scales possess the properties of lower-order scales. For example, a ratio scale possesses all the properties of interval, ordinal, and nominal scales and, as noted, additional properties as well.

The two methods which are to be described shortly—the Churchman-Ackoff value measure and the Von Neumann-Morgenstern utility function—are both *interval scales*. At this juncture one might ask why so much concern is given to discussing interval scales. The answer is straightforward. In the preceding chapter which stressed Bayesian procedures, the criterion of rationality used was the maximization of expected value (payoff) where expected payoff for some act, A_i, was defined as

$$EP\ (A_i)\ =\ \sum_{j=1}^{n}\ P_j\ V\ (A_i,\ S_j)$$

For example, if act A_H yielded the highest expected payoff of all acts, this assumed that

$$EP\ (A_H)\ >\ EP\ (A_i) \qquad\qquad\text{for all } i \neq H$$

which, in turn, means that

$$EP\ (A_H)\ =\ \sum_{j=1}^{n}\ P_j\ V\ (A_H,\ S_j)\ >\ \sum_{j=1}^{n}\ P_j\ V\ (A_i,\ S_j) \quad\text{for all } i \neq H$$

But, we can "factor out" the $\sum_{j=1}^{n} P_j$, and transpose the $V\ (A_i,\ S_j)$, giving

$$\sum_{j=1}^{n}\ P_j\ [V\ (A_H,\ S_j)\ -\ V\ (A_i,\ S_j)]\ >\ 0 \qquad\qquad\text{for all } i \neq H$$

The reader will recall that the sense of an inequality is not changed by multiplying each side by any positive constant or by adding a constant to each side. That is to say, a positive linear transformation of the form,

$$y = a + bx;\ b > 0$$

could be applied without affecting the validity of the inequation. Hence, only an *interval scale* is needed in order to use the expected payoff criterion. Of course, as noted earlier, ratio scales also possess interval scale properties and could be used if available. The next step is to examine two interval scales which have been proposed for weighting multiple objectives—the Churchman-Ackoff measure and the von Neumann-Morgenstern measure.

THE CHURCHMAN-ACKOFF VALUE MEASURE FOR WEIGHTING OBJECTIVES

As a problem setting for describing the Churchman-Ackoff value measure assume that the market planner has several product candidates (man-made fibers) each of which could be used in making industrial V-belts for heavy machinery. All products could be priced at about the same dollar-per-pound level. In this case interest centers on the objectives of the V-belt *fabricator*. What properties of a man-made fiber does he consider of value when selecting a raw material for a V-belt fabrication? Suppose that a group of leading V-belt manufacturers has listed the following characteristics (suitably defined) which it feels are desirable in a raw material for V-belts:

Durability
Ease of handling
Light weight
Low investment in fabricating equipment
Rot resistance

The market planner is faced with a dilemma. He wishes to commercialize only one of the product candidates. Some products are superior to others in some of the above characteristics but are inferior in others. How much importance should be assigned to each performance objective so that the market planner may make a reasoned selection among the product candidates for commercialization?

The Churchman-Ackoff procedure for weighting multiple objectives operates on the basis of repetitive comparisons. It represents a procedure by which the evaluator can check his originally assigned value weights for internal consistency. In terms of this illustration, suppose the market planner were to ask an executive of a leading V-belt firm to rank the qualitative characteristics listed (that is, the objectives are either obtained or not obtained) in order of importance from 1 (high) to 5 (low). He then asks the executive to perform the following steps, results of which are shown in Table 6–2.

Table 6–2

ILLUSTRATION OF CHURCHMAN-ACKOFF PROCEDURE—V-BELT EXAMPLE

Characteristic	Rank	Preliminary Weights	Adjusted	Final Weights	Adjusted
Durability................	1	1.00	.34	1.00	.31
Light weight.............	2	.70	.24	.95	.30
Low investment..........	3	.50	.17	.50	.16
Rot resistance...........	4	.45	.15	.45	.14
Ease of handling.........	5	.30	.10	.30	.09
		2.95	1.00	3.20	1.00

1. After ranking the various characteristics from high to low, assign the number 1.0 to the most important characteristic and weight the other characteristics relative to this standard. (This first step will be called the assignment of preliminary weights.)
2. Compare the importance of characteristic 1 (durability) with the combination of the other characteristics, 2 through 5 (to which weights of 0.70 + 0.50 + 0.45 + 0.30 = 1.95 were originally assigned).

(a) If characteristic 1 is more or equally preferred to the sum of
    the other characteristics, change the original weight of 1.0 to a
    value greater than 1.95 (the particular value dependent upon
    the preference now expressed) or just equal to 1.95, respec-
    tively. Proceed to step three.

(b) If characteristic 1 is less preferred than the combination of the
    other four characteristics, adjust (if necessary) the weight as-
    signed to characteristic 1 until this value is less than the sum-
    mation of the combination's weights. Next, compare charac-
    teristic 1 with the combination of characteristics 2 through 4
    and continue this procedure until (1) characteristic 1 becomes
    more or equally preferred to the relevant combination or (2)
    the last comparison, namely, characteristic 1 against the com-
    bination of characteristics 2 and 3, is reached. Then proceed
    to step three.

3. In this step compare characteristic 2 to the combination of characteristics 3 through 5.

   (a) If characteristic 2 is more or equally preferred to the combina-
       tion, adjust (if necessary) the weight assigned to characteristic
       2 and proceed to characteristic 3, etc.

   (b) If this characteristic is not preferred to the combination, go
       through the process outlined under step 2 (b) and then pro-
       ceed to characteristic 3, and so on.

In terms of the illustrative problem of Table 6–2, assume the
following outcomes:

1. The executive first compares the attainment of characteristic 1
   (durability) with the combination of characteristics 2 through 5
   (light weight, low investment, rot resistance, and ease of handling). He feels that the combination of these characteristics is to be
   preferred to characteristic 1. Since the sum of the weights originally assigned (1.95) is also greater, no adjustment is required in
   the weight (1.0) assigned to characteristic 1.

2. He next compares characteristic 1 (durability) with the combination of characteristics 2 through 4 (light weight, low investment,
   and rot resistance). He feels that this combination of characteristics is also preferred to characteristics 1. Since the summation of
   their weights (1.65) is greater than the weight (1.0) originally
   assigned to characteristic 1, no adjustment in the weight assigned
   to characteristic 1 is needed.

3. The executive next compares characteristic 1 (durability) with the
   sum of characteristics 2 and 3 (light weight and low investment).
   Again, the executive feels that characteristic 1 is not as desirable
   as the combination of 2 and 3. Since the summation of the weights
   assigned to 2 and 3 is 1.2, no change in the weight assigned to
   characteristic 1 is needed.

4. Next, the executive compares characteristic 2 (light weight) with
   the combination of characteristics 3 through 5 (low investment, rot
   resistance, and ease of handling). He prefers the combination to

characteristic 2. Since the weight (1.25) assigned to the combination of characteristics 3 through 5 exceeds the weight (0.70) originally assigned to characteristic 2, no adjustment of the latter weight is needed.

5. He next compares characteristic 2 (light weight) with the combination of characteristics 3 and 4 (low investment and rot resistance). He feels that characteristic 2 is equal to the combination. Since the combination carries an original weight of 0.95, the executive adjusts the original weight (0.70) assigned to characteristic 2 to 0.95.

6. The executive next compares characteristic 3 (low investment) with the combination of characteristics 4 and 5 (rot resistance and ease of handling). He feels that characteristic 3 is not as important as the combination. Hence the original weight (0.50) assigned to characteristic 3 remains unchanged from the original assignment of 0.50.

7. Since characteristics 4 and 5 are the last two characteristics remaining, they receive their originally specified weights of 0.45 and 0.30, respectively.

8. The final weights are "standardized" so as to total 1.0.

The effect of this procedure on the original assignment of weights (see Table 6–2) can now be compared. In this illustrative case the executive showed a rather high degree of consistency in the final weight assignment compared to the original weight assignment (both sets having been adjusted to total 1.0). Characteristic 2 has received a somewhat greater weight than originally assigned but, in general, fairly close correspondence can be noted between the preliminary (adjusted) weights and the final (adjusted) weights. Such high consistency may not always be the case; the opportunity to *revaluate initial comparisons* constitutes the essence of the procedure. The procedure itself does not lead, however, to a unique assignment of weights; other sets of weights could satisfy the relevant inequalities.

ASSUMPTIONS UNDERLYING THE CHURCHMAN-ACKOFF VALUE MEASURE

If one thinks a bit about the rationale underlying the above illustration, it is clear that several assumptions were involved:

1. It was assumed that the executive could judge the relative value of *any* combination of outcomes and could assign a number which measures the "true" relative value of each outcome combination. That is, (a) for every outcome O_j there corresponds a real nonnegative number V_j; (b) if O_j is preferred to O_k then $V_j > V_k$; and (c) if O_j and O_k are equally important, then $V_j = V_k$.

2. Additivity was also assumed. That is, given the values of, say,

outcomes O_1 and O_2 as V_1 and V_2, respectively, it is assumed that $V(O_1$ and $O_2) = V_1 + V_2$.

While the Churchman-Ackoff procedure provides a scale for weighting objectives the fact must be stressed that the successive comparisons provide only a means for checking the internal consistency of the *first* set of value weights which are assigned after the outcomes are ranked. Furthermore, in actual applications of the procedure the market planner may wish to secure independently the opinions of several persons in the firm who are in a position to render value judgments on the firm's objectives. While this procedure involves some (perhaps arbitrary) weighting scheme for deriving *composite* weights, the benefits of obtaining agreement on the relative weights of several objectives may justify the extension of the procedure to several decision makers in the organization.

After the values assigned to each characteristic are obtained, the market planner could treat this problem as any other problem utilizing the Bayesian approach. He would, of course, have to assign probabilities to the respective states of nature which would affect the attainment of each characteristic, given the commercialization of each fiber candidate. He would choose that act (commercialize a specific product candidate) which led to the highest expected value, assuming that a product's characteristics constituted the *only* outcomes of interest to the planner.

VON NEUMANN-MORGENSTERN UTILITY FUNCTIONS

Another axiomatic procedure for weighting objectives is the von Neumann-Morgenstern utility scale. Unlike the Churchman-Ackoff scale, this procedure is *not* restricted to qualitative objectives nor does it require the assumption of additivity. Utility in the sense used by von Neumann and Morgestern is not to be confused with the utility notions of classical microeconomics. The latter concept referred to the "psychic satisfaction" derived from possessing varying quantities of some good and assumed a scale measured in absolute units. On the contrary, the von Neumann-Morgenstern measure is an interval scale which is used in a rather special way to predict rankings concerning an individual's preference for certain "prizes," or outcomes, whose attainment is subject to risk. More properly, the predictions of this scale refer to the preference for gambles involving the outcomes as prizes.

Suppose the decision maker, who will be called Mr. Conservative, is viewing several investment proposals which could lead to net returns on investment of, say, 20 percent, 10 percent and −5 percent. He ranks these outcomes in order of preference as follows:

$$O_1 = 20 \text{ percent (rank 1)}$$

$$O_2 = 10 \text{ percent (rank 2)}$$

$$O_3 = -5 \text{ percent (rank 3)}$$

Up to this point he is merely dealing with a simple ordinal scale. Suppose the value 1 to O_1 and the value of 0 to O_3 are arbitrarily assigned.

$$V(O_1) = 1$$

$$V(O_3) = 0$$

Now he would like to assign a value to O_2 which preserves the original ranking.[1] Suppose the decision maker is asked to visualize a hypothetical gambling situation in which he can obtain O_1 with "true" probability $P(O_1)$ and O_3 with "true" probability $1 - P(O_1)$, that is only two possible outcomes are allowed. The decision maker is told that O_2 can be obtained with certainty (investment in a particular group of high-yield bonds for example). The decision maker is asked to tell what probability associated with outcome O_1 of the gamble would make him just indifferent between selecting O_2 for certain or the gamble which could end in either O_1 or O_3.

Suppose the decision maker (after some contemplation) says that he would be indifferent between obtaining O_2 (return of 10 percent) for certain and participating in a gamble in which he could obtain O_1 with probability $P(O_1) = 0.7$ and O_3 with probability $1 - P(O_1) = 0.3$. To find the utility index assigned to O_2 use the following equation:

$$U(O_2) = P(O_1) \cdot U(O_1) + [1 - P(O_1)] \cdot U(O_3)$$

Since $U(O_1) = 1$ and $U(O_3) = 0$ have been arbitrarily allowed, substitute in the above equation

$$U(O_2) = 0.7 (1) + 0.3 (0)$$

$$= 0.7 \text{ utiles (where "utiles" is an arbitrary label}$$
$$\text{assigned to the index number)}$$

Now that 3 points on the decision maker's utility function are determined, determine by similar calculations the utilities associated with outcomes $O_4 = 15$ percent; $O_5 = 5$ percent; and $O_6 = 0$ percent return on investment. Since O_1 and O_3 have been chosen as the out-

---

[1]Allowing for the possibility of weak ordering.

comes for this reference gamble, make sure that all additional outcomes fall within this range. Mr. Conservative's utility index numbers are summarized in Table 6-3. His utility function is next plotted
in Figure 6-1, with a curve drawn between the plotted values.

Table 6-3

ILLUSTRATIVE UTILITY INDEX NUMBERS FOR MR. CONSERVATIVE
(OUTCOMES EXPRESSED IN PERCENT RETURN)

Return on Investment	Utility Index
20	1.0 utiles
15	0.9
10	0.7
5	0.6
0	0.3
−5	0.0

Figure 6-1

ILLUSTRATIVE UTILITY FUNCTIONS—RETURN ON INVESTMENT

(MR. CONSERVATIVE VS. MR. ACTUARY)

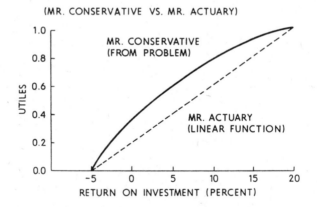

As can be noted from Figure 6-1 this freehand curve merely approximates Mr. Conservative's utility function and is based on a
limited set of hypothetical gambles. Notice, however, that the rate of
increase of Mr. Conservative's utility function tapers off as return on
investment increases. That is, Mr. Conservative's marginal utility for
additional return is decreasing. Assume the interrogation of another
decision maker, who will be called Mr. Actuary, elicits a utility function which is linear (dotted line plotted in Figure 6-1) and, hence,
of constant marginal utility. To compare the behavior of these two
individuals in selecting between two risky situations whose outcomes fall between the end points of the return on investment scale,
note that the curvilinear function describes Mr. Conservative's risk

attitudes while the linear function is assumed to describe Mr. Actuary's risk attitudes.

Specifically, suppose Mr. Conservative and Mr. Actuary are presented with the following decision problem where a choice between two investment options is to be made (Table 6–4). Option A_1 is assumed to lead to an 18 percent return under state of nature S_a and a 4 percent return under state of nature S_b. Option A_2 is assumed to lead to returns of 12 and 8, respectively, under S_a and S_b. The prior probabilities associated with the occurrence of S_a and S_b are 0.5 and 0.5, respectively.

Table 6–4

EXPECTED UTILITY CALCULATIONS—MR. CONSERVATIVE *vs.* MR. ACTUARY

						Mr. C		Mr. A			
	$P(S_a)$	S_a	$P(S_b)$	S_b	$U(A_i, S_a)$	$U(A_i, S_b)$	$U(A_i, S_a)$	$U(A_i, S_b)$	$E\ U_i(C)$	$E\ U_i(A)$
$A_1..$	0.5	18	0.5	4	.98	.48	.92	.36	.73	.64
$A_2..$	0.5	12	0.5	8	.82	.66	.68	.52	.74	.60

Suppose, as in the preceding chapter expected *monetary* payoffs for the two acts A_1 and A_2 are first calculated.

$$EP\ (A_1) = 0.5\ (18) + 0.5\ (4) = 11 \text{ percent return}$$

$$EP\ (A_2) = 0.5\ (12) + 0.5\ (8) = 10 \text{ percent return}$$

If the criterion were to choose the act leading to the maximum expected monetary payoff act A_1 would be chosen.

Now *utility* calculations are introduced into the analysis. Utilities will reflect the *individual* decision maker's attitudes toward risky situations and, hence, the act selected may *not* agree with the action chosen under the expected monetary payoff criterion.

For Mr. Conservative the utilities for each monetary type of outcome are derived by (*a*) reading the associated utility number from his curve on the chart of Figure 6–1 and (*b*) then substituting the *utility* index numbers for the payoffs originally expressed in terms of return on investment into the general expected (utility) equation.

$$E\ U_1\ (\text{Mr. C}) = 0.5\ (.98) + 0.5\ (.48) = 0.73$$

$$E\ U_2\ (\text{Mr. C}) = 0.5\ (.82) + 0.5\ (.66) = 0.74$$

Mr. Conservative, were he consistent with his attitudes toward risky situations as expressed by the series of reference gambles, would choose act A_2.

Now make similar computations for Mr. Actuary who is assumed to possess a linear utility function, the values of which are again read from his particular function which appears in Figure 6–1.

$$E \; U_1 \; (\text{Mr. A}) = 0.5 \; (.92) + 0.5 \; (.36) = 0.64$$

$$E \; U_2 \; (\text{Mr. A}) = 0.5 \; (.68) + 0.5 \; (.52) = 0.60$$

Mr. Actuary, who possesses a linear utility function, chooses the *same* act as would be chosen under the expected (monetary type) payoff criterion or A_1.

This latter correspondence is not by accident and points out a very important principle: *Use of maximum expected monetary value as a criterion of choice assumes that the decision maker's utility function is a linear (at least within the range of outcomes contained in the problem) function of the monetary measure used.*

If a linear utility function is relevant, it is not hard to see why the maximization of expected monetary value would also maximize expected utility. For example, let x equal the monetary outcome and $U(x)$ stand for the utility of outcome x; then, assuming a linear utility function

$$U \; (x) = a + bx.$$

Now if we take the expectation of both sides

$$E \; [U(x)] = E \; (a + bx)$$

$$= a + b \; E \; (x)$$

$$= a + b \; \mu_x; \; \text{where } \mu_x \text{ is the mean of } x.$$

That is, expected utility depends only upon the expectation of x (or the mean of x) since a and b are both constants. On the other hand, if $U(x)$ were, say, quadratic rather than linear, this would not be the case. Illustratively, suppose the quadratic equation $U \; (x) = a + bx - cx^2$ is used. If the expectation of both sides of this equation is taken, the result is

$$E \; [U(x)] = E \; (a + bx - cx^2)$$

$$= a + b \; E(x) - c \; E(x^2)$$

But from elementary statistics it is known that the variance of x, σ_x^2 is equal to $E \; (x^2) - [E(x)]^2$. Thus, $E(x^2) = \sigma_x^2 + [E(x)]^2$ where $E(x)$ is the mean of x, or μ_x. Hence, these expressions can be substituted in the general equation

$$E \; [U(x)] = a + b \; E \; (x) - c \; \{\sigma_x^2 + [E(x)]^2\}$$

$$= a + b \; \mu_x \quad - c \; (\sigma_x^2 + \mu_x^2)$$

In this case expected utility depends upon both the mean *and* variance of the monetary outcome, *x*, and, therefore, the decision maker's preference between two acts might *not* agree with the choice implied by the expected monetary value criterion.

ASSUMPTIONS UNDERLYING THE VON NEUMANN-MORGENSTERN UTILITY FUNCTION

Again, one may pause and reflect about the assumptions which underlie the preceding method. Somewhat informally, they can be stated as follows:

1. The decision maker is assumed to be able to make a complete and transitive ranking of outcomes. That is, if the decision maker prefers (or is indifferent to) A vs. B and prefers (or is indifferent to) B vs. C, then he prefers (or is indifferent to) A vs. C.
2. Assuming the transitive relationship, A preferred to B preferred to C, then some lottery exists with A and C as prizes in which the decision maker is indifferent between receiving B for certain and participating in the gamble.
3. If the outcomes A and B are equally desirable (substitutable) then the decision maker is indifferent between any gamble in which A is substituted for B.
4. If A is preferred to B then a lottery (involving only A and B), in which the probability of outcome A is $P(A)$, is preferred to a lottery in which the probability of outcome A is $P^*(A)$ if and only if $P(A)$ is greater than $P^*(A)$.
5. If the decision maker is offered a lottery in which the outcomes are *other* lottery tickets, his preferences will be the same as those associated with the result of reducing the compound lottery to a simple one (by application of the standard probability calculus). That is, the decision maker will value a compound lottery ticket in terms of the *final* outcomes associated with his engaging in the compound lottery.

While these assumptions may seem intuitively plausible, it is relevant to note that criticisms of each assumption can be made (and are discussed in selected references at the end of this chapter).

THE USE OF UTILITY FUNCTIONS IN ROUTINE DECISION MAKING

While theoretically it might seem that utility functions could be adopted by businessmen as a means for incorporating risk attitudes toward alternative outcomes, the fact remains that little empirical work has been done in measuring individuals' utilities for money or commodities in general. The few experiments which have been conducted raise some questions about the ability of utility functions to predict decision makers' behavior. There is also some reason to believe that these functions might not remain stable over time even if people's behavior were consistent with some underlying utility function.

Still, it would be naive to ignore the notion of utility functions completely. In most planning situations monetary measures will, perforce, be used. The reader should remember that the choice of alternative courses of action based on expected payoff (expected monetary value) implies a linear utility function over the range of outcomes covered in the problem. The analyst might well ponder the utility function of the hypothetical Mr. Actuary and see if this type of function seems to agree with the risk preferences of real decision makers. This point will be returned to later.

THE CASE FOR PROFIT MAXIMIZATION

The market planner, if only for pragmatic reasons, will probably be obliged to deal largely with monetary outcomes until much more experience, both theoretical and applied, is gained about value measures like the Churchman-Ackoff method and von Neumann-Morgenstern utility functions. This being the case, at least over the short run, one should probe into the various types of *monetary* measures and their relevance to choosing alternative plans under conditions of uncertainty.

The "rational man" of economic theory (who possessed perfect knowledge of static demand and cost functions and who desired only to maximize profits) is, of course, a gross distortion of the modern marketing manager. Not only is the manager dealing with a dynamic rather than static environment but his knowledge about his environment is far from perfect. As has been noted before, however, the term "rational" can be more generally defined to mean merely behavior which is consistent with the assumptions underlying some explicated model. If one wishes to retain emphasis on profit maximization he should (and can) expand the profit model to include consideration of uncertainty and the time horizon over which profits are anticipated to be made.

While the use of portmanteau variables like profits, cash flow, and so forth, is a crude approximation to the problems of dealing with multiple corporate objectives, these measures of effectiveness do possess the virtue of being generally known and used by businessmen in one form or another. Unfortunately the term "profits" is a very ambiguous concept. Are short range or long range profits meant? Are accounting profits or "economic" profits which reflect opportunity costs meant? Are expected profits (which reflect a probabilistic environment) meant or can profits measured in some deterministic sense be dealt with?

CAPITAL BUDGETING PROCEDURES—DESIRED CHARACTERISTICS FOR PLANNING

The market planner looking for a suitable monetary measure of effectiveness will soon find that no shortage of alternative methods exists. Monetary measures may range from incremental profit to more complex budgeting procedures like interest rate of return. A variety of different procedures exists which vary in their assumptions, method of computation, and comprehensiveness. With no attempt to cover all of these procedures, a set of desirable characteristics which a monetary measure of effectiveness should possess will first be listed and then what appears to be a reasonable candidate for further study will be described.

1. *Future Revenues and Costs.* Since the market planner is dealing with future streams of revenues and costs, a method should be used in which the earnings of each alternative represent *added* earnings (or savings). If the alternatives consist of making a new investment or not, the estimates should reflect how revenues and costs would be expected to *change* as a result of making the investments or not making it. That is, the planner is concerned with future (hence avoidable) inflows and outflows, not such things as allocation of existing overheads, book values of existing investment, and the like.

2. *The Time Pattern of Future Earnings.* Inasmuch as the market planner will usually be considering alternative courses of action, the implementation of which can lead to different configurations of revenue and cost streams, a procedure should be able to deal with different time patterns of earnings and to convert these different time patterns to some common basis.

3. *The Opportunity Cost Principle.* Associated with the preceding point is that evaluation of alternative marketing plans usually assumes the availability of alternative uses of the firm's resources. A method should reflect both an opportunity cost of capital and time value of money. For example, if one alternative involves a long range program in product development which might not pay off until five years hence, the method should reflect the lost opportunity of investing the capital required in some shorter range venture which could be earning a return before the longer range project started paying off.

4. *The Effect of Taxes.* An investment method should reflect the net impact of tax laws on earnings. For example, some items like plant and equipment can be capitalized. The depreciation allowance represents a cash flow-back which receives tax credits. Working

capital can be recovered tax-free, and items which can be expensed will receive 100 per cent depreciation credit the year expended. Hence, the differential impact of taxes on various outlays should be incorporated in the method selected.

5. *The Effect of Uncertainty.* In the real world of decision making all future revenue and cost streams represent outcomes conditional upon which alternative state of nature occurs. The method should reflect the probabilistic environment which the market planner faces.

The method proposed here does meet the above criteria. However, it is by no means the simplest monetary measure to apply.

EXPECTED NET PRESENT VALUE

The reasoning behind expected net present value is not difficult although it does require more computation and more detailed forecasting than less elaborate processes. First, assume conditions of "certainty", that is, a single stream of revenues and costs over a period which can be called the "planning horizon."

In cash flow analysis the firm is viewed as something like a giant cash register from which outlays are made and into which inflows (hopefully) appear. Suppose, for purposes of illustration, that the planner wishes to calculate the *present value* of a new plant which is expected to produce a new product over a period of five years, after which the plant will be dismantled and sold for salvage. The following symbols can be used to denote the pertinent elements of the problem:

$I_0 =$ initial plant investment at start-up.

W_0, $W_5 =$ working capital required at start-up and recovered at end of year 5.

O_2, $O_4 =$ additional cash outlays at end of years 2 and 4 respectively.

R_1, R_2, R_3, R_4, $R_5 =$ after-tax revenues plus depreciation (assumed to occur at year-end).

$S_5 =$ salvage value at end of year 5.

$r =$ annual interest rate (opportunity cost of capital) expressed decimally.

Then, present value calculations would be expressed in net present value, NPV, as follows:

$$NPV = \left[\frac{R_1}{(1+r)} + \frac{R_2}{(1+r)^2} + \frac{R_3}{(1+r)^3} + \frac{R_4}{(1+r)^4} + \frac{R_5 + S_5 + W_5}{(1+r)^5} \right]$$

$$- \left[\frac{O_2}{(1+r)^2} + \frac{O_4}{(1+r)^4} + I_0 + W_0 \right]$$

To generalize the above expression initial plant investment, working capital, and salvage value can be added to the appropriate revenue or outlay figures, yielding

$$NPV = \sum_{i=0}^{n} (R_i - O_i) (1 + r)^{-i}$$

where

$i =$ the relevant time period;
or $i = 0, 1, 2, 3, 4, 5$ in the example.

A NUMERICAL EXAMPLE

Actually, the formula looks more complicated than it is. Suppose the planner wishes to evaluate the investment proposal whose pertinent revenues and outlays appear in Table 6-5.

Table 6-5

NEW PLANT INVESTMENT PROPOSAL—INTEREST RATE EQUALS 10%

(IN THOUSANDS OF DOLLARS—ALL REVENUES AND ADDITIONAL
OUTLAYS OCCUR AT YEAR-END)

Year	Revenues, Salvage and Working Capital Recovery	Additional Outlays	Initial Plant Investment and Working Capital	Discount Function	Present Value
0.............	...	...	−800	1.000	−800
1.............	100	...	...	.909	91
2.............	300	−200	...	.826	83
3.............	600	...	...	.751	451
4.............	400	−100	...	.683	205
5.............	200	...	...	.621	124
					154

As can be noted in Table 6-5, the anticipated cash flow of this venture, discounted to the present, equals $154 thousand. This figure can be interpreted as the amount of additional cash generated by the venture over that required to pay back all outlays and earn an average annual return of 10 percent on the present value of all outlays.

Observe that several simplifying assumptions were made regarding the preceding calculations. First it was assumed that the initial outlay for plant investment took place simultaneously with plant start-up and that all revenues and additional outlays occurred at the *end* of a given year. In practice, of course, such is not the case. More realistically, a period shorter than a year could have been used for discounting to present value or continuous discounting could have been assumed. In this latter instance the general formula would change to

$$NPV = \int_{t=0}^{T} [R(t) - O(t)] \, e^{-rt} \, dt$$

where the factor e^{-rt} is the continuous analogue of $(1 + r)^{-i}$. In the continuous case each "bit" of cash inflow or outflow is instantaneously discounted to present value. The integral sign takes the place of the summation sign, the symbol t replaces the symbol i, and the symbol T replaces the symbol n associated with the discrete case.

ADDING THE FACTOR OF UNCERTAINTY

The preceding example assumed a condition of certainty with respect to future revenues and outlays. In practice, of course, a *set* of discounted cash flows (related to the conjunction of courses of action and states of nature) would be calculated. Using the prior probability assignment one could expect over these conditional payoffs and treat the problem in the same fashion as any other decision situation involving expected payoff.

However, an additional problem arises with respect to the discount function $(1 + r)^{-i}$. If desired, this can be treated as a "certainty equivalent," that is, a single (certain) state of nature. On the other hand, one may wish to treat the discount function as a random variable. Notice, however, that all of these procedures still assume that the decision maker's utility is linear with money. If one wished to use utility functions (and to assume that utility is not affected by time preferences in a manner inconsistent with application of the discount function) he could convert each year's cash flow to a utility index, discount the index to present value, and find the expected present value expressed in utility measure. But in practice, businessmen's use of this more elaborate concept is at least several years away. In subsequent chapters it will, for the most part, still be assumed that utility is linear with money.

SOME EMPIRICAL RESULTS IN THE DETERMINATION OF UTILITY FUNCTIONS

As mentioned earlier in this chapter, utility functions—while representing an intriguing area of interest for the market planner—are not yet being used on a routine basis by businessmen. In fact, hardly any field research has been conducted in even deriving utility functions of actual managers, let alone using these functions on an operational basis.

The purpose of this section of the chapter is to relate some of the results of a small-scale experimental program (conducted by one of the authors) whose objective was to derive empirical utility functions for a group of middle management personnel in a large chemical company. (Only a partial summary of the findings is presented here. A more detailed description of the research is found in the Green reference at the end of the chapter.)

Briefly stated, an attempt was made to measure risk attitudes held by a sample of middle-management personnel and, more specifically, whether their utility functions were linear with monetary outcomes in cases where the range of outcomes would not place undue strain on the firm's resources. The middle managers interviewed in this study played an important role in the decision process, both in preparing investment data and in the recommendations made to top corporate officers.

Two experimental procedures were used. First, each of twelve respondents (three each from the company's Sales, Production, Finance, and Research Departments) was presented a series of hypothetical two-outcome gambles expressed in terms of return on investment. They were asked to state the probabilities which would have to be attached to the more favorable outcome before they would be just indifferent between selection of the gamble and a reference alternative which would lead to a certain outcome.

Second, the same respondents were presented a chart on which was inscribed a complete probability distribution of outcomes associated with a reference alternative. Plastic overlays of five other probability distributions (of larger variance and/or different shape) were, in turn, superimposed on the reference curve so that the expected value of the reference curve and experimental curve coincided. Each respondent was asked to reposition—if he felt it necessary—each experimental curve until he would be just indifferent between selection of the investment alternative underlying the outcome distribution of the reference curve and that underlying each experimental curve respectively.

Some insight into the following questions was sought:
1. For this group of respondents are their utility functions linear with monetary outcomes?
2. Do particular corporate goals appear to affect individuals' attitudes toward risk and, if so, how?
3. Do individuals' personal goals appear to influence their attitudes towards risks involving corporation funds?

RESULTS OF THE STUDY

Some of the results of the experiments are portrayed in Figure 6–2. The upper panel of the chart shows two of the twelve curves which were obtained, namely, the curve of R. M. (Research Department) and the curve of W. S. (Sales Department). These curves,

Figure 6–2

ILLUSTRATIVE UTILITY FUNCTIONS FOR INDIVIDUALS R. M. AND W. S.
AND SUMMARY FUNCTIONS OF EXPERIMENTAL VERSUS REFERENCE CURVES

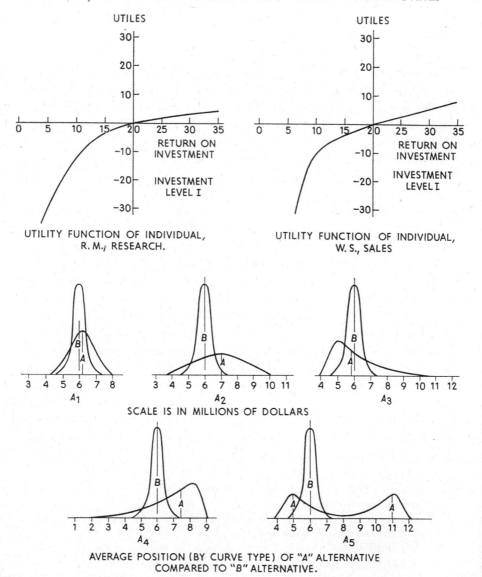

UTILITY FUNCTION OF INDIVIDUAL,
R. M., RESEARCH.

UTILITY FUNCTION OF INDIVIDUAL,
W. S., SALES

SCALE IS IN MILLIONS OF DOLLARS

AVERAGE POSITION (BY CURVE TYPE) OF "*A*" ALTERNATIVE
COMPARED TO "*B*" ALTERNATIVE.

however, are representative of the general shape of all twelve curves.

First note that the curves are *not* linear with percent return on investment. Although the required investment outlays ($1–10 million) were rather small, compared to the firm's asset position, there was a general disinclination to prefer gambles whose variance was wide to relatively sure gambles which could lead to acceptable returns.

For example, suppose (*a*) the gamble in which a 35 percent return is received with 0.5 probability and a 5 percent return is received with 0.5 probability is compared to (*b*) receiving a certain return of 15 percent. The expected monetary value of the gamble would equal 20 percent, and if R. M.'s utility function were linear, R. M. would prefer the gamble to the certain option. If the appropriate utilities are read from R. M.'s curve, however, it is found that the utility of the certain 15 percent return at −3 utiles is higher (less negative) than the expected utility of the gamble (0.5 (4 utiles) + 0.5 (−28 utiles) = −12 utiles). In terms of expected utility, R. M. would prefer the certain option of a 15 percent return.

It is relevant to note that a "goal rate of return" prevailed in the subject firm. This goal return, amounting to 20 percent, served as a rough rule of thumb for guiding investment selection. While top level managers knew that the goal return was only suggestive and, hence, was not required to be met for all projects selected, lower level managers appeared to consider the goal rate as a much less flexible lower limit. By the same token they felt that little was to be gained by exceeding this standard. That is, from the *individual's* standpoint, he was not inclined to view the chance at very high returns (if these returns were also highly risky) as preferable to satisfactory returns (close to 20 percent) if there was high assurance that the approximate goal rate could be obtained. This type of attitude toward risk appeared to be the case (regardless of the respondent's job function) even though, on an actuarial basis, the more risky option would have led to a higher expected monetary value.

The lower panel of Figure 6–2 reveals similar findings on the non-linear nature of utility functions for this sample of middle management personnel. Had the respondent's underlying utility function been linear, the expected value of all of the experimental (*B*) curves would have *coincided* with that of the reference (*A*) curve, since the only relevant parameter would then be the expectation of the distribution. The average (taken over all twelve responses) position of the experimental curves shown in the chart indicates, however, that the respondents tended to reposition the (*B*) curves so as not to do any worse than approximately $1 million less than the worst outcome that would be experienced under the referenced (A) curve. Again, no significant differences in repositioning were noted among job functions.

IMPLICATIONS OF THESE EXPERIMENTS

While one should be hesitant in trying to generalize too much from such a limited inquiry, it does appear as though the use of expected monetary value (which assumes an underlying linear utility function) may represent, at best, a fairly crude approximation to expected utility. Corporate "rules of thumb" (for example, goal rates of return) and individuals' goals may have rather marked effects on risk attitudes even when corporate assets are not imperiled by the alternative investment options under consideration. From the individual's viewpoint, however, his own success or failure in the corporate organization may be quite sensitive to the behavior of that particular portion of total assets for which he is (or feels he is) responsible. Of course, much more field research in different organizations and at different hierarchical levels in specific organizations remains to be done before even reasonably adequate generalizations can be drawn about the characteristics of utility functions.

The purpose in presenting these brief findings is to alert the reader to the dilemma which is faced in attempting to devise meaningful and operational measures of effectiveness by which alternative plans can be evaluated. On the one hand, experience with, and businessmen's knowledge of, utility functions is too brief at present for adopting the concept of expected utility as an operational criterion of choice. On the other hand, it is possible that monetary measures (for instance, expected discounted cash flow over the planning horizon) may be very gross approximations to a figure of merit which truly reflects the decision maker's goal structure. At this point one can only point out this dilemma and hope that future research will be undertaken to generate improved measures of effectiveness for decision evaluation.

SUMMARY

This chapter has attempted to relate some of the concepts of value theory to decision making under uncertainty. The nature of objectives, the difficulty of specifying objectives, and the problem of combining multiple objectives in such a way as to derive some overall measure of effectiveness were first discussed.

Next two models — the Churchman-Ackoff measure and von

Neumann-Morgenstern utility—for deriving operational measures of value were discussed. It was indicated that some rather restrictive assumptions underlie each measure and that the resultant scales are only interval scales (unique up to a linear transformation). Hence, one is not allowed to make interpersonal comparisons of utility functions since an arbitrary zero point is one of the characteristics of an interval scale.

Some of the elements of monetary measures of effectiveness and their associated limitations were next summarized. Expected discounted cash flow was selected as a monetary measure which appears to be best suited to the needs of market planning under conditions of uncertainty.

The discussion of value theory was concluded with a summary of some experimental results in deriving utility functions under field conditions. The implications of these experimental findings raise some questions about the adequacy of expected monetary value as a criterion of rationality and whether its use is justified, even in a normative sense. It was concluded that until more is known about value theory, expected monetary measures—with all of their limitations—will still represent the principal criterion for evaluating alternative courses of action.

This chapter has raised many more questions than it has answered. Value theory represents one of the least explored (and most difficult) areas of management science. Ignorance of this area can well limit the potential success of the newer decision techniques as applied to market planning. Much more behavioral research will be required before people's perception, motivation, and cognition can even begin to be understood.

The first three chapters of Part II have largely been methodological. As various functional areas of marketing planning and problem solving are discussed, the analytical tools presented in these chapters will be recalled.

Selected References

ALDERSON, WROE, AND GREEN, PAUL E. "Growth vs. Profit Maximization in Market Planning," *Growth and Profit Planner*, Vol. 1, No. 1 (February, 1963). Philadelphia, Pa.: Behavior Systems.
     Discusses some of the more general considerations involved in determining corporate objectives, particularly the relative influence of growth and profit on corporate decision making.

BAUMOL, WILLIAM J. *Economic Theory and Operations Analysis.* Englewood Cliffs, N. J.: Prentice-Hall, Inc., 1961.
     Von Neumann-Morgenstern utility functions are discussed at length. Also provides a lucid discussion of the formal properties of scales.

CHURCHMAN, C. WEST. *Prediction and Optimal Decision.* Englewood Cliffs, N.J.: Prentice-Hall, Inc., 1961.
One of the most definitive works on value theory and its relationship to science and scientists.

CHURCHMAN, C. WEST; ACKOFF, RUSSELL L.; AND ARNOFF, E. LEONARD. *Introduction to Operations Research.* New York: John Wiley & Sons, Inc., 1957.
Contains both a general discussion of value theory and a detailed exposition of the Churchman-Ackoff value measure.

DEAN, JOEL. "Measuring the Productivity of Capital," *Harvard Business Review,* January–February, 1954.
Provides an elementary and clear description of discounted cash flow, its computational aspects, and its relationship to other capital budgeting techniques.

GRAYSON, C. JACKSON, JR. *Decisions under Uncertainty.* Cambridge, Mass.: Harvard Business School Press, 1960.
Describes some of the first empirical research on deriving utility functions under field conditions (for a group of oil and gas drillers).

GREEN, PAUL E. "Risk Attitudes and Chemical Investment Decisions," *Chemical Engineering Progress,* January, 1963.
Elaborates on the experiments briefly described in this chapter.

LUCE, R. DUNCAN, AND RAIFFA, HOWARD. *Games and Decisions.* New York: John Wiley & Sons, Inc., 1957.
Von Neumann-Morgenstern utility functions are discussed at length.

MOSTELLER, FREDERICK, AND NOGEE, PHILIP. "An Experimental Measure of Utility," *Journal of Political Economy,* October, 1951.
Discusses the determination of utility functions under experimental conditions.

SPENCER, MILTON H., AND SIEGELMAN, LOUIS. *Managerial Economics: Decision Making and Forward Planning.* Rev. ed. Homewood, Illinois: Richard D. Irwin, Inc., 1964.
Provides an elementary and clear description of discounted cash flow, its computational aspects, and its relationship to other capital budgeting techniques.

Problems

1. The March Corporation, a medium size producer of ethical drugs, is contemplating entering the proprietary market by introducing a revolutionary new cold tablet. Initial research has demonstrated the capabilities of the tablet, but unfortunately the production of the tablet will require a large investment in new plant and equipment. The management of the March corporation believes an initial investment of $1 million for plant and equipment will be necessary. Subsequent necessary outlays would be $200,000 at the beginning of the second year of production and $100,000 at the beginning of the third year of operation.

a) Given that the March Corporation can expect a total cash inflow of $2 million at the end of the third year of operation, compute the present value of the cash flow for a three-year venture into the production of the cold tablet when the cost of capital is 8%, annually.

b) Explain the meaning of the above answer.

c) Given that the March Corporation can expect a total cash inflow of $1.7 million at the end of the third year of operation (other conditions remaining the same), compute the present value of the cash flow for a three-year venture into the production of the cold tablet when the cost of capital is 12%, annually.

2. The Hill Corporation, a leading manufacturer of tile floor coverings, has for some time been perplexed as to what long-range strategy should be adopted in the tile floor covering market. The Hill Corporation's director of long-range planning has, after careful research, narrowed his search for a suitable strategy to the following:

1) Concentrate production and marketing effort on linoleum floor coverings, (A_1).
2) Concentrate production and marketing effort on asphalt floor coverings, (A_2).
3) Concentrate production and marketing effort on vinyl floor coverings, (A_3).

A five-year planning period was deemed appropriate and additional research enabled the construction of the follow'ng conditional payoff matrix:

	Demand 1	Demand 2	Demand 3
A_1............	$ 2 million	$ −0.5 million	$ −1 million
A_2............	1 million	3 million	−1 million
A_3............	−2 million	0.5 million	5 million

a) Given that the prior probabilities assigned to the various demands are

$$P \text{ (Demand 1)} = 0.5$$
$$P \text{ (Demand 2)} = 0.3$$
$$P \text{ (Demand 3)} = 0.2$$

choose the act with the highest expected monetary value.

b) Use a concrete example to show that a business executive may wish to use expected utility value rather than expected monetary value as his criter'on of choice.

c) Using the following utility functions, calculate expected utility in the above problem for the three individual functions. Which act would be chosen under each utility function?

$$U_1 = \left\{ \begin{array}{l} 0.04\ x^2 \ ; x \geqslant 0 \\ -0.04\ x^2 \ ; x < 0 \end{array} \right\}$$

$$U_2 = 0.2x \qquad\qquad (x \text{ in millions of dollars})$$
$$U_3 = 0.4x - 0.04\ x^2$$

3. Define the following terms: (*a*) nominal scale, (*b*) ordinal scale, (*c*) cardinal scale, and (*d*) utile.

4. Present a critique of the Churchman-Ackoff value measure.

5. What are the drawbacks to the use of the von Neumann-Morgenstern utility measure in real life business problems?

Chapter 7

MARKET POSITION ANALYSIS

൜഻ൕ

Market position (usually defined as a firm's "share or percentage of the total market") constitutes one of the principal measurements made by business firms. Not infrequently, marketing plans are expressly formulated with a view toward either increasing the level of this variable or at least maintaining it at some desirable level. More usually, market share provides an important measure of the firm's marketing efforts and represents an *intermediate* variable for deriving cash flows required in the evaluation of alternative plans. It is this latter viewpoint regarding the need for market position measurement which is discussed here.

This chapter looks at market position analysis within the framework of a decision model. Market share (and, ultimately, sales and profit projections) constitutes one of the main classes of outcomes which the marketing planner tries to predict, given alternative courses of action. Sometimes he may employ single estimates of future market position. This procedure can be described as decision making under certainty. In other cases he may wish to use several estimates and thus consider alternative levels of market share (whose occurrence ultimately depends upon other states of nature such as changes in consumer tastes, competitive activity, and so forth). This viewpoint represents decision making under risk if the probabilities attached to alternative outcomes are assumed to be known and decision making under uncertainty if they are not assumed to be known. The first two categories are emphasized in this chapter, while a discussion of the third category is left to subsequent chapters.

The chapter starts out with a classificatory description of the major variables which influence a firm's market position and, ultimately, sales and profits. The firm's position within the framework of the industries in which it presently competes, potential industries, and the economy is discussed. Then a model for analyzing these various factors is described.

A discussion of a probabilistic model for predicting changes in market share over time, namely, the Markov process model follows. The principal properties of discrete, first-order Markov chains are described, and it is shown how they can be used to predict period-to-period changes in market position as a function of the interaction of a firm's courses of action with those of its competitors. Some of the more mathematical aspects of Markov processes are discussed in a technical appendix at the end of this chapter.

The discussion of market position is concluded with a statement of some of the limitations of market share as a measure of the firm's effectiveness. This chapter is thus introductory in nature in that it focuses upon the major outcomes of marketing decisions considered *generically* while the next four chapters are concerned with the four major classes of marketing decisions, namely, product, price, promotion, and channel decisions. In a sense this chapter serves as a bridge between the methodological framework of the first three chapters of Part II and the next four chapters which deal with specific classes of decisions.

MARKET SHARE AND MARKETING PLANS EVALUATION

Marketing courses of action are typically classified according to the following categories:

1. *Product decisions.* In this category planners are concerned with (*a*) modifications of the existing product line; (*b*) new product additions to the existing line; and (*c*) product deletions from the existing line.

2. *Pricing decisions.* In this category planners are concerned with (*a*) product life cycle pricing; (*b*) base pricing policy; and (*c*) pricing relationships among product line members.

3. *Promotion decisions.* In this category planners are concerned with (*a*) the determination of total promotional budgets; (*b*) the allocation of the total among competing and complementary activities, for example, advertising, personal selling, point-of-purchase promotion and marketing services; and (*d*) the timing and content of promotion.

4. *Channel decisions.* In this category planners are concerned with (*a*) the initial selection of channels; (*b*) the allocation of distribution among channels; and (*c*) the promotion of channels of distribution.

A breakdown of marketing decisions into the above categories is done largely for convenience and should not imply that these decision categories are unrelated. For example, in the case of new product planning, not only must various product decisions be made, such as how much and what types to commercialize, but pricing, promotion, and channel decisions must, of course, be made as well.

Two other facets of the market planning task should also be considered. First, the planner must frequently take into account the interrelationships of marketing courses of action with other decision centers in the firm such as production, finance, personnel, and research. In most instances the effectiveness of marketing plans will hinge to a large extent on the coordination of these plans with other activities, (sometimes considered as nonmarketing activities of the firm).

Secondly, and quite important from the viewpoint of this chapter, the effectiveness of the planner's courses of action will be dependent upon the courses of action pursued by his competitors. The net impact of his actions vis-a-vis those of competitors determines his firm's market share. Hence, market position is an important outcome of the decision process both in the sense of providing a performance measure and, more importantly, as an intermediate variable for deriving (in conjunction with estimates of the variables influencing total market sales) the firm's sales volume. Finally, after measuring the costs incurred to achieve changes in market position, estimates of the firm's profits and cash flow (short and long term) can be made.

MARKET POSITION WITHIN THE DECISION MODEL

No going business firm operates in a vacuum. Industrial giants and small firms alike are subject to external influences on sales and profits. In some cases the influencing factors will be of such a broad nature (for example changes in the level of the general economy) that the firm's courses of action will be limited to various means of adapting to external change. That is, the firm will be influenced by broad changes in the *socio-economic environment* in which it operates but, in general, will be too small to influence in turn this type of environment.

In its *industry environment* the firm's market positon and other relevant outcomes will be under only partial control. The firm's outcomes will be dependent upon the interaction of its courses of action (for example, price, promotion, and channel selection) with those of its competitors. Finally, in its *internal environment* the outcomes of decisions will be largely under the firm's control.

Recall that the basic problem model of Chapter 5 consisted of

$$V = f\ (A_i,\ S_j)$$

where V represented a value measure to the firm; the A_i represented factors under the firm's control; the S_j represented factors which affected the firm's value measure but which were not under its control; and f $(\cdot)$ represented the functional relationship between the A_i, S_j, and the dependent variable V.

This notion can be elaborated upon by naming some of the pertinent variables influencing the firm's value measure. For example, suppose V stands for next year's gross profits before taxes.

$$V = (s - c) \, X - F$$

By definition it can be said that profits equal the difference between s, sales price in dollars per unit, and c, variable cost (which is fixed per unit), times X, the number of units sold, minus F, fixed costs in dollars.

However, the question next arises of what factors influence X, sales volume in units. The firm's unit sales volume will be a function of its price, promotion, product properties, marketing services, and so forth, relative to competition and also a function of *total* sales of the various industries in which the firm operates. In a given industry with total unit sales I

$$X = g \, (A_1, A_2, \ldots, A_m; C_1, C_2, \ldots, C_n; I)$$

That is, X, the firm's sales volume in units, will be a function of the interaction of A_i, its courses of action, with the corresponding C_j, its competitors' courses of action, and I, total industry sales units. If the firm operates in several industries, the model of its unit sales volume, X, will, of course, have to be expanded to deal with the firm's and competitors' actions in its overall marketing area.

But how are total unit sales for even a single industry determined? Obviously these sales will depend upon both interindustry competition and the level of total economic activity. As we know, a wide variety of goods made by different industries competes for the consumer's dollar. Vacation homes and pleasure boats may compete with automobiles or fur coats. To add to the complexity, aggregate activity for the economy will be dependent upon total consumption and investment which are, in turn, shaped by a host of decisions made at the individual consumer, business, and governmental level. For our purposes, a given industry's sales volume I, in units, can be viewed as follows:

$$I = h \, (B_1, B_2, \ldots, B_m; D_1, D_2, \ldots D_n; E)$$

That is, a given industry's sales volume will be some function, h, of B_i, the composite courses of action for the firms of which it is composed, the composite courses of action, D_j, of the firms in other industries, and E, the level of total economic activity.

In summary, the planner can first start out with a very general problem model:

$$V = f\,(A_i,\ S_j)$$

and a general statement of an individual firm's profits

$$V = (s - c)\,X - F$$

Its unit sales volume, X, can be expressed as

$$X = g\,(A_1, A_2, \ldots, A_m;\ C_1, C_2, \ldots C_n;\ I)$$

while total industry unit sales volume, I, can be expressed as

$$I = h\,(B_1, B_2, \ldots, B_m;\ D_1, D_2, \ldots D_n;\ E)$$

Thus, a given firm's profits, in principle, are a function of both its courses of action, A_i, and a host of uncontrolled variables, S_j, which can be generalized as the various C_j, B_j, D_j and E of the above expressions.

From the oversimplified form shown above, it can at least be inferred that the firm's market position for each industry in which it operates is part, albeit a very important part, of a more general complex. These relationships can next be explored by means of an illustrative planning problem which involves "single estimates," or single states of nature. From this one can generalize to the case of alternative states of nature, that is, a probabilistic environment.

A DETERMINISTIC ENVIRONMENTAL FRAMEWORK

Robert S. Weinberg (see References at end of chapter) has developed some useful analytical concepts for the market planner. Essentially Weinberg assumes that the values of the parameters are known with certainty. He develops several relationships in formulating a "multiple-factor" approach to analyzing a firm's alternative plans within both a static and dynamic (time-dependent) framework. Only the former model is considered here.

Weinberg, in a fashion similar to the discussion of the preceding section, develops three structural relationships:

1. *The general-economic-activity–industry-sales relationship.* This is, in brief, the economy-industry relationship which describes how the sales of the industry(ies) in which the firm operates are associated with pertinent measures of general economic activity, for example, Gross National Product, Disposable Income, F.R.B. Index of Industrial Production.

2. *The industry-sales–company-sales relationship.* This is a structural equation which relates the firm's sales volume to the sales volume of the

industry(ies) in which it operates. As such, it reflects the interaction of the firm's marketing courses of action with those of its competitors.

3. *The sales–profit relationship.* This is a structural equation which is derived from the familiar "break-even" analysis of Walter Rautenstruch, Raymond Villers, and others. This equation relates the firm's profits to its sales volume and, as such, considers the influence of the firm's courses of action on its unit sales volume, sales price, and variable and fixed costs.

These relationships can perhaps best be explained by means of an illustrative (hypothetical) case which is next discussed.

AN ILLUSTRATIVE APPLICATION OF MULTIPLE-FACTOR ANALYSIS

The Athenian Corporation manufactures one product class—heat exchangers.[1] These capital equipment items are sold primarily to the process industries and are used in the manufacture of petroleum, chemical, pulp and paper, pharmaceutical, and beverage products. The Athenian Corporation enjoys annual sales of ten million dollars, presently has 10 percent of the total heat exchanger market, and makes a profit before taxes of two million dollars. However, in the heat exchanger industry, there is a relative newcomer—aluminum heat exchangers. Athenian is the conservative in the industry and has up to now made only steel heat exchangers. Presently 15 percent of total expenditures for heat exchangers is for the aluminum variety and 85 percent is for steel. Thus, Athenian's ten percent of the total market really represents 10/85 or 11.8 per cent of the steel heat exchanger market and 0/15 or 0 percent of the aluminum segment of the market.

Preliminary study by Athenian management has revealed that the engineering and production know-how required in fabricating aluminum heat exchangers is such that entry into this type of manufacture would require an annual addition to fixed cost of one million dollars in research and special equipment and there would be a gestation period of one year before Athenian could market a satisfactory aluminum heat exchanger. Athenian's economist has studied the relationship of total industry heat exchanger sales to variations in the expenditures for capital equipment made by the process industries. Two findings have stemmed from his analysis of historical data.

---

[1]This illustration is taken from an article by P. E. Green and S. R. Calhoun, "An Environmental Framework for Break-Even Analysis for Planning," *N.A.A. Bulletin,* Vol. 39, No. 7 (March 1958), pp. 45–51.

1. Heat exchanger sales, in total, are linearly related to changes in total capital equipment expenditures. This relationship has not appreciably changed over the past ten years. Within the relevant range of the data, a change of one million dollars in capital equipment expenditures is associated with a change of $100,000 in total heat exchanger sales. This relationship is shown in Exhibit 1 of Figure 7-1.

2. Although the ratio of total heat exchanger sales to total capital equipment expenditures has remained rather constant, a more detailed study indicates that aluminum is gaining in share of the total heat exchanger market at the rate of three percentage points annually.

Consultation with Athenian's marketing staff indicates that aluminum heat exchangers are expected to garner an additional three percentage points annually of total heat exchanger sales over the next five years, at which time the ratio is expected to stabilize at about 70:30 in favor of steel. Although Athenian's market share now represents 10 percent of total industry sales, this share shows signs of declining unless Athenian either is able to capture a greater share of the remaining steel-fabricated class exchanger market or adds the aluminum variety to its line. Present and projected industry—company relationships (under alternative plans) are shown in Exhibit 2 of Figure 7-1 and will be commented upon later.

A look into Athenian's internal cost structure shows that annual fixed cost amounts to two million dollars. The ratio of variable cost to sales equals 0.6; that is, for each dollar increase in sales, variable cost increases 60 cents. Under these conditions, the current sales–profit relationship appears as a solid line in Exhibit 3 of Figure 7-1.

If, however, Athenian Corporation could satisfactorily produce aluminum-type heat exchangers, the variable cost to sales ratio is calculated to decrease to 0.56 because of a more favorable product mix. This relationship appears in Exhibit 3 as a broken line. Notice, however, that if Athenian elected to add aluminum heat exchangers to its line, fixed costs would rise by one million dollars. Hence, the dotted line reflects the fixed cost as well as the variable cost component. Furthermore, Athenian's marketing management believes that entry into the aluminum segment could increase the firm's total sales by 20 percent over sales expected if Athenian were to remain in the steel-only segment.

EVALUATING THE ALTERNATIVES

Very broadly sketched, the preceding information represents the facts available to Athenian's management at the present time. As management considers these facts, it desires to know what Athenian's total profit picture would look like two years hence if *no* change

Figure 7-1

MULTIPLE FACTOR ANALYSIS—ATHENIAN CORPORATION

EXHIBIT 1

RELATIONSHIP OF HEAT EXCHANGER INDUSTRY SALES
TO CAPITAL EQUIPMENT EXPENDITURES (TEN YEAR PERIOD)

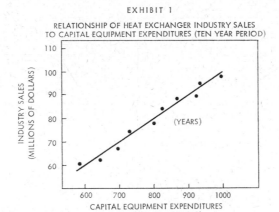

EXHIBIT 2

RELATIONSHIP OF ATHENIAN CORPORTION
SALES TO TOTAL INDUSTRY SALES

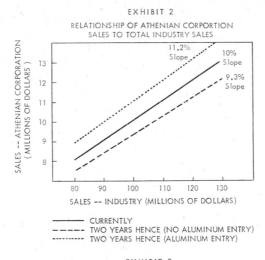

EXHIBIT 3

SALES - PROFIT RELATION

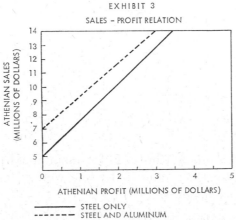

Figure 7–1 (continued)

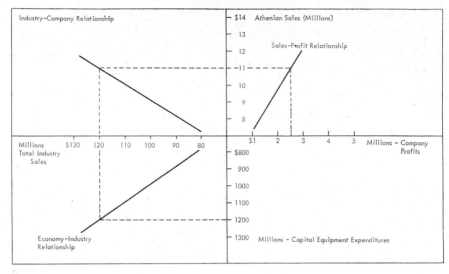

EXHIBIT 4

ATHENIAN CORPORATION PROFIT OUTLOOK TWO YEARS HENCE (NON ENTRY INTO ALUMINUM)

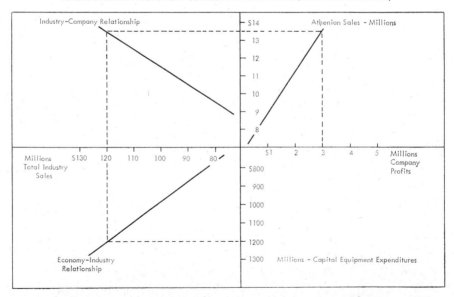

EXHIBIT 5

ATHENIAN CORPORATION PROFIT OUTLOOK TWO YEARS HENCE (ENTRY INTO ALUMINUM)

were made in the product line (and it maintained its current share of the steel-only market) and if the line were extended to include aluminum heat exchangers.

Athenian's economist then goes to work and forecasts that capital equipment expenditures will total $1.2 billion two years hence, thus yielding (based upon the economy–industry relationship) $120 million *total industry* heat exchanger sales. Since it is estimated that aluminum has now increased six percentage points to a 21 percent share, the total dollar market consists of approximately $25 million for aluminum and $95 million for steel heat exchangers. If the Athenian Corporation just holds its own in the steel heat exchanger portion, its 11.8 per cent of this part of the market will represent sales of about $11.2 million. Note on Exhibit 2 of Figure 7–1 the broken-line graph representing Athenian's nonentry into the aluminum field. This increase of $1.2 million over present sales, it should be observed, is entirely the result of an expanding total market and obtains in spite of the shrinkage (from 10 percent to 9.3 percent) of Athenian's share of it.

From Exhibit 3, it can be seen that, given a sales volume of $11.2 million derived entirely from steel heat exchangers, the corporation may expect to have profits of about $2.5 million, as against a present $2 million figure. The step-by-step tracing of the various factors influencing profits can be seen in Exhibit 4 of Figure 7–1. Starting at the $1,200 million capital equipment expenditure level, the dotted line indicates, by its intersections with the various functional relationships (*a*) total industry sales of $120 million; (*b*) Athenian sales of $11.2 million; and (*c*) Athenian profits of $2.5 million.

Now the case, two years hence, in which the Athenian Corporation has presumably entered the aluminum market can be considered. The economy–industry relationship remains the same at 10 percent of capital equipment expenditures, leading again to projected total industry sales of $120 million.

However, Athenian's industry–company relationship has changed. Based on its potential in aluminum plus the steel share, Athenian's sales are expected to amount to $13.4 million (120 percent of $11.2 million) resulting in a shift in the industry–company relationship which amounts to a *total* market share of 11.2 percent as opposed to 9.3 percent under the steel-only alternative. (These comparisons are shown in Exhibit 2.)

The sales–profit relationship shows that fixed cost has risen from $2 million to $3 million (reflecting the additional fixed cost of producing the aluminum variety) but the ratio of variable cost to sales has declined from 0.6 to 0.56. Hence, both the slope and intercept of the sales–profit relationship is changed. In terms of total profit, however, Athenian would enjoy $2.9 million on $13.4 million sales as opposed to $2.5 million on $11.2 million sales under the steel-only alternative. The results of Athenian's entering the aluminum market are shown in Exhibit 5 of Figure 7-1 which should be compared with Exhibit 4 of the same chart.

In a realistic problem situation, however, the analysis would hardly end here. The analyst would probably wish to calculate the respective sales volumes needed to break even (since fixed cost and the ratio of variable cost to sales would differ for the two alternatives). Additionally, the interim year and perhaps the third, fourth, and fifth year situations would be analyzed as well.

COMMENTS ON THE MULTIPLE-FACTOR MODEL

The preceding, highly simplified illustration of the multiple-factor model nevertheless demonstrates the essential features of the static or "snapshot" form of the procedure. From the point of view of market position analysis, it should now be clear that courses of action undertaken to increase a firm's market share and (perhaps) sales as well are typically cost incurring and thus should be considered within a broader framework which includes the firm's economy–industry and sales–profit relationships.

The multiple-factor model can be extended to deal with probabilistic and dynamic environments in addition to the deterministic, essentially static environment described above. For example, one could consider alternative economy–industry, industry–company sales, and sales–profit relationships. These states of nature could be derived from (a) the standard errors of the estimates (associated with regression procedures) or (b) the judgment of the economist, marketing manager, or financial manager, as the case might be. In addition, in dealing with long range analyses, the measure of effectiveness could be transformed into *discounted cash flow* over the *whole* planning period. Various sensitivity analyses of the specific parameters making up the model could also be run.

Rather than extend the multiple-factor model to deal with both dynamic and risk environments, this book will describe these concepts within the framework of Markov processes which are discussed in the next section.

MARKET POSITION ANALYSES WITHIN THE FRAMEWORK OF MARKOV PROCESSES

Another procedure for forecasting changes in a firm's market position involves the technique of Markov processes, named after the mathematician, A. A. Markov (1856-1922). While theoretical developments in these processes have extended over several decades, only in recent years have attempts been made to apply the Markov process to customer brand shifting behavior and to use the model to study the impact of brand shifting on the firm's market position.

The essential framework of Markov processes is probabilistic; however, it is typically assumed that the relevant probabilities are known; hence, in terms of the classification of decision models, use of the Markov framework would generally fall into the category of decision making under risk. (Later the possible extension of Markov processes to deal with the category of decisions under uncertainty will be discussed.)

Markov processes deal with a sequence of events over time which is generated by a probabilistic process with the property that the probability of the next event in a successive sequence of trials depends at most only on the present outcome and not on the particular occurrence of any of the events before that. While this property may seem restrictive, empirical research has indicated that many behavioralistic processes do appear to exhibit this property. Moreover, means are available to extend the Markov process to deal with conditional probabilities which extend over more than a single time period.

The mathematics of Markov processes go well beyond the level of this book. This section of the chapter will serve to acquaint the reader with the concept and to pique his interest for further reading in this area. In line with this objective such treatment of the subject will be largely nontechnical and illustrated by numerical examples. Some of the more technical machinery is discussed in the appendix to this chapter.

The Markov process is characterized by the following terms: system, state of the system, and a state transition. By system is meant a complex of interacting components and the relationships among them which lead to particular outcomes. For example, customer behavior could be viewed as a system in which the outcomes of interest are the various shares of the total market gained by each competing brand.

By state of the system is meant a description of the system's relevant properties. For example, if the system is defined to include the two states, "purchased firm A's product" and "purchased firm B's product," then for our purposes this may be a sufficient definition of the customer population. Or, the states could be expanded to include "purchased neither," "purchased both," "purchased firm C's product," and so on. In any case we shall be concerned with partitions over the system, that is a mutually exclusive and collectively exhaustive set of states.

By state transition is meant a change of state as, for example, when a customer who last purchased product *A* buys product *B* on his next purchase occasion. Should the customer purchase product *A* again this is still considered as a transition, in this case from state *A* to state *A*.

Suppose we are interested in the behavior of some randomly selected purchaser over time (where time is measured in equal, discrete intervals). Assume that in the beginning of the process the customer has last purchased Brand *A* and in the next purchase period he can purchase brand *A* again or switch to brand *B*. Suppose these transition probabilities are 0.6 and 0.4 respectively. If he purchases brand *B*, the conditional probabilities of switching to brand *A* or remaining with brand *B* are 0.9 and 0.1, respectively. Suppose we would like to know the probability of his being in state *A* or state *B* after, say, three transitions. The tree diagram of Figure 7–2 summarizes this process.

Figure 7–2

Tree Diagram—Two-State Markov Process

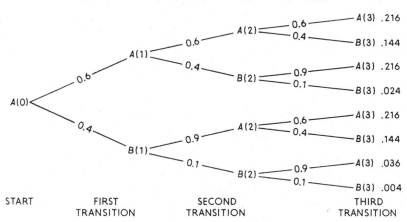

As can be inferred from Figure 7–2 the probability that the customer is in state $A(3)$, purchased brand *A* on the third transition, is $.216 + .216 + .216 + .036 = .684$, while the probability that he is in state $B(3)$ is $.144 + .024 + .144 + .004 = .316$. Since it was assumed that the states are mutually exclusive and collectively exhaustive, notice that the two probabilities sum to unity.

What would happen if the process were kept going? Would the probabilities settle down to some fixed values? What would happen if the marketing manager were able to change (by appropriate promotional or price activity) the transition probabilities? These and other questions can be explored by turning to a somewhat more realistic illustration of the Markov model.

AN ILLUSTRATIVE CASE OF MARKOV CHAIN ANALYSIS

While the preceding example has shown how the Markov model leads to changes in the state probabilities, the task is now to apply the technique to a problem of more realistic scale and to demonstrate some of the uses to which Markov processes can be put.

Assume that a manufacturer of floor preparations is interested in the progress which a recently-introduced product is making in the market. More specifically, assume that our manufacturer has introduced a new polish, E-Z Off, into the home floor-polishing market. At the end of the first year of introduction E-Z Off has captured 24 percent of the market. Brand *A*, the dominant floor-polishing brand, has 47 percent of the market, and all other brands combined (which will be called, generically, brand *C*) have the remaining 29 percent of the market. The marketing manager of E-Z Off is concerned with the trend in his product's share of the market and how alternative plans (promotion, price, and so forth) may affect his product's future market position.

Next assume that E-Z Off's marketing manager has collected consumer panel data from which he can estimate the pertinent brand switching probabilities. In consumer panel studies each participant maintains a diary of her purchases of various personal and household items (food, soaps, apparel) in which are recorded such characteristics as date purchased, store in which the purchase was made, brand of article purchased, price paid, and so on. In this way the market researcher is able to make a more or less continuous appraisal of the dynamics of consumer purchasing, for example, the frequency with which various items are purchased, the extent to which new brands are tried and then either dropped or repurchased on the next buying occasion. Furthermore, from the standpoint of making the Markov model operational, consumer panel data can be used to provide estimates of both a brand's current market share and the brand switching probabilities which are used in the model to estimate the brand's future market share if market conditions were to remain approximately the same.

Assume that E-Z Off's marketing manager has made a tabulation of the proportion of purchasers of floor polish, by brand, who, over the last two purchase periods, (*a*) remained with their old brand or (*b*) switched to a new brand. These empirically derived proportions represent estimates of brand switching probabilities for a purchaser chosen at random from the universe of floor polish purchasers. The current market shares of E-Z Off and brands A and C and the estimated transition probabilities are shown in Table 7–1.

Table 7–1

ESTIMATED SHARE AND TRANSITION PROBABILITIES
(FLOOR POLISH BRANDS)

Brand	Current Share	Last Purchase	Next Purchase			Total
			A	E-Z Off	C	
A....................	47%	A	.32	.31	.37	1.00
E-Z Off..............	24	E-Z Off	.10	.43	.47	1.00
C....................	29	C	.36	.41	.23	1.00
	100%					

As noted in Table 7–1, the estimated probability that a consumer who last purchased brand A continues to purchase brand A on the next buying occasion is .32, the probability of switching from brand A to E-Z Off is .31 and the probability of switching from brand A to brand C is .37.

The main diagonal of the table (consisting of the numbers 0.32, 0.43 and 0.23) can be interpreted as consumer "loyalty" measures. From the marketing manager's standpoint he would undoubtedly like to see E-Z Off's "loyalty" probability approach 1; that is, all purchasers of E-Z Off would continue to purchase it on subsequent buying occasions. By the same token, the marketing manager would like to increase the probabilities that nonbuyers of E-Z Off would switch to being buyers of E-Z Off. But the problem involved is that overconcentration on building repeat purchase loyalty may result in reduced funds available for attracting nonbuyers of E-Z Off. One of the primary uses of the Markov model is in tracing the implications of changes in promotional mix on future market share levels for the product under study.

Before approaching this problem, however, assume that the marketing manager is interested in making long-term projections of E-Z Off market share under present conditions. In other words, given the present market share pattern for the three brands and the estimated transition probabilities, how would market share for the three brands fare in the future?

Suppose one transition is carried out and then what would happen as the number of transitions becomes very large is shown. For purposes of illustration assume that the total universe of customers consists of 1,000 people. Also assume that all customers buy in equal quantities and with equal frequency. Given the transition probabilities, estimate E-Z Off's market share during the next purchase period. According to the transition probabilities, 43 percent of present E-Z Off customers will remain loyal. Thus, out of E-Z Off's current group of 240 customers, .43 of 240, or 103 customers, will remain loyal. In addition, E-Z Off will pick up customers from brands A and C. In the former case the number of A customers switching to E-Z Off is .31 of 470, or 146, and the number of C customers switching to E-Z Off is .41 of 290, or 119. During the next buying occasion, E-Z Off's share is estimated to be $\frac{103 + 146 + 119}{1,000}$, or 36.8 percent of the market. It should be emphasized that this is an *expected* share.[2]

In a similar manner, estimates of market share during the next buying period turn out to be 27.9 percent and 35.3 percent for brands A and C, respectively. In this illustrative case it is apparent that both E-Z Off and Brand C have gained market position at brand A's expense. It is also clear that this process could be continued by again applying the transition probabilities, arriving at a new set of share levels for two periods ahead, and so on.

If this were done, however, market share patterns for the three brands would ultimately approach an equilibrium under the conditions of illustration. As shown in the appendix, this equilibrium is obtained by solving a set of simultaneous linear equations. The results are noted in Table 7-2 and Figure 7-3.

Table 7-2

PROGRESSION OF MARKET SHARE PATTERN

(FLOOR POLISH BRANDS)

Brand	Original Shares	First Transition	Second Transition			Equilibrium Shares
A......................	47%	27.9%	25.3%	.	.	24.8%
E-Z Off...............	24	36.8	38.9	.	.	39.3
C.....................	29	35.3	35.8	.	.	35.9
	100%	100.0%	100.0%			100.0%

As the reader may note from either Table 7-2 or Figure 7-3, the market shares of E-Z Off and Brands A and B rapidly approach their equilibrium values (which theoretically obtain as the number

---

[2]For a good discussion of "vector-Markov" and "semi-Markov" models, see R. Howard, "Stochastic Process Models of Consumer Behavior," *Journal of Advertising Research*, Vol. 3, No. 3 (September, 1963), pp. 35–42.

of transitions approaches infinity). From a practical viewpoint
equilibrium shares are virtually reached by the second transition.
This is not infrequently the case when one is dealing with real
problem situations and more advanced methods are available (see
references at the end of this chapter) for calculating rate of approach to equilibrium values.

Figure 7–3

PROGRESSION OF MARKET SHARE PATTERN—FLOOR POLISH BRANDS

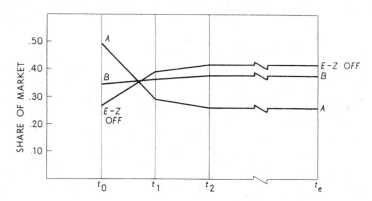

From the market manager's point of view, he can note that E-Z
Off's share might be expected to reach almost 40 percent of the
market if brand switching conditions remain approximately constant; hence the new product appears to be highly successful even
though its current share is slightly less than a quarter of the market.
But the marketing manager's job can be interpreted as evaluating
alternative courses of action which (interacting with competitive
actions) may change the entries of the table of transition probabilities. This primary value of Markov chains is examined in the following section.

USE OF THE MARKOV MODEL IN PLANS EVALUATION

In one sense the marketing manager's job may be viewed as
designing and evaluating plans whose purpose is to *alter* the probabilities in the transition matrix to some more favorable level, consistent with the net payoffs obtained by increasing his firm's market
position. Ideally, E-Z Off's marketing manager might like to see the
entries of the second column of the table of transition probabilities
(Table 7–1) equal unity and, hence, all other entries equal zero.
In practice, of course, the manager must contend with competitors

whose actions are opposed to this objective, and he must also weigh the economic consequences of such an ambitious goal.

Suppose the Markov model is next used to predict the impact of alternative strategies on E-Z Off's market position. More specifically, assume that the marketing manager is evaluating two alternative plans whose implementation would incur equal costs. The first course of action A_1 is concerned with increasing the appeal of "loyalty" type advertising and, hence, increasing the probability that an E-Z Off purchaser would again purchase this brand on her next buying occasion. The second course of action A_2 is concerned with increasing the appeal of "attraction" type advertising, that is, winning over noncustomers of E-Z Off floor polish.

In this illustration assume that the marketing manager can estimate (by consumer pretesting, perhaps) the effect of these alternative plans in terms of their net impact on the entries in the original table of transition probabilities. The new entries which the manager estimates for each action are shown in Table 7–3.

Table 7–3

TRANSITION PROBABILITIES—ALTERNATIVE PLANS
(E-Z OFF POLISH)

	Action A_1				Action A_2			
	A	E-Z Off	A	Total	A	E-Z Off	C	Total
A	.32	.31	.37	1.00	.30	.36	.34	1.00
E-Z Off	.08	.53	.39	1.00	.10	.43	.47	1.00
C	.36	.41	.23	1.00	.33	.46	.21	1.00

In comparing the entries under action A_1 with the original data of Table 7–1 the only row changed is the E-Z Off row in which the "loyalty" entry is raised by 0.10 (from 0.43 to 0.53). The two other entries of this row are decreased proportionately so as to make the row total 1.00. Under action A_2 rows one and three are changed by adding 0.05 to the middle entry of each row and decreasing proportionately the two other entries of each row in order to have the row probabilities sum to unity. In other words, A_1 adds 0.10 probability points by directly affecting the "loyalty" entry while A_2 adds 0.10 probability points by adding 0.05 to the switching probability of brand A to E-Z Off and 0.05 to the switching probability of brand C to E-Z Off.

The marketing manager is now interested in estimating the long run (equilibrium) market share levels of E-Z Off under each of these plans, given the original market share data of Table 7–1. The equilibrium shares (found by methods described in the appendix) are shown in Table 7–4.

Table 7–4

EQUILIBRIUM SHARES—ALTERNATIVE PLANS

(FLOOR POLISH BRANDS)

Brand	Share: A_1	Share: A_2
A	33.2%	35.0%
E-Z Off	44.0	42.5
C	22.8	22.5
	100.0%	100.0%

As it turns out, action A_1, which stresses the customer loyalty factor, results in a larger share level for E-Z Off than does action A_2. The manager, given equal costs of plan implementation, would select act A_1. These results, however, should not be generalized. Rather, the purpose has been to show how the manager could proceed to use the Markov model as a predictive tool in evaluating the dynamic effects of alternative marketing plans.

In the cases illustrated so far, a major simplifying assumption— that the table of transition probabilities, once set up, would remain invariant from purchase period to purchase period—has been made. More realistically, the job of the marketing manager often consists of trying, more or less continuously, to modify these probabilities by means of consumer promotion, personal selling, increased product availability, and so on. Hence, calculation of equilibrium levels may not constitute more than an academic exercise. But, in practice, share levels often approach their equilibrium levels rather quickly. Moreover, estimates for any period or periods into the future can be made by merely calculating out the relevant share levels with the appropriate transition probabilities then assumed to be operative. The fact that these probabilities will typically change over time increases the desirability of setting up a more or less continuous monitoring system by means of consumer buying panels. The nature of this type of feedback will be discussed in a later chapter.

COMMENTS ON THE MARKOV MODEL

The preceding discussion has only scratched the surface of the Markov model and its potential utility as a technique for predicting the market position of brands over time. The purpose in this section is to discuss some of the restrictive assumptions underlying the model and how these limitations can, in practice, be overcome. Comment on possible extensions of the model which go considerably beyond the scope of the material covered in this chapter will also be made.

Some of the assumptions underlying the use of the Markov model have already been commented upon: (*a*) the probability of a particular transition at a given time depends upon the current state only, not the prior history of the process; (*b*) the consumers all purchase equal quantities of the product in question; (*c*) the total customer population remains constant through time; and (*d*) the same transition probability applies to all purchasers in a given state.

In practice, all of the above limitations can be overcome by a suitable redefinition of states. For example, if the transition probabilities are assumed to depend upon, say, two previous purchases, the states can be redefined as *AA, A* E-Z Off, *AC, . . ., C* E-Z Off, *CC.* Moreover, by suitable state redefinition high-quantity buyers can be separated from low-quantity buyers. Expansion of states to include dummy "birth and death" states permits changing the level of the total buying population. Furthermore, so-called "hard-core" (high loyalty) customers can be separated and analyzed separately as can customers typified as "switchers."

This analytical "trick" of redefining states can also be used to predict the progress of new product introductions and provides a way to deal with products whose time interval between purchases is long. In the first instance, states can be redefined into buyers, triers, and nonbuyers. This enables the analyst to study the impact of re-purchasing on the product's future success as contrasted with "fad" type buying where trier rates are high but repurchase rates are low. In products when the time interval between purchases is long, con-sumer durables and some types of apparel for example, the plan-ner may wish to develop data on attitude changes as "intermediate" states prior to purchase. This extension requires, of course, that satisfactory measures of "awareness," "preference," and so on can be derived from consumer panel interviews.

Finally, the preceding discussion assumed that the relevant prob-abilities were known and that the payoffs related to choice among courses of action could be calculated independently of the model. In theory, however, the transition probabilities may be viewed as alternative states of nature and prior probability assignments could be made over these states. This could permit answers to such questions as: (*a*) how large a sample of consumers should be taken for panel studies; (*b*) how frequently should sampling be done, and so on. While research is adapting Bayesian methods to the study of Markov processes has been conducted recently, the complexity of this subject is beyond the scope of this chapter. With respect to the second question, incorporation of payoffs into the Markov structure, the work of Ronald Howard (see References) has been directed to this subject.[3]

LIMITATIONS OF THE MARKET SHARE MEASUREMENT

Although the primary emphasis of this chapter has been on models for dealing with market share changes, it must be remembered that courses of action taken to increase market position usually represent a means toward an end.

Increasing market position is typically cost incurring. Not infrequently plans which emphasize high market participation are not the most profitable plans. The planner must consider the net financial flows which stem from actions taken to react favorably on the firm's share of the market. There appears to be some support for the assertion that diminishing returns set in as firms try to gain ever larger shares of the market. This is quite apart from the government's interest in those firms which dominate their marketing area. All of which suggests that the objective of "maximizing market share" is hardly a sound one even though marketing executives may imply that this goal is (or should be) the prime concern of the firm.

The importance of market share in overall marketing planning will continue to be emphasized. However, this variable will be treated as an intermediate outcome useful for deriving discounted cash flows or other monetary measures of effectiveness.

SUMMARY

This chapter has introduced the reader to market position analysis via two models—a "certainty-equivalent" static model and a probabilistic, dynamic model.

The multiple-factor model was found to be useful in showing the structural relationships (economy–industry, industry–company, and sales–profit) which link the firm with its environment. In particular, the model shows how sales-increasing actions frequently weaken the sales–profit relationship by adding to fixed costs. That is, the

---

[3]Also see Howard, *op. cit.*, on the use of semi-Markov models and their advantages over the earlier Markov "flow" models described above.

cost of, say, a large advertising campaign or product development program must be weighed against the impact of this campaign on changing the industry–company relationship and, ultimately, on profits. The model also permits the planner to forecast profits by considering the individual effects of such influences as aggregate economic activity, industry sales, and so forth, on the firm's sales and profit picture.

The Markov model was next described as a predictive tool for studying the time changes in market position as affected by consumer brand shifting behavior. Application of this model works from transition probabilities as estimated from consumer panel data. The evaluation of marketing plans was discussed from the standpoint of their impact on changing the transition probabilities. It was then indicated how, in practice, some of the limitations of the conventional Markov model often can be overcome by a suitable redefinition of states. Newer model formulations (semi-Markov processes) are increasing the flexibility of these techniques.

Finally, a word of caution was added about viewing market position as more than a means toward the ultimate objective of profit maximization (expressed, say, in terms of expected net present value) over the planning horizon. The market share variable, however, represents an important intermediate measurement for appraising the interaction of the firm's courses of action with those of its competitors and, ultimately, in deriving company sales. This measurement will be found to play an important role in the next four chapters which deal with individual classes of market planning decisions.

Selected References

HARARY, FRANK, AND LIPSTEIN, BENJAMIN. "The Dynamics of Brand Loyalty: A Markovian Approach," *Operations Research,* Vol. X, No. 1 (January–February, 1962), pp. 19–40.

Interesting both from the standpoint of its discussion of digraph theory and its relationship to Markov processes and for the marketing applications which are described.

HOWARD, RONALD A. *Dynamic Programming and Markov Processes.* New York: John Wiley & Sons, Inc., 1960.

Discusses Markov chains (both in discrete and continuous time) from the point of view of z and Laplace transforms, a useful device for describing the transient behavior of Markov processes in closed-form expressions. Howard then develops a programming approach (policy iteration) for solving Markov process problems with "reward" or payoff vectors. Requires a fairly mature mathematical background on the part of the reader.

KEMENY, JOHN G., AND SNELL, J. LAURIE. *Finite Markov Chains.* Princeton, N.J.: D. Van Nostrand Co., Inc., 1960.

KEMENY, JOHN G., *et al. Finite Mathematics with Business Applications*. Englewood Cliffs, N.J.: Prentice-Hall, Inc., 1962.

> Both books by Kemeny *et al.* provide rigorous and lucid accounts of finite Markov processes and develop the necessary matrix and probability theory required to understand the development of the concepts.

RAUTENSTRAUCH, WALTER, AND VILLERS, RAYMOND. *Budgetary Control*. New York: Funk and Wagnalls Co., 1950.

> Discusses the use of break-even charts in setting and controlling budgets and, as such, ties in closely with the Weinberg approach.

WEINBERG, ROBERT S. "Multiple Factor Break-Even Analysis: The Application of Operations Research Techniques to a Basic Problem of Management Planning and Control," *Operations Research*, Vol. IV, No. 2 (April, 1956), pp. 152–86.

> Discusses in detail the multiple-factor model which was described in this chapter. Also covers the use of the model in a dynamic planning situation.

Technical Appendix

This technical note[4] describes the use of matrix methods in solving for equilibrium market shares as discussed in the chapter.

The matrix P is defined to consist of the transition probabilities p_{ij}:

$$\begin{bmatrix} p_{11} & p_{12} & \ldots & p_{1r} \\ p_{21} & p_{22} & \ldots & p_{2r} \\ p_{i1} & p_{i2} & \ldots & p_{ir} \end{bmatrix}$$

where $0 \leqslant p_{ij} \leqslant 1$ and $\sum\limits_{j=1}^{r} p_{ij} = 1$ for all i. The probability that a customer will switch from brand i to brand j is given by the ij-th intersection.

To illustrate the transition matrix for the two-state problem (see Figure 7–2) of the foregoing chapter, we write

$$P = \begin{bmatrix} 0.6 & 0.4 \\ 0.9 & 0.1 \end{bmatrix}$$

We next define a row vector $\underline{v}(n)$ with components $v_i(n)$. The row vector for the $(n+1)$th step is

$$\underline{v}(n+1) = \underline{v}(n) P \qquad\qquad n = 0, 1, 2, \ldots$$

Suppose the process starts out with a given row vector of market shares

$$\underline{v}(0) = (v_1(0), v_2(0), \ldots, v_r(0))$$

---

[4]This section assumes that the reader is familiar with elementary matrix methods. A sufficient reference for background material is Daniel T. Finkbeiner, *Introduction to Matrices and Linear Transformations* (San Francisco, California: W. H. Freeman and Company, 1960).

Given $v\,(0)$ and the transition matrix P, we may compute $v\,(n)$ recursively.

$$v\,(1) = v\,(0)\,P$$
$$v\,(2) = v\,(1)\,P = v\,(0)\,P \cdot P = v\,(0)\,P^2$$
$$\cdot$$
$$\cdot$$
$$\cdot$$
$$v\,(n) = v\,(0)\,P^n$$

In terms of the example, suppose the process starts out with the consumer purchasing brand A. Then

$$v\,(1) = v\,(0)\,P = (1 \quad 0) \begin{bmatrix} 0.6 & 0.4 \\ 0.9 & 0.1 \end{bmatrix}$$
$$v\,(1) = (0.6 \quad 0.4)$$

In the next transition we have

$$v\,(2) = v\,(1)\,P = (0.6 \quad 0.4) \begin{bmatrix} 0.6 & 0.4 \\ 0.9 & 0.1 \end{bmatrix}$$
$$v\,(2) = (0.72 \quad 0.28)$$

It is clear that we could continue the multiplicative process indefinitely. If we did, however, it would be found that for this type of problem rows of sufficiently high powers of the matrix converge to values such that a fixed vector results as the number of transitions n approaches infinity. Such a process is called a completely ergodic chain and the limiting state probability distribution is independent of the initial vector. We define the fixed vector v with components v_i

$$v = v\,P$$

In terms of the example,

$$(v_1 \quad v_2) \begin{bmatrix} 0.6 & 0.4 \\ 0.9 & 0.1 \end{bmatrix} = (v_1 \quad v_2)$$

$$v_1 = 0.6\,v_1 + 0.9\,v_2$$
$$v_2 = 0.4\,v_1 + 0.1\,v_2$$

Since the components of v must sum to unity, we add the equation $v_1 + v_2 = 1$ and solve the resultant system.

$$-0.4\,v_1 + 0.9\,v_2 = 0$$
$$0.4\,v_1 - 0.9\,v_2 = 0$$
$$v_1 + \quad v_2 = 1$$

We note that $v_1 = \%_{13}$ and $v_2 = \frac{4}{13}$.

Substituting these values in the equation

$$v = v\, P = (\%_{13}\ \tfrac{4}{13}) \begin{bmatrix} \%_{10} & \frac{4}{10} \\ \%_{10} & \frac{1}{10} \end{bmatrix}$$

$$= (\%_{13}\ \tfrac{4}{13})$$

Thus, if the process were to go through a large number of transitions the state probabilities would converge to 0.69 and 0.31 for the purchase of brand A and brand B, respectively, independent of starting conditions.

THE Z-TRANSFORM

A useful way to describe the transient behavior of Markov chains in closed form is by means of the z-transform (see the Howard [1960] reference).

The z-transform $f^*(z)$ is defined as

$$f^*(z) = \sum_{n=0}^{\infty} f(n)\, z^n \text{ where: } |z| < 1$$

We assume that $f(n)$ takes on values at nonnegative, discrete, integrally spaced points. Two particular functions of interest are

$$f(n) = \begin{cases} 1 \; ; n = 0, 1, 2, 3 \ldots ; \\ 0 \; ; n < 0 \end{cases}$$

$$f(n) = \alpha^n \; ; n \geqslant 0$$

For the first function, the appropriate z-transform is

$$f^*(z) = \sum_{n=0}^{\infty} f(n)\, z^n = 1 + z + z^2 + z^3 + \ldots$$

$$= \frac{1}{1-z}$$

For the second function,

$$f^*(z) = \sum_{n=0}^{\infty} f(n)\, z^n = \sum_{n=0}^{\infty} (\alpha z)^n = 1 + \alpha z + \alpha^2 z^2 + \alpha^3 z^3$$

$$= \frac{1}{1 - \alpha z}$$

Finally, we should note that

$$\sum_{n=0}^{\infty} f(n+1)\, z^n = \sum_{m=1}^{\infty} f(m)\, z^{m-1} = z^{-1}\, [f^*(z) - f(0)]$$

To show this, we first write:

$$\sum_{n=0}^{\infty} f(n+1) z^n = f(1) z^0 + f(2) z + f(3) z^2 \ldots$$

$$\sum_{m=1}^{\infty} f(m) z^{m-1} = f(1) z^0 + f(2) z + f(3) z^2 \ldots$$

But the latter expression is equal to

$$z^{-1} \sum_{n=0}^{\infty} [f(n) z^n] - z^{-1} f(0)$$

since we can write:

$$z^{-1} [f(0) z^0 + f(1) z^1 + f(2) z^2 + f(3) z^3 \ldots] - z^{-1} f(0)$$

$$= [f(0) z^{-1}] + [f(1) z^0 + f(2) z + f(3) z^2 \ldots] - [z^{-1} f(0)]$$

Hence,

$$\sum_{n=0}^{\infty} f(n+1) z^n = z^{-1} [f^*(z) - f(0)]$$

We next take the z-transforms of the equation $\underline{v}(n+1) = \underline{v}(n) P$ and write the vector z-transform as $\underline{v}^*(z)$. We then obtain

$$z^{-1} [\underline{v}^*(z) - \underline{v}(0)] = \underline{v}^*(z) P$$
$$\underline{v}^*(z) - \underline{v}(0) = z \underline{v}^*(z) P$$
$$\underline{v}^*(z) - z \underline{v}^*(z) P = \underline{v}(0)$$
$$\underline{v}^*(z) (I - zP) = \underline{v}(0)$$
$$\underline{v}^*(z) = \underline{v}(0) (I - z P)^{-1}$$

Since I is the identity matrix the transform of the state vector equals the original state vector postmultiplied by the inverse of $I - z P$. We shall proceed to find this inverse by the usual matrix methods. Suppose we continue to use the two-state matrix of the preceding chapter.

$$P = \begin{bmatrix} 6/10 & 4/10 \\ 9/10 & 1/10 \end{bmatrix} \quad I = \begin{bmatrix} 1 & 0 \\ 0 & 1 \end{bmatrix}$$

$$I - zP = \begin{bmatrix} 1 - 6/10\, z & - 4/10\, z \\ - 9/10\, z & 1 - 1/10\, z \end{bmatrix}$$

We next compute (a) the adjoint matrix and (b) the determinant of the matrix. The adjoint matrix is

$$\text{Adj } [I - zP] = \begin{bmatrix} 1 - 1/10\, z & 4/10\, z \\ 9/10\, z & 1 - 6/10\, z \end{bmatrix}$$

The determinant of the matrix is

$$|I - zP| = [(1 - \tfrac{6}{10} z)(1 - \tfrac{1}{10} z) - (-\tfrac{9}{10} z)(-\tfrac{4}{10} z)]$$

$$= 1 - \tfrac{7}{10} z + \tfrac{6}{50} z^2 - \tfrac{18}{50} z^2$$

$$= 1 - \tfrac{7}{10} z - \tfrac{3}{10} z^2$$

$$= (1 - z)(1 + \tfrac{3}{10} z)$$

$$(I - zP)^{-1} = \frac{1}{|I - zP|} \operatorname{Adj}(I - zP) = \begin{bmatrix} \dfrac{1 - \tfrac{1}{10} z}{(1 - z)(1 + \tfrac{3}{10} z)} & \dfrac{\tfrac{4}{10} z}{(1 - z)(1 + \tfrac{3}{10} z)} \\[2em] \dfrac{\tfrac{9}{10} z}{(1 - z)(1 + \tfrac{3}{10} z)} & \dfrac{1 - \tfrac{6}{10} z}{(1 - z)(1 + \tfrac{3}{10} z)} \end{bmatrix}$$

We then use partial-fraction expansion to separate each expression into the sum of two terms. For example,

$$\frac{A}{(1 - z)} + \frac{B}{(1 + \tfrac{3}{10} z)} = \frac{1 - \tfrac{1}{10} z}{(1 - z)(1 + \tfrac{3}{10} z)}$$

$$A(1 + \tfrac{3}{10} z) + B(1 - z) = 1 - \tfrac{1}{10} z$$

Letting $z = 1$:

$$A = \frac{1 - \tfrac{1}{10}}{1 + \tfrac{3}{10}}$$

$$= \tfrac{9}{13}$$

Letting $z = -\tfrac{10}{3}$:

$$B = \frac{1 + \tfrac{1}{3}}{1 + \tfrac{10}{3}}$$

$$= \tfrac{4}{13}$$

By similar operations we arrive at

$$(I - zP)^{-1} = \begin{bmatrix} \dfrac{\tfrac{9}{13}}{1 - z} + \dfrac{\tfrac{4}{13}}{1 + \tfrac{3}{10} z} & \dfrac{\tfrac{4}{13}}{1 - z} + \dfrac{-\tfrac{4}{13}}{1 + \tfrac{3}{10} z} \\[2em] \dfrac{\tfrac{9}{13}}{1 - z} + \dfrac{-\tfrac{9}{13}}{1 + \tfrac{3}{10} z} & \dfrac{\tfrac{4}{13}}{1 - z} + \dfrac{\tfrac{9}{13}}{1 + \tfrac{3}{10} z} \end{bmatrix}$$

$$= \frac{1}{1 - z} \begin{bmatrix} \tfrac{9}{13} & \tfrac{4}{13} \\[1em] \tfrac{9}{13} & \tfrac{4}{13} \end{bmatrix} + \frac{1}{1 + \tfrac{3}{10} z} \begin{bmatrix} \tfrac{4}{13} & -\tfrac{4}{13} \\[1em] -\tfrac{9}{13} & \tfrac{9}{13} \end{bmatrix}$$

If we let the matrix $J(n)$ be the element-by-element inverse transform of $(I - zP)^{-1}$, by applying the two transforms stated earlier, we get

$$J(n) = \begin{bmatrix} \tfrac{9}{13} & \tfrac{4}{13} \\[1em] \tfrac{9}{13} & \tfrac{4}{13} \end{bmatrix} + (-\tfrac{3}{10})^n \begin{bmatrix} \tfrac{4}{13} & -\tfrac{4}{13} \\[1em] -\tfrac{9}{13} & \tfrac{9}{13} \end{bmatrix}$$

Finally we take the inverse transform of

$$\underline{v}^* (z) = \underline{v} (0) (I - zP)^{-1}$$

and we get

$$\underline{v} (n) = \underline{v} (0) J (n)$$

Thus, we note that $J (n)$ represents a closed-form expression for P^n, the n th power of the transition matrix.

If we compare the results of using the z-transform with the solution obtained by solving the set of simultaneous equations, we note that the equilibrium probabilities

$$v_1 = \tfrac{9}{13} \text{ and } v_2 = \tfrac{4}{13}$$

are given by the first term of $J (n)$. Notice as n approaches infinity the second term of $J (n)$ approaches a limit of zero.

Furthermore, we can use the expression to reproduce the numerical answers which we have already computed for $\underline{v} (1)$ and $\underline{v} (2)$, given that the process starts in state v_1 (purchaser of brand A), then

$$v (0) = (1 \ 0) \text{ and } \underline{v} (n) = (\tfrac{9}{13} \ \tfrac{4}{13}) + (-\tfrac{3}{10})^n (\tfrac{4}{13} - \tfrac{4}{13})$$

For $\underline{v} (1)$, we find that

$$v_1 = \tfrac{9}{13} - (\tfrac{3}{10} \cdot \tfrac{4}{13}) = \tfrac{3}{5} \text{ or } 0.6$$

and

$$v_2 = \tfrac{4}{13} + (\tfrac{3}{10} \cdot \tfrac{4}{13}) = \tfrac{2}{5} \text{ or } 0.4$$

which agrees with our earlier results.
For $\underline{v} (2)$, we find that

$$v_1 = \tfrac{9}{13} + (\tfrac{9}{100} \cdot \tfrac{4}{13}) = \tfrac{18}{25} \text{ or } 0.72$$

and

$$v_2 = \tfrac{4}{13} - (\tfrac{9}{100} \cdot \tfrac{4}{13}) = \tfrac{7}{25} \text{ or } 0.28.$$

We note that these solutions agree with our previous results.

The reader may thus note that $J (n)$ consists of a "steady-state" part (the first term) and a transient part which approaches zero as n approaches infinity. The transient part (the second term) consists of matrices whose elements sum to zero across rows and are called differential matrices.

Finally, we show the application of the z-transform to the three-state matrix of the E-Z Off problem (Table 7–1) and derive the $J (n)$ matrix in the same manner as above.

$$P = \begin{bmatrix} .32 & .31 & .37 \\ .10 & .43 & .47 \\ .36 & .41 & .23 \end{bmatrix} \qquad I = \begin{bmatrix} 1 & 0 & 0 \\ 0 & 1 & 0 \\ 0 & 0 & 1 \end{bmatrix}$$

$$I - zP = \begin{bmatrix} 1 - .32z & -.31z & -.37z \\ -.10z & 1 - .43z & -.47z \\ -.36z & -.41z & 1 - .23z \end{bmatrix}$$

$$| I - zP | = 1 - .98z - .0468z^2 + .0268z^3$$
$$= (1 - z)(1 - .154z)(1 + .174z)$$

$$\text{Adj } (I - zP) = \begin{bmatrix} 1 - .66z - .0938z^2 & .31z + .0804z^2 & .37z - .0134z^2 \\ .10z + .1462z^2 & 1 - .55z - .0596z^2 & .47z - .1134z^2 \\ .36z - .1138z^2 & .41z - .0196z^2 & 1 - .75z + .1066z^2 \end{bmatrix}$$

$$(I - zP)^{-1} = \left| \frac{1}{I - zP} \right| \text{ Adj } (I - zP)$$

By partial fraction expansion separation we obtain

$$(I - zP)^{-1} = \frac{1}{1 - z} \begin{bmatrix} .248 & .393 & .359 \\ .248 & .393 & .359 \\ .248 & .393 & .359 \end{bmatrix} + \frac{1}{1 - .154z}$$

$$\begin{bmatrix} .619 & - .462 & - .157 \\ - .582 & .434 & .148 \\ .210 & - .157 & - .053 \end{bmatrix} + \frac{1}{1 + .174z} \begin{bmatrix} .133 & .069 & - .202 \\ .335 & .172 & - .507 \\ - .458 & - .236 & .694 \end{bmatrix}$$

$$J(n) = \begin{bmatrix} .248 & .393 & .359 \\ .248 & .393 & .359 \\ .248 & .393 & .359 \end{bmatrix} + (.154)^n \begin{bmatrix} .619 & -.462 & -.157 \\ -.582 & +.434 & +.148 \\ .210 & -.157 & -.053 \end{bmatrix}$$

$$+ (-.174)^n \begin{bmatrix} .133 & .069 & -.202 \\ .335 & .172 & -.507 \\ -.458 & -.236 & .694 \end{bmatrix}$$

We next calculate the first and second transitions and the equilibrium matrix.

First Transition

$$(.47 \quad .24 \quad .29) \begin{bmatrix} .320 & .310 & .370 \\ .100 & .430 & .470 \\ .360 & .410 & .230 \end{bmatrix} = (.279 \quad .368 \quad .353)$$

Second Transition

$$(.47 \quad .24 \quad .29) \begin{bmatrix} .267 & .384 & .349 \\ .244 & .408 & .348 \\ .239 & .382 & .377 \end{bmatrix} = (.253 \quad .389 \quad .358)$$

Equilibrium Matrix

$$\begin{bmatrix} .248 & .393 & .359 \\ .248 & .393 & .359 \\ .248 & .393 & .359 \end{bmatrix}$$

The reader will note that the solutions obtained are the same as those shown in Table 7–2.

Problems

1. The Gale Corporation's Marketing Manager was considering introducing a new product into the light duty liquid detergent market. After preliminary research had been completed, a medium size city was chosen in which to test market two possible new products. Selected consumers in the test city were asked to record purchases of two leading light duty liquid detergents already on the market and also purchases of the new products. The results of this investigation are presented in the transition probability matrix below.

Transition Probability Matrix

	L. B. #1	T. B. #1	L. B. #2	T. B. #2
Leading brand #1.......	.10	.50	.30	.10
Test brand #1..........	.20	.60	.20	.00
Leading brand #2.......	.30	.50	.10	.10
Test brand #2..........	.40	.40	.05	.15

The original brand shares in the test city were

$$
\begin{array}{ll}
\text{Leading brand \#1} = & .9 \\
\text{Test brand \#1} \quad = & .0 \\
\text{Leading brand \#2} = & .1 \\
\text{Test brand \#2} \quad = & .0 \\
\hline
& 1.0
\end{array}
$$

a) What is the "loyalty" factor for each of the four products?

b) Compute the brand shares for each of the four products for the first four transitions. (Carry computations to six places.)

c) Explain the difference between the brand share of Test Brand #1 and Test Brand #2 after the fourth transition.

d) Explain why Leading Brand #1's market share fell so drastically after the first transition.

e) Explain the rise in Test Brand #1's market share during the first transition.

2. Suppose that you are a marketing manager of a consumer packaged product and that you possess the following information:

1) As of June 30, your brand (Brand X) possesses 20 percent of the market; Brand Y possesses 50 percent of the market; Brand Z possesses 30 percent of the market.

2) A transition probability matrix:

	X	Y	Z
Brand X..........	.10	.40	.50
Brand Y.........	.80	.20	.00
Brand Z..........	.40	.30	.30

3) Each percent share of the market is worth $1,000.

The transitions take place at the end of each month. You are contemplating an advertising campaign during July which you assume will change the transition probabilities at the end of that month. You assume, however, that competitive counteraction in August will nullify the advantages gained in your July campaign.

There are two possible advertising campaigns. Campaign *A* is assumed to produce the following matrix:

	X	Y	Z
Brand X..........	.30	.30	.40
Brand Y.........	.80	.20	.00
Brand Z..........	.40	.30	.30

Campaign *B* is assumed to produce the following matrix:

	X	Y	Z
Brand X..........	.10	.40	.50
Brand Y.........	.90	.10	.00
Brans Z..........	.50	.30	.20

Which campaign would you use during the month of July? What is its net advantage over no campaign at all?

3. What are the principal limitations of the Markov model?

4. Define the following: (*a*) transition probability, (*b*) brand switching, and (*c*) equilibrium state.

Chapter 8

NEW PRODUCT DEVELOPMENT DECISIONS

This chapter is concerned with decisions related to new product development and introduction, a major subclass of all product decisions. Some of the motivations underlying product development activity, the role of new product introduction in overall marketing planning, and some traditional techniques which have been used to screen new product candidates for possible commercialization are first discussed.

Next the new product evaluation problem is framed as a multistage decision problem under uncertainty and the use of Bayesian procedures in its resolution is discussed. Decisions include whether to purchase additional information before making a terminal choice and, given that the time for making a terminal choice has been reached, whether or not to continue the new product development. The costs of decision delay are matched against the costs of uncertainty with regard to the new product's chances for success.

Next an actual application of decision theory to new product development is described and the questions which are related to *how* the product should be introduced (for example, pricing policy and size of initial facilities) within the strategic, "go, no-go" model are discussed. The use of Bayesian analysis in practice is contrasted with its use in our earlier, hypothetical problem.

The discussion of new product development decisions is concluded with a brief sketch of the problems which are encountered in allocating development funds among competing projects. Some comments are offered regarding the direction which future research on product development decision making is likely to take.

THE PRODUCT DEVELOPMENT PROCESS

The importance of product decisions in overall marketing planning can hardly be exaggerated. One need only take note of the vast sums which are being spent on industrial research and development to appreciate the increasing emphasis being given to this activity. Not only are the costs of product development increasing, but the risks appear to be mounting as well. In recent years the ratio of products successfully commercialized to total products placed on the market (let alone those that reached at least some stage in development) has been variously quoted as ranging from one in five to one in twenty.

In many business firms product lines often undergo almost continuous modification. New products may be added; the properties of existing products may be altered; and unprofitable products may be dropped from the line. The emphasis on new product additions to the line should *not* imply that decisions to modify existing products or to retire marginal products are inconsequential. Rather, it is hoped that the techniques described for coping with new product development decisions are equally applicable to other classes of decisions involving changes in the composition of the product line.

But, even defining a 'new product is no easy task. For our purpose we shall consider "new" product decisions to represent a class of decisions where (*a*) uncertainty regarding the product's technical and/or commercial success and (*b*) outlays for new plant and equipment are both high. While this obviously begs the question, this point of view does appear to distinguish between the risks attached to making minor variations of an existing product and the risks associated with developing and commercializing new or significantly improved products.

The process of product research and development can be viewed as an activity involving a flow of new or improved product candidates and information. Insofar as the information process is concerned, this flow is typically bidirectional. That is, information on consumer wants and/or needs may flow into the research department from the firm's market environment. Information on new ways to fill those wants and prototype models embodying this knowledge may then flow out of the research function. In turn, feedback information concerning the potential of the new product candidates toward filling customer wants may flow back to research.

The marketing manager may thus perform two functions. He may assist the research department by supplying suggestions for new product development, and he may assist in evaluating the potential marketing success of product candidates already under development. This evaluation may be concerned with products designed for the firm's present market configuration or products designed to fit into a diversification strategy in which the firm simultaneously departs from both its present product line and marketing strategy.

THE MOTIVATIONS UNDERLYING NEW PRODUCT DEVELOPMENT

The reasons underlying product development activity are many and varied. Some firms may operate in a type of industry (for example, fashion apparel or toy manufacture) where the life cycles of most items are extremely short. Products are likely to be purchased for a season or two and are then replaced by some new fad. Product life cycles in the drug and cosmetic industries also tend to be limited to perhaps a four- or five-year span for many items. Product obsolescence, either in the technological or psychological sense, may constitute sufficient need for more or less continuous new product development activity.

Even in industries which are not characterized by high product obsolescence the quest for new products may be intense. Profit margins on present products may be unattractive; the demand for the product line may be highly subject to cyclical fluctuations in business; excess production capacity may be evident; or the firm may need to develop companion products to bolster sales of an existing item.

The incentive for seeking new products may also rise out of recognition of a future "product gap." That is, multiproduct firms may find that the life cycles of many of their products appear to be reaching stability at roughly the same time. Unless new products are added future returns to the firm will not meet its profit and growth objectives. Some firms appear to make a conscious effort to plan both the type and timing of new products by attempting to phase in new variations of the product line when older members of the line start declining in sales and earnings.

Finally, some mention should be made of the me-too type of motivation underlying new product development activity. Judging from the high ratio of new product failures to successes it would appear that the development activity of some firms, at least, appears more motivated by the desire to "innovate," almost as an end in itself, than a more reasoned approach which attempts to estimate the gains against the cost of innovation.

EVALUATION PROCEDURES

While the ultimate question of whether or not to commercialize a new product is a financial one, it is clear that this decision is related to how, when and what to commercialize. How to commercialize concerns the selection of a plan for pricing, initial production capacity, and level and allocation of marketing effort. When to commercialize concerns the technical and marketing conditions which should be met before commercialization. What to commercialize concerns the selection of the product configuration and performance characteristics best suited to exploit end use opportunities and the deficiences of competitors' products. The marketing manager obviously plays an important role in all of these evaluations.

The development of marketing information relevant to the above questions involves a hierarchy of search and evaluative routines. For example, in the early stages of development, marketing research may establish that present product performance and cost characteristics are possibly suitable for a variety of markets. Then, more detailed screening routines may be employed to sift out the more probable potential markets from the less probable. In so doing, the matching process can also work in reverse by suggesting needed changes in the product's characteristics if it is to compete in certain desirable markets.

NEW PRODUCT SCREENING PROCEDURES—
PRODUCT PROFILE ANALYSIS

Perhaps one of the oldest procedures used to screen new product candidates is the so-called "product profile." Essentially the procedure involves matching the candidate's market, product, and profitability characteristics against criteria which, in some sense, are assumed to represent desirable characteristics which management wishes a new product venture to possess. For example, suppose several product candidates are being reviewed for the purpose of choosing those on which further development time and effort is to be spent. Budgetary limitations are such that all ventures cannot be supported. Management thus desires a procedure by which the attractiveness of the various product candidates can be ranked according to their performance on a list of desirable criteria.

To illustrate, suppose management has listed six criteria which are deemed important in appraising the attractiveness of a proposed new venture, namely, that the product (a) will use present distribution facilities, (b) possesses high profit margins, (c) will serve an industry with high growth prospects, (d) will be difficult for competitors to match or supersede, (e) will gain a large volume of sales, and (f) will require low investment in new facilities. Suppose, moreover, that management has been able to define operationally all of the above criteria and has assigned weights to the criteria which reflect their "relative desirability." (The feasibility of this assumption will receive comment later.) Finally, suppose that management is able to score product candidates on a 5-point "scale" from 4 (very high rating) to 0 (very low rating). Table 8–1 shows a hypothetical product profile listing for three products, *A, B,* and *C.*

Table 8–1
ILLUSTRATION OF PRODUCT PROFILE ANALYSIS
(TABLE ENTRIES ARE PRODUCT "SCORES" AND CRITERIA WEIGHTS)

Products	C_1	w_1	C_2	w_2	C_3	w_3	C_4	w_4	C_5	w_5	C_6	w_6	Weighted Index
A	2	.05	3	.20	1	.20	2	.10	3	.40	4	.05	2.5
B	0	.05	4	.20	4	.20	4	.10	0	.40	0	.05	2.0
C	3	.05	1	.20	2	.20	0	.10	2	.40	3	.05	1.7

As noted in Table 8–1, products *A, B,* and *C* receive index values of 2.5, 2.0, and 1.7, respectively. The reader will note that the weights w_j assigned to the criteria are "normalized" to sum to unity and that the index number merely represents a weighted average $(\sum_{j=1}^{n} w_j C_j)$ of scores on individual criteria.

The above procedure has been advocated by many product development managers as being simple, effective, and particularly applicable "when the products are at such an early stage in development that little data are available on which to make any more elaborate calculations."

While one may sympathize with the manager who is required to allocate development funds among several product candidates at *any* stage in research, it is nonetheless important to make explicit some of the assumptions on which the commonly employed product profile method is based. First, as the reader may note, there is no guarantee that the criteria weights w_j represent the "relative values" which they purport to represent. As was noted in the discussion of the Churchman-Ackoff value procedure in Chapter 6, the development of value weights is fraught with difficulty. In this case most of the criteria dealt with can be *quantified*. This poses the possibility of trade-offs among criteria. For example, while criterion C_1 may receive a weight of only 0.05 in some generalized situation, it may be that if the product were to score extremely well in meeting, say, criteria C_2 and C_3, then the weight, w_1 assigned to C_1 might be changed. Thus, consideration of rather complex multiple trade-offs may be required, and criteria weights might interact with product scores.

In addition, it is not clear what is meant by "scoring" on the 5-point scale, 0 to 4, and then finding weighted averages. If a quantified definition of each criterion can be constructed, it should also be possible to specify the appropriate ranges on the scale to which the values 0 to 4 should be assigned. But if this can be done, why should one necessarily settle for so gross a scale? The fineness of the scale gradations may, of course, be some function of the ability to specify precisely what is meant by, say, "high sales volume." For example, criterion C_5 (large volume of sales) might be redefined to consist of unit sales in the third year of commercialization. As an illustration, the product receives one of the following scores: 4, if sales $\geq$ 4 million pounds; 3, if $3 \leq$ sales < 4 million pounds; 2, if $2 \leq$ sales < 3 million pounds; 1, if $1 \leq$ sales < 2 million pounds; and 0, if sales $<$ 1 million pounds.

However, if this degree of specificity can be employed, one might well question why such a (seemingly) "rough and ready" method as product profile analysis need be employed at all. That is, why not use an evaluation procedure which attempts to relate the new venture's attractiveness to some *overall* monetary measure of effectiveness like discounted cash flow over the estimated development and life cycle of the product? Moreover, since a commitment to continue development of a new product is not irrevocable, it would seem that a desirable feature of this more elaborate model would be the incorporation of the opportunity to discontinue the product development at some future time as pertinent information regarding the product's potential success or failure improves as a function of the time and effort devoted to its development.

While product profile analysis may be criticized on the grounds that (a) the weights assigned to evaluative criteria are not necessarily independent of product scores, (b) the criteria themselves may not be independent, and (c) the procedure really assumes more about the evaluator's state of knowledge about product characteristics than appears on the surface, the fact remains that this method is quite prevalent in research and development management. Our predilection for cash flow analysis should not imply that product profile analysis is without merit but rather that its assumptions are not so simple and obvious as may first appear. But, the method *may* represent a good means for discriminating between very good and very poor product candidates. Moreover, if the method yields results which correlate well with more detailed financial analyses, one could argue that further model refinement is not worth the cost. It is in the spirit of presenting alternative procedures for evaluating new products that the problem is next discussed from a Bayesian point of view.

THE SEQUENTIAL NATURE OF NEW PRODUCT DECISIONS

In exploring other models applicable to new product development decisions, the decision maker will find the domain is conditioned by several characteristics of the development process. First, as has just been mentioned, decisions antecedent to commercialization as well as the commercialization decision itself are *not* irrevocable. That is, a decision may be made to construct, say, a pilot plant to produce experimental quantities of a new product even though some probability exists that subsequent information will result in the development being terminated prior to commercialization. Still, the value of the subsequent information may justify the cost of obtaining it. This means that the decision maker should consider future courses of action and information states as they relate to his present decision.

Second, it is also clear—by the nature of the development process—that to continue a new product's development implies at least some nonzero probability that the product will be successful, given commercialization. Inasmuch as the cumulative cash flows may assume a large negative value prior to commercialization, the decision to continue should include consideration of future cash flow over the estimated life of the product, given successful commercialization.

Third, the element of uncertainty abounds in development problems. Product properties, anticipated price and production costs, sales potential and development outlays are not known with high reliability. Typically, the reliability of the information increases as the product development approaches commercialization, but the cost of obtaining this information increases as well. Probability estimates of critical variables like length of product life cycle, total market size, market share, price, production cost, and development outlays are frequently subjective in nature and require revision as information accumulates. Somewhat paradoxically, the decision to continue a development must reflect the decision maker's estimate of his information state in future time periods and his strategy for reacting to this information.

Hence, new product development decisions can be viewed as

multistage decisions under uncertainty, where the decision maker
has the option of purchasing some types of additional information
and *must* "purchase" a minimal amount of other types of information
(for example, instructions on how to make the product) if he is to
commercialize the product at all. The problem is first considered
from the standpoint of evaluating a single new venture.

THE BAYESIAN MODEL

It is not surprising that the Bayesian model provides a framework within which the above considerations can be handled. This
model utilizes subjective and/or objective probability estimates,
modifiable by new data. The model also enables the analyst to deal
explicitly with multistage processes and then, by preposterior analysis, to choose a present course of action which has been determined
to be optimal through a recursive-type solution that considers both
future terminal decisions and information states.

In considering the Bayesian model in the context of product development decisions the analyst can address himself to two main
questions:

1. Should he make a decision *now* with respect to continuation or
   termination of the product's development; or should the decision
   be delayed pending the receipt of additional information?
2. Given when he should make the decision, should he decide to continue or to terminate the product's development?

In line with our earlier definitions, the go or stop decision is called
a terminal choice. Decisions made prior to this choice will be called
information-gathering decisions.

The next section of the chapter illustrates a simple application
of this model to a question regarding the number of project review
(information-gathering) stages which should be associated with a
new product's development. Rather than an attempt to derive a
general solution to this very complex problem, the approach will be
illustrated by considering only a zero-stage review up to (and including) a three-stage review. This range will be sufficient to point
out the principal characteristics of this class of problems.

BACKGROUND INFORMATION ON THE
PROJECT REVIEW STAGE PROBLEM

Some firms follow—explicitly or implicitly—what amounts to a
single review period in a new product's development. That is, a
new product candidate is first subjected to a critical review in the
research stage. Then a project team is selected to "run with the ball,"

in effect, to commercialize the product. This philosophy may not be patently ridiculous even when product development cycles are long and costly. First, development appraisals are costly in themselves and may also delay the total development time of the new venture. Second, if the decision maker attaches a very high probability to the new product's success, then subsequent cost-incurring reviews may not be necessary. Third, even if the decision maker assumes a high variance around the expected payoff, if future information is thought to be so unreliable as *not to reduce the cost of uncertainty significantly*, then the collection of new information may not be warranted.

Finally, it should be mentioned, parenthetically, that a psychological factor may underlie the decision to proceed toward ultimate commercialization without further review options. That is, a project team which has no option but to commercialize the product successfully may be more strongly motivated to implement this decision than one which retains the option to reconsider the advisability of continued development at some later stage. This illustrative analysis, however, will not consider this factor. In terms of this problem the single-review option (made between the *research* stage and development stage) will be labeled a zero-stage review, inasmuch as *no* reviews are made during the *development* period.

A policy of considering *multireview* periods implies that the cost of making wrong terminal decisions is high enough to outweigh the delay costs associated with venture reappraisal and that the reliability of the relevant information will improve over the time period required to reach commercialization. This expectation of improved reliability should enter into the present decision.

RELEVANT COSTS

If one adopts the viewpoint that the time spent on new product review has the effect of delaying the venture as well as incurring the costs of review itself, then the analyst must consider two classes of costs.

First, a delay in the development means that the present value of all payoffs is reduced as a consequence of deferring the start of revenues until a more distant period in the future. Second, a delay in the development may also mean a lowering of the project's present value due to the increased probability of competitors making inroads on the product's market share, this probability being related to the extent of the development's delay. These time-dependent costs, if deemed relevant, should be included in the evaluation.

In addition, the venture review, whether or not the project is delayed, is cost-incurring itself. Suppose, for example, that the unknown parameter under review concerns the level of sales, given commercialization, and that the activity associated with the venture review represents the opportunity to conduct a series of market pretests of the product. It is clear that market testing costs money and may not yield perfectly reliable information about future sales.

On the other side of the coin (that is, the option which considers *no* subsequent venture appraisals) it is obvious that under the go choice the only opportunity to consider stopping the venture arises after commercialization when, it will be assumed, the decision maker knows the true state of nature with regard to sales volume. This means that some cash outlays (for example, outlays to build the commercial facility) which are avoidable under the multireview option are not avoidable, given no opportunity for venture review once the project reaches the development stage.

AN ILLUSTRATION OF THE MODEL

In order to keep the analysis reasonably simple, while still demonstrating the nature of the Bayesian model in this type of application, only a two-states-of-nature case, namely high or low unit sales volume, given commercialization, will be assumed. Other parameters of the measure of effectiveness, for example, price, production cost, product life cycle, future construction and development outlays, salvage value, takedown costs, and discount rate, will be assumed as "certainty equivalents." While these variables could also be represented as alternative states of nature, considerable computational and expository complexity would have to be introduced without demonstrating any major new principles.

Assume that a new product candidate has emerged from research and is being considered for further development. Three antecedent, cost-incurring development stages, prior to commercialization, exist, namely, pilot plant, semiworks, and commercial plant. Three possible review stages also exist, one for each development stage. In the illustration the information stages are assumed to be represented by the anticipated results of market surveys of potential sales volume (in units). One year after commercialization it is assumed that the decision maker knows the true state of potential sales volume and has the option of keeping the new product in the line or terminating its production and closing down the plant.

Salvage value at any construction stage is assumed to just balance out-of-pocket cost of takedown. That is, the net cost of takedown at

Table 8–2

CONSTRUCTION AND INFORMATION OUTLAYS IN UNDISCOUNTED DOLLARS

Construction Activity	Outlay (Millions of Dollars)	Information Activity	Outlay (Millions of Dollars)
Pilot plant............	1	Survey 1	0.2
Semiworks.............	2	Survey 2	0.4
Commercial plant.......	10	Survey 3	1.0

any stage is zero with respect to future, avoidable costs. The reliability of survey results is assumed to increase as a function of the stage of product development, but as noted in Table 8–2, the survey cost increases as well. Surveys are assumed to indicate estimates, Z_1 or Z_2, of the true state of nature, S_1 (high sales) or S_2 (low sales). The reliability of these estimates increases with time. For example,

$$Z_1 (e_1) \mid S_1 = 0.6$$
$$Z_1 (e_2) \mid S_1 = 0.7$$
$$Z_1 (e_3) \mid S_1 = 0.9$$

where e_1, e_2 and e_3 are surveys 1, 2 and 3, respectively.

Assume that each survey delays the new product's development by one year. Assume further that pilot plant construction and operation requires two years, semiworks construction and operation requires three years, and commercial plant construction requires three years. The completion of each activity in the order named is a necessary condition for the start of subsequent activities. Finally, assume that, as a result of competitive gains in lead time during each period of delay due to surveys, cash flow, discounted to one year after commercialization, is reduced by 5 percent, if the product turns out to be successful. The opportunity cost of capital is assumed to equal 10 percent per year. (First-year cash flows are also included in the total year-after-commercialization payoff.)

Figure 8–1 shows the decision structure for this illustrative problem. Despite the many simplifications, the "game" can still end in over 70 different ways, which gives some idea of the multiplicity of outcomes which are generated in sequential decision problems.

In order to determine the optimal strategy, assume that the conditional payoff at time t_9 is $40 million, given S_1 and "go", and $-30 million, given S_2 and "go". The $40 million and $-30 million refer to the discounted value at time t_9 of all future cash flow over the product's life cycle (including the first-year flow). The decision maker's present or 0-stage prior probabilities assigned to S_1 and S_2, respectively, are 0.6 and 0.4. At time t_9 it is assumed that the decision maker will have perfect information, that is, know which state of nature is prevailing. Thus, his present prior probabilities refer to the chances of receiving *perfect* information of type S_1 or S_2 at time t_9. Moreover, at t_9 it is clear that the venture can be shut down at a *future* cost of zero if at that time this is a superior alternative to continuing the venture. Table 8–3 summarizes the expected value of the zero-stage review case as of time t_9 under conditions of perfect information.

Table 8–3

EXPECTED VALUE—ZERO REVIEW PERIOD CASE AT TIME t_9

	$P(S_1)$	S_1	$P(S_2)$	S_2	EMV
Go	0.6	$40 million	0.4	—	$24 million
Stop	0.6	—	0.4	$0 million	0
					$24 million

As shown in Table 8–3, if S_1 is observed at time t_9 the decision at that time is "go" while, if S_2 is observed, the decision is "stop" since the manager would prefer $0 million (shut down) to a loss of $30 million, were he to continue.

The expected monetary value of $24 million, however, has to be discounted to time t_0 and, from this payoff must still be subtracted the construction and/or operating costs (associated with pilot plant, semiworks, and commercial plant) also discounted to time t_0. When these calculations are made, the expected value of discounted cash flow at time t_0 is $1.3 million:

$$[24 (1.10)^{-9}] - [10 (1.10)^{-5} + 2 (1.10)^{-2} + 1] = 1.3$$

Clearly, this is superior to stopping the venture at time t_0 which carries a payoff of $0 million.

In order to evaluate the other strategies, that is, the 1-, 2-, and 3-stage review cases, appropriate posterior probabilities must be calculated. These calculations are shown in Table 8–4.

Suppose the expected payoff for the 1-stage review case is first calculated and labeled e_1. The 1-stage review will delay the venture one year. This single survey can end in sample result Z_1 or Z_2 after which the decision maker can elect to launch the development toward ultimate commercialization or terminate the development at time t_1. If Z_1, the posterior probabilities assigned to S_1 and S_2 are 0.69 and 0.31, respectively, as noted in Table 8–4. If Z_2, the posterior probabilities assigned to S_1 and S_2 are .50 and .50, respectively. However, we must also allow for the effect on present value at time

Table 8-4

CALCULATION OF JOINT, MARGINAL, AND POSTERIOR PROBABILITIES

e_1	$P(S_1)$	$P(S_2)$	Marg.	$P(S_1 \mid Z_i)$	$P(S_2 \mid Z_i)$
$P(Z_1)$.........	.36	.16	.52	.69	.31
$P(Z_2)$.........	.24	.24	.48	.50	.50
	.60	.40	1.00		

e_2	$P(S_1 \mid Z_1)$	$P(S_2 \mid Z_1)$	Marg.	$P(S_1 \mid Z_{ij})$	$P(S_2 \mid Z_{ij})$
$P(Z_1)$.........	.48	.09	.57	.84	.16
$P(Z_2)$.........	.21	.22	.43	.49	.51
	.69	.31	1.00		

	$P(S_1 \mid Z_2)$	$P(S_2 \mid Z_2)$	Marg.	$P(S_1 \mid Z_{ij})$	$P(S_2 \mid Z_{ij})$
$P(Z_1)$.........	.35	.15	.50	.70	.30
$P(Z_2)$.........	.15	.35	.50	.30	.70
	.50	.50	1.00		

e_3	$P(S_1 \mid Z_1$ (e_1) and $Z_1 (e_2))$	$P(S_2 \mid Z_1$ (e_1) and $Z_1 (e_2))$	Marg.	$P(S_1 \mid Z_{ijk})$	$P(S_2 \mid Z_{ijk})$
$P(Z_1)$.........	.76	.02	.78	.97	.03
$P(Z_2)$.........	.08	.14	.22	.36	.64
	.84	.16	1.00		

	$P(S_1 \mid Z_1$ (e_1) and $Z_2 (e_2))$	$P(S_2 \mid Z_1$ (e_1) and $Z_2 (e_2))$	Marg.	$P(S_1 \mid Z_{ijk})$	$P(S_2 \mid Z_{ijk})$
$P(Z_1)$.........	.44	.05	.49	.90	.10
$P(Z_2)$.........	.05	.46	.51	.10	.90
	.49	.51	1.00		

	$P(S_1 \mid Z_2$ (e_1) and $Z_1 (e_2))$	$P(S_2 \mid Z_2$ (e_1) and $Z_1 (e_2))$	Marg.	$P(S_1 \mid Z_{ijk})$	$P(S_2 \mid Z_{ijk})$
$P(Z_1)$.........	.63	.03	.66	.95	.05
$P(Z_2)$.........	.07	.27	.34	.21	.79
	.70	.30	1.00		

	$P(S_1 \mid Z_2$ (e_1) and $Z_2 (e_2))$	$P(S_2 \mid Z_2$ (e_1) and $Z_2 (e_2))$	Marg.	$P(S_1 \mid Z_{ijk})$	$P(S_2 \mid Z_{ijk})$
$P(Z_1)$.........	.27	.07	.34	.79	.21
$P(Z_2)$.........	.03	.63	.66	.05	.95
	.30	.70	1.00		

t_{10} due to competition (reduction in cash flow of 5 percent if the product is successful) and a period's deferral of the start of revenues. At time t_9 the expected value of the optimal strategy from that point forward is $23.8 million (Panel A of Figure 8–1) if Z_1 is observed and $17.3 million (Panel B of Figure 8–1) if Z_2 is observed. Discounting these payoffs back to time t_3 leads to discounted payoffs of $3.9 and $0.24 million under Z_1 and Z_2, respectively. Already it is

Figure 8–1A

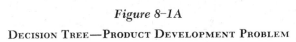

DECISION TREE—PRODUCT DEVELOPMENT PROBLEM

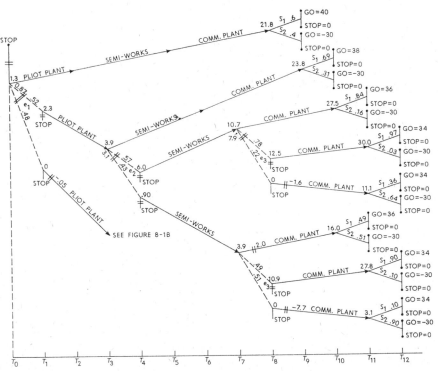

clear that the decision maker would stop if Z_2 is observed at time t_1; in so doing, he could avoid the outlay for the pilot plant at time t_1. If Z_1 is observed, however, the expected payoff at time t_1 is $2.3 million; that is, it is preferable for the decision maker to continue the development toward ultimate commercialization.

Next, the decision maker must apply the appropriate marginal probabilities for Z_1 and Z_2 (0.52 and 0.48) to the conditional expected payoffs of $2.3 million and $0 million, which represent optimal action at time t_1 under Z_1 and Z_2, respectively. This calculation results in an expected gross payoff of $1.17 million which, discounted to time t_0, is \$0.87 million, clearly less than the payoff associated with the zero-stage review strategy.

Similar calculations would pertain to the evaluation of the 2-stage and 3-stage reviews. Figure 8–1 (Panels *A* and *B*) summarizes the pertinent payoffs and probabilities. The procedure is to select that branch which leads to the highest expected payoff from that point forward. The problem is then solved by backward recursion similar to the sequential problem of Chapter 5.

Figure 8–1B

DECISION TREE—PRODUCT DEVELOPMENT PROBLEM

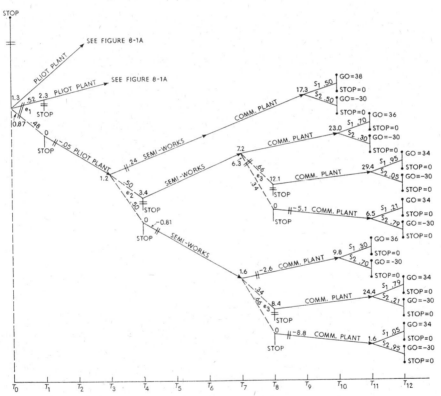

Note that in this particular problem the zero-stage review represents the superior alternative. That is, the decision maker would make *no* market surveys, but at time t_0 would proceed sequentially with the construction of pilot plant, semiworks, and commercial plant. At time t_9 he would either continue the venture (if S_1 turns out to be the underlying state) or terminate the venture (if S_2 turns out to be the underlying state). In this hypothetical illustration the value of additional information was lower than the cost of obtaining it.

AN ACTUAL CASE ILLUSTRATION

The reader will recognize that the preceding hypothetical example represented a Bayesian preposterior analysis in which the decision maker appraised the expected value of the additional information (anticipated to be derived from further market surveys) before conducting the surveys. As was demonstrated, in this particular case the expected value of the additional information did not justify the costs associated with decision delay and conducting the surveys.

An actual case application of the Bayesian approach to a product development problem is now considered. It is hoped this illustration will point out (a) some of the problems encountered in deriving prior probability distributions, (b) the usefulness of (if not necessity for) employing computer simulation in developing the appropriate conditional payoffs for large-scale problems, and (c) the use of models in checking the consistency of decision makers' judgments about unknown events. The reader will observe quite a few differences between the well-structured (if tedious) example just covered and the use of Bayesian procedures in real problems.

This study was performed for the Commercial Development Division of a major chemical producer. The interest in relating this account, in almost narrative fashion, is to contrast the structuring of a real decision problem with the hypothetical case just covered. While the data of the problem are disguised, all relationships among the variables have been kept intact.

THE PROBLEM AND ITS SETTING

In the Commercial Development Division of the subject firm a new product (here called, ingloriously, Product X) had been under development for several years. Development had reached the semiworks stage, and some preliminary product evaluation (via potential customer tests of the material) had already been made. Moreover, estimates of future year-by-year sales potential, if the product were commercialized, had been prepared for the twenty major end uses then contemplated. These forecasts depended, of course, on the particular pricing policy which might be followed.

Unfortunately, high uncertainty regarding the new product's potential marketing success was held by the personnel responsible for ultimate commercialization. The main questions at the time the study was undertaken were (a) should a decision be made now (either to commercialize or terminate the venture) or should this decision be delayed until more market data had been assembled and (*b*) given the decision to commercialize (now or later), what should be the initial size of the commercial facility and what pricing policy should be followed. It was apparent that these questions would have to be answered conjointly.

PRELIMINARY PROBLEM STRUCTURING

Structuring of the problem proceeded through a series of discussions with Product *X*'s development manager and his marketing personnel. On the question regarding the choice of a suitable measure of effectiveness, expected net present value[1] (opportunity cost of capital equal to 10 percent annually) was selected as the primary payoff measure. However, in keeping with the firm's established practices, other financial summary measures (for example, return on investment for selected years) were also computed. Based on projections of the product's life cycle, given successful commercialization, a planning horizon of thirteen years, as measured from the decision point to proceed rather than actual plant start-up, was chosen.

As just discussed above, the course of action labeled commercialization was dependent upon two classes of tactical decisions: (*a*) size of initial commercial facilities and (*b*) type of pricing policy to follow. With respect to the first tactical class, equipment indivisibilities suggested two alternative plant sizes that made a difference, namely, (*a*) 10 million pounds and (*b*) 25 million pounds of initial annual plant capacity. With respect to the second tactical class, pricing policies appeared to be bracketed by three alternatives: (*a*) a so-called Base Case pricing which reflected gradual price reduction over time for the purpose of eventually building up Product *X*'s sales to a 100 million pound annual level, (*b*) a Case A policy which represented high maintenance of profit margins at the expense of foregoing potential sales that could be effected only at very low price levels, and (*c*) a Case B policy which represented a penetration type of pricing where high profit margins would be traded off in order to achieve quickly and sustain a high sales level. Figure 8–2 summarizes the nature of these pricing alternatives over the planning period.

DEVELOPING THE PRIOR PROBABILITIES

Inasmuch as the effectiveness of each combination of pricing policy and initial plant size might be expected to differ as a conse-

---

[1] It is thus implied, as described in Chapter 6, that the firm's utility (in the von Neumann-Morgenstern sense) is linear with money.

quence of Product X's unit sales over the future, three alternative forecasts of sales potential, given each price policy, were used. These alternative unit sales forecasts were developed in several stages. First, a single year-by-year forecast had already been prepared, under each price policy, for each of the twenty separate end uses by the appropriate marketing representative responsible for each market.

Figure 8-2

PRODUCT X AVERAGE PRICE BEHAVIOR

UNDER ALTERNATIVE PRICING STRATEGIES

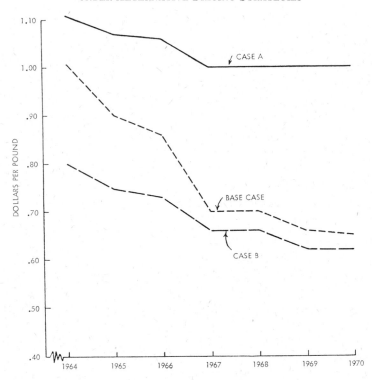

To develop alternative forecasts and the subjective probabilities assigned thereto, each marketing representative was confronted with a chart which showed, for a given pricing policy, the sales poundage which he had already forecasted as a most probable estimate. He was then asked the following questions:

1. In line with your best judgment on the market situation (standard ground rules were stated) for this product, what chances would you assign that unit sales in this market will be at least as high as those indicated on the chart?

2. Now, suppose market conditions did not turn out well for the product. Will you now prepare a pessimistic estimate (to be drawn on the original chart) such that, in your judgment, unit sales of the product would have a 90 percent chance of being this high or higher?

3. Now, suppose market conditions turned out quite well for the product. In your estimation what would be the upper bound on unit sales such that you would assign only a 10 percent chance that sales could go this high or higher?

4. Now, I am going to draw two sales curves, one equidistant between your original forecast and the pessimistic forecast and one equidistant between the original forecast and the optimistic forecast. What are the chances that sales will equal or exceed these respective forecasts?

The reader will note that a rough probability distribution can be derived from this series of questions under the Base Case pricing policy. Figure 8–3 shows the sales estimates given for one of the

Figure 8–3

ESTIMATES OF ALTERNATIVE SALES LEVELS—MARKET A

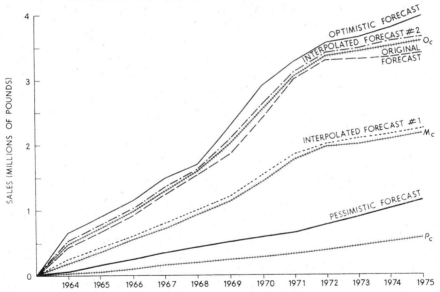

end uses, Market *A*, under Base Case pricing assumptions. Suppose that the marketing representative answered the above questions as follows: (1) 20 percent; (2) the line labeled pessimistic; (3) the line labeled optimistic; (4) 50 percent and 12 percent, respectively. Notice that the answers to the last question provide a crude check on the consistency of the decision maker's judgments.

Note that the marketing representative had in this instance originally prepared what, upon examination, turned out to be an

optimistic original forecast. That is, when confronted with the problem of assigning a subjective probability to meeting or exceeding
the original forecast, the marketing representative's degree of belief
was only 0.2 or 20 percent, rather than, say, 50 percent. This judgment carried through the remainder of the questioning. Note, how-

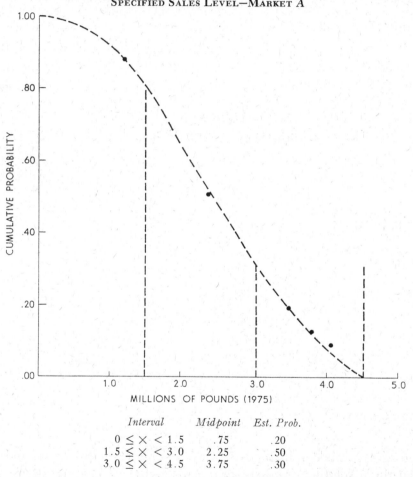

Figure 8–4

CUMULATIVE PROBABILITY OF EQUALLING OR EXCEEDING
SPECIFIED SALES LEVEL—MARKET A

MILLIONS OF POUNDS (1975)

Interval	Midpoint	Est. Prob.
$0 \leq X < 1.5$	.75	.20
$1.5 \leq X < 3.0$	2.25	.50
$3.0 \leq X < 4.5$	3.75	.30

ever, that the slopes of the forecasts roughly correspond throughout
the forecast period. The task now is to graph the crude probability
distribution derived from this series of questions. This plot is shown
in Figure 8–4. The chart is an estimated cumulative probability
curve which has been faired in between the five dots derived from
the estimates for 1975 (year-end). Inasmuch as the general shape
of all curves was approximately the same (that is, the curves differed

chiefly in terms of asymptotes), the estimates for 1975 were deemed representative enough to be used in estimating the prior probabilities. Notice that Market A sales can range from 0 to an estimated 4.5 million pounds.

From this distribution can be derived prior probabilities for three forecasts which can be labeled "pessimistic," "most probable," and "optimistic." But now these labels refer to *calculated* values. This is done by dividing the sales range of Figure 8-4 into thirds: 0 to 1.5; 1.5 to 3.0; and 3.0 to 4.5 million pounds and noting the midpoints: 0.75; 2.25; and 3.75 million pounds, respectively. All of the probability over each interval is then assigned to its respective midpoint. For example, 0.20 of the total probability falls in the 0 to 1.5 million pound range and, hence, the midpoint of 0.75 million pounds is assigned this probability. In effect, "partial expectations" of the probability distribution are taken by assigning all of the probability in a given interval to the interval's midpoint. While, theoretically, the range of the variable *could* be divided into as many intervals as we please (and the "precision" of the results thereby increased) in this particular study three alternative forecasts were thought by the sponsors of the study to be sufficient to describe the uncertainties of the market situation while remaining comprehensible to the personnel taking part in the study. These three forecasts, label O_c (optimistic), M_c (most probable), and P_c (pessimistic), are sketched in Figure 8-3. The subscript c refers to the fact that these forecasts are calculated from the original estimates. These latter forecasts for Market A now represent the estimates used in all further calculations; probabilities assigned to P_c, M_c, and O_c were 0.20, 0.50, and 0.30, respectively.

Three forecasts (under each of the three pricing policies) for each of the twenty different end uses were developed in a manner similar to that shown for Market A. The three alternative forecasts were then separately aggregated into three *total* market forecasts for each price policy. The subjective probabilities at the total market level were found by taking weighted averages of the probabilities assigned to individual markets, using the poundage levels in each market as appropriate weights of the market's importance. As a cross check on the aggregation procedure, the marketing development manager independently estimated probabilities for all markets combined. The results agreed well with the probability estimates derived by the weighting procedure. As an illustration, Figure 8-5 shows the most probable or M_c sales forecast under each pricing policy for a portion of the planning period (1964-70).

In order to construct a computer model of this problem, other ground rules had to be established. First, the matter of capacity additions *subsequent* to the initial facility had to be explored. In view of the indivisibilities of equipment it was decided to consider three discrete steps beyond the initial plant size of either 10 million or 25 million pounds. These additions involved resultant total ca-

Figure 8–5

PRODUCT X SALES POTENTIAL
UNDER ALTERNATIVE PRICING STRATEGIES
(MOST PROBABLE FORECAST M_c)

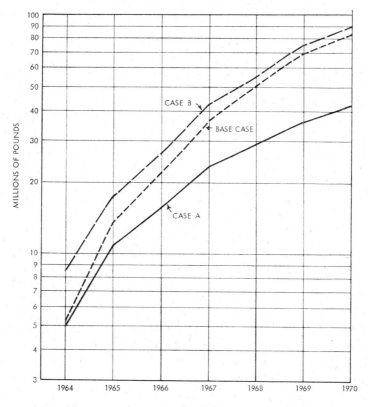

pacities of 50, 75, and finally 100 million pounds (if needed), in sequence. Next, inasmuch as the lead time from decision point to capacity addition start-up covered two years, it was decided to test the effect of delays in demand recognition and the possible inter-action of these delays on present courses of action. Time delays ranged from zero (that is, no potential sales lost due to delayed expansion) up through a maximum of three years operation under capacity limitation (which thus included the year in which recognition of sales potential exceeding existing capacity was made). A second constraint, however, was that the *first* capacity addition could not be started until one year after operation of the initial facilities had begun. This constraint was merely descriptive of the way decisions of this type would have been ordinarily made.

COMPUTER SIMULATION AND STUDY RESULTS

At this juncture in the study it was clear that the length of the planning period and the large number of variables to be included (markets, prices, production costs, initial and subsequent plant and equipment outlays) represented a calculational burden of no mean proportions in just developing the conditional payoffs under each course of action and state of nature combination. To compute net present values for all combinations of 2 initial plant sizes, 3 pricing policies, 3 sales forecasts, and 4 capacity addition delay levels (number of years of capacity limitation) would require 72 different sets of cash flow calculations, each embracing a 13-year planning period.

Fortunately, recourse could be had to a 7070 computer. A generalized model was developed in FORTRAN programming language, and the relevant inputs to the program were prepared on punch cards. Figure 8-6 shows the FORTRAN program which was used. Simplified algebraic coders like FORTRAN permit drastic reductions in programming time for problems of this type.

The program was first set up for making an initial set of 72 runs. Then, subsequent runs were made in which such factors as number of markets materializing and the opportunity cost of capital were varied. Payoff matrices (in terms of net present value over the planning period) were then prepared from the computer output.

The results were first analyzed under the "no capacity restriction" option for each combination of (*a*) initial plant size and (*b*) pricing policy, under each of the three sales forecasts associated with each price policy.

The main findings of the computer simulation can be conveniently summarized in terms of the payoff matrix shown in Table 8-5 for the case of "no capacity limitation" and cost of capital equal to 10 percent.

Table 8-5 shows the conditional payoffs in net present value for each plant size–pricing strategy combination under each alternative sales level. In this case, capacity limitation was not experienced beyond that (possibly) associated with the initial plant size. (Additional payoff matrices covering other delay times in making capacity additions were likewise prepared.)

Figure 8–6
FORTRAN Program
(Product Development Program)

```
    NP-1 COMPUTER RISK SIMULATION    AUGUST 61 PAUL GREEN
    DIMENSION PM%20, 10"P%20, 10",SD%20, 10", TSD%10", TPM%10", AVP%10",
    1CP%2", GP%10", FAC%2", FACB%2", CEO%10,2", FINV%2", FNP%10", ROI%10",
    2FD%2", CFL%10", DFL%10", A%10", SDFL%2"
210 FORMAT%7H1  CASE 13.5H   F4.1,20H MKT. GROWTH PLANT"
200 FORMAT%12.9F7.3"
201 FORMAT%212"
202 FORMAT%16F5.2"
203 FORMAT%2F4.1,4F6.3"
204 FORMAT%10F6.3"
211 FORMAT%11OHO                           1964        1965
1      1966       1967       1968        1969       1970"
212 FORMAT%29H    TOTAL SALES %MM POUNDS"  7F12.2"
213 FORMAT%29H    TOTAL SALES %MM DOLLARS" 7F12.2"
214 FORMAT%29H    AVERAGE PRICE %$/POUNDS" 7F12.2"
215 FORMAT%29H    TOTAL COSTS%MM DOLLARS"  7F12.2"
216 FORMAT%29H    GROSS EARNINGS           7F12.2"
217 FORMAT%29H    NET EARNINGS             7F12.2"
218 FORMAT%29H    RETURN ON INVESTMENT     7F12.2"
219 FORMAT%29H    DISC. CASH %ANNUAL"      7F12.2"
220 FORMAT%25HO        DISC. CASH FLOW F9.2"
221 FORMAT%7HO CASE 13.5H       F4.1,20H   MKT.  GROWTH PLANT"
250 FORMAT%8F7.3"
    READ INPUT TAPE 1,200, NPROB, F1,F2, FINV%1", FINV%2", FINVE, TAX,
    1FD%1", FD%2", FDE
    READ INPUT TAPE 1,250, F3, F4, FINVH, FDH, F5, F6, FINVG, FDG
    READ INPUT TAPE 1,204,%A%J", J#1, 10"
    DO 300 M#1, NPROB
    READ INPUT TAPE 1,201, NT, NM
    DO 101 J#1, NM
101 READ INPUT TAPE 1,202,%PM%J, K", P%J, K", K#1,NT"
    READ INPUT TAPE 1,203,CP%1", CP%2", FAC%1", FACA%2"CFACB%1, FACB%2"
    WRITE OUTPUT TAPE 2,210,M, CP%1"
    DO 300 MM#1,2
    F1#F1NV%MM"
    DEP#FD%MM"
    1SW#0
    DO 198 K#1,NT
    TSD%K"#0.0
    TPM%K"#0.0
    DO 102 J#1,NM
    SD%J, K"#PM%J, K"*P%J, K"
    TSD%K"#TSD%K"&SD%J, K"
102 TPM%K"#TPM%K"&PM%J, K"
    AVP%K"#TSD%K"/TPM%K"
    1F%1SW"103,104,103
103 1F%K - 1SW"107,110,110
104 1F%TPM%K" - CP%MM""105,105,106
105 CEQ%K, MM"#FACA%MM"&FACB%MM"*TPM%K"
    GO TO 108
110 1F%TPM%K" -50.0" 320,320,319
319 1F%TPM%K" -75.0" 321,321,322
320 CEQ%K, MM"#F5&F6*TPM%K"
    F1#F1NVG
    DEP#FDG
    GO TO 108
321 CEQ%K, MM"#F3&F4*TPM%K"
    F1#F1NVH
    DEP#FDH
    GO TO 108
322 CEQ%K, MM"#F1&F2*TPM%K"
    F1#F1NVE
    DEP#FDE
    GO TO 108
106 1SW#K&3
    CEQ%K, MM"#FACA%MM"&FACB%MM"*CP%MM"
107 TSD%K"#AVP%K"*CP%MM"
108 GP%K"#TSD%K" -CEQ%K, MM"
    FNP%K"#TAX*GP%K"
    RO1%K"#%FNP%K"/F1"*100.0
    CFL%K"#FNP%K"&DEP
    DFL%K"#CFL%K"*A%K"
198 CONTINUE
    SDFL%MM"#0.0
    DO 190 K#1,NT
190 SDFL%MM"#SDFL%MM"&DFL%K"
    WRITE OUTPUT TAPE 2,211
    WRITE OUTPUT TAPE 2,212,%TPM%N", N#1, NT"
    WRITE OUTPUT TAPE 2,213,%TSD%N", N#1, NT"
    WRITE OUTPUT TAPE 2,214,%AVP%N", N#1, NT"
    WRITE OUTPUT TAPE 2,215,%CEQ%N, MM", N#1, NT"
    WRITE OUTPUT TAPE 2,216,%GP%N", N#1, NT"
    WRITE OUTPUT TAPE 2,217,%FNP%N", N#1, NT"
    WRITE OUTPUT TAPE 2,218,%RO1%N", N#1, NT"
    WRITE OUTPUT TAPE 2,219,%DFL%N", N#1, NT"
    WRITE OUTPUT TAPE 2,220,SDFL%MM"
    WRITE OUTPUT TAPE 2,221,M, CP%2"
300 CONTINUE
    STOP 7777
    END
```

Table 8–5

Net Present Value—Millions of Dollars over the Period 1962–75

| | Alternative States of Nature | | |
Courses of Action	Most Probable	Optimistic	Pessimistic
10-Million-Pound Plant			
Base Case..............	10.7	27.3	−40.4
Case A.................	14.2	30.4	−28.9
Case B.................	8.7	21.7	−46.7
25-Million-Pound Plant			
Base Case..............	12.9	35.6	−37.9
Case A.................	17.1	37.6	−28.4
Case B.................	10.0	26.4	−40.2

As could be inferred, *given* the wisdom of commercialization at all, the study uncovered a dominant course of action with respect to *both* plant size and pricing policy. That is to say, under each alternative demand level the largest positive payoff (or least negative payoff) was associated with the 25-million-pound plant size and Case A (high margin) pricing strategy.

In view of this fortunate result, the cost structure of the 10-versus 25-million-pound plant was examined more closely. As it turned out, the economies of scale were so large that the reduced risk of initial capacity limitation (under the 25-million-pound plant alternative) more than overbalanced the slightly higher fixed costs of operation in the early years of commercialization, even under the pessimistic forecast, which was still high enough to prompt one capacity addition beyond the initial level.

Figure 8–7 shows the year-by-year cumulative cash flow (in terms of net present value) for each pricing policy under (illustratively) the most probable forecast case and with an initial plant size of 25 million pounds annual capacity. One can note how the trends of cash flow compare over time as a function of pricing policy.

Figure 8–8 shows the impact of delays in recognition of the trend in demand and the resultant impact on the number of capacity-limited years of operation. Delays experienced in making plant additions lower payoffs signilcantly under each pricing alternative. Again, this chart covers, illustratively, the 25-million-pound initial capacity alternative under the most probable forecast of potential sales. (Similar charts were prepared for the other cases.) In this problem the opportunity costs of lost sales clearly outweighed the costs associated with temporary underutilization of capacity.

At this point the preliminary results can be briefly recapped.

First, due to (*a*) sizable economies of scale and (*b*) fewer lost sales under possible capacity limitation, given the second constraint that a plant addition could not be started until after one year's sales experience were available, the 25-million-pound plant size yielded

Figure 8–7

PRODUCT X NET PRESENT VALUE
UNDER CAPITAL COST OF 10% ANNUALLY
(25-MILLION-POUND INITIAL PLANT—MOST PROBABLE SALES FORECAST)

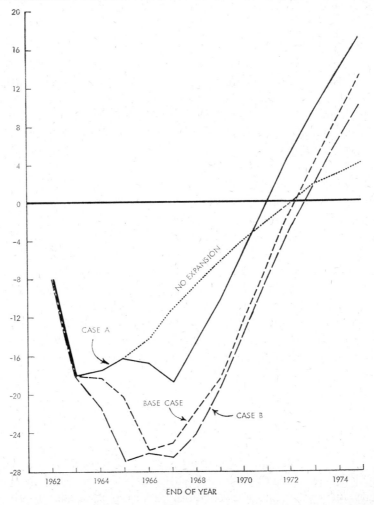

the largest payoff under all sales forecasts and under all pricing policies. Second, the Case A pricing policy dominated the other pricing policies, here again under all sales potential forecasts and under both initial plant sizes. Third, it was clearly to the firm's advantage not to delay capacity additions (if required); potential lost sales opportunities outweighed the costs associated with a temporary low level of capacity utilization stemming from making a capacity addition too early.

Figure 8-8

EFFECT OF ANTICIPATION OF CAPACITY ADDITIONS ON PRODUCT X PROFITABILITY (25-MILLION-POUND INITIAL PLANT—MOST PROBABLE SALES FORECAST)

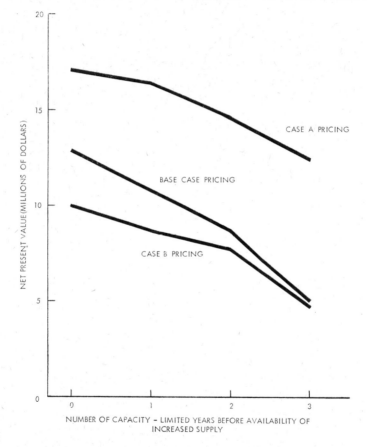

However, the main consideration at this point concerned *the wisdom of commercialization at all, at the present time.* In other words, given commercialization now, the Case *A* pricing policy and 25-million-pound initial plant size represented the best tactical alternative. As Table 8-5 indicates, though, *if* the pessimistic forecast occurred and *if* the venture were continued, unprofitable operations even under the best tactical alternative would still result.

It became apparent then that the questions of (*a*) given the desirability of acting now, should the product be commercialized or not and (*b*) should this decision be delayed, pending the accumulation of better information, still had to be answered. That is, the marketing group's *probabilities* associated with the three forecasts had to be applied to the *conditional* payoffs and the worthwhileness of delaying the decision had to be evaluated.

DECIDE NOW VERSUS DELAY

As covered earlier, the so-called most probable, optimistic, and pessimistic forecasts had been developed in the manner summarized in Figures 8–3 and 8–4. On an overall (total) market basis the resultant subjective probability assignment, under the Case A pricing policy, turned out to be

$$O_c \text{ (optimistic)} \quad = 0.10$$
$$M_c \text{ (most probable)} = 0.55$$
$$P_c \text{ (pessimistic)} \quad = 0.35$$

At this juncture the main question could be evaluated: should a decision be made now (to commercialize or terminate the venture) or should this decision be delayed pending the receipt of better market information over, say, the next year.

Figure 8–9 summarizes the results of this analysis. At point "O" on the left hand margin of this chart, three alternative decision paths are shown, namely, build, delay, and do not build. Following the build path first, one sees that, under the most probable or optimistic forecasts, an expected payoff (net present value, 1962–75) of $20.3 million results under the best tactical alternative—Case A pricing and 25 million pounds of initial capacity.[2]

However, it is clear that, if commercialization were effected now and if the *pessimistic* forecast actually occurred, the firm would not continue to operate the venture over the *whole* planning period and thus incur a significant loss. Instead, a stop loss action could be taken. It was calculated that this negative payoff would amount to only —$15.4 million rather than the —$28.4 million shown in Table 8–5 for the Case A pricing and 25-million-pound initial plant size alternative, under the pessimistic forecast. The —$15.4 million figure reflects the investment outlay, cost of further product development

---

[2]As can be noted, to simplify the analysis a partial expectation has been taken so as to reduce the problem to a two-state case. The figure of $20.3 million was obtained by taking a weighted average of $10/65 \times 37.6 + 55/65 \times 17 = \$20.3$ million.

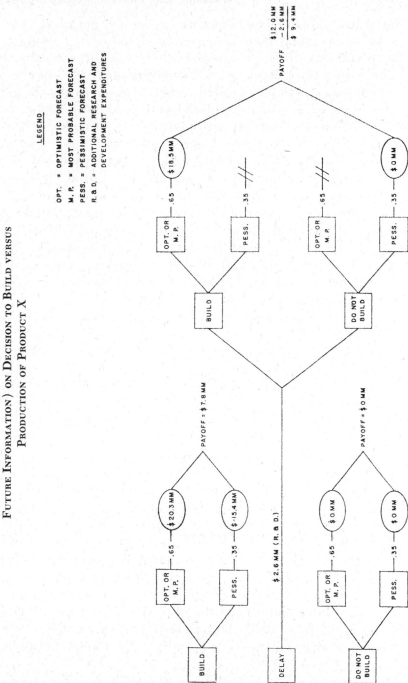

Figure 8-9

INFLUENCE OF DELAY (UNDER PERFECT
FUTURE INFORMATION) ON DECISION TO BUILD VERSUS
PRODUCTION OF PRODUCT X

LEGEND

OPT. = OPTIMISTIC FORECAST
M.P. = MOST PROBABLE FORECAST
PESS. = PESSIMISTIC FORECAST
R.&D. = ADDITIONAL RESEARCH AND
DEVELOPMENT EXPENDITURES

in the 1962–63 period, and revenues generated during a three-year period of operation (the assumed time required to recognize that the pesssimistic forecast was prevailing) less salvage value stemming from a tax write-off on the undepreciated value of the plant and equipment. On an expected payoff basis, *given* the decision to act now, it is. clear that the build path leads to a higher payoff ($7.8 million) than the do not build payoff ($0 million). This latter path is thus blocked off in Figure 8–9.

However, if one traces out the path labeled delay it may be seen that specific gains and costs are associated with this choice as opposed to the choice to commercialize now. From the avoidable cost standpoint an extra year of development expense ($2.6 million) is involved. In addition, the payoff under the most probable–optimistic forecast combination drops from $20.3 million to $18.5 million, a reflection of the fact that all revenues are produced one year later along the time axis, given commercialization one year later; hence their net present value is less.

If perfect information regarding the two-state sales situation could be secured in the one-year delay period, the expected payoff through delay, at $9.4 million, would exceed the $7.8 million payoff associated with commercialization now.

However, information about future sales is rarely, if ever, perfect. The function which this model serves is to indicate how reliable the new information would have to be in order to justify delaying the decision to commercialize Product X now. As it turned out, under the original prior probability assignment, a one-year delay of the decision would have to lead to a reliability level of 90 percent in the sense of correctly calling the pessimistic forecast as opposed to the optimistic most probable combination.[3]

RECEPTION OF STUDY RESULTS

At this point the substance of the study findings could be related to Product X's development manager. In essence the results indicated that (*a*) if the decision is to be made now, commercialization offers the better option, and the Case A pricing policy–25-million-pound initial plant is the best tactical alternative; and (*b*) if the decision is delayed one year pending the receipt of additional

---

[3]This value, 90 percent, is obtained from the following equation (when P equals the chance of correctly calling the appropriate state of nature).

$$7.8 + 2.6 = .65 (18.5) P + .35 (-14.0) (1 - P)$$
$$15.3 = 16.925 P$$
$$P = 0.90 \text{ or } 90 \text{ percent}$$

market test data, a reliability level of 90 percent would have to be attached to the new information in order to make this option equal in desirability to the commercialize now alternative.

When these findings were reviewed by development management, it is of interest to note that the tactical conclusion (namely, given commercialization, the best option to take is the Case A pricing policy–25 million-pound initial facility) was accepted by Product X's development group.

However, less unanimity existed with respect to the wisdom of commercializing now versus delay of this decision until one year hence. Although the group felt that a reliability level of 90 percent (required to make the delay strategy break even with the act now strategy) would be hardly attainable, management did not feel confident enough to proceed on the marketing data which currently existed. Assuming that the model adequately reflected the real situation in other respects, management's adoption of the one-year delay option can be viewed as either an imputed subjective probability attached to the pessimistic forecast, which was higher than the 0.35 probability used in the analysis, or a utility function which was nonlinear with money.

When management was asked what reliability level could be achieved through a one-year delay, they intuitively felt that a reliability of 70 percent could be obtained. From this estimate may be derived an imputed subjective probability of 0.50 to be attached to the occurrence of the pessimistic state of nature (opposed to the original assignment of 0.35).

This difference in probability estimates was pointed out to the marketing people responsible for supplying data outputs. When informed of this discrepancy the marketing sponsors felt that their original estimates had probably erred on the optimistic side; that is, they were willing to change their prior probabilities to agree with the imputed value. As the reader may surmise, however, a pertinent piece of information in this study was the conditional loss associated with the occurrence of the pessimistic state of nature. It is possible that utility notions interacted with the subjective probabilities of the study's sponsors.

Parenthetically, the group sponsoring this study was a newly organized section whose desire was to do all they could to make sure that their first project would be successful. Since the reader may question the value of such "fluid" subjective probabilities, the position that the Bayesian model is a *normative* one which states what choice the decision maker should make if he agrees with the assumptions underlying the model should be restated. In this instance the computer program served to measure the risk associated with proceeding under the pessimistic state of nature. In our judgment the high disutility attached to the occurrence of the pessimistic state of nature prompted the decision to delay the development. The model was useful, however, in apprising the marketing personnel of both the conditional outputs and the impact of their probability estimates on expected payoff. *A model, in general, can do no more than show the implications of the assumptions underlying it.* And, prior to the study, the marketing personnel were unaware of these implications.

After a little more than one year of further market evaluation the decision was finally made to commercialize the product, using the tactical option (25-million-pound plant and Case A pricing) which was found to be optimal in the original study.

COMMENTS ON THE CASE STUDY

The reader will note that the actual case illustration, similar to the hypothetical problem, involved a preposterior analysis. That is, the anticipated effect of changes in the decision maker's future information state was used to help answer the question of whether or not the decision should be delayed. The reader will also note, however, that the approach and content of the real case study differed rather markedly from the hypothetical problem.

In the hypothetical problem it was assumed, among other things, that the decision maker's prior probability distribution was given. It was learned from the real case study that the *development of prior probabilities can be a time-consuming and formidable task.* Even at that, it was necessary to make several simplifying assumptions for the purpose of making the analysis reasonably tractable and to provide inputs and outputs simple enough to be easily comprehended by the marketing specialists who were associated with the investigation.

This odd mixture of conceptual simplification, on the one hand, and expanded operational detail, on the other, carried over to the computation of conditional payoffs. In dealing with 20 end uses, it is clear that the computational problem becomes tedious if no mechanical means is available to handle the calculations. A set of 72 calculational runs each comprising a planning period of some 13 years would become prohibitive if recourse was not made to an electronic computer. Fortunately, a computer program of some generality can be prepared rather quickly for problems of this type by using one of the simplified algebraic programming techniques like IBM's FORTRAN. Moreover, the computer program can be used as a "simulator" in which such inputs as market composition, growth rates, cost of capital, and so forth, can be systematically varied, if desired, in order to perform sensitivity analyses of the relevant parameters.

A further contrast between the hypothetical and real problem situations concerns the manner in which the conditional probabilities (that future sample results will indicate the true underlying sales volume parameters) were determined. As noted, in the hypothetical case it was assumed these conditional probabilities $P(Z_i$ $(e_j) \mid S_k)$ were known for each contemplated market survey. In the real problem situation the required conditional probabilities were "solved for" by finding *how reliable future information would have to be* in order to justify delaying the decision until one year in the future.

With all of the difficulties attached to using Bayesian techniques in actual problems, the preceding comments still demonstrate, however, one of the principal values of this type of formal analysis, namely, to determine the financial implications of various marketing and production assumptions by providing the decision maker with a manipulatable "if . . . then" model for studying the effect of changes in his assumptions and for checking their internal consistency.

ALLOCATING THE PRODUCT DEVELOPMENT BUDGET

All of the illustrations so far have treated the decisions underlying new product devlopment as rather particularized activities. That is, the problem of allocating a limited development budget among several product candidates competing for funds and/or manpower has not been explicitly considered.

In a sense the allocation problem has been approached by assuming that the firm's "opportunity cost of capital" (which was inserted in the net present value formulation) reflected a financial cutoff point. If the venture earned an expected return greater than, say, ten percent, it would be accepted; otherwise, it would be rejected. This assumes that the firm has *other* projects which could earn this rate of return. From a more realistic viewpoint, this criterion may not be adequate.

First, even the determination of an appropriate opportunity cost of capital is difficult and involves questions of its stability over time and, at a given time, the differential risks associated with competing projects. The decision maker may well prefer a new product venture which carries a high probability for making a modest return to one whose return is highly variable, even though the expected monetary value of the latter project is higher. This involves questions of utility, a subject discussed in Chapter 6.

Second, limited availability of capital may preclude the funding of all new product ventures, even though a satisfactory return (according to past standards) could be forthcoming. This would suggest that projects might be ranked in decreasing order of return, the cutoff point on project selection being determined by availability of funds. In other words, rather than using some opportunity cost of capital as an input, the analyst would solve for the appropriate interest rate of return which would lead to an expected net present value of zero over the estimated planning period of the project. This sub-category of discounted cash flow procedures is known as the "yield" or "interest rate of return" method.

Third, limited capital may not be the only—or even major—constraint in the allocation problem. Limitations of research facilities, trained manpower, and other scarce resources may impinge on project selection. These considerations can represent additional constraints on the allocation process and thus make the evaluation procedure that much more complicated.

Finally, questions pertaining to the possible interdependence among product development ventures and the *future* demand for resources add to the complexity of resource allocation. As one could surmise, the use of Bayesian procedures in product development is hardly sufficient for coping with the many ramifications of determining the total size and mix of the product development budget.

Numerous techniques (for example, the differential calculus in the presence of constraints, linear programming, and dynamic programming) have been proposed for dealing with the allocation problem. Discussion of these procedures will be deferred until Chapter 10. The purpose here has been to show how Bayesian analysis provides a useful technique for coping with the high uncertainty which is associated with new product decisions and how the activity of product development can be viewed as a multistage decision problem (including information steps) and where present choices should be made which reflect the opportunity to make future choices under changed information states.

It would appear that future research or new product decision making will emphasize (a) the role of information in reducing the cost of uncertainty and (b) the sequential nature of development decisions. Empirical research will be required to estimate the appropriate conditional probabilities (that is, the $P(Z_i \mid S_j's)$) at various stages in the product's development. This, in turn, means that more careful record keeping or "logging" of development projects will be needed if we are to develop information useful not only for the current venture but for future development projects as well. If uncertainty is a key feature of research and development activity, then we must attempt to measure how uncertainty is reduced as the new product proceeds through development as well as the cost incurred in reducing this uncertainty.

SUMMARY

This chapter has emphasized techniques for making new product development decisions, as a major subclass of all product decisions, on the assumption that many of these techniques can also be used to evaluate plans for modifying the existing product line or dropping marginal products.

The mechanics of product profile analysis were first described as a simple and quick procedure for screening new product candidates. While some of the apparent virtues of the procedure were criticized, the fact remains that preliminary analysis of this type can be useful in discriminating between projects worthy of further review and those which appear to be poor risks for further development.

The product development process was then described from the point of view of Bayesian analysis, and it was shown how these techniques can be useful in treating the new venture as a sequential decision problem under uncertainty. A hypothetical problem was constructed in which the costs of additional project review were matched against the value of additional information in reducing the costs of uncertainty. Next, an actual case was covered in some detail so as to show some of the problems encountered in making the procedures operational in real situations. As noted, a computer simulation of the venture was found to be useful in handling the heavy calculational load associated with developing the table of conditional payoffs.

Finally, some of the limitations of the Bayesian model were described, and it was indicated that the allocation problem under uncertainty, with its many ramifications, is indeed a complex one, requiring much additional research of both a conceptual and empirical nature.

Selected References

BANKS, SEYMOUR. "Why People Buy Particular Brands," *Motivation and Market Behavior* (ROBERT FERBER AND HUGH G. WALES, eds.). Homewood, Ill.: Richard D. Irwin, Inc., 1958.

Discusses the specific use of multiple regression and discriminatory analysis in the measurement of consumer attitudes toward product attributes.

BROWN, GEORGE H. "Measuring Consumer Attitudes toward Products," *Motivation and Market Behavior* (ROBERT FERBER AND HUGH G. WALES, eds.). Homewood, Ill.: Richard D. Irwin, Inc., 1958.

Interesting from the point of view of methodology and content. Like the Banks chapter above, this describes the various influences on product sales (such as availability, extent of consumer knowledge, price, and product attributes) and the use of attitudinal measurements generally in estimating consumer attitudes regarding new products.

HOWARD, JOHN A. *Marketing Management*. Homewood, Ill.: Richard D. Irwin, Inc., 1957.

The chapter "Product Decisions" discusses the source of product change, qualitative criteria for new product evaluation, marketing testing of new products, "add-drop" policy with respect to product line decisions, and product acquisition.

LAZO, HECTOR, AND CORBIN, ARNOLD. *Management in Marketing*. New York: McGraw-Hill Book Co., 1961.

The chapter "Product Planning—the Heart of Marketing" describes marketing organization for new products, the motivations underlying product innovation, and the pretesting of new products. A check list for evaluating new products is also included.

TERRY, HERBERT. "Comparative Evaluation of Performance Using Multiple Criteria," *Management Science*, Vol. 9, No. 3 (April, 1963), pp. 431–42.

Describes the potential role of game theory in evaluating product performance, discusses weighting procedures (similar to "product profile" analysis) in some detail, and offers a critique of this class of evaluative procedures. A useful bibliography is appended.

Problems

1. The Warren Manufacturing Corporation is presently engaged in the manufacture of industrial heating and air-conditioning equipment. Mr. Carr, the president of the corporation, has been considering expanding the corporation's market by entering the home air-conditioning market. In his attempt to make a decision Mr. Carr has developed the following information:

1) Possible acts:

    a) Enter the home air-conditioning market immediately with an initial expenditure of $0.5 million and a subsequent expenditure at the beginning of the third year of operation of $0.2 million, (A_1).

    b) Do not enter the home air-conditioning market, (A_2).

    c) Delay a terminal decision for one year and conduct a marketing research survey that will be 80% reliable, that is, $P(d_1 \mid D_1) = 0.8$; $P(d_1 \mid D_2) = 0.2$ and $P(d_2 \mid D_2) = 0.8$; $P(d_2 \mid D_1) = 0.2$. (e_1). If Mr. Carr decides to enter the home air-conditioning market after the one-year delay, conditional revenues will be reduced by 5% due to competitive inroads and will also carry a one-year delay penalty. Necessary outlays will be delayed one year but will be the same amount as under act A_1. The home air-conditioner survey will cost $0.1 million.

2) Possible demands and conditional revenues attained at the end of the five-year planning period (assuming no delay) are:

Acts	Demand 1	Demand 2
A_1...............	$5 million	$-4 million
A_2...............	0 million	0 million

3) Prior probabilities:
   a) Demand 1 = 0.6
   b) Demand 2 = 0.4

4) Opportunity cost of capital = 10%
   a) Compute the expected net present value for act A_1.
   b) What is the value of perfect information?
   c) Compute the expected net present value for strategy e_1.
   d) Construct a decision tree showing the appropriate strategies.

2. Criticize the product profile procedure for screening new products.

3. Discuss the similarities and differences between the hypothetical case and the actual case illustrated in the chapter.

4. Can you suggest a possible way to handle the problem of dependencies among investment options?

Chapter 9

PRICING DECISIONS

Another major class of marketing planning decisions concerns product and/or service pricing. As was noted in the preceding chapter, the pricing decision cannot usually be considered independently of other classes of decisions, for example, product or promotional decisions. While, for expository reasons, separate attention is given to this set of decisions, in actual planning situations pricing strategy will probably be considered in conjunction with other classes of decisions related to marketing.

The chapter begins with an overview of several types of pricing decisions such as base pricing, pricing relationships among product-line members, defensive pricing, and so on. The various procedures by which businessmen decide upon prices are discussed and these methods are contrasted with the marginal analysis of economic theory. The problem of estimating the firm's demand schedule is also commented upon.

Some of the principal quantitative procedures (for example, regression analysis of time series, cross-sectional analysis and experimentation) by which demand elasticities can be estimated are described. An illustration of one of these techniques is explained in some detail.

The use of Bayesian decision theory combined with field data is then described in a setting involving demand estimation for a product (synthetic fibers) possessing a derived demand. Concepts of equal-profit contours, long-range effects of price, and the independent influences of marketing channels on price are discussed in this illustration.

The chapter concludes with a description of the principal limitations of present analytical procedures in estimating price–volume relationships and suggests some techniques which may be used to a greater extent in the future in studying the interaction between pricing and other sets of courses of action which the firm has at its disposal.

OVERVIEW OF THE PRICING DECISION

In the large multiproduct firm of today, *the* pricing decision is a gross oversimplification of the many courses of action subsumed under pricing. Pricing problems can be associated with

1. *New product introduction.* In this category the firm may be introducing a product sufficiently different from competitive products to warrant a fair degree of discretion in setting initial (and subsequent) price. Problems concern the strategy to be adopted over the product's anticipated life cycle. For example, should the firm follow a "skim the cream" strategy in which the product is initially priced high and then lowered over time, or should a "penetration" strategy be adopted to discourage competitive imitation of the product?

2. *Basic price of existing line.* Should the firm aim at being a prestige producer with higher-than-average price for the industry (coupled with product differentiation), or should it assume other pricing postures, for example, pricing at or somewhat below prevailing industry pricing?

3. *Pricing relationships within the line.* Should the firm attempt to differentiate product-line members and thus segment its market, or should it aim for standardized, volume markets with one-price policies?

4. *Discount structures.* How should discounts to various accounts be set? That is, what should be the firm's policy with respect to quantity and functional discounts?

5. *Defensive pricing.* How should the firm react to competitive price moves? Should competitors' price reductions be met, or should the firm attempt to "hold the line" with respect to price, while making further attempts to differentiate its product?

6. *Price and nonprice interaction.* How should the firm plan its promotional and marketing-service policy in conjunction with the stance it wishes to assure with regard to pricing policy?

It is clear that a firm which (through either its relative size in the industry or its uniqueness of product) is capable of exercising some freedom of action regarding pricing may encounter a wide variety of pricing problems.

No attempt will be made to explore all of these pricing issues but, rather, the major analytical tools available for coping with pricing situations will be concentrated on. In preparation for this discussion (*a*) the economist's overall view of pricing, (*b*) some of the ways in which businessmen appear to set price, and (*c*) the economist's marginal analysis approach to price determination will be briefly reviewed.

ECONOMIC THEORY VERSUS BUSINESS
APPROACHES TO PRICING DECISIONS

Most of the work of the economist in the area of price setting has been concerned with the two extreme cases, namely, perfect competition and monopoly. In the first instance, most closely approached by agricultural markets, the problem of an *individual* firm's setting of price is, by definition, nonexistent since no single firm is large enough to influence the price. The industry's price becomes the firm's price. In the second instance, which again is only crudely approached in a real-world setting, the individual firm is presumed to have full control over price in the sense that the demand for the firm is the demand for the industry. In point of fact, however, virtually no product is without substitutes; the term monopoly is largely a matter of degree and the pricing freedom which a monopolist enjoys is governed by the closeness of available substitutes and their prices relative to the price of his product.

At some point along the line between these two extremes fall actual competitive situations. These more realistic situations are identified under two categories:

1. Monopolistic competition, where a single firm is able to achieve a measure of independent pricing by differentiating its product from competitive products.

2. Oligopoly, where the number of sellers are so few that any single firm, whether selling a standardized or differentiated product, must consider the reaction of competitors to a change in price. Most competitive situations in manufactured materials fall under this category.

Under each one of the situations just described, the "rule" as given by economic theory for the maximization of an individual firm's total profits is to charge that price and produce that output which will "equate marginal revenue with marginal cost."

By marginal the economist means the revenue received and cost incurred through the sale of the last unit. So long as revenue received from the last unit exceeds its cost of production, it would pay the businessman to increase output up to the point where marginal revenue just equalled marginal cost. This procedure will be illustrated a bit later.

But at this point, one should take stock of the assumptions and information required for application of marginal analysis.

1. Marginal analysis assumes that the individual firm, at any point in time, desires only to maximize total profits; other business goals are not considered.
2. Marginal analysis, being a static concept, ignores the time dimension.

3. In order to derive both marginal revenue and marginal cost, the demand at various prices and total cost at various outputs must be known.

The limitations of this analysis are readily apparent. A firm may not wish to set a price which will maximize short-run earnings if, in so doing, longer-term earnings (through the intervention of new competitors, government, or unions) may be jeopardized. In addition, a pricing decision which ignores the time dimension may merely produce a bunching of sales (in early response to, say, a price cut) without any additional increase in total sales over a longer time period; the sales might have occurred anyway. Finally, total costs at various levels of output can usually be only crudely estimated; demand at alternate prices represents an even more difficult task for measurement.

Economic theory as applied to the individual firm does, however, serve to *systematize* the approach to pricing policy. Moreover, modification of theory to reflect business practice more accurately is not only desirable but necessary. The point of view taken here is that the interaction of theory with business behavior provides an analytical framework more powerful than each taken separately.

HOW BUSINESSMEN SET PRICE

If an accurate description of pricing presents a challenge to the theoretical economist, the businessman is confronted with just as perplexing a problem in formulating pricing policy.

Surveys taken of the various policies which businessmen follow in pricing their products have indicated that price policies are much more cost oriented than demand oriented. This tendency is reflected in the industry practices of cost-plus, rate-of-return, administered pricing, and so on, in which some "normal" margin of profit (conditioned by competition) is added to full production costs of the product in question.

In the light of the information typically available to the businessman, these practices are usually justified on the following grounds:

1. Businessmen, as a rule, know much more about product costs than consumer demand.
2. These methods are relatively quick and easy to apply inasmuch as product costs are typically calculated anyway.
3. By and large, these practices are "safe."

In addition to motivations stemming from the uncertainty of demand and competitors' reactions, there appear to exist real or imagined notions on the part of some businessmen that a "normal" margin meets ethical or moral considerations and in the long run is the most prudent course of action to take in safeguarding the economic health of the organization.

Cost-plus pricing in its simplest form involves the determination of full, allocated cost of production plus the addition of a fixed percentage mark-on. As such, this practice reflects historical rather than future costs at past rather than anticipated output levels and employs full rather than the incremental costs of the economist.

Rate-of-return pricing is a procedure which is somewhat less arbitrary than cost-plus. The margin to be added is determined from corporate policy regarding the planned rate of return on investment. Total cost of a period's average production is estimated and the ratio of invested capital to production cost is computed (capital turnover). Multiplication of this ratio by the desired rate of return yields the markup on cost which is required. This method represents an improvement over cost-plus in that recognition of changes in output rate is implied in the use of a standardized output over the price-planning period. In contrast, however, to the economic theorist's criterion of maximizing profits, rate of return still employs the concept of some planned "normal" rate of return.

Intuitive pricing rather than representing a distinct method, is by nature, a flexible procedure, borrowing from cost-plus or similar policies and modifying these practices based on the "feel" or judgment of the market which the price setter possesses. This practice probably enters to some degree in most pricing decisions.

Administered pricing, where prices remain fixed over rather long periods of time, represents the result of business motives which are aimed at preserving a semblance of industry peace more than an active approach toward maximizing short-term profits. Administered prices are generally found in industries comprised of relatively few sellers where products are not highly differentiated and where "price leadership" is dominant. Strategic action on the part of an individual firm to maintain or increase its market share is primarily of a nonprice nature and involves promotion, quality control, and customer services of various types. Administered pricing, by providing at least short-term stability, serves to lend more assurance to day-to-day sales, production, and inventory planning.

It is apparent that the business methods described above are not strict alternatives; that is, one may find administered pricing based primarily on a cost-plus formula. Furthermore, the policies may vary in degree. The margin over cost need not necessarily be fixed for all products of a multiproduct firm or, for that matter, the same product at different points in time. In addition, "normal" margins undoubtedly differ from industry to industry.

Nevertheless, certain common elements appear to stand out which distinguish business practice from economic theory:

1. Businessmen appear to rely on costs much more formally than demand when making pricing decisions. This is in large measure due to their better ability to estimate this side of the coin.

2. The costs chosen, however, are primarily full, historical costs rather than the incremental, future costs of the theoretical economist.

3. The competitive role seems to be taken into account more on a defensive than offensive basis; that is, the implication may be "leave well enough alone."

4. Emphasis appears to be more on safeguarding a "normal profit" than accepting the assumed greater risk associated with the policy of price setting for maximum profits.

When one considers that economic theory assumes much more than the businessman typically knows about consumer demand, the reactions of competitors, and his firm's future costs, pricing policies as currently practiced can hardly be expected to mirror the tenets of economic theory.

CONTRIBUTIONS OF ECONOMIC THEORY
TO PRICE DETERMINATION

It has just been noted that disparities between formal price theory and business practice exist. One may now inquire as to what elements of economic theory appear useful in actual pricing policy and how these elements might be adapted to fit practical situations. Businessmen have already made a start in this direction.

In recent years, businessmen's use of *break-even analysis* has, within the limitations of current accounting procedures, approximated the incremental cost concept of the economist. But, less progress has been made in the area of estimating demand response to price and competitors' reactions, both of which can influence the firm's marginal revenue.

The contribution of economic theory to business decision making unfortunately rests more on the recognition of the demand relationship to price than on providing a means for its measurement. That businessmen typically use cost-oriented approaches to pricing policy is some evidence of the great amount of uncertainty connected with determining how sensitive demand is to price. And yet, this measurement is critical to any formal method for evaluating the role of price in profit maximization.

Also related to the derivation of the marginal revenue curve as formulated by the economic theorist are the actions of both *present and potential competitors,* since the actions of present competitors can affect the firm's market share and total sales associated with a price change and the recognition of potential competitors may serve to limit the pricing freedom of even a monopolist. A price increase may or may not be followed by present competition and/or may serve as an umbrella for potential competition to become active competitors. A price decrease may be matched (or exceeded) by present competitors, thus reducing the firm's revenue if total industry demand is not stimulated enough to offset this possibility. However, the price reduction could deter potential competition from becoming active competitors.

Although not directly related to the actions of the individual firm, economic theory recognizes the shift which can occur in the firm's *industry* demand curve, stemming from events largely independent of the price setter's actions. Changes in disposable income, population changes, and general business conditions can play a pronounced effect on shifting industry demand and yet are subject to little control by the individual firm.

THE MECHANICS OF MARGINAL ANALYSIS

As viewed by the theoretical economist the problem of finding the best combination of price and output becomes a straightforward application of the marginal analysis. That is, the firm will choose that price and output combination in which the revenue received from the marginal unit equals the cost of producing the marginal unit. Application of this rule assumes, of course, that the firm wishes only to maximize profits and also knows its demand and cost schedules.

A simple illustration, mathematical and graphical, can be used to demonstrate the use of the economist's marginal analysis in price and output determination. Assume that the firm's price (average per unit) schedule, over the relevant output range, is given by the linear equation

$$P = 500 - 0.1 \, Q$$

where Q is, say, monthly production in units and P is price per unit in dollars. Notice that for each additional unit marketed the average price for all units sold will drop by 10¢ per unit. For example, if the firm markets 100 units per month it can get $490 per unit, while if it markets 200 units per month it receives only $480 per unit.

Suppose the firm's total cost function on a monthly basis is given by

$$C = 40,000 + 100\ Q$$

This linear equation states that C, total cost in dollars, is equal to fixed cost plus variable cost. That is, if the firm produces no units, its fixed cost will equal $40,000 per month. Furthermore, for each unit produced, total cost will increase by $100.

The total revenue function per month is merely price times quantity, or

$$PQ = (500 - 0.1\ Q)\ Q$$
$$= 500\ Q - 0.1\ Q^2$$

Marginal revenue and marginal cost are found by differentiating[1] the total revenue and total cost equations with respect to Q.

$$\text{Marginal revenue} = \frac{d\ (PQ)}{d\ Q} = 500 - 0.2\ Q$$

$$\text{Marginal cost} = \frac{d\ C}{d\ Q} = 100$$

According to the marginal analysis, total profits are maximized when marginal revenue is set equal to marginal cost (assuming second order conditions are satisfied).

$$\frac{d\ (PQ)}{d\ Q} = \frac{d\ C}{d\ Q} = 500 - 0.2\ Q = 100$$

$$Q = 2,000 \text{ units}$$

Thus, at a production level of 2,000 units per month, price per unit will be

$$P = 500 - 0.1\ Q = 500 - 200 = \$300 \text{ per unit}$$

and total profit π per month will be

$$\pi = PQ - C = [500\ (2,000) - 0.1\ (2,000)^2] - [40,000 + 100\ (2,000)]$$
$$= \$360,000$$

The mathematical relationships which were used to represent the demand schedule, total cost and revenue, and marginal revenue and cost are shown graphically in Figure 9-1. Looking first at the upper panel of the chart one can note that the marginal-cost line intersects the marginal-revenue line at an output of 2,000 units. At this intersection the product's price is $300 per unit, the price to be

---

[1]The rule for differentiating an algebraic function of the form x^n is nx^{n-1} and can be applied term by term. The derivative of a constant is equal to zero.

charged in order to obtain maximum profits. In the lower panel are
plotted the firm's total-revenue and total-cost lines. At an output of
2,000 units the firm receives a total revenue of $600,000 less total
costs of $240,000 or a total profit of $360,000 which agrees with the

Figure 9–1

MARGINAL AND TOTAL REVENUE
AND COST RELATIONSHIPS

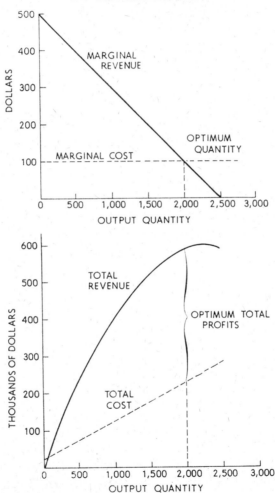

results of the preceding arithmetic. Notice that the *difference* between the total-revenue and total-cost lines is greater at an output
of 2,000 units than at any other output shown in the graph.

So much for this brief analytical treatment of output and price
determination. From a pragmatic standpoint the problem is to de-

termine the relevant demand and cost relationships. In practice the determination of the demand relationship becomes particularly difficult and requires, at the very least, consideration of the firm's product and purchaser characteristics vis-a-vis those of its competitors.

EMPIRICAL DETERMINATION OF DEMAND RELATIONSHIPS

It should be clear from the foregoing illustration that in order to apply the techniques of marginal analysis the firm must have knowledge of its demand schedule, that is, the number of units which it can sell at alternative prices. In practice, however, the firm typically knows only one point on its demand curve, namely, the number of units being sold at a single price.

Several techniques have been suggested for estimating price–volume relationships. Each of these techniques has its own limitations, and it seems fair to say that the empirical determination of demand schedules (particularly at the individual firm level) is still fraught with difficulty.

1. *Questionnaire methods.* This class of procedures involves a variety of approaches: (*a*) In the case of new-product-demand estimation, a sample of consumers may be shown the new product in an array of existing products with tagged prices and asked to position the new product in this array. (*b*) The consumer may be given a description of the new product and asked to state whether he would desire the product or a stipulated amount of cash (the amount of money being varied according to a predesigned plan). (*c*) In the case of existing products, the consumer may be asked whether she would continue to buy the product if the price were increased by x cents, prices of competing products remaining the same. (*d*) In the case of nonbuyers, she may be asked whether she would switch to the product if its price were lowered by y cents, prices of competing products remaining the same.

2. *Regression analysis.* This set of techniques typically involves two principal approaches, namely, analysis of the relationship of past sales to price changes over time and cross-sectional analysis of sales and prices where regional differences in price exist at any point in time. For example, demand curves have been estimated for various agricultural products by means of regression analyses of quantity consumed and relative prices over time. Demand curves have been estimated for fuel oil by the use of regression analysis of regional consumption of fuel oil as a function of its price relative to competing fuels.

3. *Experimentation.* In more recent years attempts have been made to estimate demand curves by experimentally manipulating price in actual purchase situations. For example, pricing experiments have been conducted in supermarkets, department stores, and other retail outlets where the price of the experimental brand was manipulated and actual consumer purchases, under controlled conditions, were tabulated. In

some instances the purpose of the experiment was to estimate the additional volume which a price reduction might be expected to produce (if other prices remained invariant) while in other instances the experimenter was interested in the national brand's "loyalty power," that is, the price to which the test brand would have to be lowered before sales of the nationally-known brand would be significantly lowered.

All of the preceding techniques possess limitations, particularly when the problem involves estimation of an individual firm's demand schedule. Questionnaire methods reflect the dubious assumptions that (a) consumers can perceive how they would act if prices were changed and (b) that they would, in fact, act this way under a real purchase situation. Regression techniques applied to time series are frequently of little value because (a) both demand and supply may be changing over time, (b) price changes may have been too infrequent and too narrow to yield a range of volume response to price broad enough for planning purposes, and (c) other factors (changes in consumer tastes, product quality, promotion) may have influenced sales volume. Regression techniques applied to cross-sectional data are subject to similar limitations of (a) lack of enough variability in regional prices to establish a meaningful demand schedule and (b) regional differences in consumer attitudes and competitive practices also influencing sales for the product through shifts in the demand curve.

Price experimentation is also subject to the problems of adjusting for the effect of other variables on the product's sales and the systematic and sampling error that is associated with experimentation techniques generally. Furthermore, a major problem exists in attempting to extrapolate the results of an experiment to an across-the-board pricing action. Competitors are likely to retaliate if a price reduction is initiated, thus nullifying the conditions existing at the time the experiment was conducted. In this case the analyst will be required to separate "industry" effects, that is, sales garnered from competing product groups, from "brand" effects, or sales garnered from other brands of the same product group. While competitors may not respond in kind to an across-the-board price increase, they may elect to make the consumer more aware of brand price differences, thus changing the conditions which were in effect when the pricing experiment was conducted. This problem of "scaling up" the results of an experiment is a particularly acute one in marketing, generally, and in pricing analysis, specifically.

We shall not attempt to illustrate all of the various techniques for estimating empirical demand relationships which have been outlined above. The next section, however, will describe the use of regression analysis in a problem of estimating the industry demand for cellulosic fibers while the following chapter will provide an illustration of an experimental design technique in measuring the response of sales to advertising. A guide to other applications of demand estimation techniques is provided at the end of this chapter.

AN ILLUSTRATION OF REGRESSION ANALYSIS IN DEMAND ESTIMATION

Regression analysis of time series data has frequently been used to estimate price elasticities of demand, that is, the percentage change in sales in response to a small (say, 1 percent) change in price. Usually these analyses have been made using industry rather than individual company data.

The following analysis (which was made for a large producer of synthetic fibers) uses multiple regression to estimate the functional relationship between United States per capita consumption of rayon-acetate fiber (used in apparel, home furnishings fabric, and so forth) and the independent variables, personal disposable income (deflated, per capita) and rayon-acetate fiber price relative to prices of cotton, a closely competing fiber. Annual data were available for each of the three variables over the period 1928–57 (war years were excluded from the analysis).

A *priori*, one might expect that per capita consumption of rayon-acetate fiber would increase as personal disposable income increased and that consumption would decrease as the price of rayon-acetate fiber relative to cotton increased. That is, the "income elasticity" of demand would be presumed to be positive while the "price elasticity" would be presumed to be negative.

A multiple linear regression analysis was applied to the logarithms of the original data. This model assumes an estimating equation of the following general form:

$$\log Y_c = \log a + b_1 \log X_1 + b_2 \log X_2$$

Translated into "antilogs," this implies

$$Y_c = a X_1{}^{b_1} X_2{}^{b_2}$$

where Y_c = calculated annual per capita consumption (in pounds), X_1 = real personal disposable income per capita (in dollars), X_2 = ratio of rayon-acetate-fiber price to cotton-fiber price, and a, b_1 and b_2 are coefficients calculated by least squares.

Figure 9–2 shows the actual time series of per capita rayon-acetate consumption compared to the time series calculated by application of the relationship derived from the multiple regression technique. The estimating equation used to derive the calculated values was

$$Y_c = 10.12 \, X_1{}^{0.6154} \, X_2{}^{-1.1494}$$

Figure 9-2

RAYON-ACETATE CONSUMPTION PER CAPITA (TEXTILE YARN AND STAPLE)
(1928–57 EXCLUDING WORLD WAR II PERIOD)

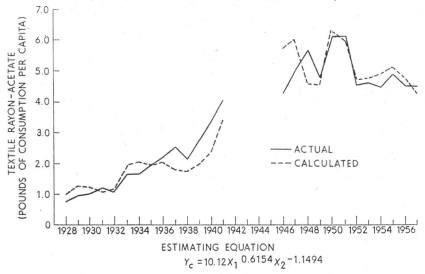

ESTIMATING EQUATION

$$Y_c = 10.12 X_1{}^{0.6154} X_2{}^{-1.1494}$$

Y_c = ESTIMATED PER CAPITA RAYON-ACETATE CONSUMPTION
X_1 = REAL PERSONAL DISPOSABLE INCOME PER CAPITA
X_2 = PRICE RATIO: RAYON-ACETATE / COTTON

As can be noted from the chart the calculated series appears to agree reasonably well with the actual time series of rayon-acetate per capita consumption. The values of coefficients, b_1 and b_2 (found by application of the least squares regression procedure to the logarithms of the original data) are + 0.6154 and − 1.1494 and can be viewed as measures of average "demand elasticity" for income and price, respectively.[2]

As real income per capita changed 1 percent, there was associated with this change a 0.6 percent change in rayon-acetate consumption

---

[2]The rate of change of $y = f(x)$ when both changes are expressed in proportional terms is $\dfrac{d(\log y)}{d(\log x)} = \dfrac{x \, dy.}{y \, dx.}$ In the general case, if both x and y were plotted on logarithmic paper, the gradient of the tangent to the curve would be $\dfrac{d(\log y).}{d(\log x).}$

per capita in the same direction. Thus, a less than proportional change in rayon-acetate consumption resulted from a real per capita income percentage change; rayon-acetate consumption was rather inelastic with respect to changes in real income.

A change in the price ratio of rayon-acetate to cotton fiber of 1 percent was associated with an almost proportional change in the opposite direction $(-1.1$ percent) for rayon-acetate consumption. Demand "elasticity" was almost unitary.

The economic interpretation of these coefficients and the information which they shed on anticipated volume responses to subsequent changes in rayon-acetate price, relative to cotton, is subject to several reservations. It is true that each coefficient carries the algebraic sign that common sense would suggest. One would expect that as income went up, consumption would increase and that as relative price went down, consumption would increase. In addition, other economic studies have indicated that the demand for clothing (a major market for rayon-acetate) is rather inelastic to income changes over the long run and that derived-demand products, differentiated to some degree, are generally not highly elastic to price changes.

However, a general limitation of this type of analysis is that it is extremely difficult to isolate the static demand curve postulated by economic theory. By this is meant that *both* demand and supply were probably changing throughout most of the period of analysis as new uses for rayon-acetate were exploited in the early years and as excess production capacity came in during the latter years of the period. The estimation of an average price elasticity serves to cloud the particular effect that a price change might exert in the growth period of the product as opposed to its effect in a more stable period. These reservations severely limit the usefulness of the calculated elasticity coefficients. One can only broadly infer that, on the average, rayon-acetate consumption was not highly elastic to either income or fiber price relative to cotton.

While regression analysis can be useful in gaining some insight into demand relationships, care must be exercised in using the results of these studies for specific pricing action. For example, one cannot use regression analysis, as such, to infer causality. In the above case it might make just about as much sense to say that "rayon-acetate-fiber price declines as consumption per capita goes up" as to infer the converse of that assertion. Correlation procedures show only association, not causation. The apparent relationship between consumption and price may be due to the effect of a third variable which influences both variables but was not included in the formal analysis.

BAYESIAN DECISION THEORY IN PRICING DECISIONS

The foregoing comments on the limitations of empirical procedures for estimating demand schedules apply as well to the use of decision theory in pricing problems. The "state of the art" in pricing analysis is still not highly developed.

Reasons for discussing the use of Bayesian procedures in pricing problems are that (*a*) these techniques focus upon the decision characteristics of the problem rather than demand-schedule estimation, per se (*b*) the pricing problem which has been chosen to demonstrate the procedures provides an illustration of how field data can be combined with judgmental data to estimate pertinent demand relationships, and (*c*) the use of a realistic marketing example can show better the dynamic characteristics of pricing action and the sequential nature of decision making in this area. The illustration refers to price problems associated with the marketing of the newer synthetic (typically called "noncellulosic") fibers.

The content of this section of the chapter is partly descriptive, partly normative. First, some of the characteristics of the textile fibers industry will be briefly discussed insofar as these characteristics influence the empirical determination of price–volume relationships. Second, some of the problems encountered in demand estimation and the decision models developed to deal with these uncertainties will be outlined. Finally, a numerical problem illustrating the techniques in a hypothetical pricing illustration will be described in some detail.

CHARACTERISTICS OF THE TEXTILE FIBERS INDUSTRY

The textile fibers industry is both vast and complex; within the confines of this chapter no attempt will be made to cover even superficially its many aspects. For our purposes this industry may be viewed in terms of three major product groupings, the natural fibers (for example, cotton and wool), the cellulosic fibers (rayon and acetate), and the newer noncellulosic fibers (polyamides, acrylics, and polyesters).

Both the noncellulosic and cellulosic categories may be described as oligopolistic industries. Cross-elasticities of demand are very high within each respective segment but, with few exceptions, are relatively low between segments. This is to imply that a firm which lowers the price of some noncellulosic fiber might expect rapid retaliation by other producers of the noncellulosic fiber. However, in most cases, prices of cellulosics would not be affected. Expansion of the market through the impact of a price reduction at the non-cellulosic *industry* level thus has meaning in terms of generic demand for noncellulosic fibers, although intramarket shares by fiber producers might not be changed.

The marketing of both noncellulosic and cellulosic fibers follows a long and intricate distribution chain. Fiber producers typically market only the fiber, which must in turn be spun, woven, dyed, cut, sewn, wholesaled, and retailed before reaching the hands of the ultimate consumer. Fibers used in nonapparel markets like tires, conveyor belts, and upholstery fabrics follow only slightly less elaborate channels. It follows that the demand for textile fibers is a derived demand. The cost of the fiber in some apparel uses may amount to only 10 to 15 percent of the retail price of the garment. The ultimate impact of price changes at the fiber-producer level may thus be influenced by the actions of many links in the long distribution chain. Both the magnitude of a fiber-producer-initiated price change on retail prices and the timing of this impact can be estimated only imperfectly by the fiber producer.

In essence, a noncellulosic fiber producer can anticipate that a price reduction will be matched by noncellulosic producers. Principal uncertainties concern the quantitative impact on generic demand for the fiber, from which the fiber producer can estimate his participation in this increase. In the case of apparel markets, increased demand as a function of lower price can arise from two principal sources: (*a*) the fiber's penetration of lower retail price brackets (the relatively high price of noncellulosic fibers has restricted their ability to compete across all price lines in many apparel markets) and (*b*) the fiber's increased share of retail-price brackets in which it is already being used.

PROBABILITY MODELS IN PRICING ANALYSIS

The preceding description has pointed out some of the characteristics of a textile fiber producer's marketing environment. A quantitative formulation of these descriptive aspects as they relate to estimating price–volume relationships for a specific fiber-producing firm is now presented, with short-range analysis considered first.

Assume that a major noncellulosic fiber company is considering the possibility of making a price reduction on a fiber principally used in a single apparel market, which we shall call market *A*.[3]

---

[3]In less simplified situations, more than a single end use would be involved. Moreover, the marketing analyst would have to consider cross-elasticities of demand among members of his own product line, should the price of only one fiber type be changed.

Their marketing analyst would like to determine the extent of the price reduction, if required at all, which would maximize short-range (say, next year's) profits. The analyst can typically gather historical data of the following types: (a) total market size in pounds of all fibers sold in this end use, (b) a breakdown of total market pounds by retail-price bracket, (c) market share enjoyed by the generic noncellulosic fiber (his firm's brand plus competing firms' brands) by price bracket for the price lines in which his firm currently competes, (d) an estimate of the functional relationship between fabric cost and retail-price points of garments using the fabric, (e) his firm's share of generic noncellulosic sales, and (f) his firm's costs of production as a function of the fiber's sales volume in units.

First assume that all of the above variables can be estimated without error, that generic demand instantaneously adjusts to a price reduction, and that all past relationships unaffected by the price reduction will persist into the future. The unrealism of these simplifications will be pointed out as the major uncertainties of the problem are later discussed.

Figure 9–3 shows the first idealization in quadrant form. The most recent annual unit sales of the fiber are assumed to amount to 2 million pounds, the fiber having been priced at $1.65 per pound. Profits amounted to $0.2 million. Suppose the marketing analyst is first interested in exploring possible price reductions which will result in enough additional volume so as to meet at least his firm's current annual level of $0.2 million profits. The 2-million-pound sales volume, in oversimplified terms (that is, holding constant the level of total demand, competitive prices, relative promotion, and so on) represents *one point* on an estimated, but really unknown, demand curve. However, using his knowledge of the behavior of production costs with volume changes, the analyst can prepare a curve of equal profits. It is clear that this equal-profit contour represents the sales needed in order to *maintain* net profits at the $0.2 million level for each contemplated price reduction.

The other quadrants indicate how the analyst may forecast actual (as opposed to "break-even") sales volume. First, the lower left quadrant shows the average relationship of the retail price of garments to the cost of the fiber used in the garments. This relationship is a reflection of both fiber cost, fabric and garment fabrication costs, and distribution markups. For example, at the current fiber price of $1.65 per pound, the fiber is used only in garments retailing at $6.00 and over; but, if fiber price were reduced to $1.35 per pound, the fiber *could*, if the price decrease were passed along, be used in garments retailing at slightly under $5.00. The cumulative distribution of noncellulosic market potential (upper left quadrant) shows the total pounds of fiber which could be used in garments priced at $1.00 or more. In practice, of course, this distribution is discrete rather than continuous.

Figure 9-3

PRICE-VOLUME RELATIONSHIPS IN MARKET A

(First Approximation)

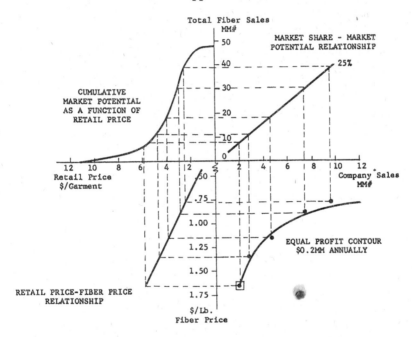

Next, the marketing analyst has data on market share which his firm's fiber enjoys for the retail-price brackets in which it currently competes. The net share is derived from his firm's share of generic demand for the specific noncellulosic fiber. Assume, on a weighted-average basis over all relevant price brackets, that this net share amounts to 25 percent. On the oversimplified assumption that a price reduction would not change, on a weighted-average basis, the firm's aggregate share level derived from combining its new share in present retail-price brackets with the share levels anticipated in newly-opened price brackets, the analyst can then derive estimated sales for the firm at each price level. The dotted lines thus trace out a simplified demand schedule (heavy black dots). Should these dots fall to the left of the equal-profit contour, it is clear that these price reductions would *not* generate enough additional sales to maintain current profit levels. If some dots fall to the right of the equal-profit contour, these price reductions should be considered for further review. Finally, the reader should note the character of the cumulative distribution of total noncellulosic market potential, particularly the steepness of this curve in the lower- or "popular"-price brackets. Typically, unit garment sales by retail-price bracket are heavily skewed, indicating that a given fiber price reduction in the high end of the retail distribution would open up much less poundage potential than an equal reduction near the middle of the distribution of garment unit sales and, hence, fiber poundage sales by retail-price point.

So much for this first approximation. Now examine, in turn, the reasonableness of the assumptions of (*a*) linearity of the retail-price–fiber-price relationship and market-share–market-potential relationship, (*b*) the essentially static nature of the premises under Figure 9–3, and (*c*) the use of single estimates of the retail-price–fiber-price relationship and market-share–market-potential relationship.

PRICE AND VOLUME RELATIONSHIPS

Figure 9–4 shows that both the retail-price–fiber-price relationship and market-share–market-potential relationship may not turn out to be strictly linear. Nonlinearity of these relationships may significantly affect the price–volume relationships. To illustrate, the relationships of Figure 9–3 have first been reproduced. Now looking at curve (*a*) in the lower left quadrant, note the influence of the fabrication trade on moving a high-priced fiber into lower retail-price brackets. This independent action can be accomplished by either the use of more open constructions, that is, less fiber per square yard, or a reduction of value added in finishing and tailoring cost. This is to say that the distribution chain—should the fiber have sales appeal—could, in effect, compound the impact of a price reduction. On the other hand, they could elect to increase fabric weights and keep the fiber in the same price brackets as before through offering improved fabric quality and/or making an attempt to increase their profit margins.

Similarly, curve (*b*) in the upper right quadrant may sometimes represent the behavior of weighted-average market share as a function of cumulative market potential. It could be the case that the particular attributes of the noncellulosic fiber appeal more to medium-retail-price-bracket customers than to higher-price-bracket customers. If so, this interaction indicates that, if new potential is opened via a fiber price reduction, the effect may again be compounded. Also, the converse could be true. In this expository case, the combined effect of the nonlinearities in these two relationships is to change substantially the resultant volume change for a given price reduction. The change is noted in the lower right quadrant.

Figure 9–4

PRICE–VOLUME RELATIONSHIPS IN MARKET A
(Effect of Nonlinearity)

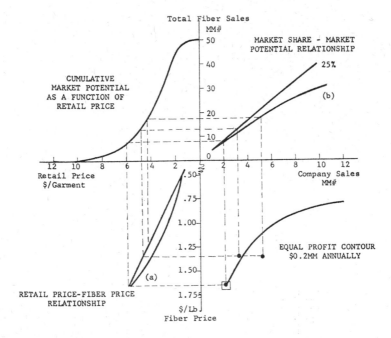

RELATIONSHIPS OVER TIME

Not only may nonlinearities in the current relationships be present, but the analyst might also be concerned with time shifts in both the retail-price–fiber-price relationship and market-share–market-potential relationship in considering the longer-range implications of a proposed fiber price reduction. (Fortunately, in this class of goods, cumulative market potential by retail-price bracket–on a relative basis–changes very slowly over time). Time shifts in the retail-price–fiber-price relationship are a function of fabrication learning on the part of the distribution chain, a reduction in innovative profits for those mills which first work with the fiber, and the

ultimate motivation on the part of the trade and fiber producer
alike to increase unit volume, consistent with satisfactory profit
levels. Time shifts in market share, at given relative prices, are a
function of advertising and promotion levels, increasing consumer
familiarity and satisfaction with the properties of the fiber, and similar nonprice factors.

Figure 9–5

PRICE–VOLUME RELATIONSHIPS IN MARKET A
(Effect of Time Shifts)

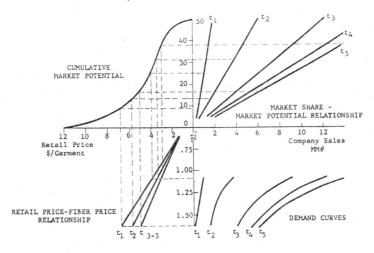

ALTERNATE SALES–PRICE CURVES
(Market A)

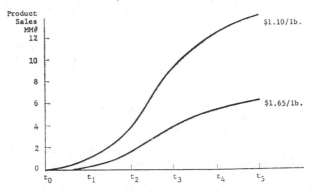

Figure 9–5 shows a conceptualization of this behavior for two
hypothetical fiber prices, namely, $1.10 per pound and $1.65 per
pound. At time t_1, say the first period after introduction, the retail-
price–fiber-price relationship reflects learning time on the part of

the fiber fabrication and distribution chain and innovative profits associated with early introduction of a new type of fiber for this market. The market-share–market-potential relationship reflects consumer learning time as well. Assume, however, that price remained at $1.65 per pound for several periods into the future. *Independent* actions on the part of the fabrication and distribution chain could effect lower retail prices for garments containing the fiber. These shifts are noted in t_2 and t_{3-5}. At some point in time this· type of shifting tends to stabilize.

Also, affective and cognitive learning by consumers—as a function of advertising and product improvements—can shift the market-share–market-potential relationship. The combined impact of these relationships may produce the type of unit-sales curve (fiber price equal to $1.65 per pound) shown in the lower panel. Notice, however, that the $1.10 per pound price—with the same type of time shifts—produces appreciable differences in unit sales. Also, note the changing slope of the demand schedules as a function of time.

UNCERTAINTY OF ESTIMATES

One more complicating feature has to be introduced before the construction of a Bayesian model for this type of problem is considered. Heretofore some *single* estimate for both the retail-price–fiber-price relationship and the market-share–market-potential relationship has been assumed. As tempting as this assumption may be, the fact that these relationships cannot be estimated perfectly provides the rationale for the decision theory approach which is later explained.

Figure 9–6 shows (in exaggerated fashion) the impact of variances around these relationships. A contemplated price reduction to, say, $1.35 per pound might conceivably permit the fiber to be sold in garments retailing as low as $3.95 per garment or might produce only a slight impact on retail price. Moreover, the change in market share, conditional upon the impact of the fiber price reduction in both present and potential retail-price brackets, may differ markedly. The combined impact of these relationships could thus result in sizable sales poundage effects. It follows that the marketing analyst must contend with alternative repercussions (or "states of nature," in decision theory parlance) in appraising the volume impact related to alternative price changes.

One should also note the basic differences in the makeup of the two shaded areas shown in Figure 9–6. The range shown for the retail-price–fiber-price relationship reflects the phenomenon that several differently priced fabrics may be sold in middle to high retail-price brackets but as the retail price of the garment decreases the variance around prices of fibers used in the fabrics decreases. Some minimum fixed cost of fabrication and distribution is required; that is, at the low end of the retail-price scale the garment manufacturer is able to exercise little flexibility between material cost versus fabrication and distribution cost.

Figure 9–6

Price–Volume Relationships in Market A
(Effect of Uncertainties)

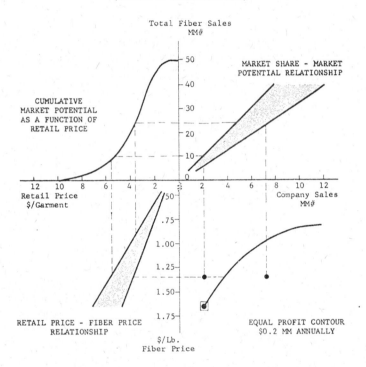

The shaded area under the market-share–market-potential relationship reflects a possible range of the manager's subjective judgments. At the assumed current price of $1.65 per pound the fiber is competing in garments priced in the $6.00-and-over range. Should price decreases of various amounts be contemplated, the manager's task is to estimate a new weighted-average market share covering both old and newly-opened retail-price brackets. One would then surmise that the precision of this estimate would tend to decrease as a greater number of new price brackets are opened; hence the increase in range of aggregate share as a greater portion of the total market is opened to penetration.

THE USE OF BAYESIAN PROCEDURES

At this juncture the reader can appreciate the complexity of the task of estimating price-volume relationships. In concept, however, this type of problem is typical of decision making under uncertainty. In other words, the decision maker has to combine his more or less objective information on total market potential by retail-price bracket, costs as a function of volume, and similar data (which he feels can be estimated with reasonably high precision) with his more subjective judgments regarding the nature of the retail-price–fiber-price relationship and the market-share–market-potential re-lationhip. A very simplified version of this problem can now be structured by using Bayesian analysis.

Suppose that this mythical fiber is currently selling at $1.65 per pound and has captured 25 percent of the poundage of total fibers used in garments selling at $6.00 and over. Moreover, we assume that $0.2 million in profits has been earned by this fiber (in our single Market *A*) over the last year and that next year's sales at this price will also generate $0.2 million profits. From the equal-profit contour could be calculated the expected sales at some reduced price which would have to be made in order to provide equal profits under these static assumptions.

Further assume a total market size and composition by retail-price bracket for the coming year which is equal to last year's. (In practice, however, all of the above assumptions could be relaxed). Our principal unknown sets of states of nature are (*a*) the retail-price–fiber-price relationship and (*b*) the market-share–market-po-tential relationship.

Suppose that we wish to evaluate our expected net profits under two alternative prices, namely, $1.45 per pound and $1.25 per pound. To estimate first the possible new retail-price brackets which could be opened, the analyst would examine (*a*) the possible impact of the fiber price reduction on grey-fabric prices, (*b*) the impact of reduced grey-fabric prices on finished-fabric prices, and (*c*) the impact of reduced finished-fabric prices on new retail-price brackets which a fiber price reduction might possibly open.

Table 9–1 summarizes the manager's probability judgments about these alternative states of nature for each of the assumed price reductions.

As the foregoing table indicates, the lower price of $1.25 per

Table 9–1

POSSIBLE NEW RETAIL PRICE BRACKETS OPENED AND
PROBABILITY OF ATTAINMENT AS A FUNCTION OF FIBER PRICE

Fiber Price	$6.00 & Over	$5.00 & Over	$4.00 & Over	$3.00 & Over	$2.00 & Over	$1.00 & Over
$1.45/pound.....	1.00	.80	.50	.10	.00	.00
1.25/pound.....	1.00	.95	.75	.15	.05	.00

pound would be expected to offer a higher probability of opening new retail-price brackets for the fiber. However, the manager must still state his probability judgments regarding, now, the conditional probability of attaining different possible aggregate market shares, given that the fiber reaches each of the possible price brackets included. Aggregate share will be derived by considering possible share in each bracket (including retail-price brackets in which the fiber already competes), weighted by the relative importance of each bracket in terms of potential unit sales. Assume that the manager admits the following classes of aggregate market share, where probabilities of attainment are based upon the midpoint of the lowest retail-price bracket reached. As a reference point, current aggregate share under the prevailing price is 25 percent of the available potential. These conditional probabilities are noted in Table 9–2.

Using the Bayesian approach, first find the conditional expectation of share level Y, given the midpoint X of the lowest retail-price bracket reached under each fiber price. The results of these calculations are shown in the last two columns of Table 9–2. For example, under price equal to $1.45 per pound, the share 29.3 percent is the conditional expectation, given the midpoint of the lowest retail-price bracket to be $5.50. That is

$$29.3 = .35\ (32.5) + .65\ (27.5) + .00\ (22.5) + .00\ (17.5)$$

and so on for each conditional expectation.

Next, expect over these conditional expectations by applying the marginal probabilities assigned to the midpoint X of the lowest retail-price bracket reached (derived from Table 9–1). These calculations yield expected market shares of 28.1 percent and 29.3 percent, respectively, for the $1.45 and $1.25 per pound cases. Thus the standard formula

$$E\ [E\ (Y \mid X)] = \sum_{x} E\ (Y \mid X)\, f\ (X)$$

for finding expectations of conditional expectations is used.

Table 9-2

CONDITIONAL PROBABILITY OF ATTAINING SPECIFIC CLASS OF AGGREGATE MARKET SHARE, GIVEN ATTAINMENT OF (LOWEST) RETAIL-PRICE POINT

Midpoint or Lowest Retail Price Bracket (X)	Share Levels (Y) and Price Alternatives								Expected Value $E(Y \mid X)$	
	30–34.99%		25–29.99%		20–24.99%		15–19.99%			
	1.45/ lb.	1.25/ lb.	1.45/ lb.	1.25/ lb.	1.45/ lb.	1.25/ lb.	1.45/ lb.	1.25/ lb.	1.45/ lb.	1.25/ lb.
5.50	.35	.70	.65	.30	.00	.00	.00	.00	29.3%	31.0%
4.50	.30	.60	.55	.30	.15	.10	.00	.00	28.3%	30.0%
3.50	.25	.55	.55	.25	.15	.20	.05	.00	27.5%	29.3%
2.50	.20	.50	.55	.25	.20	.20	.05	.05	27.0%	28.5%
1.50	.15	.40	.40	.25	.25	.25	.20	.10	25.0%	27.3%

Cumulative sales potential, sales volume for the firm, and net profits are next derived, the results being noted in Table 9–3.

Table 9–3

SUMMARY FINDINGS UNDER EACH PRICE ALTERNATIVE

(All Figures in Millions)

	Comulative Sales Potential	The Firm's Sales		Costs and Profits	
Fiber Price	Pounds	Pounds	Dollars	Costs	Net Profits
$1.45/pound......	17.1	4.8	$7.0	$4.9	$2.1
1.25/pound......	23.5	6.9	8.6	6.3	2.3

As Table 9–3 indicates, next year's expected profits under *both* price reduction alternatives substantially exceed last year's profit level of $0.2 million under the prevailing price of $1.65 per pound.[4] Moreover, the lower price ($1.25 per pound) generates slightly larger net profits. These results are shown graphically in Figure 9–7.

Figure 9–7

PRICE–VOLUME RELATIONSHIPS IN MARKET A

(Application of Decision Model)

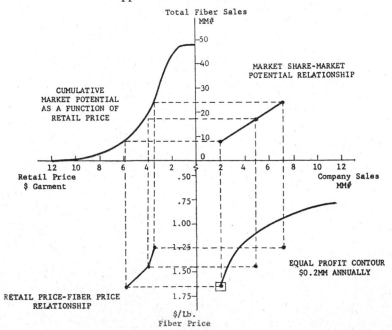

---

[4]In the foregoing exposition demand elasticities have been greatly exaggerated in order to illustrate the procedure graphically. In practice high elasticities are the exception rather than rule in this industry.

It is clear, however, that the manager obviously does not have to assess only two price alternatives. Athough this expository case has been restricted to this number, in practice other alternatives could be evaluated within the general framework outlined. Moreover, sensitivity analyses could be made of the behavior of any of the price alternatives under changed assumptions regarding either the probabilities and/or the range of admissible retail-price points under both the retail-price–fiber-price relationship and market-share–market-potential relationship. In an even more elaborate analysis, recognition could be given to emphasis on longer-range expected profits and the use of discounting. Moreover, by following up the results of a price change, Bayesian prior probabilities can be converted to posterior probabilities (assuming estimates of appropriate conditional probabilities can be derived.)

THE OUTLOOK FOR FUTURE RESEARCH IN PRICING ANALYSIS

The "state of the art" insofar as the planning of pricing strategy is concerned is still in need of much further development. While the marginal analysis of economic theory provides a normative model for making price decisions, in practice little is known about the relevant functions, particularly the demand schedule. Descriptively, the prevalent use of cost-based, administered pricing is probably indicative of the uncertainties associated with attempting to price by means of the marginal analysis as well as the risks attached to the impact of competitors' actions. By the use of "conventional practices" in pricing matters, firms try to assure themselves of greater certainty with respect to their environment, meanwhile electing to compete along nonprice lines like advertising, marketing services, and product improvement.

Nor do the techniques discussed earlier (regression analysis, experimentation) provide any easy, foolproof basis for measuring the firm's elasticity of demand with respect to price. The complex interaction of price with other marketing actions and the time-dependent nature of demand preclude any simple approach to optimal pricing action.

It seems reasonable to assume that future research on demand analysis will continue to use experimental procedures, but of an order of complexity much higher than exists today. Markov processes, as discussed in Chapter 7, will probably receive greater attention as a descriptive framework within which pricing experiments can be conducted. It is also likely that the techniques of system simulation and experimental gaming will receive increasing emphasis as researchers attempt to gain a better understanding of the interaction of price and nonprice courses of action. It is also possible that some of the more sophisticated models of *n*-person, nonzero sum game theory may find at least experimental application. But with all of these potential research avenues, pricing decisions will probably continue to reflect a large measure of the intuitive and adaptive approach by which they are characterized at present.

SUMMARY

This chapter has shown the relationship of pricing decisions to other marketing planning decisions and has pointed out some of the major problems of analysis. First the various classes of pricing decisions were discussed and the marginal analysis techniques of the economist were contrasted with what appears to be industry practice in setting price.

Next some of the procedures, namely, questionnaires, statistical analysis, and experimentation, which have been used in attempting to measure demand elasticity were discussed and some of the major limitations which these techniques possess were pointed out.

A Bayesian model was then formulated which incorporated field information with managerial judgment in estimating pertinent demand relationships and the use of equal-profit contours in making crude evaluations of alternative pricing actions was demonstrated. It was noted that these procedures have limitations as well, particularly when extended to deal with the dynamic character of demand changes through time.

The chapter concluded with some speculative comments regarding the directions in which future research on pricing decisions is likely to take.

Selected References

ALLEN, R. G. D. *Mathematical Analysis for Economists.* New York: Macmillan and Co., 1938.

> Provides basic material on the marginal analysis approach of economic theory and emphasizes the mathematical aspects of marginal analysis.

CASSADY, RALPH, JR. "The Time Element and Demand Analysis," *Theory in Marketing* (W. Alderson and R. Cox, eds.). Homewood, Ill.: Richard D. Irwin, Inc., 1950.

> Discusses some of the limitations of marginal analysis as it pertains to industrial pricing decisions and is concerned with enriching the economist's framework to deal better with the dynamic character of price changes.

EITEMAN, WILFORD J. *Price Determination in Oligopolistic and Monopolistic Situations.* Ann Arbor, Mich.: Bureau of Business Research, 1960.

> Discusses some of the limitations of marginal analysis as related to industrial pricing decisions and describes the role of uncertainty in demand analysis. Discusses some operational techniques for arriving at "optimal" prices.

GREEN, PAUL E. "Bayesian Decision Theory in Pricing Strategy," *Journal of Marketing*, Vol. 27, No. 1 (January, 1963).
    Describes an application of decision theory to the development of a long-range pricing strategy for an industrial product.

HAWKINS, EWARD R. "Methods of Estimating Demand," *Journal of Marketing*, Vol. 21, No. 4 (April, 1957).
    A survey of the various procedures (and their limitations) which have been applied to demand estimation.

PESSMIER, EDGAR A. "An Experimental Method for Estimating Demand," *Journal of Marketing*, Vol. 37, No. 4 (October, 1960).
    Reports the results of a simulation experiment designed to measure the demand for certain convenience goods.

SPENCER, M. H., AND SIEGELMAN, L. *Managerial Economics: Decision Making and Forward Planning*. Rev. ed. Homewood, Ill.: Richard D. Irwin, Inc., 1964.
    Provides basic material on the marginal analysis approach of economic theory. Discusses empirical studies in demand analysis as well as providing coverage of conceptual material.

Problems

1. The Kathy-Ann Doll Corporation is currently engaged in the production and marketing of the Kathy-Ann mechanical doll. The company is approaching the end of its fiscal year and is interested in setting optimum price and production rates for the coming year. In an attempt to apply the marginal approach to the solution of the optimum price–volume relationship for the Kathy-Ann mechanical doll, Mr. Huff, the company's chief economist, estimates that the following relationships hold:

1) Demand function or the Kathy-Ann mechanical doll on an annual basis:

$$Q = A - BP$$

Where

P = price per unit in dollars
A = 22,000 units
B = 1000 (units)/dollar

2) Cost function for the Kathy-Ann mechanical doll on a yearly basis:

$$C = D + EQ$$

Where

C = total yearly cost in dollars
D = fixed cost = \$5,000
E = variable cost per unit = \$15 per/unit
Q = quantity produced per year

a) What is the optimum price (under the marginal analysis approach) to charge for the Kathy-Ann mechanical doll, in the next fiscal year?

b) What is the optimum quantity (under the marginal analysis approach) of dolls that should be produced in the next fiscal year?

c) What is the total revenue that will be received by the corporation in the next fiscal year if the marginal approach to the optimum price–volume relationship is used?

d) What is the total profit that will be received by the corporation in the next fiscal year if the marginal approach to the optimum price–volume relationship is used?

e) What would the corporation's profit be if the price of the Kathy-Ann mechanical doll were $20.00 in the next fiscal year?

2. The Webb Company is currently engaged in the production and marketing of textile fibers used in the production of retail garments. The garments are marketed on a national scale. Since the company is considering a cut in textile fiber price, Mr. Sloan, the company's financial advisor, developed the following estimates of market response to pricing policies. (See Figure 9–3):

$$1.\ RPG = 4 \times FPP$$
$$2.\ TFS = 0.1 \times RPG^3 - 1.5\ RPG^2 + 50$$
$$3.\ CFS = 0.3 \times TFS$$

Where

FPP is fiber price per pound (dollars)

RPG is retail price per garment (dollars)

TFS is total fiber sales (millions of dollars)

CFS is company fiber sales (millions of dollars)

The company's costs are

Fixed cost = $2 million

Variable cost = $.40 per pound.

a) What is the relationship between company sales and price per pound for a fixed profit of $0.2 million?

b) What is the estimated profit when the price is $.50/pound, $1.00/pound, and $2.00/pound?

3. Describe the following: *a*) perfect competition, *b*) monopolistic competition, *c*) oligopoly, *d*) monopoly, *e*) marginal approach to pricing, *f*) cost-plus approach to pricing, *g*) rate-of-return approach to pricing, and *h*) administered approach to pricing.

4. Present a critique of the use of each of the following techniques for estimating demand relationships: *a*) questionnaire method, *b*) regression analysis, and *c*) experimental method.

Chapter 10

PROMOTIONAL DECISIONS AND THE EFFECTIVENESS OF SALES EFFORT

Of increasing importance to the task of marketing planning are decisions related to promotional effort, that is, advertising, packaging, displays, marketing services, and so on. This chapter is concerned with two broad (and interrelated) questions: (*a*) how much to spend, in total and among alternative activities, for promotion and (*b*) what procedures are available for measuring the response of sales to promotional stimuli. It will be seen that the current state of technique development does not permit definitive answers to either of these questions.

The general nature of promotion decisions, their relationship to other marketing decisions, and the difficulties inherent in measuring the consequences of alternative promotional plans are first described.

A description follows of the use of normative models, for example, the marginal analysis and dynamic programming techniques, for finding the "optimal" total budget and promotional mix under conditions of certainty. Then the influence of uncertainties on the relevant parameters is discussed and the difficulties encountered in determining the dynamic characteristics of sales response to promotional stimuli are commented upon.

The chapter concludes with some speculative comments on the direction of future research in this area. A technical appendix discusses briefly the underlying mathematics of various allocation procedures, for example, the calculus with Lagrange multipliers and dynamic programming, which have been proposed for dealing with the problem of promotional budget allocation.

PROMOTIONAL ACTIONS AND NONPRICE STRATEGY

No completely satisfactory and agreed-upon definition of promotion exists among either marketing practitioners or academicians. For purposes of this chapter "promotion" will be defined as any marketing effort whose function is to inform or persuade actual or potential consumers about the merits of a (given) product or service for the purpose of inducing a consumer either to continue or to start purchasing the firm's product or service at some (given) price. As such, promotion could include advertising, personal sales effort, packaging, point-of-purchase display, public relations, and so on.

The term "nonprice" strategy will be used to include all promotional activities and, in addition, tactics whose objectives are to adapt the *functional* properties of the product (for example, quality, size, performance attributes) to meet consumer wants. These definitions, while not completely satisfactory, do appear to agree reasonably well with prevailing conceptions about the two terms.

Nonprice activities (including promotion) share a common purpose, namely, to effect a favorable shift in the firm's demand curve through a change in the consumer's perception of the product. That is, at some given price, to the extent that nonprice actions are effective, it is assumed that consumers would demand more units of the product than they would have before. Ultimate measures of effectiveness, for example, profits, must then be determined by measuring the revenues and costs associated with alternative courses of action.

Nonprice competition has achieved a major role in today's oligopolistic industry and, at times, offers many advantages over direct price competition:

1. In contrast to direct price competition, nonprice action tends to produce indirect effects whose impact is harder to fathom by competitors and may thus be less susceptible to immediate retaliation. A strong advertising campaign, the introduction of a patented product feature, or a new package design produces less immediate impact on competitors. Hence, competitors must make efforts to evaluate the particular feature and decide upon the best way in which to retaliate.

2. But time is required in this evaluation process. Also, trademark restrictions, "sold-out" TV time, and so on, often prohibit immediate retaliation. Competitors may be put on the defensive with limited means for responding to the action.

3. Nonprice strategy can also provide a selective competitive weapon, subject to "stop-loss" action (if unsuccessful), which can be used in market segments which require bolstering without "spilling over" into stronger product-market areas where the firm is already doing well.

4. Nonprice competition appears less likely to lead to unstable, chaotic industry conditions and the chain-like competitive reaction often associated with direct price competition.

This is not to say that nonprice action is always preferable to price competition. It is to say, however, that means *other* than pricing action should at least be considered in the attempt to strengthen the firm's sales and market position.

As noted above, one important distinction between price and nonprice action is that nonprice activities, such as promotion and changes in product attributes, influence sales through a *shift* in the whole demand curve while price action involves a *movement along* the demand schedule. Thus, a firm may combine nonprice action with price action which could then involve a simultaneous shift in the total curve and a movement along the curve as noted in Figure

Figure 10-1

EFFECT OF SCHEDULE SHIFT AND PRICE REDUCTION
ON QUANTITY DEMANDED

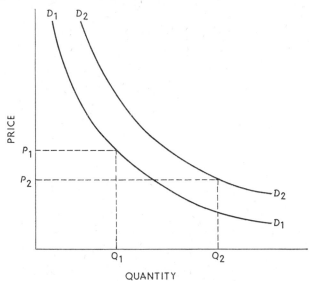

10-1. It is assumed in this illustration that the firm chose to couple a nonprice tactic (a stronger advertising campaign) with a slightly reduced price (in keeping with the image created by the new ad campaign). Figure 10-1 summarizes the combined impact of both actions.

While the apparent ease with which diagrams can be drawn might suggest that such problems are well structured, the fact remains that the actual determination of how much to spend, say, in total promotion and how to allocate the promotional budget among alternative means is an extremely involved problem for the following reasons:

1. *Interdependencies among promotion, product, price, and channel decisions.* Not only promotional expenditures but product design, pricing, and product availability can affect the firm's sales of the product.

➤ 2. *Multiproduct decisions.* Many firms produce a variety of products with various interrelated demands. An increase in promotion on one product may increase (or decrease) the sales of another of the firm's products.

3. *Competitors' interactions.* In making promotion decisions, the firm must not only consider other marketing actions of its own but also the effect on its sales and earnings through competitors' marketing actions, promotional or otherwise.

4. *Complexity of courses of action.* The allocation of a promotional budget among types (personal sales, broadcast promotion, point-of-purchase), among media (TV, radio, newspapers), among vehicles within media, and so on, can become exceedingly complex, if only due to the sheer number of possible alternatives.

5. *Difficulty of measuring sales response.* Before total budget and allocation problems can be solved, estimates must be obtained of sales response, as a function of level and mix of promotional effort. These measurements are difficult and costly to make, to say the least. Sales response will be some function of not only relative promotional effectiveness but also of relative price and availability, consumer incomes, previous promotional expenditures, and so on, insofar as these factors also influence industry sales and/or the firm's market share.

The preceding caveats should serve to point out the extremely tenuous basis on which promotional decisions can be approached scientifically. The determination of total budget size and the allocation problem is difficult on two major bases: (*a*) model building and (*b*) measurement of relevant parameters.

Discussion of the model-building phase will concentrate on the contributions which the marginal analysis and mathematical programming can make to total budget determination and allocation decisions. Discussion of the measurement phase will deal with experimental design techniques and the analysis of variance.

MARGINAL ANALYSIS AND "OPTIMAL" PROMOTIONAL DECISIONS

As was demonstrated in the preceding chapter, the marginal analysis provides a theoretical framework which is useful in answering basic allocation questions. In terms of promotional decisions, the questions might be phrased as follows:

1. How much should we spend on total promotion?
2. Given alternative ways to spend our promotional dollars, how should they be allocated among broad types of promotion, territories, media, and so on?

In the preceding chapter the rule, "equate the marginal revenue of the activity with its marginal cost," was used to answer the first question. To answer the second question the rule, "allocate funds among activities to levels where the marginal gain per dollar cost among all activities is equal," is used.

It will be seen that, in practice, application of the preceding rules assumes that quite a bit about the relevant revenue and cost functions is known (or assumed). A firm's sales depend, among other things, not only on the firm's promotional effectiveness relative to that of competitors but on relative price, product attributes, past promotional efforts, ability to supply, consumer tastes and incomes, and so on. Attempting to net out the effect of promotion, alone, is a difficult job, to say the least.

In this section of the chapter no attempt will be made to construct a global model which contains the many factors noted above. The purpose, rather, is to demonstrate the use of analytical techniques in fairly simple cases under certainty with regard to response functions. A discussion of some of the statistical techniques which have been used in an attempt to measure sales response to promotional effort will follow.

AN ILLUSTRATION OF TOTAL BUDGET DETERMINATION

Assume that a firm is desirous of determining how much it should spend on total promotion in order to maximize short-range profits. Assume that the firm knows its sales (units) response to promotion and this function takes the following form:

$$Q = a + \sqrt{bX}$$

where Q = sales units per time period, X = dollars of promotion, and a and b are parameters. A plot of this function is shown in Figure 10-2 for various values of X and with parameters a and b assumed to equal 500 and 100, respectively.

First, note from the chart that the firm still sells 500 units with no promotion, a reflection, perhaps, of past promotional efforts, consumer loyalty, and the like. Also, observe that equal increments of promotion lead eventually to smaller increments in sales, a reflection of the concept of diminishing returns which is usually assumed, incidentally, by economist and businessman alike.

Suppose that the firm's net profit, π is given by the equation:

$$\pi = PQ - [VQ + F + X]$$

where P = price in dollars per unit (assumed to be a constant);

Figure 10-2
ILLUSTRATION OF DIMINISHING RETURNS
ON ADDITIONAL PROMOTIONAL EXPENDITURES

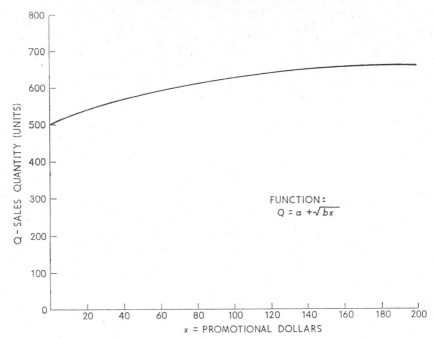

FUNCTION:
$Q = a + \sqrt{bx}$

x = PROMOTIONAL DOLLARS

Figure 10-3
BEHAVIOR OF TOTAL REVENUE, COST, AND PROFIT
AS A FUNCTION OF PROMOTIONAL EXPENDITURES

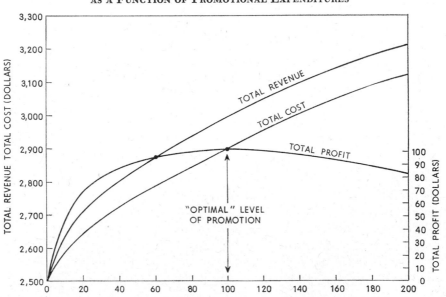

V = variable cost per unit exclusive of promotion; and F = fixed cost. Substituting the expression for Q, the total profit equation is then

$$\pi = P\,(a + \sqrt{bX}) - V\,(a + \sqrt{bX}) - F - X$$
$$= (a + \sqrt{bX})\,(P - V) - F - X$$

This function is plotted in Figure 10-3 for various values of X assuming that $P = \$5.00$ per unit, $V = \$3.00$ per unit, and $F = \$1,000$. Total revenue, PQ, and total cost $(VQ + F + X)$ are also plotted on the same chart, as a function of the amount of sales effort, X.

By standard calculus methods one can find the "optimal" amount to spend on promotion by differentiating the profit equation with respect to X, setting the derivative equal to zero, and then checking to see that second-order conditions are met. (Detailed calculations are shown in the appendix to this chapter.)

As can be inferred from the diagram of Figure 10-3, profits are maximized when $100 is spent on promotion. Total revenue, PQ, is $3,000 and total cost $(VQ + F + X)$ is $2,900, leaving a maximum profit, π, of $100. Notice that the difference between total revenue and total cost is greatest at an expenditure level of $100 for promotion.

Note must be made of several assumptions which underlie the use of the calculus in the above problem. First, it has been assumed that the values of all of the relevant variables were known exactly. Secondly, functions were chosen that were all "well behaved", continuous, and differentiable. Third, it has been assumed that the function had a maximum which did not lie on the boundary of the domain of the function. Finally, one should remember that the calculus only identifies local maxima or minima. In the case of "ill-behaved" function one would have had to examine all local extreme points in order to find *the* maximum or minimum. These difficulties become even more cumbersome when one is required to deal with several variables.

ALLOCATING PROMOTIONAL FUNDS
AMONG COMPETING ACTIVITIES

The preceding illustration involved the application of the marginal analysis to the determination of the "optimal" *total* promotional budget. At that, it was observed that the use of the calculus makes several rather restrictive assumptions about the nature of the response functions. When the scope of the problem is expanded to deal with allocation decisions, the conceptual and computational job becomes much more complex, often rendering application of the calculus less useful than alternative techniques.

While rule two, "allocate funds among activities to levels where the marginal gain per dollar cost among all activities is equal," is sound in principle, when one deals with practical allocation problems it may be extremely difficult, if possible at all, to use the calculus. Difficulties soon appear from a computational standpoint, even assuming that all functions are "well behaved" and that second-order conditions are met, that is, that a "true" maximum can be arrived at.

The use of the calculus in the problem of allocating promotional expenditures among several activities will not be explored in detail. The relevant mathematics for this case are covered in the appendix. It is well to point out here, however, that in allocating funds among alternative activities by means of the calculus, one may be faced with two types of problems. In one case, there may be no practical constraints on the total resource being allocated; while in the other case, there may be limitations on the amount of the resource available (for example, just so much promotional money may be available for allocation). If so, one can make use of another mathematical device, namely, the Lagrange multiplier technique. Use of this procedure is also explained in the appendix.

In summary, the calculus can be used in special cases for finding both that total promotional budget and its allocation among alternative activities which maximizes total profit. Moreover, by use of special techniques (Lagrange multipliers) the method can be extended to handle resource constraints of various types. Another very useful technique for making allocation decisions which overcomes many of the disadvantages of the calculus is now presented.

DYNAMIC PROGRAMMING IN BUDGET ALLOCATION

In recent years mathematicians have developed a series of techniques known as mathematical programming for making optimal allocations. A particularly useful subset of this class of techniques is dynamic programming, named by its developer, Richard Bellman (see References).[1]

The principal advantages of dynamic programming over other allocation techniques are that (*a*) the functions need not be linear or even continuous and (b) the procedure can be readily extended

---

[1]The mathematics underlying dynamic programming is discussed in the technical appendix to this chapter. In Chapter 11 another programming technique, linear programming, is discussed.

to deal with probabilistic as well as deterministic variables. The approach can perhaps be best explained by means of an illustrative application in which the payoff functions are nonlinear and discrete rather than continuous. The problem will be deliberately oversimplified so the dynamic programming solution can be compared more easily with the solution obtained by enumeration of all feasible allocations.

Assume that an advertising manager wishes to place three full-page advertisements in conjunction with a forthcoming promotional campaign for a new product. He has four different magazines at his disposal. These "activities" are labeled 1, 2, 3, and 4. Assuming that he wishes to allocate exactly three pages of advertising among four magazines, Table 10–1 summarizes the twenty possible allocations.

Table 10–1

POSSIBLE ALLOCATIONS: THREE ADVERTISEMENTS
AMONG FOUR MAGAZINES

									Allocations										
Magazine *1*	*2*	*3*	*4*	*5*	*6*	*7*	*8*	*9*	*10*	*11*	*12*	*13*	*14*	*15*	*16*	*17*	*18*	*19*	*20*
1.... 0	0	0	3	1	1	1	2	2	2	1	1	1	0	0	0	0.	0	0	0
2.... 0	0	3	0	0	0	2	1	0	0	1	1	0	1	0	0	2	1	1	2
3.... 0	3	0	0	0	2	0	0	1	0	1	0	1	1	1	2	1	2	0	0
4.... 3	0	0	0	2	0	0	0	0	1	0	1	1	1	2	1	0	0	2	1

As can be noted from Table 10–1, the manager has twenty possible selections in allocating exactly three advertisements to four possible magazines. For example, in allocation 1, he can place all three advertisements in magazine 4 and none in magazines 1, 2, and 3. Now assume that the manager can also estimate the behavior of net profit as a function of the number of advertisements placed in each magazine. These profit response functions are listed in Table 10–2 and are graphed in Figure 10–4.

As noted in Table 10–2, the various entries refer to total net profits (revenue minus cost) as a function of the number x of advertising pages placed in the ith magazine. In magazine 1 of total return first increases and then decreases as (it is assumed) diminishing returns set in. In magazine 4, however, the net payoff continues to increase as the number of advertisements increases. Notice further that the return functions are both discrete and nonlinear.

Figure 10–4

RESPONSE FUNCTIONS FOR FOUR HYPOTHETICAL MAGAZINES—
DYNAMIC PROGRAMMING ILLUSTRATION

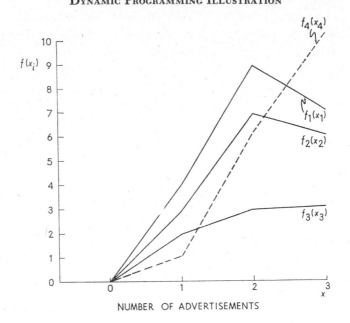

NUMBER OF ADVERTISEMENTS

Table 10–2

FUNCTIONAL RELATIONSHIP OF NET PAYOFF
TO NUMBER OF ADVERTISEMENTS

Number of Advertisements Placed in ith Magazine	$f_1(x_1)$	$f_2(x_2)$	$f_3(x_3)$	$f_4(x_4)$
x = 0............	0	0	0	0
x = 1............	4	3	2	1
x = 2............	9	7	3	6
x = 3............	7	6	3	10

In applying the dynamic programming model one would typically proceed in stages, that is, by first allocating the three advertisements among two magazines, then among three, and finally among four magazines. Consider the two-stage allocation first. If only two magazines were considered and the payoffs were assumed to be additive and independent, one could easily derive the total payoff associated with the two-magazine allocation, as shown in Table 10–3.

Table 10–3

TWO-MAGAZINE ALLOCATION

	Magazine 1	x_1	0	1	2	3
Magazine 2		$f_1(x_1)$	0	4	9	7
x_2	$f_2(x_2)$					
0	0		[0]	[4]	[9]	7
1	3		3	7	[12]	
2	7		7	11		
3	6		6			

The boxed entries in each diagonal of Table 10–3 show the maximum payoff associated with allocating 0, 1, 2, 3 advertisements between the two magazines. For example, the maximum total payoff associated with allocating exactly three advertisements is obviously the largest of the following numbers: $(f_1(0) + f_2(3))$, $(f_1(1) + f_2(2))$, $(f_1(2) + f_2(1))$, $(f_1(3) + f_2(0))$. As noted from Table 10–3 this maximum is 12 units. Each boxed entry represents the largest of each diagonal set of numbers. However, a more succinct way to summarize the results is

$$F(3) = \max_{0 \le x \le 3} [f_1(x) + f_2(3 - x)]$$

where x is an integer, 0, 1, 2, or 3, and F = net profits. More generally, to find the maximum payoff for A advertisements among two magazines,

$$F_2(A) = \max_{0 \le x \le A} [f_1(x) + f_2(A - x)]$$

Where $A = 0, 1, 2, 3$ and F_2 indicates the value of the function for the 2-stage allocation.

Now, however, the analyst would like to extend the problem to deal with the next stage, magazine 3. In this case it is clear the problem can be viewed as allocating 0, 1, 2, or 3 advertisements to magazine 3 and the rest to magazine 1 and/or 2. But the optimal assignment for magazines 1 and 2 is already known. Thus, the boxed return numbers of Table 10–3 can be used. The results are shown in Table 10–4.

Table 10–4
THREE-MAGAZINE ALLOCATION

Magazines 1 and 2	A	0	1	2	3
Magazine 3 $F_2(A)$		0	4	9	12
A-x $f_3(A\text{-}x)$					
0 0		$\boxed{0}$	$\boxed{4}$	$\boxed{9}$	$\boxed{12}$
1 2		2	6	11	
2 3		3	7		
3 3		3			

Again the highest payoffs on each diagonal of Table 10–4 are boxed. These numbers represent the optimal assignment of 0, 1, 2, or 3 advertisements to three magazines. Next, magazine 4 is introduced into the problem; the results are shown in Table 10–5.

Table 10–5
FOUR-MAGAZINE ALLOCATION

Magazines 1, 2, and 3	A	0	1	2	3
Magazine 4 $F_3(A)$		0	4	9	12
A-x $f_4(A\text{-}x)$					
0 0		$\boxed{0}$	$\boxed{4}$	$\boxed{9}$	$\boxed{12}$
1 1		1	5	10	
2 6		6	10		
3 10		10			

As it turns out, the assignment does not change. The optimal allocation is to assign two advertising pages to magazine 1 and one advertisement to magazine 2. Mathematically phrased, a particular case of the following general equation has been solved:

$$F_n(A) = \operatorname*{Max}_{0 \leq x \leq X} [F_{n-1}(A) + f_n(A - x)] \; ; \; n = 2, 3, \ldots$$

As can be inferred from the above, the general equation provides a means to solve the problem recursively. (Mathematical details are covered in the technical appendix). Furthermore, an absolute, not relative, extremum has been obtained. Finally, the functional forms need be neither continuous nor linear.

If, however, one wished to enumerate the payoff related to each of the 20 possible assignments, it would be seen that this solution agrees with the answer obtained by application of this step-by-step procedure, as shown in Table 10–6.

Table 10–6

ENUMERATION OF ALL POSSIBLE RETURNS

Magazine	*1*	*2*	*3*	*4*	*5*	*6*	*7*	*8*	*9*	*10*	*11*	*12*	*13*	*14*	*15*	*16*	*17*	*18*	*19*	*20*
1....	0	0	0	7	4	4	4	9	9	9	4	4	4	0	0	0	0	0	0	0
2....	0	0	6	0	0	0	7	3	0	0	3	3	0	3	0	0	7	3	3	7
3....	0	3	0	0	0	3	0	0	2	0	2	0	2	2	2	3	2	3	0	0
4....	10	0	0	0	6	0	0	0	0	1	0	1	1	1	6	1	0	0	6	1
	10	3	6	7	10	7	11	12	11	10	9	8	7	6	8	4	9	6	9	8

Table 10–6 is derived from Table 10–1 by merely inserting the functional values for each possible allocation. Notice that the optimal assignment is still two advertisements in magazine 1 and one advertisement in magazine 2, leading to a total profit of 12 units. In real problems, of course, the direct enumeration of all possible allocations would become hopelessly complex, while by application of dynamic programming one need only deal with finding the optimal policy for each stage as one moves from stage to stage.

Although this illustration was deliberately oversimplified, the technique of dynamic programming provides a very useful and flexible procedure for handling multistage problems under either deterministic or probabilistic conditions. And, in this problem it is interesting to note that the calculus could not have been used inasmuch as discrete, not continuous, return functions were being dealt with.

The reader may also notice a rather interesting analogy between the dynamic programming problem just covered and the technique which was used in Chapter 5 to solve sequential decision problems under uncertainty. Both make use of a recursive procedure in which the problem is solved one step at a time and then the next stage is attacked.

GENERAL CHARACTERISTICS OF ALLOCATION PROCESSES AND THEIR RELEVANCE TO PROMOTIONAL MIX DETERMINATION

While the use of analytical tools in the determination of the firm's promotional mix has been covered only briefly, one may already note that the problems attendant with using mathematical tools are considerable.

First, any analytical method employed (for instance, the calculus or dynamic programming) must consider the large number of *possible* alternatives which are typically associated with the allocation of promotional expenditures. For example, suppose the problem involves the allocation of a fixed print media budget among alternative vehicles, say, ten different journals. If the choice concerns the inclusion (or not) of any given journal, it is clear that allocation can be made in $(2)^{10}$ different ways or 1,024 possibilities. If problems of frequency, timing, and size of advertisement are relevant, the possible allocations can easily extend into the millions.

Second, the determination of suitable response functions constitutes a major problem in its own right. Up to now it has been assumed that these functions (sales, profits, and so forth) are given. In practice, by far the most difficult part of the allocation procedure is to estimate the form and parameters of the response functions, a problem which frequently involves the use of experimental design techniques.

EXPERIMENTAL DESIGN PROCEDURES IN MEASURING PROMOTIONAL EFFECTS

Most people view an experiment as a type of activity in which the researcher tries to hold constant all variables influencing the experiment's outcome except the variable which he is interested in studying. In marketing such opportunities are rarely, if ever, possible.

In recent years, however, statisticians have developed procedures which enable the experimenter to measure pertinent outcomes in cases where all variables cannot be controlled in the strict sense of the word. For example, suppose the researcher is interested in which of two package designs has greater sales appeal, that is, will result in greater sales volume. If the two package designs are called A and B and S_A and S_B stand for the sales of package designs A and B, respectively, then the researcher may be interested only in the difference between S_A and S_B or S_A-S_B.

Suppose the researcher attempts to carry out his experiment in two groups of stores over a certain time period. Obviously, sales in each group of stores will be a function of not only the factors under the researcher's control (that is, package designs) but uncontrolled variables as well, such as store traffic, T; competitive activity, C; weather, W; and a host of other variables. If the researcher is interested only in the sales *difference* due to package design, he might set up the following model which assumes that the effects of each variable on sales are additive:

$$S_i = S_A + S_T + S_C + S_W + \ldots \text{etc.}$$
$$S_j = S_B + S_T + S_C + S_W + \ldots \text{etc.}$$
$$S_i - S_j = S_A - S_B + 0 + 0 + 0 + \ldots \text{etc.}$$

That is, if the researcher can so design his experiment that the effects of other variables largely cancel out, he can use the actual sales difference of the ith store and the jth store as an estimate of the true sales difference which he would get if the experiment were repeated a large number of times.

Of course, the influence of store traffic, competitive activity, weather, and so on, may not be equal across each group of experimental stores. These differences can result in a tangling of the affects among the variables influencing sales. If the differences among individual pairs of stores $S_{i,A} - S_{j,B}$ are quite consistent over all pairs, then our confidence in the effect of the "treatments" A versus B would be higher than if these differences varied considerably from store pair to store pair. Moreover, the statistician can make use of various tricks (randomized blocks, switchover designs, covariance) in an attempt to net out the influence of variables under study. A major advance in statistical technique consists of randomizing the treatments over experimental units (so as to provide some protection against the introduction of systematic error) and the use of control groups.

To illustrate, suppose the experimenter groups the experimental units (stores) by sales volume prior to running the experiment. Assume that stores are classified as low, medium, and high sales volume and that there are two stores in each class. The experimenter could then assign package designs A and B at random to the two stores within each given size class. Suppose, unknown to the experimenter, that

1. Independent of package design, sales volume of the product would equal 10 units, averaged over all classes of stores.
2. The effects of store size (low, medium, and high) on sales are −2, 0, and +2 units, respectively.

3. The sales effect of design *A* is +3 units; effect of design *B* is −3 units.

Under these artificial conditions, Table 10–7 shows the results of the experiment, if *no other* variables influenced sales.

Table 10–7

HYPOTHETICAL SALES RESPONSES

	Low	Medium	High	
	Sales Volume Class			
Design *A*	11	13	15	39
Design *B*	5	7	9	21

As inferred from Table 10–7, the average treatment difference, S_A −S_B, is equal to 1/3 (39-21) or 6 units which, of course, equals 3 − (−3) or 6 units. That is, the effect of store class cancels out. Suppose, however, that only treatment *A* had been assigned to low-volume stores, only treatment *B* had been assigned to high-volume stores, and each treatment had been assigned to medium-volume stores. Results are shown in Table 10–8.

Table 10–8

ALTERNATIVE EXPERIMENTAL DESIGN

	Low	Medium	High	Total
	Sales Volume Class			
Design *A*	11	13	–	24
Design *B*	–	7	9	16

It can be inferred from Table 10–8 that the average sales difference, S_A −S_B, is equal to 1/2 (24-16) or 4 units rather than the "true" difference of 6 units. Obviously, the true difference has been understated because the effects of store size have not been balanced out. That is, what has been assumed to be a difference in treatments in this latter case reflects difference in sales volume class as well.

As oversimplified as the preceding illustration is, it does serve to point out the necessity for achieving balance in experimental design. Only in the category, "medium-volume class" has this been done in the design whose results are shown in Table 10–8.

ANALYSIS OF VARIANCE

Many experimental design models are of the above general type with the addition of one important ingredient, experimental error.

That is, in *real* situations other variables in addition to store size can be expected to influence a product's sales, independent of package design. The experimenter could hardly control all of these variables (for example, competitive activity, weather) even if he wanted to. He must usually resort to a statistical model which allows for the possible effects of uncontrolled variables on the outcomes of the experiments.

For example, suppose the researcher would like to test four package designs, *A, B, C,* and *D*. Moreover, he also feels that size of store is an important variable on sales; hence he wishes to take this factor into account by grouping all stores into, say, four size classes. Assume, further, that he feels that time effects are important as well. He would like to use each treatment for one week in each store and, hence, must extend the experiment over four weeks.

An appropriate model for this experiment is the so-called Latin Square design where each observation is assumed to be the algebraic sum of the named variables above plus experimental error:

$$X_{ijk} = \mu + A_i + B_j + C_k + E_{ijk} ; \quad \begin{aligned} i &= 1, 2, \ldots, a \\ j &= 1, 2, \ldots, b \\ k &= 1, 2, \ldots, c \end{aligned}$$

where X represents sales response to the ith package design, jth store class, and kth week. The E_{ijk} represents an additive factor due to the effect of "all other" variables. The model assumes that the mean effect of experimental error E_{ijk} is zero and that the observations are drawn independently from a normal universe with a constant variance, σ^2.

Statisticians have developed the technique of analysis of variance, abbreviated ANOVA, for dealing with models of the above type. The particular model above is known as a "fixed" model in which we assume that the overall mean μ, the treatment A_i, the store class B_j, and the week effect C_k are all fixed with respect to the model's parameters. Only the experimental error component E_{ijk} is a random variable with mean zero and a constant variance. Because of the influence of the E_{ijk}, individual cell values will reflect experimental error as well as the effect of the fixed factors. This experiment can be simulated by assuming the following values for the model components:

$$\mu = 20$$
$$A_1 = 5; A_2 = 1; A_3 = 0; A_4 = -6; \quad \Sigma \; A_i = 0$$
$$B_1 = 3; B_2 = 2; B_3 = -1; B_4 = -4; \quad \Sigma \; B_j = 0$$
$$C_1 = -2; C_2 = 0; C_3 = 1; C_4 = 1; \quad \Sigma \; C_k = 0$$

Table 10-9
RESULTS OF SIMULATED LATIN SQUARE DESIGN

Week	B_1	B_2	B_3	B_4
C_1	A_3	A_4	A_2	A_1
C_2	A_2	A_1	A_3	A_4
C_3	A_4	A_3	A_1	A_2
C_4	A_1	A_2	A_4	A_3

Experimental Results—Individual Effects

Week	B_1	B_2	B_3	B_4
C_1	$20 + 0 + 3 - 2 - 1 = 20$	$20 - 6 + 2 - 2 + 3 = 17$	$20 + 1 - 1 - 2 + 0 = 18$	$20 + 5 - 4 - 2 + 1 = 20$
C_2	$20 + 1 + 3 + 0 + 0 = 24$	$20 + 5 + 2 + 0 - 2 = 25$	$20 + 0 - 1 + 0 + 4 = 23$	$20 - 6 - 4 + 0 - 1 = 9$
C_3	$20 - 6 + 3 + 1 + 2 = 20$	$20 + 0 + 2 + 1 - 1 = 22$	$20 + 5 - 1 + 1 + 0 = 25$	$20 + 1 - 4 + 1 + 6 = 24$
C_4	$20 + 5 + 3 + 1 - 5 = 24$	$20 + 1 + 2 + 1 + 1 = 25$	$20 - 6 - 1 + 1 - 2 = 12$	$20 + 0 - 4 + 1 - 7 = 10$

Experimental Results—Combined Effects

Week	B_1	B_2	B_3	B_4	Row Total
C_1	20	17	18	20	75
C_2	24	25	23	9	81
C_3	20	22	25	24	91
C_4	24	25	12	10	71
	88	89	78	63	318

Now, however, some values for E_{ijk} need to be added. To simulate the effect of experimental error, one can make use of a table of random normal numbers (see the Snedecor reference at the end of the chapter) and assume that the relevant universe of "uncontrolled effects" has a mean of zero and a variance of 25. That is, a large urn can be visualized in which has been placed a large number of chips with a specific number written on each. The numbers are normally distributed with a mean of zero and variance of 25; hence one would expect about 95 percent of the chips drawn to have numbers within the range of $\mu \pm 2(5)$ or -10 to 10, and so forth. Suppose this drawing yields the numbers (rounded to nearest integer): -1, $+3$, 0, $+1$, 0, -2, $+4$, -1, $+2$, -1, 0, $+6$, -5, $+1$, -2, -7. The mean of *this sample* is $-2/16$ with a *sample* variance of only 9.5, a reflection of sampling variation.

With the above assumptions the experimenter is now ready to prepare Table 10–9 which shows how the "data" would look to one who was unaware of the values of the variables.

From the upper panel of Table 10–9 first note that each treatment (package design) appears once in each row (C_k) and each column (B_j). The individual effects from this dummy experiment are next shown; now the effect of sampling variation can be observed. Finally, the lower matrix shows the combined effect of each component and the marginal totals. Notice that the grand total is 318 rather than 320 (or 16×20) inasmuch as the sum of the sample E_{ijk} was equal to a minus two rather than zero.

Next the standard ANOVA technique can be applied by calculating the relevant sums of squares and mean squares for package design, store class, and display week. Calculations and summary numbers are shown in Table 10–10.

Table 10–10 shows the mechanics of developing the relevant sums of squares, mean squares and *F-ratios*. Using the notion of fixed factors, A_i, B_j, C_k, Table 10–11 indicates the "components of variance" which are being estimated.

By following through each of the calculations shown in Table 10–11 one can see how the various components of variance are estimated. Notice that the E_{ijk} effect is such as to lead to only *estimates* of (what are known to be) the "true variances" for the A_i's, B_j's and C_k's.[2]

---

[2]In the fixed effects model, the only *true* variance is that due to sampling error. Other "components of variance" really are estimates of the non-centrality parameters measuring departures of the observations from the various null hypotheses.

Table 10–10

ANALYSIS OF VARIANCE—PACKAGE DESIGN EXPERIMENT

Source of Variation	Degrees of Freedom	Sum of Squares	Mean Square	F Ratio
Package Designs—A_i........	3	206.25	68.75	6.71; $p < .05$
Store Classes—B_j...........	3	109.25	36.42	3.55; $p > .05$
Display Weeks—C_k.........	3	56.75	18.92	1.85; $p > .05$
Error....................	6	61.50	10.25	
Total...............	15	433.75		

Correction Factor: $C = \dfrac{(318)^2}{16} = 6320.25$

Total: $(20)^2 + (17)^2 + \ldots + (10)^2 - C = 433.75$

Rows: $(C_k): \dfrac{(75)^2 + (81)^2 + (91)^2 + (71)^2}{4} - C = 56.75$

Columns: $(B_j): \dfrac{(88)^2 + (89)^2 + (78)^2 + (63)^2}{4} - C = 109.25$

Treatments: $(A_i): \dfrac{(94)^2 + (91)^2 + (75)^2 + (58)^2}{4} - C = 206.25$

Error: Total − Rows − Columns − Treatments = 61.50

Table 10–11

VARIANCE COMPONENT ANALYSIS OF THE PACKAGE DESIGN EXPERIMENT

Source of Variation	Degrees of Freedom	Mean Square	Parameters Estimated
Package Designs—A_i...............	3	68.75	$\sigma^2 + 4\,K_A^2$
Store Classes—B_j....................	3	36.42	$\sigma^2 + 4\,K_B^2$
Display Weeks—C_k.................	3	18.92	$\sigma^2 + 4\,K_C^2$
Error...........................	6	10.25	σ^2

$$K_A^2 = \frac{A_i^2}{a-1} = \frac{(5)^2 + (1)^2 + (0)^2 + (-6)^2}{3} = 20.67$$

$$K_B^2 = \frac{B_j^2}{b-1} = \frac{(3)^2 + (2)^2 + (-1)^2 + (-4)^2}{3} = 10.00$$

$$K_C^2 = \frac{C_k^2}{c-1} = \frac{(-2)^2 + (0)^2 + (1)^2 + (1)^2}{3} = 2.00$$

Treatment mean square = 68.75 estimates $25 + 4\,(20.67) = 107.68$
Column mean square   = 36.42 estimates $25 + 4\,(10.00) = 65.00$
Row mean square   = 18.92 estimates $25 + 4\,(2.00) = 33.00$
Error mean square   = 10.25 estimates 25

The preceding calculations can be used to test the following null hypotheses:

H_o: All four package designs have the same effect on sales under the conditions of the experiment.

H_o:' All four store classes have the same effect on sales under the conditions of the experiment.

H_o:" All four display weeks have the same effect on sales under the conditions of the experiment.

The F ratios of Table 10–10 (with an alpha risk equal to .05) reveal the following:

H_o: Reject at alpha risk equal to .05.

H_o:' Accept at alpha risk equal to .05.

H_o:" Accept at alpha risk equal to .05.

That is, the sampling variance has been great enough to conceal the "true" effects of the B_j and C_k factors; only the A_i factor is "significant" at the alpha risk level equal to .05.

The presence of sampling variation (the E_{ijk}'s) has really complicated the experimenter's life. Note that when sampling variability is high, due to the effects of uncontrolled variables, even *real* differences do not show up to be significant, a warning for marketers who wish to conduct experiments on promotion types and levels.

CAUTIONS IN THE USE OF EXPERIMENTATION IN MEASURING RESPONSE TO PROMOTION

It has already been noted that the effect of sampling variability can mask the true response of sales to changes in promotional levels and types. Moreover, as may be recalled from elementary statistics, sampling error varies inversely with the *square root* of sample size. Even though one tries, through proper randomization techniques, to reduce the effect of systematic error, unless he uses extremely large sample sizes, the effect of uncontrolled variables may be quite discouraging to the researcher who wishes to estimate the response of sales to changes in promotion. Needless to say, marketing experiments can be quite expensive to conduct.

Second, it has been previously mentioned that sales response possesses a dynamic character, that is, changes over time in response to a whole series of variables. Marketing experiments of the type illustrated in the preceding section are usually limited to a "snapshot" of the market. By the time results are in, it is possible that relationships between sales and controllable variables may have changed.

Next, the possibility of other types of systematic error entering into the results of the experiment should also be considered. Experimental "units" (for example, store managements, consumers, and so on) may exhibit behavior different from that normally exhibited just because they are aware that an experiment is going on. Furthermore, in promotional experiments it is difficult to "wall in" the test zone. Consumers may talk to their neighbors; store managers may consciously or unconsciously take certain courses of action (for example, local promotion) which can bias the study's results.

Finally, the statistician's mystique of testing hypotheses—as illustrated in the Latin Square design—is not directly addressed to the central issue of why one conducts experiments and makes measurements in the first place, namely for gathering pertinent information for decision making purposes. As was noted in Chapter 5, the value of sample information may not be worth the cost of obtaining it.

This problem is again approached in the next section of this chapter, as marketing experimentation is viewed within a Bayesian framework.

MARKET EXPERIMENTATION WITHIN A BAYESIAN FRAMEWORK

The foregoing illustration on the use of the analysis of variance model in market experimentation has pointed out some of the statistical problems encountered in using experimental techniques in this substantive area. In this section of the chapter the approach to experimentation via a Bayesian framework is contrasted with that of traditional hypothesis testing involving analysis of variance models. As before, the illustration of the Bayesian approach is oversimplified and strictly apochryphal, the primary purpose being to emphasize the differences in approach.

The Alpha Vending Co. was a small firm specializing in the sale of soft drinks vended by machine. Its chief competitor, Beta Vending, had been increasing its share of the market, largely at Alpha's expense. Mr. Alpha, company president, asked his sales manager, Mr. Martin, for an explanation of the persistent decline noted in his firm's market share. Mr. Martin believed that the principal reason for their competitor's gains stemmed from the fact that Beta's vending machines were much more appealing to the consumer. With lavish chrome trim and colored lights which simulated a flow of bubbles, the attractiveness of Beta's machines were in marked contrast to the rather drab and strictly functional appearance of Alpha's machines. Since both firms offered the same variety of drinks and product quality was also comparable, Mr. Martin could offer no other reason for Beta's comparative gains.

Mr. Alpha addressed himself to the problem of improving his firm's "point-of-purchase" display, namely, the appearance of the vending machine itself. He speculated that by adding a more modern plastic front to his machines, a music box which played a thirst-inducing jingle, and a special slot which provided a fortune cooky with each drink, he could recapture his lost market share. With obvious glee he summoned Mr. Martin to his office and explained his new strategy.

Mr. Martin listened patiently to the new scheme and promised to report back to Mr. Alpha as soon as he had obtained some information bearing on the problem. After several consultations with vending machine engineers, he told Mr. Alpha that costs incurred in machine conversion, including lost profits on sales which could have been made during the conversion period, would amount to $48,000, a cost of $480 per machine for the 100 machines which Alpha owned. Moreover, the gross margin per dollar of sales would decline from 30 percent to 25 percent, due to higher materials cost (the fortune cookies) and more expensive machine maintenance. But if smaller cups and a weaker syrup solution were used, present margins could be maintained.

Mr. Alpha insisted on the maintenance of present quality and quantity. He then asked Martin just how much the monthly increase in sales per machine would have to be in order to justify the conversion expense and the lower gross margin. After careful calculation Mr. Martin replied that monthly gross sales would have to increase $200 (over next year's forecasted level of $200 per machine) just to break even.[3] This assumed that a one-year payoff of added investment was required. His interest in a short payout period resulted from the fear that Beta Vending would probably imitate the innovation relatively quickly if a marked reversal occurred in the trend of their share.

Mr. Alpha, a bit sobered by the financial implications of his

---

[3]The breakeven value of (μ_b) of $400 sales per machine per month, on the assumption of 100 machines in operation, is found by the equation:

$$.25\ \mu_b = .30\ (\$200) + \frac{\$48,000}{12 \times 100}$$

$$.25\ \mu_b = \$60 + \$40$$

$$\mu_b = \$400$$

In terms of differences, an increase of $200 over the next year's $200 monthly sales level, anticipated without conversion, would be required.

strategy, still felt that the idea had merit. He proposed an experiment as follows: (*a*) take 15 of Alpha's present vending machines as prototypes and convert them to the new design; (*b*) choose 15 other Alpha machines as a control; (*c*) select at random 30 different machine locations; place the 15 converted machines in half of these locations and the control group in the second half, positions being selected at random; (*d*) after recording sales for each machine for one month, place the converted machines in locations in which the control machines had been installed and vice versa; then record sales for each machine during the second month; (*e*) at the end of the two-month period, for each machine location, subtract the observed sales of the control machines from the observed sales of the converted machines; and (*f*) calculate the mean difference of sales over all locations.

Under Mr. Alpha's direction the experiment was carried out. The average increase in sales of the converted machines amounted to $190 per machine per month.[4] The sample standard deviation of the sales differences, which was based on 30 observations, amounted to $82. Noting that the sample mean difference was $10 under the $200 increase required to break even, Mr. Alpha was still perplexed as to which course of action to adopt.

Mr. Martin replied that he could render assistance. First, he asked Mr. Alpha what betting odds he would have chosen, before undertaking the experiment, regarding the possible real difference in sales if the new strategy were adopted across the board. Mr. Alpha replied that in his judgment he could not conceive of any chance that the mean sales difference could be negative, that is, that present Alpha machines could outsell the newer design. Upon further reflection he felt that he could quantify his betting odds in even more explicit terms, as shown in Table 10–12.

Mr. Martin replied that, if Mr. Alpha had acted on the basis of his prior judgments alone, he would have proceeded with the conversion of all machines to the new design since the mean difference would have exceeded the $200 increase per machine deemed necessary to break even. But with the sample results available, Mr. Martin wondered if the conversion of the machines was still desirable. Mr. Martin first addressed himself to the question: how likely was

---

[4]A more interesting but more complex question is whether or not the experiment should have been undertaken at all. That is, would the expected gain of the information be worth the cost incurred to get the information? Questions of this type involve preposterior analysis of the type covered in Chapter 5.

Table 10–12

MR. ALPHA'S PRIOR PROBABILITIES FOR VENDING MACHINE PROBLEM

Prior Probability Assignment	Mean Sales Difference: New vs. Old (Dollars per Machine per Month)	Expected Value
0.00	Under 100	$ 0.00
0.10	100–150	12.50
0.30	150–200	52.50
0.50	200–250	112.50
0.10	250–300	27.50
0.00	Over 300	0.00
		$205.00

it that he would get the experimental results he did get under each one of the states of nature Mr. Alpha thought possible to occur?

To answer this question, Mr. Martin first calculated the conditional probability of getting the sample difference, $190, under each possible state of nature, using the midpoints of the ranges shown in Table 10–12. The results are noted in Table 10–13.

Table 10–13

CONDITIONAL PROBABILITIES FOR VENDING MACHINE PROBLEM

Possible Differences	Midpoint	$Z = (\bar{x} - \mu)/(\sigma_{\bar{x}})$	Ordinate	$P(\bar{x} \mid \mu)$
$100–$150............	$125	$(190 - 125)/15$	.00004	.00004 $\Delta \bar{x}/15$
150– 200............	175	$(190 - 175)/15$	.23200	.24200 $\Delta \bar{x}/15$
200– 250............	225	$(190 - 225)/15$	.02833	.02833 $\Delta \bar{x}/15$
250– 300............	275	$(190 - 275)/15$	.00000	.00000 $\Delta \bar{x}/15$

Mr. Martin first calculated the standard error of the mean ($\sigma_{\bar{x}}$) by the conventional formula:

$$\sigma_{\bar{X}} = \frac{\sigma}{\sqrt{n}}$$

Since his sample size n equalled 30, he was willing to assume that the population deviation was equal to the sample measure ("large sample" theory) and was also willing to disregard use of a finite multiplier. Hence,

$$\sigma_{\bar{X}} = \frac{82}{\sqrt{30}} \approx 15.$$

The fourth column of Table 10–13, labeled "ordinate," represents the height of the standardized normal curve at each Z value shown in the third column. The last column, $P(\bar{x} \mid \mu)$, represents the conditional probability of getting the sample difference, $190, given the midpoint of each admissible interval of mean sales differences. This probability is a product of "height" (ordinate) times "width" ($\Delta \bar{x}/15$) of the density function.

Mr. Martin was then ready to apply Bayes' theorem in a fashion similar to its use in Chapter 5. He derived Table 10–14 by combining Mr. Alpha's prior probabilities (Table 10–12) with the conditional probabilities calculated in Table 10–13 and then calculated the posterior probabilities.

Table 10–14

POSTERIOR PROBABILITIES FOR VENDING MACHINE PROBLEM

State of Nature	Prior Probabilities	Conditional Probabilities	Joint Probabilities	Posterior Possibilities
$125......	.10	.00004 $\Delta \bar{x}/15$	.000004 $\Delta \bar{x}/15$	.00
175......	.30	.24200 $\Delta \bar{x}/15$	.072600 $\Delta \bar{x}/15$	.84
225......	.50	.02833 $\Delta \bar{x}/15$	.014165 $\Delta \bar{x}/15$	.16
275......	.10	.00000 $\Delta \bar{x}/15$	.000000 $\Delta \bar{x}/15$	.00
			.086769 $\Delta \bar{x}/15$	1.00

Next Mr. Martin applied the posterior probabilities of Table 10–14 to the admissible states of nature and derived a new expected value based on the combined judgmental and sample evidence:

$$E.\ V. = .00\ (125) + .84\ (175) + .16\ (225) + .00\ (275) = \$183.$$

To Mr. Alpha's dismay, the expected value of the new strategy turned out to be less than the $200 mean sales difference required to justify the conversion strategy. Hence, he chose not to make the machine conversion.

CONTRASTS BETWEEN BAYESIAN AND TRADITIONAL APPROACHES TO MARKET EXPERIMENTATION

As oversimplified as these hypothetical illustrations were, it is of interest to point out that the Bayesian approach emphasized the decision aspects of experimentation, including the following:

1. The conditional payoffs related to the alternative courses of action and states of nature pertinent to the problem.
2. The prior experience of the decision maker.
3. The incorporation of sample results with prior experience and beliefs.

From the standpoint of promotion planning, however, it would seem that the major advantage of Bayesian techniques over traditional experimental models is that the former procedure provides a framework for "bounding" the problem, that is, for estimating whether additional information is needed at all, and if so, what type of information to collect and how much to spend for it.

Traditional analysis of variance models have a much longer history than do Bayesian models and, consequently, their underlying structure is more fully developed. It is to be expected that future developments in Bayesian statistics will provide counterparts for the varied models which already exist in the analysis of variance class of techniques.

FUTURE RESEARCH IN THE ALLOCATION OF PROMOTIONAL EXPENDITURES

As mentioned in the introduction to this chapter, the problem of total promotional budget determination and its allocation among alternative promotional activities is still largely unsolved. While several allocation models have been proposed (for example, the calculus, mathematical programming techniques) the fact remains that these models assume that quite a bit is known about the response of sales to promotional levels and types.

As was noted in the brief description of analysis of variance models, experimental (and systematic) error may be quite high in experimental and general measurement tasks which are conducted in marketing environments. It would thus appear that future research in promotional allocation problems will deal as much (if not more) with techniques for measuring sales response as with the allocation models themselves.

With respect to the latter research area, however, it is interesting to note that several research projects are currently under way in the construction of models for allocating advertising expenditures among media. The large advertising agencies appear to be spearheading these efforts. Early models which have been developed use such techniques as linear programming, Markov chain analysis, and computer simulation. (See references at the end of this chapter.)

The measurement of sales response to promotional activity is also getting increased research attention by large industrial firms and retailers. Studies are being conducted in a more or less continuous fashion on sales response, often employing panel data and Markov analysis in addition to more classical experimental designs like factorial layouts, randomized blocks, and Latin Squares.

With regard to future research in the measurement of sales response to promotion and the problem of expenditure allocation, it would appear that several new techniques will be used to an increasing extent. Some progress is being made in learning theory; psychologists are gaining sharper insights into how people perceive and remember. It would appear that "laboratory-scale" experimentation coupled with panel data might provide a framework for measuring response to promotional activity at a reasonable cost. From the standpoint of allocation models, much of the newer research in mathematical programming is concerned with multistage problems under conditions of risk and uncertainty, the type of environment faced by the marketer. Moreover, recent work in operational gaming and simulation models should provide some insight into the behavioral process of search, choice, and implementation of courses of action.

While future research in this area appears promising, this is not to imply that all promotional decisions will be reduced to mere calculational routines, but, less ambitiously, that quantitative analysis may permit the decision maker to concentrate his attention on those aspects of promotional decision making which cannot be reduced to straightforward computation, simple or complex.

SUMMARY

This chapter has viewed the problem of total budget and mix determination within the framework of choice models and measurement of sales response. A simple illustration of the calculus in answering the question of how much to spend on total promotion was first discussed. The limitation of this technique became readily apparent as the problem of promotional mix determination was described. It was then shown, via a simple advertising illustration, how the technique of dynamic programming can be used to make allocations when the nature of the response function does not permit the use of standard calculus techniques.

Some of the problems attendant with measuring response to promotional stimuli were discussed and the traditional approach to experimentation was illustrated by means of a discussion of the Latin Square design. This approach was contrasted with a simplified illustration on the use of Bayesian analysis in experimentation.

The chapter concluded with some speculative comments on the directions which future model building and measurement research may take in the substantive area of promotional decisions.

Selected References

ALLEN, R. G. D. *Mathematical Analysis for Economists*. New York: Macmillan & Co., 1950.
   Gives the reader excellent material on the use of the calculus in microeconomic theory. A classic in this field which covers marginal analysis, partial differentiation, Lagrange multipliers, and the calculus of variations.

BELLMAN, RICHARD E. *Dynamic Programming*. Princeton, N.J.: Princeton University Press, 1962.
   Definitive, but mathematically advanced, work on dynamic programming.

BELLMAN, RICHARD E., AND DREYFUS, STUART E. *Applied Dynamic Programming*. Princeton, N.J.: Princeton University Press, 1962.
   Mathematically advanced work which emphasizes solution techniques in dynamic programming.

COX, D. R. *Planning of Experiments*. New York: John Wiley & Sons, 1958.
   Lucid, introductory material on experimental design.

FRANK, RONALD E. "Brand Choice as a Probability Process," *Journal of Business*, Vol. 35, No. 1 (January, 1962).
   Discusses the Markov model as a framework for analyzing consumer purchase behavior.

GREEN, PAUL E. "Bayesian Decision Theory in Advertising," *Journal of Advertising Research*, Vol. 2, No. 4 (December, 1962).
   Represents an extension of the hypothetical experiment discussed in this chapter.

ST. GEORGES, JOSEPH. "How Practical Is the Media Model?" *Journal of Marketing*, Vol. 27, No. 3 (July, 1963).
   Comments on the use and limitations of the media allocation models now being used by the major advertising agencies.

SNEDECOR, GEORGE W. *Statistical Methods*. Ames, Iowa: Iowa State College Press, 1956.
   Provides clear, introductory material on experimental design. Illustrates several analyses of variance models by means of "dummy" experiments, similar to the approach followed in this chapter.

TINTNER, GERHARD. *Mathematics and Statistics for Economists*. New York: Rinehart & Co., 1953.
   Gives excellent material on the use of the calculus in microeconomic theory. In addition to coverage of the calculus as applied to economic problems has a section on statistical methods.

VAZSONYI, A. *Scientific Programming in Business and Industry*. New York: John Wiley & Sons, Inc. 1958.
   A good introduction to programming techniques in general. The notation used in the dynamic programming example of this chapter follows Vazsonyi's treatment of this subject.

WEINBERG, ROBERT. *An Analytical Approach to Advertising Expenditure Strategy*. New York: Association of National Advertisers, Inc., 1960.
   Excellent material on the use of the calculus in microeconomic theory. Provides a highly readable section on marginal analysis as well as several illustrations of his multiple factor model.

WILSON, C. L., AND MANELOVEG, H. "A Year of L. P. Media Planning for Clients," *Proceedings of the Midwest Conference of the Advertising Research Foundation* (November, 1962).
   Comments on the use and limitations of the media allocation models, now being used by the major advertising agencies.

Technical Appendix—Chapter 10

This section of the chapter describes briefly (*a*) the mathematics underlying the problem of determining the "optimal" total budget described in the text, (*b*) the general nature of allocation processes, (*c*) the use and limitations of the calculus in solving allocation problems, and (*d*) the structure of mathematical programming techniques.

MATHEMATICS UNDERLYING THE DETERMINATION OF THE TOTAL PROMOTIONAL BUDGET

The reader will recall the equations which represented the response function and profit function:

$$Q = a + \sqrt{bX}$$

Where

$$Q = \text{sales units}$$
$$X = \text{promotional dollars}$$

a, *b* are parameters to be estimated (*a*, *b* > 0)

$$\pi = P\,(a + \sqrt{bX}) - V\,(a + \sqrt{bX}) - F - X$$
$$= (a + \sqrt{bX})\,(P - V) - F - X$$

Where

$$\pi = \text{total profits}$$
$$P = \text{price in dollars/unit}$$
$$V = \text{variable cost in dollars/unit}$$
$$F = \text{fixed cost in dollars}$$

To find the optimal promotional expenditure X which maximizes profits differentiate the profit equation with respect to X, set the derivative equal to zero, and solve for X. Then take the second derivative of the profit equation and check to see if this expression is negative.

$$\frac{d\,\pi}{d\,X} = \frac{b}{2\,\sqrt{bX}}\,(P - V) - 1 = 0$$

$$\frac{b\,(P - V)}{2} = \sqrt{bX}$$

$$\frac{b^2\,(P - V)^2}{4} = bX$$

$$X = \frac{b\,(P - V)^2}{4}$$

Let

$$b = 100;\ P = \$5;\ \text{and}\ V = \$3$$

$$X = \frac{100\,(5 - 3)^2}{4}$$

$$X = \$100\ \text{(optimal promotional expenditure)}$$

Second Order Conditions

$$\frac{d^2\pi}{dX^2} = \frac{-b^2(P-V)}{4\sqrt{(bX)^3}} \left| \frac{d\pi}{dX} = 0; \; X = \frac{b(P-V)^2}{4} \; \text{at} \frac{d\pi}{dX} = 0 \right.$$

$$= \frac{-b^2(P-V)}{4\sqrt{b^3(\frac{1}{4})^3 b^3[(P-V)^2]^3}}$$

$$= \frac{-b^2(P-V)}{4b^3 \frac{1}{8}(P-V)^3}$$

$$= \frac{-2}{b(P-V)^2} < 0, \text{ since } b \text{ is positive}$$

THE GENERAL NATURE OF ALLOCATION PROCESSES

Allocation processes play a dominant role in both microeconomic theory and operations research. Descriptively, an allocation process can be viewed as follows:[5]

Suppose a certain quantity of resources, for example, money, men, machines, and so on, are available. Each resource can be used in a variety of ways which will be called activities. Insufficient resources exist for performing each activity in the most efficient way. As a result of assigning resources to activities a certain payoff is derived. The payoff may or may not be expressible in terms of the units in which the resources are measured. Moreover, the payoff may be either deterministic or probabilistic. The magnitude of the payoff depends upon the type and quantity of the various resources used in the various activities. The basic problem is that of allocating resources to activities in such a way as to maximize (or minimize) the total payoff.

The basic assumptions underlying most allocation models are

1. The payoffs from different activities can be measured in some common unit, for example, dollars.
2. The return from any activity is independent of the allocation of resources made to other activities.
3. The total payoff can be computed as the algebraic sum of the individual payoffs.

Some of the models which have been proposed to deal with the general problem of allocation can next be examined.

THE USE AND LIMITATIONS OF THE CALCULUS

Optimization problems in the calculus can be viewed under two categories: (*a*) unconstrained solutions, and (*b*) constrained solutions. The method of unconstrained optima is based on the familiar procedure of taking partial derivatives of the payoff function with respect to each variable, setting the derivatives equal to zero, and solving the resulting set of simultaneous equations. When solutions are constrained, the

---

[5]The treatment of this section follows that of Bellman and Dreyfus, *op. cit.*, pp. 4–13.

Lagrange multip'ier is used to find relative extrema. To illustrate the unconstrained case, consider the following function:

$$V(X_1, X_2, \ldots, X_n) = f_1(X_1) + f_2(X_2) + \ldots + f_n(X_n)$$

The partial derivatives, $f_i'(X_i)$ are set equal to zero.

$$f_i'(X_i) = 0, \ (i = 1, 2, \ldots, n)$$

and the resultant set of equations is solved. Second order conditions must, of course, be met.

If a constraint of the form, $X_1 + X_2 + \ldots + X_n = X$ is relevant, the maximand with λ, the Lagrange multiplier, is formed as follows:

$$V(X_1, X_2, \ldots, X_n) = f_1(X_1) + f_2(X_2) + \ldots + f_n(X_n) \\ - \lambda(X_1 + X_2 + \ldots + X_n - X)$$

In this case the following equations are formed:

$$f_i'(X_i) - \lambda = 0, \ (i = 1, 2, \ldots, n)$$

and the resultant set plus the derivative of the constraint equation is solved. A necessary condition for a maximum or minimum is that all first order partials are zero. Sufficient conditions are more difficult to state inasmuch as the function may involve a saddle point rather than a maximum or minimum.

As an illustration, consider the following function in two variables. (Assume that second order conditions are met.)

$$V = 4x + 17y - x^2 - xy - 3y^2$$

Suppose, first, that the variables x and y are not constrained.

$$\frac{\partial V}{\partial x} = 4 - 2x - y = 0$$

$$\frac{\partial V}{\partial y} = 17 - x - 6y = 0$$

$$\text{Max}(x) = 7/11$$
$$\text{Max}(y) = 30/11$$

Now assume that the following constraint is imposed: $x + 2y = 7$. Using the Lagrange multiplier λ, we form the equation

$$V = 4x + 17y - x - xy - 3y - \lambda(x + 2y - 7)$$

It is also clear that $(x + 2y - 7) = 0$. Next, we differentiate V with respect to x and y and add the conditional equation, $x + 2y - 7 = 0$.

$$\frac{\partial V}{\partial x} = 4 - 2x - y - \lambda = 0$$

$$\frac{\partial V}{\partial y} = 17 - x - 6y - 2\lambda = 0$$

$$\frac{\partial V}{\partial \lambda} = -7 + x + 2y = 0$$

Rel. Max $(x) = 1$

Rel. Max $(y) = 3$

$$\lambda = 1$$

Notice in this case that when the domain over which x and y are allowed to vary is constrained, the values of x and y which maximize the function V change.

To employ the method of the calculus and Lagrange multipliers it is clear that the function must possess continuous partial derivatives, a condition which may represent a poor approximation to many real problems. Moreover, several other deficiencies are associated with the method of the calculus.

First, the vanishing of derivatives represents only a necessary, not sufficient, condition for finding extrema. Horizontal points of inflection will satisfy this condition as well. This means that in multidimensional cases many possible combinations of values may have to be computed in order to identify extrema.

Further, in addition to the problem of approximating discrete functions by continuous functions (in order to use the calculus), some functions, while continuous, are not differentiable. Other functions may only be differential, piecewise. This latter set increases the complexities involved in finding extrema.

Next, an important set of functions consists of linear functions. Calculus is of no help here since the relative extrema must be located at boundary points on the function's range.

Finally, the calculus (being based on continuous variation) is quite sensitive to small errors of measurement. Errors in the values identified as extrema may be much worse than errors in the initial measurements.

In summary, the classical methods of the calculus presuppose a number of considerations which rarely approximate the data available regarding multidimensional systems.

MATHEMATICAL PROGRAMMING TECHNIQUES

Mathematical programming is a term used to describe a variety of optimization techniques—linear programming, quadratic programming, dynamic programming, and so on. In this section two subsets of this class of procedures, linear programming and dynamic programming, are described briefly. (See Chapter 11 for a special application of linear programming—the transportation method—to a problem involving the routing of materials from warehouse to distribution.)

Linear programming, an important subset of mathematical programming techniques, involves the special case of optimizing a linear function subject to a set of linear constraints. We wish to maximize (minimize) the following:

$$V = \sum_{j}^{n} c_j\, x_j$$

Where

$$x_j \geqslant 0 \text{ and } \sum_{j}^{n} a_{ij}\, x_j \leqslant b_i\,;\, i = 1, 2, \ldots, m;$$
$$j = 1, 2, \ldots, n;$$

and the a_{ij}, b_i, and c_j are given parameters.

This tool assumes, of course, that all functions are linear. Nonlinear functions can sometimes be handled by special techniques, convex programming, for example. Care must also be exercised in the choice of constraints; some types of redundant constraints will lead to what are known as degenerate situations.

The original linear programming formulations assumed that all values in the effectiveness and constraint functions were known and fixed. Current variations of linear programming permit varying the parameters (parametric programming) or using probability distributions of the parameters (stochastic programming). Linear programming has also been extended to deal with dynamic processes (optimization over a set of time periods), basically by extending the static or one-period case.

Probably the least restrictive of all allocation models is the technique of dynamic programming. Functions need not be linear or even differentiable. Furthermore, the technique can be readily expanded to deal with probabilistic as well as deterministic variables. Dynamic programming is particularly well adopted to deal with multistage decision problems. Consider the arbitrary function

$$V(x_1, x_2, \ldots, x_n) = f_1(x_1) + f_2(x_2) + \ldots + f_n(x_n)$$

where $x_i \geqslant 0$ and $\sum_{j}^{n} x_i = X$

As was noted in the illustration of this chapter, dynamic programming approaches this problem by means of a recurrence relation and the use of functional equations. Since multistage decisions usually concern the time variable, it is not surprising to find that dynamic programming is particularly applicable to time-dependent processes, either deterministic, probabilistic, or adaptive. While both the calculus and linear programming would attack the multistage problem by using one gigantic set of equations (if the stringent assumptions underlying these methods were met), dynamic programming solves the overall problem by solving one step of the problem at a time.

With respect to the above problem it is first to be noted that the maximum, V, depends upon both X and n. We thus introduce:

$$G_n(X) = \text{Max } V(x_1, x_2, \ldots, x_n)$$

where $n = 1, 2, \ldots n;\, x_i \geqslant 0;$ and $\sum_{i} x_i = X.$

Moreover, $G_n (0) = 0$; $n = 1$, 2, etc., provided that $f_i (0) = 0$ for each i.

Also $G_1 (X) = f_1 (x)$ for $x \geqslant 0$.

The basic functional equation becomes

$$G_n (X) = \underset{0 \leq x \leq X}{\text{Max}} [f_n (x_n) + G_{n-1} (X - x_n)]$$

Bellman's Principle of Optimality expresses the above situation thus: "An optimal policy has the property that whatever the initial state and initial decision are, the remaining decisions must constitute an optimal policy with regard to the state resulting from the first decision."[6]

Problems

1. What is the "standard error of the mean?" What size sample would be necessary from a normal distribution, with $\mu = 25$, $\sigma^2 = 6.25$, to be 95% "confident" that your results would be within 1% of the true mean?

2. The Leggums Company, a medium-size producer of nonalcoholic cocktail mixes, is not presently engaged in commercial advertising. The Leggums Company plant is operating near capacity, but the product manager feels that an increase in sales may result from commercial advertising. The production department estimates that the incremental cost of production can be closely approximated by the following:

Incremental cost = (constant) × (incremental sales quantity)

$$I_c = C_1 \times Q^2$$

where Q is the change in units in quantity sold. The advertising manager feels the dollar volume of sales would change directly with the amount spent for commercial advertising:

Incremental quantity = (constant) × (advertising expenditure)

$$Q = C_2 \times X$$

where X is advertising expenditures (in dollars).

a) Given P, the selling price, find the expression for the incremental profit associated with initiating commercial advertising. (Note: There is no fixed cost in this expression.)

b) If $C_1 = .0008$, $C_2 = 2.5$, and $P = \$2$ what is the incremental profit when $X = \$500.00$?

c) What is the value of X that maximizes profit?

3. Distribution, Inc. supplies construction contractors in the Philadelphia area with small orders and odd lots of construction materials and accessories. The dispatch manager, Mr. Lome, has designed six delivery loops which, with minor deviations, cover all the major building areas in the city. Mr. Lome would like to allocate fourteen trucks his company

---

[6]Richard Bellman, "Some Applications of the Theory of Dynamic Programming—A Review," *Journal of the Operations Research Society of America*, August, 1954, pp. 275–88.

has to the six routes so as to maximize the gross margin on sales for all routes, per day. He estimates that operating cost for these trucks is $90.00 per day per truck, and the gross margin on sales for each route is shown in Table 10–15.

Table 10–15

GROSS MARGIN ON SALES
(In Hundreds of Dollars)

Number of Trucks per Route	Routes					
	1	*2*	*3*	*4*	*5*	*6*
1	14	16	12	13	17	15
2	18	19	17	16	17	16
3	21	20	11	18	17	17
4	22	20	24	19	17	17
5	23	20	26	19	17	17

a) Assign the fourteen trucks to delivery routes, maximizing the dollar total of the routes.

b) If new trucks can be operated for $177.00 per day per truck, should any new trucks be purchased? If so, how many should be purchased, and where should they be assigned?

c) Assign the fourteen trucks to routes 1, 2 and 3. Add route 4 to the system and compute the change in assignments. Add 5, then 6, in the same manner.

d) Convert Table 10–15 to an incremental value matrix. Assign the fourteen trucks to delivery routes using this information. Does this answer agree with your answer to the first part of this question? Why or why not? (Example: the incremental value of $X_{21} = 18 - 14 = 4$; incremental value of $X_{31} = 21 - 18 = 3$, etc.)

Chapter 11

CHANNEL DECISIONS AND THE LOGISTICS
OF DISTRIBUTION

A properly designed product, effectively promoted at an attractive price, may go for naught if means have not been established to make the product readily available to interested consumers. This chapter is concerned with the selection and control of distribution channels, the fourth major class of marketing decisions.

Channel decisions may also interact with product, price, and promotion decisions. The major types of marketing channels and channel decisions which a firm may face with respect to both established and new products will be discussed and then the relationship of channel decisions to other classes of decisions will be shown. Next one of these decisions, choice between using a manufacturer's own sales force versus an independent distributor to handle a packaged consumer product, will be illustrated within the framework of decision making under uncertainty.

Distribution channels also give rise to logistical problems in production scheduling, inventory, and transportation. Some of the analytical techniques which have been developed to deal with this class of problems will be briefly discussed and one of the techniques, the so-called "transportation method" of linear programming, will be illustrated within a supply problem context.

The chapter concludes with some speculative comments regarding future research in the planning and control of distribution channels.

THE CHARACTERISTICS OF CHANNEL DECISIONS

A marketing channel can be defined as a path or route through which a firm's product or service reaches the ultimate consumer.

Typically, the word "channel" is applied to the whole configuration
of middlemen who assist in the distribution of the good or service.
Figure 11–1 shows in tree diagram form some of the many possibilities by which a producer may distribute his product. For example,
vacuum cleaners may be sold to sales agents who, in turn, sell to
wholesalers who, in turn, sell to retailers. Or, vacuum cleaners may
be sold through company-owned retail outlets, mail order establishments, or on a door-to-door, direct-to-consumer basis.

Figure 11–1

AN ILLUSTRATION OF SOME POSSIBLE DISTRIBUTION CHANNELS

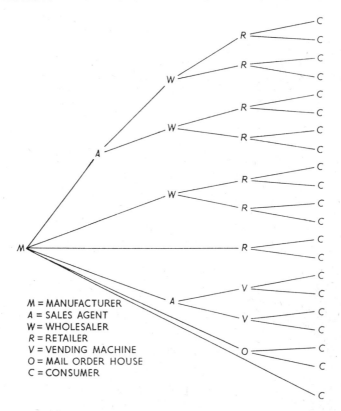

M = MANUFACTURER
A = SALES AGENT
W = WHOLESALER
R = RETAILER
V = VENDING MACHINE
O = MAIL ORDER HOUSE
C = CONSUMER

When one speaks of distribution channels, he commonly refers
to the physical flow of the product. The marketing planner of a
manufacturing firm should bear in mind, however, that channels
also involve flows of money and flows of information. A manufacturer's use of brokers may be associated primarily with information
flow since brokers typically do not bind their principals. A so-called

full-function wholesaler may carry inventory, grant credit, subdivide stock, and deliver merchandise. His function may thus involve information, financial, and physical product flows.

Distribution channels may be relatively simple (direct from producer to conusmer) or exceedingly extensive and complex. A manufacturer of a popular consumer packaged item may use 75 wholesalers and upwards of 15,000 retailers. A manufacturer of synthetic fibers for apparel uses may face a long and intricate chain of spinners, weavers, converters, cutters, wholesalers, and retailers before his product reaches the ultimate consumer.

Manufacturers of industrial products, for example, heavy electrical machinery, machine tools, tanks, and pressure vessels, usually sell directly to the industrial buyer. These products are typified by high unit price, product features tailored to individual buyer needs, a relatively small number of potential buyers, high technical information requirements, and application engineering, both prior and subsequent to the sale. It is not surprising that direct sale from manufacturer to industrial consumer is the usual channel selected for products of this type.

"Off-the-shelf" items like small motors, valves, and fittings may follow a somewhat longer channel involving mill supply houses as a link between producer and industrial buyer. Information needs are typically lower, and unit value of the item may be small as compared to the custom equipment handled on a direct producer-to-industrial-buyer basis.

Channels for high-ticket, consumer durable products like electrical appliances and furniture may involve direct manufacturer-to-retailer selling or manufacturer-wholesaler-retailer channels. Outlets may be manufacturer controlled or not. Consumer nondurables like packaged foods, toiletries, various apparel items, and cigarettes may involve a diversity of channels including mail order, vending machines, and door-to-door canvassing.

Various product and customer characteristics, for example, product unit value, perishability, degree of standardization, number of potential consumers, degree of follow-up service required, and so forth, have been proposed to explain the channel differences that exist between product classes. But the fact remains that anomalies exist under almost any classification scheme, a reflection of the diversity of activity on the part of individual producers toward carving out a distribution niche for the specific product and thus achieving differentiation on the basis of type of channel used in distribution.

While most planning problems in this area concern the selection of some best channel from already existing alternatives, sometimes the manufacturer may wish to design a new channel and thus add to the existing channel structure. Once a channel is selected, the maintenance and modification of the channel gives rise to a series of problems over time. For example, a manufacturer may find that a direct, producer-to-retailer channel provides the best alternative for introducing a new product. Subsequent sales expansion, however, might eventually require the employment of wholesalers in areas which cannot be efficiently served by the firm's own sales force. Moreover, the selection of a general channel configuration is usually not a sufficient answer to his problem. The manufacturer must decide on *which* agents and wholesalers to use, whether or not he wants to grant exclusive franchises, and so on.

Nor can channel decisions usually be considered independently of product, price, and promotion decisions. The manufacturer must consider trade discount policy, product design, quality and packaging, and promotional activity within the framework of the distribution channel. To illustrate, a large manufacturer of synthetic fibers not only has sales personnel calling on primary customer groups (spinners and weavers) but also employs technical service sales representatives and promotional effort at each major link in the chain toward the ultimate consumer.

Not only must the traditional marketing planning decisions of product, price, and promotion be considered in relationship to the channel framework, but many other classes of decisions, for example, warehouse capacity, inventory levels, and production schedules, must be considered as well. For example, the manufacturer may have to decide upon the best routing for his product from plants or company warehouses to wholesalers' depots. Information flow through the channel may provide an important source of data regarding such activities as production forecasting, inventory control, and product transportation.

Finally, the marketing planner should not overlook the possibility of the firm's assuming some or all of the functions of the distribution channel by integrating toward the ultimate consumer in some product lines. In the ethical drug field, for example, the importance of wholesale houses appears on the wane as manufacturers choose to sell a greater proportion of their products directly to retail pharmacists, hospital dispensaries, and the prescribing physician himself, when the nature of the product (for example, vaccines) makes direct sales to physicians an efficient alternative.

COSTS AND VALUES IN CHANNEL DECISIONS

From the viewpoint of the manufacturer, distribution channels provide the means to increase product availability and to gain additional sales effort on the part of members of the channel. The decision to select one channel configuration over another should be based as much on long-range sales and profit considerations as are the internal decisions which the firm makes. That is, the marketing planner must consider anticipated revenues and costs stemming from alternative channel selections.

But the manufacturer faces a difficult and complex job in making choices among alternative channels. First, he is dealing with a subtle combination of conflict and cooperation in his relations with channel members. The manufacturer's objective may be to maximize his firm's profits, while channel members (wholesalers, retailers, and so forth) may be interested in maximizing their own establishment's profits. Any specific branded item typically competes with other brands for the distributor's attention, including the private brands of large supermarket chains, department stores, drug chains, and so on. The manufacturer must convince the channel member that greater profits can be made through carrying his particular brand than without it. But first, he, the manufacturer, must have demonstrated to himself the worthwhileness of using this particular channel member.

The distributor, however, is also evaluating the relative merits of carrying a specific manufacturer's brand versus other brands which are all competing for display space and/or selling time. Since the distributor is also competing with other distributors, failure to carry the brand could result in high opportunity losses, given the brand's success. It is clear that this interesting combination of conflict and cooperation can lead to rather involved negotiations between manufacturer and distributor, particularly with regard to new brands whose consumer demand is yet to be ascertained. To obtain satisfactory distribution, manufacturers of a new product may have to offer many types of inducements (for example, "free goods," discounts below established brands, advertising allowances, and so on) in order for the distributor to stock the item prior to launching the introductory campaign. Nor can the manufacturer necessarily relax after the product has become established. He may be more or less continuously competing for display space and dealer "push" with other branded items of the same product class and with other classes of products, as well.

In addition to the presence of conflict and cooperation which characterizes manufacturer–distributor relationships, channel decisions, once made, typically involve long-term commitment. It is not easy to change distribution channels, once they have been set up. Costs of transition are usually high and renegotiation is time consuming.

Finally, the manufacturer must frequently contend with a high degree of uncertainty regarding channel efficiency and dealer reaction. Distributors may make choices to stock certain brands largely on the basis of incomplete criteria like gross margin per item, rather than on some more comprehensive measure like return on investment, which reflects stock turnover as well as profit margin. Channel members may be unskilled in forecasting the product's demand, leading to the possibility of alternate product shortages and gluts and a resultant serious impact on the manufacturer's production scheduling and inventory levels (see the Forrester reference at the end of the chapter).

ANALYTICAL TECHNIQUES IN DISTRIBUTION CHANNEL PLANNING

The marketing planner interested in the application of analytical tools to channel decision making will find few really comprehensive models capable of predicting the consequences of alternative channel selections. While game theory has been developed (see the Shubik and Luce and Raiffa references) to cope with relatively well-structured conflict problems, the fact remains that the subtle interplay of conflict and cooperation in the relationships between manufacturer and channel members is exceedingly difficult to model within presently formulated game theory. In the language of the game theorist, the manufacturer is typically faced with an "n-person, nonzero sum" conflict situation. Game theory has much less to contribute to this problem class than in "games" involving strictly opposed interests by, say, two competitors.

Perhaps the most direct approach to the channel selection problem involves a more or less direct assessment of revenues and distribution costs associated with alternative channel configurations. In some cases the marketing planner may possess several alternative routes for distributing the product while, in other cases, his "degrees of freedom" may be nil. That is, to sell the minimum required volume of the product he may be forced to use a specific established channel. In this case his decisions concern the pricing and promotion tactics to employ in negotiating for channel acceptance of the product, rather than choice among alternative routes.

Analytical models do exist, however, for a wide variety of problems which arise after channels have been established. Production scheduling and inventory control theory may be used to guide decisions regarding the supply of product to the distribution channel. Network models (PERT and other critical path procedures) may be employed to assist in the scheduling of new product introductions and various techniques may be used to minimize transportation costs from supplier to primary channel links.

In this chapter, decision theory in channel selection and the use of linear programming (the transportation method) in the allocation of company warehouses to distributor-customers are discussed as illustrative cases of quantitative techniques. Other techniques, for example, queueing theory, inventory control theory, production smoothing, and so forth, may also be applicable to specific facets of distribution. Their discussion, however, would exceed the scope of this chapter. (See the Manne, Balderston, Miller and Starr references for discussion of these techniques areas.)

BAYESIAN DECISION THEORY IN CHANNEL SELECTION

Many channel decisions are of the "make versus buy" class, for example whether the firm should perform some part of the distribution process or whether the task should be "farmed out" to independent agents. In actual practice these decisions might be very complex, involving such considerations as comparative operating costs, sales effects on the product under study, effects on other products of the manufacturer, repercussions on other links in the distribution channel, and so on.

The problem which will be selected for illustration will be highly simplified. The purpose in choosing a relatively simple illustration is twofold. The first objective is to show that this general class of problems can be framed within a Bayesian model of the type described earlier and thus round out the functional areas in which decision theory can be applied. The second objective is to introduce the concept of continuous prior distributions by means of a numerical illustration which is straightforward enough for simple exposition of this notion. Heretofore it has been assumed that the relevant states of nature were discrete; in fact, only a small number of states were usually assumed so as to make the problem easier to solve. In practice, however, the decision maker may visualize a large number of possible states of nature. When his continuous prior distribution can be represented by a mathematically tractable function (for example, a normal or Gaussian distribution) it is easier to apply the methods of continuous probability. If the decision maker's prior distribution cannot be so represented, the planner can always resort to a discrete analog of the underlying continuous distribution, using methods similar to those illustrated in the preceding chapters.

In this section, then, a Bayesian application is discussed in which the decision maker's prior distribution can be approximated by a normal distribution. It will be shown how such measures as the expected value of perfect information can be calculated under these conditions.

Assume that a manufacturer of a consumer packaged product has been using a sales agent to distribute his product to various retail food outlets, such as supermarket chain, independent food outlets, and so on. The sales agent's commission for performing this service amounts to 6 percent of the sales price per case to retailers. That is, assuming the price to retailers is $10.00 per case, the sales agent receives 60c for each case sold.

The manufacturer has been considering the possibility of replacing his sales agent by an intracompany sales force. According to preliminary estimates, the cost incurred in distributing the product by means of his company's own salesmen would amount to only 50c per case, once the sales force was trained. Moreover, the manufacturer feels that use of a company sales force could result in a larger volume of sales than the sales agent is currently producing. Current sales, using the agent as distributor, amount to 100,000 cases, on an annual basis.

The manufacturer's marketing planner is asked to study the problem. He first looks at the costs associated with transition from sales agent to company sales force. His estimates indicate that the fixed costs of hiring and training a group of salesmen (and phasing out the sales agent's services) are quite significant, amounting to $25,-000. That is, if the salesmen did *not* produce additional business, it would take approximately two and a half years (ignoring the time value of money) to recoup the original transition costs on the basis of reduced selling costs alone:

$$\$10 \ (.06 - .05) \ 100,000 \ \text{cases/year} = \$10,000/\text{year}.$$

The manufacturer believes, however, that use of a company sales force would produce additional sales. But, considering the vagaries of the market place and the possibility that the product may be superseded by newer products, he wishes to use a short time horizon (one year) in considering the payback of his original investment of $25,000.

The marketing planner next finds that the sales units required to justify the switch from sales agent to company salesmen amount to 250,000 cases over the one-year planning period:

$$\$10 \ (.06 - .05) \ S_b = \$25,000; \ S_b = \text{breakeven sales}$$

$$S_b = 250,000 \text{ cases}$$

Any sales beyond 250,000 cases would, of course, make the transition more attractive, while if sales were less than 250,000 cases, an opportunity loss would be sustained. If S_b continues to stand for total sales required to break even (250,000 cases) and S represents actual sales in cases, the result is:

$$\$ \ .10 \ (S_b - S) \text{ if } S \leq S_b$$

$$0 \qquad \text{if } S > S_b$$

as the manufacturer's conditional opportunity loss, assuming that he makes the transition from sales agent to company salesmen. For example, if sales are only 200,000 cases during the first year, the manufacturer suffers a conditional loss of $.10 (250,000 − 200,000) = $5,000. Notice that if actual sales S are only 100,000 cases (the amount anticipated by maintaining the sales agent's services) the conditional opportunity loss is equal to $15,000, since the salesmen would produce a $10,000 additional contribution to profit and overhead (through the 5 percent cost of their services versus the 6 percent sales agent commission) but their services would involve a transitional outlay of $25,000.

Now assume that the marketing planner attempts to elicit from the decision maker some sales estimates, given the use of company salesmen rather than the present sales agent. The decision maker estimates that first year sales, with the company sales force, would average 275,000 cases. He believes, however, that a 50-50 chance exists that sales could be less than 225,000 cases or more than 325,-000 cases.

Now suppose it is assumed that the decision maker's estimates can be represented by a normal distribution. It will be recalled from elementary statistics that about one half of the area under the normal curve lies between the mean ± 0.67 standard deviations. Figure 11–2 shows the normal curve for this specific problem.

Note in Figure 11–2 that the decision maker has provided two pieces of information, namely, a mean sales estimate (275,000 cases) and a probability equal to 0.5 that true sales lie between 225,000 and 325,000 cases. Thus, one half of the total area under the curve must lie outside these limits. This information can be used to solve for the standard deviation of this normal distribution, as follows:

$$.67 \ \sigma \ (S) = 50{,}000 \text{ cases}$$

$$\sigma \ (S) = 75{,}000 \text{ cases (approximately)}$$

It will also be remembered from elementary statistics that

1. About 68 percent of the total area under a normal curve lies between the mean ±1 standard deviation.
2. About 95 percent of the total area under a normal curve lies between the mean ±2 standard deviations.
3. About 99.7 percent (practically all) of the total area under a normal curve lies between the mean ±3 standard deviations.

In this case the implication is that the decision maker cannot, for all practical purposes, conceive of first-year sales falling below 50,000 cases or being higher than 500,000 cases (275,000 ± 3 (75,000)), given the use of a company sales force.

Figure 11–2

NORMAL PRIOR DISTRIBUTION OF SALES
(Sales in Thousands of Cases)

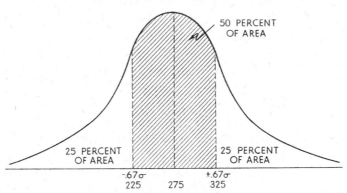

Inasmuch as the mean sales estimate of 275,000 cases exceeds the breakeven requirement of 250,000 cases, the decision maker would (ignoring utility and time value of money considerations) change over to the company sales force.

Notice, however, that *should* sales turn out to be lower than S_b, the breakeven value of 250,000 units, the decision maker would suffer an opportunity loss. Also, notice that the size of this loss increases the further away that actual sales S are from breakeven sales S_b. For example, if $S \leq 225{,}000$ cases (an event which can happen with probability .25), an opportunity loss of *at least* $2,500 would be incurred. If actual sales $S \leq 125{,}000$ (the mean minus two standard deviations), an opportunity loss of *at least* $12,500 would be incurred.

Now suppose that the decision maker could obtain additional information of "perfect reliability" regarding true sales, assuming a changeover to company salesmen. It will be recalled from Chapter 5 that the value of this information is conditional upon whether or not the decision would be *changed* on the basis of the new information. That is, the conditional value of perfect information can be summarized as follows:

$$CVPI = \quad 0 \text{ if } S > 250{,}000 \text{ cases}$$

$$CVPI = \$ \ .10 \ (S_b - S) \text{ if } S \leq 250{,}000 \text{ cases}$$

That is, if the perfect information indicated sales exceeding 250,-000 cases, the decision would not be changed from that taken in the absence of new information. If the perfect information indicated sales less than 250,000 cases, however, the *value* of this information would increase as the difference between true sales and break-even sales increased. This relationship is shown (along with the prior distribution) in Figure 11–3.

Figure 11–3

CONDITIONAL VALUE OF PERFECT INFORMATION

(Sales in Thousands of Cases)

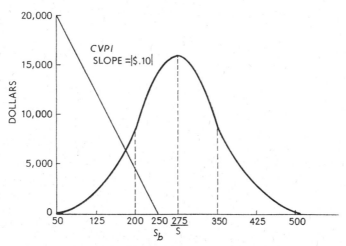

In Figure 11–3 the expected value of perfect information is shown to increase linearly as the actual sales parameter moves to the left of the breakeven sales level of 250,000 cases. EVPI equals zero, however, for all sales levels exceeding 250,000 cases since, in these cases, the original decision would not have been changed, given the new information. Note that the slope of the CVPI line equals \$.10, corresponding to the additional 1 percent commission saved on each \$10 of sales per case. Finally, it is inferred that if sales actually amounted to zero cases, the *opportunity* loss through switching over to the company sales force would involve \$25,000. That is, this alternative would produce a loss of \$25,000 *more* than the loss sustained under using the sales agent.

To derive the *expected* value of perfect information one would have to multiply the conditional value of perfect information by the probability that true sales, given by the perfect information, would be a value falling respectively within each one of a set of tiny intervals in the range 0–250,000 cases; making such an approximation would be laborious, to say the least.

Fortunately, a short cut procedure, permissible through the use of a normal distribution of prior probabilities, can be used. (See the Schlaifer reference in Chapter 5.) The formula is

$$EVPI = C \, \sigma \, (S) \cdot N \, (D)$$

where C = absolute value of the slope of the *CVPI* line; $\sigma(S)$ = the standard deviation of the normal prior distribution; and D of $N(D)$ is a measure of the absolute distance of the mean of the decision maker's prior distribution from the breakeven value, expressed in terms of the number of standard deviations of the prior distribution.

$$D = \frac{\mid S_b - \bar{S} \mid}{\sigma \, (S)}$$

$$= \frac{\mid 250{,}000 - 275{,}000 \mid}{75{,}000}$$

$$= 0.33$$

Table 11–1 shows $N(D)$, a loss function for the standardized normal curve. It shows the value of $N(D)$ for $D = 0.33$ to be .2555. The expected value of perfect information can now be calculated as follows:

$$EVPI = C \cdot \sigma \, (S) \cdot N \, (D)$$

$$= .10 \, (75{,}000) \, (0.2555)$$

$$= \$1{,}916.25$$

In other words, the decision maker could afford to spend up to approximately \$2,000 for perfect information which would indicate true sales, given the changeover to a company sales force for distributing the product to retailers. If the decision maker could not obtain perfect information (the more usual case) it is clear that the expected value of imperfect information would be less than

$2,000. The $2,000 figure thus provides an upper limit on how much to spend for information. (For a discussion of the expected value of imperfect information, see **Chapter 5** for the discrete case and the Schlaifer reference for the continuous case.)

Table 11–1

N(D)—Loss Function*

D	.00	.01	.02	.03	.04	.05	.06	.07	.08	.09
.0	.3989	.3940	.3890	.3841	.3793	.3744	.3697	.3649	.3602	.3556
.1	.3509	.3464	.3418	.3373	.3328	.3284	.3240	.3197	.3154	.3111
.2	.3069	.3027	.2986	.2944	.2904	.2863	.2824	.2784	.2745	.2706
.3	.2668	.2630	.2592	.2555	.2518	.2481	.2445	.2409	.2374	.2339
.4	.2304	.2270	.2236	.2203	.2169	.2137	.2104	.2072	.2040	.2009
.5	.1078	.1947	.1917	.1887	.1857	.1828	.1799	.1771	.1742	.1714
.6	.1687	.1659	.1633	.1606	.1580	.1554	.1528	.1503	.1478	.1453
.7	.1429	.1405	.1381	.1358	.1334	.1312	.1289	.1267	.1245	.1223
.8	.1202	.1181	.1160	.1140	.1120	.1100	.1080	.1061	.1042	.1023
.9	.1004	.09860	.09680	.09503	.09328	.09156	.08986	.08819	.08654	.04891
1.0	.08332	.08174	.08019	.07866	.07716	.07568	.07422	.07279	.07138	.06999
1.1	.06862	.06727	.06595	.06465	.06336	.06210	.06086	.05964	.05844	.05726
1.2	.05610	.05496	.05384	.05274	.05165	.05059	.04954	.04851	.04750	.04650
1.3	.04553	.04457	.04363	.04270	.04179	.04090	.04002	.03916	.03831	.03748
1.4	.03667	.03587	.03508	.03431	.03356	.03281	.03208	.03137	.03067	.02998
1.5	.02931	.02865	.02800	.02736	.02674	.02612	.02552	.04294	.02436	.02380
1.6	.02324	.02270	.02217	.02165	.02114	.02064	.02015	.01967	.01920	.01874
1.7	.01829	.01785	.01742	.01699	.01658	.01617	.01578	.01539	.01502	.01464
1.8	.01428	.01392	.01357	.01323	.01290	.01257	.01226	.01195	.01164	.01134
1.9	.01105	.01077	.01049	.01022	$.0^2 9957$	$.0^2 9698$	$.0^2 9445$	$.0^2 9198$	$.0^2 8957$	$.0^2 8721$
2.0	$.0^2 8491$	$.0^2 8266$	$.0^2 8046$	$.0^2 7832$	$.0^2 7623$	$.0^2 7418$	$.0^2 7219$	$.0^2 7024$	$.0^2 6835$	$.0^2 6649$
2.1	$.0^2 6468$	$.0^2 6292$	$.0^2 6120$	$.0^2 5952$	$.0^2 5788$	$.0^2 5628$	$.0^2 5472$	$.0^2 5320$	$.0^2 5172$	$.0^2 5028$
2.2	$.0^2 4887$	$.0^2 4750$	$.0^2 4616$	$.0^2 4486$	$.0^2 4358$	$.0^2 4235$	$.0^2 4114$	$.0^2 3996$	$.0^2 3882$	$.0^2 3770$
2.3	$.0^2 3662$	$.0^2 3556$	$.0^2 3453$	$.0^2 3352$	$.0^2 3255$	$.0^2 3159$	$.0^2 3067$	$.0^2 2977$	$.0^2 2889$	$.0^2 2804$
2.4	$.0^2 2720$	$.0^2 2640$	$.0^2 2561$	$.0^2 2484$	$.0^2 2410$	$.0^2 2337$	$.0^2 2267$	$.0^2 2199$	$.0^2 2132$	$.0^2 2067$
2.5	$.0^2 2005$	$.0^2 1943$	$.0^2 1883$	$.0^2 1826$	$.0^2 1769$	$.0^2 1715$	$.0^2 1662$	$.0^2 1610$	$.0^2 1560$	$.0^2 1511$
3.0	$.0^3 3822$	$.0^3 3689$	$.0^3 3560$	$.0^3 3436$	$.0^3 3316$	$.0^3 3199$	$.0^3 3087$	$.0^3 2978$	$.0^3 2873$	$.0^3 2771$
3.5	$.0^4 5848$	$.0^4 5620$	$.0^4 5400$	$.0^4 5188$	$.0^4 4984$	$.0^4 4788$	$.0^4 4599$	$.0^4 4417$	$.0^4 4242$	$.0^4 4073$
4.0	$.0^5 7145$	$.0^5 6835$	$.0^5 6538$	$.0^5 6253$	$.0^5 5980$	$.0^5 5718$	$.0^5 5468$	$.0^5 5227$	$.0^5 4997$	$.0^5 4777$

*Reproduced, with permission from Schlaifer, R., *Probability and Statistics for Business Decisions* (New York: McGraw-Hill Book Co., Inc., 1959).

Before leaving this illustration one should note that *EVPI* is a function of the absolute value of the *CVPI* line (0.10 in this illustration), the standard deviation of the decision maker's prior distribution and the absolute distance of the prior mean from the breakeven point. As common sense would suggest, the higher the opportunity loss of wrong decisions, the more one should be willing to pay for additional information about the consequences of his decisions. Moreover, the surer he is of the relevant consequences (small standard deviation of the prior distribution) and the better his preferred alternative is (distance of mean from breakeven value), the less valuable additional information becomes. Finally, one should remember that additional information assumes value *only if it changes the choice* which he would have made in its absence.

CHANNEL LOGISTICS AND THE TRANS-PORTATION METHOD OF LINEAR PROGRAMMING

An earlier section of this chapter discussed briefly some of the interrelationships between marketing channel control and decisions regarding production scheduling, inventory levels, and product routing. In this section one such problem is illustrated—the scheduling of a product from multiple company warehouses to product distributors so as to minimize shipping costs, subject to meeting distributor requirements and restrictions on warehouse capacity. This problem can be handled by the so-called "transportation method", a special case of linear programming.

Linear programming is another mathematical tool which can be useful in assisting the planner in allocating scarce resources among activities competing for those resources. As such, it can be used in many allocation situations, such as promotional mix decisions (similar to those discussed in the preceding chapter), product mix determination, and so on. Like the techniques of the calculus and dynamic programming, linear programming has its own set of assumptions. Moreover, any extensive inquiry into the details of the procedure would presuppose a much more technical background on the part of the reader than is assumed here. The transportation method, however, is a particularly simple case of linear programming which does not require extensive mathematical background to discuss and which can be useful in problems associated with maintaining the efficiency of distribution channels.

A trivial illustration will acquaint the reader with the nature of the problem and provide an intuitive grasp of it. Assume that a manufacturer has only two company warehouses, W_1 and W_2, and only two wholesale distributors, D_1 and D_2, the capacities and requirements of which are known with certainty. Moreover, the manufacturer knows the costs to ship x units of product from each warehouse to each distributor. These "data" are shown in Table 11–2.

Table 11–2

SHIPPING COSTS AND WEEKLY SALES CAPACITIES
AND REQUIREMENTS

Warehouses	Distributors		Warehouse Capacity
	D_1	D_2	(units)
W_1.....................	1	3	9
W_2.....................	5	8	4
Distributor Requirements (units)....	5	8	

The cell entries of Table 11–2 indicate the cost to ship one unit of product from each warehouse to each distributor. For example, to ship one unit of product from W_1 to D_1 costs $1. What are the feasible shipping schedules which could be designed which would not violate the conditions of the problem? If x_{11} equals the quantity shipped from W_1 to D_1 note that x_{11} can equal 1, 2, 3, 4, and 5, respectively. Any other integer for x_{11} would violate some of the restrictions. Table 11–3 summarizes the total shipping cost for each unit of product assigned to the x_{11} cell.

Table 11–3

TOTAL SHIPPING COSTS AS A FUNCTION OF X_{11} ASSIGNMENT

	1	2	3	4	5
Total Cost	45	46	47	48	49

Table 11–3 implies that the lowest total shipping cost is associated with shipping 1 unit from W_1 to D_1; 8 units from W_1 to D_2; 4 units from W_2 to D_1 and 0 units from W_2 to D_2. This, in essence, is the nature of the transportation problem. As will be seen, however, as the number of possible routes is expanded, a procedure will be needed which does not require the exploration of the total cost of all possible combinations.

Let us now expand the scale of the problem and introduce another notion which is more realistic—that total warehouse capacity and distributor requirements may not coincide. Assume that the manufacturer has three warehouses and four distributors, the weekly capacities and requirements of which are known. Also assume that the costs of shipping a unit of product from each warehouse to each distributor are known. These data are shown in Table 11–4.

Table 11–4

SHIPMENT PROBLEM—THREE WAREHOUSES AND FOUR DISTRIBUTORS

Warehouses	Distributors					Warehouse Capacity
	D_1	D_2	D_3	D_4	D_5	
W_1	13	9	4	11	0	60
W_2	20	10	7	2	0	30
W_3	3	12	16	24	0	20
Distribution Requirements	15	23	38	16		

The cell entries of Table 11-4 represent, as before, the direct costs to ship one unit of product from any warehouse to any distributor. By "direct" is meant incremental shipping costs (not warehouse overhead) which could change as a consequence of the decision under consideration. It is assumed, of course, that these costs are linear; for example, if it costs $13 to ship one unit of product from W_1 to D_1, it costs $26 to ship two units, and so on. Notice that in this new example the total capacity of the warehouses (60 + 30 + 20 = 110 units) exceeds the total weekly requirements of the distributors (15 + 23 + 38 + 16 = 92 units). That is, some excess capacity exists in one or all of the warehouses. To allow for this overage, a dummy distributor "D_5" is inserted which really represents unused capacity in each of the warehouses; "cost of shipment", then, is equal to zero for the dummy distributor case. This artifact will permit the use of a standard computational routine for finding the lowest cost allocation of warehouse capacity to distributors.

At this stage a little mathematical notation is introduced and the problem formulated. First, let x_{ij} stand for the quantity of product shipped from the ith warehouse to the jth distributor. Let c_{ij} stand for the cost of shipping one unit of product from the ith warehouse to the jth distributor. The values of the various c_{ij}'s ($13, $9, and so on) are shown in Table 11-4.

Now the problem may be stated as finding the values of the various x_{ij}'s which minimize total cost:

$$TC = 13\, x_{11} + 9\, x_{12} + 4\, x_{13} + 11\, x_{14} + 20\, x_{21} + 10\, x_{22} + 7\, x_{23}$$
$$+ 2\, x_{24} + 3\, x_{31} + 12\, x_{32} + 16\, x_{33} + 24\, x_{34}$$

Subject to conditions:

$$x_{11} + x_{21} + x_{31} = 15$$
$$x_{12} + x_{22} + x_{32} = 23$$
$$x_{13} + x_{23} + x_{33} = 38$$
$$x_{14} + x_{24} + x_{34} = 16$$
$$x_{11} + x_{12} + x_{13} + x_{14} \leq 60$$
$$x_{21} + x_{22} + x_{23} + x_{24} \leq 30$$
$$x_{31} + x_{32} + x_{33} + x_{34} \leq 20$$
$$x_{ij} \geq 0$$

The above formulation may look a bit formidable at first glance, but the so-called transportation method involves a calculational routine which can be handled quite simply. The above equations and inequalities, however, represent a typical illustration of the general linear programming problem which, more succinctly, would state:

$$\text{Minimize} \quad TC = \sum_{j=1}^{n} c_j x_j$$

$$\text{Subject to:} \sum_{j=1}^{n} a_{ij} x_j \leq b_i \ (i = 1, \ldots, m)$$

$$x_j \geq 0 \ (j = 1, \ldots, n)$$

In this particular problem the c_j's and x_j's have been double subscripted as a convenient way to express the table of shipping costs. Notice, particularly, that negative quantities are not shipped. All x must equal or exceed zero. One final note is pertinent before the problem summarized above is solved. Linear programming (as suggested by the nature of the preceding equations) represents only one technique of a still broader class of tools known as mathematical programming. By dealing with the transportation method alone, a special case of a subset of a still much larger group of techniques is, in effect, being applied.

Now after this brief digression, examine Table 11–4 again and consider the problem at hand—to find the allocation of product from warehouses to distributors which minimizes total shipping costs, subject to the constraints on warehouse capacity and distributor requirements. What would be the lowest shipping cost if there were no effective ceiling on warehouse capacity? If warehouse capacity were unlimited, then obviously each distributor's requirement would be satisfied from that warehouse in which shipping costs were lowest. In terms of the data all of D_1's requirements would be shipped from W_3, all of D_2's requirements from W_1, and so on. Under this rather unrealistic case the total cost would amount to

$$\$3 \ (15) + \$9 \ (23) + \$4 \ (38) + \$2 \ (16) = \$436$$

The total cost figure of $436 provides a floor to whatever minimum total cost schedule can be derived which satisfies the restrictions on warehouse capacity.

Now we are ready to start applying the transportation method to the solution of the problem summarized in Table 11–4. This procedure involves a step-by-step series of calculations which converges on the minimum total cost solution. That is, one first starts out with a feasible solution (one that satisfies the constraints) and then systematically improves the solution until a solution is reached which represents minimum total cost. An initial feasible solution might be that which is shown in Table 11–5.

Table 11–5

First Feasible Solution—Shipping Problem

	D_1	D_2	D_3	D_4	D_5	Capacity
W_1	\$13 / 15	\$9 / 7	\$4 / 38	\$11	\$0	60
W_2	\$20	\$10 / 16	\$7	\$2 / 14	\$0	30
W_3	\$3	\$12	\$16	\$24 / 2	\$0 / 18	20
Requirements	15	23	38	16		

A study of the first feasible solution of Table 11–5 will reveal that all distributor requirements are met and that warehouse capacities are not exceeded; as a matter of fact, W_3 is left with 18 units of unused capacity. The particular schedule of Table 11–5 represents only one of a large number of possible schedules and has been selected arbitrarily. No information has been considered as to whether this particular selection represents a lowest-cost schedule or not. However, the total cost of this allocation can be calculated by summing the products of the shipping cost per unit (shown in the upper left corner of each cell) times the quantity shipped.

$$TC = \$13\ (15) + \$9\ (7) + \$4\ (38) + \$10\ (16) \\ + \$2\ (14) + \$24\ (2) = \$646$$

Notice that this cost, \$646, exceeds rather substantially the cost floor of \$436. One might wonder whether this gap might be closed by selection of some other cost schedule which still meets the constraints.

Table 11–6 is next set up to search for this schedule.

Table 11–6

Determination of Implicit Prices

	D_1	D_2	D_3	D_4	D_5	Implicit Ware-house Prices
W_1	13 / $a_1 + b_1 = c_{11}$	9 / $a_1 + b_2 = c_{12}$	4 / $a_1 + b_3 = c_{13}$	11	0	$a_1 = -23$
W_2	20	10 / $a_2 + b_2 = c_{22}$	7	2 / $a_2 + b_4 = c_{24}$	0	$a_2 = -22$
W_3	3	12	16	24 / $a_3 + b_4 = c_{34}$	0 / $a_3 = c_{35}$	$a_3 = 0$
Implicit Price to Distributor	$b_1 = 36$	$b_2 = 32$	$b_3 = 27$	$b_4 = 24$		

A series of "implicit cost" factors a_1, a_2, and a_3 and b_1, b_2, b_3, and b_4 and the seven cell equations which link these factors together have been set up in Table 11-6. Look first at the W_3D_5 which represents excess capacity in warehouse W_3. Adding, say, an additional unit to W_3 capacity (which already contains 18 units of excess capacity as shown in Table 11-5) would be worth zero dollars. That is, the implicit price of a_3 is equal to zero, since excess capacity already exists in W_3. Now look at cell intersection W_3D_4 containing the equation $a_3 + b_4 = c_{34}$ or $0 + b_4 = 24$. If D_4 requirements were to increase by one unit, then warehouse W_3 would have one less unit of excess capacity which, as has just been seen, is valued at a \$0 implicit price. Hence, a net implicit price rise of \$24 would result. Thus, b_4 receives the implicit price of \$24.

In a similar manner use the result of previous equations to solve for $a_1 = -23$, $a_2 = -22$, $b_1 = 36$, $b_2 = 32$, and $b_3 = 27$. Notice that a_1 and a_2 are negative. This is so because an increase in, say, the capacity of W_1, would be utilized by increasing the level of W_1D_3 (\$4) and, hence, decreasing the capacity of D_3 (\$27). The net result is $4 - 27$ or -23, the implicit price (or opportunity cost) of a unit of W_1 capacity.

After implicit prices for the various warehouse capacities and distributor requirements are calculated, one can compute the implicit prices for each cell of the table. In all cases where cells are nonempty (that is, represent the initial allocation) the implicit prices are equal to the unit cost coefficient c_{ij}. These implicit prices are shown in the lower right corner of each cell in Table 11-7.

Table 11-7

NUMERICAL VALUES OF IMPLICIT PRICES—
FIRST FEASIBLE SOLUTION

	D₁		D₂		D₃		D₄		D₅		Warehouse–Implicit Prices
W₁	13	13	9	9	4	4	11	1	0	-23	-23
W₂	20	14	10	10	7	5	2	2	0	-22	-22
W₃	3	36	12	32	16	27	24	24	0	0	0
Distributors–Implicit Prices	36		32		27		24				

The implicit prices will be labeled in the lower right corner of each cell $\overset{*}{c}_{ij}$. Note, however, that all $\overset{*}{c}_{ij} = c_{ij}$ for those cells in which entries were made during the initial assignment.

To improve the initial allocation, first scan all of the cell entries in order to determine which, if any, implicit prices exceed the original unit shipment costs, such that the differences $\overset{*}{c}_{ij} - c_{ij} > 0$. There are only three entries—W_3D_1, W_3D_2, and W_3D_3—in which this is the case.

$$\overset{*}{c}_{31} - c_{31} = 36 - 3 = 33$$

$$\overset{*}{c}_{32} - c_{32} = 32 - 12 = 20$$

$$\overset{*}{c}_{33} - c_{33} = 27 - 16 = 11$$

Note that cell W_3D_1 provides the greatest reduction in opportunity loss if this cell is chosen in the construction of feasible solution 2. Each unit so allocated should reduce total cost by (36-3) or $33. Now the plan for adjusting the initial solution is starting to take form. It is desirable to introduce x_{31} into the allocation. It is clear, of course, that if in order to do this some other activity has to go out.

Table 11–8 is constructed to find out which activity is to be replaced by x_{31}.

Table 11–8

ADJUSTING FEASIBLE SOLUTION 1

	D_1		D_2		D_3		D_4		D_5	Capacities
W_1	13	$15-\theta$	9	$7+\theta$	4	38	11		0		60
W_2	20		10	$16-\theta$	7		2	$14+\theta$	0		30
W_3	3	θ	12		16		24	$2-\theta$	0	18	20
Requirements	15		23		38		16				

Table 11–8 shows the original allocation, now to be changed by choosing some quantity θ to go into cell W_3D_1. The problem is to find which original nonzero entry now becomes zero, to be replaced by an entry in cell W_3D_1. Notice first that if a plus quantity θ is inserted into cell W_3D_1 other cells have to be adjusted to retain the marginal totals.

Next look for the smallest value (containing a negative θ) as the cell activity to eliminate. Of the values $15 - \theta$, $16 - \theta$, and $2 - \theta$, the value $2 - \theta$ is the smallest; hence, the value of this cell is to be reduced to zero and the two units originally assigned to W_3D_4 now go to W_3D_1. When this is done (and corresponding adjustments made in the other cells) feasible solution 2, shown in Table 11–9, results.

Table 11-9

FEASIBLE SOLUTION 2

	D_1	D_2	D_3	D_4	D_5	Capacities
W_1	13 / 13	9 / 9	4 / 38	11 /	0 /	60
W_2	20 /	10 / 14	7 /	2 / 16	0 /	30
W_3	3 / 2	12 /	16 /	24 /	0 / 18	20
Requirements	15	23	38	16		

Now compare the allocation of Table 11–9 with the initial location shown in Table 11–5. Next calculate the total cost of the revised schedule of Table 11–9.

$$TC = 13\ (13) + 9\ (9) + 4\ (38) + 10\ (14) + 2\ (16) + 3\ (2) = \$580$$

Notice that total cost has been reduced by $\$646 - 580$ or $\$66$ which, incidentally, corresponds with the opportunity cost per unit, $\$33$, associated with cell W_3D_1, multiplied by the two units assigned to that cell.

The method is not complete. One keeps applying the preceding routine until he arrives at an allocation in which all $\overset{*}{c}_{ij} - c_{ij} \leq 0$. To check feasible solution 2 construct the usual table of implicit prices, Table 11–10.

Table 11-10

IMPLICIT PRICES—FEASIBLE SOLUTION 2

	D_1	D_2	D_3	D_4	D_5	Implicit Price– Warehouse
W_1	13 / $13-\theta$ [13]	9 / $9+\theta$ [9]	4 / 38 [4]	11 / [1]	0 / [10]	$a_1 = 10$
W_2	20 / [14]	10 / $14-\theta$ [10]	7 / [5]	2 / 16 [2]	0 / θ [11]	$a_2 = 11$
W_3	3 / $2+\theta$ [3]	12 / [-1]	16 / [-6]	24 / [-9]	0 / $18-\theta$ [0]	$a_3 = 0$
Implicit Price Distributors	$b_1 = 3$	$b_2 = -1$	$b_3 = -6$	$b_4 = -9$		

In Table 11–10 several steps have been combined, since they represent repetition of previous discussion. After calculating the implicit prices of each cell note that $\overset{*}{c}_{ij} - c_{ij}$ is positive in only two cases: cells W_1D_5 and W_2D_5.

$$\overset{*}{c}_{15} - c_{15} = 10 - 0 = 10$$

$$\overset{*}{c}_{25} - c_{25} = 11 - 0 = 11$$

Choose the larger of these numbers and, as before, place θ in cell W_2D_5. As before, make adjustments for this inclusion in other affected cells. Note that the cell carrying the smallest value with negative θ is cell W_1D_1 with the value $13 - \theta$. Make this assignment zero, adjust other cells accordingly, and derive feasible solution 3 shown in Table 11–11.

Table 11–11
FEASIBLE SOLUTION 3

	D_1	D_2	D_3	D_4	D_5	Capacities
W_1	13	9 / 22	4 / 38	11	0	60
W_2	20	10 / 1	7	2 / 16	0 / 13	30
W_3	3 / 15	12	16	24	0 / 5	20
Requirements	15	23	38	16		

Next calculate the cost of feasible solution 3 as follows:

$$TC = 9\,(22) + 4\,(38) + 10\,(1) + 2\,(16) + 3\,(15) = \$437$$

The cost of feasible solution 2 has been reduced by $\$580 - 437$ or \$143. Notice that this equals $\$11\,(13)$ or the opportunity cost assigned to each unit of W_2D_5 times number of units. Note also that the present cost of \$437 is only one dollar more than the lower limit on total cost (\$436) which was calculated in the absence of constraints on warehouse capacity. It would not be surprising if the current solution represents the minimum cost solution of this problem. Indeed, such is the case when the implicit prices of feasible solution 3 are prepared as shown in Table 11–12.

Table 11–12
IMPLICIT PRICES—FEASIBLE SOLUTION 3

	D_1	D_2	D_3	D_4	D_5	Implicit Price– Warehouses
W_1	13 / 2	9 / 9	4 / 4	11 / 1	0 / -1	$a_1 = -1$
W_2	20 / 3	10 / 10	7 / 5	2 / 2	0 / 0	$a_2 = 0$
W_3	3 / 3	12 / 10	16 / 5	24 / 2	0 / 0	$a_3 = 0$
Implicit Price– Distributor	$b_1 = 3$	$b_2 = 10$	$b_3 = 5$	$b_4 = 2$		

Inspection of Table 11–12 to see if some $\overset{*}{c}_{ij} - c_{ij}$ is positive, shows that no such entry exists. Feasible solution 3 represents the optimal solution to this problem.

ADDITIONAL COMMENTS ON
THE TRANSPORTATION METHOD

This discussion of the transportation method was necessarily introductory and brief. Aside from the rather tedious method of solution, no mathematics more difficult than simple algebra was encountered. Mention should be made, however, of a few features of the transportation method which have not been described here.

First, the reader might wonder if some procedure exists for finding a *first* feasible solution which, by application of the method, can be improved upon until an optimal solution is reached. A good rule of thumb is to start with the lowest shipping cost (in this problem, $2 per unit) and assign units until some constraint is reached. Then proceed with the next lowest cost, and so on. Indeed, if this procedure is followed in this problem one derives the lowest cost solution right at the start. More usually, only a few additional iterations will be required if this procedure is followed.

A second consideration involves the problem of "degeneracy" in which a problem involving, say, n constraints can be satisfied by fewer than n nonzero activity levels. (The Charnes and Cooper reference describes methods for coping with this problem).

Finally, the *general* linear programming problem has not been discussed at any length nor the various techniques (for example, simplex procedure) which have been designed to solve linear programs. (Useful, highly readable books on this subject are the Baumol and Manne references at the end of this chapter.)

FUTURE RESEARCH IN CHANNEL DECISIONS

Despite the interest of many marketing theorists in the area of distribution channel analysis relatively little has been done on models of interest to the manufacturer who is responsible for evaluation and control of alternative channels.

Perhaps the most interesting research on distribution channels concerns the derivation of measures of efficiency as viewed on a social, rather than individual firm, scale. The work of Breyer and Cox and Goodman has been directed to this problem. Also, the senior author of this book has formulated a functional theory of distribution channels. Recent work by Balderston has been concerned with the development of channel models and the derivation of conditions for market equilibrium (see respective references).

Viewed from the standpoint of the individual firm, most research on channel selection and control has involved distribution cost analyses and "make versus buy" decision models.

It appears likely that future research at the individual firm level will continue to stress distribution cost analysis but, in addition, it appears that research efforts will also begin to cope with those aspects of channel decision making which deal with the dual role of conflict and cooperation. Recent experiments in negotiation and nonzero sum game theory suggest that research along these lines may be fruitful in at least providing insights into some of the most complex problem areas faced by the marketing planner. These problems become all the more bewildering when the planner has to consider the interaction of the decisions made by channel members with his own firm's decisions regarding packaging, trademarking, pricing, and merchandising.

SUMMARY

This chapter first discussed the nature of distribution channels and the types of problems associated with channel selection and control, as viewed by the manufacturer. Some of the interrelationships between channel decisions and other classes of marketing and nonmarketing decisions faced by the firm were indicated.

Discussion followed of some of the process characteristics of channel decisions, namely, the presence of conflict and cooperation among channel members, the emphasis on long term commitment in channel selection, and the manufacturer's lack of control over decisions where outcomes are affected by the actions of channel members. Various technical approaches—game theory, distribution costing, production scheduling, and inventory control—were briefly described in relation to channel selection and channel logistics.

An illustration was given of the application of Bayesian analysis to a problem in channel selection in which the decision maker's prior probability distribution could be represented by a normal distribution and a linear opportunity loss function. The conditional and expected value of perfect information for this class of problems was computed.

Next a logistics problem associated with distribution channels—choice of a lowest cost allocation between warehouse and distributor-customers—was used to show how the transportation method of linear programming can be applied to this class of problems.

The chapter concluded with some speculative comments regarding the paths which future research might take in channel selection and control.

Selected References

ALDERSON, WROE. *Marketing Behavior and Executive Action.* Homewood, Ill.: Richard D. Irwin, 1957.
Develops the subject of distribution channels along functional lines.

BALDERSTON, FRED E. "Communication Networks in Intermediate Markets," *Management Science*, Vol. 4, No. 2 (January, 1958).
Illustrates the growing use of mathematical analysis in the study of distribution channels. Discusses equilibrium conditions in the producer-distributor complex.

BAUMOL, WILLIAM J. *Economic Theory and Operations Analysis.* Englewood Cliffs: N.J.: Prentice-Hall, Inc., 1961.
Lucid, nontechnical introduction to linear programming and other operations research techniques as related to economic theory.

BREYER, RALPH F. *Quantitative Systemic Analysis and Control: Study No. 1— Channel and Channel Group Costing.* Philadelphia: Published by the author, 1949.
Primarily concerned with developing measures of distribution channel efficiency.

CHARNES, ABRAHAM, AND COOPER, WILLIAM W. *Management Models and Industrial Applications of Linear Programming.* 2 vols. New York: John Wiley & Sons, 1961.
Contains an excellent and comprehensive, though technical, treatment of linear programming.

COX, REAVIS, AND GOODMAN, CHARLES S. "Channels and Flows in the Marketing of Housebuilding Materials." Philadelphia: Published by the authors, 1954.
Primarily concerned with developing social measures of distribution channel efficiency.

FORRESTER, JAY W. *Industrial Dynamics.* New York: John Wiley & Sons, 1960.
Illustrative of the growing use of mathematical analysis in the study of distribution channels. Illustrates the interconnections between system components as they affect inventory and production levels.

LUCE, R. DUNCAN, AND RAIFFA, HOWARD. *Games and Decisions.* New York: John Wiley & Sons, 1957.
A definitive work on the subject of game theory and its underlying assumptions. Describes various zero sum and nonzero sum solutions, including Pareto optimality and the Nash equilibrium solution to cooperative games.

MANNE, ALAN S. *Economic Analysis for Business Decisions.* New York: McGraw-Hill Book Co., 1961.
Nontechnical introduction to linear programming. Excellent book for becoming acquainted with the field.

MILLER, DAVID W., AND STARR, MARTIN K. *Executive Decisions and Operations Research.* Englewood Cliffs, N.J.: Prentice-Hall, Inc., 1960.
Clear and nontechnical introduction to linear programming and related techniques. Illustrates the use of linear programming in a promotional mix problem.

SHUBIK, MARTIN. *Strategy and Market Structure.* New York: John Wiley & Sons, 1959.
Deals with various aspects of game theory, including nonzero sum games. Attempts to explain some actual business phenomena—for example, conditions in the automobile industry—within a game theoretic framework.

Problems

1. The Major Electric Company manufactures a full line of home appliances. Presently the company uses independent wholesalers and retailers. Mr. Gunn, the marketing vice-president, feels that a sales increase could be obtained by leasing local warehouses and staffing them with company personnel, thereby offering better back-up facilities for retailers. The distribution cost group estimates that cash outlays for setting up the warehouses would amount to $2.3 million but the company could effect a cash inflow of 10 percent on sales. Mr. Gunn estimates that sales to retailers will be $25 million and will bet even money that this figure is between $21 million and $29 million.

   a) What is the breakeven point on sales, assuming a one-year payback period?

   b) List the *CVPI*.

   c) What is the expected value of perfect information?

   d) The marketing assistant vice-president will bet even money that sales will be between $23 million and $27 million. What are his *CVPI* and *EVPI*?

2. Major Electric has established warehouses in New York, Philadelphia, and Washington. Sales are above expectations, and some shipping volume must be switched between warehouses. Each warehouse supplies its local market, but there are six important in-between retailers whose orders can be shipped from any warehouse. All product volume can be expressed in terms of cubic feet of storage and trucking space. The following is the shipping cost matrix in dollars per 1,000 cubic feet,

From \ To	R_1	R_2	R_3	R_4	R_5	R_6
Wn...........	3	4	7	5	6	8
Wp...........	6	5	3	2	1	4
Ww.........	8	8	5	7	4	2

The capacity (in units of 1,000 cubic feet) available at each warehouse after considering the local market is

Wn	*Wp*	*Ww*	Total
90	40	80	210

The requirement (in units of 1,000 cubic feet) of each retailer is

R_1	R_2	R_3	R_4	R_5	R_6	Total
20	30	20	50	40	40	200

a) Find the optimum shipment schedule and its cost.

b) If extra warehouse space is available in Philadelphia at $2 per 1,000 cubic feet, how much, if any, should Major Electrical rent?

Chapter 12

CONTROL DECISIONS

~~~~~~

This chapter, which concludes Part II, marks a return to methodological matters similar to Chapters 4 through 6 in this section of the book. The term "control" might appear to be a simple one and to suggest a procedure which permits adjustment of courses of action to changes in environmental conditions for the purpose of optimizing some outcome of the system. It will be seen, however, that control decisions (and their underlying methodology) are far from trivial; this area offers provocative possibilities for further research.

The chapter begins with a simplified portrayal of the control process by using as a frame of reference the decision model described in Chapter 4. Some of the difficulties associated with the control of marketing actions are next discussed. A classification scheme which permits discussion of such concepts as marketing system feedback and stationary versus nonstationary environmental conditions is used. Note is made that Bayesian information processing provides a useful means for adapting decisions to changes in the decision maker's information about his environment.

Next some of the basic concepts underlying statistical control are discussed by drawing upon the control chart technique. It is shown how traditional quality control techniques can be modified by the introduction of explicit measures of the costs of wrong decisions. This modification is applied to an illustration drawn from distribution cost analysis.

The chapter concludes with a more speculative discussion of control systems as applied to marketing, with comments upon such concepts as (a) the cost versus value of control procedures, (b) the high "noise" level which appears to be associated with marketing environments, and (c) the apparent instability of marketing systems. The paths which future research may take in the interesting but complex area of marketing control are discussed.

THE FUNDAMENTALS OF CONTROL

Marketing decisions are forever susceptible to change. In marketing a new product, for example, it is clear that initial decisions with respect to sales effort allocation, total budget setting, and even the decision to keep the product on the market are not final. Control is a procedure consciously initiated to monitor environmental changes for the purpose of detecting significant differences between actual and desired events so as to make appropriate adjustments in the course of action being pursued.

Consider the common household thermostat. The goal of the home owner is to keep the room temperature within tolerable limits. The furnace may either be producing heat ("on" position) or not producing heat ("off" position). Temperature fluctuations in the room serve to activate the thermostat when upper or lower limits are reached. As room temperature drops below a preset level, the furnace goes on. As the heat from the furnace increases the room's temperature, the upper limit of the thermostat is reached and the furnace is turned off. The limits of the thermostat are set far enough apart so that the furnace will not be continually going on and off and thereby adding to the annoyance and expense of the home owner.

The concept of control permeates the work of the marketer as well. Consider the principle of "management by exception." According to this principle managers address their efforts to only those matters which are "out of control." For example, if the sales performance of some product is accomplishing preset goal levels, no change is made in the course of action currently being pursued. The same concept, considered in a hierarchial sense, implies that problems are only funneled up to the executive when lower level personnel do not possess the authority (or sufficient information) to resolve them. In a still somewhat different context, control may be initiated in the implementation of courses of action, in which case the manager compares the actual stage of implementation with the desired stage and, if significant differences exist, takes corrective action.

As pervasive as the concept of control is, the subtleties underlying this notion present challenging and complex problems. For example, the manager's perception of environmental changes is subject to error. He may assume that a significant change has taken place (and act on this assumption) when, in fact, no significant change has occurred, and vice versa. Moreover, control procedures incur costs of initiation and maintenance. The problem of deciding whether a course of action should be (or, in some cases, can be) controlled can become exceedingly complex, particularly in the marketing area.

CONTROL AS VIEWED WITHIN THE PROBLEM SITUATION MODEL

The reader will recall in Chapter 4 a description of problem situation models of the type

$$V = f(A_i, S_j)$$

where

V = a measure of the value to the decision maker of the action which is chosen

A_i = the factors which are subject to some control by the decision maker, that is, alternative courses of action

S_j = the factors which affect outcomes and, hence, the decision maker's value but which are not under his control

f $(\cdot)$ = the functional relationship between the factors, A_i, S_j, and the dependent variable V

He can also recall that the decision maker's task was to choose some A_i which optimized V. The realism and accuracy of the problem model (and the decision maker's choice) was dependent upon inclusion of (a) the relevant environmental variables S_j (b) the correct functional relationship between the dependent variables V and the variables, A_i and S_j, and (c) the correct numerical values of the parameters S_j. If any of these conditions were to change, some course of action other than the one chosen might be preferable.

Consider as an illustration a simple situation in quality control. Suppose one is interested only in keeping the average diameter of the product of a machine, which is producing metal washers, within some preset limits. Also assume that the form of the probability distribution characterizing the process and other relevant parameters remain constant over time but that the mean is subject to change from "assignable" causes (for example, the machine going out of adjustment).

The courses of action may be simply: A_1 = keep the machine running and A_2 = stop the machine and search for and correct the assignable cause. In this illustrative case only the values of some of the environmental variables which influence the process mean are subject to change. Even at that, certain conditions must be met if one is to talk meaningfully about the possibility of control:

1. The values of the parameters underlying "in control" operation must not be so broadly set as to cover all possible conditions.
2. The available courses of action must be "rich" enough to allow the decision maker to do something about an out-of-control situation.

If neither of the above conditions is met the possibility of control cannot be considered. In terms of the quality control illustration if *any* average diameter washer is acceptable, then there is no need to control the process. Or, if the mean diameter exceeds some desired diameter and yet no possibility exists for correcting the condition, then the process is not subject to continuous control. That is, while the machine could be shut down under these conditions, under the above restrictions the machine would never be started up again. Even in this simple illustration it is clear that a system is needed which meets the following requirements:

1. Is capable of defining and detecting a significant change in the state of the process.
2. Is capable of prescribing an action which will move the process back into some desirable state.
3. Represents the lowest cost combination of system installation, system maintenance, adjustment (including the cost associated with machine downtime), and the costs of wrong decisions. Included in the evaluation, of course, is the alternative of no control system at all.

At this juncture the complexities involved in control models are probably becoming apparent. However, the questions arise of how to approach the problem of control when the machine is subject to tool wear over time or if the variance or the whole probability distribution of output is subject to change. These questions are hardly simple ones. It is apparent that some type of classification system is needed for viewing decisions over time, a condition implied by the concept of control.

A FRAMEWORK FOR CLASSIFYING DECISION TYPES

Related to the discussion of the previous section (and earlier chapters, as well) Ward Edwards (see reference at the end of this chapter) has proposed a useful taxonomy for classifying time-dependent decisions. As descriptors, Edwards uses the following:

1. Stationary versus nonstationary environment.

　　2. Environment affected versus unaffected by previous decisions.
　　3. Decision maker's information affected versus unaffected by the
　　　　results of earlier decisions.

While eight combinations of the above descriptors are possible,
only five are used here, since some combinations are internally
inconsistent.

　　Suppose we examine these five combinations and relate them to
previous discussion in this or earlier chapters.

　　1. Stationary environment; neither environment nor decision maker's
information is affected by the results of earlier decisions. This is the
static, "one-shot" type of decision which was considered under the discussion of various "standard gambles" in which the decision maker was
to imagine himself in a series of betting situations. Each problem situation was assumed to start anew.

　　2. Stationary environment; environment unaffected by decisions; but
information is affected by earlier decisions. This situation was encountered in the use of preposterior analyses when one of the alternatives
available to the decision maker concerned *delaying* a terminal decision
until additional information about the relevant states of nature was obtained by, say, conducting a market survey.

　　3. Nonstationary environment; environment and decision maker's information are unaffected by decisions. In this instance the decision maker
is not able to learn. The best he can do is "keep flexible" and try to react
as best he can to current events. He must deal with an unstable, unpredictable environment.

　　4. Nonstationary environment; environment unaffected by decisions;
but information controlled by decisions. In this case the decision maker
must "learn" the relationship of environmental variables to time. Decisions to obtain information about the environment are concerned with
finding the relationship of these variables to the time variable.

　　5. Nonstationary environment; environment affected by decisions; information affected by decisions. This is perhaps the most complex category of sequential decision making, in which the decision maker's action
interacts with environmental variables (for example, a price reduction
which invites retaliation by competitors and the probability of their taking subsequent price action, and so forth).

The three remaining cases can be listed, namely: (*a*) stationary
environment; environment affected by decisions; information affected by decisions; (*b*) stationary environment; environment affected by decisions; information unaffected by previous decisions;
and (*c*) nonstationary environment; environment affected by decisions; information unaffected by previous decisions. It is clear that
combination (*a*) is internally inconsistent since an environment
which can be affected by decisions must be nonstationary. Cases
(*b*) and (*c*) are internally inconsistent since the presence or ab-

sence of an environmental change can only be defined realistically in terms of the decision maker's information about it. Table 12–1 summarizes the above descriptions.

Table 12–1

SUMMARY OF CLASSIFICATION FRAMEWORK—DYNAMIC DECISION MAKING

Type of Environment	Environment Affected by Decisions		Environment Unaffected by Decisions	
	Information Affected	Information Unaffected	Information Affected	Information Unaffected
Stationary.........	(*a*)	(*b*)	Case 2	Case 1
Nonstationary......	Case 5	(*c*)	Case 4	Case 3

Now that a classificatory framework has been introduced to show the possible types of situations facing the decision maker, the familiar concepts of statistical control can be placed within this taxonomy and the limitations of present control techniques discussed. The traditional notions of statistical control (as, say, used by quality control analysts) usually assume a stationary environment prior to the initiation of control. After control is initiated, typically one parameter of the environment, for example, the mean of the process, is assumed to be subject to change over time while other parameters, for example, the variance, are assumed to remain constant over time.

The statistician thus defines a "stable" distribution as one whose parameters and distribution form remain constant over time. In terms of the preceding framework, common statistical control procedures assume that the distribution form (for example, normal, binomial, and so forth) is stationary and so are all parameters (save the one being controlled) assumed to be stationary. Decisions to adjust the process (for example, remove assignable causes of out-of-control conditions such as operator error or machine wear) do affect some of the environmental variables. Hence, in the case of a single process parameter such as the process mean, the statisical control analyst deals with Case 5 above, but with respect to all other environmental factors he is assumed to be dealing with Case 1.

The above situation can be contrasted with that of the marketing planner who must deal with decisions where values of the parameters, the functional relationship between them and the decison maker's measure of effectiveness, and the relevancy of environmental variables can all change over time (nonstationary) and, in many cases, where his decisions affect the environment and his information about the environment. This situation is represented by Case 5 and can become exceedingly complex to analyze.

The Bayesian approach which has been employed in earlier chapters is, strictly speaking, applicable to only stationary environments. However, more than one *level* of stationarity can be conisdered. If the parameters can be defined with respect to time, and if *these* definitions are assumed to remain invariant with time, then a second-level stationarity could be assumed. It is clear, in theory, that super-rules could also be constructed for controlling the second-level rules if need be, and so on. In practice, however, such extensions are difficult to make

The problem of control in marketing planning will be reexamined after some of the more traditional uses of statisical control have been explored.

THE FUNDAMENTALS OF STATISTICAL CONTROL

Statistical methods in quality control go back some twenty-five years (see Shewhart reference at end of the chapter) and currently are used by virtually every major industry in the control of production processes and the quality of incoming and outgoing products. In more recent years statistical methods have been extended to deal with various financial matters, for example, auditing of accounts, cost control, and budgetary procedures. They have also been used in the forecasting of sales and in the determination of salesmen's compensation.

In this section of the chapter the use of statistical methods in the control of distribution costs will be demonstrated by means of the control chart technique. First the more traditional use of control charts in controlling distribution costs will be shown while a discussion of decision theory in this type of application will be reserved for the next section of this chapter.

The control device of the statistician is the so-called control chart on which is plotted some output of interest, for example, the weekly cost of some business activity. Suppose the marketing planner was interested in setting up a control on weekly traveling expenses for a group of salesmen. Even on the (unrealistic) assumption that each salesman makes roughly the same territorial coverage each week, one could expect individual differences among salesmen in any given week and differences among weeks for any given salesman. These differences can arise from a host of individual causes (car breakdown, weather variations, variations in the amount of customer entertainment, and so on) which, it will be assumed, operate independently over time.

Assume, for expository purposes, that the marketing planner is interested only in controlling the average weekly sales expense for the group of salesmen. Since the number of salesmen is quite large (say, over a thousand), the total cost of compiling expense data on every individual salesman for each week is also assumed to be large. Suppose that the marketing planner would prefer to take a random sample of salesmen's records each week and, on the basis of his sample evidence, decide whether salesmen's expenses for the whole group are in control or not

Assume that the marketing manager has collected past data for several weeks on the expenses of *all* salesmen for the purpose of estimating the form and parameters of the system. After all past assignable causes have been eliminated, the planner notes that his distribution of weekly sales expense can be represented by a normal distribution with a mean expense, $\mu = \$150$ and a standard deviation, $\sigma = \$30$. Figure 12-1 shows this theoretical distribution, as estimated from past data.

Figure 12-1

NORMAL DISTRIBUTION—SALESMEN'S WEEKLY EXPENSES

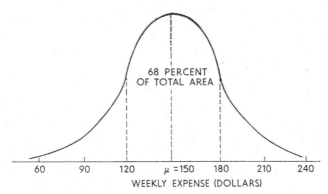

68 PERCENT OF TOTAL AREA

| 60 | 90 | 120 | μ =150 | 180 | 210 | 240 |

WEEKLY EXPENSE (DOLLARS)

Note from Figure 12-1 that about 68 percent of the area of the curve lies between $120 and $180 ($\mu \pm \sigma$). Similarly, about 95 percent of the area lies between $\mu \pm 2\sigma$ and about 99.7 percent of the area lies between $\mu \pm 3\sigma$. It is assumed, of course, that the planner chooses to treat the parameters of his past data as the "true" mean and standard deviation.

Now assume that the planner wishes to construct a control chart for monitoring weekly sales expense for the total group of salesmen. He is willing to assume that both the distribution form (normal)

and the variance remain constant over time. That is, he wishes to set up a control chart for the mean only. Further assume that the expense of sampling his population of salesmen is such as to warrant taking a random sample of nine salesmen each week and computing the mean from the sample of salesmen.

The reader will recall from elementary statistics the concept of the standard error of the mean (also discussed in Chapter 10). This statistic, in effect, is the standard deviation of a random sampling distribution. That is, if one were to take a very large number of random samples of size n from some normally distributed universe, the grand mean of the sample means would equal μ and the various sample means would also be normally distributed with a standard deviation given by

$$\sigma_{\bar{x}} = \frac{\sigma}{\sqrt{n}}$$

In terms of the present example, the grand mean of all sample means of size $n = 9$ would equal $\mu\,(x) = 130$ and the standard deviation of these sample means would be

$$\sigma_{\bar{x}} = \frac{30}{\sqrt{9}} = \$10$$

The distribution of the mean and the original distribution for comparison are plotted in Figure 12–2.

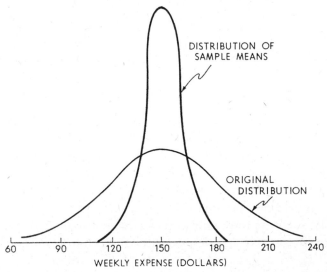

Figure 12–2

SALESMEN'S WEEKLY EXPENSE—ORIGINAL DISTRIBUTION
AND THE DISTRIBUTION OF SAMPLE MEANS BASED ON $n = 9$

DISTRIBUTION OF
SAMPLE MEANS

ORIGINAL
DISTRIBUTION

60   90   120   150   180   210   240
WEEKLY EXPENSE (DOLLARS)

As can be inferred from Figure 12–2, the planner would expect practically all sample means based on $n = 9$ to fall within \$120–\$180, which is the range given by $\mu \pm 3\,\sigma_{\bar{x}}$. Suppose now that the planner would like to set up a control chart for monitoring weekly sales expense. He wishes to assume only a 5 percent chance (approximately) of alerting marketing management to a change in mean weekly sales expenses when no change has, in fact, occurred. (In terms of the discussion in Chapter 5, he is willing to place the risk of an alpha-type error at approximately .05.) The resultant control chart, along with some assumed weekly average expense figures, is shown in Figure 12–3.

Figure 12–3

TYPICAL CONTROL CHART FOR SAMPLE MEAN

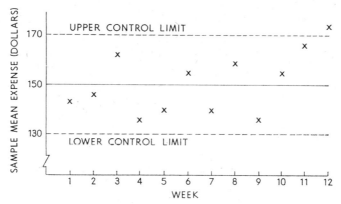

A review of the data shown in the control chart of Figure 12–3 indicates that the control limits have been set at $\mu \pm 2\,\sigma_{\bar{x}}$ or \$170 for the upper control limit and \$130 for the lower control limit. This involves an alpha risk of approximately 5 percent. Viewing the time path of the data, note that average weekly expense (the sample mean) stays within the control limits during the first several weeks. At week 11, mean sales expense moves rather close to the upper control limit and, at week 12, exceeds the upper control limit. Presumably at this time the planner would alert marketing management to this situation and an investigation would be launched into determining some assignable cause for the deviation.

The preceding description, in oversimplified form, demonstrates the basic principles and mechanics underlying control charts. As the reader might already have surmised, however, several questions underlie the traditional approach to control chart preparation:

1. Why was the particular alpha risk, 0.05, used?

2. How are beta risks (the risk of assuming the process to be in control when it really is not) handled?
3. How are the costs of installing and maintaining the control system in the first place, incorporated?

Typical control charts of the type just described are not sufficient to provide explicit guidance toward answering the above questions. Some of these questions are considered in the next section of the chapter as some of the concepts of decision theory as applied to statistical control are discussed.

DECISION THEORY IN STATISTICAL CONTROL

The preceding exposition of the typical control chart (such as used in quality and cost control) left open the reasons underlying the choice of a particular risk level (0.05 in this case) for making an alpha error, that is, acting as though the process were not in control when, in fact, it was in control. The point of interest now is to see how control limits may be set which reflect both the chances and costs of examining systems for possible assignable causes when the system is really "in control" versus "out of control."

The example of the preceding section can serve as a focal point for further elaboration. Suppose now that the same process statistics apply as before but the analyst is interested in setting control chart limits which reflect the costs associated with investigating, say, unfavorable deviations (sales expenses above the mean of $150). Table 12–2 summarizes some (hypothetical) cost figures for the sales expense problem.

Table 12–2

CONDITIONAL COSTS OF INVESTIGATING UNFAVORABLE DEVIATIONS
(Sales Expense Problem)

Acts	S_1: System in Control	S_2: System Out of Control
A_1: Investigate deviation..............	\$5	\$5 + D
A_2: Do not investigate deviation........	\$0	\$2 D

The assumed costs in Table 12–2 indicate that if *any* sales expense above the $\mu = \$150$ line is investigated a cost of $5 will be incurred if the system is really in control and the deviation is just due to sampling variation. This cost reflects merely the time required to conduct the investigation. If the unfavorable deviation is not investigated, and if, indeed, the system is not out of control, the cost incurred is zero.

If the unfavorable deviation is investigated *and* the system is really out of control, it is assumed that the usual $5 investigatory cost will be incurred, plus, however, a correction cost equal to the dollar value of the unfavorable deviation D. If, however, an unfavorable deviation is not investigated, and if the system is really out of control, it is assumed that the delays incurred in responding to the true situation mount as a function ($2 D), of the size of the unfavorable deviation D through belatedly correcting a situation which should have been investigated via the control chart technique.

The figures in Table 12–2 are, of course, conditional cost figures. Still required are the probabilities that various unfavorable deviations (which could be observed) will arise. For example, suppose one set up the following list of possible unfavorable deviations: $D_i = \$5; 10; 15; 20; 25$. That is, if an unfavorable deviation of $D_1 = \$5$ or ($\$155 - \$150$) were observed on the control chart (for sample size $n = 9$), would it pay to investigate this unfavorable deviation?

Before answering this particular question, however, let us try to approach the problem somewhat more generally by defining the following conditional probabilities:

$$P (D_i \mid S_1) = p_i$$
$$P (D_i \mid S_2) = 1 - p_i \qquad \text{where: } D_i = \bar{x}_i - \mu \geqslant 0$$

That is, the probability of getting an unfavorable expense deviation, D_i, given that the system is in control ($\mu = 150$) can be labelled as p_i; and the probability of getting this deviation, given that the system is not in control ($\mu \neq 150$), can be labelled as $1 - p_i$ since, clearly, the system's mean is either equal to or not equal to 150.

Next, the expected costs associated with taking acts A_1 (investigate) and A_2 (do not investigate) can be determined as follows:

$$EC (A_1 \mid D_i) = 5 p_i + (5 + D_i) (1 - p_i)$$
$$EC (A_2 \mid D_i) = 0 p_i + 2 D_i (1 - p_i)$$

Now, if $EC (A_1 \mid D_i) = EC (A_2 \mid D_i)$ it matters not whether the analyst investigates or does not investigate the deviation. Presumably the analyst will investigate in all cases where $EC (A_1 \mid D_i) < EC (A_2 \mid D_i)$ and will not investigate in all cases wherein $EC (A_1 \mid D_i) > EC (A_2 \mid D_i)$. The next step is to determine the critical probability which would just make the expected costs of the two acts, A_1 and A_2, equal. This can be done by setting the two above equations equal to each other and solving for the value of p_i which will be called the critical value p_c.

$$5\,p_i + (5 + D_i)\,(1 - p_i) = 0\,p_i + 2\,D_i\,(1 - p_i)$$
$$5\,p_i + 5 + D_i - 5\,p_i - p_i\,D_i = 2\,D_i - 2\,p_i\,D_i$$
$$p_i\,D_i = D_i - 5$$
$$p_c = p_i = \frac{D_i - 5}{D_i}\,;\ \text{where } D_i \geqslant 5$$

Notice that the constraint on D_i must be changed to values equal to or greater than \$5.00 so as to preserve the conventional restriction (nonnegativity) on probabilities. (Obviously, the analyst will not wish to investigate a deviation where the cost of investigation exceeds the cost of the deviation itself.) For example, if D_i is only \$5.00 (that is, the sample mean is \$155), this deviation would not be investigated. If, on the other hand, D_i is very large, say, \$200 (that is, the sample mean is \$350), then $p_c = \dfrac{\$195}{200}$ or virtually equal to unity, and it would obviously pay to investigate this large a deviation.

Now critical probability values can be calculated for $D_1 = 5$; $D_2 = 10$; $D_3 = 15$; $D_4 = 20$; and $D_5 = 25$. For example, for $D_2 = 10$

$$p_c\,(D_2) = \frac{10 - 5}{10} = 0.5$$

This value is plotted in Figure 12–4 along with other critical probability value for deviations D_2 through D_5 (calculated by similar methods) and a smooth curve is faired in between the points.

Figure 12–4 indicates that an unfavorable deviation of, say, \$20 (that is, \$170 $-$ 150) should be investigated if the conditional probability of getting this large an unfavorable deviation is less than or equal to 0.75, given that the process is really in control. If this probability exceeds 0.75, however, it does not pay to investigate the deviation.

The next step, then, is to calculate the conditional probability.

$$P\,(D_4 \geqslant 20\ |\ S_1)$$

First recall from Chapter 5 that the conditional probability, say, $P\,(A\,|\,B)$ is defined as follows:

$$P\,(A\ |\ B) = \frac{P\,(A \text{ and } B)}{P\,(B)}$$

Figure 12-4

INVESTIGATORY CHART WHICH ILLUSTRATES COSTS OF SEARCH
AND CORRECTION OF ASSIGNABLE CAUSES

(Sales Expense Example)

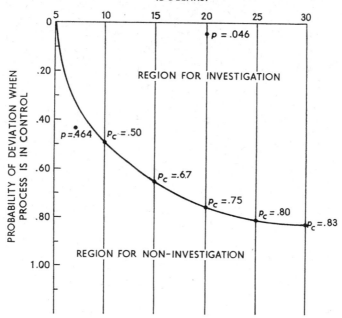

Also recall, from earlier discussion regarding the standard error of the mean, that this statistic is normally distributed, with mean $= \mu$ and standard deviation,

$$\sigma_{\bar{x}} = \frac{\sigma}{\sqrt{n}}$$

In this illustration, $\mu = 150$ and $\sigma_{\bar{x}} = 10$. The probability of getting an unfavorable deviation, $(\bar{x} - \mu > 0)$ is equal to 0.5. Thus, $P(B) = 0.5$. The probability of getting an unfavorable deviation of \$20 or more is found by consulting a table of the standardized normal cumulative distribution function (Table 12-3) for

$$Z = \frac{\bar{x} - \mu}{\sigma_{\bar{x}}} = \frac{170 - 150}{10}$$

$$Z = 2$$

The probability of getting a Z value greater than or equal to 2 is found in the single tail of the standardized unit normal distribution and is equal to approximately .023. Thus, the probability of D_i equalling or exceeding \$20, given that the deviation is unfavorable, is

$$P\,(D_4 \geqslant 20 \mid S_1) = .023/.50 = .046$$

This value is plotted in Figure 12–4 and it will be noted that the analyst would definitely investigate an unfavorable deviation of \$20.

Table 12–3

THE STANDARDIZED NORMAL CUMULATIVE DISTRIBUTION FUNCTION

.5	0.00	0.01	0.02	0.03	0.04	0.05	0.06	0.07	0.08	0.09
0.0	0.5000	0.5040	0.5080	0.5120	0.5160	0.5199	0.5239	0.5279	0.5319	0.5359
0.1	0.5398	0.5438	0.5478	0.5517	0.5557	0.5596	0.5636	0.5675	0.5714	0.5753
0.2	0.5793	0.5832	0.5871	0.5910	0.5948	0.5987	0.6026	0.6064	0.6103	0.6141
0.3	0.6179	0.6217	0.6255	0.6293	0.6331	0.6368	0.6406	0.6443	0.6480	0.6517
0.4	0.6554	0.6591	0.6628	0.6664	0.6700	0.6736	0.6772	0.6808	0.6844	0.6879
0.5	0.6915	0.6950	0.6985	0.7019	0.7054	0.7088	0.7123	0.7157	0.7190	0.7224
0.6	0.7257	0.7291	0.7324	0.7357	0.7389	0.7422	0.7454	0.7486	0.7517	0.7549
0.7	0.7580	0.7611	0.7642	0.7673	0.7703	0.7734	0.7764	0.7794	0.7823	0.7852
0.8	0.7881	0.7910	0.7939	0.7967	0.7995	0.8023	0.8051	0.8078	0.8106	0.8133
0.9	0.8159	0.8186	0.8212	0.8238	0.8264	0.8289	0.8315	0.8340	0.8365	0.8389
1.0	0.8413	0.8438	0.8461	0.8485	0.8508	0.8531	0.8544	0.8577	0.8599	0.8621
1.1	0.8643	0.8665	0.8686	0.8708	0.8729	0.8749	0.8770	0.8790	0.8810	0.8830
1.2	0.8849	0.8869	0.8888	0.8907	0.8925	0.8944	0.8962	0.8980	0.8997	0.90147
1.3	0.90320	0.90490	0.90658	0.90824	0.90988	0.91149	0.91309	0.91466	0.91621	0.91774
1.4	0.91924	0.92073	0.92220	0.92364	0.92507	0.92647	0.92785	0.92922	0.93056	0.93189
1.5	0.93319	0.93448	0.93574	0.93699	0.93822	0.93943	0.94062	0.94179	0.94295	0.94408
1.6	0.94520	0.94630	0.94738	0.94845	0.94950	0.95053	0.95154	0.95254	0.95352	0.95449
1.7	0.95543	0.95637	0.95728	0.95818	0.95907	0.95994	0.96080	0.96164	0.96246	0.96327
1.8	0.96407	0.96485	0.96562	0.96638	0.96712	0.96784	0.96856	0.96926	0.96995	0.97062
1.9	0.97128	0.97193	0.97257	0.97320	0.97381	0.97441	0.97500	0.97558	0.97615	0.97670
2.0	0.97725	0.97778	0.97831	0.97882	0.97932	0.97982	0.98030	0.98077	0.98124	0.98169
2.1	0.98214	0.98257	0.98300	0.98341	0.98382	0.98422	0.98461	0.98500	0.98537	0.98574
2.2	0.98610	0.98645	0.98679	0.98713	0.98745	0.98778	0.98809	0.98840	0.98870	0.98890
2.3	0.98298	0.98956	0.98983	0.9^20097	0.9^20358	0.9^20613	0.9^20863	0.9^21106	0.9^21344	0.9^21576
2.4	0.9^21802	0.9^22024	0.9^22240	0.9^22451	0.9^22656	0.9^22857	0.9^23053	0.9^23244	0.9^23431	0.9^23613
2.5	0.9^23790	0.9^23963	0.9^24132	0.9^24297	0.9^24457	0.9^24614	0.9^24766	0.9^24915	0.9^25060	0.9^25201
3.0	0.9^28650	0.9^28694	0.9^28736	0.9^28777	0.9^28817	0.9^28856	0.9^28893	0.9^28930	0.9^28965	0.9^28999
3.5	0.9^37674	0.9^37759	0.9^37842	0.9^37922	0.9^37999	0.9^38074	0.9^38146	0.9^38215	0.9^38282	0.9^38347
4.0	0.9^46833	0.9^46964	0.9^47090	0.9^47211	0.9^47327	0.9^47439	0.9^47546	0.9^47649	0.9^47748	0.9^47843

Next check to see whether an unfavorable deviation of \$7 would prompt investigation. Follow the same procedure.

$$P\,(D_i \geqslant 7 \mid S_1) = \frac{.232}{.5} = .464$$

Note in this instance that the probability value .464 falls in the region of noninvestigation.

To understand these results, go back and calculate the costs associated with each act, A_1 and A_2, for the unfavorable deviations of \$20 and \$7, respectively.

For the $20 case:

$$EC\ (A_1) = .046\ (\$5) + .954\ (\$5 + \$20)$$
$$= .23 + 23.85$$
$$= \$24.18$$
$$EC\ (A_2) = .046\ (\$0) + .954\ (2 \times \$20)$$
$$= \$38.16$$

The act A_1 (investigate) clearly entails the lower cost; hence the analyst will choose to investigate an unfavorable expense deviation of $20.

For the $7 case:

$$EC\ (A_1) = .464\ (\$5) + .536\ (\$5 + \$7)$$
$$= 2.32 + 6.43$$
$$= \$8.75$$
$$EC\ (A_2) = .464\ (\$0) + .536\ (2 \times \$7)$$
$$= \$7.50$$

The act A_2 (do not investigate) clearly involves a lower cost; hence the analyst would choose not to investigate an expense deviation of this magnitude.

It is clear that the foregoing procedure could be extended to deal with favorable expense deviations as well. (See the Bierman, Fouraker, and Jaedicke reference at the end of this chapter). The analyst might wish to investigate favorable deviations as well as unfavorable ones either for the purpose of rewarding the salesmen for good performance or for seeing if the basis on which past controls were set up (mean and standard deviation of assumed population) is still indicative of current conditions.

Note should be made of the fact that in the foregoing problem it was assumed that the process was just as likely to be in control as out of control. This assumption is implied by the assumption that $P\ (D_i\,|\,S_1) = P\ (S_1\,|\,D_i)$. For example, suppose $D_i \geq 20$. Then, according to the model,

$$P\ (S_1\,|\,D_i \geq 20) = \frac{P\ (D_i \geq 20\,|\,S_1)\ \cdot\ P\ (S_1)}{P\ (D_i \geq 20\,|\,S_1)\ \cdot\ P\ (S_1) + P\ (D_i \geq 20\,|\,S_2)\ \cdot\ P\ (S_2)}$$

$$= \frac{.046\ (.5)}{.046\ (.5) + .954\ (.5)}$$

$$= .046,\ \text{or as shown in this illustration}$$

The above assumption (equal prior probabilities for S_1 versus S_2) could have been relaxed without changing the essentials of the method.

While it has been shown how the cost of errors associated with investigating an unfavorable deviation (when the process is in control) and failing to investigate an unfavorable deviation (when the process is out of control) affects the decision rule, explicit consideration has not been given to the cost of the control system itself. This situation is considered in the next section of this chapter.

THE COST OF CONTROL

When the cost attached to maintaining the control system is introduced as well as the costs attached to decision errors, the control problem becomes quite complex. First, one must have some prior idea as to how frequently the course of action might change in the control period as well as the cost of maintaining the system. A very simple illustration will show just some of the complications which arise.

Suppose the analyst is dealing with a sales expense situation as before and that all expense figures per week exceeding $200/salesman are considered bad while all expenses per week equal to or less than this amount are considered good. Suppose, as before, $S_1 =$ system in control and $S_2 =$ system not in control. Assume that the analyst will merely look at a random sample of ten sales expense records, classifying them as g (good) or b (bad) according to the above definitions. If he sees one or more bad records (a sample outcome which will be called Z_2), he assumes that the system is out of control. He also assumes that, a priori, the system will be in control 60 percent of the time and out of control 40 percent of the time. Moreover, he assumes that the proportion p_1 which defines an in-control system is .05 and the proportion p_2 which defines an out-of-control system is .30. (For example, if just 5 percent of all expenses would be classified as b then the system is considered in control.) Finally assume that the cost of maintaining the system (sampling and tabulating) amounts to $20/week.

The cost of investigating errors is given in Table 12–4.

Even with the very simple assumptions made above, the problem of deciding whether to adopt a control system is not trivial. As an illustration, however, assume that the analyst wishes to see if the system would pay for itself. His alternative is not to use any control system at all, that is, not to investigate.

Table 12–4
COST OF INVESTIGATING ERRORS

Acts	S_1: System in Control	S_2: System Out of Control
A_1: Investigate..............	10	20
A_2: Do not investigate.........	0	100

If the analyst decides not to investigate, the cost of this decision is conditional upon whether the system is in or out of control.

$$EC \text{ (No Control)} = .60 \text{ ($\$0$)} + .40 \text{ ($\$100$)} = \$40$$

That is, for any particular week, the analyst faces an expected cost of \$40 if he never sets up a control system and, it is assumed, never investigates.

The weekly cost of using the control system will be equal to

$$EC \text{ (Control System)} = P(S_1) \cdot P(Z_1 \mid S_1) \text{ ($\$0$)} + P(S_1) \cdot P(Z_2 \mid S_1)$$
$$\text{($\$10$)} + P(S_2) \cdot P(Z_2 \mid S_2) \text{ ($\$20$)} + P(S_2) \cdot P(Z_1 \mid S_2)$$
$$\text{($\$100$)} + \$20$$

Notice that a rather large expression has been introduced to compute in just this simple dichotomous, one-stage case. Moreover, one must now determine $P(Z_1 \mid S_1); P(Z_2 \mid S_1); P(Z_2 \mid S_2);$ and $P(Z_1 \mid S_2)$. These are the conditional probabilities of getting

$$Z_1 = \text{zero } b\text{'s; } (n = 10; p_i)$$
$$Z_2 = \text{one or more } b\text{'s; } (n = 10; p_i)$$

The conditional probability of getting no "bad" records, given that underlying state S_1 (probability of a bad record $p_1 = .05$) is equal to the probability of getting all good items where N_g is the number of good items.

$$P(N_g = 10 \mid 1 - p_1 = .95, n = 10) = {}_{10}C_{10} (.95)^{10} \cdot (.05)^0 \approx .60$$

Hence, the conditional probability of getting at least one "bad" record, given that the system is really in control, is $1 - .60$ or $.40$. Thus,

$$P(Z_1 \mid S_1) = .60$$
$$P(Z_2 \mid S_1) = .40$$

Similarly, the conditional probability of getting no "bad" records ($N_b = 0$) given that the underlying state S_2 (probability of a bad record $p_2 = .30$) is

$$P(N_g = 10 \mid 1 - p_2 = .70, n = 10) = {}_{10}C_{10} (.70)^{10} \cdot (.30)^0 \approx .03$$

Hence, the conditional probability of getting at least one "bad" record, given that the system is really out of control, is $1 - .03$ or $.97$. Thus,

$$P\,(Z_2 \mid S_2) = .97$$
$$P\,(Z_1 \mid S_2) = .03$$

Now, if the appropriate values are substituted in the *EC* (Control System) equation,

$$EC\ \text{(Control System)} = .60\,(.60)\,(\$0) + .60\,(\,40)\,(\$10) + .40\,(.97)\,(\$20) \\ + .40\,(.03)\,(\$100) + \$20$$

$$= \$11.36 + \$20$$

$$= \$31.36$$

Notice that in this case the cost of control system more than pays for itself. The expected cost of the system is only $31.36, clearly less than that associated with foregoing the use of a control system.

Notice, however, that in this simple illustration such considerations as (*a*) the proper frequency of control, (*b*) the duration of the control system, and (*c*) the best type of control system to set up have been neglected. With regard to the latter point, it is quite possible that some other control rule might be superior to the one chosen (investigate if the number of "bad" records exceeds zero in the sample of ten; otherwise, do not investigate).

Control systems that approach any degree of realism can thus become exceedingly difficult to analyze. It is little wonder, perhaps, why so many actual applications of control embody the less complex—if less sophisticated—control charts which do not explicity consider the cost of wrong decisions and the cost of maintaining the control system, itself.

FUTURE RESEARCH ON CONTROL DECISIONS

The problems discussed in this chapter, even with deliberate attempts to oversimplify, nevertheless show some of the complexities associated with the design and evaluation of marketing control systems. It is not difficult to imagine the problems encountered in attempting to extend these techniques to strategic-level problems in marketing plans control. Yet this area is where the larger payoffs of applied research appear to lie.

The marketing planner must deal with changes in environmental variables over time and with the way in which these changes can affect the efficiency of current actions with respect to product, price, promotion, and channels. Contingency planning, for example, is just such an attempt to design a strategy which contains within it a set of decision rules for reacting to new information. Moreover, judged by the recent activities of some of the nation's most progressive companies, it would appear that the time is not very far distant when the planner will be provided with a continuous flow of data on customer purchase rates, brand switching, and so forth.

Future research on marketing control systems is thus likely to emphasize the nonstationary characteristics of the decision parameters and the more or less continuous use of marketing experimentation, either in simulated or real-world environments. It is also probable that the design of control systems will be aided by computer simulation of alternative strategies and future developments in interactive models. For example, tests of alternative promotional mixes may well be conducted in conjunction with operating systems inasmuch as one of the continuing problems which a marketer faces is this: "What is a superior course of action when some important environmental variables change?"

It appears probable, then, that future research in marketing control will deal to an increasing extent with (*a*) multiple nonstationary parameters, (*b*) the cost of wrong decisions, (*c*) the cost of control maintenance, and (*d*) the relationship of the effectiveness of alternative courses of action to changes in the functional form and parameter values of environmental variables. In addition to increased investigation of more "global" control models, it seems likely that greater attention will be given to applying what is already known about statistical control to such tactical problem areas as distribution cost analysis and sales forecasting. Some of the recent work in exponential smoothing[1] is quite amenable to the use of statistical control techniques.

SUMMARY

This chapter has raised many more questions than answers concerning the use of control techniques in marketing.

It first discussed a framework for viewing dynamic decisions and discussed some of the conditions underlying the notion of control. It indicated that most of the work in control systems has assumed a stable system for all parameters save one, for example, the arithmetic mean of a process. It discussed a typical control chart applica-

---

[1]Robert Brown, *Statistical Forecasting for Inventory Control* (New York: McGraw-Hill Book Co., 1959).

tion to a sales expense problem and pointed out some of the limitations of the technique.

It next described via a simplified case how some of the concepts of decision theory (the risks and costs of wrong decisions) can be used in a control framework for the purpose of attempting to evaluate the worth of investigating deviations from anticipated system performance.

The control problem was carried an additional step by a simple illustration which included the cost of control maintenance. The question in this section was whether or not the gains from control justified its cost. Some of the perplexing issues involved in the design of alternative control systems were then pointed out. Finally, some speculative comments were offered concerning the direction which future research on marketing control systems may take. It was indicated that these efforts will probably make use of techniques drawn from decision theory and computer simulation of complex, interactive systems.

Selected References

ACKOFF, RUSSELL L. "The Concept and Exercise of Control in Operations Research," *Proceedings of the First International Conference on Operational Research*, (Oxford, 1952). Baltimore: Operations Research Society of America, 1957.

> A provocative treatment of some of the more subtle issues underlying control techniques; a model is presented which embodies such notions as the cost of wrong decisions and the cost of control maintenance.

BEER, STAFFORD. *Cybernetics and Management.* New York: John Wiley & Sons, Inc., 1959.

> A lucid introductory work on the general problems of control for man and machines.

BIERMAN, HAROLD; FOURAKER, LAWRENCE E.; AND JAEDICKE, ROBERT K. *Quantitative Analysis for Business Decisions.* Homewood, Ill.: Richard D. Irwin, Inc., 1961.

> Provides the basis for the decision theory approach to control problems which is described in this chapter.

COWDEN, DUDLEY J. *Statistical Methods in Quality Control.* Englewood Cliffs, N.J.: Prentice-Hall, Inc., 1957.

> Offers a definite treatment of statistical methodology as applied to problems in quality control.

EDWARDS, WARD. "Dynamic Decision Theory and Probabilistic Information Processing," *Human Factors* (April, 1962).

> Provides both a framework (discussed in this chapter) for analyzing dynamic decisions and a summary of the research efforts (stochastic learning models, Bayesian information processing, dynamic programming) being undertaken in this area. Edwards also discusses some recent developments in probabilistic information processing and the potential applicability of Bayesian techniques to this field.

LONGMAN, DONALD R., AND SCHIFF, MICHAEL. *Practical Distribution Cost Analysis.* Homewood, Ill.: Richard D. Irwin, Inc., 1955.

> Represents a comprehensive treatment of distribution cost analysis. It would appear that some of the techniques discussed in this chapter might find useful application to this area of the marketer's interest.

SHEWHART, W. A. *Statistical Method from the Viewpoint of Quality Control.* Washington, D.C.: U.S. Department of Agriculture, 1939.
A "classic" in the field of statistical control and still offers interesting reading to anyone interested in control problems.

SIELAFF, THEODORE J. *Statistics in Action.* San Jose, Calif.: The Lansford Press, 1963.
Offers a set of readings in control, including statistical sampling for accountants, statistics in auditing, and controls on accuracy in clerical work.

Problems

1. The Wilson Company is a subassembler for a large computer manufacturer located in the western section of the United States. Mr. Latta, the quality control engineer, is presently concerned with the value of inspecting versus not inspecting the subassemblies. Mr. Latta possesses the following information:

$$\text{Probability of defect } A; P(A) = .0014$$
$$\text{Probability of defect } B; P(B) = .0022$$
$$\text{Probability of defect } C; P(C) = .0650$$

The occurrences of defects A, B, and C are independent.

The cost of inspecting for and correcting defect A; $C(A) = \$40.00$
The cost of inspecting for and correcting defect B; $C(B) = \$80.00$
The cost of inspecting for and correcting defect C; $C(C) = \$12.00$

Any defect not corrected means that the complete assembly will be defective. The cost of incurring a defective assembly in production is $23,000 in downtime and wasted labor.

The probability of finding a defect if present is 0.92 for defect A, 0.95 for defect B, and 0.93 for defect C. This is, $P(a|A) = 0.92$; $P(b|B) = 0.95$, and $P(c|C) = 0.93$.

a) What inspections should be made?

b) If the subcontractor guaranteed (that is, will reimburse purchase price of $15,000 per assembly) that there would be no more than one type B defect per thousand subassemblies, would this change your answer to part *a*)?

c) Assume that defect A can only be present if C is present (and $P(A \mid C) = .0215$). The marginal probabilities, $P(B)$ and $P(C)$, are as given above. What inspections should be made under these conditions?

2. Distinguish between the following terms: *a*) stationary versus nonstationary environment, *b*) environment affected versus environment unaffected by previous decisions, and *c*) decision maker's information affected versus unaffected by the results of earlier decisions.

3. Give at least two decision situations in which traditional control charts would suffice as measurements of variation.

4. How can decision theory be used as a "better" control device than control charts?

Part III

PLANNING PROBLEMS

๛๛๛๛๛๛๛๛๛๛๛๛๛๛๛๛๛๛๛๛๛๛๛

The ten chapters in Part III discuss the way in which various kinds of structures and sequences are developed in order that they may be subjected to the kind of evaluation which completes the solution to a planning problem. Part III might be regarded as consisting of four subdivisions. These sections are concerned with design, techniques of market planning, the end-products of planning, and an overview of the planning function. They consist respectively of one chapter, three chapters, four chapters, and two chapters.

The initial presentation of design principles for market planning is contained in a single chapter. The four end-products of planning are named, and two kinds of design principles are set forth. On one side are principles of optimization, and on the other side, structural principles of design. The optimizing principles name the goals to be accomplished through planning, and the structural principles are concerned with the means for accomplishing these ends. One deals with function, and the other, with the structure appropriate to function. In addition, there are aesthetic principles of design which appear to govern all insights into structure, whether for a poem, a painting, a musical composition, or a marketing plan.

The remainder of this chapter deals with the art and technique of the planning process. It introduces the idea of the planning dialog as a continuing interchange between the staff planner and line executives at several levels. This leads on to a discussion of standard planning assignments, such as the plan for a single campaign, a repetitive planning process, and the contingency plan to be ready for an event which may never happen. Finally there are admonitions to the planner for the continuing formalization of the arts of planning. He must be concerned with the evolving discipline of planning. He must also press for a clear definition of each planning assignment. This understanding is called the planning contract to emphasize its formal content.

The next three chapters are concerned primarily with the first of the end-products of planning, namely, marketing campaigns. These chapters deal with starting points for planning, what the future holds, and how the planner undertakes to influence the future. The planner starts with goals or objectives, but he also starts with the resources which make it feasible to pursue these goals. The chapter is largely concerned with balancing what is desirable and what is feasible. The concept of the preplan audit is introduced to illustrate the matching of goals and resources. Matching is also basic to other concepts such as the review of the marketing mix and the selection of appropriate promotions, month by month.

Forecasting is intimately related to planning since it attempts to project the future level of sales or profits. This chapter emphasizes the use of interrelated growth curves to evaluate market potentials as compared to predicting the ups and downs of the business cycle. There is a brief discussion, however, of exponential smoothing, one of the newer tools of short-range forecasting. The chapter is concluded with a discussion of the problem of forecasting structural change. There are no fully developed formal procedures, but several useful clues are presented for forecasting the shape of things to come.

Finally in this group of chapters there is a discussion of the search for effective strategies. A strategy is a core idea from which a marketing plan is evolved. The consideration of possible strategies leads to the development of alternative plans for evaluation. Sometimes the marketing strategist is playing a game against an active opponent such as a major competitor. More often the business contest is more like a race in which each contestant is trying to make best use of his own resources and gives only limited attention to his rival. Various ways of generating strategies are considered, such as examining the strengths and weaknesses of competitors and distinguishing between offensive and defensive strategies and the appropriate occasions for the use of one or the other.

The next group of four chapters deals with the principal end-products of planning, namely, marketing campaigns, marketing facilities, marketing organization, and marketing systems. Campaigns are mounted by marketing systems using facilities and organization. A campaign is planned in time and facilities are planned in space while organization planning involves the design of a structural hierarchy and a communication network. The most embracing form of planning or re-planning is the design of a complete marketing system for operational efficiency.

These four chapters exemplify the functional and structural principles of design which were summarized in Chapter 13. In each case the design procedure moves through several stages, beginning with a generalized sketch of major relationships and ending with the concrete facts of calendar time, physical location, the personnel constituting an organization, and the actual products and customers with which the operating system deals. The most embracing systems concepts are those of the two dimensions of market adjustment. The horizontal dimension is concerned with decisions to serve segments of the market or to withdraw from these segments, taking account of current and prospective profits. The vertical dimension is concerned with channel efficiency, defining the channel to include the various components of the internal sales organization as well as external factors such as distributors and dealers. The projection of future costs and profits and the continued search for a shorter route to market are held up as ideals to be approximated by the systems planner.

The last two chapters present an overview of the planning process. Chapter 21 is concerned with testing, installing, and operating under a completed plan. This is a very crucial stage in the process since the whole planning activity is at stake and not merely the individual plan. To test a plan is to find ways of demonstrating in advance that the plan will work. To install a plan is to prepare a climate of acceptance and to translate the analytical model into the detailed marching orders for the organization, which may be called the administrative model.

Finally, Chapter 22 presents perspectives on the planning process. Various definitions are suggested to illustrate first one phase and then another of the complexities of market planning. The positioning of the planning function in the organization and various aspects of its management are discussed. The chapter closes with what is called a paradigm of planning. A paradigm is an analytical outline or summary. In this case it serves as a condensed version of the entire discussion of planning problems.

Chapter 13

DESIGN PRINCIPLES FOR MARKET PLANNING

A firm has a marketing problem when it faces uncertainty about vital marketing facts or about the reaction of the market to a marketing plan. Problems of the first type can be solved by providing a reliable answer to a question of fact or reaching a conclusion about some basic issues of marketing policy. This result is achieved by gathering evidence and evaluating it, employing the principles of decision theory which have been presented in Part II.

Problems of the second type, or planning problems, have an additional requirement. Plans must be designed before they can be evaluated. The evaluation of plans can call for advanced techniques, including computer simulation, but the concept of design places planning problems in a very different category. The chart shows this simple but fundamental relationship. Planning problems are a subclass of all marketing problems in which design must come first, followed by evaluation.

PLANNING
PROBLEMS

OTHER MARKETING PROBLEMS

THE PRODUCTS OF PLANNING

Planning in marketing has four primary end-products. The term plan is probably most readily associated with a campaign or program designed to accomplish some result over time. But campaigns use marketing facilities which also need to be carefully planned. There is also the larger problem of production facilities which must be planned with the requirements of the market in mind. Organization is the third end-product of planning. The professional management consultant has tended to concentrate more on this area of planning than any other. Finally, it is possible to plan an entire marketing system which embraces facilities, organization, and the procedures for using them.

These four end-products of planning are not isolated notions but are obviously closely connected. Their relationship can be shown in a simple chart which is really a single sentence connecting the four products of planning.

SYSTEMS | mount | CAMPAIGNS | using | FACILITIES | and | ORGANIZATIONS

OPTIMIZING PRINCIPLES

This chapter is concerned with design principles for planning in marketing. These design principles can be classified under several headings, the first being principles of optimization. For each of the four end-products of planning there are optimizing principles for making best use of the relevant resources. These principles will be discussed first as they apply to campaigns and then for facilities, organizations, and systems.

In planning a campaign the target or goal is the optimal use of time. Campaigns include a wide range of programs from new-product introduction to short-run promotional programs to middle-range or long-range strategic programs.

To say that the target in a campaign is the optimal use of time means that the plan is concerned with the relations between time and the outputs of the system. In optimizing this selection either time or the proposed outputs are taken as given. If time is given, such as a calendar or fiscal year, then the goal is to maximize outputs over the period. More precisely, the aim is to maximize net outputs or the excess of outputs over inputs. If the proposed outputs are given, such as the completion of a building, a research project, or a product introduction, then the goal is to minimize the time required. This objective is subject to constraints as to cost and risk. That is equivalent to saying that the project will be completed as expeditiously as possible without prohibitive cost or undue risk. Once again the real target is net outputs. The planner takes account of costs and risks but weighs them against the urgency attached to the completion of the project.

Crash programs have become familiar in the development of new weapons, but the concept is not unknown in marketing. Crash programs in the introduction of a new product are expensive, but the attempt is to establish a solid market position before those already in the field can organize their defenses. The general principle still holds, however, that there are compelling reasons for moving ahead as rapidly as possible with a product introduction subject only to the constraint of keeping costs and risks within tolerable limits.

In designing marketing facilites, the planning emphasis is upon optimal use of space. This is true whether the planner is designing a supermarket, a warehouse, a sales office, or geographic coverage of the United States. There are several ways of optimizing the use of space, the clearest contrast pertaining to a warehouse versus a self-service store. In laying out a grocery warehouse, for example, the emphasis is on convenience of order assembly. Convenience varies inversely with the number of steps the warehouseman has to take or rather with his movement qualified by the weight and bulk of the good he has to handle. The planning target in the warehouse is to minimize movement.

In laying out a supermarket the planner is still concerned with the optimal use of space, but the optimizing principle is quite different. Since he wants to give the customer a chance to see the entire display, he wants her to move up and down every aisle in the store. Ideally he wants the traffic at each point in the store to approximate 100% of the traffic entering the store. Instead of minimizing movement, as in the warehouse, he is trying to maximize exposure. The self-service store serves as a sort of illustrated catalog. The customer should look at the entire catalog to be sure she has everything she needs. Occasionally she visits the store to pick up a few emergency needs, but if she is well acquainted with the store, its catalog aspect also serves her well for these occasional purchases.

ORGANIZATIONS AND SYSTEMS

The optimizing principles for organizations and systems cannot be stated quite so simply. Both entities occupy space, but they also have histories. People in organizations continue to change, and the adaptive processes in a behavior system never cease. The ability to decide and to perform are the essential adaptive functions.

The indicated goal of an organization is to optimize decision power. The measure is to make sound decisions and to make them promptly enough so that the system can adapt to the circumstances of the environment. The successive decision points in a sequence should lead to the choice of the better alternatives or the better gambles in terms of expected values. Over time the desired result is to maximize expected values. One way this goal can be attained is through providing adequate information channels flowing into the central decision center and mature judgment in dealing with the issues for decision. This formula would apply particularly to the formulation of basic marketing policy for the system.

The other side of the picture begins where the formulation of policy leaves off. The corresponding principle of optimization is to minimize departures from policy. Assuming that the policies adopted are the right ones, it is essential that they should be observed in order to maximize expected values. These two principles are scarcely alternatives for each other but differ slightly in emphasis, depending on whether the key problem of policy is thought to lie in its formulation or its execution. The second principle of minimizing departures from policy is especially important in a very large organization in which many decisions are necessarily made at subordinate levels.

The goal for a system is to optimize its operational effectiveness. In considering how this can be done it is convenient to think of a system as operating in both a horizontal dimension and a vertical dimension. In the horizontal dimension the given firm is one of several competitive agencies for providing goods and services. Internally products compete for resources and may differ substantially in the rate of return on these resources. Management can direct its efforts from the less profitable to the more profitable products in its line. It can serve those customers which it can serve most profitably and discourage sales to other customers. In the process of carrying out these policies a firm abandons to its competitors some of the business which it can do only at a loss. The result is an improved adjustment among products and services competing for the resources of the firm and improved external adjustment among tasks performed by the firm and its competitors. The system operates in the horizontal dimension to maximize competitive adjustment.

In the vertical dimension the firm seeks good coordination with its supplier and its customers. The manufacturer with a merchandising plan tries to induce his dealers and distributors to cooperate with the plan. Much depends on the ability of all factors in the channel to operate as a unit. Channel cooperation and competitive adjustment react on each other. Manufacturers are linked to their retailers through the need for cooperation and hence are brought to have a stake in the competitive adjustment among retailers. Again the two principles are not alternatives but would have a different emphasis in various systems. In one case the emphasis might be on competitive adjustment if the company had an extensive product line with relatively little promotional effort behind any individual product. At the other extreme might be a case with a maximum requirement for channel cooperation if the company had relatively few products and a large promotional budget for each one.

SUMMARY OF PRINCIPLES OF OPTIMIZATION

Later chapters will provide a more detailed discussion of planning principles and procedures for each of the four end-products of planning. Following is a summary in tabular form of the principles of optimization which have been discussed. Two principles are listed under each of the four major headings.

PRINCIPLES OF OPTIMIZATION

Campaigns optimize use of time.
    (*a*) Maximize outputs for specified period.
    (*b*) Minimize elapsed time, subject to constraints on cost and risk.
Facilities optimize use of space.
    (*a*) Minimize movement.
    (*b*) Maximize exposure.
Organizations optimize decision power.
    (*a*) Maximize expected values.
    (*b*) Minimize policy exceptions.
Systems optimize operational effectiveness.
    (*a*) Maximize competitive adjustment.
    (*b*) Maximize channel cooperation.

STRUCTURAL PRINCIPLES OF DESIGN

In addition to optimizing principles in planning, there are structural principles of design. The principles of optimization start from a conception of how an entity functions and name the variables for which a maximum or minimum value is sought. Structural principles are concerned with the pattern of activity which must be devised in order that a plan may function optimally. To introduce these structural principles a table is presented, showing three planning levels for each of the end-products of planning.

End-Product		Planning Level	
Campaigns	Sequence	Duration	Dates
Facilities	Proximity	Area	Site
Organizations	Hierarchy	Duties	Personnel
Systems	Objectives	Model	Operations

In each case these planning levels move from the general to the specific. The first step in planning a campaign is to consider the order of the steps or stages in the sequence of activity. From the consideration of the before-and-after relationship the planner moves to a determination of the amount of time required. Finally he comes to grips with the calendar and sets starting and closing dates for the proposed activity. There is a structural principle corresponding to each of the twelve cells in this table. How these principles can serve as guideposts in structuring a plan will be shown for each of the end-products of planning.

THE STRUCTURE OF A CAMPAIGN

The place to begin in arranging a sequence is with what may be called the principle of precession, which may be stated as follows: "First arrange the sequence in what appears to be the rational order of steps, starting with the end-result and working backward." The reason for working backward is that the planner wishes to include only those steps which are necessary antecedents for the end-result or for some other step in the sequence. A necessary antecedent is a step which must take place in order that some later step can happen at all. For example, merchandise must be shipped to retail stores before merchandise displays can be built. The consumer package for a new product must be designed before it can be reproduced in advertising. Any therapeutic claim appearing on the package must be cleared with the Pure Food and Drug Administration before the package is printed.

The duration of a campaign is determined by a procedure which may be called sequence manipulation. It is not aimless trial and error but an orderly process of checking the sequence to bring it closer to optimality. The steps in this process are as follows:

1. Place a time estimate on each activity in the sequence.
2. Check for possible eliminations since some of the steps which seem like necessary antecedents may have been accepted only because they have been traditional.
3. Check for steps which might be added, not because they are essential but because they facilitate subsequent steps. The facilitating step A_1 may be inserted before A if the cost of A alone is greater than the cost of $A_1 + A$.
4. Check for the possibility of advancing or postponing a step in the sequence where it seems likely that it may affect the cost of subsequent steps.
5. Consider the possibility of saving time by having steps run concurrently.

Determination of starting and closing dates involves a decision on strategic timing. The date should be late enough so that a state of readiness has been adequately prepared. An obvious example is that a product should be ready for market before attempting introduction. This is not a simple decision since there are degrees

of readiness which must be balanced against the need to come on
the market before all competitive advantage has been drained away
because rivals have introduced similar products. Often a product
is geared to the calendar as in the case of a farm or garden product
which should be introduced in the spring. If the product is too late
for the season, it may be necessary to wait a year with increasing
risk that a competitor will come out at the same time. The question arises as to whether a crash program should be used to get
ready in time rather than letting the season pass. A crash program
will not pay unless there is a good chance of getting ready in time
without too great a hazard of premature introduction.

THE STRUCTURE OF A FACILITY

Facility planning is carried through the stages of coping with
proximity, area, and site. Design principles can serve as guideposts
at each stage. There are many types of facilities to be planned in
marketing. In addition, the marketing perspective should enter into
the planning of production facilities. Engineers are needed to lay
out the plant, but marketing should help determine the size and
the location of plants and the extent to which modification should
be foreseen even before construction starts.

The first principle of spatial planning can be called the principle of access. It states that the planner should establish a control
center and plot efficient lines of traffic flow connecting all portions
of the space with the control center. The choice of the control center differs according to the nature of the facility. In the supermarket
it is the check-out counter. In the warehouse it is the shipping dock.
In the sales office the spatial layout should reflect the organization
structure allowing easiest access to the chief executive to those who
have occasion for the most frequent contact. In planning geographic
coverage, the traffic flows extend over large areas following high-
ways and air lanes. The plan for the movement of goods need not
be identical with the plan for the movement of personnel because
the traffic channels are not identical.

In any case the traffic channels are either controlled or diffuse;
either an ideal path is created for all flows through the system, or
provision must be made for a kind of an average path among many
diverse paths. The ideal path is the usual pattern in the plant or
warehouse. Setting up such a path is similar to setting up a sequence of steps for a campaign. The path must be channeled to prevent cross traffic and the consequent traffic jams. The planner must
work with an average path in retail stores, sales offices, or in planning geographic coverage. Where there are many individuals who

can initiate trips through the system there should be maximum convenience for the modal trip and as much convenience as possible for trips which depart from the mode in varying degrees.

The assignment of amounts of spatial area to activities is an exercise in functional balance. The planner starts out with some gross estimate of the space required, often derived from experience with similar problems. He works for functional balance between types of space and tries to hold the total required within cost limits. There are always service or access areas as compared to occupied areas. Service areas are usually aisles or passageways providing access to occupied areas. At one time, the aisles in a grocery warehouse had to be nine feet wide to accommodate the turning radius of the forklift trucks. The forklift truck was redesigned to turn in a six-foot aisle with a sharp reduction in the total amount of warehouse space required. The amount of occupied space was adjusted to the most efficient design of a pallet for handling goods. The new forklift truck made possible a substantial saving in the size of warehouse required and the cost of its construction.

The aisles in a supermarket should be wide enough for advantageous display and to facilitate the customer's assembly of her order. Halls and passageways in office planning are subject to similar considerations. The problem of functional balance is complicated by the existence of specialized functional areas such as the broken-package room in the warehouse or the meatcutting room behind the partition in the supermarket.

Obsolescence for a facility begins to set in the day it is completed. This fact poses the basic planning issue of current efficiency versus flexibility. If it is built for maximum efficiency when completed, it will probably be less efficient a year later. If it is built for maximum efficiency a year or two after completion, it may suffer some competitive handicap in the interim. There are various ways of adjusting a facility to growth and change, none of them wholly satisfactory. A large tract can be acquired initially and occupied gradually from one adjacent plot to the next. A variant is to scatter the buildings over the whole area initially, leaving room for groups of similar units in the intervening spaces. This method was used at the Fairless Steel plant of U.S. Steel outside Philadelphia. Buildings are built with a strong enough skeleton so that upper floors can be added. Movable partitions are used to give flexibility in changing the use of space to fit changes in organization. New communication devices make it easier to get along in space that is physically separated into two or more locations.

Spatial planning for marketing facilities encounters on a smaller scale many of the same problems as city planning. In fact, the proper planning of warehouses and retail shopping centers can be regarded as a significant part of the city planning job although carried out by business planners. The time dimension must not be forgotten either in planning a city or in planning a marketing facility.

THE STRUCTURE OF ORGANIZATION

The first concern of the organization planner is to analyze the hierarchy or chain of command. There are various questions which might be raised in the critical review of an organization chart. Perhaps the most fundamental pertains to the shape of the power pyramid. It can be relatively flat with few levels of control and many subordinates reporting to the top executive. On the other hand, it can have numerous levels of control in order to reduce the span of control. In developing an appropriate chain command, the first care of the planner is to balance span of control against levels of control. Suppose there are 240 field salesmen in a sales organization. A very flat pyramid would be one with twenty men under each of twelve district managers who report to the salesmanager. A somewhat steeper pyramid would have two levels above the salesmen with a 5-6-8 structure. Finally a very steep pyramid with three levels of supervision would be a 3-4-5-6 structure.

The hypothetical cases suggested here allow for a larger span of control at lower levels. The assumption is that there is a greater functional diversity at the top of the pyramid and greater similarity toward the bottom. The thing that makes a large span of control difficult is the need of the top executive to coordinate distinct and separate decision domains under the command of his various subordinates. If employees are performing exactly the same kind of task a single foreman can supervise a whole roomful of people. In marketing, however, salesmen are often scattered over a wide territory and work by themselves much of the time. It is difficult to define a performance standard which can be applied uniformly. The issue of span of control versus level of control is only a clue to be followed in working toward a solution. Many different patterns emerge as most suitable for one organization or another.

From the organization hierarchy the planner proceeds to the specification of duties for each position. At this stage it becomes apparent that organization is not simply a matter of superior and subordinate. In many staff positions the individual is likely to spend a large part of his time with his opposite number in other departments. Any position in the firm can be specified in terms of lines of communication and the place of the individual in the network of information flows. The network of communication channels bears little resemblance to the organization chart.

Taking account of the predominant place of communication in organization activities, a principle may be stated with respect to the assignment of duties to positions in the hierarchy. "Assign duties in such a way as to minimize ambiguities in communication." This rule will be found on reflection to have considerable substance. It implies that the description of duties will inform the incumbent of each position as to the kind of orders he is to expect from his superior and what kind of instructions he is expected to give his subordinates. The description will define working relations with persons in other departments. It will specify the common standard by which the individual is to be measured. The common avoidance of multiple authority over anyone in the organization is generally necessary to avoid the ambiguity of apparently conflicting instructions from two different bosses. The same principle is at work in determining the content of messages in business. Men within the same specialty normally have more occasion to talk among themselves than to communicate with men in other specialties. Cross-channel communication tends to be limited to the essential facts about work accomplished or to be initiated.

The final stage of specificity in planning organization is to name the personnel who are to fill the various posts in the hierarchy and to function in accordance with the duties prescribed. Ordinarily the planner's responsibility is terminated at this point, and the responsible executive issues orders to effectuate any personnel changes within the hierarchy. At this point considerations of motivation and morale become paramount. Individuals receiving promotions within the hierarchy are generally strongly motivated to perform effectively in the new position. The morale of others who have not been promoted must also be considered. Sometimes a promotion has to be delayed because of indications that it would be extremely unpopular with others in the organization. Much depends on handling these changes, once they have been decided upon, with firmness and tact. The principle with respect to personnel in the case of organization overhaul may be stated as follows: "Assign personnel in such a way as to preserve the pattern of motivation." There is always some risk of losing valuable men in the process of reassignment. Thus the organization planner must be ready with further moves if all assignments are not accepted.

Organization changes include formal changes in official status and informal changes in the balance of power as time goes on. Some persons exceed expectations, and others do not develop as rapidly as expected. The case is somewhat different from the planning of facilities with the organization changing steadily while facilities remain relatively static until they are changed by a sudden jump. Organization is dynamic and continues to change but not always in an adaptive direction. No organization structure is perfect, but one form of organization may be preferable to another. Each possible form of organization tends to give special prominence to some organization features and to suppress others. A sales organization may be organized by products, by territories, or by industries. It cannot give equal recognition to all three. The structural principles which have been suggested are directed to the development of the most effective working compromise.

THE STRUCTURE OF A SYSTEM

System planning begins with the consideration of objectives. Desirability must be balanced against feasibility. Objectives must be stated operationally in terms of expected outputs or in terms of the state of affairs at some future date taken as a target. This state of affairs can be described as the desired market position for a product, an attained percentage of market coverage, or annual rates of sales and profits. The test of feasibility attempts to define the limits set by the resources which the firm can command. For maximum growth the firm must generate in the current period the resources it will require as inputs in the next period. Various patterns of growth need to be considered to get a first approximation of the one which is most likely to maximize operational effectiveness because it meets the criteria of feasibility and desirability. To shape the structure of a marketing system is the most ambitious goal of market planning.

The next step in planning a system is to build a model of the system in operation. A general model will be suggested in a later chapter which is perhaps only an ideal not generally attainable at this time. The practical question is to determine a suitable level of aggregation which will cast most light on the basic structure of the system. Several highly aggregated models of a marketing operation have been suggested by market planners. One of these models can be taken as a place to start and the model disaggregated in successive steps until it is possible to simulate the flow of decisions in detail. Such a model can be used to promote understanding of the present system and to project possible improvements into the future.

The final step is to provide procedures for scheduling and coordinating the specific campaigns which are being executed by the system. These campaigns may be regarded as the fundamental outputs of the system. Compromises must be made among these campaigns or programs to achieve optimal effectiveness. The plan for the system begins to take on the concrete detail of a complete set of directions for system operation. It covers all of the separate campaigns, product by product, with a determination of the priority ratings for each. If each campaign has been separately evaluated the combination of campaigns should determine the requirements for manpower and other resources.

The planning or replanning of a whole marketing system is to be undertaken only at intervals. Usually the market planners will be concerned with specific campaigns on major products. Or they will be concerned with changes in facilities or organization. Only in the more advanced companies will it be possible to project future operations through the use of a comprehensieve model of the system. Most will still be at the stage of using a highly aggregated model to provide some sense of direction.

SUMMARY OF STRUCTURAL PRINCIPLES

For convenient reference the structural principles of design are summarized herewith. The name of the principle or the design issue is matched against the appropriate structural feature.

STRUCTURAL PRINCIPLES

Campaigns
    Sequence   –Principle of precession
    Duration   –Sequence manipulation
    Dates   –Strategic timing

Facilities
    Proximity   –Principle of access
    Area   –Functional balance
    Site   –Current efficiency versus flexibility

Organizations
    Heirarchy   –Span of control versus levels of control
    Duties   –Minimize ambiguity
    Personnel   –Preserve motivation

Systems
    Objectives   –Desirability versus feasibility
    Model   –Determine level of aggregation
    Operations   –Schedule and control specific programs
                       or campaigns

THE ELEMENTS OF STRATEGY

The discussion of design principles in market planning has proceeded to this point with no reference to the term strategy. Yet strategy is indeed at the heart and core of planning. Later an entire chapter will be given to the search for effective strategies. A strategy is the core idea out of which a plan is developed. Design principles represent the successive stages through which a plan is carried in giving progressively more concrete form and expression to the central concept of strategy. Full treatment of strategy will be reserved to the later chapter but the subject will be introduced here to show how it is related to the various design principles.

Strategy is not a simple concept as is shown by the various attempts to define it and to distinguish it from tactics. Both of these terms drawn from the military field have apt parallels in business activity and particularly in marketing. In terms of war, strategy applies to a commander's comprehensive vision of how a battle can be fought and won. Tactics refers to the execution of commands in actual fighting on each front or sector. Strategy is concerned with the initial distribution of troops and the assignment of specific objectives within the overall plan for victory. Grand strategy is a conception guiding the course of a campaign or even of the war as a whole. Lincoln was responsible for the grand strategy by which the Civil War was eventually won by slicing through the Confederacy at vital points with the closing of the Mississippi by the combined actions of Grant and Farragut, followed by Sherman's march through Georgia to the sea.

There are important connections between strategy and tactics which also have a parallel in marketing. Tactics is not merely the way the fighting turns out, but it is the way the men have been trained to fight and to handle the weapons with which they have been equipped. It is the application of weapons by men properly trained in their use on the field of battle. Officers are trained in tactical use of men and weapons, but only a few ever achieve the status of serving as master strategists. Yet there is the need to see the pattern of action as a whole at each level in turn, and even a reconnaissance patrol can have a plan of action which will help to determine its success or failure.

At the broadest level of consideration tactical developments determine the strategic possibilities. Hannibal's strategy at Cannae by which he enticed the Roman legions to attack up a steadily narrowing ravine would have little application for armies equipped with artillery and tanks. Gustavus Adolphus was a tactician before he was a strategist and developed improvements in small arms which rendered rather futile the strategies of the Imperial commanders opposing him. It is tactical advantage which has made first one nation and then another a great military power. Great strategists are important too, primarily because they have the genius to take maximum advantage of the tactical means available.

The parallel to marketing is obvious because there have been such drastic changes in marketing technology in recent years; the emergence of television and the advance of other advertising media, the development of new types of retail institutions and the changes in the physical handling of goods are examples. The marketing strategist today is charged with making optimal use of these new tactical means. The success of his campaigns depends on how he employs the technology of marketing almost as much as it depends on the differential advantage derived from product characteristics. Research and planning are modern tools of marketing which he must also learn to use well. A marketing plan incorporates a strategic idea but success will depend on the effective use of all tactical means, including formal planning. Indeed as competitors match each other in other directions, excellence in planning may frequently be the deciding factor.

Strategy in marketing is compounded of several elements. Most important is the concept of strategic timing already discussed as an aspect of the design of campaigns. A second is the concept of the state of readiness to be discussed more fully in Chapter 16. Finally, there are the dimensions of differential advantage which can be exhibited in many different directions. Differential advantage can be relatively permanent in nature or it can be something which will assure a competitive edge for only a brief period. Something which provides only a momentary advantage can be called a stratagem. A stratagem may decide the outcome of an entire battle in the military sphere, but it is less likely to be decisive for a war between great nations. Stratagems are seldom conclusive in marketing, but a succession of clever stratagems may give a good merchandiser what amounts to a continuous competitive edge.

The state of readiness, which has also been called internal strategy, is embodied in the planning of facilities, organizations, and systems. Campaigns are preeminently the area of external strategy in which a firm seeks to maintain an edge in competition. Campaigns are concerned with both momentum and long-run advantage and with the timing of all strategic moves. The simple requirement for facilities, organizations, or systems is that they should be ready when needed. While these structural elements may be in existence, it is essential that they should be in a condition of effectiveness equal to the occasion. If a facility or an organization needs to be replaced or modified, the chief executive cannot delay too long in taking remedial action. The most brilliant strategies embodied in campaigns will fail if the state of readiness has not been properly prepared.

The four aspects of strategy which have been suggested here are strategic timing, the state of readiness, basic strategy or market posture, and the lesser strategic concepts which are called stratagems. It is the stratagem which fits most neatly in the framework of game theory in which either side must act in the face of uncertainty concerning the actions of the other. Market posture illustrates the special case which game theorists call a game against nature. The strategist chooses a market posture without regard to the action of competitors since he faces more fundamental uncertainties with respect to the reaction of the market to his products.

In playing a game against nature, the strategist will have relatively greater concern for the state of readiness which gives him operational effectiveness. He is not so much trying to outwit individual opponents as to maintain his basic competitive edge and make the most effective use of the resources he brings to the marketing task. He tries to stay flexible and to take advantage of the mistakes of his competitors and the openings they leave for the exertion of his full marketing power. But strategic timing in the use of marketing stratagems can continue to enhance the strength of his market posture.

AESTHETIC PRINCIPLES OF DESIGN

As long as planning is an art rather than a science, it appears that aesthetic principles of design would have some bearing on market planning. Such principles as balance and symmetry will at least have the merit of suggesting areas to be considered in fleshing out a plan. A campaign which is extended over time would bear the closest resemblance to a musical composition. It will have a beginning and a conclusion and the development of major theme and subordinate themes in between. It will have a tonal texture resulting from the coordination of all the instruments or voices at each point in the composition.

The Gestalt principle of closure will find application in all aspects of planning whatever the end-product. Planning always starts from the consideration of some totality such as a campaign or a facility and works toward a steadily more concrete embodiment of an abstract design idea. Missing pieces will begin to be suggested by their very absence. The principle of closure simply asserts that the mind can only come to rest in terms of a complete pattern and creates in imagination the elements needed to complete the pattern. There are other aesthetic principles which are involved in the process of seeking closure. If there is a control center, for example, as in designing a facility, the traffic lines should radiate out into the space to be controlled with a minimum of cross traffic and a maximum convenience of access to the center. In fact, some of the principles of structural design which have been enumerated are in effect aesthetic principles applied to the specific subject matter of market planning.

Market planning may be described as an art which is on its way to becoming a science or at least an art which applies many of the tools of science. If an executive is making a plan for himself, it will inevitably take on something of his personal style. To some extent he acts in a particular way because he finds it easier or more convenient to act in that way. A staff planner who is working for a marketing executive will come to understand something of the executive's style and perhaps cast the plan in that style to the degree possible. On the other hand, the demand for formal planning is in itself an acknowledgement that the activities of many different personalities will have to be coordinated to make the plan work. A plan of operation which strikes field salesmen as utterly unrealistic will be honored more in the breach than the observance. The element of personal style will be further minimized if the plan is made for one executive who will in turn have to present it to his superior for approval. It can be predicted that planning will become more and more scientific as more and more people are affected by it. The discussion which follows undertakes to show how planning principles are put to work in the context of interactions within the company.

THE PLANNING PROCESS

To specify the planning assignment is to make a plan for planning. The planner in marketing tries to deal with each activity he plans for as a well-ordered process. The discussion of design principles has suggested this movement from optimizing principles to concrete plan through the application of the structural principles of design. He shoud be prepared to treat planning as a well-ordered activity and to seek a clear understanding and agreement as to what is required in any given planning assignment. The statement of the assignment is itself the vehicle for getting the planning process under way. It is obviously appropriate for the planner to try to find out what is expected of him in the given instance. The executive who makes the planning assignment, in the course of setting goals for the staff planner, is obliged to consider his own objectives. He must know what he wants to do in order to tell the planner what to do.

This statement does not exclude the case of the executive who is in doubt as to the direction he wants to take. If his objectives are vague, then one of the goals of planning is to clarify them. His initial state of mind may fit one of several descriptions. He may know exactly what he wants to accomplish and be willing to disclose his objectives in order to provide definite targets for the staff planner. Just as in designing the layout of physical space he may require several preliminary sketches before the detailed plan is produced. The executive may stop short of full disclosure of his objectives for good reasons such a security considerations. Rather than tip his hand as to the precise strategy he is contemplating, he may expect the planner to proceed on the basis of general rather than specific objectives. Finally, he may not be ready to make his goals specific until he has a preliminary test of what is feasible. The planning assignment should then be conducted in such a way as to afford the executive a range of choice rather than proceeding on the basis of a choice already made.

THE PLANNING DIALOGUE

The planning processes might be pictured with some justice as a dialogue or interchange between the executive responsible for action and the staff planner. Even more aptly, it may be described as a three-way conversation with the planner acting as intermediary between the executive and those at subordinate levels who are responsible for carrying out the plan. The expected outcome of the dialogue is that the executive will talk himself into adopting a specific course of action. The conversation between executive and planner becomes fruitful because their viewpoints are distinct but complementary. The executive is in a position something like the driver on a hazardous road. He must always concentrate on taking the next step successfully even though this may involve some sacrifice in breadth of perspective. The planner can give uninterrupted study to the route as a whole because he does not have his hand on the wheel.

The planning dialogue or trialogue is a formal interchange which should move progressively toward the visualization of a preferred course of action and its ultimate adoption as the official company program. The formal dialogue contrasts sharply with informal talk about courses of action which has an unfortunate tendency to move in circles. The initial step of specifying the assignment charts the path which discussion is to follow. It describes the end-product which the planner is to deliver in the form of a written document. This document in turn is only a working tool for the executive who is concerned with the real end-product of a change in marketing operations.

The conversation of the planner with personnel at subordinate levels is concerned with what are the most feasible methods for achieving the objectives of the chief executive. The latter may have some suggestions on the strategies by which objectives are to be attained and, indeed, is often the senior strategist in the organization. The planner talks to personnel at subordinate levels for help in determining the most feasible methods of attaining the objectives tentatively established by the chief executive. If he is positive after exhausting every possibility that these goals cannot be reached, he goes back to the chief executive for new instructions and a modification of stated goals.

A procedure which has been found very useful in this early stage of planning is what might be called Bayesian-type interviews at both the top level and subordinate levels. Each executive is presented with a list of alternatives which appear reasonable to him. He is then asked to rate the completed list according to the probability of success. Often he can even be induced to give odds for success or failure on each course of action. In addition to the value of this procedure in turning up possibilities, it reveals striking differences of opinion which will need to be reconciled to make any plan fully effective.

The evaluation of an acceptable plan is geared to the calendar. The statement of the assignment should name a date by which the new plan of operation is to be in effect. Working back from this date, deadlines should be set for the submission of the plan and the critical review, and for the agreement on the general direction to be pursued in the evaluation of a comprehensive plan. Agreement on the statement of the assignment is an essential prelude to all other steps and by giving precise form to the planning problem forecasts the nature of the solution.

The interchange which has been called the dialogue of planning can deal with three broad subjects. One is the content of the planning assignment, including the situation the plan is expected to meet and the issues to be resolved in preparing a plan for action. Next is the discipline of planning and the growth of understanding by participation in the planning dialogue. Finally, there is what might be called the planning "contract" or definition of mutual commitments under which the planner must operate. The content of the assignment will be considered first and most fully since the dialogue of planning differs greatly among several types of planning situations.

THE CONTENT OF THE ASSIGNMENT

The planning assignment will generally fall under one of the four headings already discussed, namely, campaigns, facilities, organizations, and systems. The market planner will be most concerned with campaigns which can be either short run or long run. A campaign can pertain to the promotion of old products or the introduction of a new product. It can be a firmly committed plan or a contingency plan. With respect to the other aspects of planning, the market planner may enter the situation in several different ways. He may work on a plan for a marketing facility with architects and engineers. He may be a member of a team for a general overhauling of the organization or work on a special assignment inside the marketing organization only. Because of the political implications of organization planning, outside consultants are frequently used for their objective judgment. The overhauling of the marketing system can be undertaken periodically inside the marketing organization, but there will often be implications for other functions in the business which will have to be resolved at the highest level. A production facility will ordinarily be planned by production personnel, but the need to plan it to the market will often dictate the presence of a market planner on the planning team.

THE INITIAL PLAN

Planning itself is on trial when the assignment is to make an initial plan. Formal planning may be new to the company and is certainly new with respect to a particular activity or segment of the business. The planner must find out at once just how much of the marketing organization is to be covered. If it pertains to the structure and function of the advertising department, at what points, if any, does it touch the sales force? If it is a plan for the marketing of major household appliances, can this activity be separated completely from the marketing of small appliances made by the same company? Will the plan be placed in effect only west of the Mississippi, and is it legally and practically possible to market nationally under two separate programs and policies?

There is a common principle relating these questions. A plan will affect the behavior of identifiable individuals and operating units and, indeed, is intended for that purpose. An elementary precaution in preparing an initial plan is to know for whom the plan is being made.

There are some related questions wtih respect to executive responsibility. Will the executive making the assignment direct the execution of the plan? If the plan is designed to establish a more effective pattern of behavior for a subordinate, to what extent is the latter expected to participate in the planning dialogue? Is the plan prepared for use in a given executive position regardless of who occupies it, or does it assume the participation of the present incumbent? Does the executive making the planning assignment have full authority to adopt the plan, or does he expect to sell it to his superior after it is completed?

Questions inevitably arise as to the value of planning and must be answered by the planner. Probably the most persuasive argument, if not the most logical, is that other organizations are doing it. The other organization using formal planning may be another division of the same company, competitors in the same industry, or companies in other fields who are similarly situated as to the scale and complexity of their marketing operations.

A still more significant issue is how much difference the plan will make in the behavior of the organization and in the results achieved. If the plan contemplates too sharp a break with past behavior patterns, it may encounter resistance from those affected. If it does not promise measurable improvements in results, it will not be worth undertaking at all. Opponents of planning may raise the issue of timing, conceding that formal planning is on the way but arguing that it is not needed just yet. Some key individuals may be about to retire, opening up the opportunity to bring in new men with new methods.

Up to this point the interchange between management and planning staff is concerned with the activities to be covered by the plan if, indeed, there is to be formal planning at all. The planning dialogue also begins to make some preliminary soundings as to the scale and character of the program which the planning effort will produce. The dialogue at this point can best proceed in terms of the inputs and outputs of the marketing system to which the plan would apply.

Among the outputs of primary concern are sales, profits, and increased capacity of the marketing organization itself to meet an expected increase in competition or the challenge of enlarged opportunity. These are all positive or desired outputs but systems sometimes have negative outputs or undesired effects which partially offset the positive outputs. Examples would be the loss of prestige and profit margins which might be involved in bringing out a popular-priced model of a product already established at a higher level or the problem of moderating conflict between unlike trade channels selling the same product. A marketing plan might have the general goal of maximizing positive outputs, minimizing negative outputs, or arriving at some workable compromise between the two.

A plan might also attempt to set some limits on the inputs of investment and marketing expenses. Usually the goal would not be to minimize dollar expenditures unless the business was running at a loss and the current objective was simply to survive until conditions became more favorable. The drive for efficiency in marketing can usually be expressed as minimizing inputs relative to outputs, or, in the more precise formulation of the economist, equating marginal costs and marginal returns.

Seldom are the data on demand and cost available in sufficient detail to enable the planner to proceed with all the rigor of marginal analysis. He must rely on systematic trial and error to approach a balance between planned inputs and expected outputs that seems right to him intuitively. One purpose of the planning dialogue is to develop some benchmarks to guide this trial-and-error process. For example, agreement might be reached concerning two restrictions to be imposed on the plan. One restriction specifies the minimum results required to justify any special effort. The other limiting condition is the maximum effort that management would be willing to undertake, in view of the uncertainty of results and other financial requirements.

The determination of both minimum results and maximum effort must start with the subjective judgments on the part of the responsible executive. The chart in Figure 13–1 suggests the way in which such judgments could be used by the planner in trying to feel his way toward a quantitative functional relationship between the incremental yield of the program and the incremental costs. The scale on the vertical axis represents marketing results as measured by dollars of sales. The scale on the horizontal axis represents effort as measured by dollars of sales expenditure. One point on this scale is labeled minimum results. The planner would mark the minimum results figure on the vertical scale and then estimate the effort required to produce these results. This pairing of input and output is indicated on the chart by the point, X_1. Proceeding in the same way the planner would mark the maximum effort figure on the horizontal scale and estimate the results which should be obtained. This pairing of input and output is indicated on the chart by the point, X_2. The dotted line drawn through these two points represents the planner's final guess as to the functional relationship between effort and results.

Figure 13–1

ESTIMATED RESULTS FROM MAXIMUM EFFORT

AND

COSTS FOR MINIMUM RESULTS

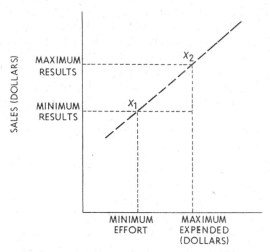

X_1 = THE AMOUNT OF EFFORT NEEDED TO OBTAIN MINUMUM SALES RESULTS
X_2 = THE RESULTS OBTAINED IF MAXIMUM EFFORT IS MADE

To summarize this section, the interaction between management and the staff planner would take the form of statements and comments, of questions and answers, with the initiative being exercised on either side. In the dialogue concerning an initial plan, questions arise with respect to the merits of market planning in general. The planner has a chance to answer these and to raise some questions of his own to define the limits within which he is expected to work. Topics of basic interest to both sides are favorable and unfavorable outputs of an activity and inputs relative to outputs. The use of the term "planning dialogue" does not imply anything mysterious but only the process of orderly discussion by which an agreement is reached. There is an implicit agenda for this dialogue, and the planner should make sure that all relevant points are covered. In seeking a clear statement of his assignment, he stimulates management to clarify its own requirements.

APPLICATION OF DESIGN PRINCIPLES

The design principles discussed earlier in this chapter have been temporarily lost from view in discussing the planning dialogue. They would come into play at about this point in the process after there had been a first set of estimates of the range of expenditure contemplated. The simplest example might be the periodic revision of a plan in being rather than an initial plan. The order in which successive design steps might be taken is as follows:

1. Determining feasibility range by maximum-minimum method.
2. First guess of optimal point within the feasibility range.
3. Tentative selection of core strategy. (If market posture was not to be revised, then the core strategy might consist of one or more strategies for reinforcing market posture.)
4. Developing the sequence of steps for putting the strategy to work, using the principle of precession and sequence manipulation.
5. Final estimate of optimal point of feasibility range.
6. Refinement of sequence and dealing with question of strategic timing either for the campaign as a whole or for individual steps in the sequence.

The reader will recognize that both optimizing and structural principles are taken into account in this list as well as methods for generating strategies. In practice, the planner moves back and forth among these steps adjusting each in turn until he finally feels that he has arrived at a workable plan. The illustration pertains to campaigns rather than the other end-products of planning, namely, facilities, organizations, and systems. Furthermore, it pertains to only one type of campaign, namely, that which is subject to periodic revision. A similar list might be prepared for any of the other end-products of planning, but there would then be greater emphasis on internal strategy or the state of readiness. The planning dialogue will now be further illustrated with respect to three types of campgaigns, namely, the periodic revision, the one-time campaign, and the contingency plan.

THE PERIODIC REVISION

There is one obvious difference in the situation involving a periodic revision as compared to an initial plan. Planning as such is probably not on trial to the same extent in the latter case, but critical attention centers on previous plans and their apparent contribution or lack of contribution to progress in the relevant activity. Special topics in the planning dialogue will include the accuracy of the last forecast and its bearing on the new one to be prepared, performance in relation to the past expenditure budgets and the extent to which the plan foresaw the true problems of coordination and provided for them within the program.

The periodic revision, with the advantage of some experience under the previous plan, might be carried out with little or no interchange with top management working primarily with executives at subordinate levels. But it is contrary to the interests of the company and certainly those of the planner to permit periodic revision to settle into the pattern of the routine exercise. Management may have to take greater initiative than ever to prevent this from happening. Questions should be raised if past plan and past performance were too far apart in either direction. If performance fell short there is evidence that either the plan or its execution were at fault. If performance runs far ahead of plan, it would look as if the planner was overcautious and suggest that performance under the plan might be deficient in relation to a better appraisal of the opportunity.

The planning group would be well advised to undertake its own evaluation of what it had contributed through the previous plans. The touchstone is whether the executives for whom the plan was drawn actually used it. Plans which are not fully activated leave those involved lukewarm as to the value of planning. Evaluation after the fact should reveal whether the fault was in the basic conception of the plan, in the language in which it was presented, or in a failure to provide sufficiently detailed suggestions for installing it and operating under it.

With all of the factors which must go into the drafting of a plan, the actual outcome could scarcely be expected to be optimal in its first version. Thus, at every periodic revision, the chances are that opportunities to improve over the last plan will be revealed. The initial plan was intended to show improvement over unplanned activity. A revised plan must strive for the more severe standard of providing an advance over the last plan.

In operational terms, a plan revision might be regarded as one step in the continuing effort to approximate the best answer through successive corrections. This would be an application of the cybernetic principle of feedback. In fact, however, markets do not stand still, and an adequate revision may require something more than a moderate correction of the last plan. Critical review of this previous plan may suggest the need for striking out in quite a new direction rather than merely inching forward from a position already achieved. It may be that objectives previously formulated have been attained fully or to such a degree that the greater urgency lies somewhere else. The possibilities for new market trends and for genuinely new marketing strategies are sufficient to be given some attention during the most casual plan revision. This is the phase of planning in which both management and planning staff should be alert to keep the dialogue going. Communication is not an end in itself, but communication about planning is to be preferred to communication about the problems which arise because the planning effort has lost its vitality.

Table 13–1 summarizes the treatment of planning for recurrent activities contained in the last two sections. A contrast is drawn between initial plans and periodic revision in one direction and between the focal points of interest for management and planning staff in the other. In both cases the contrasts are only matters of relative emphasis. The two types of planning are successive stages in the planning dialogue, and the interests of the two participants are completely consistent and complementary.

Table 13–1

POINTS OF EMPHASIS IN THE PLANNING DIALOGUE
WITH RESPECT TO RECURRENT ACTIVITIES

	Initial Plan	Periodic Revision
	The incremental values of formal planning	Past plan versus performance
Management	Maximizing favorable outputs; minimizing unfavorable outputs	Maintaining vitality of planning effort
		Marginal adjustment versus new directions
	Segment of activity covered by the plan	Departures from past plan: under and over
Planning Staff	Executive responsibility for activating plan	The open opportunity for improvement
	Subjective feelings concerning maximum efforts and minimum results	

THE ONE-TIME CAMPAIGN

The prototype of the nonrecurring activity is the one-time campaign. A one-time campaign, such as the introduction of a new product, is a unique sequence of behavior directed at a limited objective which is of critical importance at just this point in the life history of the organization. The campaign is designed to take advantage of a passing opportunity or to meet an impending threat. The marketing campaign is directly comparable to the military campaign in the requirements it places upon a planning staff. The planner has only one chance to be right in planning for a unique event. There is no opportunity for successive corrections through periodic revisions or for tuning up an operating system until the parts are all in adjustment. The uniqueness of the occasion also tests the mettle of the executive who must cope with it, but he is presumed to bring to the situation the resourcefulness and presence of mind demanded in meeting the unexpected. It is the planner who must show that systematic analysis can assist the executive in facing the decisive moment.

There are several possibilities open to the planner; one is to redefine the problem so that it is amenable to established principles of design and the outcome can be predicted with a reasonable approach to certainty. In one actual case, the problem was to shift a product from drug channels to grocery channels in a single week after the intention to do so became known. Once it was recognized that only food brokers could provide such immediate access to grocery distribution, the rest of the problem was largely procedural. The unique event of shifting channels was restated as the repetitive process of lining up one broker after another but compressing the process to a single week as compared to the actual two or three years formerly thought to be needed for such an adjustment. The whole thrust of planning was toward making this time compression possible.

The restructuring of the problem which made it soluble grew directly out of the planning dialogue. The answer was one of several considered but merely needed to be stated to be recognized as the right one. Two principles with some general application were involved, one that of breaking the problem up into smaller pieces which could be handled by repetitive procedures. The other was to compress the time required by overt action so that the issue was settled before effective counteraction could take shape.

Another principle in designing a unique campaign is to strike where the opposition is weakest, to develop a beachhead at a favorable spot and to spread out from there. Appraising one's own strength and the weaknesses of competition is again a function of the planning dialogue. The subjective judgments of the executive are crucial in this area since his confidence, based on his belief in the capacity of his organization, is itself a vital factor in organization strength.

A campaign needs a coordinating idea like the battle cry in military action. Coordinated action has emotional roots as well as logical foundations. The individual on the battle line may redouble his efforts with the prospect of common victory. The sales leader must inspire as well as instruct. The expert in the arts of planning may design the campaign around the man as a play is sometimes designed around a star football player. There is adventure in tackling a strange situation under a competent leader. When dealing with such a man, it is fortunate if the planner catches the contagion of his vision and then embodies it in an integrated program.

CONTINGENCY PLANS

If campaign plans are related to situations which happen only once, contingent plans are designed for eventualities which may never happen at all. While a contingency may have only a low probability of happening, it is of such a nature as to be taken most seriously when it does arise. Contingency plans are a common feature of military planning. The archives of a general staff are said to contain detailed programs for a number of extremely unlikely military events even including a sneak attack by an ally. There would be no time to get ready if one of these contingencies should actually occur. The hope for national survival may hang on having a plan which can be activated at once.

Fortunately business contingencies involving life or death issues are not so numerous. The contingent threats worth planning for are massive moves believed to be under consideration by major competitors. Crash programs for introducing new consumer products or radical innovations in marketing methods are examples of such threats. It is more difficult to picture contingent opportunities that justify advance planning. One of the better examples is the speculative presentation which an advertising agency might prepare on the rumor that a major account is about to be open.

Planning situations might arise which would call for sets of contingency plans, one covering each of the major possibilities. Such contingency plans might be regarded as appendices to a plan which provided a detailed program up to the point where contingencies intervened. Thus a manufacturer of furniture or home furnishings might foresee each marketing step quite clearly up to the point where his new line was displayed at the annual merchandise show.

According to the character of reactions at the show, he might have to be ready for prompt and specific action in a direction which up to that point was only one of several contingencies.

Once more there are characteristic areas for subjective judgments on the part of the executive. The planner is again obliged to take them into account and to find means of including them in a quantitative analysis. The subjective evaluation of contingencies has two phases. First, there is the hunch that the probability of an event is large enough to be taken seriously. Secondly, there is the evaluation of the importance of the contingency, arising from the nature of the consequences should it occur. Techniques are available to the planner for translating these judgments into expected utilities or perhaps expected disutilities.

Table 13-2 summarizes some of the high points in planning for nonrecurrent activities. The two main types of such plans are the one-time campaign for the event which occurs but once and planning for contingency events which may not occur at all. It becomes clearer than ever that the executive must exercise command in a world of active forces and that the planner undertakes his analysis in the mirrored world of structured variables. Each world takes on depth and meaning from its counterpart.

Table 13-2

Points of Emphasis in the Planning Dialogue
with Respect to Nonrecurrent Activities

	Campaign Plans	Contingency Plans
Management	Improving within the plan	Probability and importance of a contingency
	Emotional appeal of a coordinating idea	
		Readiness for action under mass attack
	Confidence in organizational capacity	
Planning Staff	Redefining the problem	Stockpiling plans
	Finding an opening	Expected utilities and disutilities
	One chance to be right	

THE PLANNING DISCIPLINE

The planning dialogue may seem to deal primarily with specific assignments and only incidentally with the discipline of planning, the concepts and techniques by which assignments are formalized and executed. Yet this secondary but more general theme of the discipline of planning has a cumulative result. Each side learns to ask better questions and to give better answers. The planning discipline cannot develop in isolation and be ready for application as needed. It must spring from the continuous interaction of the principal participants.

The first essential is a growing vocabulary in which the planning dialogue can be conducted. Important distinctions continue to be blurred because the need for drawing these distinctions is not generally recognized. One of the most disturbing forms of confusion is that in which several parties to a conversation mistakenly believe that they are talking about the same thing. A significant example is the quite different ways in which the term long-range planning has been applied.

One hope for this book is that it will make it easier to talk about planning in marketing. It is also intended to facilitate the dialogue which is itself an important ingredient of planning. This chapter is particularly concerned with that subject as it pertains to the major types of planning assignments and the corresponding principles of design. The aim in part is to provide a sort of agenda for these conversations in somewhat more organic form than the usual check list.

The evolving discipline of planning will recognize an expanding body of planning principles. Some of these may apply to a wide variety of planning situations, some to particular planning assignments, and some to steps in the planning process. Some will be nothing more than suggested procedural rules. Some principles state formulas for optimizing some planning variable through the use of quantitative data. Others are structural principles showing how to provide the framework within which the effort to optimize can function. Planning as a whole functions to evoke the systematic and orderly from the vague and unorganized. The first big step along the way is to identify the planning assignment.

THE PLANNING CONTRACT

There is a final stage of agreement about the nature of the planning assignment. This discussion is something like a negotiation of a planning contract just as it might take place between management and an outside planning consultant. Such a contract describes what the planner has agreed to deliver and gives the time and cost required to complete the task.

Some organization experts regard the essence of management as the continuous negotiation between the chief executive and his principal subordinates. This relationship holds with respect to the director of planning as well as for others reporting to top management. The bargain or contract between them evolves an exchange of commitments as in all other administrative relationships. The subordinate commits himself to perform a function in satisfactory fashion or according to specified standards. His superior commits some part of the company's resources to support the function and to reward faithful performance.

In addition to the overall exchange of commitments with respect to the planning function, there are specific "contracts" governing individual assignments. This internal contract is embodied in the formal statement of the assignment. Typically this planner will be required to prepare this statement and submit it for approval. This procedure is similar to the submission of a proposal by an outside consulting group. Detailed written reports are always required of the outside consultant, and they are coming to be a universal requirement for the inside planner. In fact, formal planning procedure may demand successive drafts of a plan for convenience of review and criticism. These drafts become the vehicle for the planning dialogue, for the interplay of ideas and comment between the planner and the responsible executive.

Estimates of time and cost are also part of the planning contract on any assignment. The time available for planning is always constrained by the presence of deadlines for decision. The need for timeliness stands opposed to the desire for adequacy. A plan that is complete and perfect in every detail scarcely can ever be ready in time to do any good. There is a point of optimum compromise between adequacy and timeliness which should be embodied in the planning assignment.

The cost of planning should be absorbed through the increase in effectiveness of the activity governed by the plan. Any planning expenditures which contribute to effective action are theoretically justified. The cost includes the time of planning staff and of any market surveys or analysis to provide the planner with the information he needs. More and more the planning staff should exercise some control and direction over the flow of marketing information. The extent to which information is actually used in formulating plans is a good test of whether it is needed.

The statement of assignment should also name the persons directly responsible for carrying it out. It should state the conditions under which the planner can be discharged from his responsibility and credited with a completed task. In short, the statement of assignment might be regarded as an administrative plan for preparing the specified marketing plan.

Selected References

BASS, FRANK M. *Mathematical Models and Methods in Marketing.* Homewood, Ill.: Richard D. Irwin, 1961.
    A rationale for design principles, primarily with respect to marketing campaigns, is suggested by description of models for consumer behavior and business behavior.

BAUMOL, W. J. *Economic Theory and Operations Analyses.* Englewood Cliffs, N.J.: Prentice-Hall, Inc., 1961.
    Discusses decision making in relation to various types of structured situations, laying some foundations for design principles.

CHURCHMAN, C. WEST. *Prediction and Optimal Decision.* Englewood Cliffs, N.J.: Prentice-Hall, Inc., 1961.
    This author is a philosopher as well as a management specialist. He deals with the philosophy of values in a way that is highly suggestive for a treatment of design principles in planning.

MILLER, D. W. AND STARR, M. K. *Executive Decision and Operations Research.* Englewood Cliffs, N.J.: Prentice-Hall, Inc., 1960.
    Has the special merit of showing that OR models applicable to business are reducible to a small number, each with a wide area of application.

Problems

1. Discuss the optimization principles as applied to campaigns, facilities, organizations, and systems. Select a marketing example of each of the above end-products of planning and show how the optimization principle might apply.

2. Define and discuss the principle of precession and the principle of access.

3. Distinguish between strategy and tactics. Give a marketing example to illustrate the difference between the two terms.

4. Contrast in detail the planning assignment involved in the initial plan and in the periodic review of a plan.

5. Discuss the role of aesthetic principles of design in market planning.

Chapter 14

RESOURCES AND OBJECTIVES

This chapter and the three which follow are concerned with the planning of campaigns, extending over some period of time, which most readily comes to mind when we speak of market planning. For that reason four chapters are devoted to the planning of campaigns and only one chapter each to the planning of facilities, organizations, and systems. Planning in these latter fields has an implicit time dimension also and is linked to the planning of campaigns through the relations between external strategy and internal strategy or the state of readiness.

There are various ways in which the discussion of marketing campaigns might have been organized. A distinction could be drawn between long-range, short-range, and middle-range campaigns, with somewhat arbitrary distinctions for the classification of time periods. Campaigns could be differentiated by purpose such as new-product introduction or optimizing the return from existing products over a stated period. They could be distinguished by structure as has been done in the last chapter in recognizing the differences between recurring and nonrecurring plans and between contingent and noncontigent plans.

All of these distinction are recognized and treated however briefly at appropriate points in the text. The overall structure has been shaped in another way and a word on the relationship among these four chapters may be helpful in the beginning. This chapter describes the continuing process of weighing resources and objectives against each other using criteria of desirability and feasibility. Forecasting as a planning technique, the subject of Chapter 15, is designed to show what would happen in the absence of a plan or under fixed assumptions as to the nature of the plan. The chapter on the search for effective strategies deals with ways of generating the fundamental ideas which are central to any plan. Finally, the chapter on the design of marketing campaigns suggests the detailed procedures for putting these elements together in the plan for a campaign.

One widely-accepted view of planning divides the process into two simple stages. First the planner is to obtain a clear statement of objectives from the responsible executive. He should then concentrate on mobilizing the means and resources for obtaining these goals. This advice has merit but the planning process often fails to fit into such a neat and simple sequence. The clarification of objectives is very fundamental indeed and may sometimes be the most important result of the whole planning effort. The attempt to clarify objectives starts with the first discussion of the planning assignment, but it may not end until the final plan is accepted.

It is more productive to talk about weighing resources and objectives and finally arriving at a satisfactory matching of means and ends. An exception might be made for a short-range program designed to attain limited and immediate objectives. Here the company is probably operating well within the feasibility boundary, and the executive may be prepared to specify precise objectives. For somewhat longer-range strategic planning it might be just as valid to start with resources and move toward objectives as the other way around. The question posed for the planner could be, "Given the company's available resources, what objectives would be most appropriate for it to adopt?" The opposite approach is to say, "Given the company's stated objectives, what resources will be required to attain them?"

The viewpoint adopted here is that neither of these extremes is the ideal starting point for strategic planning. Rather resources and objectives should be balanced against each other without assigning a hard and fast priority to either. The planner needs to obtain a feeling for the possibilities open from either end as a prelude to recommending a course of action. This chapter will consider this balancing of means and ends and then discuss some further steps in the clarification of objectives.

THE PREPLAN AUDIT

A systematic procedure for this early stage of strategic planning has been called the preplan audit. It is concerned with income and outgo no less than an accounting audit, but it balances potentials as well as actual results. The preplan audit for a going concern regards its position in the market as a major asset even though it can hardly be measurd in dollar figures in a financial balance sheet. The unique market position of the firm is a resource to be used to the fullest advantage in planning. Improvement in market position can be a major objective of a plan. One aspect of the preplan audit considers the balance between the needs of consumers and the production capacity of the firm. These relationships are portrayed in Figure 14-1. The dotted area at the bottom of the first bar symbolizes potential consumers for the firm's present product line who are not now being reached. The dotted area at the top of the second bar represents goods which the firm might sell to its present customers but which it does not now supply. The current business of the firm corresponds to the overlap between the two solid bars.

Figure 14-1

THE STRUCTURE OF RELATIONSHIPS IN THE MARKETING AUDIT

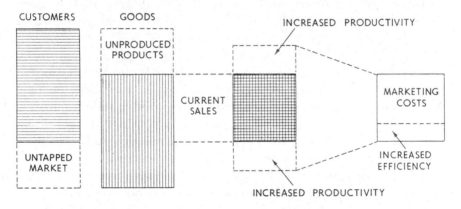

The marketing audit is directed ultimately either toward increased productivity of marketing or increased efficiency. That means getting more sales for the same marketing expenditure or the same sales volume at a lower cost. The solid part of the third bar in the chart represents current sales. The dotted portions at either end represent increased sales achieved either through selling additional products to present cutsomers or by selling existing products to new customers. The fourth bar represents the current level of marketing costs. The dotted lines spreading to the left represent the goal of obtaining greater volume per marketing dollar. The small segment at the bottom of the fourth bar represents the possible savings in marketing costs through greater efficiency.

Obviously no simple bar charts can do justice to either an accounting audit or a marketing audit. This is particularly true for

the marketing audit which is really a search for significant relationships, some of which may have to be evaluated largely in qualitative terms. The ultimate aim of the audit is to point the way toward
making the most of the firm's opportunities in the market. Opportunity arises out of the combination of consumer need and the resources available for meeting it. Market opportunity is cultivated
through marketing effort, designed to make the most effective use
of the resources available to satisfy need.

Thus the double balance which is fundamental to the marketing
audit is the balance between needs and resources and the balance
between opportunity and effort.

The preplan audit balances these elements against each other,
but the balance is expressed as a state of adjustment rather than in
accounting equations. Needs and resources may be imperfectly
matched. The resources which are being utilized might find more
effective use for some other purpose. The reverse is true also,
namely, that other resources might exist which could give greater
satisfaction with respect to this set of needs.

The businessman who recognizes an opportunity may approach
it from either one direction or the other. He may observe an unsatis-
fied consumer need and set out to satisfy it even though he may
start with only a part of the resources required for that purpose.
One of the functions of the enterpriser is to mobilize the resources
required to meet actual or potential consumer demands. In other
cases the businessman may start out with materials or products
which can function in specified ways. He then tries to find consumer
or industrial users who need to have this function performed and
who may be dissatisfied with the products now in use. Sometimes
the potential consumers must be awakened to the fact that the need
exists. In other words, the need must be transformed into an active
want. The prospective consumer must also be convinced that the
product offered will actually serve the need.

A current marketing opportunity matched by appropriate marketing effort is the essence of a marketing operation. The main function of an audit is a critical review of the matching of opportunity
by effort. The purpose of the new plan will be to improve on the
application of effort to opportunity. This is clear from the underlying relationship between needs and resources which generates
market opportunity.

DIMENSIONS OF DIFFERENTIAL ADVANTAGE

The unique position of a firm in the market can be defined in
terms of its differential advantages with respect to competition. It

is believed that every firm must enjoy an advantage over all competition with respect to some segment of the market in order to survive and prosper. Differential advantage may exist in one or more dimensions particularly with respect to product features, production economies, or locational advantages. These dimensions of differential advantage should be reviewed in the preplan audit to understand where the firm is today and what its outlook is for the future.

With respect to any given class of products there are several different dimensions of product qualities, and a choice must be made as to how these aspects of value are to be combined in the products offered on the market. This can be illustrated in so simple a product as paper napkins for table use, which can differ as to softness, tearing strength, and decorative finish. These various aspects of product quality can be represented as dimensions in a product space. Each dimension would represent variation along a range for some specific characteristic. The combination of qualities desired by any potential consumer can be represented as a point in the product space. If a considerable number or prospective consumers desire a similar combination of qualities, this results in a cluster of points in the product space. The firm which brought out the product in the first instance presumably selected a combination of product features with some knowledge of the cluster to which this combination would appeal and the probable responsiveness of consumers expressed in potential demand for the product. In conducting a preplan audit it might be considered that the planner was reviewing the firm's initial decisions in the light of possible changes in consumer requirements since the decisions were made. It frequently happens that quite a different combination of qualities is demanded after a product has been on the market for a period. For example, balloon tires came along to give greater comfort in addition to the basic utility of the older type of tires.

Another aspect of differential advantage consists of production economies. A firm can make a place for itself in the market by supplying a generally acceptable product for less money as compared to offering a product which is in some respects better or different from that which is generally used. There are two principal ways in which a firm which is technologically advanced can maintain an edge over its competitor. One is by innovation in product design or appeal, and the other is by innovation in the processes of manufacture or marketing. A firm which has an established leadership position in its field may make a strategic choice to push more vigorously in one of these directions or the other. The same firm which first established its market position in terms of product innovation may be best equipped at a later stage to maintain its differential advantage by technological advance in the production processes.

A third dimension of differential advantage consists in favorable location. A firm which does not claim to make a better product than its competitors may yet gain an advantage for a geographical segment of the market by reason of favorable location. Geographical advantage starts with lower costs of transportation in serving customers but it does not end there. A firm which is well located may also be able to give faster and more satisfactory service. The problem of location is not peculiar to firms serving only a part of the American market. This issue must also be faced by firms selling on a national scale and competing with smaller competitors who are dispersed geographically. It must still decide what combination of advantages will form the basis of its competitive efforts. As a general rule it cannot hope to match all of its small competitors in geographic advantage to the extent of locating a plant next door to each of them. To do so would generally mean losing the production advantages which arise out of its more concentrated operations. It must choose some combination of geographic and technological advantage as a basis for its efforts over time to hold its place in the market.

Locational advantages are fundamental in the competition among retailers and wholesalers but also essential for some types of manufacturers. Effective locational advantage does not necessarily reside in the widest possible dispersion of plants or retail stores. For any given economic activity some sites are more strategic than others. In retailing for example, several decentralized locations might have the greatest convenience appeal whereas a store in a centralized location in the same market could offer a broader selection to a greater number of people.

These several dimensions of differential advantage should be reviewed in a preplan audit. The combination of advantages by which the firm was able to establish itself in the market may not be the one which gives the best chance for survival and success in the future. The audit provides an occasion for reflective consideration of what the firm is prepared to offer to consumers and the appeals it wishes to rely on for market expansion. While due weight must be given to the history of the firm by which it has reached its present position in the market, there is some range of choice as to the position which it will continue to occupy. Specifically there are questions to be asked as to whether the firm should have more products or fewer products and whether future opportunity lies in the direction of advanced designs at high prices or relatively standardized products at economy prices.

REVIEW OF THE MARKETING MIX

After considering again the nature of the market opportunity, the next step in the marketing audit is a critical review of the marketing effort which is being expended in the cultivation of opportunity. Marketing effort takes several forms including advertising, personal salesmanship, sales promotion, and technical or merchandising services. The proportions in which these several elements are combined is commonly referred to as the marketing mix. One approach to the evaluation of marketing effort is to examine the marketing mix and to compare it with such yardsticks as what is being done by competitors or what might seem to be required by the marketing task which lies ahead.

Figure 14–2 is designed to illustrate the sharp contrasts which can occur with respect to marketing mix for different products or departments even within the same company. The upper half of the chart represents a hypothetical combination of types of effort for one product. More than half the total expenditure is for consumer advertising. Personal selling directed to trade buyers is a smaller component but still of substantial importance. Only a small part of the total expenditure goes for technical service.

The latter type of service is usually directed toward showing the buyer how to install a product or to use it effectively. The lower half of the chart shows a very different marketing mix for another product. While advertising still represents a substantial part of the total expenditure it is third rather than first in importance. Personal selling is correspondingly increased and now accounts for about half of the total expenditure. The most marked change is with respect to technical service which is relatively much more important than for product A. There are real cases in marketing for which the differences are just as great as those indicated in this chart. Quite often marketing mix can be broken down further and examined in considerably greater detail.

The contrast suggested in this chart might readily be found between a consumer product and an industrial product even though both were manufactured and marketed by the same company. Equally striking differences can be found in the marketing mix appropriate to different products growing out of differences in the physical characteristics of products or in the nature of their end use.

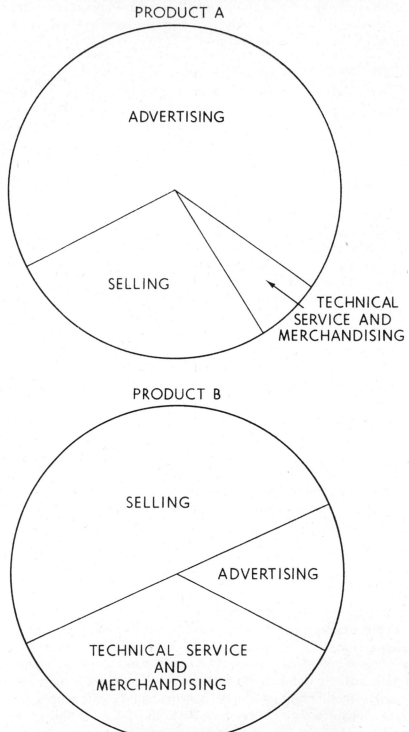

Figure 14–2

Differences in Marketing Mix for Two Products

PRODUCT A

ADVERTISING

SELLING

TECHNICAL
SERVICE AND
MERCHANDISING

PRODUCT B

SELLING

ADVERTISING

TECHNICAL SERVICE
AND
MERCHANDISING

A study was made of a paper manufacturer selling three classes of products to industrial consumers. The sales task was found to be quite different with respect to printing paper, packaging materials, and insulation materials sold to the construction industry. A similar pattern of diversity in marketing mix was observed in a study for the agricultural division of a large chemical company. This division sold several classes of products all containing antibiotics, yet there was sufficient difference in the way the products had to be sold and used to call for a substantially different marketing mix from one product class to another.

In the pattern of marketing effort for any given product group, it will generally be found that one component is dominant while others are complementary. For many consumer products the dominant effort is that of influencing consumer buyers through advertising. Other forms of marketing effort in such cases are directed toward getting the full benefit from advertising. Salesmen have the function of presenting such products to trade buyers and persuading them that they can make money on the product because the consumers will buy it. Thus, their real job may be to sell wholesalers and retailers on the power of advertising rather than to sell them on the product itself. The third category of marketing effort, which can cover many types of activity, is sales promotion. Expenditures for sales promotion are entirely complementary to the basic efforts to influence consumers on the one hand or the trade on the other. Promotions can be divided into those that are oriented toward the consumer and those that are oriented toward the trade. A dollar spent in sales promotion can be justified because it enhances the effectiveness either of advertising dollars or of sales dollars.

In industrial selling it frequently appears that personal selling is the dominant component of the marketing mix and that advertising is useful as a complementary activity. To sell an installation of machine tools, for example, a salesman may engage in a process of investigation and negotiation extending over many months. He must learn a good deal about the production problems of the customer and be prepared to present in very specific terms the economic advantages of buying his products rather than those offered by competitors. He is unlikely to encounter any prospects who have made up their minds about a machine tool purchase primarily on the basis of advertising. The function of advertising in such cases is to facilitate the job of the salesman. Advertising may help the salesman in a variety of ways. It may induce prime prospects to identify themselves through inquiries prompted by advertising. It may help to build confidence in a supplier so that the salesman presents his sales message in a more favorable atmosphere. Advertising may point up the competitive issues thus prompting buyers as to the questions to be asked of the salesman and putting the salesman on notice as to the kind of answers he will be expected to provide.

The complementary function of advertising can be illustrated by a hypothetical example. Suppose that the management of a marketing organization was considering an advertising expenditure that might cost 10 percent as much as the cost of the sales force. Conceivably such an expenditure would increase the productivity of the sales force by more than would result by an expansion of 10 percent in personal selling effort. If so, it would be justified as a complementary form of effort even though no sale could result directly and solely from the advertising expenditure. In the following illustrative chart, Figure 14–3, it is assumed that the proposed advertising expenditure would increase the average efficiency of the existing sales force by 20 percent while the same expenditure for additional salesmen would yield less than a 10 percent incre-

Figure 14-3

HYPOTHETICAL CASE OF COMPARATIVE YIELD

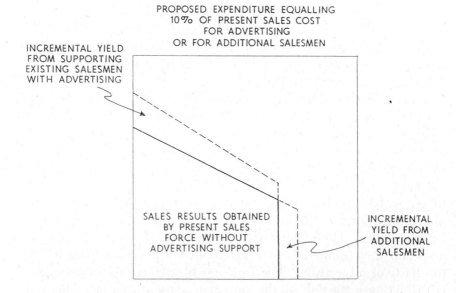

mental return. As indicated by the chart salesmen are not equally effective, and it might be expected that new sales trainees would show less than the average return for some time to come. Under the conditions illustrated in the chart, management would doubtless decide in favor of the advertising expenditure. In general the last units of expenditure allocated to advertising and to direct selling should be so calculated as to produce the same incremental return.

Rough calculations would ordinarily suffice for the kind of preliminary judgments about marketing mix required for a preplan audit. It is sometimes useful, however, to consider what would be required for a more complete analysis and to utilize the available data within that framework.

ALTERNATIVE STATEMENTS OF PROFIT OBJECTIVES

The discussion of corporate objectives usually starts with the familiar proposition that every firm is in business to make money. The business executive would usually agree that in some sense he is trying to maximize his profits as assumed by economic theory. Having granted so much he is likely to qualify his statement as meaning long-run profits rather than short-run profits. He may want to hedge further and say that he is trying to maximize benefits arising from the company's operations, and, while the major item is profits, that the desired benefits include other economic and noneconomic values. The conception of benefits to be maximized can readily become extended still further to include benefits for company employees and others rather than being restricted to benefits for owners or stockholders.

A policy of maximizing immediate dollar profits can be expressed in the form of a standard break-even chart as shown in Figure 14-4. The volume of sales is indicated by the diagonal crossing the chart from one corner to the other. Production cost is shown by the area between the base line and the slanting line above. This line starts well above the base line at the left hand margin to represent the component of fixed cost. Marketing cost is represented by the area just above production cost and has a curved line as its upper boundary. The shape of this curve reflects the assumption of diminishing returns from marketing expenditures intended to increase the sale of goods. Net profit is represented by the area which indicates the excess of dollar sales over total costs.

The point *A* represents the volume of sales at which the maximum profit would be obtained.

Assuming that the marketing executive had the data which

would enable him to draw such a chart, the decision he would make to maximize profits is clearly indicated. He would plan on the sales volume represented by the distance from 0 to *A* along the base line. This is the point at which the net profit zone, measured vertically, is at a maximum.

Figure 14–4

Break-Even Chart Showing Alternatives
as to Profit Objectives

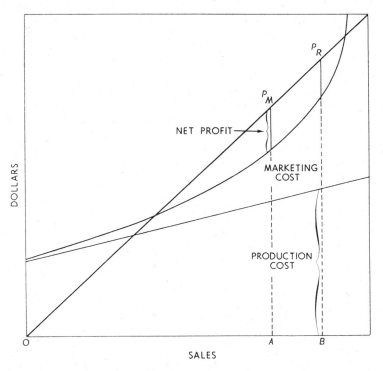

The same chart illustrates a contrasting profit policy and one which many firms are believed to follow. That is to set a minimum in profit dollars to be earned and to seek the greatest sales volume which is consistent with that profit requirement. Assume that the required minimum earnings would be represented in this case by the line segment marked P_R. The sales target corresponding to this profit goal is indicated by the line 0 to *B*. In general it would be anticipated that seeking maximum sales under a profit constraint would lead to a greater marketing effort and a larger sales volume than maximizing immediate profits.

The policy-making executive who used the second formulation of his profit goals would probably defend it as an approximation to the maximizing of long-run profits. Increase in the size of a business broadens the base on which it can earn a margin of profits. There may be other reasons for regarding growth as a goal of business enterprise, but at this first level of consideration it may be regarded as a corollary of profit maximization. The formula of maximizing sales under a profit constraint is analyzed at length by W. J. Baumol in *Business Behavior, Value, and Growth.*[1] Dr. Baumol contends that this policy is actually followed by many business firms and shows that it results in as close an approach to true profit maximization as can usually be achieved in the realistic situation confronting the policy maker.

GOALS OF GROWTH AND STABILITY

The desire for immedite profits is usually qualified in various ways by other economic objectives such as the desire for growth. It is a reasonable presumption, as already mentioned, that a large firm will make more money in the future than a small firm. Management is willing to give up something in the way of immediate dividends if the result 10 years ahead may be to earn a profit on a $50 million volume rather than on a $20 million volume. Dollar earnings may be regarded as the product of volume and a rate of profit. The volume of sales on which profits are earned is generally more expansible in a growing economy than the profit rate.

There are other economic values to be obtained from growth beyond the direct expansion of the profit earning base. The growing company offers opportunities for increasing responsibility and compensation for its executives. Thus it is able to compete on a favorable basis for the kind of executive talent it requires. The internal tensions which might be generated between rival individuals and operating groups are relaxed if the company is moving ahead so fast that everyone is mainly preoccupied with adjustment to expanding operations. The growing company attracts favorable attention from suppliers, customers, and investors. Ideas and opportunities are brought to such a company automatically where others might have to spend great effort in seeking them out. The momentum of growth helps to compensate for mistakes and carries the company forward even while errors are being corrected.

Corporate objectives often involve some combination of growth and profit goals. A firm may wish to achieve maximum growth subject only to the limitation of maintaining a minimum ratio of profits

---

[1] W. J. Baumol, *Business Behavior, Value, and Growth* (N.Y.: Macmillan Co., 1958).

to sales. This is a somewhat different formulation from that of Dr. Baumol in which the profit constraint is stated as a dollar amount. Sometimes the sales goal is stated as maintaining a certain percentage of sales for the industry as a whole. In a particular instance management might say that its goal was to maintain a 15 percent share of market and to earn 5 percent on investment after taxes. These goals might be considered as complementary, a certain position in the market being thought to be a prerequisite for maintaining the target earnings.

The usual notions of market position and market share turn out to be fraught with thorny difficulties when an attempt is made to state precise company objectives. To calculate a market share makes it necessary to set boundaries for the market. The firm which undertakes to measure its relative importance in its industry takes on the job of defining the industry. Antitrust cases which turn on the question of market share have disclosed that neither government nor industry in most instances has any accurate knowledge of market share figures or even any clear basis for specifying what is meant by market share. These limitations do not hold to quite the same degree with respect to market position. The position occupied by a firm can be described in terms of its unique advantages without requiring that the boundaries of the competitive area be defined. A firm's market position rests on the fact that it constitutes the best route by which certain suppliers can reach the market and by which certain customers can get the goods which they demand. Something can be said about the magnitude and the strength of the firm's market position without reference to competitive share. Most firms in formulating their profit policy make explicit or implicit assumptions as to the related goals of maintaining or enhancing their position in the market.

In planning for growth a firm may first set some desired future level of business somewhat arbitrarily and then test the feasibility of this goal by looking at the probable sources of growth. In general growth must come either from increased business on present products, from the development of new products from within the company, or from the acquisition of other companies with established products. These three sources will vary as to the amount of growth which can be expected from each over a stated period and in the degree of risk pertaining to such growth expectations. Growth from the present product line could generally be projected with the greatest reliability. Growth from new products to be introduced by the company is problematical except in those cases where there is an established cycle of development and introduction of somewhat related products. A pharmaceutical company, for example, based on past experience, might be able to predict with some reliability the number of pharmaceutical specialties it would introduce over the next five-year period and the probabilities of success with these products. Growth based on the acquisition of existing companies is particularly difficult to estimate. It is hard enough to find suitable companies whose operations are really complementary to those of the acquiring firm. Other uncertainties arise as to the willingness of the selected company to sell out on an acceptable basis and the legal obstacles to mergers of substantial size. In evaluating possible patterns of growth, management will doubtless be influenced by its preference as to the types of problems it is willing to confront in the future.

Figure 14-5

GROWTH AND STABILITY
EXPECTATIONS FROM CONTRASTING POLICIES

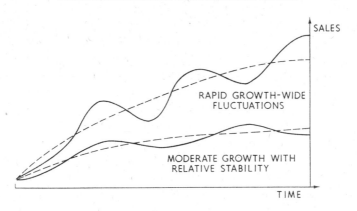

The adoption of goals of growth also involves decisions as to the source of investment funds to finance the growth pattern. On the one hand management may assume that it can finance its growth plans by plowing earnings back into the business. On the other hand it may have to go into the capital markets if the facilities needed for growth cannot be paid for out of current earnings. These are questions of financial planning that extend beyond the range of the marketing functions. Company decisions in these areas, however, may be a determining influence as to the character of the marketing plans which will be appropriate. As in other matters of company policy affecting objectives, the planner in marketing will need to know something about top-management thinking, or make some assumptions about company goals in order to develop alternative plans for consideration.

Sometimes the policy-making executive gives considerable weight to the objective of minimizing risks or at any rate keeping the degree of risk within tolerable limits. This requirement may serve to qualify in substantial degree the desire for growth and profits. Confronted with a choice, management may prefer a satisfactory profit rate with moderate risk to the expectation of high profits and larger risk. To push for the most rapid possible growth rate might be to incur the risk of wide fluctuations in sales. Figure 14-5 illustrates the possible outlook for the firm under constrasting policies, one pointing toward more growth and the other toward greater stability.

NONECONOMIC OBJECTIVES

There are a number of noneconomic considerations which can have a substantial effect on the formulation of company objectives. Some of these spring from executive preferences as to the way they would like to work or the kind of organization to which executives and other personnel would like to belong. Fundamental, of course, is executive temperament with respect to the taking of risk and habits of judgment and analysis in the weighing of risks. The question of company image is quite as important on the inside as on the outside, and the individual's pride and satisfaction in his work rests on what he believes to be the public reputation of his company. If he has confidence in the company's prestige, he draws psychic satisfactions in all of his contacts from the credit which he feels is reflected upon himself. Opportunities for maximum profit may be passed up because of his conception of what the company ought to be.

Many useful things get done because of a mixture of motives. Whether acting on his own behalf or as head of a large company, an individual often has both private and public reasons for the action he takes. He gives $50,000 to the Community Chest or to the local university because he believes that business has a responsibility to support such institutions. At the same time he would not feel justified in making so large a contribution unless the gift reflected credit on his company. Similar mixtures of motives pertain to the marketing function in business. An objective may be defined as an end-result which will satisfy one or more motivations. Any effort to clarify company objectives inescapably becomes involved with the weighing of motives which cannot all be laid out neatly on a monetary scale.

Ordinarily the market planner need not become too involved with noneconomic objectives even though it is useful for him to know they are there. It is the province of top management to determine company action with respect to these objectives. At lower levels of responsibility it is appropriate that objectives should be defined more sharply in terms of the economic goals of profits and efficient operation. If the company is inefficient at the operating level, the means will not be available at the top level to support noneconomic objectives.

The target variable to be maximized at the operating level might be designated as disposable surplus or the margin over current operating costs. Some part of the surplus may not show up in the statement of earnings because top management has disposed of it in other ways. It is within its discretion to allocate some of these funds to product and market development or to contributions to various projects which can be written off as business expense.

Strategic planning can seldom tie down objectives completely as prerequisites for planning. More typically clarification of objectives proceeds throughout the planning assignment. The recommended approach is the weighing of resources and objectives against each other. A systematic procedure for this purpose is called the preplan audit. When the audit is completed the planner can take a more detailed look at objectives. They may be classified as alternative formulation of profit goals, economic objectives other than profits, and noneconomic objectives.

SHORT-RANGE PROGRAMMING

For any firm operating under a three- to five-year plan the year requiring the most detailed attention is obviously the one immediately ahead. The appropriate planning activity for the year which is about to start is called short-range programming. In the middle range, as already discussed, the main concern is with the broad strategic concepts guiding the matching of resources and objectives in the face of competition. In the short range, planning is directed toward the step-by-step outline for specific execution.

Looking at the year ahead as the first segment of a middle-range plan a company operating under formal planning will decide on the markets to be covered and the amounts to be spent for marketing activity. The chief issue remaining is how to use these short-term resources with maximum effectiveness. Some part of the total may be held in reserve to meet contingencies, particularly if some major competitor is expected to take the initiative in introducing new products or marketing methods. The greater part of the budget must be committed to specified uses or the plan cannot serve its fundamental purpose of maximizing effective impact. Ideally, each individual engaged in executing a marketing program carries out his own assignment with vigor and precision because he is confident that the other parts of the plan will be carried out in similar fashion. Thus, the plan as a whole succeeds because everyone concerned with a segment of it understands the plan and believes in it.

The statement that a plan starts with objectives and then considers the means for carrying them out is quite valid for short-range programming. This is in contrast with strategic planning in which both objectives and resources should be examined critically, and where one of the fruits of planning is the clarification of objectives. But given the short-range objectives of marketing, the goal of maximizing effectiveness may be served by detailed administrative planning. The administrative version of a plan says that specified individuals or organization units will carry out activities as outlined on particular dates and at particular places.

A military example may be suggestive at this point. The invasion of Europe in the Second World War was doubtless considered first in terms of an analytical or strategic model visualizing the main impact of the Allied attack and of the lines of defense which might be adopted by the Germans. Consideration was doubtless given to several possibilities as to the best place to establish a beachhead and the difference this would make in the joining of the conflicting forces. When the decision was made to land in Normandy, the general staff began the process of translating a strategic conception into a sequence of field orders. The plan now took the form of instructions to commanders who could be identified by name and for the movement of specified army corps, divisions, and regiments. The Air Force was told just what was expected in saturation bombing of the beaches. Precise schedules were set for the landing craft to move in. The attacking troops were given instructions as to regrouping their forces on the beaches and preparing for the further advance. A variety of specialists in communication, supply, and medicine moved in behind after thorough briefing on what was expected of them.

The administrative version of a marketing plan is designed to secure the same kind of precision in execution. In practice, this completeness of administrative detail is ordinarily worked out in advance only in those cases in which a marketing campaign takes on the character of a blitz—attempting to smother opposition before it can get organized. Such meticulous procedure is especially pertinent in the introduction of a new product which has genuine advantages in performance but which must gain a foothold against strongly entrenched opposition. The premium on coordinated effort is only slightly less in the detailed programming of special promotions involving saturation advertising, trade cooperation, and the physical movement of special promotional packages. In the average case there is ample room for improvement in the efficiency of such activities through more detailed administrative planning.

IMMEDIATE OBJECTIVES

Administrative planning as visualized in this chapter can be interpreted in the general framework of matching means and ends. But the objectives to be sought and the means to be employed are quite detailed, limited, and specific. Broad objectives such as increasing sales volume or attaining a desired rate of profits are not involved directly. The targets are more immediate objectives which are believed to be way stations on the road to the final goal. Standards of performance for short-range programming can usually be stated in terms of these immediate objectives. A divisional sales manager, for example, starts the year with the specific objective of getting coverage in retail stores selling 75 percent of the given class of products as compared with an existing 60 percent of coverage. He sets a budget to cover the effort required to achieve this result and at the end of the year compares the level attained with the target level established in advance.

In the sale of a consumer product, the limited objectives sought during a given year are likely to include such goals as the following:

1. To achieve greater coverage in the present channels of trade.
2. To induce retailers now handling the product to push it more vigorously through larger inventories and displays or advertising cooperation.
3. To introduce the product into new markets or new channels of trade.
4. To get more consumers to try the product.
5. To increase the rate of retention or the percentage of tryers who continue as regular users.
6. To decrease the rate of loss to other brands.
7. To increase the rate of use among regular users of the product.

Any or all of these limited objectives could mean an expansion of the sales base for profits. Some of them might be more worthwhile than others in a given case or might represent a greater yield for the dollars expended. Individually they would not be essential conditions for success but bear some analogy to a row of hills or fortified

points facing a military commander. Some he may be determined
to take by frontal assault, while others are bypassed. The commander is looking for the least costly route to his ultimate destination. The selection among intermediate objectives, however, is not
independent of means to be employed. Whether a highway or a river
was the best path to the destination would obviously depend in part
on the type of vehicle or vessel available for the movement of troops
and supplies.

Similarly, the choice of intermediate objectives in short-range
market programming depends in part on the resources available.
For these reasons it is useful to try to get some general view of the
possible limited goals and how they are related to each other.
Figure 14–6 is an attempt to provide such a picture. It is confined to
the objectives which have already been listed, showing how each one
is designed to expand the business, but in somewhat different directions.

Figure 14–6

LIMITED OBJECTIVES FOR A MARKETING PROGRAM

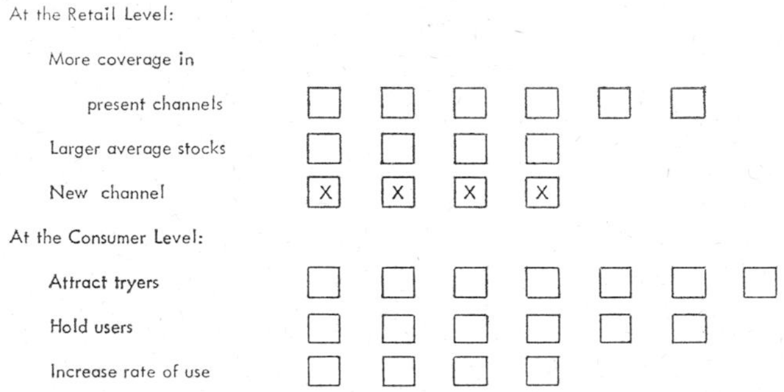

At the Retail Level:

    More coverage in
       present channels   ☐ ☐ ☐ ☐ ☐ ☐

    Larger average stocks   ☐ ☐ ☐ ☐

    New channel   ☒ ☒ ☒ ☒

At the Consumer Level:

    Attract tryers   ☐ ☐ ☐ ☐ ☐ ☐ ☐

    Hold users   ☐ ☐ ☐ ☐ ☐ ☐

    Increase rate of use   ☐ ☐ ☐ ☐

The weighing of immediate objectives takes the form of choosing
the most feasible and economical route to the ultimate destination
while taking account of the resources at hand. Once the route has
been chosen, the next concern of administrative planning is the
effective employment of means in gaining the limited objectives as
specified. Further speculation as to the best route should cease at
this point and attention be devoted completely to the details of
procedure, scheduling, and coordination. Intermediate objectives
must be taken as fixed targets for the program period, but they are
always subject to revision on the basis of experience. In fact, the
meaning of experience for the line executive in marketing consists,
in part, of acquiring an intuitive feeling for the amount of response
which can be expected in applying the readily available types of
effort to immediate objectives.

COMPONENTS OF MARKETING ACTIVITY

The elements to be coordinated in a short-range marketing program are those which could influence either the consumer buyer or factors in the channels of trade by which the producer reaches the consumer. In general these forms of effort are advertising, which is largely directed toward the consumer; personal selling, which is directed toward dealers and distributors; and promotions, which can be oriented toward either. A consumer-oriented promotion would be exemplified by a coupon contained in one package which entitled the purchaser to a price reduction on another package. A trade-oriented promotion could take many forms, one of the simplest being the free goods deal in which the retailer may get one case free with a purchase of ten.

A special sales drive or promotion often has many components which have to be coordinated in order for the program as a whole to be effective. A concrete case might be a campaign in which the main purpose was to get new tryers for the product, but a related objective was to introduce the product into some additional metropolitan markets where it had not previously been stocked by retailers. The plan adopted might call for the use of a special introductory size to be purchased at a price below that of the regular size and carrying a coupon which would provide a ten cent credit on a purchase of a regular package. The retailer might be offered three cases of the introductory size free with a purchase of a dozen cases of the regular size. The manufacturer would perhaps be getting his sampling job done more cheaply and more selectively than if he had distributed free samples on a house-to-house basis. He would be obtaining additional advantages, if the deal was successful, such as inducing retailers to put in an initial stock adequate for an impressive display.

Many elements calling for close coordination would ordinarily go into such an introductory campaign. The special package would have to be designed, produced, and filled, and supplies made available as needed market-by-market. There would usually be an accompanying advertising campaign in local media such as newspapers. This advertising would either be placed directly or through the retailer, financed in whole or in part by the manufacturer. Sales materials would be developed for use by the salesmen in persuading retailers to accept the deal. Success stories from other markets; the usual proofs of advertising support, both local and national; point-of-sale display materials and instructions on how to use them are among the elements typically found in such a promotional package.

Various methods of tying one element to another are often devised. For example, the proposed newspaper advertising might show a mass display of the product as it would appear in the retail store, partly for consumer appeal and partly as one means of convincing the retailer of the advantages of building such a display.

Despite the range of experience with such promotions, the instances in which they are carried out with real efficiency are in the minority. There are several reasons for this, including retailer resistance or indifference. Certainly one of the reasons is the lack of adequate planning and the failure to recognize the exacting nature of the planning job. Ordering new packages is delayed too long because the person responsible did not make sufficient allowance for the time required for creating the package design. On the other hand, the final order for packages can be given too quickly and before fully thinking out the basic issues as to special promotional copy, size of the package, its functional features, and the most appropriate ways of relating the special package to the regular package.

In this matter, as in other phases of the program, various suppliers need to be given standby notice some time in advance of the final order. Sometimes there are specific things suppliers can do to make ready, as for example, being sure they will have a supply of the appropriate paper stock when the order is received. In the case of advertising, preliminary stages of copy development and layouts can be well advanced if there is effective liaison between an advertiser and his agency. Some primary contractors in the defense industries issue multiple-stage orders to suppliers which may go through as many as five phases to initiate design, production, shipment, and so on. The multi-stage order is a promising tool of coordination in integrated planning of promotions.

One of the greatest wastes in any aspect of consumer goods marketing is in careless planning of point-of-sale materials. Very expensive display pieces are created and delivered to retailers often with no assurance that a piece will be used even once. Inventories of such materials stored in the basements of various types of retail stores have turned up staggering amounts of expensive commercial art which is not yielding any benefits for the manufacturer and is merely absorbing storage space for the retailer. Sometimes the control of promotional materials is so loose that the salesman gets credit for the number of pieces delivered without any accounting for the number effectively used. The waste of the material is bad enough, but the real loss is in the failure of the promotional plan to have the impact for which it was conceived. Various remedies have been tried, such as having detail men, employed by the manufacturer, build displays of merchandise, and leaving special display materials in the store only when they have been built into such displays.

Various devices are used to make the retailer aware of the financial value of a display piece. Sometimes he is offered a chance to buy the item at cost rather than receive it as a gift. In other instances it is understood that this display is the property of the manufacturer, who can pick it up when a promotion is over and perhaps move it to another store or even to another city. Some retailers make a charge for setting up a display in a window or in a store. While this is an additional cost, it at least offers some assurance that the display will be used. The charge made by the retailer might compare favorably with what the manufacturer would otherwise be spending to get displays, taking account of the relatively low probability of success on some products. This component of short-range programs is often ignored or minimized in planning. It is emphasized here both because of the direct opportunities for saving and because the determination to get more value out of point-of-sale material by the manufacturer will provide a thread of coordination running through the whole program. This is by contrast with other situations in which it seems wise to build the effort around the objective of getting the most out of media advertising.

In many aspects of marketing the planner has to take account of legal limitations on the strategies and procedures which can be adopted. This problem is present in the offering of merchandising help to retailers. The basic rule, however, is that these aids must be made available to all on a proportionate basis. It is still possible for the seller in his own interest to devote more effort to helping those who are fully cooperative than to trying to persuade those who are indifferent.

Many of the same considerations apply in the handling of premiums or inducements to the consumer. Detailed and meticulous planning is needed in maximizing the effect on new prospects as compared to lavishing trial packages on regular users. The amount in the trial package should be sufficient to give the prospect a chance to convince himself that the product is a good one. The redemption rate on premium offers needs to be carefully calculated and redemptions made promptly and in a manner convenient for the consumer without becoming an irritating burden for the retailer. Premiums should be judiciously selected both for their general appeal and for favorable association with the image that the company is trying to project. The purpose to be achieved should be a genuine and serious one rather than merely to keep a sequence of offers running. It is true that a special offer helps to give the salesman a fresh approach in calling on his accounts, but it is well for him to have something to talk about besides the offer.

Large scale advertising generally involves detailed and precise programming. The importance of the budgets involved, and the need for coordinating the actions of the advertiser, the advertising agency, and the advertising medium make planning mandatory. Television programs or issues of a magazine appear on scheduled dates and advertising must meet a series of deadlines to make these dates. Most agencies have plan boards with representatives from each functional department, and some have three or four separate planning groups entering into a campaign at different stages. Thus, one planning group might consider the concept of overall marketing strategy to be implemented through advertising; a second might be concerned with selection of appeals and their embodiment in copy themes; while a third planning group develops recommendations as to the media in which the advertising will appear and the allocation of the budgeted expenditure to reach the type of audience desired.

Advertising was once regarded as a great sales force which could be planned and executed as a distinct and separate enterprise. The trend has been toward increasing recognition that advertising is only one component to be coordinated with other factors in marketing. Agencies have set up merchandising departments or have tried to penetrate more deeply into market planning. Advertisers, on the other hand, have developed a level in middle management called product managers. The product manager may actually work in the advertising department in the cases where advertising makes up the larger part of the total marketing budget. Their responsibility for planning and coordination embraces all aspects of the product and its marketing program including advertising. The product manager in some companies is regarded purely as a staff planner with an advisory relationship to the field sales organization. In other instances he has line responsibility as the name product manager implies. This can be true even though he does not give orders to the field salesmen but has to sell them his program. This relation to his company's salesmen is similar to that of the old line sales manager who had to sell his merchandising program to independent distributors or wholesalers.

SCHEDULING SPECIAL PROMOTIONS

To illustrate this detailed scheduling activity suppose that a marketing organization has decided to put on four major promotions during the year. This would mean four somewhat independent but obviously related decision problems. A promotion would be chosen in each quarter that was appropriate for the given season and that would make the greatest contribution to the results for the year. Promotions should be avoided which created obvious handicaps for subsequent efforts. Part of the planning function is to foresee and evaluate unfavorable side effects.

The wide range of choice among alternations in this type of programming creates a need for systematic procedure. The artistic and intuitive touch of a gifted merchandiser may be needed to conceive of novel and effective promotions. Some simple planning devices can be useful in selecting among such ideas and combining individual promotions into a successful merchandising year.

The scheduling of special promotions and sales drives should reflect some general principles of program design. A good type of promotion in retail stores, for example, is one which gets active consumer response but does not provoke retailer resistance because of some of the features of its operation. There are standard types of tried and true promotions which retailers in a given trade recognize by name and evaluate accordingly. They are reluctant, however, to proceed with the same promotion indefinitely or to have it repeated too frequently. Even within the standard types of promotion there is room for variety and novelty to enhance the appeal for both consumers and the trade. The planners choice takes account of both proven effectiveness and novelty appeal. Often this simply means going back to a promotion that was effective some time past and will now appear fresh and novel again.

A considerable amount of historical information can be used in this type of planning if it is brought together in convenient form. Table 14–1 is a simple illustration of how this is sometimes done. The upper part of the chart shows the division of annual sales by months for a five year average and also for the past year. The lower part of the chart shows the months for the past five years in which certain standard promotions were going on. The letter *O* in a cell represents ordinary operation while each of the other letters designates some special promotion. The vacant row at the top is left for filling in the choice of promotions for the current year.

Obviously this chart as shown does not include all of the data which might be considered. This is a situation in which the planner might make good use of transparent overlays for visual comparison. Thus an overlay for the panel at the top might show what happened to monthly sales during 1957 to help the planner in evaluating promotion *K* which occurred only in that year. Other overlays could show whatever is known about the promotions or sales results of principal competitors.

Table 14–1

PLANNING TABLE
FOR SELECTING PROMOTIONS

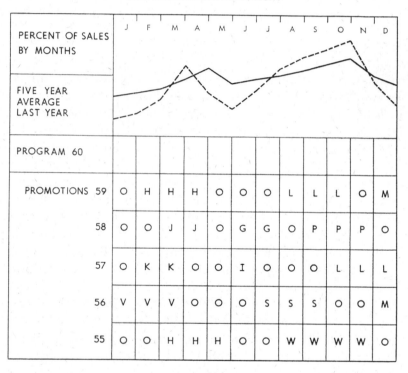

	J	F	M	A	M	J	J	A	S	O	N	D
PERCENT OF SALES BY MONTHS												
FIVE YEAR AVERAGE LAST YEAR												
PROGRAM 60												
PROMOTIONS 59	O	H	H	H	O	O	O	L	L	L	O	M
58	O	O	J	J	O	G	G	O	P	P	P	O
57	O	K	K	O	O	I	O	O	O	L	L	L
56	V	V	V	O	O	O	S	S	S	O	O	M
55	O	O	H	H	H	O	O	W	W	W	W	O

In selecting promotions, the planner should take account of both the desired results and the possible adverse reactions. This is one area in which limited and sharply defined objectives should always be a part of the planning process. A promotion may be designed to get additional retail stores to stock a product, to induce retailers to increase their inventories, or to induce consumers to try the product who might not be reached in other ways or for other reasons. Promotions that are under consideration should be evaluated against the stated objectives and not merely by their scope or attention-getting value.

There is a great deal of lost motion and wasted effort in the field of sales promotion because of the failure to consider and foresee consequences which may not be in line with the stated objectives. One of the most common side effects is a sharp slump in sales after a promotion is over. In other words, a special promotion sometimes appears to mean nothing more than an acceleration of business that would have been obtained in the normal course of affairs a little bit later. Under certain circumstances even this acceleration can be worthwhile, but it must be remembered that it is achieved at the cost of a price cut or special promotional expenses or both. Depending on the nature of the trade involved, however, there may not be a clear choice between promotion or no promotion but only a choice among possible promotions. One value of a promotion is in giving salesmen a specific reason for calling on customers and something to talk about when they get there. While in theory it might be better to have continued sales effort of a more stable kind, in practice it might be difficult to obtain day-in day-out sales efforts without promotion.

This discussion of detailed programming is confined at this stage to sales promotion activities. Many of the same kind of planning issues arise, of course, with respect to advertising programs. For the present purpose, however, it is more convenient to use the illustration of sales promotion which is usually planned inside the company. The planning responsibility for advertising is often shared by the company's advertising department and its advertising agency.

ACCEPTANCE OF SHORT-RANGE PROGRAMS

A short-range program is generally submitted for approval and must have the endorsement of superior authority before it goes into effect. Sometimes the approval is purely nominal and merely signalizes the fact that the planning assignment has been completed and the responsibility of the planner discharged. The criterion for acceptance may merely be that a plan which appears workable and sufficiently detailed has been completed on time. In other cases more rigid standards may be applied before a plan is accepted as satisfactory. If short-range programming is regular and periodic, approval of a program can constitute the mass production of decisions within the framework of established administrative procedure.

Reference has already been made to the use of a company-wide forecast as the coordinating instrument, as compared to centralized planning. One version of the forecast is a consolidated statement of the various operating units as to what they believe they can accomplish during the year. If the means of accomplishing the stated goals are set out in some detail, the statement by each unit approaches the character of a short-range program. Acceptance of the forecast as a target figure can be made conditional on the approval of the program which supports the forecast. Even when the line executive is planning for himself, as frequently happens in the case of short-range planning, there is still the point of decision which might be called acceptance of the program. That is the point at which the executive is satisfied that the program as conceived will work and he can now turn his attention to carrying it out.

A slightly more advanced procedure related forecasts and programs to budget requests. An annual review of marketing budgets provides the occasion for top management to get a cross-sectional picture of what is going on. The review should cover what happened under the last plan and offer an explanation of any major deviations between budget and performance either in failing to hit the target or in turning back unexpended funds. The new budget request should be supported by a written statement of what is to be done with the money and with evidence that the proposed program will achieve the indicated results. The procedure of budget approval is one way of gaining some assurance that programs have been thought through to an extent that gives some assurance of success.

Several alternatives are open to management if the supporting plan does not appear promising. It can be sent back with requests for further clarification. The planner may be commended for his promotional ideas but be required to translate them into an administrative version of a program with names and dates and places. The budget figure may be approved for a lower figure than that requested on the ground that the immediate objectives at stake do not justify the suggested expenditure. The budget may be increased on the ground that the objectives are really vital but that greater effort will be required to accomplish them. If the budget approved is greater than that requested, the proposal will doubtless be referred back for further work on how the larger budget is to be spent.

The most systematic evaluation of a single marketing program is one that considers it as one of the components in a larger system of action. A large company committed to formal planning will have detailed programs for many products or product groups. All of these programs together make up the schedule of activities for the year ahead. The product programs must be related constructively to each other to constitute an effective total program. The total program for the year must form an appropriate first phase of what is to be accomplished during the next three to five years. Product programs running concurrently can interact in several ways. Most obviously they impose limitations on each other because they compete for such scarce resources as advertising space or the time of salesmen. Two programs can get in each other's way more seriously because they make conflicting claims on distribution channels or because they represent inconsistent policies. It is true that success with one product can often smooth the way for another, but it is also true that the success of one product can block the way of another with a brighter future. Internal competition among products made by the same company can be constructive for both, or the tactics employed can be mutually destructive and react against the company as a whole. One way to state the purpose of detailed planning, product by product, is to make all the separate efforts additive in their results rather than tending to cancel each other out. Unless the review of individual plans is conducted with an awareness of company-wide objectives, it can turn out that the whole is less than the sum of the parts.

The total program for the year must in turn be considered in relation to the objectives which have been set for three to five years ahead. Starting from the initial base, the planned activities are designed to apply a growth multiplier to sales and profits. This aspect of planning was discussed in Chapter 3. The present point is that the growth factor for the company as a whole is the end-result of growth achieved by a collection of individual product plans. The perspective of growth provides another means of raising questions about the contributions to be made by individual product plans.

Table 14–2 is intended to indicate the interplay of the various considerations in evaluating a single product plan. For illustration,

Table 14–2

CONTRIBUTION OF PRODUCT PLANS
TO STRATEGIC COMPANY OBJECTIVES

Product Plans	Planning Horizon—Three Years			
	t_0	t_1	t_2	t_3
V	—	V_1	—	V_3
W	—	W_1	—	W_3
X	X_0	X_1	X_2	X_3
Y	—	Y_1	—	Y_3
Z	—	Z_1	—	Z_3
Company Plan	K	$a(K)$	$b(aK)$	$c(abK)$

attention is called to the detailed program for the product X, which is up for evaluation. The strategic goal for the company as a whole is represented by the expression in the lower right corner. From one point of view this is the sum of the goals for the five products as shown in the right-hand column. From another viewpoint it is the result of increments of growth applied to K, which is the total result achieved in the base year. The plan to be evaluated is that pertaining to product X for t_1, which is the year immediately ahead.

The review can be said to revolve around two questions which both are concerned with the contribution of the plan X_1 to the strategic plan for the company. Will the plan make the optimum contribution to the expansion of the company represented by multiplying the base K by the growth factor a? Will the growth of product X under the plan make an adequate contribution to the total growth achieved by applying the successive factors a, b, and c? To answer both questions to the best advantage means that plan X_1 should be designed to produce a favorable effect on product X without an offsetting detrimental effect on the other plans which are running concurrently.

To summarize this discussion of short-range programming, it is the phase of planning in which the planner must start from a clear statement of objectives and use the means available with maximum effectiveness in relation to these goals. The objectives sought are very specific immediate objectives rather than general considerations such as maximizing profit. The end-product of short-range programming is a detailed outline of proposed activities sometimes approaching the precision of an operating manual. All forms of marketing effort including advertising need to be coordinated by means of the short-range program. Strategic planning for periods of three to five years becomes effective only through execution under a series of short-range programs.

Selected References

BENEDICT, TRUMAN. "The Staff Man in the Decision-making Process," *Advanced Management*, May 1960.

> Makes a plea for multiple bosses for the staff planner, which is equivalent to recommendations in the text that the staff planner should have close ties at various levels.

FREY, ALBERT W. *The Effective Marketing Mix.* Hanover, N.H.: Amos Tuck School of Business Administration, Dartmouth College, 1956.

> Stresses integration and coordination by assigning single responsibility and arriving at predetermined goals.

HAGEN, EVERETT E. *On the Theory of Social Change; How Economic Growth Begins.* M.I.T. Center for International Studies. Homewood, Ill.: The Dorsey Press, 1962.

This treatise on the problems of underdeveloped countries makes the point that planning can start either from resources or objectives, a view which holds quite as well among firms in the American market.

OXENFELD, ALFRED AND SCHUCHMAN, A. *Qualifying and Improving Marketing Performance*. Report #32, American Management Association, 1959.

A comprehensive view of various types of marketing audits, including types similar to the pre-plan audit.

Problems

1. Discuss in detail the objects, methods, and advantages of the pre-plan audit.

2. Select a product that will allow you to evaluate the differential advantage this product enjoyed but which has been cancelled out in the years since its introduction. Discuss the product, tracing the above-mentioned product life cycle.

3. Discuss the economic values to be obtained from company growth. Discuss the principal methods of company growth, enumerating the relative merits of each. Discuss the dangers involved in using the goal of profit maximization as the only goal of the company.

4. Explain how detailed administrative planning can be used to promote the goal of maximizing marketing effectiveness once the short-range objectives of marketing have been chosen.

5. Contrast the planning involved in preparing for minor changes with the planning involved in preparing for major structural changes.

Chapter 15

FORECASTING FOR PLANNING

Forecasting of sales and of other outcomes, such as prices, costs, and net earnings, is one of the foundation stones for planning in marketing. In most companies, forecasting is undertaken first and may be carried to a fairly advanced stage before formal planning procedures are adopted. For some period in the history of a firm, forecasting may serve as a partial substitute for central planning. A sales goal based on the forecast is accepted as feasible by the various divisions or operating units of the company. Each unit is then expected to conform its individual activities in such a way as to make the maximum contribution to the stated goals.

Forecasting plays a fundamental role in planning, whether it remains decentralized or becomes fully coordinated. Under decentralized operation, the management of a division may participate in preparing the forecast and setting the short-term goals for its own sales and profits. The division then submits a budget for approval describing the expenditures that will be required to reach the stated goals. The budget request may be supported by a plan, in such detail as may be required by central management, showing how the resources requested will be used to achieve the operating goals.

Under centralized planning, forecasts of sales and costs might be prepared for the entire company. A marketing plan or program for the whole company would then be developed. This procedure might be appropriate if the major impact of marketing effort was represented by a massive advertising expenditure under centralized control. Another situation favorable to fully coordinated short-range planning would be one in which maximum economy of physical handling appeared to be the major marketing problem in a highly competitive market.

In some cases of long-range planning, the entire procedure could be expressed as an extension of forecasting. The planner attempts to foresee the environment of action in which future operations must take place. He forecasts the outcome of significant trends that are presumably beyond the control of executive decision. Within the limits set by these trends, he then attempts to predict the results of major decisions open to the company.

The discussion of forecasting which follows will not attempt to deal with all the issues appropriate to a treatise on forecasting techniques. The purpose here is to discuss forecasting in terms of the kind of results which can be most useful for planning. The choice of forecasting techniques in a given instance can be determined by considering the requirements for planning. Some illustrations of forecasting techniques, however, are provided in order for the reader to see their relationship to planning requirements. Also, an important aspect of forecasting—the costs of forecasting—is discussed.

THE PROJECTION BASE

Forecasting is an attempt to foresee the future by examining the past. The validity of forecasting depends on the assumption that a pattern or relationships observable over a past period can be expected to continue into the future. Whether this can be done depends in part on the length and breadth of the record which is available for examination. The requisite length of the record, or number of years over which it extends, obviously bears some relationship to the length of the period for which the forecast is to be made. If the forecast is to be made for one year only, a five-year past record might be sufficient. One of the principal components in a month-by-month forecast over the year is seasonal variation. A five-year past record should provide a reasonably good picture of the seasonal pattern and whether this pattern is relatively stable or is itself changing. A record of this length might also be adequate to take account of the ups and downs of the business cycle for the purposes of a one-year forecast.

If a five-year forecast is to be made, it would usually be desirable to have a past record of ten to fifteen years. Both the cyclical element and secular trend could show marked differences within a five-year period. For forecasts over any longer future periods, such as ten to twenty years, not much would be gained by going back more than a quarter of a century. For any longer period, the statistical record is likely to be fragmentary and some of the relevant trends have gone through qualitative shifts as well as quantitative changes.

What the record lacks in length may sometimes be compensated for by breadth and depth. The term "breadth" in this instance refers to the scope of related information which might be used in forecasting the particular series such as the sales of a given product or firm. Thus, sales records on each of the major household appliances would provide breadth for a forecast on automatic washing machines as compared to past records for washing machines alone. "Depth" implies the extent of the detail in which the particular series is recorded, which might permit a more penetrating study of functional relationships. Referring again to washing machines, depth would be provided by past records, by trading areas, by family income, or by new and replacement sales.

In the more formal forecasting procedures, there is usually an attempt to derive a forecasting equation from a study of some past period and to use this equation in estimating the required values for a future period. The simple (linear) form of such an equation would be

$$ax + by + cz + k = w.$$

In this formula w is estimated sales; x, y, and z are the factors believed to be associated with sales. The coefficients a, b, and c are the respective weights given to these factors, and k is a constant derived from say, a multiple linear regression. (See Chapter 9 for a description of multiple regression applied to demand forecasting.) Sometimes a past period is divided into two parts. The equation is derived from the study of one of these periods, and then it is tested by seeing how well it could have predicted the results in a subsequent period. That is one reason for the requirement that the length of the past record should be longer than the future period to be forecasted. The past record must serve both for formulating the forecasting equation and for testing it.

Any attempt to predict the future is fraught with uncertainties and should never be represented as more than systematic guessing. Perhaps its main justification in ordinary business practice is that it provides an orderly and organized foundation for the guesses about the future which the business executive and the staff planner are obliged to make in any case. The information which the executive is most familiar with consists of the facts which have made the deepest impression on him. These are likely to represent a very biased sample, inadequate to form the basis for predictions. The canvas of available data needs to be pushed far enough to determine what the key variables are likely to be and to make some judgments as to the statistical reliability of the record. Even in so simple a matter as forecasting the seasonal pattern of sales, the analyst runs into serious discrepancies of data arising from accounting practices.

INTERRELATED GROWTH CURVES

A market planner is usually most interested in secular trend or long-run growth curves as compared to short-range fluctuations in sales. His first approach to studying the curve of growth for a product or a company is to consider its relationship to other secular trends in the economy. He thus regards the product for which he is forecasting as a component of a larger aggregate and tries to make at least a preliminary forcast in this way. In studying consumer markets, the economic determinants of greatest interest to the planner are population, consumer income, and ownership of major assets. A vast amount of published work is available on forecasts for these factors which the planner can utilize in making his more detailed forecasts.

Population statistics in their various aspects are the most fundamental for the market outlook. Twenty-five years ago it was assumed that total population could be predicted with great reliability for a country or a sizeable region. The population experts reecived a rude jolt when the trend turned up sharply again after the decade of the thirties. Nevertheless, there are some very important aspects of population figures which can be predicted accurately enough for most marketing purposes. For example, it is possible to tell quite closely how many men and women in the United States will be forty years old five years from today. The number who are thirty-five years old today is known, and there is also good information on the mortality experience which can be expected to reduce the size of this age group over the next five years. A very important marketing statistic is the number of young men and women who will reach marriagable age and set up new households over any future period for which a forecast is being made. In the short run this can be done quite accurately by taking account of the aging of the appropriate population groups, their expectations for survival, and the current trends as to the percentages in these age groups contracting marriages. One of the most hazardous population predictions is the number of babies that will be born in the next year or the next five years. But, predicting the number of women of child-bearing age during the period can be made with high confidence, since those women are already here and will enter the forecast period with known survival rates.

Increasing use is being made for forecasting purposes of available figures on major consumer assets. For example, the number of automobiles in use at any given time can be regarded as a population which can be treated in much the same way as a human population. Actuarial studies analyze the births and deaths of human beings to predict the net increase or decrease of population. Similarly, the market analyst watches the trends on new car purchases and on scrapping of old cars to predict how many automobiles are likely to be in use at a given date. The automobile registration figures are something like a perpetual census which gives direct guidance to several industries. In predicting the tire market, for example, the manufacturer has a special interest in those cars which have been registered for three years and which are nearing the point of having to replace some or all of their tires. Home ownership and the age of homes owned similarly provide basic trends to which the growth trends of many products may be related.

Many consumer products are directly complementary to other products. An excellent example is the development of low-sudsing detergents for use in automatic washing machines. The use of this packaged product depends directly on the number of automatic washing machines installed in homes, and reliable figures have been available for some years on washing machine populations. As a result it was possible to predict the annual sales of these products within a very narrow range of error even during the period of their most rapid and dynamic growth. These relationships are illustrated (conceptually) in the following chart (Figure 15–1).

Figure 15–1

POPULATION OF A DURABLE GOODS ITEM AS
FORECASTING BASE FOR RELATED PRODUCT
(Conceptual Chart)

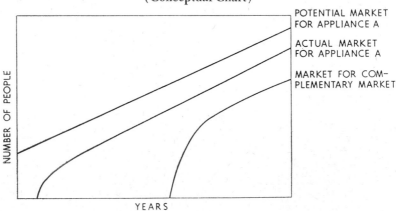

Major studies which have been made and which are of service to the market forecaster deal with the structure of the American economy and the pattern of relationships between the various components of the consumer's budget. Expenditures for food, clothing, durable goods, and consumer services have been studied over a long term of years, and close correlations have been found with the level of consumer income and its distribution by size of income groups. Of equal importance as a foundation for forecasting in industrial marketing are the input-output tables which have been calculated for several benchmark years. This way of viewing the national economy divides the total economy into a number of segments and for each of these segments shows how much it receives from or supplies to each of the other segments.

Public services of all kinds constitute a growing segment of the entire economy. Government agencies at all levels are major purchasers of many types of goods and in addition influence other markets in many ways as through relief and old age benefits and subsidies to farmers and other groups. One important resource for the planner is the budgets of public bodies which can help him in forecasting future expenditures. There are also some increasingly reliable studies on the purchasing intentions of consumers with respect to durable goods and of industry with respect to plant and equipment.

COMPONENTS OF GROWTH

In studying the growth curve for a product, the forecaster may analyze it from the inside rather than looking at its external relationships to other trends. In the case of consumer durable goods, one of the most important distinctions is between new purchases and replacement purchases. For a period after a new appliance is developed, all of its sales are new sales in the sense that the families buying the appliances have never owned them before. Sales to new users will predominate during the period that the normal saturation level for the product is being established. The percentage of families using the product may level off at 25 percent or 50 percent, or it may approach the present situation of the automobile with nearly every family owning one. Long before saturation is reached, the emphasis will shift to replacement sales, and most of the prospective purchases will be found among those who already own a unit and wish to replace it with a new one. This situation with respect to new buyers and replacement buyers is pictured in the next chart (Figure 15-2).

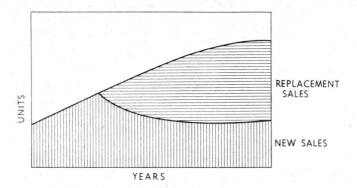

The lower portion of the chart shows new sales rising to a peak and sinking to lower levels in subsequent years. At the beginning all purchasers are new purchasers, but this element in demand reaches a peak and then begins to slide off. Meanwhile the older units in the hands of consumers have depreciated to the point where their owners are ready to replace them. For a considerable period thereafter the replacement segment of the market continues to increase in relative importance. Obviously the market never swings completely to replacement sales since there are always new users and new families coming into the market who have never owned the item before. Finally, a point is reached at which new and replacement sales are in equilibrium with each other and with the population trend. At this point new sales vary directly with the number of individuals or the number of families who reach the point of becoming prospects, and the outlook for replacement sales varies with the number of units which have been in use for a certain number of years before.

A somewhat similar situation exists with respect to the prospective market for a packaged product. Here the two principal components in the curve of growth are the increasing number of users and the increase, if any, in the average rate of use. This distinction is important both for forecasting purposes and for other aspects of planning. The number of users for a product may reach a point of saturation but still leave considerable room for expanding the market on the basis of increasing the average consumption per user. Thus the increase in the amount of meat consumed in recent years is due partly to the steady growth in population and partly to rising consumer income which has enabled consumers to indulge their preference for meat as compared with other foods.

Another important distinction particularly related to market planning for a product is the rate at which a product gets new users on a trial basis as compared with its experience in the retention of these consumers or the shift of their preference to other products. In attempting to forecast for individual brands, it is important to study all available information on the rate of competitive shifts during any given operating period between this brand and others. So long as these rates remain stable, it is possible to estimate the share of the market which the particular brand will be able to get and to hold.

Suppose, for example, that brand A loses 15 percent of its users to competitive brands during any given period. Suppose, further, that the brand gains users from competition, these brands losing 10 percent of their users in the given operating period. The interchange would be in equilibrium when brand A has 40 percent of the market. If it now stands at 50 percent, its market share will fall at a predictable rate to the equilibrium level. Similarly, if brand A has only 20 percent of the market, its share of the business should double over a foreseeable period. The latter statement might seem like a paradox since brand A loses at a higher rate than its competition. It is really a simple matter of arithmetic as can be seen by looking at the equilibrium case in which there are 40 users of a brand A to 60 users of all competitive brands. During a given operating period, product A would lose 15 percent of its 40 users or 6 users. During the same period other brands would lose 10 percent of their 60 users which would also be 6. The interchange would be in balance and hence the market shares would remain the same. The tendency toward equilibrium, assuming stable loss ratios for either side, is illustrated in the next chart (Figure 15–3). The two points marked on the horizontal time scale would represent the predicted time to reach some high proportion of the equilibrium level under the stated assumptions as to initial shares and comparative rates of loss. The point D indicates the date by which the market share of brand A might decline to (close to) the 40 percent level if it starts with 50 percent. The point S indicates the date by which brand A would approach market equilibrium under the reverse assumption of starting at 20 percent. (See Chapter 7 for further details on the Markov process underlying this behavior.)

Still another way to break down a growth curve is to regard it as

Figure 15-3

TENDENCY TOWARD MARKET SHARE EQUILIBRIUM
ASSUMING TWO DIFFERENT STANDING LEVELS FOR BRAND A
(Conceptual Representation)

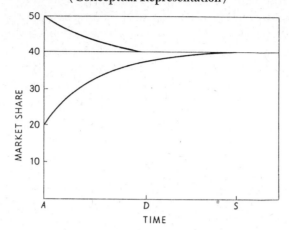

the accumulation of separate growth curves for significant segments
of the total volume. Suppose a product is now being sold nationally
that was originally sold state by state or region by region. There
is reason to assume that it may have achieved its most rapid expansion and then tended to level off in one region after another. The
next chart (Figure 15-4) is intended to illustrate a hypothetical
situation in which the overall trend for the product follows the
standard S-shaped curve of growth.

Figure 15-4

POSSIBLE COMPOSITION OF A GROWTH CURVE FOR A FIRM
(Saturation points are quickly reached region by region, but the
growth trend is impressive for the market as a whole)
(Conceptual Representation)

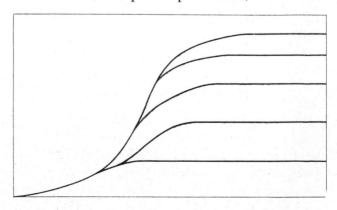

It is assumed in this case that the business spread slowly across the country, one major marketing region being opened up each year. It could be that the trend of the business followed the S-shaped curve in each of these regions individually. The first region might then be in a later stage of the growth curve than any of the others. It would be quite possible, however, to get something like the logistic curve for the total volume even though the business had already become static in most sales regions. Simply opening up new markets gives the appearance of an increasing rate of growth for the business as a whole. In other words, the growth is soon realized in each case, but the base on which growth increments are added each year is being steadily expanded. Sales presently level off segment by segment and may reach a fixed level in each of the older markets. There is an appearance of continuous growth for the volume of business as a whole merely because some of the more recently opened markets have not yet reached full maturity. This type of analysis could lead to an extremely useful prediction as to when a rapidly growing business might be expected to approach a ceiling. An accurate forecast of this kind could make a great difference in marketing plans either through keeping costs in line with the expected volume or through finding a way to penetrate the apparent ceiling, thus starting a new cycle of growth.

CYCLICAL AND SEASONAL PATTERNS

Much of business forecasting has been preoccupied with trying to foresee the peaks and valleys of the business cycle. This emphasis arose in part from the special interests of security buyers. The relative attention given to the cycle is somewhat out of proportion for the purposes of the planner in marketing. Nevertheless foreseeing turns in the business cycle is of considerable importance, second only to the analysis of long-run growth trends. Some market planners are in a relatively favorable position with respect to the business cycle because the segment of the economy which concerns them lags behind the general movement of the cycle rather than following it. Thus, when the general level of business activity turns down they still have a period of grace within which to get ready for the drop in the level of their own activities. There are other types of enterprise in which a fair share of the business is counter-cyclical. Thus, in the building materials industry, leading firms are anxious to obtain their share of the home repair and remodeling markets. Sale of building materials for this purpose tend to go up when sales of materials for new houses go down. For these and similar considerations the forecaster inside the company has an important function in interpreting the meaning of the business cycle for his particular firm.

The company forecaster concerned with market planning is likely to rely on authoritative forecasts from public sources and specialized services for his judgment as to what will happen to general business. With the multitude of services available, he must be a critical buyer as well as a skillful user. Behind each of these services there is likely to be a theory of how the economy works, often leading to a set of techniques which distinguishes it from other services. The company forecaster using such information is concerned both with the general validity of a given service and with its applicability to his particular industry or firm. Thus, some forecasters follow the theory that all business fluctuations are self-generated oscillations developing within the economic system. This approach might be particularly valid and useful for a market planner working in an industry which was itself marked by self-generated oscillations, as for example, wide swings in the level of inventories. Other forecasters emphasize the regularity of cyclical movements of various durations and expect the business outlook at any given time to reflect the result of piling several of these so-called "sine waves" on top of each other. Others look for the particular strategic factors which may be at work in the current business cycle, interpreting each cycle as a unique constellation of forces. The latter approach might appeal particularly to those inside forcasters who felt equipped to enumerate the strategic factors presently impinging on their own field and to weight these along with the favorable and unfavorable factors of more general character in reaching a final judgment.

The forecasting of seasonal requirements is especially critical for market planning in many consumer goods lines. To generate his own sales, the manufacturer must gear his operations to the merchandising year of the retailer. Some products, such as children's toys, are manufactured throughout the year but are mostly shipped a month or two before the holiday season. Many other products which sell throughout the year nevertheless have strong seasonal peaks related to Christmas giving. Items as different as whiskey and sterling silver have sales twice as large in December as in the average month. Quite a number of products sell rather evenly throughout the year except for moderate peaks in retail sales in the spring and in the fall. The manufacturer must plan backward from retail requirements in order to schedule his advertising and personal selling.

There are other lines, such as apparel, in which there can be a disconcerting amount of variation in the seasonal pattern from year to year. Sales may be disappointing because of such factors as unseasonable weather. A new style may catch on beyond the expectations of the producer, and he is thereafter engaged in frantic efforts to supply the unexpected demand. Once the season is under way, the problem is hardly one of forecasting but of an evaluation of the market from day to day in order to sense the trend as quickly as possible. What is going on in the style centers may be used in effect to forecast the demand which may be expected to develop in the smaller markets. For some products, such as domestic fuel oil, the traditional seasonal pattern is not nearly accurate enough. A number of the oil companies study long-run weather cycles and try to predict fuel requirements for the given year in terms of degree days. One advantage of nationwide operation in many types of consumer products is that the country as a whole is likely to have a more stable seasonal pattern from year to year than might be found in a single region.

SHORT-RANGE FORECASTING AND EXPONENTIAL SMOOTHING

It is frequently useful to the forecaster to have some assurance that cyclical turning points have been reached. Time series can frequently show a sharp upward or downward movement which later is found to be only a random fluctuation in the series. Even more importantly, in the short-range forecasting of individual product varieties (for example, package sizes, colors) the labor involved in making hundreds of individual short-range forecasts can become immense.

For a number of years, "mechanical" forecasting techniques have been used to make projections, particularly when the analyst is dealing with a large set of time series values. For example, a moving average of the type

$$\bar{S}_i = \frac{1}{m} (S_i + S_{i-1} + S_{i-2} + \ldots + S_{i-m+1})$$

where $\bar{S}_i$ = average sales; S_i, $S_{i\text{-}1}$, etc. = actual sales in the ith, $(i\text{-}1)$th, etc. period; m = number of periods making up the moving average ($m = 1, 2, \ldots$, etc.), has been used to smooth time series for purposes of projecting some future value of the series. For example, a 5-period moving average of the "sales" data: 18, 22, 21, 17, 28, 30, 32, would be

$$\bar{S}_i = \tfrac{1}{5}\,(28 + 17 + 21 + 22 + 18) = 21.2$$
$$\bar{S}_{i+1} = \tfrac{1}{5}\,(30 + 28 + 17 + 21 + 22) = 23.6$$
$$\bar{S}_{i+2} = \tfrac{1}{5}\,(32 + 30 + 28 + 17 + 21) = 25.6$$

Frequently the analyst "centers" the average on the middle term of the series before computing the next period's average by dropping the first term of the old series and adding a new term.

In more recent years, however, a more modern form of time series "tracking" has been developed, exponential smoothing. Exponential smoothing (see the R. G. Brown references at the end of the chapter) permits smoothing of the data and also tracks the time series in a manner not unlike the moving average. Exponential smoothing techniques are particularly useful for short-range forecasting for, say, inventory control where literally hundreds of items must be forecasted and where the requirements for accuracy do not preclude recourse to a mechanical procedure. This class of techniques lends itself easily to computer storage and the calculation of monthly, weekly, or even daily sales projections.

Figure 15–5

TURNING POINT "TRACKING" DEVICE
PRODUCT Y MONTHLY SHIPMENTS

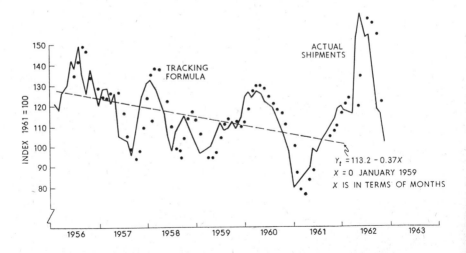

As an illustration of one form of exponential smoothing, Figure 15–5 portrays the monthly sales (in index form) of product Y over the period 1956–63 and the one-month-ahead forecasts prepared by the use of the exponential formula

$$\overset{*}{S_i} = \alpha\, S_{i-1} + 2\,(1-\alpha)\,\bar{S}_{i-2} - (1-\alpha)\,(\bar{S}_{i-3})$$

$\overset{*}{S_i}$ = forecasted sales in month i

S_{i-1} = actual sales in the preceding month $i-1$

$\bar{S}_{i-2}$ = smoothed sales (calculated by application of the formula) up through two months preceding the forecast month

$\bar{S}_{i-3}$ = smoothed sales up through three months preceding the forecast month

α = smoothing constant $(0 \le \alpha \le 1)$ which in this illustration was set equal to 0.5

To illustrate the formula, suppose one is interested in making a one-month-ahead forecast $\overset{*}{S_i}$. Actual sales currently $(S_{i\text{-}1})$ are 100 and the calculated values $\bar{S}_{i\text{-}2}$ and $\bar{S}_{i\text{-}3}$ are 95 and 90 respectively. Substituting in the formula

$$\overset{*}{S_i} = 0.5\,(100) + 2\,(0.5)\,95 - 0.5\,(90)$$
$$= 50 + 95 - 45$$
$$= 100$$

Now suppose that actual sales for the month forecasted turn out to be 110 units. To calculate the forecast for the next month S_{i+1}, one substitutes

$$\overset{*}{S}_{i+1} = 0.5\,(110) + 2\,(0.5)\,100 - 0.5\,(95)$$
$$= 55 + 100 - 47.5$$
$$= 107.5$$

Figure 15–5 shows application of the smoothing formula of the type just described. In addition, a linear trend of the form $y = a + bx$ has been calculated by least squares and is graphed as a dashed line in the chart.

Examination of this chart shows fairly definite cyclical turning points, for example, early 1959 and late 1960, as well as some rather extreme but short-run fluctuations of the type occurring in 1956. If the fluctuations of the series where truly random, deviations of the actual series from the tracking formula would tend to cancel out, that is, a short run of plus deviations would tend to be cancelled out by a series of minus deviations.

For example, one could examine the behavior of forecast error near the January, 1959 cyclical trough by looking at the cumulative deviations (in percentage error) of actual versus forecasted. This is shown in Table 15–1.

Table 15–1

ACTUAL VERSUS FORECAST SHIPMENTS OF PRODUCT Y
(October, 1958 through April, 1959)

Time Period	Actual Sales	Forecast Sales	Percentage Deviations $\dfrac{\text{Forecast} - \text{Actual}}{\text{Actual}}$	Cumulative Percentage Deviations
October, 1958	109.7	112.6	2.6	2.6
November	105.1	115.7	10.1	12.7
December	101.6	112.0	10.2	22.9
January, 1959	95.5	105.0	9.9	32.8
February	97.5	96.8	−0.7	32.1
March	97.6	93.1	−4.6	27.5
April	98.7	93.5	−5.3	22.2

As Table 15–1 indicates, forecast sales are consistently overestimating actual sales over the period October, 1958 through January, 1959 (the cyclical trough of the actual series). Cumulative percentage deviations are building up until February, 1959 when a reversal takes place.

In more detailed formulations of exponential smoothing, it is sometimes possible to set up control limits by which the analyst can determine whether a significant reversal in the trend of the series has taken place (again see the Brown references at the end of the chapter). In addition, exponential smoothing techniques can be developed to deal with seasonal components and for tracking not only linear trends (as illustrated above) but curvilinear trends as well. The purpose here, however, is merely to give the reader some introductory illustration of these techniques and to point out areas of application where "mechanical" techniques can be helpful.

This is not to suggest that mechanistic extrapolation is superior to methods based on the anlysis of the variables affecting the time series under study—quite the contrary. But in cases where the nature of the forecasting job does not justify detailed study or where forecasting error can be "insured against" (by the use of, say, safety stocks in inventory control), mechanistic techniques may be entirely adequate. More will be said on the costs versus gains of increased forecasting accuracy in the next section of this chapter.

THE COSTS OF
FORECAST ERROR

Without question a large portion of management's time is spent in making forecasts, either of an explicit or implicit type. All decisions imply some prediction about the course of future events. Forecasts may be made for ascertaining the possibility of change in the course of action currently being pursued or for determining the likelihood that each course of action under evaluation will attain specific objectives.

The costs of forecast error will naturally vary with the decision under study. For example, in inventory control a poor forecast (in the sense that a wrong decision was made) may carry a relatively small cost if rapid feedback in the next period could establish that an error was made and a subsequent decision could be made to achieve balance in the inventory level. On the other hand, a poor forecast which led to the decision to introduce a new product when it should not have been introduced could carry a sizable economic consequence.

All forecasts realistically involve error and cost something to produce. The forecaster's "most probable" estimate of the future may, in fact, be highly improbable, and the cost of forecast error may be quite different, depending upon whether the forecast errs on the high side or low side. The problem becomes one of ascertaining how erroneous the forecast may be before the relative effectiveness of one course of action compared to other alternatives is vitiated. Chapter 5 showed how "indifference probability" calculations could shed some light on the permissible variation in the probabilities attached to alternative outcomes. This notion can be expanded upon by considering the activity of forecasting within the formal framework of decision theory. Such techniques are frequently called "probability forecasting."

As the first illustration, consider a production planner at the plant level faced with three production alternatives whose effectiveness partially depends upon the state of product sales three months after the decision must be put into effect. The problem is deliberately oversimplified in order to illustrate the technique as concisely as possible.

Figure 15–6 summarizes the situation faced by the production planner in the month of May. Product sales been continuously declining prior to this month and the relevant questions facing the production planner are (a) whether a sales trough has been reached and (b) if so, what might be the pace of the cyclical upturn in product sales.

If state S_1 in August should prevail, the planner knows that production for inventory must be begun in May so as to reduce the risk of lost sales to competition through failure to meet demand (assuming safety stocks are geared at some current average demand level). Similarly, the occurrence of states S_2 and S_3 would dictate his following other production policies. The cost of misjudging the market is shown in the table under the graph. For example, if sales were to reach S_1 in August and action A_1 were taken (which is based on an S_1 sales level) the plant would incur no cost of an incorrect decision. However, if A_1 were taken and sales level of only S_2 were realized, costs of carrying excess inventory (capital tie-up, storage) would be incurred.

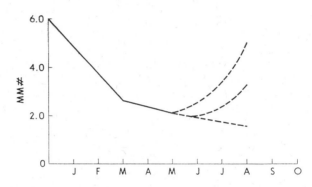

Figure 15-6

PROBABILITY FORECASTING

(Discrete Case)

On the other hand, if the product planner took the extremely conservative approach A_3 (that is, he planned for a sales level of S_3) and if S_3 did not obtain, costs of lost sales to competition would be incurred. If S_3 did occur, however, no cost through forecast error would be incurred. The critical element of this problem, however, is that these costs are asymmetrical. Suppose that costs of underproduction (lost sales for example) were approximately three times the cost incurred through overproduction (carrying costs of excess inventory). These assumed costs are reflected in the tabular entries.

COST OF WRONG DECISIONS

(Cell Entries)

Actions	Possible State of Sales		
	S_1	S_2	S_3
A_1..........	0.0	−7.8	−10.8
A_2..........	−19.5	0.0	− 3.0
A_3..........	−27.0	−7.5	0.0

If it is assumed that the planner must choose one of the three courses of action and can only assign an equal chance to each of the three possible sales states obtaining, what action should the planner take? Using methods similar to Chapter 5, it can be shown that under the "givens of the problem, the planner's best choice is A_1 (upping production to reach an expected level of S_1 in August). However, had the probability of occurrence of S_1 been, say, only one chance in five rather than one chance in three (assuming that the balance of the probability was split equally between S_2 and S_3), action A_2 would have been preferable. As would be supported by intuition, act A_3 is least desirable. It would require an *extremely high probability* of occurrence of S_3 to make act A_3 superior to the other acts.

In the second illustration of the costs of forecast error, one can use the context of a new product planning situation in which a decision is to be made concerning the addition of production capacity in anticipation of an overall sales increase arising from a new addition to the product line. If it is assumed that the marketing strategist's best estimate of the amount by which potential sales in the year ahead will exceed current capacity is 5 million pounds, the result is a single point or, "most probable" forecast. However, on the assumption that the planner also recognizes that potential sales might well deviate from this estimate, a range of sales forecasts can be derived based on his judgment of the likelihood that sales volume may assume other values.

Figure 15-7 shows the planner's estimates of the amount by which potential sales might exceed current capacity. As the chart indicates, he is virtually certain that potential sales will exceed current capacity by at least 2 million pounds and is virtually certain that the excess of potential sales over present capacity will not exceed 8 million pounds.

However, again the costs of erroneous decisions are not symmetrical. If the capacity addition is underbuilt relative to potential sales, lost sales will be incurred either through shifts to a competitive product or to deferment of sales to the future (with a resultant loss in present value of earnings and the contingency of competitors sharing in those future sales). If the capacity addition is overbuilt relative to potential sales, costs of carrying idle capacity will be incurred until sales increase (it is assumed) in the future.

In this simplified example, assume that the cost of foregone earnings through lost sales is larger than the carrying cost of idle facilities, say, $.50 per pound lost versus $.30 per pound of excess capacity. Under these assumptions, the solution to the problem is quite simple. It involves merely finding the ratio of $.30 to the sum of $.30 and $.50. The resultant ratio, 0.375, can then be plotted on the vertical axis of the cumulative probability chart and extended

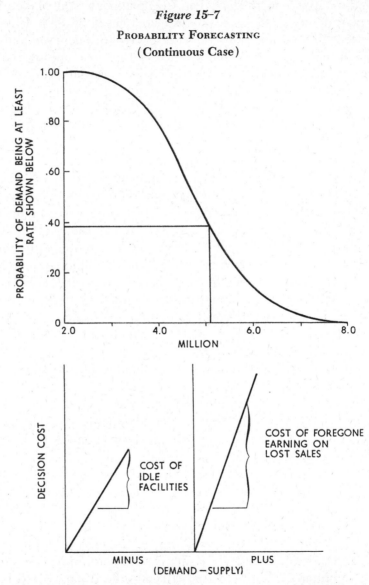

Figure 15–7

PROBABILITY FORECASTING

(Continuous Case)

until it intersects the curve; the resultant capacity addition figure of 5 million pounds can then be read off the horizontal axis of the chart. This is the capacity addition which minimizes total expected costs.

Both of the above examples were deliberately oversimplified to show application of the technique unencumbered by more realistic, yet complicated, detail. In practice, however, the concept of probability forecasting is a very general one, capable of being used in more complex situations, although methods of solution would become much more tedious than those shown here. Its logic rests on the basic intuitive notion that the costs of incorrect decisions through forecast error are rarely symmetrical.

In summary, the planner can view the activity of formal forecasting as another type of information gathering which is cost incurring and whose estimates are subject to error. It may well turn out to be the case that the gains of improved accuracy do not justify the cost incurred to achieve them. Or, even if they do, practical limits to improved accuracy usually exist, and the decision maker will still have to make his choice under some uncertainty with respect to the consequences attached to the various alternatives being evaluated.

FORECASTING STRUCTURAL CHANGE

Planning for innovation involves preparing to serve consumers who are not yet in the market with resources which are not yet available. This is not an easy assignment, but it can be facilitated by organizing the evidence for changes of the sort described in the last section. Forecasting major changes calls for something more than merely extrapolating trends that are already clearly under way. The chief interest is in the sharp breaks in established trends through which novel features arise in the cultural pattern and opportunities are created for new goods and services. The process of acquiring long-range perspective is vitally dependent on developments in a type of forecasting to which quantitative techniques are only beginning to be applied.

Some concepts related to this type of forecasting will be presented even though most of them can be employed only in an intuitive way at present. It is assumed here that the forecasting techniques to be developed would rest on a fairly sophisticated model of the economy, or one of its major sectors, but that additional procedures would be introduced to predict changes in the structure itself. In general this would mean examining the relationship among diverse trends and the constraints under which trends were expected to operate, in order to deduce the probable consequences as to the nature and timing of changes in the market structure. The term market structure is intended here to embrace more than the economic concept of the pattern of competitive relationships. Of at least equal importance for the present purpose would be the changing pattern of consumer demand and changing channels and methods of distribution.

It is useful at this point to recall Schumpeter's distinction between invention and innovation. The proposed forecast techniques would relate to innovation rather than invention. Invention is the creation of a device, operating method, or form of organization, designed to function in a certain way. Innovation characteristically occurs somewhat later when the pressure of need or the lure of profit causes the invention to be put to work on a significant scale.

THE OVERLOADED SYSTEM

One basic reason for innovation of a new pattern of behavior or a new operating system is that the existing system has become so overloaded that it is approaching the point of breakdown. Expressed in terms of trends, this might be described as the disparity between the trend as to capacity and the trend as to demands made upon the system. Capacity may be static or at best increasing slowly while the burden of use is increasing at a much more rapid rate. The problem of the overloaded system is illustrated by the constant increase in traffic congestion in urban areas despite continued efforts to provide increased highway capacity. When the pressure of increased use is on some system such as the highway network, any new facility often appears to generate increased use rather than to bring relief to the extent expected.

In the area of marketing facilities, this trend toward the breakdown of an overloaded system may begin to show up presently in the supermarket where the limitation on shelf space and the rising pressures from manufacturers of both food and nonfood products to get their products on these shelves may have to be solved eventually by drastic changes in the pattern of grocery distribution.

Something like this happened years ago in department stores, which once seemed to embrace the ideal of having adequate stocks of all products and brands that their customers could possibly want. The multiplication of items seeking distribution through department stores long ago demonstrated the impossibility of realizing such a goal. Stores are now necessarily selective from among the many items offered, and financial control imposes drastic limitations on the inventories carried. This in turn forces significant policy changes on suppliers of department store lines of merchandise and innovations in marketing channels to find new routes to the consumer. Suppliers who correctly foresaw what was happening to the department store undoubtedly derived from this knowledge a significant competitive advantage.

ECONOMIES OF SCALE

Economies of scale are often treated as if they arise automatically from the fact of large-scale operation. To some extent this is doubtless true as in the case of the growing firm which may be able to spread certain fixed costs over a large volume. For the present purpose, it is important to note that economies of scale often are the result of adopting new methods which are appropriate for a large volume of business but could not have been adopted economically at a smaller volume.

In many aspects of marketing it appears that there is a range of methods or patterns of operation, each appropriate at some level of sales volume but not at others. In advertising, for example, a nationwide television program would be no more appropriate for a small regional mail-order house than a direct mail campaign would be for a national manufacturer of cigarettes.

In some fields it is possible to discern a regular progress in technological advance related to increasing sales volume. Thus, grocery warehouses today nearly all have systematic methods of information handling, and most of these use punch card equipment, while some of the largest and most advanced use electronic computers.

The first stage based on the so-called tub files of IBM cards developed about 30 years ago and is still the most appropriate method in many warehouses. As these individual operations become larger, many of them will doubtless go into the second stage of using mark sensing cards as they are now employed by Penn Fruit and many others. Penn Fruit, on the other hand, as its volume continues to grow, can be expected at some time in the future to go into the third stage now illustrated by some very large individual warehouse operations such as Jewel Tea in Chicago and Dominion Stores in Canada. This idea of the technological procession should be especially useful in predicting what may happen in less advanced countries, or in smaller markets in the United States, as increased scale of operation presents them with the same opportunities for economies which have already been explored in the more advanced areas. Among the larger companies in the United States a major problem is often that of preserving the advantages of mass production in the face of all the forces which tend to dissipate them.

TECHNOLOGICAL ADVANCE AMONG USERS

One of the constraints on the use of any new idea or device is the ability of prospective users to understood and operate it. Attempts to introduce complicated farm machinery in backward rural areas have encountered difficulties which illustrate this point. This same thing is also often true in household goods. What is needed in much of rural Latin America is not a gas range or even a kerosene stove so much as an improved charcoal brazier. Sometimes markets appear to develop almost overnight because the technological skills and awareness of prospective users have suddenly surpassed the minimum level which makes profitable exploitation of the market possible. Very likely the tremendous leap forward in the mechanization of the American farm in the decade 1940–50 resulted in considerable part from just such changes in the readiness of the market.

COMPLEMENTARY PRODUCTS

The study of interrelated growth trends could turn out to be the most fundamental starting point of all. Many products come into existence because they are useful complements to some existing product. A well-known example is the rise of the low-sudsing detergent as a result of the development of the automatic washing machine. The marketing of a new expendable product often leads to the successful marketing of specialized equipment for supplying or using it. The adoption of a satisfactory applicator may in turn remove some constraints on the use of the expendable product and result in accelerated market growth. Complementary relationships are widely prevalent in today's markets, sometimes involving several stages. Thus, the building of new homes expands the market for central heating and air-conditioning systems. The installations of such systems expends the market for various items marketed by other suppliers such as automatic controls and the appropriate fuels.

THE MOMENTUM OF SPECIALIZATION

One tendency that has appeared many times both in biological and cultural evolution is for specialization in a given direction to lead progressively to still further specialization. In the biological field this tendency sometimes gets out of hand, specialization proceeding far beyond any functional value. An illustrative case is that of a species of elk whose horns finally grew so large that they apparently contributed to the extinction of the species. The trilobite and some other fossils are believed to represent the dead end of specialization in certain evolutionary lines.

Something like this appears to happen frequently with products and ways of living although the mechanisms involved are obviously quite different. Thus, in the manufacture of automobiles the momentum of specialization has been exhibited in such matters as increasing horsepower and the profusion of chrome fittings. The competitive principle appears to be that if a certain feature will attract customers then giving them more of the same will have even greater attraction. It might be possible to predict such trends and their final leveling off by taking account of the principle of limited possibilities with respect to competitive appeals and the relative cost of more fundamental changes. Some students of the automobile industry feel that the competitive value of step-by-step change is about to become exhausted and that the time for truly radical innovation is approaching. It would be of tremendous value to be able to forecast with reasonable accuracy the onset of this new change of direction.

SIMPLIFICATION AND STANDARDIZATION

As opposed to the momentum of specialization there is a countertrend which sometimes seems equally powerful. This is the tendency to simplify and standardize products in fields in which specialization and differentiation has perhaps gone to extremes. The swing toward the small car is a current example of such a reaction.

A very important marketing phenomenon, with respect to many products, is that of simplifying a product to a point where it is foolproof in the hands of the ordinary user. At one stage the products available in a certain field may be complex to the point of requiring the skilled specialist for their operation. The number of specialists available as customers is strictly limited. If automatic controls can be built into the product or if a simpler model will produce reasonably good results in the hands of an amateur, simplification provides a way of breaking out of the limited field into the general market.

COST VERSUS INCOME

In examining trends which may lead to innovation, a very important relationship to consider is that of the cost to own or operate a product as compared to its yield in user satisfaction. Historically, a very powerful factor in precipitating innovation has been rising labor costs. This factor operates today with increasing force in the field of marketing. Employees of retail and wholesale establishments and other small businesses once seemed content to work for less money than factory employees. These wage differentials are being reduced today with the result of many laborsaving innovations both in goods handling and information handling. There are other rising costs which lead to innovation in products and in processes. One of the most obvious is the rising cost of certain natural materials which has helped to open the market for synthetic goods and materials in one field after another. The impact of the tax structure on innovation is a broad subject in itself and can doubtless operate both favorably and unfavorably.

THE STRUGGLE FOR DOMINANCE IN DISTRIBUTION

Relative control over access to the market tends to shift from time to time between manufacturers and the intermediary distribution agencies. One of the most significant aspects of modern advertising is that the massive appeal to consumers on behalf of certain products has given their manufacturers greater power over the market relative to wholesalers and retailers.

There are other measurable trends today which may shift control in the other direction in important segments of the economy. These trends are important as such because the achievement of dominance in either direction can have sudden and dramatic effects. The whole pattern of marketing could become quite different if distributors were calling the signals rather than manufacturers. At the same time, if we place any confidence in the principle of countervailing power, we must anticipate that the approach to dominance by any one factor will precipitate innovation in competitive strategies and tactics on the other side.

INSTITUTIONAL DRIFT

The viewpoint adopted here is that structure generally follows function in competitive markets. This view is different from institutionalism in which the emphasis is on the evolution of one structure into another. It would not be wise, however, to ignore the fact that institutions in some degree do have a life of their own and that once a pattern is established certain stages in its development may appear to make the institution less serviceable for its original function. If the factor of drift is tending to make a segment of the marketing system less effective, it may be anticipated that this will eventually prepare the way for innovations that look toward more satisfactory performance of the original function. The factor of drift or inertia in existing channels of trade undoubtedly helps to make a place for the so-called discount house.

THE LOGIC OF GROWTH

In developing techniques for forecasting structural change, critical attention should be given to whatever is known or assumed about the principles governing growth. For example, logistic curves have been fitted to the growth trend for many industries or products. Raymond Pearl some years ago attempted to rationalize the logistic curve for his own field of biology in a book called *The Biology of Population Growth*.[1] He offered some persuasive reasons for the sudden spurt of growth after a period of time and for the eventual leveling off which produced the so-called S-shaped curve of growth.

While considerable reliance has been placed on this type of curve in considering market growth, there is doubt that it can be rationally justified or that the principles proposed by Pearl can be translated from biology to marketing.

With respect to the first stage of relatively slow growth, there is more than one plausible explanation. One is that the enterpriser may have jumped in before the market was really ready for innovation and that rapid growth begins as soon as a real market opportunity exists.

In another situation it might mean that while the market is ready, it takes a period of trial and error before the sponsor of the product learns how to market it or commands the resources for that purpose. Similarly, the slowing down of growth might be due to either internal or external reasons. After a period of spectacular growth, such as many companies or products have enjoyed in the United States, the executive personnel may become complacent and experience a slower rate of growth simply because they are not working as hard as before.

The external notion of market saturation seems plausible, but it turns out to be very difficult to define with any precision in any particular case. Thus, if the growth of a product is dependent on the market growth of some other product and this in turn is dependent on still broader factors, there is some ambiguity as to the definition of the market which is becoming saturated. Certainly, if there is any dependable tendency for growth to follow the S-shaped curve, it becomes very important to find ways of predicting the spurt of growth or its final leveling off. If these points of inflection in the market growth curve could be known, it might be very useful in predicting innovations in related areas.

---

[1]Raymond Pearl, *The Biology of Population Growth* (New York: Alfred A. Knopf, Inc., 1925.)

SUMMARY

The role of forecasting in planning varies widely according to the phase of planning and the way that planning is organized in the company. Short-range programming may be most concerned about the seasonal pattern which is likely to account for greater sales variation from month to month than would result from cyclical and secular trends. Long-range planning can ignore the seasonal pattern and generally has relatively little interest in the business cycle. It is chiefly preoccupied with secular trends and with the forecasting of critical points which may lead to major innovations. Middle-range planning utilizes forecasting in its full content although perhaps with least emphasis on the seasonal pattern. Over a three- to five-year period substantial fluctuations can occur as a result of cyclical and secular changes. The ultimate interest of middle-range or strategic planning is in growth trends. However, cyclical movements can be very significant for strategic timing in the attempt to outguess competition.

It has also been pointed out that forecasting sometimes functions in the place of centralized and organized planning. In these cases there are often two versions of the forecast, one being what the central staff group regards as the most realistic prediction and the other the summation of what the various sales divisions have undertaken to sell during the operating period. The kind of thinking which takes place throughout the company to produce these twin estimates is itself a form of planning. It may be the preferred form in cases where management is trying to get full participation in planning from line sales executives and is trying to avoid or delay the creation of a separate staff group for planning.

Forecasting is preoccupied with the potentiality of markets and feasibility with respect to marketing effort. It looks ahead to see what is most likely to happen, assuming the present strategies and marketing mix and to see what could happen under various assumptions as to a modified marketing program. It is in connection with the latter point that forecasts usually get translated into individual goals for separate segments of the business such as product divisions or sales regions.

It will be obvious that the approach to forecasting techniques visualized here is very eclectic. The forecasting of general business activities end where the hard part begins for most market planners, that is, in the development of specific forecasts for the industry or company. The forecast which is most serviceable for planning is the one which comes to grips with the factors for growth and stability in the given case. Of particular significance, of course, are the variables which can be controlled or influenced by planned marketing effort. Emphasis on these factors distinguishes forecasting undertaken for planning purposes from an attempt to predict without reference to changes in strategy.

Of some importance to the "economics" of forecasting are the gains vs. costs of attempting to improve forecasting accuracy. Our concluding illustrations of this chapter showed how some of the techniques of decision theory can be used in making choices where the costs of wrong decisions were asymmetrical and where the sensitivity of choice among alternatives to forecast error can be determined.

Another kind of forecasting of special interest for planning has also been discussed. This is the attempt to predict turning points in basic trends or structural changes in the competitive environment. Such forecasting must rely largely on qualitative judgments rather than quantitative analysis. Its primary sphere is in truly long-range planning. In this domain, planning does not generally move very far beyond a qualitative forecast and an attempt to derive some of the consequences for action from this perspective. Tested techniques for forecasting structural change do not yet exist but some beginning in this direction has been considered.

Selected References

BRATT, ELMER C. *Business Forecasting.* New York: McGraw-Hill Book Co., 1958.
  Deals with forecasting problems and techniques at successive levels from gross national product to broad categories of expenditure to specific industries.

BROWN, ROBERT G. *Smoothing, Forecasting and Prediction of Discrete Time Series.* Englewood Cliffs, N.J.: Prentice-Hall, Inc., 1963.
  Treats the subject of exponential smoothing at a level requiring greater than elementary mathematical preparation on the part of the reader.

BROWN, ROBERT G. *Statistical Forecasting for Inventory Control.* New York: McGraw-Hill Book Co., 1959.
  An introduction to the subject of exponential smoothing.

CRAWFORD, C. M. *Sales Forecasting of Selected Firms.* Urbana, Ill.: University of Illinois, 1955.
  Description of forecasting methods employed by a number of firms and some suggestions for further development of techniques.

ESTES, B. E., JR. "Problem Areas in Industrial Forecasting," *Proceedings of 41st National Conference, American Marketing Association,* (Chicago, 1958).
  An evaluation of contrasting methods of forecasting industrial sales—breaking down from gross national product, building up from forecasts of end use.

ETHE, SOLOMON. "Forecasting in Industry," New York, *National Industrial Conference Board,* 1956.
   Chiefly concerned with the preparation of short-range forecasts and their uses. Three illustrations from company experience are included.

FABIAN, TIBOR. "Mathematical Approaches to Marketing Problems," *Marketing and the Computer* (W. ALDERSON AND S. J. SHAPIRO, eds.), ch. 3, part II. Englewood Cliffs, N.J.: Prentice-Hall, Inc., 1963.
   Provides a brief and elementary discussion of exponential smoothing. It also discusses econometric models in forecasting and provides a short description of brand switching models and their relationship to forecasting.

MACGOWAN, A. C. "Techniques in Forecasting Consumer Durable Goods Sales," *Journal of Marketing,* October 1952.
   Surveys short-range forecasting techniques in 56 companies and appraises their relative value.

ROSENZWEIG, JAMES E. "The Demand for Aluminum: A Case Study in Long Range Forecasting," *University of Illinois Bulletin,* Vol. 63 (April, 1947).
   Represents an extensive treatment of statistical techniques (logarithmic, Gompertz, and logistic trend fitting, regression equations) which he used to forecast aluminum demand over the period 1954-65. In addition to using statistical techniques the author develops an additional forecast by the process of building up estimates from the major aluminum using markets. Results of the various approaches are compared.

WIENER, NORBERT. *Extrapolation, Interpolation and Smoothing of Stationary Time Series.* New York: John Wiley & Sons, Inc., 1949.
   Treats the subject of exponential smoothing at a level requiring greater than elementary mathematical preparation on the part of the reader.

Problems

1. Contrast the role of forecasting in a centralized and decentralized operation.

2. Explain what is meant by the S-shaped curve of growth.

3. Discuss the relative advantages and disadvantages of the use of exponential smoothing versus a mechanical procedure as a method of forecasting.

4. Discuss the importance of foreseeing turns in the business cycle versus the forecasting of long-run growth trends.

5. Discuss the main external economic influences that a forecaster will want to consider in predicting a curve of growth for his company.

Chapter 16

THE SEARCH FOR EFFECTIVE STRATEGIES

Every marketing plan embodies a core-idea or marketing strategy. A plan is a detailed program for making a strategy effective. The choice of a strategy is a basic decision as to the matching of ends and means in marketing. The generation of strategies is one of the most creative aspects of planning, and the choice of strategy is the crucial decision determining the shape that a plan will take.

The term "strategy" is too often loosely applied to any move which the speaker regards as clever or important. There are two somewhat distinct but not inconsistent definitions of strategy as the term has been used in economics and marketing. John R. Commons distinguished between strategic and routine decisions. The strategic decision in his view was the one which exercised a general or controlling influence and established the framework within which decisions of lesser importance would be made. The choice of a strategy in planning is a strategic decision in this sense.

The second connotation of strategy arises whenever the planner or the organization he represents is viewed as being engaged in a contest. Game theory developed as a branch of mathematical economics to explain how the business strategist might behave in trying to get the best of a competitor. This chapter will not utilize game theory in any formal sense. Yet the procedures which will be suggested for generating and evaluating marketing strategies will make use of some of the simple tools and concepts of game theory.

The emphasis, however, will be on the creative process of generating strategic ideas rather than on the mathematical techniques for evaluating them. It is not possible, of course, to provide a rigid framework for the creativity of the marketing strategist. This chapter is directed rather toward suggesting a variety of approaches which may speed up the process by bringing some measure of system into the search for strategic ideas.

COMPETITION VIEWED AS A RACE OR GAME

The games which have been of greatest interest to the economist or social scientist in trying to understand conflicts of interest, or competition among a few large firms, are those which involve a combination of skill and chance. In a game of pure skill, such as chess, it would be theoretically possible for the chessmaster to be fully informed on the outcome of all possible moves. If human affairs, such as economic competition, are to be compared to a game, it is the kind of game in which each player must act on the basis of imperfect knowledge. He is striving to outguess one or more opponents and perhaps a course of events which is beyond the control of any of the players.

One very simple game is that of matching pennies. The first player places his coin with either heads or tails up, and the second tries to guess what he has done and to match this action in placing his own penny. The second player scores a point if both pennies have the same face up while the first player scores a point if they do not. The diagram (Figure 16–1) shows the payoff-matrix for this game.

Figure 16–1

PAYOFF MATRIX FOR SIMPLE GAME

FIRST PLAYER	SECOND PLAYER	
	HEADS	TAILS
HEADS	-1	1
TAILS	1	-1

The usual notation shows positive numbers when the score is in favor of the first player whose alternatives moves are represented by the two rows. Similarly, the negative numbers represent scores favorable to the second player whose alternative plays are represented by the columns. In this simplest of all games there are four possible outcomes each represented by one of the cells in the table. The upper left-hand cell indicates that the first player has played heads, that the second player has matched him by playing heads and that the second player has scored a point. The kind of game situation considered and the resulting payoff-matrix can become much more complicated. The basic principle remains the same for strategic choice in marketing or any other field. That is to say, the outcome of the game is determined by the choices of the two players with neither being able to predict with certainty the choice of the other.

There are continuing efforts to extend game theory and to make it pertinent to a greater range of real life situations. The matching of pennies is a game for two persons only, and there are many marketing situations in which the strategist must take account of a number of opponents or competitors rather than a single opponent. Matching of pennies is also a game in which what one player wins the other player loses, and it is therefore called a zero-sum game. There are many situations in real life which cannot be forced into this category but in which there are sufficient incentives to make the players cooperate in some respects even while they are competing in others. For these and other reasons game theory has not been able to show many dramatic applications to marketing strategy so far.

Stimulating and suggestive as game theory is for consideration of strategy in the abstract, there is one limitation more than any other which has blocked its application to market planning. Certainly every marketing organization knows that it is engaged in a contest, but the contest may not be readily interpreted as a game. In many cases the marketing strategist feels that his main problem is to manage his own resources effectively regardless of what competition may do. There have been attempts to extend game theory in this direction through the notion that the strategist is playing a game against nature. This notion would appear to strain the conception of a game rather far, although it is intended to represent the fact that the player confronts uncertainties arising from impersonal hazards as compared to those depending on the decisions of opponents.

An alternative formulation, which may be more congenial intuitively to the marketing strategist is that the contest in which he is usually engaged resembles a race, while at other times it may seem to be a combination of a race and a game. Suppose that two players, A and B, are each trying to reach distinct but related goals. They are engaged in a contest in the sense that each is trying to get there first, but the fact that A reaches his goal does not exclude B from reaching his even though he may get there a little later. The payoff situation might be compared to that of an athletic event in which a dozen contestants are entered in a mile race but prizes are given only for first, second, and third place. In actual competition there may be prizes for all even though twelfth prize is much less desirable than first prize. A simple example would be the opening up of a new area of opportunity, such as a gold field or the opening of Oklahoma territory for homesteading. Most of the men who raced across the line at the starting gun were able to stake out some kind of a claim, but those who got there first tended to get the better claims.

Many real life situations give each player a choice as to whether he will behave as if he were in a race or as if he were playing a game. That is to say he may on the one hand apply himself completely to overcoming natural obstacles and mastering the complexities of getting the best results from the resources under his command. On the other hand, he may seek an easier or more direct route to his destination even though this may bring him into direct conflict with other players and thus introduce additional uncertainties into his own planning. In marketing this might mean the choice between continuing to cultivate a market in which the firm was strongly entrenched as compared to aggressive efforts to enter a field currently occupied by others.

Figure 16-2

CONTEST COMBINING ELEMENTS OF RACE AND GAME

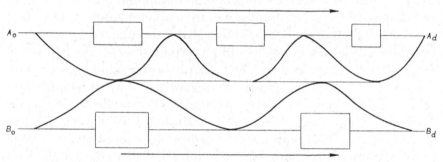

A and B each tries to reach his own destination. Each has the choice of coping with natural obstacles only or of risking interference from the other.

Figure 16-2 is an attempt to show a schematic representation of this type of situation. The player A can move directly down the line toward his destination even though he has three moderate hurdles to get over on the way. Similarly B can move directly toward his destination even though he has two rather major obstacles to deal with. Either one or both can choose to try the available detours although in doing so they may run into interference and opposition from the other. This situation might be regarded fundamentally as a race with a fringe element of gaming or trying to outguess an opponent. Alternatively it might be regarded as a game in which one of the choices available to each opponent was to behave as if he were merely engaged in a race.

SETS OF ALTERNATIVES

The notion of constructing a matrix is fundamental for any consideration of strategy even though it may not be possible to evaluate the alternatives in terms of simple numerical values. In marketing, as in military strategy, the core of the strategic idea is likely to be very simple. In the days of pitched battles the commander could either attack or defend. If he were attacking a fortified city, he could try to take it by storm or lay seige to it and starve out the inhabitants. It is still important, nevertheless, for the commander to be sure that he is looking at the right payoff matrix and that it covers all of the basic choices available. Thus an opponent might appear to be taking up the defensive or entrenched position, which turns out merely to be a screen to mask a strategic retreat. The seige of Troy provides a legendary illustration of extending a matrix to include an alternative which had not been seen until an inspiration occurred to Ulysses. The Greeks neither starved out the Trojans nor stormed the walls of Troy but used the Trojan horse to trick the defenders into opening the gates.

In marketing, as in war or on the football field, strategies may emphasize power or deception according to the practical means at hand. Napoleon used speed of movement and his superiority in artillery to overwhelm his opponents before they could get organized for effective defense. George Washington and the Roman general Fabius Maximus were necessarily more concerned with counterstrategies because of the lesser means at hand. Hannibal, who was possibly the greatest military strategist of all time, was brilliant in both offense and defense. In either case he usually succeeded in tricking his opponent into taking the unfavorable position. He thus kept an army in the field against the superior forces of Rome for many years. At the battle of Cannae he annihilated the Roman legions by allowing them to break through the center of his line where he had deliberately placed his weaker troops.

In generating strategies for consideration the market planner will find it useful to think of his present marketing operation as located in a kind of strategy space. It represents a combination of various kinds of activities which in total are designed to gain an advantage over competition. To move from point to point in this strategy space means to adopt a new combination because it is expected to yield a greater competitive impact. There is an infinite number of possible combinations, and it is not practical to evaluate all the possibilities with equal detail. The notion of a strategy space with a limited number of dimensions helps to simplify the problems of generating and evaluating strategies. The market planner first tries to identify the principal dimensions or degrees of freedom for modifying his present operation. Even along a single dimension the possibilities are too numerous for separate consideration. As an analytical device, the planner may start with simple dichotomies or polar extremes along one dimension or another of strategy space. An example would be to consider the implications of giving up advertising completely as compared to increasing the advertising budget to the absolute ceiling which was economically feasible. Each pair of extremes can lead to the construction of a matrix of strategic choices, and the intermediate or mixed cases can be considered later.

Freedom to vary along some of the dimensions of strategy space may turn out to be more apparent than real. For one reason or another there may be little room for variation or change along a given dimension. Discretion as to price may be restricted to a narrow range by competition. Product features may have become highly standardized with little promise of breaking out into a new era of technological improvement. Promotional expenditures in the given case may be limited because of legal regulations or because of the lack of appropriate advertising media. All of these limiting factors enter naturally into an orderly process of generating strategies for consideration.

To summarize, the market planner first tries to get an adequate conception of the strategy space in which the marketing organization is operating. That means that he tries to identify the various dimensions or directions in which a revised operation could differ significantly from the present operation. The dimensions of pricing, product features, and promotional methods, which have already been mentioned, are found in every marketing actuation. Other ways in which marketing operations can vary such as the choice of channels may assume primary importance in a particular situation. Having decided what the dimensions are the planner will consider how much difference it would make to move in one direction or the other along the line. In some cases he may discover that the freedom to vary around the point on the line represented by current operation is negligible and can be ignored as a source of alternative strategies. Suppose he ends up with a half dozen significant dimensions for variation. The next step is to construct a game matrix for each of these possible variations considered separately.

CONSIDERATION OF COMPETITIVE COUNTERMOVES

To complete the matrix a planner will have to consider at least the more obvious counterstrategies on the part of his competitors. As a start in this direction, he may list three types of possibility open to the competitor. The first is to ignore the action recommended by the planner for his own company. The second is to imitate it as in matching a price cut. And the third is to take a quite different action from that of the planner, such as adopting a different product feature or promotional appeal. As a further step toward completing the matrix, the planner may want to include the company's present position along the given dimension as well as the extreme deviations in one direction or the other. After separate consideration of each matrix, the planner now begins to compare them with each other in terms of relative cost, risks of competitive retaliation, and combinations which would represent shifts along two or more dimensions of strategic space in looking for a better combination of factors. This type of preliminary evaluation should lead presently to not more than two or three distinctive ways of framing the company's basic strategic problem. The final step is to consider several intermediate stages or quantitative variations within each matrix which is given serious consideration. The next chart (Figure 16-3) illustrates another way of looking at strategies and counterstrategies in comparing two major dimensions of marketing action.

Figure 16-3

COMPANY STRATEGIES FOR INCREASED CONSUMER APPEAL
AND
COMPETITIVE COUNTERSTRATEGY

OWN MOVES	OPPONENTS MOVES		
	REDUCE PRICE	IMPROVE QUALITY	NO CHANGE
REDUCE PRICE	SAME	REVERSE	IGNORE
IMPROVE QUALITY	REVERSE	SAME	IGNORE
NO CHANGE	SEIZE INITIATIVE	SEIZE INITIATIVE	SAME

(Instead of payoff values, the cells show the competitors' possible reactions to the company's moves.)

Much of what is described here must proceed in intuitive and qualitative terms in the present state of the art. That is to say that techniques are not available for comparing an infinite number of variations in strategic choice. The practical procedure is the intuitive sifting of possibilities until a few alternatives are left for quantitative evaluation. One device which can be used in this final stage is illustrated in Figure 16-4. While strategy space has a number of dimensions, any two dimensions can be considered as lying in the same plane. The chart visualizes the process of weighing two possible changes against each other: one in the number of dollars spent for advertising and the other in the number of dollars spent for product improvement. The point labelled *A* on the chart represents the position in strategy space of the present operation. The dotted line is the feasibility boundary which is set by such considerations as a budget limitation for the two factors combined. The chart as drawn shows that there is some room for increase in either direction by moving out to the feasibility boundary. The deeper question is the choice of a most favorable point along this curve. The chart is intended merely to display the range of possibilities, while the choice of an optimum point would be made through other considerations. In general these considerations would be factors facilitating qualitative or quantitative judgments as to the relative desirability of combinations which were equally feasible.

Figure 16–4

TWO ASPECTS OF MARKETING STRATEGY

(Represented as a Plane in Strategy Space)

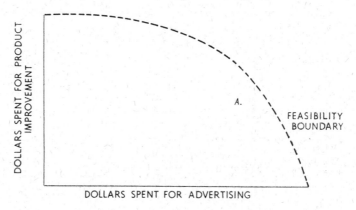

DOLLARS SPENT FOR ADVERTISING

POSSIBLE CHANGES IN CURRENT POLICIES

Another way to generate new strategies is first to formulate the operating assumptions under which the organization is working and then to challenge these assumptions. Marketing executives may be making optimistic assumptions as to potential demand for their products or about the effectiveness of their sales organization even though these assumptions no longer hold under changed conditions. Similarly they may be making pessimistic assumptions and observing restrictions on the possibilities for action which were true in an earlier day but no longer hold. Often it may take substantial marketing research to check these operating assumptions and either support them or disprove them. In order to get a plan accepted, the evidence which explodes an operating assumption may have to be very persuasive if marketing executives have long been acting as if this assumption were true.

Aside from restrictions arising from assumptions about the nature of the action environment, a marketing organization may be observing some self-imposed restrictions. Such policy restrictions may rule out certain types of available business as undesirable in itself. These could be restrictions covering prospective customers with inferior credit ratings or classes of trade whose business methods are not acceptable to the marketing organization. All such restrictions merit review from time to time since they may no longer serve the same purpose they did when they were first instituted. Some of them may have been designed to minimize adverse reactions in the market. Some of them may have been safeguards against excessive cost, waste, or friction among departments within the marketing organization. Meanwhile some of these problems may have been alleviated or may no longer stand high on the priority scale for management consideration. Some business practices may have started for reasons which are now long since forgotten, and are continued today purely as a matter of habit or inertia. It is often useful to stop and think how the business might be handled today if it were possible to design its procedures from scratch and without regard for a heritage of traditional methods.

THE SEARCH FOR NEW OR UNUSED OPPORTUNITIES

Any marketing firm which engages in planning probably owed its original existence to some unique advantage in its products or services. The planner cannot rest content with existing adavntages since his function is to find a way of improving upon them. He may well raise the question of whether the company has taken full advantage of its natural opportunities even though it has developed them sufficiently for survival. Similarly he may raise the question as to whether the original conception of the firm's competitive advantages could not be modified in the light of subsequent market changes. From this viewpoint the search for marketing strategies can be interpreted as an attempt to define missed opportunities. Among the fruitful areas for this search are those of neglected markets, unutilized capacity, and unrealized economies of scale.

In finding its niche in the market a firm or a product must relate itself to what is already there. It may simulate an existing operation or product as closely as possible, or it may find significant ways in which to deviate from it in order to appeal to some other segment of the market. The market niche may also rest on a complementary relation to existing products or operations. Sudsless detergents developed as complementary products whose success is related to that of the automatic washing machine. Food brokers come into being to provide complementary service for food manufactures who are unable to cover wholesale buyers adequately through their own sales organizations. These are questions which are never settled once and for all but must be brought up for review and revision from time to time in dynamic markets.

The competitive advantage of the firm may be increased by developing new product features or expanding the product line. It may be increased on the other hand by simplifying the product line to bring about more economical production and the possibility of lower prices. The economics of production and transportation sometimes make it advantageous to locate near raw material sources and in other cases to locate near final markets. The net competitive advantage of any firm consists of some combination of the distinctive features of its products and services, of its technological advantages in the production and physical handling of goods, and of the geographic advantages of location. This bundle of advantages must be reconsidered from time to time as the basis for new and more effective strategies.

Another source of possible strategies is the review of unutilized capacity. This may enable a firm to take on new products and particularly companion products. Unutilized capacity may be more than just the idle time of machines. Thus a firm may be the main source of employment in a small city but give employment primarily to male workers. New departures have sometimes arisen simply from making use of the womanpower in the same community. Sometimes unutilized capacity is available because of the seasonal swing in marketing and production with respect to a company's present line. Both manufacturers and retailers have taken on many new items to provide increased activity in what was previously the off-season. Obviously these possibilities must be reviewed critically to make sure that they really fit in with the existing operation. Sometimes the new activity, which is expected to take up the excess, turns out to require new production or marketing operations for which the firm was not equipped.

Economies of scale arise from the installation of methods of operation which would not have been appropriate at a lower volume of output. Opportunities for such economies appear in marketing as well as in production. Planners should be on the watch for the emergence of possibilities of this kind. The firm which has been selling exclusively through food brokers reaches the point where it has the option of selling through its own sales force. The product which has been established through specialty stores eventually achieves a volume level at which it becomes attractive to low-margin mass retailers, such as supermarkets. A firm which has been advertising only through newspapers presently achieves broad enough distribution to consider the possible economies of national advertising media. A company whose marketing costs are heavily weighted with paper work reaches the point at which it is ready to look at the possibilities of electronic data processing.

Obviously all of these possible changes could be looked upon as separate problems, and many of them will deserve very intensive consideration in themselves. The virtue of looking at them within the framework of market planning is that a number of them may be ripe for consideration within any given operating or planning period. Serious as the problems may be individually, there are also higher order problems as to which of the specific problems are most urgent and whether there are other considerations relevant to the timing of the possible changes. For example, it would be time lost to give detailed consideration to the improvement of a marketing function, such as brokerage service, if on broader grounds that function was presently to be eliminated altogether.

STRENGTHS AND WEAKNESSES OF COMPETITORS

Another place to search for possible strategies is in the area of the strengths and weaknesses of principal competitors. Even a very large and formerly dominant competitor may be vulnerable at crucial points and open to well-planned attack. Even a relatively new and as yet secondary competitor may have elements of strength which will lead to dominance, and this should stimulate the older firms toward the timely preparation of defensive measures.

Looking first at the vulnerability of the large competitor, its weaknesses may be found either at the level of consumer acceptance, in market coverage through distribution, or in factors internal to the marketing organization itself. Consumers sometimes appear to have a generalized desire for an alternative choice even though they are reasonably well satisfied with the existing product or service.

Since moods and circumstances vary, no product can give its users the same satisfaction on every occasion of use. After a period in which only one product of a given type is available, there is likely to be a substantial body of consumers ready to respond to a clever and well-timed appeal on behalf of a competitive product. This tendency may be reinforced by the intangible aspects of the corporate image which suggests that the new company is somehow a more suitable supplier of the given product.

A large firm can easily become vulnerable at the level of trade support. Some classes of wholesalers and retailers may feel that their interests are no longer given adequate consideration even though, in their opinion, they had much to do with the original success of the firm. The firm may have been slow in broadening its product line to meet the trade requirements. Distribution margins may have shrunk to the point where they no longer interest the trade. The firm's reputation for fair dealing may have suffered from its practice in allocating goods during times of scarcity. The firm may be so closely and exclusively affiliated with certain classes of trade as to open the way for a competitor to supply the same type of product to a competitive class of trade.

A competitor may be in a crucial period of his history because of a variety of internal factors. He may have been overextended in certain products or markets and may have difficulty in financing the required readjustment. Management may be excessively conservative as in the case of a dominant personality who has built the company and is not prepared to give way to a new regime. New management may have taken over very recently and still be uncertain as to its future course. The large firm may be in the hands of a bureaucracy whose prime objective is to maintain the status quo.

The canvass of competitive strengths and weaknesses here is only designed to provide signposts for the marketing planner in search for fresh and effective strategies. These suggestions cannot take the place of creative and imaginative thinking but only provide a more organized framework in which the search for strategies can take place. The core-idea is likely to come from the best marketing brains in the company, but the procedures outlined here can shortcut a good deal of preliminary floundering.

OFFENSIVE AND DEFENSIVE STRATEGIES

It has seriously been suggested that in marketing as in military strategy it is useful to distinguish the characteristic features of offense and defense. Great commanders, marketing executives, or athletes in various sports often exhibit a predilection for one stance or the other. One boxer leads aggressively, and another counterpunches. Some tennis players stay back at the base line, and others rush the net whenever possible. Some football teams are known for their stonewall defense, and others for their brilliant scoring plays. Some executives are eager to seize the initiative in competition while others prefer to wait until the competitor has disclosed his intentions.

There is no general argument for the superiority of one view over the other, or even a given company's commiting itself fully to offense or to defense in its marketing strategies. Nevertheless it is an issue that is worthy of serious consideration by the planner in marketing, and an awareness of the issue will sometimes help him in reaching a sharper and more prompt decision. The factors which might have to be considered are the predilections of the executives who will carry out the plan, the energy and precision with which the marketing organization can execute an aggressive program, the relative resources of the competing firms and the stage that each has reached in its life history, and the extent to which freedom to take the initiative may be limited by the requirement of coordination with others in the market, such as dealers and distributors.

First of all the planner should recognize certain inherent advantages in one approach or the other. The offensive strategist counts on the element of surprise to catch his opponent off balance. He launches his attack at a time which seems most advantageous for his side. He has presumably developed a detailed plan of action and hopes to make significant inroads on the competitor's position before encountering organized opposition. In marketing, as in warfare, the strategist may try to mask his real intentions as long as possible, feinting an attack in one direction while he is really preparing to launch his major offense at another point. Such tactics may be indispensable in order to gain a beachhead in the face of an entrenched position. The parallel to military action is not complete since the marketing strategist is not always free to choose startling innovations but is restricted by legal limitations and considerations of trade relations and consumer attitudes. On the other hand, there are special advantages in gaining a reputation for being progressive and the first in the field to undertake new developments.

The defensive leader who occupies a strong position has the opportunity of watching for his opponent's mistakes and taking advantage of them. For that matter, in marketing, the firm with smaller resources can sometimes let its larger competitor incur all of the costs of pioneering a new field and then seize some of the benefits for itself. It can offer to do the same thing for less after its competitor has made the investment in showing how to do it. It can add minor refinements to a basic innovation or add improvements in processing or marketing to what someone else has accomplished in basic design. The small firm, with a less rigid and ponderous organization, is more free to adopt hit and run tactics resembling the pattern of guerilla warfare.

The analogy to military offense and defense is suggestive but should never be pursued too far. Commercial competitors do not meet head on in quite the same sense as armies. The planner is often working in a middle ground of strategy. The fact that his company undertakes formal planning at all, means that it is in some degree taking the offensive. The exception would be purely contingent plans which were kept in readiness to be activated only in case of a major move by a competitor. But while firms with growth ambitions are in a sense on the offensive, there is a defensive aspect too in the tendency to keep a close watch on competition with an eye to meeting any new moves. In general, the issue posed here is closely related to the sense of timing which is so important to good marketing strategy. When a major marketing shift is brewing in any field, it is a question of prime importance as to whether to seize the initiative or to wait until competitors have absorbed the initial developmental costs and the outlook has been at least partially clarified.

The military analogy has been used so far as if the essential aim of strategy was the management of single battles. Actually the true strategic unit for planning, both in war and commercial competition, is the campaign. Indeed terms like advertising campaign and introductory sales campaign are often heard in business. A campaign is formulated around specified objectives and the mobilizing of resources to attain them. In business as in war one side may first mount a successful campaign and push its opponent back into its own heartland. Meanwhile the side which has just suffered reverses may be planning its counterattack and presently gain back all it has lost and more. This ebb and flow of the fortunes of war has a close parallel in the struggle between large firms. Generally, they survive, though temporarily defeated, and show remarkable capacity for recuperation and retaliation.

PLANNING FOR GROWTH AND PROFITS

The generation of marketing strategies will now be considered within the framework of continuous plan revision. The concept of business strategy is inherently dynamic because strategies are intended to bring about changes in outcomes. The new strategy is itself a new conception of the best way of bringing resources to bear on objectives. In planning for growth and profits during a period, the planner considers inputs of resources during the early part of the period which should lead to accelerated growth or increased profits before the period is over. The strategies adopted must, of course, be measured by these intended results and must take account of uncertainties which may be encountered during the period. If expenditures are made today which affect growth and profits some years hence, some orderly attempt must be made to balance the cost against the expected payoff.

The notion of the planning horizon exercises a basic influence on the choice of strategies. The horizon marks the furthest point in time for which it is useful to predict the outcome of marketing actions taken now. Strategic planning is generally regarded as dealing with a period one to five years ahead. It may lie near the lower limit in highly competitive consumer goods markets. At times it may exceed the upper limit and be more like seven or eight years in advanced industrial and defense products which require this longer cycle from product idea through development to market introduction.

Since marketing is concerned with short-range programming as well as with longer-run strategic planning, there are actually two kinds of horizons to be observed. One horizon deals with how far ahead we can see, and the other, with how far ahead we can jump. More precisely, the second concept of the horizon means how far ahead we can see with sufficient certainty that we are willing to jump. Jumping in this case means making an irrevocable commitment of resources to limited objectives such as occurs in short-run programming.

In strategic planning the strategies initially chosen are under continuing scrutiny. They are constantly being revised and modified leaving only the basic market posture unchanged over time. Contingency planning is often a necessary bridge between reluctance to commit resources irrevocably and the need to be prepared if certain changes in demand or competition should take place. Suppose a company is sure that its principal competitor will choose between alternative strategies A and B. It may then be well advised to make a plan conditional on move A and another conditional on move B. It may be too late to start planning after the competitor's choice has been made. If the issue is really crucial, the company should be ready to snap the appropriate plan into place and start issuing the corresponding orders the moment the die is cast. Even without the contingency factor, the dynamic aspect of long-run strategy requires looking back over past performance of the firm to assay its potential for the future. What follows builds on the notion of a preplan audit as presented in Chapter 14 but becomes somewhat more specific in pursuing the search for effective strategies.

INTERPRETATION OF COMPANY HISTORY

The review and revision of a five-year plan will often go back further into the course of events through which the company attained its present position. The company which is progressive enough to be giving serious attention to planning is usually one which has done a reasonably good job in the past. The planner is well advised to look for the reasons behind the past success before he undertakes to show the company how it could do better in the future.

It should not be assumed, however, that the course the company has pursued was necessarily the right one because it has been crowned with a measure of success. The results might have even been better with a truly effective marketing program. It is more important to be aware of difficulties which might face the future operation because of mistakes in the past. Some operating procedures may be continued simply because they have become habitual and not because they represent the best out of several alternative possibilities. Patterns of behavior are the result of accident as well as of design, and a policy or procedure may tend to be perpetuated simply because it got started that way.

One way to judge the validity of a company's marketing practices is to try to imagine how the company might operate if it had to start from scratch today. Looking at each phase of the company's marketing function, the planner can consider how it would be performed in an ideal marketing system created for the purpose. Would the ideal marketing system utilize the same type of dealers and distributors as the actual ones? Are the men who make up the majority of the sales force there primarily by right or seniority? Do present salesmen truly represent the type which the company would employ today to carry out the same type of sales assignment? Does the company's advertising campaign direct the right appeals to the right kind of people? Is the total advertising expenditure in scale with the real opportunities for stimulating demand and the real necessities for meeting competitive tactics?

With respect to all of these questions it will be useful to undertake historical analysis of what has happened and functional analysis of what ought to happen. The comparison of results obtained from the two points of view can be very illuminating as to the strengths and weaknesses of the company's position. Organization units are created or develop gradually in accordance with some conception of how a marketing function should be performed. Even though this structure was well adapted to its purpose at first, it may have been rendered obsolete by new methods available today or by subsequent changes in the nature of the marketing objective. On the other hand any ideal functional arrangement created in the abstract runs the risk of overlooking crucial controlling factors and should be checked against the historical background to make sure that it is realistic.

The history of a firm may also be reviewed in terms of the stage it has reached in the life cycle. It is a well-established fact that the growth of business firms tends to follow the S-shaped curve of growth. There is a logical basis for the prevailing shape of this curve. Figure 16–5 provides a schematic representation of the growth curve of a firm and of significant stages in its life history related to this hypothesis concerning the pattern of growth.

In its early history there is a threshhold of effective marketing effort which must be passed before the firm begins to enjoy rapid growth. This threshhold may result from the new firm's lack of knowledge. The executives of the firm may understand what needs to be done to promote market development but simply lack the funds to invest in an adequate effort. In other cases an initial period of slow and uncertain growth results from imperfect knowledge as to the precise product features or promotional appeals which will provoke a maximum of consumer response. Presently, when management has learned what needs to be done and has accumulated the funds with which to do it, a period of rapid expansion may begin.

At the upper end of the scale a tendency toward market saturation is encountered, and sales may begin to level off. This ceiling on further growth is a perfectly natural and inevitable phenomenon. A product may grow much more rapidly for a period than the spendable income of consumers, but obviously this disparity cannot continue indefinitely. There was a time, for example, when the number of central heating systems was increasing at a faster rate than the construction of new homes, because systems were being installed in many older homes as they were remodeled. Obviously there was a limited number of older houses suitable for such modernization. It could be expected that a time would come in the history of the industry when the annual number of housing starts would form an effective ceiling on the market for central heating systems.

It is usually not too difficult to determine the stage which a company has reached in its life cycle. This judgment is very important to a plan review and revision since characteristically different marketing policies are appropriate to each of these stages. If the time has come when a company may be expected to pass from one stage to the next, it should prepare to change the pattern of its marketing efforts correspondingly.

Figure 16–5

LIFE HISTORY OF THE FIRM

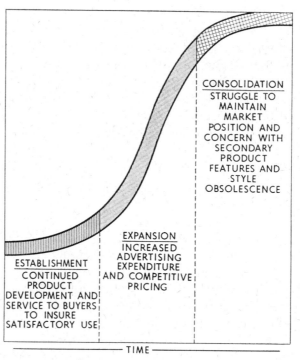

(CURVE REPRESENTS HYPOTHETICAL EXPECTATIONS OF GROWTH)

In the first stage the basic problem is to become established in the market. It is of crucial importance that the product should be satisfactory to some solid core of users in the market in order that their reactions should have a favorable effect on other potential users. This means that the emphasis in this stage is likely to be on continuing research and product development and on the kind of services to buyers which will increase the probabilities of effective and satisfactory use. Price appeal is of less importance at this stage as the product is being sold to a limited market. These consumers are likely to be those of higher-than-average income who can afford to buy a new product even though the initial price is high. Similarly there is only a limited function for advertising during this period of establishment. The company cannot afford to invest in massive advertising so long as serious limitations in the quality of product cause many people who try it to have an adverse reaction. To advertise it widely before it has been reasonably well perfected will cause people of limited purchasing power to expect too much of it, creating obstacles to future acceptance.

The second stage of the life cycle may be called the stage of expansion. This is the period during which advertising and price appeal will find their maximum usefulness for increasing sales. Advertising expenditures are likely to be large throughout the period. They will be greater relative to the volume of sales in the early part of this expansion period. This is the time for the product to become known to the whole body of consumers who might logically be expected to use the product. As the period of expansion proceeds the price of the product is likely to be gradually lowered. Price appeal logically follows large initial advertising since a conception of value must be created before a low price will seem like a bargain. Also as expansion proceeds the field is likely to attract an increasing number of competitors. The lowering of prices then becomes a sound competitive strategy to reduce the penetration of newcomers into the market.

The third stage may be called the period of consolidation. Substantial advertising will be continued, but its goal will be that of protecting competitive position rather than creating new users for the type of product. Renewed attention will be given to product design and to product features. At this stage, innovations are likely to be restricted to secondary features in an attempt to render obsolete the items owned by consumers and to induce them to buy again. Really major improvements, should they be discovered during this period, could initiate a new cycle of growth and another period of rapid expansion.

The concept of a standard curve of growth may be unacceptable to an ambitious management but many large companies have been obliged to accept the final levelling off as the growth rate slows down. The reconciliation of philosophies lies in regarding a large company as consisting of a number of enterprises. The company as a whole can maintain its growth rate if it can establish a sufficient number of successful new enterprises. As growth slows down or ceases in each of the older enterprises, marketing strategy turns increasingly toward new products and new markets.

STRATEGIC TIMING IN MIDDLE-RANGE PLANNING

Another major consideration in plan review and revision is that of strategic timing in relation to major events which may occur while the next plan is in effect. The dates of these events are known with various degrees of probability, and relevant information may have accrued since the last annual plan revision. Two types of situations are to be considered. The first is that in which specific market changes or other external events and conditions can be pretty accurately anticipated. Figure 16–6 and the following discussion refer to this case.

Figure 16–6

THE TIMING OF ACTIONS IN RELATION TO
CONTROLLING EVENTS AND DECISIONS

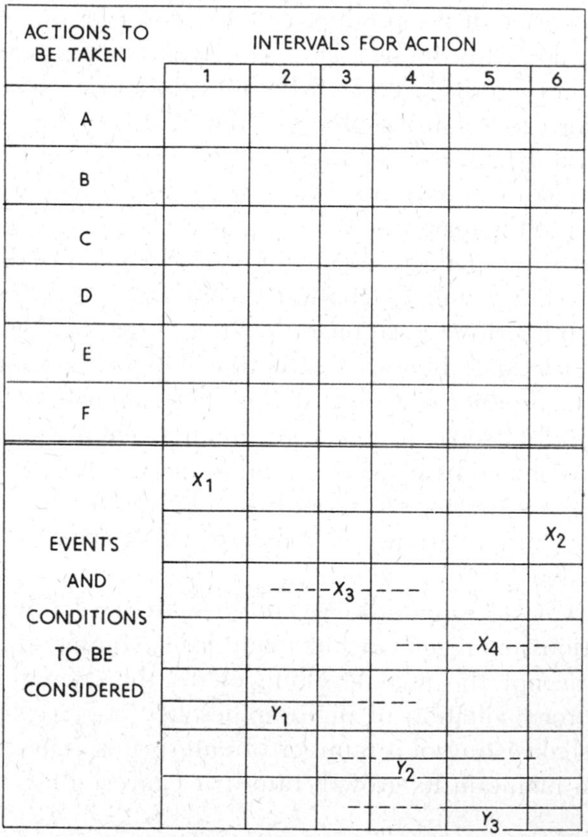

ACTIONS TO BE TAKEN	INTERVALS FOR ACTION					
	1	2	3	4	5	6
A						
B						
C						
D						
E						
F						
EVENTS AND CONDITIONS TO BE CONSIDERED	X_1					
						X_2
		----X_3----				
				----X_4----		
		Y_1 ---				
			---- Y_2 ----			
			-----		Y_3	

The letters A to F in the left-hand stub represent the actions or decisions which are to be scheduled for action during the interval which is under consideration. The lower half of the chart reflects the planner's information or best guesses concerning crucial dates which a plan must take into account. An X standing alone means a date that is already definitely fixed, such as the completion of a new plant or the expiration of a patent or franchise. The symbol X with dotted lines to either side refers to an event for which the date is only approximately known. The location of the X is the best guess, while the dots to either side represent the range of possibilities. A solid line represents a condition which is pretty certain to prevail over a period. Here again, the dots represent the additional period during which the condition may prevail. In the actual use of such a planning chart it would be further specified in relation to the given situation. Thus, the symbols X_1, X_2, X_3, and X_4 would refer to separate events, and Y_1, Y_2, and Y_3 to separate conditions. This simple device is merely a convenient way of taking account of a whole array of expected events, conditions, and contingencies in scheduling each proposed action in turn.

There are several types of events and conditions to be represented in this kind of approach in addition to the more obvious types which have been suggested. One of the most important is the continually changing scale of a growing company, and at a given point in its history it may be appropriate to consider economies of scale which become available for the first time. That is to say that a marketing organization has just recently become big enough to make it feasible to use certain techniques which could not be used economically in a small operation. The change of scale may happen suddenly through the introduction of new products or the opening of new markets, or it may have happened gradually, allowing more discretion as to when the change is to be made.

In using this type of planning chart, the first step might be to take the proposed action A and consider its most advantageous placing in relation to the anticipated events and conditions scheduled in the lower half of the chart. Suppose that as a first try action A was placed in interval 4. This would mean that it would definitely follow event X_1 and would probably be after X_2 but before X_3. The action would also be taken at a time when condition Y_2 was definitely prevalent, with the probability that condition Y_3 would exist at the same time. This should lead readily to a judgment as to whether action A should be delayed or advanced in time. The specific nature of the expected events and conditions would, of course, be taken into account.

The same type of preliminary trial and correction would be carried out for the other proposed actions. The final result would be a
sequence of the six actions which emerged from the attempt at external adjustment. Up to this point, interdependence among these
acts by the company is ignored. Later chapters will deal with the
internal problem of sequencing activities which affect each other.

Figure 16–7 is a suggested device for dealing with another variety of timing problem. Here it is assumed that no dates are fixed
in advance, but that two competitors are going to introduce similar
products during the period under consideration. Each tries to outguess the other as to the timing of the introduction in one segment
of the market after another. The segments could be regional markets or types of consumers classified on other lines than geographi-

Figure 16–7

TIMING OF COMPETITIVE ENTRY
INTO SEGMENTS OF THE MARKET

MARKET SEGMENTS	INTERVALS FOR ACTION					
	1	2	3	4	5	6
1		A				B
2				A		
3			BB	A		

cal. It is assumed that the manufacturer of product *A* is somewhat
further advanced in technical development and introduces his product first. Several questions of strategy in timing are then posed to
the producer of product *B*. While product *A* has been introduced in
segment 1, product *B* might be introduced in segment 3 on the judgment that it would be some time before the first competitor got
around to this segment. The *BB* is meant to indicate real concentration in segment 3 to try to get a solid foothold ahead of the stronger
competitor. The maker of *B* might pass up segment 2 entirely, feeling that he is not strong enough to meet his competitor everywhere.
While the second competitor tries to beat his rival to the punch in
segment 3 by launching a strong effort in interval 3, he might
attempt entry in segment 1 later on. Here he assumes that his rival
has developed the market in segment 1 to the point where there
is room for a second supplier. Thus, his sense of timing in entering
segment 1 in interval 6 is in sharp contrast with his thinking in
trying to anticipate his rival in going into segment 3. Obviously,
this is only one of the many possible competitive situations and is

merely illustrative of a simple procedure for thinking through questions of strategic timing.

TRIANGULATION IN MARKET PLANNING

The term "triagulation" as used here means bringing three basic factors into adjustment over the time period covered by the plan. The method presented is nothing more than systematic trial and error within an appropriate framework. More formal techniques for dynamic programming are under development but nothing is yet available to handle anything as complex as a marketing plan for a large company.

The three factors to be triangulated are goal, opportunity, and effort. These factors can be expressed in many cases as desired revenue, "normal" sales, and the cost of marketing expenditures designed to augment sales from the normal level to the desired or optimal level. The "normal" level year by year is the expected sales without increased expenditure to prompt market growth. The excess of sales over this benchmark level varies as a function of growth expenditures. The complication in finding the optimum relationship between expenditures and results arises from the fact already mentioned that the growth expenditures incurred in one year largely pay off in a subsequent year. The next two charts illustrate the way in which the analyst searches for a favorable adjustment between the three basic factors.

In the phase of market planning here called triangulation the need is quite apparent for coordination with production and investment planning. Suppose a forecast of future market opportunity induces management to build a new plant. Keeping the new plant operating at a satisfactory level is often taken as the immediate marketing goal. The market planner should remember that this is only an approximation. His task is to estimate the payoffs to be derived from efforts to accelerate market growth. It is the responsibility of others to determine how the company should supply the market.

The opportunity for a product in any future year cannot be expressed as a single figure either in units or dollars. Rather it is a demand function estimated for that date, indicating the number of units which can be sold at various price levels. When a product is successfully introduced it can be assumed that the opportunity will expand even without expenditures to stimulate growth. Expressed in the terms first suggested by Chamberlin,[1] this means that the

---

[1] E. H. Chamberlin, *Theory of Monopolistic Competition* (1st ed.; Cambridge, Mass.: Harvard University Press, 1934).

demand curve will shift to the right and upward from year to year or
that a greater number of units can be sold at the same price. For
many consumer products, however, there is little reason to assume
that the demand curve will shift in this way. That is to say that the
improvement in demand is not in the direction of persuading present
customers to pay more for the product but in interesting a more
massive consumer market in buying it at all. Figure 16–8 shows a set
of demand curves as they might exist for a series of years. The first
dates at the bottom are the years to which the curve is assumed to
apply without advertising, while those in the second row reflect the
results of growth expenditures.

Figure 16–8

EXPANDING MARKET OPPORTUNITY
DEMAND CURVES FOR SUCCESSIVE YEARS WITH
AND WITHOUT GROWTH EXPENDITURES

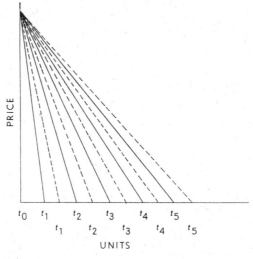

The dotted lines in the chart are meant to represent the shifting
of the demand curves applying to each of the five years achieved
as the result of growth expenditures in the first year only, between the dates t_0 and t_1. Ideally, the amount of growth expenditure in the first year should be determined by estimating the
resulting increase in net profits over the five years. There are
too many unknowns to make this a useful speculation. Instead it is
recommended that the payoff be estimated by the following rule
for approximation: Select the figure for growth expenditure which
is the smallest percentage of the estimated incremental sales. In
other words the best gamble may be the growth budget which seems

likely to produce the greatest amount of growth per dollar expended. To determine the incremental sales for this type of estimating, it would usually suffice to hold price constant during the five years. Alternatively, if data were available from production planning to show how cost would change from year to year, the planner might assume a price that would pass these economies on to the consumer. One of the reasons for making growth expenditures is to generate enough demand to permit volume production at a lower price.

The calculation described is sufficient if the only aim is to recommend growth expenditures for next year's marketing budget. If it is desired to set up a five-year operating statement, however, a similar calculation can be made for the several succeeding years. The impact of growth expenditures in each case is considered only for the period preceding t_5. Having adopted a planning horizon, no payoffs should be anticipated for years lying beyond it. The payoffs within the planning horizon accrue mainly toward the end of the period while growth expenditures are shown as being concentrated toward the beginning of the period.

Figure 16-9

MARKETING EXPENDITURES
FOR CURRENT OPERATION AND GROWTH

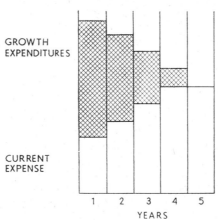

Current expense is shown in Figure 16–9 as rising steadily over the period. It is assumed that sales would rise and that the current costs of making the sales would rise accordingly. Growth expenditures on the other hand are shown as tapering off and reaching zero in the final year. The amounts indicated for growth may not be the total spent for this purpose. In the plan revision only those expenditures are included which take effect within the planning period. The margins over these arbitrarily limited costs are the outputs from the earlier inputs. Some part of this surplus may also be allocated to growth expenditures in a later plan revision when new years are added to the end of the series.

The first trial allocation of expenditures to years is subject to successive amendments in the search for the best adjustment. Funds might be moved from the initial year to later years because all the money needed to promote growth is not available from sales revenue or other sources. This is equivalent to setting the target levels ahead and taking longer to achieve them. On the other hand, new conditions such as information about competitive moves might force an acceleration of expenditures. For example, launching a contemplated new product might be more costly or even impossible a little later because of competitive moves.

Selected References

ANSOFF, H. I. "Strategies for Diversification," *Harvard Business Review*, September–October, 1957.
> Discusses a procedure for posing alternative strategies and estimating their relative profit potential.

LAMB, HAROLD. *Hannibal: One Man against Rome*. New York: Doubleday, Inc. 1958.
> A concise presentation of the strategies or battle plans of one of the greatest military leaders of all times.

LUCE, ROBERT DUNCAN AND RAIFFA, HOWARD. *Games and Decisions; Introduction and Critical Survey*. New York: John Wiley & Sons, 1957.
> Development without mathematical treatment of basic concept of strategy. Very suggestive for the search for marketing strategies.

SHUBIK, MARTIN. *Strategy and Market Structure*. New York: John Wiley & Sons, 1959.
> Utilizes concepts of strategy as developed in game theory, including some extreme forms which are called games of ruin or, alternatively, games of survival.

Problems

1. Contrast the notion of competition viewed as a race and as a game. Discuss each in respect to its value in aiding the businessman to evaluate strategies.

2. Contrast the relative merits of offensive and defensive strategies in marketing. Use marketing examples to illustrate both types of strategies.

3. Discuss the importance to the marketing planner of knowledge of the stage which a company or product has reached in its life cycle.

4. Discuss the use of "triangulation" in marketing planning.

5. Discuss the importance of strategic timing in middle-range planning.

Chapter 17

DESIGNING MARKETING CAMPAIGNS

‿◦‿

The most characteristic end-product of planning in marketing—the one which most readily springs to mind at the mention of planning—is a marketing campaign or program. The three preceding chapters are all preparatory to the discussion of the planning of campaigns. The process begins with the attempt to balance resources and objectives against each other, and this weighing of the feasible against the desirable continues throughout the planning process. Next there is a discussion of forecasting which is, in effect, the attempt to foresee what would happen without a plan or with no change in existing plans. Finally there is the search for effective strategies which relate resources to objectives, form the central core or idea of a plan, and enable the planner to revise his forecasts upward with a satisfactory probability of hitting his target.

The present chapter will return to the discussion of design principles and attempt to develop them in somewhat more specific terms as they apply to the design of campaigns. A campaign consists of the three elements of program, schedule, and budget. A program is a sequence of activities. A schedule relates this sequence to calendar time and specifies the actions of the various participants. The budget relates the sequence of activities to the resources which have been mobilized to support the program. A well-conceived budget is the final proof that the stated objectives can probably be attained within the limits of the available resources.

There are basically two kinds of campaigns to be discussed, one in which the time for completion is the principal unknown and the other in which the time period is determined in advance by such considerations as the planning horizon. A prime example of the first type of plan is a campaign for introducing a new product or entering a new market. The second type is illustrated by the programming of all marketing activity for a stated operating period. The application of design principles will be considered for each of these types of campaigns. Some of the special problems of new product introduction will then be discussed because of the importance of this phase of marketing in the American economy. There can be little doubt that a market economy requires a stream of innovations which, in turn, places a high premium on skillful planning of introductory campaigns.

ECONOMIZING TIME

For the first type of planning a primary objective is to save time. A specific result has been stated in advance, and the immediate goal is to accomplish this result in the shortest time possible. The optimizing principle has been stated as follows: To make optimal use of time subject to constraints of cost and risk. Time is of the essence because of the possibility, or even strong probability, that competitors are getting ready to come out with the same product or with a slightly different answer to the same consumer problem. The objective is to get established in the market first and to secure the great promotional advantage of being first in the field.

The ultimate constraint on expenditure is the maximum the company can afford to spend. At the other extreme is the minimum campaign which might be launched if cost were the only consideration. The actual cost will usually be somewhere above this minimum because of the expectation of increased benefits for the future. Risk is a constraint because there is always the chance that the product is not the best answer to the consumer problem. In particular, it is risky to come out with the product too quickly when it might have gone through further refinement in the laboratory. There is the risk that a premature product introduction may spoil the market for an indefinite period. For this reason it is better to think of product research and development and the market introduction as part of a continuous process. Certainly it is desirable to accelerate research and development to advance as much as possible the date when a model of the product is judged to be fully ready for the market.

STRUCTURAL PRINCIPLES OF DESIGN

The three structural principles of design are sequence construction, sequence manipulation, and sequence dating. The construction of a sequence is achieved by working backward from a desired end-result and putting in every step which is regarded as a necessary antecedent for the end-result or any of its antecedents. This is called the principle of precession. The sequence which results from this process indicates only the logical order of steps. The problem of how much time is required for each step is to be dealt with later. In working backward from the end-result it will be found that some steps have a single necessary antecedent while others may have two or more. That is to say that Step C cannot happen until both A and B have occurred. Further examination may show that B cannot happen until A has happened. In other instances B is not dependent on A, but the two can go on concurrently, the only requirement being that both A and B should precede C.

Sequence manipulation offers a means of testing the sequence as originally constructed. A sequence is constructed by looking for necessary antecedents and tested by consequences. The consequences of each step in a sequence can be either instrumental or detrimental. An instrumental step has a favorable effect on the costs or risks of the steps which follow. A detrimental step has an unfavorable effect on the costs or risks of the following steps. When a tentative sequence has been constructed, the planner raises four questions to test it for optimality. He takes the sequence to be optimal when he can no longer improve it by invoking any of the test questions. The questions are as follows:

1. Can any step be eliminated because it turns out that it is not truly a necessary antecedent and because it has detrimental effects on some of the steps which follow?
2. Even though a step is a necessary antecedent to the end-result, can it be postponed to a later point in the sequence, thereby avoiding detrimental effects on steps which would otherwise follow it?
3. Can any additional step be added which would have an instrumental effect on later steps without increasing either the total elapsed time or the total cost?
4. Can any step be advanced in the sequence in such a way as to reduce the costs or the elapsed time of steps which would otherwise precede it?

The second of these steps is the one which shows the greatest promise and might be called the principle of postponement. To eliminate detrimental consequences for early steps in the sequence, it seems only natural to postpone the step that is being questioned until after these steps have occurred. It is good to begin with the effort to postpone a step, and it will sometimes turn out that it can be dispensed with altogether. In a marketing sequence, sorting operations are among the steps to be questioned. A sort may occur too early in the sequence and hence increase the cost of later steps.

Similarly, in adding steps which have instrumental effects on those that follow first consideration should be given to additional sorts which may prepare the goods or materials being marketed for more efficient application of the later steps. Thus, the sorting out of apples or potatoes by size may result in a higher average market price than would be obtained for run-of-the-field products. There are other sorting operations, by contrast, where placing them too early in the sequence will increase subsequent transportation and storage costs.

CRITICAL PATH SCHEDULING

The concept of critical path scheduling was first developed by DuPont in collaboration with Remington-Rand. The problem which led to the development of this technique was the planning and control of large petro-chemical facilities. Since 1957 it has been applied to many planning problems from hospitals to shopping centers and from research and development projects all the way through to the introduction of the new product on the market. A variation of this method known as PERT was pioneered by the U.S. Navy and is said to have saved two years in the development of the first Polaris submarine. This type of scheduling is now generally required of all defense contractors. It has many applications in marketing and can be used in applying the design principles which have been enumerated in both the construction and the testing of sequences of marketing activity.

The critical path method takes its name from the key concept which this type of planning involves. A tightly connected sequence of activities, each a necessary antecedent for those which follow, may be called a chain. The longest chain in the network of activities constitutes the critical path. This path is critical because it is the one which determines the duration of the entire program. There are other activities which are not on the critical path and which represent slack or float. Once the critical path has been determined, it is clear that only by finding some means of shortening this path can the total elapsed time for the program be shortened. The simplest possible critical path network is the one shown in Figure 17–1.

The network is made up of the three activities *A*, *B*, and *C*. They are plotted proportional to time. The diagram shows that *B* and *C* are on the critical path since *C* cannot begin until *B* is completed and together they represent a continuous duration from the starting date to the completion date. The activity *A*, on the other hand, allows slack since it does not have to begin until sometime after the starting date in order to be completed before activity *C* must begin. It is clear that no further saving of time with respect to *A* can make any difference in the total elapsed time. Any saving in time must come out of activity *B* or activity *C*. For example, if the elapsed time for *B* depends on the size of the work force, it can be speeded up by employing more men.

Figure 17–1

THE SMD PLANALOG

To Stanley Mendell goes the credit for simplifying the critical path method by making it possible to plot all activities proportional to time. Using his method, the network only needs to be plotted for the critical path to be immediately visible as well as the parts of the network where slack exists. Mendell invented a plotting device called the SMD planalog which can readily be used for networks

Figure 17–2

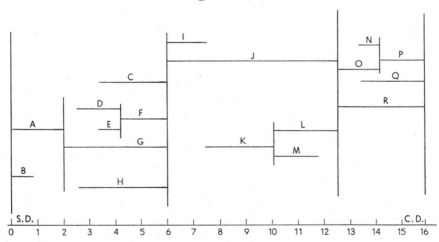

embracing as many as 600 activities. Shown in Figure 17–2 is a network of only eighteen activities as it would be plotted on the planalog.

The total elapsed time indicated on the chart is 16 weeks. Only four activities are on the critical path, namely, those numbered A,

G, J, and R. Before the planalog was invented the network would
have been drawn in some such fashion as that shown in Figure 17–3.

The numbers above each arrow now represent the elapsed time
in weeks for the completion of each activity. The critical path still
consists of four successive activities lasting two weeks, four weeks,
six and a half weeks, and three and a half weeks. The two diagrams
mean the same thing but the advantages of the first one with activities plotted proportional to time should be obvious. The advantages
of the planalog method are enhanced by the ease with which a
sequence can be manipulated in the course of such adjustments as
trying to shorten the critical path. Critical path scheduling can also
be managed through computer programs, but it is easier to explain
by reference to the planalog.

Figure 17–3

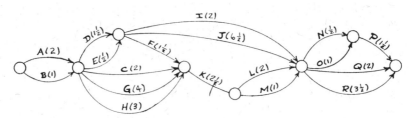

There are three basic elements or modules making up a set of
planalog equipment. First there are the aluminum channel boards
with parallel tracks or slots in them. They are about two feet long
by six inches wide, but an indefinite number can be joined together
either lengthwise or side by side. Next are the gauges of various
length which are placed in the slots of the channel board to represent periods of time. The smallest gauge may represent a single
week while the larger gauges and their combinations can represent
much longer periods. Finally there is the unit called a fence, which
is a thin piece of metal fitted perpendicularly across the channel
board. The original critical path diagrams consisted of nodes connected by arrows. Mendell's basic insight was that he could stretch
a node out perpendicularly to form a fence and thus make it possible to plot the longitudinal lines representing activities proportional to time.

An advertising planning problem and the way it was solved
with the help of the planalog will now be described. The problem
was to determine whether to take an advertising account offered at
the beginning of 1963 on the condition that the campaign should
break in all media by Labor Day. The media to be used included

newspapers, magazines, radio, television, and point-of-sale displays. All of the planning was to culminate in a meeting with the wholesale trade for the purpose of selling them on the campaign in the hope of getting their enthusiastic support. The preparation of newspaper copy and its approval was regarded as a necessary antecedent to all other activities as a way of establishing and maintaining a consistent theme for all media. The first element of logical connection was shown by placing a fence after the gauges representing newspaper copy and approval with all other media planning to follow. At this point the chart as plotted on the planalog looked something like this:

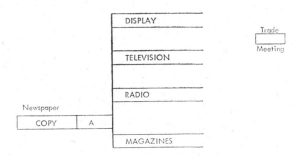

Everything now depended on whether planning could be completed for the other media in time for the trade meeting which would have to take place early in July. All copy should be available in approved form by that time, but experience had shown that magazines would take longer. Hence the practical goal was to arrive at the trade meeting with approved copy for display, television, and radio in addition to newspapers but not waiting for the completion of magazine copy. The planner next took account of the fact that radio largely uses the sound track developed for television. This relationship is shown by putting in a fence following the TV script and allowing TV film production and the completion of the record for radio use to run concurrently.

TV SCRIPT	TV PRODUCTION
	RADIO RECORD

The trade meeting would be followed by a period of retail selling to get retailers to accept the displays. Obviously the displays must be forwarded before the end of this period of retail selling so that installation could be made at once. When the time had been estimated for the preparation of all media copy, for the forwarding of copy and display material, for the trade meeting, wholesale and retail selling and display installation, it turned out that the program would have to extend to the middle of November, as indicated by the critical path. The planner now began to take some risks to see whether the critical path could be shortened to save the all-important five weeks. The preparation of display copy and the printing of displays loomed large on the critical path. The first gamble was to put display printing after the trade meeting, but not enough time was saved. Television was now on the critical path, but after all possible excess time was squeezed out of television and radio, display was once more on the critical path, and the program was still three weeks too long. The final diagram, set up on the planalog, is shown

Figure 17–4

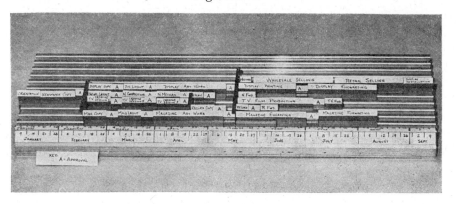

in Figure 17–4, and the agency decided not to take the account if it was still necessary to meet the Labor Day deadline. The agency had felt that they had already taken some substantial risks and did not dare push it any further. To be stretched so tight and still be not quite able to make the deadline was a very uncomfortable position to be in.

In the chart most of the labels are self-explanatory. The letter *A* always stands for approval of the immediately preceding step. The letters *FWD* stand for forwarding where there is not enough room to spell it out.

Actually the whole episode ended happily for the agency, but that is somewhat beside the point. The real point is that the agency head, with his traffic manager beside him, was able to get an answer in an afternoon which would otherwise have taken two weeks of intensive conferences with various department heads.

PLANNING WITHIN THE HORIZON

In the other major type of campaign the amount of time available is already given rather than the time required being one of the unknowns to be determined by planning. Actually the application of structural principles is reversed in this type of campaign. The planning horizon is estimated to be at some point in the future, such as two to five years ahead. Thus, the planner begins with calendar time rather than ending with it. The order of consideration is date, duration, and sequence rather than sequence, duration, and date. This is the type of planning in which it is particularly important to begin with the desired state of affairs as of the horizon date and plan backward to the present moment.

A somewhat different formulation of structural principles might be set up to supplement those already stated. First, establish or reestablish the horizon date by checking past forecasts for reliability. There is no use in pretending that the horizon lies five years ahead if past experience shows that it is impossible to see ahead with any precision beyond three years. Second, estimate the upper and lower limits of the gross and net revenues which can be generated during the period from the present date to the horizon date. Third, consider the possible strategies and programs for using the spendable portion of gross and net revenues over the period. It has already been stated that this is the type of planning which is most appropriate for the whole marketing effort as compared to planning the introduction of new products.

Planning within the horizon is frequently done at as many as three different levels of intensity. Suppose that a firm has a five-year horizon, meaning that market trends are predictable for five years ahead. It may further be supposed that no market expenditure made during the current year will have effects carrying over beyond next year. Thus the period from two to five years ahead would be in general predictable but not controllable. This situation would appear to call for contingency planning with respect to the more remote period. An attempt should be made to anticipate major market developments or changes in competitive strategy and to prepare countermeasures to meet them. Contingency plans should not necessarily be specified fully but certainly to the point of knowing the direction in which to move and the general character of the movement required if these contingencies should occur.

The more immediate future might be divided into a fully committed program and a provisionally committed program. There are some built-in rigidities which make it difficult to modify programs upward or downward in the short run. Advertising commitments in particular may run three to six months ahead. Thus the near term is governed by a plan already in operation. Planning decisions are being made meanwhile about expenditures three to six months ahead. It is always possible, of course, to hold some part of current expenditures in reserve to meet conditions as they develop. The deployment of a sales force can perhaps be adjusted more rapidly than the allocation of advertising expenditures.

The remainder of this chapter deals with some of the special problems associated with new product introduction, the invasion of new markets, or the initial entry of a new firm into the market. One of these problems is the coordination of product research and development with market research and development. These several aspects of innovation are of fundamental importance in our type of free market economy. Economic rewards in an enterprise economy, according to one school of economists, are primarily the profits of innovation. Profits are paid to the innovator because of society's pressing need for his services. There is, of course, a common need for the continuous improvement and proliferation of products. There is also a need for constant innovation to sustain the level of economic activity. New processes, new products, and new marketing strategies are all ways of putting modern technology to work in attaining an improving standard of living for everybody.

NEW PRODUCTS AND NEW MARKETS

In bringing out a new product or cultivating a new market, a company can be faced with a set of problems which lie outside the range of its past experience. Many new ventures fail, and one of the reasons is the lack of adequate planning. A systematic planning approach would reduce failures in two ways. First, the exercise of foresight would make it possible to avoid costly mistakes after the campaign had started. Second, the attempt to construct a practical plan might reveal insurmountable obstacles so that the project could be abandoned before large sums had been wasted on an impossible task.

The terms new products and new markets raise the question of how new is new. For planning purposes the degree of newness is measured directly by the anticipated effect on consumer behavior patterns. A truly significant new product is one that brings about a major departure from customary behavior by a substantial number of consumers. A market is new, including a market for a new product, if it obliges the company serving it to make major adjustments and to employ new marketing methods and channels. Often a new company is formed to exploit what appears to be a new opportunity in the market. Short of the wholly new venture, a marketing project can be quite new to the company launching it even though it is not new to the consumer or to industry.

The broader term product research and development has generally replaced the term product research. More recently some companies have begun to talk about market research and development rather than the narrower notion of market research. The viewpoint adopted here is that development of products and markets should be closely coordinated throughout to assure the success of new ventures.

In the establishment of a new marketing operation there is little question about the need for planning. The executives managing a going concern may be justified in keeping formal planning to a minimum and relying on the momentum of growth as the primary basis for coordination. When a new operation is contemplated, no such momentum exists. Not only must the broad structure of the operation be considered but also operating details which may later be reduced to routines. Since there is no historical pattern of behavior, the planner is called upon to visualize such a pattern in advance.

Any proposed new operation must attract the interest and support of someone who can provide it with capital funds. The plan of operation is essential in showing what outputs are expected, what inputs will be required, and in demonstrating step by step how the operation will use the inputs to obtain the outputs. The plan may have to be presented to an internal management group, to a small group of major investors, or to the general public if the operation is to be financed by an issue of securities. In any of these cases, the plausibility of the plan and the persuasiveness of its presentation will determine whether it will attract the support it needs to become an established fact.

TYPES OF NEW VENTURES

There are several types of new ventures and a corresponding variety of planning assignments. All of these assignments involve marketing as a fundamental consideration, although some extend considerably beyond the range of marketing as narrowly defined. Three types of new ventures deserve special consideration. The first of these is a separate enterprise involving a new entry into the market by a new marketing organization. The second is a major entry into a new field of endeavor by an established organization.

An example would be a chemical manufacturer who decided to set up a separate division to develop and market products for agricultural use. Other examples would involve major attempts to reach new groups of consumers or to integrate forward into other levels of distribution. One case might be a petroleum company making a major entry into foreign markets or attempting to develop its own retail outlets in the domestic market as compared to disposing of its output at the refinery level. Finally there is the development and introduction of a single new product by an existing company or a division of a large company. A large part of the accumulated planning experience in marketing pertains to new product introduction. Special attention will be given to new product planning here, not only for its intrinsic importance, but as a special case of the marketing aproach in the planning of new ventures.

The planning of a new enterprise is perhaps more generally regarded as falling in the area of finance rather than that of marketing. The crucial question at this stage is whether any potential investors have enough confidence in the project to put up the initial capital. Actually, this is a special phase of marketing in which the promoter is attempting to sell potential investors a chance to make money. In the past he has sometimes been much more interested in whether investors would buy shares of the company than whether consumers would buy its products or services. The plan, or prospectus, was designed to make investors visualize the possibilities of large earnings easily achieved rather than presenting realistic details of what would be required to establish the new product in the market. The trend in public regulation as well as in greater understanding by the investing public puts an increasing premium on well-conceived marketing plans for new ventures. Informed investors want evidence that the output of an operation can be sold, and the mere decision to build a plant is no guarantee that a going operation can be evolved.

The creation of a new division or a new area of operation within a company is not unlike the promotion of a separate new enterprise except that the prospective source of funds is now the management of the existing company. The proponents of the new operation must have a persuasive plan including evidence that the new division can market its output at a profit. In some respects there are obstacles confronting a new venture launched inside a company over and beyond those facing a separate new enterprise. Unless the product line of the new division is completely distinct, there is some overlapping area of competition with existing divisions. On the other hand, if the proposed operation is entirely new, resistance may arise on the grounds that the company is not qualified to operate in the new field and has a better chance of increasing its profits by expanding its present operations. The existing divisions are usually active competitors for any investment funds to be allocated by top management even when the operations as such are not competitive. Special obstacles also arise when the new operation represents an effort to integrate forward into new levels of distribution. In taking such a step, the company will almost inevitably be in competition with some of its existing customers. Tensions will be generated both as between the company and its customers and also among individuals within the organization whose attitudes and interests are differentially affected by the new activity.

Even in the introduction of a single new product, some of these same considerations arise in persuading management that the new product has a good chance of becoming a profitable venture. The introduction of a new product means diverting funds from existing products and raising questions as to whether the firm is really equipped to market it. Even a relatively minor innovation such as a new grade or quality of a product already in the line may raise such issues because of its impact on marketing channels and methods. Thus, whatever the new venture, it presents a threefold problem to the planner. He must devise a way of establishing a foothold in the market for an activity which departs in some degree from what existed before. He must present a persuasive picture of probable success in order to get the resources for making the attempt. Finally he must be prepared to bring about adjustments within the marketing organization and its distribution channels to offset the disadvantages which may be caused by any deliberate departure from established marketing programs.

In every type of new venture there is need for some familiar framework within which planning can take place. If an entirely new product is to be planned, the planner must look to consumer behavior for the planning framework. In fact, even the proposed modification of an existing product should be referred to the relevant consumer activity as the framework for planning, but this becomes even more obvious when there is no existing product to serve as a point of departure. Either the completely new product or the modified version of an existing product comes into being in order to serve some segment of demand more adequately. The same considerations hold for the entry of an entirely new firm into a competitive field. The entry of the firm is justified by the expectation that there is some group of customers who would be served more effectively than they were by the firms previously in existence. The term "consumers" here must be defined broadly to include all present and future participants in a particular type of activity. It is not good planning to set up a new firm to serve past markets which may already be in a state of decline by the time the firm begins to operate. The planner is called upon to visualize the future course of a given activity and the opportunity it will offer for the profitable use of the firm's resources.

There are some offsetting advantages in planning for a new enterprise or a new product. First of all, the planner is assured of more serious attention from the first because of the obvious necessity of some type of planning for the genuinely new venture. The planner is not hampered by restrictions imposed by the history of an operation. He is free to consider what would be best on analytical grounds rather than having to compromise with an unsatisfactory plan of operation simply because it is customary. The resources to be employed are in relatively liquid form and can be structured according to the best available judgment as to market requirements. There is an opportunity to explore the technological possibilities for genuine innovation more fully than may ever be true again once an operation of some type has been established. In summary, the planner engaged in the design of a new venture must find a constructive balance between two considerations. On the one hand he must find a specific framework or context in the real world since an innovation, no matter how sweeping, is always an addition or modification to some existing pattern. On the other hand, a successful new departure must offer a significant break with the past to gain a foothold and enjoy a growing market.

A somewhat related considerations is what might be called the degree of specificity in a new product. Since the needs and tastes of consumers vary, a new product may have to be very precisely specified to meet the exact requirements of any small segment of the market. Some of these specifications may have to be dropped if the product is to appeal to a larger number of consumers. This is partly because the extra features will make it necessary to charge a higher price. More generally it is because the wider market may feel at home with a simpler product or one which represents only a moderate departure from products which are already familiar.

Figure 17-5 attempts to picture these opposing market forces which must be reconciled in new product planning. The degree of specificity is indicated on the horizontal axis and increases from left to right—the higher the specificity the greater the preference of some prospective buyers over anything else in the market. Strength of preference is shown on the vertical scale at the right. Number of prospective users, as shown on the scale at the left, decreases as degree of specificity increases. Neither extreme is likely to be the right position for a new product. The new product needs to be different enough to create genuine preference on the part of some prospective users and yet not so specialized as to restrict demand to an inadequate market base.

Figure 17–5

SPECIFICITY IN NEW PRODUCT DESIGN

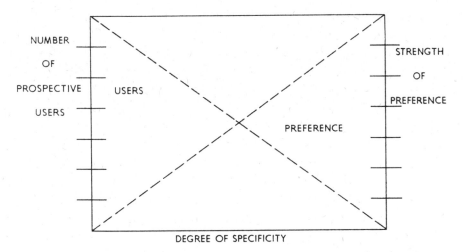

A SYSTEMATIC APPROACH TO NEW PRODUCTS

The general view taken in this book emphasizes the matching of needs and resources as the essence of planning. New product development is the process of carrying out this matching of means and ends on a conceptual and experimental basis before the product has been designed and often before the need has been fully specified. The matching process starts in the domain of possibilities and potentials. Sometimes a marketing organization is handed a product prototype and is told to find a way to market it. Sometimes it is the other way round, the starting point being the marketer's hunch as to something people need or can be induced to want. The task then is to design an acceptable product. A third approach to new products which is advocated here, is intended to coordinate both types of thinking through successive stages of development. Five such successive stages will be discussed, beginning with the generation of ideas for new products. The exposition of these five stages builds on the work of B. F. Bowman, an experienced product planner.

The planner is most likely to stress the technical side if his company is strongly oriented to basic scientific research and operates in a field of rapidly advancing technology. Chemical companies produce many products as by-products, and an obvious move toward improving their profits is to find fields of application for these by-products. Sometimes these efforts are so successful that what was

Table 17–1

GENERATION OF IDEAS

Technical Research (*Resources Calling for Use*)	*Marketing Research* (*Needs Calling for Satisfaction*)
By-products	Study of own and competitive products
New materials	with respect to consumer complaints
New mechanical or electrical systems	Nonusers among prospects
General technical possibilities	Projected rate of use
Miniaturization	Study of consumer activity with respect
Automation	to economy, ease and convenience, im-
Precision standards	proved results

originally regarded as the by-product now becomes the main product. The term by-product can also be applied to the results of basic research since new product possibilities are sometimes discovered accidentaly through investigation directed toward quite different objectives. The term serendipity is used to characterize this process of accidental discovery. Actually systematic planning should increase the chances that such happy accidents will occur. For example, they are more likely to happen if someone who is strongly oriented toward application is in close touch with the research program in the laboratory.

A somewhat different approach to new products results from studying the characteristics of new materials and new mechanical or electrical systems. A material or a system may be well established for certain uses, but the product planner or innovator considers other areas of application and appropriate modifications in the product for these uses. Basic products such as aureomycin may become the foundation of a whole family of products by successive adaptations for one use field after another.

Still another approach from the resource side is through the application of some generalized technical possibility to a product prototype. One of these general processes which occurs in technological advance is miniaturization. Once designers have found a mechanical answer to a given problem, the next stage is likely to be finding a way to do the same thing in smaller and smaller units. Thus, in the electrical field, transistors and printed circuits have replaced more cumbersome apparatus and have greatly increased the area of product application. Automation is another technical possibility which can be applied to either industrial equipment or consumer products. It achieves its most startling effect on sales in the consumer field by making a complex product simple to operate and relatively trouble-free. In the industrial field specialized operators may be available to handle complex equipment, but automation procedes as a means of reducing labor costs. Other generalized steps toward product design include the development of precision standards and interchangeability of parts to increase consumer confidence and decrease service difficulties.

On the marketing research side, the generation of new ideas can be promoted by the study of existing products and the study of the consumer activity to which the product is related. The study of existing products would utilize a sales history of the company's own products and analyze apparent market response to any changes in product features, price, or promotional appeals. The same type of study might usefully be made of competitive products although under the obvious limitations as to the availability of comparable data. Another place to look is at the record of consumer complaints which can be analyzed in such a way as to suggest new product features needed to overcome the principal complaints. Market investigation at this stage should cover nonusers as well as users in order to pinpoint the obstacles to use. Among the users may be some with an abnormally low rate of use whose attitudes are usually somewhat different from those of nonusers. In some cases these might be prospects with an urgent need for a product of the particular type but with a strong objection to some features of the available product.

The study of consumer activity would often be guided by general conclusions as to types of improvement which might appeal to the consumer. One of these, of course, is the ever-present requirement of economy. While there may be a perverse tendency to regard high prices as desirable as a symbol of prestige in some product classifications, most people most of the time are interested in getting more for their money. A second general consideration is that of convenience and ease of use, advantages which have been vital ingredients in the success of hundreds of consumer products. Finally, there is the broad category of improved results. This may take the

form of eliminating some unsatisfactory feature such as service difficulties, or it may take the form of adding refinements, variety, or
aesthetic appeal.

Stage two begins with the assumption that stage one has produced an exhaustive list of new product possibilities. The obvious
next step is to apply appropriate screens to this list of possibilities in
order to select one or several items for further development. In some
actual cases, the list available at the termination of stage one has run
into hundreds of items. Elimination through the application of successive criteria is essential to reduce such a list to a limited number
of ideas worthy of serious development efforts. Table 17–2 suggests
some of the screens to be applied on the technical and marketing
sides.

Table 17–2

SELECTION FOR DEVELOPMENT

Technical Research (Production Screens)	Marketing Research (Marketing Screens)
Technical difficulties such as side effects	Consumer awareness of need
Processing problems	Rate of product obsolescence
Economic limitations	Relation to existing product line
Availability of men and facilities	Relation to existing sales organization and distribution channels

It may turn out that while a product is theoretically feasible,
some serious technical difficulties remain. An illustration would be
the undesirable side effects which are sometimes produced by a
drug or chemical product. Some of the first synthetic detergents, for
example, produced serious corrosion in some of the metals used in
automatic washing machines. There are processing problems to be
overcome in moving from the laboratory to the pilot plant and finally
to full scale production. There are economic limitations in processing and packaging which make it necessary to redesign a product or
to make it from cheaper materials. Also to be considered is the
availability of plant facilities and skilled manpower. Sometimes the
available resources are not exactly matched to the production task
so that some retooling or retraining is required.

On the marketing side it is essential to apply some measure of the
state of development of the market as a whole. A need may exist,
or improved performance may be possible, but the marketer must
evaluate consumer awareness of need. Unless there would be ready
acceptance of the product in some segment of the market, an educational program would be required which might strain the re-

sources of the firm in putting over the new product idea. If the innovator is attempting to enter a well-established field in which individual products have a limited life, he needs to have some measure of the rate of product obsolescence. The average life of a product design or style varies greatly from one field to another. A firm may not want to enter a field with a single design unless it is equipped to follow up this original entry with new designs and product improvements to keep pace with changing requirements.

A new product must also be evaluated in relation to the established pattern of the company's marketing operation. There are questions as to how the product fits into the existing product line and whether it complements existing products or in some way conflicts with their sale. The planner must also consider whether the existing sales organization is equipped to sell the new product and whether it will have adequate incentives to do so. This issue extends to the distribution channels for the product and whether it should be sold by existing dealers and distributors or whether new and separate channels will have to be created. It is not uncommon for a new product to get only lukewarm support from the company's distributors and dealers or even its own sales force.

The third stage is the more intensive research and development of the products which have survived the successive screens applied in stage two. It is this third stage that will produce the final product design and the first conception of a marketing plan for selling it. Some of the major considerations on the technical and marketing sides are listed in Table 17–3.

Table 17–3

DEVELOPMENT PROJECTS

Technical Research (*Fitting the Product to the Market*)	*Marketing Research* (*Fitting the Marketing Process to the Product*)
Performance requirements	Market potentials
Alternative formulations or designs	Marketing requirements
Adaptability to machine production	Cost and profit targets
Styling and packaging	Market share goals
Patentability	Competitive developments
	Selling techniques

On the technical side, the process is that of incorporating in a practical design the product idea which was selected as feasible and desirable as a result of stage two. Instead of attempting to outline the engineering procedures in product design, the table lists some reference points which should be familiar to the planner. The place to start is with performance standards calculated to gain market acceptance. Several different formulations or designs will be considered. The criteria for selection among these alternatives include factors of production economy and of consumer appeal. Patentable features help in gaining a foothold but from a marketing viewpoint the main hope is in entering the market ahead of competition. Overall strategy sometimes requires that a particular development project be terminated before the basic problem is fully solved. The aim is to preempt a market position and to get some feedback from actual consumer use as the basis for further refinements. In some areas products for a given use are constantly evolving and a new product presumably represents the best formulation of what basic research can offer at the time. The terms "basic" and "applied" must be taken in a relative sense and in an industrial laboratory both may be directed toward specific product uses. Thus, applied research on a packaged household chemical might refer to the degree of concentration and physical form of a particular chemical compound, while basic research continues to seek quite different chemical formulas designed for the same purpose.

On the marketing side, effort at this stage is directed toward defining more precisely the particular niche which the product can be expected to occupy in the market. It involves attempts to estimate the potential market for the whole class of products and to weigh the factors which will determine market shares within the product group. It is concerned with product possibilities under various assumptions as to market shares and the costs associated with each level of attainment. The alternatives considered from a marketing viewpoint will be crucial at this stage in determining the final formulation or choice of product features in the laboratory.

The fourth stage is concerned with testing the conclusions about technical feasibility and potential demand which were arrived at in stage three. Up to this point the matching of consumer needs and available resources has been carried through several conceptual stages but still without direct contact with the realities of plant operation or competition in the market place. The two aspects of a testing program are suggested in Table 17–4.

On the technical side, production planning now undertakes the task of devising the sequence of steps which will constitute the working process in a full-scale operation. To arrive at this point, the design of the production process may pass through the successive stages of laboratory development, pilot plant production, and preliminary operation in the production plant. The successive stages in process design are accompanied by engineering analysis to determine costs and control methods and to establish the final product specifications.

Table 17–4

TESTING

Technical Research (Can it be made?)	Marketing Research (Can it be sold?)
Process development	Pilot marketing:
Pilot plant production	Panel tests
Preliminary plant production	Consumer tests
Process costs	Market tests
Control methods	Review of previous evaluations
Ingredient specifications	Appraisal of sales potentials and marketing plans

Simultaneously, the planner will be involved in a step-by-step evaluation of the full-scale marketing plan. The laboratory tests of the production process will result in limited quantities of the product such as are required for the preliminary series of panel and consumer tests. The pilot plant should produce sufficient quantities for the more extensive market tests in the home or the retail store. Here again successive stages of pilot marketing are accompanied by a program of analysis to get the greatest benefit from the experimental results.

Upon the completion of this extensive testing program on the technical and marketing sides, the planner now turns to product introduction. The launching of a new product requires the closest coordination between production and marketing to get the maximum initial impact without excessive waste or disruption of established operations. Some of the larger considerations involved in planning a successful introduction are displayed in Table 17–5.

Table 17–5

PRODUCT INTRODUCTION

Technical Research (Initial Production Operation)	Marketing Research (Establishing Market Position)
Production scheduling	Introduction method:
Product specifications for procurement	Crash program
	Growth out of earnings
Quality control	Market by market
In-plant training	Trade cooperation and building
Review of production methods and costs	market channels
	Continuing analysis of initial results

On the technical side, estimates must be made as to the requirements for initial inventories, working back from the deadline for the appearance of merchandise on retailer's shelves. Production schedules must be established to provide for the introductory sales campaign and for the most probable rate of replenishment or re-orders when the product begins to move. Quality should also be maintained during this period at a level which will promote product acceptance, but not at a level so high that is cannot be maintained economically later on. The other steps enumerated are those of integrating the new product fully into normal plant operations. As in previous stages, the running analysis of results accompanies and facilitates the step-by-step installation of the new operation.

On the marketing side, the planner is engaged in the installation and adjustment of the marketing plan which has been evolved during the preceding stages. His responsibilities during the introduction period will be related to the fundamental choice which has been made as to the introduction method. Among the possibilities available are those listed in the table. By a "crash program" is meant a massive expenditure to establish the product across the market immediately. Reference has been made to this type of investment in market position in previous chapters. The alternatives are the gradual growth through promotion financed out of earnings and the introduction of the product, market by market. Either of these latter possibilities gives some period of time for adjustment and revision of the marketing plan in operation. The crash program imposes maximum responsibility on the market planner to be right the first time. The market-by-market approach gives the organization a chance to perfect its marketing plans and operations as it moves on from one market to another. Among the crucial elements under either type of program are the factors involved in gaining trade co-operation for the new product. This process must be conducted in such a way as to lay a sound foundation for building marketing channels over time rather than merely attempting to get the maximum sales response during the introductory period.

COORDINATED PRODUCT PRESENTATION

The coordination of marketing programs begins with the unified presentation of each product. There is obviously a special need for coordination in the case of a single-shot campaign such as the introduction of a new product. Since it will only happen once, there is only one opportunity to get it right. This is in contrast to planning for a repetitive activity in which there is a period for detailed adjustment or "de-bugging" to work out a smoothly balanced operation.

One aspect of coordination will be considered here because it is so central to the problem of new product introduction. That is the need for an integral relationship among the several facets of the new thing which is offered to the consumer. Having decided that it will get into a new field, a company must decide on the posture it expects to take in the field. This is partly a question of whether the product is to be a relatively stripped-down version of its particular class of products or whether it is to be a deluxe model with all of the available extra features. The face which the new product presents to the prospective user is more than a question of product design. There are several elements which go into a specific posture before the user. These can generally be related to the three major facets of product, price, and promotion. The gist of all this can perhaps be suggested in another way. Any new offering to the consumer involves a design problem considerably broader than the physical structure of the product itself. It is the responsibility of market planning to work out a balanced pattern or package embracing these various aspects of the new offering.

Most obviously a low price may restrict the maker to a streamlined product on cost grounds. Similarly a high price may be justified to the consumer on the basis of some distinctive features that set the product apart from anything already available. Actually this situation is considerably more complicated than this sketch suggests. Several distinctive combinations of attributes could be offered at the same price. Thus, even with so simple a product as paper napkins there are such attributes as size, finish, wet strength, and absorbency. Two models might combine these attributes in quite different degrees and yet have similar costs or be salable at the same price, although probably to quite different consumers.

Price is not a simple, indivisible factor but is made up of various elements. A flat price to every buyer might be suitable in one product situation where another would require a base price with extra charges for delivery, installation, or accessories. Trade prices to distributors and dealers present special problems in designing a price structure. Elements in the price structure reflect the costs of marketing the product and of the services which facilitate the sale.

The term promotion is meant to embrace all the appeals made for the product in advertising or other sales efforts. This is not merely a matter of gaining the favorable opinion of the prospective user but of trying to project a specific type of product image which fits in with the other aspects of market posture. Quite often the problem of design in this field is to avoid some negative connotation such as that faced by low-sudsing detergents when they were first intro-

duced, or to overcome psychological obstacles to product acceptance such as those encountered in introducing certain cosmetics
for men.

Some of the more effective product design and development specialists recognize the importance of designing a product in the
market. These designers try to proceed from the use situation rather
than from general aesthetic considerations. The same general principle should be applied to the total product posture and not to the
physical product alone. This is one of the reasons for marketing
research and development being in the picture from the beginning
of a new product project. It also emphasizes the need in the usual
case for a project coordinator who can keep a close rein on all the
diverse elements in the new offering, including product, package,
price structure, trade channels, and promotional appeals.

SUMMARY

The introduction of new products is one field in which formal
planning and coordination have been going on for some time. A
conscious awareness of techniques of planning is still needed in this
field as in other phases of marketing. Especially is it essential to
coordinate the successive stages of technical and marketing research and development. Of key importance also is the concept
of integrated design for the market posture of the new product
offered to the consumer.

The idea of a new venture is generalized to include situations
in which new markets are to be cultivated or new marketing machinery created, even though the product itself may not represent
a major innovation. The point of view is expressed that the test
of newness is the degree of modification in behavior patterns which
a new product brings about. It is a new product in the planning
sense if consumers act differently because it is available or if marketing organizations must break with old patterns of behavior in supplying it. There are forces of inertia in both consumer behavior and
business behavior which delay the acceptance of innovation. Once
a meritorious product obtains a foothold, it gains momentum from
the contagion of favorable reactions. A systematic approach to
product development and introduction can vastly improve the number of successes among new product ventures.

Selected References

JOHNSON, S. C. AND CONRAD, JAMES. "How to Organize for New Products,"
Harvard Business Review, May–June 1957.
A case study from the makers of Johnson Wax on how to organize for the
effective development and launching of new products.

LARSON, G. E. *Developing and Selling New Products.* Washington, D.C.: U. S. Department of Commerce, Small Business Administration, Government Printing Office.
> Lays out a program of marketing introduction for the typical new product.

MILLER, ROBERT W. *Schedule, Cost and Profit Control.* New York: McGraw-Hill Book Co., 1963.
> A simple presentation of the principles of PERT or critical path scheduling to the design of sequences in a campaign.

PHELPS, D. M. *Planning the Product.* Homewood, Ill.: Richard D. Irwin, Inc., 1959.
> A standard work on the marketing characteristics of products by a leading authority in the field.

PLANALOG, INC. Suburban Station Bldg., Philadelphia.
> For more detailed information about the use of the planalog in designing marketing campaigns.

Problems

1. Discuss critical path scheduling and its application to marketing. Indicate, using a marketing example, how the critical path might be shortened.

2. Contrast Mendell's SMD planalog with the usual network presentation. Discuss the advantages of the former device in critical path scheduling.

3. Explain how the planning of a new enterprise differs from the planning of a new product introduction.

4. Discuss the generation of new product ideas from a marketing point of view.

5. Discuss and contrast the available marketing strategies during the introduction period of a new product.

Chapter 18

DESIGNING MARKETING FACILITIES

The design of marketing facilities is an effort to apply an optimizing principle to the use of space. There is more than one version of the optimizing principle because there are several ways of using space to accomplish a marketing objective. In any case, efficient use of space may be described as the functional goal of the facility plan. There is also a set of structural principles through which an appropriate setting or framework is provided for the activities which are to take place in the designated area. The types of marketing facilities to be considered include warehouses, retail stores, retail shopping centers, sales offices, and the pattern of geographic coverage for a national organization, including the routing of salesmen and delivery trucks.

In planning a facility, the emphasis is mainly on spatial relationships. For example, given the assignment of planning the layout of a grocery warehouse, how much space should be allotted to various functions or product inventories, and how should these allocated spaces be related to each other? Yet there is often a time dimension in spatial planning related to the activity which is to take place in the area being planned. Each point in the area considered may owe its special significance to the fact that it is a station in a behavior sequence. In some cases there is a prescribed path which everyone using the space must follow. In other cases there is a range of possible paths, and the planner must consider an average or prevailing path and the probable dispersion of actual paths around this mean.

The first task in spatial planning is to set up the sequence of activities which is to take place along the path or paths which gives access to the space. Figure 18–1 represents seven stations for the corresponding steps in an operating sequence. Here a second task has already been performed since the sizes of the squares vary according to the estimated amount of space required for each step. Both the numbers and the arrows represent the direction in the flow of activities. The third task, coming to grips with the actual site, is also suggested in the chart. In the lower half of the chart, the same space allocations have been arranged within a compact area. The shapes of the areas have been changed in order to fit them in and still preserve the same sequence. This is one way of adapting the flow of activities to the area available. There are usually some limitations as to the shape of the space that could be used for any given

Figure 18–1

HYPOTHETICAL CASE OF SPATIAL PLANNING

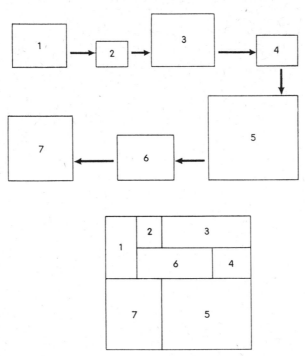

step. When the steps are numerous, it becomes very difficult to preserve the requirements as to proximity, size, and shape of areas without considerable waste in the total space. This problem is complicated, of course, if the space actually available has peculiar outlines or is divided into two or more parcels.

The three elements of proximity, size, and shape are present in every problem of spatial planning, but they appear in a variety of forms from one planning task to another. The concept of proximity or nearness seems deceptively simple so long as the problem concerns the arrangement of the steps of an operating sequence along a single path. In a more complex spatial pattern, nearness becomes a relative factor requiring choices among alternatives. There are several basic patterns of spatial arrangement which will be illustrated in the discussion of specific tasks of spatial planning in marketing.

First, there is the single open path to accommodate a process with inputs at one end and outputs at the other. The example which will be discussed is the flow of goods through a warehouse. The inputs at one end of the path are typically car lots of individual products received from suppliers. The outputs at the other end are smaller quantities of single items or assortments of a number of items, going out to satisfy customers' orders.

The next pattern is the closed loop in which the path returns on itself. Examples in marketing are the routes followed by salesmen, out and back to the sales office, or delivery trucks out and back to the warehouse. Quite commonly a number of closed loops radiate from a center, as in the two examples given. These routes may be fully determined, following a standard path out and back. They may be subject to variation around the fixed nucleus, both as to the exact course followed and the incidence of trips over one loop or another. This pattern of space use might be called a probabilistic network of nucleated closed loops. Some of the planning tasks discussed in this chapter involve that type of pattern including the internal arrangement for a self-service store such as a supermarket. Spatial planning in marketing assumes that a primary use of space is for paths along which goods or people will move. The planner also needs the related notion of stations occurring along a path. A station is a point at which the physical flow is arrested and certain functions are performed. In marketing flows the primary functions to be performed at stations along the way are storage, display, the sorting of goods and negotiations between buyer and seller. The amount of activity is relatively slight at some stations as, for example, dead storage in a warehouse for a product of infrequent sale. A station may be looked upon as a portion of the total area and sometimes there is an intricate pattern of movements over paths within the area. The broken package room is such a station within a grocery warehouse. It accommodates movements for the assembly of single packages similar to the movements for the assembly of cases which take place along the main assembly line in the warehouse.

The allocation of space by the planner in terms of size and shape can be made in terms of the requirements for paths and stations and their reaction upon one another. The width of a path should be ample for the free flow of traffic along it. Yet this result should not be accomplished at the expense of the space needed for adequate performance of functions at the various stations. The discussion of internal warehouse design will refer to the engineering steps by which the space required for paths through the assembly area was reduced from 60 percent to 40 percent of the area.

Proximity or nearness as the most essential factor in spatial planning is vitally related to the pattern of use and the size and shape of areas required for paths and stations. Proximity is best measured not in yards but in time and effort required to move from one point to another. The effort involved in moving goods is generally taken to be a function of weight times distance. In this sense a ton of goods two miles away from its destination is closer than five tons only one mile away. Ton miles is a recognized measure of bulk movement but a parallel measure which might be called pound feet could be used to measure nearness to the loading dock in a warehouse.

The goal of proximity must be pursued judiciously, or it can become self-defeating. A planned shopping center is an attempt at convenient grouping of a number of stores. If too many stores enter this agglomeration, some of them will be quite far apart and convenience in shopping begins to be dissipated. Similarly, traffic congestion whether on a highway or along an aisle in a warehouse increases the operating distance between two points even though their physical positions have not changed. Thus, determining the shortest path for goods to move through a warehouse requires some real skills in spatial planning. The operating distance must be measured in time and effort. The design should minimize the chance of congestion on the path or of any station along the route becoming a bottleneck and thus interrupting the flow. The problem of optimal allocation of space will now be considered for several types of marketing operations.

THE DESIGN OF MERCHANDISE WAREHOUSES

The last twenty-five years have seen an enormous advance in the physical handling of goods as they move through the channels of distribution. The advancing technology of goods handling is a large subject in itself, and there will be no attempt to more than sketch the broad outlines of the subject here. Only one aspect of goods handling will be described as an example of spatial planning in marketing. This is the design of merchandise warehouses such as might be operated by a wholesaler of groceries or some other classification of packaged consumer products. This phase of marketing technology has been carried further in the grocery field than anywhere else. The weight and bulk of the merchandise handled create a special need in this field, and the relatively small number of items and their physical similarity facilitate systematic handling as compared to some other merchandise lines.

The design of grocery warehouses today is a highly specialized aspect of distribution engineering. The principle is fully accepted that the planner should first design the operations to be carried out in the warehouse and then design the building itself as a shell to contain these operations. Special types of equipment which include forklift trucks, drag lines, merchandise pallets, and electronic systems for invoicing and inventory control have gradually evolved to make the handling of groceries as automatic as possible. The principles on which such spatial planning is based developed out of work on this subject by the United States Department of Commerce going back to the middle 1920's. The chart reproduced here in Figure 18–2 has the historic interest of being the first conception of a streamlined grocery warehouse prepared by W. H. Meserole, who later came to be recognized as the greatest authority on the subject. Mr. Meserole has designed hundreds of warehouses since that time which differ mainly in size and complexity of operation and in the mechanical means employed in facilitating the warehouse operation.

The problem of arrangement visualized in this chart involves the three previously mentioned elements of sequence, size, and shape of operating areas. These are universal elements in problems of spatial planning. There are two other elements of equally broad application which are also illustrated by this layout. One is that space is often assigned in two stages rather than one. The first stage is the gross allocation to different functions representing distinctive ways of using space. The second stage is the assignment of stations for the sequence of steps to be handled in one of these functional areas.

In this particular problem there are six distinctive functional areas. Most fundamental of these is the assembly line indicated by the two rows of small blocks running from front to back on either side of the floor plan. This is the assembly line which the order picker traverses in assembling the order for a particular customer. Order assembly is the basic function performed in the grocery warehouse, and everything else is designed to facilitate this basic function. In this plan merchandise comes in at the railroad siding

Figure 18–2

RAILROAD SIDING

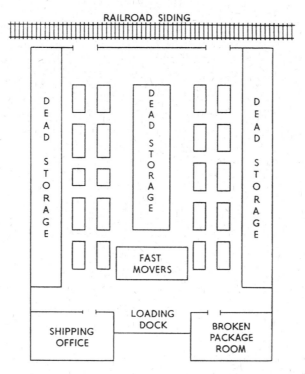

FLOOR PLAN—This plan illustrates a suggested arrangement for a one-story grocery warehouse. It incorporates such features as special dead-storage space, express lanes for fast-moving merchandise, complete rotation of stock, ease in keeping stock records, and other advantages discussed in the text. The same principles can be adapted to a multiple-story warehouse.

at the back, flows through the warehouse and out into trucks waiting at the loading dock. Certain conditions must be maintained for the goods handling machine to operate effectively, and several supplementary functions are therefore required which are also indicated on the chart.

In some types of warehouses storage might be regarded as the major function, but the purpose of dead storage is to facilitate assembly in the type of warehouse pictured here. It would not be efficient for the order picker to work directly from the main stocks held in dead storage. For one thing, he would have to cover too much ground in getting the order together. For another, merchandise in dead storage is piled to the ceiling to conserve space whereas maximum accessibility for order picking must be maintained along the assembly line. If there was a smooth flow of all items stocked into the warehouse, they could go directly into the assembly line. The wholesale grocery house receives many items in carload lots at infrequent intervals so that it is convenient to place these supplies in dead storage and draw on them as needed for the assembly line. The broken package room is for items which are ordered in less than case lots and which would not be practical to place in the assembly line once they had been removed from the original cases. The broken package room is usually a compact area in which the order picker takes individual boxes or cartons from bins which are arranged in a systematic fashion similar to the assembly line. The shipping office is the area in which invoices are prepared and the other clerical routines of goods handling take place.

Coming back to order assembly as the basic function of the warehouse, it should be noted that there will be hundreds or even thousands of items in the assembly line. Each of these has a definite station at which the item is always kept. Also fundamental for planning an efficient assembly line is a principle for selection of stations for the items. That principle is to locate each item in such a way as to minimize the total time and effort involved in assembling the average customer order. To illustrate this principle in its simplest form, first assume that the only factor affecting the cost of handling is the weight of the item. The assembly line might then be arranged so as to minimize the number of foot-pounds expended or the average distance that a pound of merchandise has to be moved in the process of order assembly. To accomplish this, items of greater than average weight and frequency of purchase would be placed near the loading dock. Items of lesser weight and frequency of purchase should go further back in the warehouse. Actually, the decision is not as simple as this because there are other factors besides weight to be given consideration. The combination of bulkiness and great frequency would also tend to move a product toward the end of the assembly line.

There has been an increasing degree of integration between the wholesale warehouse with its suppliers on the one hand and its customers on the other. Suppliers can facilitate the operations of the wholesaler by palletizing the merchandise at the factory. That means putting a number of cases on a movable platform so that a forklift truck can remove the pallet load from the freight car and transfer it directly into dead storage. In the case of corporate or voluntary chains, pallet loads of some products may be moved directly into the truck for delivery to the retail store.

Another aspect of integrated operations pertains to the order form passing from the retail store to the warehouse. This order form is laid out in precisely the same sequence as the merchandise on the assembly line in the warehouse. Thus, the same form or a duplicate of it guides the order picker in filling the order. This is a vast improvement over old-fashioned methods in which orders received from retailers were in no particular sequence and had to be rewritten and broken down into segments to be sent to the various departments. Grocery warehouses in those days typically occupied five or six floors as compared to the streamlined one-story warehouse today.

Clerical routines are integrated with physical handling in the modern warehouse by other means such as the use of punch-card tabulating equipment. In its simplest form this control system uses a file of such cards in which each card represents an item of merchandise. When cases are withdrawn from the inventory, corresponding cards are withdrawn from the card files. These cards then go into the tabulating machine which turns out the printed shipping invoices and at the same time calculates the changes in inventory for each of the items affected. There are now more advanced systems in which orders prepared by retail store managers are direct inputs activating the computer.

The principle of minimizing movement guides the whole functional design as well as the arrangement of stations for each function. The shipping office and the broken package room are each assigned to a compact space to minimize the movement required in carrying out their respective functions. Dead storage areas and order assembly areas parallel each other, thus facilitating the placing of supplies in dead storage near the point where they will ultimately be used in the assembly line. The internal arrangement of the assembly line in turn is intended to minimize movement in carrying out the primary function of order assembly. This principle of minimizing movement is always involved in spatial arrangements when the space is devoted to some physical operation such as order assembly. It will be seen that quite a different principle applies in planning display space as in a retail store.

While the type of spatial planning described here has been carried further in the grocery field, there has also been progress in dealing with the more complex handling problems of such lines as drugs and department store merchandise. Here the problem is complicated by the greater number of items, by the great variety in the physical character of the items, and by the fact that there is a large percentage of movement of individual packages rather than of the

original shipping cases. These factors naturally increase the cost
of physical distribution and impede the development of mechanical
handling methods which have progressed so far in the grocery field.
That progress will come is certain, however, and relatively speaking, the problems presented by these fields are no more forbidding
than those in the grocery field appeared a generation ago.

PLANNING THE USE OF DISPLAY SPACE

The use of space in a retail store is quite a different problem
from the use of space in a warehouse. Some of the same principles
still hold such as those concerned with sequence, size, and shape
of functional areas. There is a sharp contrast in the optimizing principle which applies in the use of space for display as compared to
order assembly. The optimum layout of a warehouse seeks to minimize the movement in the performance of the operating functions.
The optimum layout in a retail display seeks to maximize exposure
of the goods which are offered for sale. In a warehouse the operating personnel uses some areas with maximum frequency and others
with much less frequency. These differential frequencies are essential to the task of minimizing movement from area to area. In a
retail display space, layout is directed toward equalizing traffic
densities throughout the area.

In an operation such as order assembly, management has an
obvious interest in saving steps for its paid employees. Quite the
reverse is true when consumers assemble orders for themselves in
a self-service store. Management obviously wants to increase the
average size of an order, and to do this it would like to expose each
customer to all the merchandise in the store. This ideal aim is seldom realized even in such self-service stores as the modern supermarket. Nevertheless, it is good planning to lay out the display area
so as to approximate this ideal aim rather than obstructing it. The
arrangement of check-out counters, gondolas, and the relation of
the various departments to each other have a decided effect on the
path taken by the average shopper in making a purchase. The
objective is to achieve an even distribution of traffic throughout the
store approaching as nearly as possible to 100 percent of the total
coming through the front door.

As in the case of the grocery warehouse, the demonstration of
these arrangement principles can well begin with the consideration
of a prototype. This is the full scale model of a small self-service
store set up by the Department of Commerce in 1929 in connection
with the Louisville Grocery Survey. The floor plan of this store is

shown in the left-hand portion of Figure 18-3. This store was arranged on the assumption that the typical purchase would consist of a half dozen or more items of which some would be staples and others luxury or specialty foods. At that time many staples were still sold in bulk and required special wrapping or packaging. It was planned that these operations by the sales clerk should take place at a service counter in the rear. Thus the staple products and the clerical services needed for some of them were used to pull the customer all the way back into the store. Other products were arranged on open display shelves or islands along the aisles leading to the rear. The luxury items which the store was most eager

Figure 18-3

ARRANGEMENT OF SELF-SERVICE STORES

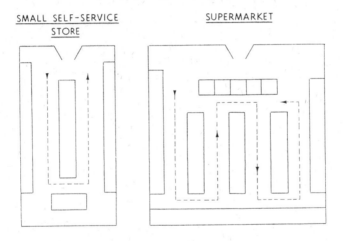

SMALL SELF-SERVICE STORE

SUPERMARKET

to sell were likely to be found in displays near the front where the customer would see them upon entering the store. There was likely to be some especially attractive display such as fresh fruits and vegetables on the right as the customer entered, with the cashier's station located on the left side. The customer who went down one aisle to the service counter and back the other aisle to the cashier would have had a chance to be exposed to every item in the store in following this pattern. These small and simply arranged self-service stores which followed this prototype came pretty near to achieving 100 percent traffic throughout the store. This small unit was a relatively efficient marketing machine thirty years ago with a smaller number of items to be displayed and a smaller average size of purchase. Once the self-service principle took on, it was rapidly expanded with stores of larger size having a wider and wider selection of products. The supermarkets first got major attention through price appeal during the great depression, but their real advantage to both consumer and producer turned out to be their efficiency in offering goods with an increased breadth of selection.

Some years later the principal remaining need for clerical service to the customer was solved by the introduction of precut meats. It now became typical for the customer to circulate through the store requiring no service until she came back to the check-out counter in the front. The increase in the size of the store was accompanied by an increase in the number of aisles and hence opened up a wider variety of possible paths which the customer might follow. Nevertheless, good arrangement still allowed for an ideal path by which the customer could be exposed to all the merchandise in the store as she passed each display once and only once. This ideal path is shown in the right-hand portion of Figure 18-3. This layout has four aisles as compared to the two aisles of the small self-service store. The ideal customer path is shown in dotted lines on each layout. The most efficient supermarkets today follow an arrangement similar to that illustrated in this sketch. Some customers may traverse only two of the aisles, others may traverse them in a different order than that shown, and some may go back again to a display which they first passed up without purchase. Nevertheless, the fact that the arrangement was made with an ideal path in mind leads to greater effectiveness than might otherwise be obtained.

Some of the difficulties which may be created by inferior arrangement are illustrated in Figure 18-4. On the left-hand side is the layout of a store with an odd number of aisles. In this layout no ideal path is possible. To put it another way, the path which would traverse all of the aisles ends in the far corner of the store and would thus require the customer to come out past displays that had already been visited. While this extra exposure is not without value, it is certainly inferior to the initial exposure to the display of each item in turn.

The right-hand side of the chart illustrates a widely used type of arrangement based on transverse aisles rather than longitudinal aisles. From the standpoint of the principles which have been discussed here, the transverse arrangement is definitely inferior to the longitudinal arrangement. No ideal path is feasible in a transverse arrangement. That is to say that a substantial retracing of steps is required after the customer has followed a path which takes her past all of the displays.

It should be further noted that the transverse arrangement creates a greater differential in shelf space values from the standpoint of the chance of their being seen by a customer entering the store. Thus the first gondola gets a degree of exposure not afforded to any one display in the longitudinal arrangement. Similarly, the fronts of the other gondolas in a descending scale have greater exposure than the displays on the back of each gondola because they are exposed first to the customer moving back into the store. This layout may have some value to the operator who is trying to maximize the sales of some products and minimize the sales of others. If he was doing this deliberately, he could exaggerate the effect still further by assigning relatively large shelf space to products displayed on the front of a gondola while crowding in many more displays into the comparable area along the back of a gondola.

Figure 18-4

DIVERGENT TYPES OF SUPERMARKET

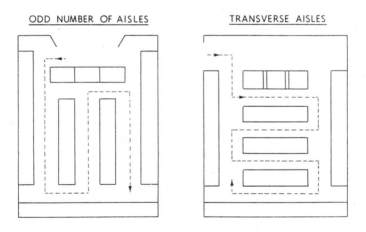

ODD NUMBER OF AISLES   TRANSVERSE AISLES

Some supermarket operators have observed that the longitudinal arrangement will prevail when two or more supermarkets are competing with each other at neighboring locations. In fact, some national chains which leaned toward the transverse arrangement have been known to adopt the longitudinal arrangement to match the prevailing pattern in specific shopping centers. This competitive phenomenon reflects the fact that the longitudinal arrangement is more efficient from the standpoint of the shopper. It will also accommodate a greater number of shoppers without creating congestion. The longitudinal arrangement moves the traffic back into the store more rapidly and distributes it more evenly over the total space. In the transverse arrangement shoppers with their carts are constantly moving in and out of the main aisle through which others are moving toward the back of the store. Thus they are compelled by the arrangement itself to get in each other's way, whereas a constant stream of customers following the ideal path could move through a store with an even number of longitudinal aisles with no intersection of their individual paths. This ideal result will never be achieved because of the diversity of paths but it can be approximated in one case while it is impossible in the other.

At this point the two optimization principles in the use of space appear to require some reconciliation. It turns out that the management cannot ignore the viewpoint of the individual moving through the space even though the individual is a customer and not a paid employee. The path must be efficient at least for the ideal aim of moving past all of the separate displays. If the operator attempts to go further in manipulating the stream of traffic, he is likely to create undesirable congestion and get less than optimum use of the display area. By striving too hard to control the character of the purchase, he may end up by decreasing the total amount of exposure, particularly if he is confronted with competitors who make it easier for the consumer to shop.

The discussion so far has used the arrangement problem in the self-service food store for illustration. The problem is different in other types of stores, depending on such factors as the number of items typically purchased on a single shopping trip. Thus the drug store services customers who typically buy one or two items at a time as compared with the twelve or fourteen which are typical in the modern supermarket. If the drug store tried to use items of frequent purchase to pull customers all the way back into the store, the tobacco department would always be in the rear. Actually it is usually in the front. The customers of this department typically buy a single item, such as a package of cigarettes, on a single trip. They require maximum convenience and, given the option, would tend to desert the store which made them walk all the way back to buy. Even if they could be induced to walk back, little could be gained from the standpoint of the operator since there is little chance of their buying other items, and the additional traffic would simply create useless congestion. It is more to the point for the fountain and the prescription department to be located farther back since customers patronizing these departments are going to be in the store for a longer time, with greater chance of exposure to other items. It is still possible to use the arts of store planning and display to disperse traffic through a drug store, but the operator must depend more on the power of display itself rather than on the placement of staple items.

The arrangement and display problems of a department store are still more complex, but the same principle still holds as to maximum exposure, subject to proper regard for consumer convenience. There has been an increasing tendency to place departments and to classify merchandise to suit the requirements of groups of customers rather than according to the physical nature of the goods. Thus, some stores now tend to put all dresses of the same size on the same rack rather than grouping them by style or price class. Since it is the size which determines fundamentally whether a given shopper can use a dress, it is generally more convenient for the shopper who wants a given size to find all of the items of that size together. The department store falls somewhere between the food store and the drug store with respect to the number of items likely to be purchased on a single trip. Certain departments tend to be placed on the first floor because the average shopper in these departments is not so likely to be interested in any other item on a given trip. The departments generally represent decreasing frequencies of shopper visits from one floor up to the next one. There is not much point in putting departments of most frequent visit at the top since customers going up to these departments in an elevator are not exposed thereby to the merchandise on the lower floors as they pass them. On the other hand, services of various kinds such as restaurants and the credit department are likely to be placed on upper floors as a way of using space less valuable for merchandising purposes.

The same principles of optimizing use of space apply to specialty stores. Even in a store where all merchandise is relatively expensive, such as a jewelry store, there are some departments selling merchandise more luxurious than others. Thus the diamond department is usually up front as the prestige department by which the store can register an impression of quality on its customers. Watches too are likely to be toward the front, although frequently watch repairs are to the rear, thus requiring the person who comes in for service to move past all of the merchandise displays to reach the repair department. Sterling flatware is a relatively staple item and a relatively large consumer of space; therefore it usually tends to be toward the middle or toward the rear of the store. Specialty stores in the downtown area have a particular problem of equalizing store traffic because of the attitude of the typical shopper in a crowded downtown section. There is often a tendency to dash in and out of a number of stores rather than getting full exposure to the displays of any one. Here is a case where the visual power of displays in the rear of the store must be given maximum effect along with any staple or service requirements that can be used to draw customers to the rear.

PLANNED SHOPPING CENTERS

Another area of spatial planning is in the development of new retail shopping centers. Many new shopping centers have been created in this way, some in what was previously open country miles from the city. The combined merchandising power of the participating retailers may be great enough to create their own traffic. In the most successful cases there has been a whole complement of services and entertainment facilities as well as retail stores to attract customers to the location. A strong enough attraction must be generated to reverse the established tendency for the shopper to travel toward the center city to reach either a subcenter or the downtown area. A major inducement, of course, is the possibility of reaching a satisfactory shopping center without encountering higher density traffic and of finding ample parking on arrival.

Planning of the shopping center has evolved some principles and yardsticks which seem to be widely applicable. One yardstick is the ratio of parking space to the selling area making up the retail center. The appropriate ratio for a given center can be calculated by estimating the number of customers who will arrive by car during the peak hour and multiplying by the amount of parking space required per car. Generally, it has seemed essential for parking space to be visible and immediately accessible from the main artery. It is difficult to induce shoppers to use perfectly good parking space behind the stores. An exception might be a multi-story parking facility which was tied in directly with a major store. Many centers have developed with buildings in an L-shaped formation with a large parking area between the buildings and the street. This standard pattern is especially prevalent for those planned centers which are built to capitalize on the traffic of a main artery. The centers which undertake to generate their own traffic are more diversified in design and innovations are continuously occurring to give them greater drawing power.

A middle position in planning outlying centers is to put in large enough facilities immediately to reach an acceptable minimum level of shopping traffic, but at the same time counting on substantial future growth. The original hard core of retail facilities would usually include one or more supermarkets and a branch department store. Such a plan should start from a reasonable forecast of what the center might look like ten years ahead. The initial development should be made in such a way as to constitute the first step toward the more fully developed center. This means leaving space for the projected expansion of the major enterprises which form the original hard core. It also means preserving rigid standards for any secondary enterprises, selecting them for their place in the eventual pattern rather than for contribution to immediate volume.

THE LOCATIONAL PATTERN

The location of warehouses, stores, and retail shopping centers present problems which will be commented on only briefly here. The concept of the nucleated network can now be extended to the service area of the central unit, such as a warehouse supplying a cluster of retail stores. Each store is a node or station along the loop constituting a delivery route and the planner enjoys considerable flexibility in determining the sequences to be followed. Suppose, however, that the customers call for goods as in a cash-and-carry wholesale warehouse, a retail store, or a shopping center. There is now a loop corresponding to each customer with two nodes, one at the customer's location and one at the service center.

The planner must now take account of all of these customer paths and locate his store or warehouse so as to minimize effort on the part of the customers he hopes to serve. The ideal location is not necessarily at the geographical center of the area which may not correspond with the vortex of customary paths. On the other hand, it may not be precisely in the vortex partly because such a site might not be available. More important theoretically, leaving out the question of availability, is the problem of entry into the service location from the various directions of approach. Thus the planner needs to think in terms of customer convenience in reaching the location versus convenience in entering or using it. The preferred location represents the best compromise of these and other factors.

A recent study of the location pattern for chain supermarkets raised the question of whether a particular chain would go into a neighborhood primarly because his competitors were already there or primarily because they were not there. The question was difficult to answer because of the overriding tendency of supermarkets as a group to be distributed in relation to the purchasing power of the community. That is to say that if purchasing power is high in a neighborhood, the volume of food business and also the number of supermarkets will be higher than average. Sometimes several stores are found in the same block, and at other times they are scattered as if they had tried to avoid direct competition.

The question concerning location strategy makes sense if a distinction is drawn between the advantage of location and differential advantage in merchandising power. If locational advantage is the primary consideration, the planner would concentrate on finding neighborhoods within his trading radius which were not adequately served by competitors. This was doubtless the ruling principle in the earlier stages of supermarket development. Today many areas are described by experts in the field as "over stored" in relation to community purchasing power. At the present time it would be hard to find an urban community without supermarkets, but a given chain might be prepared to expand into the community nevertheless. The rationale for putting in new stores in direct competition with others would be a belief in the chain's superior merchandising power. It might reason that the important thing was to blanket the areas with stores so that everyone who read the newspaper advertising could find a convenient store in which to buy from this chain. It would locate its stores in relation to the lanes of consumer traffic and without regard to the proximity of competitive stores. There are two contrasting optimizing principles at work. In one case the chain would be trying to make an optimal selection of one site after another, judging each on its own merits. In the other case it would be striving to complete a locational network so as to maximize the use of its merchandising power for a given metropolitan area.

Planning for a branch sales office is quite unlike the planning of a large general office. In the latter case internal traffic is the paramount consideration, and the same basic principles can be applied as in the planning of a warehouse or a supermarket. In the general office, where many indivduals must work together, the planner is attempting to optimize controlled or purposeful communication. The structural principles employed are the same as in other types of spatial planning. Access comes first and must be related to central and secondary control centers. Functional balance must be achieved among uses for executive offices, clerical offices, conference rooms, and various service areas.

In the branch sales office personnel is presumed to spend a limited amount of time in the office and more time on customer calls. The primary problem is location in a convenient city for coverage of the territory or sales district and location in a part of the city that facilitates travel by the means most commonly employed, whether train, plane, or automobile. The planner should think of the branch sales office as a node or control point in the channel of communication from headquarters to customers. A firm schedule for hours to be spent in the office as well as out will facilitate communication from headquarters by telephone or personal visit. Sales districts have tended to become somewhat larger where there is a substantial flow of technical information from headquarters to facilitate that link in the communication channel. There is an obvious connection between this type of spatial planning and the planning of a marketing organization to be discussed in the next chapter.

MARKET SEGMENTATION FOR COORDINATION AND CONTROL

Breaking down the national market into workable segments is a prerequisite for the deployment of manpower or other resources and for the enforcement of standards thereafter. The segments most generally used are geographic areas. The basic problem is to divide the country into geographical units which can be handled on a more or less uniform basis. The smallest units may be salesmen's territories each designed to occupy the full time of one or more salesmen. These units in turn may be grouped into sales districts or marketing regions corresponding to higher levels of marketing responsibility or to other aspects of the marketing operation.

The determination of territorial units must take account of sectional diversity from one section of the country to another. These elements include varying densities of population, per capita incomes, and other factors affecting demand for a given product. Ideally it should be possible to assign every salesman a territory with the same expectation of return and the same costs as every other territory. In practice this is impossible because of travel time and other elements of cost which run relatively much higher in some parts of the country than others. Thus, the total population as of 1960 is about the same for the states of Ohio and Texas. Yet if each state constituted a sales territory, the salesman in Texas would have to travel about four times as far to cover his territory. There has been a significant shift of population toward the western half of the United States, and this shift is still continuing. Nevertheless, there are some real limits on any future shift because of the large extent of mountains and deserts in the western states.

There is a very basic optimization principle to be employed in dividing the market of the United States into any type of administrative areas for marketing. At bottom this is the economic principle of equating marginal costs with marginal returns. Management usually desires to cover the country as intensively as possible in order to maximize its sales. There is a limit on the number of sales territories that would be economical, however, corresponding to the point at which the additional cost of putting another salesman in the field would be more than the additional revenue which this salesman would produce. This principle will probably be a little more obvious to marketing management when expressed in organization terms. If a company has too few salesmen, it will not be possible to call on all prospects or to call on them with adequate frequency. If the company has too many salesmen, there is no room for the individual salesman to improve his performance and relatively little incentive for him to try. Thus planning market coverage may need to start out from a fundamental judgment as to the right number of salesmen. In fact, it will usually start one step further back with a consideration of the optimum number of distributors if the company does not plan to sell retailers directly. In determining the right number of distributors, the opposing factors of coverage and incentive are similarly involved.

In considering market coverage the planner must deal with the problem of making a meaningful analysis of statistical data on a geographical basis. States or counties can be ranked by population size, by spendable income, or by some other factor bearing on the market for a given product. Statistical correlations can also be calculated relating one or all these factors to past sales of a product or a product type. Statistical studies of this kind leave out one factor which is crucial for laying out sales territories, namely, the factor of proximity. Thus there are some similarities, for example, between Lancaster County, Pennsylvania, and Yakima County, Washington in their outstanding importance in agricultural production. They cannot, of course, be covered by the same salesmen since they are at opposite ends of the country. This and related analytical problems will be discussed in the next section.

The most elementary difficulty in relating statistics to geography arises from the fact that such units as states are so completely unalike as to area, population and income, or any other factor affecting marketing potential. Neither does a state have any functional significance for marketing since it is purely a political entity with boundaries established by historical accident. Suppose the planner wishes to display certain market information on an outline map of the United States of the usual 8½ × 11 working size. He may wish to color in red those areas that are believed to provide the best market for the specified product. In the particular case this might mean that New Mexico and the District of Columbia would fall in this class of preferred markets. It happens that their populations were almost identical as of 1960. Yet New Mexico is one of the larger states and would form a large patch of red on the map. The District of Columbia, on the other hand, is an area of less than ten miles square and therefore would scarcely be more than a pencil point on the same map. It is difficult for the analyst using such visual methods to correct for the bias inherent in such geographical disparities.

Some years ago a very popular device was the distorted map. That is to say, maps were prepared in which the size of the state did not reflect its physical area but some other value such as population or spendable income. Such maps have a certain value simply in calling attention to the concentrated markets in more densely populated areas. They were not particularly helpful in developing trading areas or sales territories. In planning market coverage the analyst must be constantly aware of size, shape, and proximity of areas as well as of their relative importance as potential markets.

A much more effective planning device for some purposes is that of dividing the country into areas that are equal by population or by some other general measure of market potential. Considerable use has been made in planning, of a map dividing the country into ten areas of equal population. Such a map has to be revised from time to time because of the relative population decline of areas such as New England and the corresponding relative increase in the West and Southwest. The map shown in Figure 18–5 is based on an estimated population as of the beginning of 1962. While each area is very close to 10 percent of the continental population of the United States, other considerations have entered where the deviation from this standard was very small. Thus state boundaries have been followed wherever possible as in regions 6, 7, and 8. It is desirable, of course, to minimize the extent to which any totals have to be calculated starting with county figures. On the map, as shown, only two states have been split; namely, New York and Pennsylvania.

In devising this map an effort was made to keep the regions as compact as possible. The principal exception would be region 10, the Mountain region. In this map there is some geographical and historical basis to justify the division of the country along the lines shown. About half of the total population is located in the five easternmost areas. This has long been the most densely settled part of the country and will continue to be even though it is declining in

Figure 18–5

TEN REGIONS WITH APPROXIMATELY EQUAL POPULATION
ESTIMATES FOR 1962

relative importance. Region 8 alone is more than half as large as these five eastern regions combined. Region 9 is nearly twice as large.

The planner might use this map as a tool in laying out sales territories. Suppose a decision had been made to divide the country into 100 territories which would be an average of ten for each region. This number might be about the right allocation for a region with average population density, but it would need to be adjusted elsewhere. It might take 13 or 14 salesmen to cover region 9 because of the distances to be traveled. By contrast, 6 or 7 salesmen might be able to cover region 2 with equal intensity. In the latter case half of the salesmen would doubtless be occupied within New York City itself. It is clear that it is not possible to make assignments with perfect equity if the entire national market is to be covered. Some salesmen will have a smaller potential than others and will have to be away from home for longer periods to cover it. The value of the suggested device is as a means of giving effect to equality of tasks as one of the criteria.

Within a region the planner carves out the required number of roughly equal segments of the market, taking account of such further considerations as compactness and ready access from some major center in which the salesman will probably reside. Thus in region 8, the possible centers would include Dallas, Houston, Oklahoma City, Tulsa, and New Orleans. The chief problem from a travel viewpoint would be presented by Western Texas. This portion of Texas is sparsely settled and might be covered by a salesman residing in one of the smaller cities such as Amarillo. For some other type of product dependent mainly on an urban market, these places might be covered by occasional visits of salesmen working out of Dallas or New Orleans. At one time the planner would have given considerable weight to rail connections in assigning sections of territory, but the main consideration today would be the highway network around the city chosen as a center.

The principle of using equal area maps has been illustrated in terms of total population. Other series could be used when regarded as more appropriate for particular products. Current data or up-to-date estimates are available for urban population, spendable income, and retail sales, either total or classified by nine groups such as food, drugs, or general merchandise. One of the standard sources is in the annual "Survey of Buying Power" published by *Sales Management*. These figures are available by counties as well as state totals. The map shown would require subtotals for only two split states.

WHOLESALE AND RETAIL TRADING AREAS

In selecting intermediaries such as wholesalers, the planner must often go back to facts about the coverage of territory out of each wholesale center. This is particularly important if exclusive franchises are to be given to wholesalers and a selection is to be made so as to cover the complete national market. Even when an open distribution policy is followed, it may still be desirable to limit calls on wholesalers to the minimum number of trading centers required for total coverage.

More than thirty years ago the U.S. Department of Commerce prepared and published its *Atlas of Wholesale Grocery Territories*. The territories shown are chiefly of historical interest today because of continuing changes in the geography of grocery distribution. The principles employed in mapping territories remain unchanged. First a selection of centers had to be made, employing objective criteria as to the amount of wholesaling done and the completeness of the assortments and services offered. The service criterion would today include overnight delivery to any point in the territory. To accomplish this result, smaller trading centers would have to be included in the western states than on the thickly settled Eastern Seaboard. Thus Amarillo, Texas or Grand Junction, Colorado are more essential trading centers in some respects than much larger places in the East.

Once the selection of centers has been made, the problem is the allocation of territory among them. On the line connecting any two neighboring centers a point must be chosen as determining the boundary between them. This will tend to be the midpoint in time and cost rather than by physical distance only. This distinction has tended to disappear as the highway network around each center has been extended and has taken on increasing relative importance. Wholesale territories which were once elongated, following stretches of transcontinental railway, have become more compact.

SPECIAL PROBLEMS IN PLANNING COVERAGE

Some sales organizations have coverage problems which are considerably more complex than the assignment of territories and districts which has been discussed. Such problems arise in handling special types of markets or customers such as industrial plants, construction projects, and governmental agencies. Some problems lie in the peculiar character of the geographical pattern of these markets and others in the nature of the sales task. The latter consideration may lead to the use of several types of salesmen or to the segmentation of the market on other than geographical lines.

Industrial consumers in some categories are dispersed almost as broadly as household consumers. In other industrial classifications they may be limited to a single geographical region or to major metropolitan markets. This introduces special difficulties of relating statistical information to geography. There is a tendency, for example, for a firm which already has coverage of the industrial market in a given number of cities to want to add salesmen or distributors in additional cities. Analytical studies often show that what is needed is more diversified coverage in the same markets rather than coverage in additional markets.

An even more fundamental problem of choice in planning industrial coverage is whether to specialize salesmen by area, by product, or by type of industry. The argument for specialization by industry is based on the assumption that the needs of a given industry are highly specialized and that the salesmen who are well acquainted with one industry cannot deal so effectively with another. Some chemical firms, for example, have a special group of salesmen to cover the rubber industry, which is a field with its own peculiar technology and a tightly knit set of contacts. This type of argument becomes less compelling as major companies broaden their fields just as the rubber manufacturers have branched out into plastics and many other types of products.

Another possibility in industrial market coverage is to have salesmen specialize in handling individual products or product groups. The argument for this approach is particularly strong when a product is in a period of development and introduction. It is at this point that detailed technical knowledge of the product is most vital in promoting its sale. It is not efficient generally to depend on specialized salesmen once the product is widely known and generally accepted. Since this is the case, it will not often be possible to set up a specialized sales force for temporary use during the period of introduction. Major companies have solved this problem in various ways. One is to have a separately organized sales development department whose job is to deal with one new product after another during the stage of introduction. Another is to depend on the regular sales staff to introduce a new product but to provide them with the support of a technical specialist who can be sent out from headquarters to help them with special sales problems.

Many large companies maintain separate sales forces for several product groups or divisions. The controlling consideration here is a judgment as to the number of products which an individual salesman is able to know well enough to sell and service with equal efficiency. In particular cases a company may sell two products which have competitive or directly conflicting claims, as, for example, a coffee and a coffee substitute. In such cases a salesman could scarcely be expected to present both products with equal conviction and enthusiasm. Another consideration which tends toward dividing the sales assignment by product groups is that two groups of products may be sold to essentially different groups of customers and prospects. Thus, if two salesmen are going to call on different classes of people and talk about quite different products, it can turn out to be more efficient than strictly territorial assignments.

Selling to the construction field is closely related to industrial selling, but there are some significant differences which affect the planning of marketing coverage. For one thing the contractor works on a project basis, and his projects may be scattered across the country or at least over a large geographical region. The generation of leads has special importance in the construction field, and various continuing services have been established to fill this need. As in industrial selling, there may be a number of people involved in specifying the materials and components which are to go into a construction project. In the case of construction there is the further complication that the group affecting the sale, including the contractor, the architect, and the client, changes from one job to the next. This situation is met in part by detailed planning for each major project. Several types of selling are usually involved, including service selling to the contractor with a regular schedule of sales calls. At the same time major products are covered by specialized approaches to other specifiers such as the architect or the client for whom the building is being built.

Selling to governmental agencies partakes of all the difficulties which have been mentioned for both industrial and construction markets. In addition, there are problems of regulation and government procedure to be met. The individual salesman must be, among other things, a procedural specialist. Government regulations can present difficulties either because they are strictly enforced or because of laxity in administration. In the latter case the salesman always faces the hazard that his competitor will be the beneficiary of the departures from the fixed legal requirements. There are various policies to be adopted in covering such a market, but perhaps the wisest in the long run is to keep a close watch for deviations while trying not to become involved in them. In all these special fields good market coverage must be guided by current and reliable information about market developments. To a considerable extent what is needed in dealing with contractors and with industrial and governmental purchasing agents is an effective intelligence service as well as marketing research in the ordinary sense.

SUMMARY

Spatial planning attempts to provide a favorable environment for marketing activities usually involving intensive occupancy by either goods or people. There is an appropriate optimizing principle for each type of facility. The aim in the warehouse is to minimize the movement of goods and hence the cost of order-handling. In retailing, the aim is to maximize the movement of customers and hence their exposure to goods. In the retail shopping center the optimizing principle might be stated as maximizing the time in the presence of goods as compared to time spent traveling and parking. Appropriate optimizing principles can be stated for each type of spatial planning situation. The structural principles for achieving effective optimization are to be sought in the successive planning stages dealing with proximity, area, and site.

There is a time dimension in all spatial planning, since the operation to be carried on in an area is usually changing constantly. Any physical facility may start to become obsolete from the day it is completed. Thus it is usually wise for the planner to think of what space will be needed ten years ahead as well as in the immediate future. There are various ways of preserving flexibility or at least taking the need for change into account. One of the virtues of the one-story warehouse which has not always been recognized is the relative ease of expanding or rearranging it, so long as an ample site was acquired in the first instance. The long-run goal for the spatial planning of any activity is that the activity which takes place in the space should be housed in a way that approaches optimality as close as possible over the longer period. The planning of changes and the timing of the occupation of new facilities is a more or less continuous preoccupation of the planner in a growing business.

Selected References

Louisville Grocery Survey, 1930–32, and *National Drug Store Survey*, 1932–34. Washington, D.C.: U.S. Department of Commerce, U.S. Government Printing Office.
   Sections dealing with store layout and design principles in grocery stores and drug stores.
MESEROLE, W. H. *Streamlined Wholesale Grocery Warehouses.* Washington, D.C.: Industrial Series No. 18, U.S. Department of Commerce, 1945.
   Presents principles of spatial arrangement in grocery warehouses. A classic in its field.
MESEROLE, W. H. "Warehouses and Computers," *Marketing and the Computer.* (WROE ALDERSON AND STANLEY SHAPIRO, eds.). Englewood Cliffs, N.J., Prentice-Hall, Inc., 1963.
   Discusses food distribution facilities and the use of computers in operation and control of an integrated system.
Seven Common Profit Leaks in Truck Transportation. Pontiac, Mich. Transportation Productivity Research Department, General Motors Corp., Truck and Coach Division, 1962.
   Experiences in the design of truck fleets to meet specific requirements.

Problems

1. Contrast the optimizing principle which applies to the use of space for order assembly and for display.

2. Using the principles of optimal display outlined in the chapter, contrast the use of transverse aisles and longitudinal aisles in a supermarket.

3. A certain department store is known to conduct 88c sales periodically. In this type of sale various household items are sold at 88c regardless of their regular selling price. These items are displayed in the center aisle on the first floor of a three-story building. Discuss the advantages and disadvantages of this type of display policy.

4. Discuss the use of equal areas of population maps as an aid to the planner who is interested in market segmentation for purposes of coordination and control.

5. Discuss the arguments for specialization of industrial salesmen by area, by product, and by type of industry.

Chapter 19

DESIGNING MARKETING ORGANIZATIONS

~~~~~~

Of the four end-products of planning, the most intriguing design problems in many ways are encountered in the design of organizations. Sometimes a new generation of leadership is required to bring about the fundamental changes in organization structure which are required by the new functions and new opportunities in the business. This is the area in which the company is most dependent on outside consulting organizations for help. A major reorganization is both technically difficult and politically sensitive. It is hard to be a part of an organization and at the same time maintain an objective attitude toward organization changes.

This book deals with planning in marketing, and this emphasis will be maintained. Nevertheless there are organization problems which must be considered in a broader framework than marketing. Thus it is scarcely feasible to confine the discussion to marketing organization aside from the other business functions. To some extent the chapter will be looking at general organization problems but from a marketing perspective.

OPTIMIZING PRINCIPLES

In the chapter on design principles two separate principles were stated for optimizing the decision power of organizations. The first principle was that of maximizing expected values. This is not a principle which can always be applied in precise quantitative fashion because of the difficulties in measuring the expected values of an organization. Yet it would be possible to identify organizations which would rank relatively high or relatively low in decision power. At the upper end of the scale are firms which tend to act promptly and effectively and to bring the coordinated impact of the total organization to bear when faced with a major issue. Such an organization would be in touch with the facts which constituted the problem situation and would move swiftly in gathering other information necessary for action.

Organizations with low decision power would be of several types. In one case inertia and procrastination delay decision. In another, internal conflict makes it difficult to act effectively. In another, weak leadership is unable to inspire confidence in its goals and policies. In still another situation, management lacks the information which might enable it to act with assurance.

The second optimizing principle is actually only another way of stating the first principle. It says that departures from policy should be minimized if the organization is well designed. This means that policies should be realistically adapted to the facts of the operating environment to merit observance. But it also means that faithful adherence to established policy should be inculcated. A good policy is one that does not invite frequent exceptions. A competent executive is one who is skilled in interpreting policy to meet the particular situation. Thus an organization designed to minimize policy exceptions would be one in which decision power tended to be maximized. The first emphasizes the initial generation of decision power and the second its preservation in the face of the usual temptations to deviate from established practice.

STRUCTURAL PRINCIPLES OF DESIGN

The first principle mentioned with respect to the design of an organization hierarchy is the need to balance span of control against levels of control. If span is increased, a more horizontal structure results. If the number of levels is increased, the tendency is toward a more vertical structure. In the first case the top executive is attempting to participate in underlying decisions on every front. In the second case there is a screening of issues for decision at each level with the top executive involved primarily in questions of essential strategy.

Actually the situation is a good deal more complex in the design of organization hierarchy. Instead of a single principle of design, there are several design principles competing for the attention of the designer. Possibly the most basic has to do with the type of structure to be adopted rather than with span versus levels. There are three principle possibilities. The structure may be divided primarily by business functions, by product lines, or by customer groups. The division along functional lines usually serves very well for a small or middle-sized company, and a few very large ones retain this basic structure. That is to say that there is a single production department, a single marketing department, and a single finance department. As the company expands and becomes more oriented to an advancing technology, a research and development department rounds out the basic structure.

Even at this early stage of development, all three aspects of structure are necessarily recognized in the design. While the primary division is by functions, the functional departments other than finance may in turn be broken down by product lines with product managers set up in the marketing department and with some coordination along product lines in both production and research and development. Finally the field organization in marketing recognizes groups of customers whether divided by region or by consuming industry.

As the company becomes larger and more diversified, the functional structure often yields to a primary division by product lines. If these product lines are made in separate plants and marketed to substantially different customers, it is customary for each product division to be granted a considerable degree of autonomy. It is usually assumed that they can be regarded as separate profit centers and held responsible separately for return on investment. Under a structure by product divisions each division in turn is usually structured by functions with its own marketing, production, and research and development. Finance is now split between managerial accounting, at the divisional level, and central financial control at the top. Research and development may also come to be divided between basic research attached to central headquarters and development and application in the product divisions. Organization by customer group may again be either by region or by consuming industry.

Finally there is the type of organization which has a number of semi-independent regional divisions each geared to serving customers in its market. This structure is customary in the container and packaging field and also in retailing. The partition of operations in each of these regional units usually runs along functional lines. Product considerations are minimized relative to customers and functions. In retailing, the product line is largely determined by the regional buyers subject to overall product line policy emanating from the central headquarters. In the container field the product aspect is fused with service considerations for the customer in such a way as almost to disappear as a separate basis of organization. Research on new materials and methods is likely to remain a central staff function at headquarters.

In summary it can be said that every organization gives recognition in some form to function, products, and customers. The level at which they are appropriately recognized depends on the size and type of organization. On the marketing side in particular all three aspects of structure usually appear. Since marketing as such is basically involved in matching customer needs with products and services, these two aspects are fundamental. But further than that, there is nearly always a breakdown by subfunctions such as field sales, advertising, and marketing research. Within marketing the breakdown by subfunctions usually takes precedence over product considerations and customer considerations but there still remains a problem of balance. Thus a fundamental structural principle of design can be stated both for marketing and for business organization in general. "First try to strike a balance between function, product, and customer considerations, recognizing each at an appropriate level in the organization."

In finding this condition of balance the planner recognizes that the greatest need for integration is at the lower levels of organization. When he makes the first partition at the top into product divisions, it is on the assumption that marketing, production, and research and development will have to work very closely together within each product division to achieve their targets in return on investment. When he makes the first partition along functional lines, it is on the assumption that the company cannot be broken down by true profit centers, because many products can be made on the same machines and sold by the same salesmen so that the greatest need is for maximum flexibility in assigning men and machines to various parts of the total task.

There are some executives who feel that the partitioning of companies into autonomous product or regional divisions has gone too far and that the notion of a profit center is spurious at least for their companies. It is admitted, however, that if functional organization is to be restored to its place at the top, there must be a maximum use of the new devices for communication and control such as electronic computers. This pattern might tend to minimize the role of middle management with a more direct and mechanized connection between the top level of management and the detailed activities for every product or customer group.

The issue of centralization versus decentralization is important, but it is hard to say whether it is an independent issue, since it overlaps with the two design principles which have already been stated. Centralization tends to correspond with a vertical power pyramid, and decentralization, with a relatively flat power pyramid. In other words, the first requires more levels of control, and the second, a greater span of control. There is also a relationship between the centralization–decentralization issue and the placing of primary emphasis on function, product, or customer considerations. Functional partition at the top is usually associated with centralization, and partition by product lines or customer groups, with decentralization. As organizations expand through diversification, there may be adjustments in all of these aspects of design to meet the new requirements. For example, it might shift from functional to product partition, add new levels of control, decentralize some functions, and centralize others.

Finally, the establishment of an appropriate balance between line and staff is a classic issue in designing the organization hierarchy or power pyramid. Organizations differ greatly as to the relative importance of these two phases of the business and the level at which staff work is concentrated. One point of view which has been expressed as a formula is, "Decentralize line operations and centralize staff." These design decisions will depend on the conception of the separate roles of line and staff or, more specifically, what is the primary function of staff. A somewhat novel viewpoint will be expounded here, namely, that staff provides a secondary channel which is often essential for effective operation. Staff should not be regarded as a consulting or advisory group standing to one side of the main stream and connected only with the office of the executive to which it reports. It is a secondary line of communication between an executive and his subordinates, but it is not a line of command. It is an analytical channel through which the more difficult decisions are generated rather than a channel for announcing decisions already taken.

The proper positioning of staff activities in marketing can be illustrated by marketing research and by marketing planning. Marketing research is a secondary channel for communicating with customers. Management asks questions through this channel and receives answers which are probably more reliable than would be obtained by gathering salesmen's opinions. Salesmen can be reliable sources of information on particular problems in the field or on the prospects for maintaining or increasing volume in their territories. It is not their function or their natural bent to probe for reasons why or the factors underlying demand. Nevertheless, the top executive is often obliged to rely on the opinions of the line organization which are quickly available. He may get a better answer from his market research staff, but it will probably take months rather than hours.

A planning staff in the marketing department should be regarded as a secondary line of communication between the top marketing executive and his line organization. The planner standing between the two gets a feeling for desirable goals from his superior and talks to line executives at lower levels before deciding what is feasible. This is a very different conception from that of being closed off in an advisory group to which only the top executive has access. The planner should be encouraged or, indeed, directed to talk to persons further down the ladder in the course of developing a plan. The secondary channel is again a way of getting better answers even though it will take longer to get them. Line executives may be sufficiently decisive and prepared to take action as soon as the word is received from the top. Once a plan has been prepared and installed, the line officers can move with greater assurance by acting in accordance with a plan.

A word may be said at this point about the use of committees in business organizations. A committee is the most appropriate means for communication horizontally just as a staff unit is the most appropriate channel for secondary or analytical communication in a vertical direction. Committees are most effective if they are made up of independent and coequal members. They can be used to establish agreement and coordination among the various functions in support of any plan of action. They are less likely to serve any useful purpose if they are drawn from various levels of responsibility with the subordinates of a given executive sitting with him as full-fledged members of the same committee. Some organizations which have made good use of committees appoint a staff man as committee secretary. In the intervals between meetings the staff man prepares data as requested to be presented at the next meeting. The members of the committee make use of these data in arriving at decisions and instruct the secretary on what more they will need to know in order to reach a decision.

INTEGRATION OF LINE AND STAFF

Staff personnel might be said to provide the connective tissue in an organization in which line personnel constitutes the skeleton. It is easier to represent a skeletal structure in graphic form so that the usual organization chart tends to emphasize the line disproportionately. The natural way to display the line structure is in the form of a power pyramid reflecting authority and responsibility. The staff structure could best be shown as a flow chart in which the staff man receives information from one source and passes it on, perhaps, after subjecting it to analytical processing. In the case of the staff planner he may obtain information from both sources and present his final results to both parties. In any case, information flows usually can be shown as complete feedback circuits while the line structure emphasizes delegation of authority from top to bottom.

Figure 19–1 shows various ways of positioning staff in an organization conceived primarily in terms of a line structure. A three-level organization is shown which might represent the central executive office, product divisions and sectional units within the divisions. The three structures bear letter designations for convenient reference.

Figure 19–1

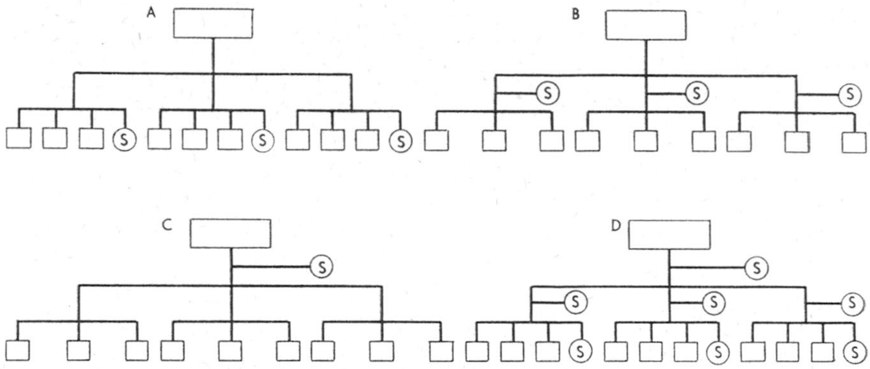

In *A*, staff appears only at the section level, in *B* at division level, in *C* at headquarters only, and in *D* staff activities appear at all three levels. There are arguments for each of these structures in given situations. *A* might be a case in which staff was concerned with market research only in divisions which had quite distinctive marketing problems. In *B* the presumption would be that the staff group was concerned with coordinating the activities of the section through planning. In *C* all staff activities are concentrated at headquarters. Since staff is concerned with information, there is argument for putting it at the center where all flows of information converge. But in this structure the division heads may be hampered by the lack of anyone to whom they can make analytical assignments. Quite often staff is found at two points in the structure or even at all three. The concern of management now is the possibility that staff activities will get out of hand, representing a continuing rise in overhead costs. It is more difficult, at least in theory, to assess the value of staff activities than to measure performance of the line. If staff units are kept small, wherever they are placed, they can often be justified on the basis of the amount of time saved for the responsible line executive who might otherwise feel compelled to undertake protracted analytical projects for himself. Eventually it may be possible to place more satisfactory yardsticks on staff activities. In principle it should be possible to compare the cost of obtaining information with the benefits through increasing the probability that the correct decision will be made.

DUTIES AND PERSONNEL

The other structural principles mentioned in the chapter on design were concerned with duties and with the assignment of specific personnel. The usual aim is to define duties clearly and concisely so that each man will know where his responsibility begins and ends. It is not always possible to realize this ideal. It is certainly better to have some overlapping in responsibilities than to leave gaps between positions with no one knowing exactly where a given responsibility falls. The technique of management through conflict is sometimes nothing more than making overlapping assignments in the hope that one party or the other will exercise the given responsibility and the issues will be thoroughly threshed out as each man moves in on an area which the other regards as his sole prerogative.

There is often considerable redundancy built into an organization but with the understanding that the man with secondary responsibility takes over only when the other is not available. Redundancy is a necessary characteristic in sales organizations, partly because of the amount of travel entailed. The assumption of extra functions may work in either direction. The subordinate may be expected to assume responsibility for some types of decisions when the boss is out of town. The field supervisor or district manager, on the other hand, should be equipped to back up his salesmen and make some decisions for them when they are not available. A formal design principle was stated for the assignment of duties to positions, namely, that duties should be assigned in such a way as to minimize ambiguity in communication. Perhaps this statement requires the refinement that the flow of commands and information should be uninterrupted and the freedom from ambiguity is one of the requirements for maintaining good connections from one level to the next.

The final design principle enumerated was concerned with the assignment of specific individuals to the jobs called for in the hierarchy and with the duties specified for each position. The assignment of individuals is the final step in making the organization structure progressively more definite. The need for able men to fill each position is paramount, but it would not be good design to start with individuals and build the organization around them. This can be done in small organizations, but chaos would result in a large organization if the structure and the duties of each position were not determined first.

In assigning specific personnel, the formal principle says that it should be done in such a way as to preserve morale and motivation. This means that the individual assignment should take account of the individual's assessment of his own capabilities and the evaluation of the individual by others. If the individual is disappointed in his assignment, it may be a blow to his morale. If the individual is pleased with the assignment, it may harm the morale of others who are his rivals or who do not expect him to measure up to the job. If the organization has been relatively stable for some time, the natural progression through career planning for personnel may ease some of the difficulties of promoting an individual or of promoting him over the heads of others. If there has been a drastic shake-up as to structure and duties, each candidate for major responsibility may need to be considered in relation to individuals available from the outside. Sometimes the rivalry between two men inside the company is so great that to advance one of them means an almost certain loss of the other. In this instance management may look outside in the hope of keeping both men. This may be a prudent but temporary solution, since it may only postpone the need to choose between them for greater advancement. The reverse situation is one in which a single individual inside is the obvious candidate for preferment but management is not quite sure he is strong enough. The rivalry here is between the inside man and the best available man from outside. In this case it may be wise for management to make the comparison before settling for the man already on the staff.

KINDRED ACTIVITIES

In the structural design of an organization, the primary objective is to place those activities or segments of activities together which belong together. Stated in this form, the principle seems almost trivial, but it is difficult to apply in practice because of distinct and even conflicting considerations as to the activities which should go together. On the one side, it is desirable to place together all activities which are similar in character. On the other hand, it is desirable to place together those activities which require a specially close coordination. The second principle tends to bring together activities which are unlike in character but complementary in function. The crucial judgments in organization design are those which go into resolving such conflicts and determining the extent to which one principle must be allowed to prevail over the others.

The argument for placing similar activities together is that this facilitates carrying them out with the greatest degree of efficiency. This is true if the activities can be reduced to a standard pattern to facilitate instruction supervision or mechanization. If the activities, while similar in intent, differ so much in detail that they cannot be reduced to routine, there is much less to be gained through assigning them to a single organization unit. Progress in routinization has been much slower on the marketing side of business than in manufacturing production. Some routines cannot operate effectively except by full cooperation of buyer and seller. The seller or his agent such as a salesman has to be prepared to make flexible adjustments to conditions imposed upon him by customer preferences or unforeseen contingencies.

Despite these obstacles, there are large areas for routinization or even mechanization in marketing. In the last thirty years the merchandise warehouse has moved a long way in the direction of becoming an automatic goods handling machine. The voluminous paper work which accompanies marketing activity has been standardized and systematized through the use of billing machines and more advanced office equipment. The last ten years has witnessed something approaching a revolution in these types of routine data handling through developments in electronic computers. The next ten years should see vast changes in the distribution and handling of goods, and the processing of information which make up such a large part of the daily activities of marketing organizations.

The difficult problems of organization structure arise in such areas as personal selling and advertising and their relationships to each other. If a sales organization is large enough to be broken down into a number of units, it is a difficult problem of classification to decide which sales tasks should be grouped together. One way is to make each organizational unit responsible for selling a commodity or a group of commodities. Another is to have salesmen deployed by type of customers or industries to which they sell. The complication in sorting out similar tasks is that they may be alike or unlike along several different dimensions. Planning judgment is involved in deciding which of these dimensions of the sales task have the greatest importance in their impact upon efficiency.

Often there are some simplifying factors which enable the planner to get ahead with the first steps in design. For example, products of class one may be sold only to customers of type A so that a whole class of sales negotiations and transactions is set aside both by product and customer characteristics. It will generally be impossible to give recognition to all of the product and customer differences which might have some bearing on efficiency. Here it may be useful to come back to the nature of the sales task itself and to classify according to the types of selling effort involved. One classification found useful in planning industrial sales organizations recognizes three distinct types of selling. These are called prestige selling, application selling, and service selling. Prestige selling prevails in those areas in which there is actually little technical difference in products and the sale depends largely on the customer's image of the firm he would like to buy from. The salesman is encouraged to behave and to select his ties and automobiles in such a way as to reflect the desired corporate image. Application selling involves an analysis of the customer's problem in using the product and recommendations which will enable him to use it as effectively as possible. Service selling rests on frequency of call, prompt adjustment of complaints, and all the steps that are needed to provide maximum convenience of supply.

Another way of analyzing the sales task is by the result which it is expected to produce. Many salesmen are interested in obtaining immediate orders for their products. Other salesmen, such as the detail man in the pharmaceutical industry, do not take orders at all. Their job is purely promotional and is designed to induce physicians and hospitals to buy the company's products. Another important distinction is between the regular marketing of a product and introductory marketing. In many large companies introductory marketing is the function of a sales development department which is quite distinct from the sales department. The goal of a sales development department is to get customers to try a new product under favorable circumstances. The regular salesman is attempting to become or remain a dominant source of supply or to take any steps available to induce customers to increase their volume of purchases.

The problems of organizing for the advertising function are

somewhat parallel to those pertaining to the sales organization. Internal operating problems are simplified somewhat by the use of
advertising agencies, but the problems of communication are correspondingly increased. The relation between the advertising department and the sales departments usually depends in part on the relative size of the expenditures for these two types of marketing effort.
If personal selling has the larger budget, advertising may be regarded as facilitating the task of the salesman and the advertising
department may become subordinate to the sales department. If
advertising is regarded as the primary means of moving the company's products, the task of the salesman may be that of getting as
much as possible out of the advertising expenditure. Domination
of one department by the other is one way to achieve coordination.
Market planning is likely to reside in the dominant department, and
then the subordinate department is expected to conform to the plans
so generated. If market research and planning come to be recognized
as major functions, they will provide a more objective approach to
the coordination of various forms of marketing effort. Both marketing effort and analysis are placed under the direction of the chief
marketing executive with adequate procedures and controls for
making sure that the marketing dollars are spent in accordance with
the marketing plan.

The ever-present need for coordination must bring all marketing
activities together at some level and may bring quite dissimilar
activities together even in small organization units. Coordination is
at a premium when maximum speed is required to stay ahead of
competition. Thus some national companies are organized on the
basis of semiautonomous local units partly to obtain close coordination and speedy performance involving customer contacts on the
one hand, and plant production on the other. The decision as to
whether the plant can handle an order or as to whether it can meet
a desired delivery date may be made much faster than if it had to
be cleared through several departments at a national headquarters.

Among the other circumstances which call for coordination of
diverse functions by small units is that of distance and difficulty of
communication between a branch and a home office. Until recent
years the West Coast offices of many marketing organizations
tended to operate on a semiautonomous basis. The same thing continues to be true of branches operating in foreign countries. Another
situation calling for close coordination is that of crash programs or
crew operations territory by territory. Varied talents are brought

to bear to accomplish specified objectives in a brief period of time and the organization structure is much different from that ordinarily employed in more regular and continuous marketing operations.

COMMUNICATION AND ORGANIZATION STRUCTURE

Communication is such an essential feature of organization structure that the planner might well begin by observing the flow of information within the firm. A picture of the lines of communication in a going concern and the amount and character of communication provides a graphic and reasonably accurate reflection of what the organization is and how it operates. The authority of an executive position is frequently portrayed by enumerating the individuals who report to this executive. This is another way of saying that his status in the operation can be specified by outlining the information which comes to him and what he does about it when he receives it.

The need for communication grows directly out of the size and complexity of organization and increases as the extent of functional specialization increases. The last phase stressed functional specialization as a source of organizational effectiveness. Distinctions are drawn among activities so that each of them can be systematized and reduced to orderly procedures. With this progressive differentiation of structure, the various parts have decreasing contact and knowledge of each other. Indeed, one of the values of specialization is that it should not be necessary for everybody to know everything about the organization in order to make it work. It is the function of the organization planner to specify the items of information which nevertheless must be transmitted from one unit to another as well as specifying the flow of information with respect to points outside the organization. Internal communication as an aspect of organization planning will be considered first.

A need for communication between operating units arises primarily because of three aspects of organization structure. The output of one unit may be an input for another unit. Two units may make complementary contributions to the same end-result. Two units may have conflicting claims on the same resource. These three types of operating communication will be considered briefly. Separate units may be concerned with a sequence of steps so that some formal notice is required to terminate a task for unit *A* and initiate the corresponding task for unit *B*. The relationship between sales development and regular sales operation which has already been mentioned is one good illustration. The sales development department may indicate that it has carried out its prescribed task of introducing the product. This information may go to the sales department on an informal basis even though formal clearance may involve an executive responsible for both organizational units. A sales department is often required to provide the production department with estimates of market demand over a month or several months ahead. The production department, on the other hand, may notify sales that a particular order is ready for shipment or that circumstances have arisen which have prevented it from being filled. The sales department may request the personnel department to recruit a specified number of new salesmen, and personnel notifies sales when these men are ready to enter sales training.

Examples of this kind could be multiplied endlessly, but the key point for the organization planner is that all such communications are operating signals designed to secure action. The goal of the planner is to specify communication methods which will avoid failures of the expected action. Without formal procedures, failures occur because one individual forgets to communicate; the second forgets that he has received the message or does not have the necessary details before him when the time for action has come. Internal communications need to be specific as to time and place for the action required and as to the person expected to carry it out. Without procedural planning, requests may be misdirected to individuals without authority to act and may be stalled without acknowledgement because the recipient is not clear on the proper disposition.

The difficulty with internal communication is likely to be lack of clear signals for action rather than any paucity in the amount of communication. In fact, a common failing is overabundant communication. Lengthy memoranda are submitted in a spirit of self-justification, and the key facts calling for action may be lost in a mass of verbiage. Content analysis of communications flowing through marketing organizations reveals a vast number of messages describing a problem without containing a request or recommendation for action. An initial message of this kind often generates a chain of similar messages so that a decision that is pushed up to the top may be one which should have been settled at or near the lowest level of responsibility. Too often orders are issued without any regular check as to whether action has been taken or even as to whether the message has been received.

As compared to the operating signals designed to coordinate a sequence of activities, internal communication also embraces situations in which the interests or activities of two organization units

run parallel to each other. One situation is that in which two or
more units are making competitive claims on the scarce resources
of the company. They are rival claimants for manpower, for a
share of the budget for annual marketing expenditures, or for the
capital funds available for investment in facilities or development
projects. A typical instance is that in which the sales departments of
several product divisions must all submit budgets to the top marketing executive covering the required expenditures for the year
ahead. When the allocation of such funds is treated on an informal
basis, the largest share is likely to go to the department head with
the greatest personal persuasiveness. A top executive is often left
with a difficult task of justifying his decision to disappointed claimants.

The market planner can contribute to more effective operation by
formalizing the procedure for budget allocations. The information
supporting requests should be standardized to facilitate the task
of making relative judgments. In particular, each claimant should
be required to present a marketing program indicating the way in
which the funds are to be used. Supporting documents should provide the factual data from company records or from market surveys
which were decisive in determining the marketing strategy and the
program for carrying it out. The same kind of specific detail should
be required in each case to provide a basis for matching one claim
against another.

While the basic procedural objective is to promote more effective
allocation, there are auxiliary benefits which flow from such formal
procedures. The annual or semiannual review of detailed marketing
programs gives management a picture of what is going on in each
division without spending an inordinate amount of time in obtaining
it. It is a good method for promoting general acceptance of formal
planning and for setting up a standard of what is required for an
acceptable plan. It gives staff groups a point of entry for offering
their services to the heads of operating units. When plans are rejected or criticized, professional help in planning will be more wel-
come next time. If the factual basis for the plan is challenged, there
will be an incentive to undertake marketing research in time to be
used in preparing the next program.

Adequate planning can remove the allocation of funds for investment or current expenditures from the area of competitive pressure
among divisions. The more appropriate perspective is that the treatment for each request for funds is the negotiation of reciprocal commitments between top management and the operating executive. He

should not be given a budget merely on the grounds of awarding him his fair share of what is available. Rather, the amount allocated should be weighed against what he wishes to accomplish with it and the evidence he produces that this result could actually be achieved. The marketing program and its appropriateness to the proposed task with supporting data are the chief means for justifying the budget request. Top management and the operating executive are engaged in striking a bargain, and both should feel committed to live up to it so long as there seems to be any prospect of success. The buying or negotiating approach should prevail over the rationing approach in the allocation of funds. The objective of top management is not to win a hollow victory by getting the best of the bargain but to negotiate toward a point of balance between the result expected and the resources made available with respect to each operating unit. This procedure provides the best hope for maximum overall effectiveness in the application of marketing effort.

A third basic situation with respect to internal communication is that in which several types of effort must be coordinated to achieve a common result. Problems frequently arise in the introduction of new products as to the coordination of the movement of initial stocks into retail stores and the appearance of advertising which will send consumers into the stores to buy. Lack of coordination can lead to unfortunate results in either direction. The retailer soon becomes restive if merchandise lies on his shelf with no call from the consumer. The consumer is frustrated and builds up a bias against the product if he fails to find it in the retail stores where the advertising tells him to look.

Coordination will not always be perfect even with the best of intentions. On the other hand, if each unit proceeds without regard for the other, it will be pure coincidence whenever good timing is achieved. The planning of communications can cut down the risk of poor coordination and reduce the lapse of time before one side catches up with the other. Ideally, one of the units involved should call the signals in the attempt to get coordinated effort. Should this be the advertising department, for example, it should take responsibility for saying when the goods should actually be in the store. Perhaps this instruction should state the ideal date and also set the tolerable limits around this date. The unit responsible for physical movement of goods should indicate in turn what the chances are of meeting specified delivery dates. The movement of goods is not always under control, particularly if intermediate handling is involved. Planned communication should make some allowance for contingencies and indicate what is the next best thing if performance stops short of the goal. Suppose, for example, that only half of the specified supply was available for the introductory sale in a given market. Should it be placed in half the stores originally planned to have it, or should each store get only half of the scheduled initial stock? The difference in results could be substantial, depending on the character of advertising support and retail displays specified in the marketing program.

In all the situations described, it is desirable to reduce business communication to a succession of unambiguous operating signals. If a message designed to produce action leaves the issue in doubt, one of two things must be wrong. Either the message does not make clear the action which is intended, or the recipient has not been instructed in how to interpret it. An operating signal should tell the recipient which of several possible courses of action he is expected to take. To be effective in action, the recipient must have in mind, before he receives the message, a comprehensive list of the possible courses of action. The message should leave no doubt as to which course of action his senior officer expects the recipient to take. In relatively simple and repetitive cases the message may be transmitted on a prepared form which lists all the recognized possibilities with only a check mark against the indicated action to complete the message.

While the planner is directly concerned with formal communication, he cannot ignore the existence of informal communication within an organization. A large amount of communication may be going on which does not constitute signals and, in fact, interferes with operating signals being heard or given the attention they require. Groups of people thrown together in business, as elsewhere, find many things to talk about besides the task at hand. The communication theorists might be tempted to classify all of this informal communication as noise or interference, and there are cases in which it needs to be minimized.

Informal communication has its constructive side and may even prepare the individual involved to receive and accept operating signals from each other. To act on a signal the recipient must have confidence in his superior officer. Informal communication an generate confidence and, in any case, serves to build up each individual's understanding and evaluation of those with whom he works. Now famous experiments in industrial relations have shown that broad tolerance with respect to informal communication can step up the productivity of a working group.

The informal organization structure in any system interacts significantly with the formal structure. The informal structure develops out of the stream of social action, much of which takes the form of communication not related to operations. A group acts more effectively in some respects according to the strength of individual feelings of belonging to the group. A large part of informal conversation is in the intangible area of individuals endeavoring to establish a position and acceptance within the group.

Operating signals are related to current activities. Some other types of communication have a bearing on the group's capacity to act. This conditioning for action takes the form in part of preparing the individual for the acceptance and correct interpretation of operating signals. The modern approach to industrial or personnel relations might be regarded as planning a place for this constructive phase of nonoperating communication. If a group is to act effectively, the capacities of each individual have to be known with reasonable accuracy to his superiors and also to his associates. One might state a general communication principle as follows: The effective group will communicate in such a way as to disclose the potential capacity of the individuals who make it up. Communication which will actually achieve this result will obviously include a substantial component of social interaction which is not directly related to the task at hand.

Informal contacts between the firm and parties outside the firm will not be explored in detail in this chapter. Communication in this sense comes close to being the essence of marketing. Communication with customers or with suppliers is the subject matter of much that has gone before and is implicit in any discussion of marketing.

AUTHORITY AND RESPONSIBILITY

Every business and every marketing department has a power structure as well as an operating structure. The element of power relations is a universal component of all organizations, formal or informal, and including business firms, public institutions, households, and purely voluntary nonprofit organizations. There is a status gradation among the several positions in an organization, and some individuals compete for the positions of higher status. In the business world these positions are endowed with broad authority and responsibility affecting the activities of other individuals in the firm.

It is the hierarchy of positions graded by authority and responsibility which is pictured in the conventional organization chart. Some subtle shadings of structure cannot be reflected in these charts.

A weighty topic of discussion in some organization planning meetings is the question of whether two boxes on a chart should be
joined by a solid line or a dotted line. In other words, does the individual in the subordinate position take his orders from the other
individual, or does he simply report certain aspects of his activity
for purposes of information? The fine art of preparing organization
diagrams will not be discussed here as it has been treated exhaus-
tively in other places.

From the standpoint of the planner in marketing, the static structure of the organization is of less interest than the structure of
decision-making process. This is not a question of rank in the power
structure but of who must reach a decision before somebody else
can decide. This process can move either up or down or sideways
in an organization. Sometimes a major decision reached at the top is
implemented by a series of decisions of less sweeping character
at descending levels in the organization. Before this master decision on what to do can be made, however, a whole series of decisions on the nature of the task and the requirements for meeting
it may have been generated from the bottom up. That is to say
that each small unit was called upon to estimate requirements or
forecast the market outlook, and these judgments were combined
into a broader synthesis by successive steps moving upward in the
organization hierarchy. There are other types of lower-level decisions which can also have a vital effect on the master policy decision.
The subordinate executive decides day by day what information to
transmit to his superiors and what questions to refer to them for
their judgment. A timorous subordinate may attempt to conceal a
bad situation and a rash subordinate may try to deal with it entirely
on his own responsibility. In either case, some phase of an operation
may reach the verge of catastrophe before it comes to the attention
of top management. In other cases, where top management is too
indulgent in listening to the problems arising at lower levels, too
much time is consumed by trivia, thereby leaving not enough time
to cope with major issues. Part of the answer is that management
cannot adopt a purely passive position but must take the initiative
from time to time in finding out what is really going on at lower
echelons.

The sidewise flow in the decision-making process may involve
relations between line and staff or between two operating executives. In the line and staff relation the staff analyst may have the
surer judgment as to the nature of the problem and the general
character of the remedy which is indicated by information and

analysis. However clear the issue may look to him, he must always remember the distinction between an analytical conclusion and a commitment to action. The line executive might have the more immediate intuitive grasp of the action situation both with respect to the resources he can bring to bear and the prospects for competitive counteraction. The responsible executive who makes the final decision necessarily takes account of the factors other than the objective data which have been collected and analyzed. Among factors entering into his decision, one is his own subjective attitude toward risk. This psychological attitude toward risk can be known directly only to the executive himself.

In organizations in which the staff has achieved full recognition, major decisions tend to be joint decisions in which line and staff participate. The same thing is obviously true in the other type of horizontal relationship in which two line executives are confronted by a common problem. In any matter calling for joint decision, the organization planner has two primary tasks to perform. One is to suggest the procedure, for example, of a standing committee by which such decisions get made. Another is to try to establish a situation in which all parties to the decision are looking at the same body of basic facts. Too often in a top marketing committee, time is dissipated in arguing about facts which should be beyond dispute. The sales manager and the advertising manager, for example, may each be more interested in getting across his version of what he thinks the situation is than in moving toward a joint decision on the basis of the record. Obviously there is room for complementary views as to the nature of the problem, but at least the essential core of pertinent factual data should be the common property of all parties to the decision.

INFORMATION FLOWS AND DECISION MAKING

Some organization theorists conceive of decision making as a process with a sequence of steps. Here the choices to be made by the organization planner have to do with the most efficient structuring of the whole process and the question of how far the process should be carried out at each stage. One authority speaks of three general types of transformation which can take place at any point in the decision-making process. These three types of transformation are called routing, integration, and specification. A routing problem is one in which an individual is simply required to decide upon the routing of the matter requiring decision. He may refer the matter to his immediate superior, or he may route it to a staff unit and ask for their analytical judgment. Routing decisions can be made with respect to matters moving either vertically or horizontally within an organization structure.

The action of integration is one of the ways of interpreting or transforming information on the way to reaching a decision. Typically, the individual performing this function would be receiving information from several different sources and reaching a conclusion as to the general significance to be attached to the information as a whole. Most typically, this type of transformation occurs as information flows upward in an organization structure. An example would be a sales manager who received reports of a similar kind from Denver, Los Angeles, and San Francisco and concluded that the company was facing a special type of problem west of the Mississippi. Having reached this decision, he might decide on a program of action to meet this condition. At this point he either puts the program into operation by his own authority or submits it to his superior with a request for approval.

The reverse type of interpretation or transformation generally pertains to and is typical of messages moving downward in an organization structure. Specification is the step-by-step process of amplifying orders at each level until they finally become explicit instructions to individuals. An example would be the announcement of a new promotion plan or price policy in which some leeway was allowed for adaptation to conditions in each sales district and in which the regional sales manager specified objectives to be accomplished by individual salesmen. The salesmen, in turn, might be required to lay out the more detailed specifications for themselves and turn back to their immediate supervisors a schedule indicating how they were going to cover their major customers to assure achievement of the marketing plan.

Characteristic organization difficulties arise with respect to all three types of information handling. By giving consideration to the structure of the organizational process, the organization planner can minimize these difficulties. On the simple matter of routing, it is usually desirable to mechanize the process as completely as possible. In routing to subordinates an executive might well turn over the task to an administrative assistant. Because of his own position of authority he is too likely to violate the structure of authority which he may have laboriously established if he undertakes routing himself. Routing to superiors should be covered by an explicit manual of instructions which helps the subordinate classify the particular item and gives him a clear answer in borderline cases. This type of routing manual is likely to become increasingly important under the trend toward multiple supervision in which the same individual functions in several capacities and reports to a different superior in each instance. With respect to both generalization and specification, these transformations also go by default unless the responsibilities have already been established in the organization manual. Individual items of information tend to be referred upstream so that the whole problem of the integration of information to support decision is passed on to top management. Similarly a plan of action moving downstream may not be implemented in proper fashion unless very explicit arrangements have been made for this function. There are two ways in which this could happen. Either the executives at each level know in advance what is required of them in the way of specifying the operating details of a plan, or the plan itself includes instructions to them to develop more detailed instructions.

The organization planner should not deal exclusively with either the structure of authority or with the structure of the decision-making process. Generally speaking, however, greater emphasis should be given to the decision-making process since that is the side that is more frequently neglected in organization planning.

DYNAMIC ORGANIZATION PLANNING

For simplicity of exposition, organization planning has been discussed as if the objective was to create an ideal organization as of a given point in time. Actually the organization planner needs to be acutely aware that organizations are constantly changing and that every organization plan is necessarily a compromise. That is to say that there are various values and criteria which are sought in organization planning but that it is never possible to give full expression to all of these considerations. With respect to marketing organization, it is only a slight exaggeration to say that the best organization plan starts to become obsolete the day it is installed. All organization planning might be futile if it were not for the possibility of taking direct account of the dynamic character of organization. Three principal aspects of dynamic planning will be mentioned.

First of all, a good job of organization planning should describe the proposed organization structure at several different stages and not as of a single point in time. The ultimate structure should pertain to a point from one to several years in the future. The development of an organization plan, say for a date three years ahead, should rest on the determination of a marketing program to be activated over a period of several years. The planning sequence determines sales goals, a program required for reaching the goals, and specifies the kind of organization capable of carrying out the program.

The proposed marketing organization three years hence may differ quite strikingly from the one now in existence. Therefore, the next step in dynamic organization planning is to picture one or more transition stages by which management can move from the present organization to the proposed future organization. Even if reorganization is carried out in an emergency spirit, it will take some time to put an organization plan into effect. That is the reason for the statement that ultimate plans should be made for a period to become effective at least one year in the future. Even if management feels obliged to take some drastic steps within the next two or three weeks, it can take these steps more wisely against the background consideration of what the organization should look like next year. Any organization plan which requires substantial expansion of personnel must allow time for recruiting and training. And an organization plan which calls for substantial reduction should allow time for judicious selection and orderly severance to preserve the morale of the reduced organization.

Organization changes are somewhat easier to carry out on the personnel side if the plan looks some distance ahead rather than consisting of a set of emergency measures. Individuals dislocated from their present positions may have more patience in awaiting the final outcome if they are given a comprehensive picture of what the company is trying to do. People naturally respond with better spirit to the preparation for a new task than to a criticism of the way the task was previously performed. If the emphasis is on getting ready for future operations, criticism of the past may enter only indirectly and as a way of pointing up what may be expected from other methods.

Another approach to the dynamics of organization is through career planning. An organization is made up of individuals, and one of its dynamic aspects is the flow of people into the organization and within the organization structure as well as out of the organization through death or resignation. Career planning can begin by working backward from the official dates of retirement of executive personnel and from the expectations of probable losses from other causes. For each executive who is scheduled to retire within the next year a judgment should already have been made as to the persons inside the company who are capable of succeeding him, or an outside search should already have been started if the inside candidates are not available. It is remarkable how often in a company without systematic planning it is suddenly discovered that top management is over age and no likely replacements are in sight. This can precipitate a very serious crisis in the affairs of a company, since it poses a challenge for recruitment and management which is almost impossible to meet.

The systematic approach in career planning is to work out replacement tables for every executive in the organization and to keep these constantly up to date. This needs to be done regardless of age, health, or the likelihood that the individual will withdraw from the company. While the young and able executive may have no intention of leaving, the death or resignation of an older man may start a whole sequence of organization changes. The retirement of a president may result in five or six changes in position as someone is promoted to fill his spot and positions following at each succeeding level are filled by promotions. In some of the more comprehensive systems of career planning each man is backed up by first, second, and third choice replacements in much the same way that the first team on a football squad is backed up. These replacement tables evaluate each executive as to the job or jobs at the next level which he is qualified to fill and also provide a priority list as to the men who are most qualified to succeed him.

This phase of organization planning will also require a determination as to the number and type of trainees who should be coming in at the bottom of the executive ladder each year. In a large organization a number of men will be required simply to offset the natural attrition of executive turnover. Additional men will be required to support any company growth plans derived from market planning. While it may be the best practice for the personnel department to recruit and indoctrinate the additional personnel at this level, the planner in marketing is responsible for specifying the number and type of personnel that will be required.

A final aspect of dynamic planning is the continuous study of the relationship between function and structure. The point has already been made that structure should follow function. In marketing this means starting with the marketing job to be performed by the company and then determining the size and structure of the organization needed to carry out this task. There are times, however, when it is appropriate to consider finding new jobs for an organization to perform before cutting it back to the size of the job at hand. An effective sales organization is a resource which may have cost the company considerable money to build. It can be good management planning to keep such a resource usefully employed just as management looks for new uses for excess capacity in other directions.

The organization planner needs to be aware of the natural history of organizations and their tendency to persist or to change in accordance with an inner logic of their own. Thus, while the planner prefers to move from function to structure, he must be aware of the tendency for one structure to evolve into another. Vigorous executives are likely to have their individual preferences as to the kind of organization they would like to see their company become. An organization may take on a more authoritarian structure or a more democratic structure, depending on the preferences of top management. Since all organization is a compromise, the tendency to take on a definite character is likely to bring out the weaknesses of that form of organization and create some sentiment for going into reverse. The opportunities for individuals in advancing their own status are sometimes associated with the intuition that it is time for a change in business, no less than it would be in politics.

It is the professional obligation of the organization planner to maintain a detached view and to promote the type of organization that will have the best operating results. In doing this he may sense deepseated organization trends which he cannot control but which he must accept as fundamental conditions of the problem. There is no point in recommending organization plans which are clearly inconsistent with the inevitable evolution of the company. In organization planning the fundamental decisions will be made at the highest level of responsibility. The organization planner undertakes to recommend the kind of organization required to carry out a marketing program. He may restrict himself to the one feasible plan which he thinks is likely to be accepted, or he may present several alternatives pointing out the respective merits of each. If the organization planner is a consultant drawn from the outside, this presentation of alternatives may be an intermediate stage leading to a final company recommendation. The outside consultant is often in a better position to take a firm stand with respect to organization structure.

Selected References

ETZIONI, AMITAI. "Two Approaches to Organization Analysis," *Administrative Sciences Quarterly*, September, 1960.
  Two kinds of models are compared in terms of what they can contribute to the improvement of organization survival models and effectiveness models.
GOULDNER, ALVIN W. "Organizational Analyses," in *Sociology Today* (ed. by R. K. Merton, *et al.*) New York: Basic Books, Inc., 1959.

Traces the development of the rational model and the natural systems model in organization theory and stresses the need for synthesis today.

HAIRE, MASON. *Modern Organization Theory.* New York: John Wiley & Sons, 1959.
Planner will be interested in some of the chapters discussing the form of organization as well as organization objectives.

MARCH, J. G. AND SIMON, H. A. *Organizations.* New York: John Wiley & Sons, 1958.
From scientific management to management science. Various approaches to the creation of viable and efficient organizations.

THOMPSON, J. D., *et al. Comparative Studies in Administration.* Pittsburgh, Pa.: University of Pittsburgh Press, 1959.
Has several chapters of special interest to organization planners.

Problems

1. Contrast the following optimizing principles for the design of organizations: (*a*) maximizing expected values and (*b*) minimizing departures from policy.

2. Contrast the orthodox view of the role of line and staff with the view taken by this book.

3. Compare and discuss prestige selling, application selling, and service selling.

4. Discuss and give examples of the following types of transformations: (*a*) routing, (*b*) integration, and (*c*) specification.

5. Discuss the three principal aspects of dynamic planning described in this chapter and the proper functions of each.

Chapter 20

DESIGNING MARKETING SYSTEMS

~~~~~~

The supreme planning task in marketing is the planning of a marketing system. Planning a marketing system embraces all of the other tasks of planning campaigns, facilities, and organization. A system generates marketing campaigns and makes use of facilities and organization. A plan for a marketing system begins with a general statement of objectives, proceeds through an examination of the feasibility constraints within which these objectives must be sought, and culminates in the specification of a schedule of outputs for the system.

Campaigns can be regarded as beginning and ending with the accomplishment of a particular phase in the growth of a company such as the introduction of a major new product or completion of a shift in distribution channels. The progress of a campaign can also be measured by arbitrary calendar dates such as the opening and closing of a fiscal year. The results to be achieved during the period can be specified in terms of salable outputs or in terms of a new state of affairs to be accomplished with respect to the system itself. Such a goal might be to accomplish a target percentage of coverage with a new product, to attain a dominant market share, or to staff the sales organization with personnel to match a new conception of the marketing task.

A primary tool for planning or replanning a marketing system is marketing cost analysis. The purpose of this procedure is to show the sales results for the period broken down into smaller segments to facilitate detailed judgments of the way the system is operating. Generally the business is segmented into product classes and customers grouped by territories or other criteria. For both products and customers gross profits, operating costs, and net profits are shown separately. This method involves the regrouping of expenditures by functional cost groups and the allocation of each cost group to the various segments of the business.

Marketing cost analysis has been severely criticized by skeptics who did not bother to understand it. Its pragmatic virtue is that it works, and no firm ever carried out an intensive analysis of this kind without reaping substantial benefits. This chapter offers some extensions and refinements of the method which may possibly lead to more general application. One of these refinements is to draw a basic distinction between effort variables and response variables in putting the results of marketing cost analysis to work. A major extension contemplates cost projections rather than stopping with the analysis of past results.

ELEMENTS OF MARKETING COST ANALYSIS

Marketing costs analysis begins with the reshuffling of the marketing cost data found in the company's records to form functional cost groups. In the standard accounting records, expenditures are grouped according to the person receiving payment rather than according to the function performed. Ten to fifteen functional cost groups will usually suffice, although some analysts will use as many as thirty to thirty-five. This more meticulous procedure is not likely to pay for the extra work and care. With thirty or more cost groups some of them are likely to constitute less than 1 percent of total marketing costs. Since the whole process of allocating marketing costs lies in the realm of approximation, it is pointless to break costs down to that extent.

The development of appropriate functional cost groups is guided by a general conception of the nature of a marketing operation. Some costs represent the actual work performed in moving goods to customers. All costs of this kind can be labeled cost of work. Some costs represent the cost of the capacity which must be available for performing the work. Maintaining inventory on the one hand or the goodwill of customers on the other are typical of capacity costs in marketing. Capacity costs are the costs which must be incurred in advance of the movement of goods and as a necessary condition for such movement. In addition to work and capacity there is the broad function of control with corresponding functional costs. Thus, all functional costs can be classified under three broad phases of operation, namely, work, capacity, and control.

Having established functional cost groups, the next problem is to find appropriate factors for allocating each cost group. We can now invoke another general principle related to the way in which the business is divided up into segments for the application of marketing costs. For analytical purposes a business can be divided up by product classes, since one goal of marketing cost analysis is to show which products are profitable or unprofitable. Another possibility is to break the business down by customer types or by territorial grouping of customers. Finally, these two forms of segmentation can be combined, resulting in a breakdown by transaction groups. A transaction group includes all sales of a given product class to a particular customer type. Functional cost groups are oriented to products, to customers or to transactions, according to whether they are determined primarily by product characteristics, by customer characteristics, or can be charged directly to transaction groups. Finally, there are some costs which are not oriented to any of these segments but to the company as a whole.

The two factors of cost orientation and phase of operation can now be used to establish a cross classification for all functional cost groups. The table is three by four, which means that there are twelve cells in the table, but most of the cells are empty. The two methods of classification turn out to be very closely related.

Cost Orientation	Phase of Operation		
	Work	Capacity	Control
Transactions..............	x		
Products.................		x	
Customers................		x	
Company.................			x

SEGMENTS OF THE BUSINESS

The procedure for dividing the total sales volume of the firm into segments has already been mentioned. Following the method which has been outlined, the business could be broken into thousands of segments or only 50 to 100. For illustration, we will consider a 10 by 10 matrix, breaking the volume of business into 100 segments. That would mean 10 product classes, 10 customer types and 100 transaction groups. This could well be adequate for the first analytical cut in quite a large business. In the illustrative table the letter x is used to show that there is some business of the type indicated by the crossing of the product class and the customer type. The cell is left vacant if there were no transactions in the given category. That would mean that the company does not sell all classes of products to all types of customers. It might have a line of products which it sold only to department stores. Or it might have a line which is sold nationally except for the South.

Product Classes	Customer Types										Totals
	1	2	3	4	5	6	7	8	9	10	
Class # A..........	x	x	x	x	x	x	x	x	x	x	
B..........	x	x	x	x	x	x	x	x	x	x	
C..........	x	x	x	x	x	x	x				
D..........	x	x	x	x	x						
E..........	x	x	x	x	x						
F..........	x					x	x	x	x	x	x
G..........	x			x	x	x	x	x	x	x	
H..........	x					x	x	x	x	x	
I..........	x							x	x	x	
J..........	x							x	x	x	
Totals.........											Grand Total

For the sake of simplicity, further illustrations will assume a four by four grid. It will be further assumed that none of the cells are empty so that there are 16 transaction groups. One table like this would show sales volume for each transaction group. Another would show cost of goods sold, and the calculated difference, group by group, would be gross profit. We now wish to subtract costs from gross profit to obtain net profit.

To arrive at this result we must allocate each of the functional costs to the various segments into which the business has been divided. The method will be illustrated for several categories of functional costs. First is billing cost, which seems to be measured pretty directly by the number of invoice lines. Invoices can be sorted by territories to distinguish between types of customers. For each customer type a count can then be made of the number of times a product appears on the invoice. We would thus have 16 subtotals corresponding to the 16 transaction groups. A calculation would be made to show each of the 16 subtotals as a percentage of the grand total for invoice lines. The total cost of billing would be entered in the lower right hand corner. It would be spread among the 16 cells on the basis of their proportionate share of invoice lines.

BILLING

	1	2	3	4	Totals
A...........	x	x	x	x	
B...........	x	x	x	x	
C...........	x	x	x	x	
D...........	x	x	x	x	
Totals...					Ⓧ

A slight variation in this procedure would be followed in allocating a product-oriented cost such as inventory storage. The total cost of storage would be entered in the right-hand corner as before, but it would first be allocated among the four product classes. In many instances an appropriate factor for allocating to products would be the percentage of warehouse space occupied. Next we must have a reasonable basis for allocating the four subtotals to customer types. If the product line were fairly simple so that each case of goods occupied about the same amount of space, it would be equitable to allocate the storage cost for the product group A to the four customer types on the basis of the proportionate number of cases shipped to each type.

INVENTORY STORAGE

	1	2	3	4	Totals
A............					x
B............					x
C............					x
D............					x
Totals...					Ⓧ

The final illustration, showing another slight variation in procedure, pertains to the salesmen's salaries and expenses. This is a good example of a customer-oriented cost group. These are generally accounted for on a territorial basis so that customers may have to be grouped by territories first before proceeding to other classifications such as grouping customers by trade. Assuming that customer type here refers to territories, the sales costs would be obtained directly from accounting records, both for the grand total and for each of the four territories. To allocate to products under each customer type, some measure of the selling time spent on each product would be needed. For relatively simple cases the proportionate number of invoice lines would be an acceptable basis for allocating the sales cost for customer type 1 among product classes A, B, C, and D.

SALESMEN'S SALARIES AND EXPENSES

	1	2	3	4	Totals
A............					
B............					
C............					
D............					
Totals...	x	x	x	x	Ⓧ

Suppose we assume a very simple business in which the only costs are billing, inventory storage, and selling. This is an artificial situation and only adopted for simple illustration. The costs shown in each cell would be totaled from the three tables shown above and entered on a cost summary table. The figures in the cell would be added vertically to give total costs by customer type. They would be added horizontally to give total costs by product class. Each of the figures shown on the summary cost table would then be subtracted from the gross profit table to give net profits by transaction groups, product classes and customer types.

FUNCTIONAL COST GROUPS AND ALLOCATION FACTORS

Returning to the previous cross classification of functional cost groups, a standard set of cost groups will now be suggested which will serve for many marketing cost studies and provide a point of departure where greater detail is indicated. Following this listing of cost groups by cost-orientation, allocation factors will be suggested which will serve in the simpler cases.

Transaction oriented
    Billing
    Order handling
    Delivery
Product oriented
    Procurement
    Inventory storage
    Inventory investment
    Inventory variety
    Product advertising
Customer oriented
    Institutional advertising
    Consumer deals
    Selling
    Trade deals
    Credit administration (and bad debts)
Company oriented
    Marketing overhead
    General overhead

1. *Billing*—to transaction groups by invoice lines.
2. *Order handling*—to transaction groups by cases shipped. (In the more difficult situations standard handling units would be computed showing the case equivalents of a barrel, bag, etc.)
3. *Delivery*—to transaction groups by the product of weight and rate. (In the more difficult cases distinctions might have to be drawn between rail rates and truck rates and the weight of the product might have to be qualified by commodity classification.)

4. *Procurement*—to products by number of purchases. To customers by annual volume.
5. *Inventory Storage*—to products by space occupied. To customers by cases shipped.
6. *Inventory investment*—calculated at 6 percent and allocated to products by average inventory value. To customers by annual volume.
7. *Inventory variety*—to product classes by number of items in the class. To customers by number of separate items ordered during a year. (This cost group would be formed by taking part of the three preceding groups on a judgment basis.)
8. *Product advertising*—to products directly. To customers by media circulation in each territory.
9. *Institutional advertisting*—to customers by media circulation in each territory. To products by gross profit dollars.
10. *Consumer deals*—in the simpler cases combined with (9) and allocated on the same basis.
11. *Salesmen's salaries and expenses*—to territories direct. Customers may be further broken down within territories by size of city in which the customer is located. This would require a special study of how much time the salesman spends in each type of place. Further breakdown such as by size of customer would require information on the frequency of call on each class. The allocation to products would be made by invoice lines on the assumption that each item absorbs some of the salesman's attention when he is in the presence of the customer.
12. *Trade deals*—in the simpler cases combined with (11) and allocated on the same basis.
13. *Credit administration and bad debts*—to territories (customer type) by average amount outstanding. To products by annual volume.
14. *Marketing overhead*—to transaction groups by all other marketing costs.
15. *General overhead*—to transaction groups by gross profit dollars.

DISPUTES OVER ALLOCATION OF OVERHEAD

One of the more unprofitable debates in the marketing cost field concerns the issue of whether administrative overhead should or should not be allocated to product classes and customer types. Many analysts have a strong preference for allocating only those costs which are more clearly traceable. When this total is subtracted from gross profit the remainder is sometimes called net contribution rather than net profit.

Some recent studies reported on this basis claim that the analysts have restricted themselves to direct charges. Yet it hardly seems accurate to speak of direct charges if an allocating factor has been used, such as space in a store or warehouse or the average inventory on hand. Apparently what some analysts mean by direct charges includes the use of allocating factors that they feel comfortable with on the basis of intuition.

There are some real advantages in allocating all marketing costs. It provides for cross checks against total gross profit and operating costs. It results in a figure which can be compared with the net profit for the business as a whole or with the net profits of other businesses which have a more specialized product line or operate in a smaller territory. Marketing costs studies should lead to decisions of several kinds, including pricing decisions. These are not arrived at so readily if only net contribution has been calculated.

To feel comfortable about allocating administrative overhead, two steps should be taken. First, every element of administrative overhead which is directly related to some operating function should be transferred to the appropriate functional cost group. It is assumed, of course, that salaries of production executives who might be regarded as part of overhead have been charged with the cost of goods sold. Secondly, the allocation of administrative overhead should be on the basis of factors which are relatively neutral from the standpoint of the final results. The two factors recommended for (14) and (15) above are of this character.

Allocation by all other costs has little effect on the result which would be obtained without allocation. It has the virtue, however, of directing the attention of the top marketing executive to the goal of keeping costs down and reminding him that marketing overhead is an incremental cost to be added to every marketing dollar expended. Gross profit dollars is also a relatively neutral basis of allocation. If the general executive can provide the leadership which generates gross profit dollars and can count on his subordinates to control costs, the generation of net profits will be assured.

WHY NOT ALLOCATE BY DOLLAR SALES?

It will be noted that allocation by dollar sales volume is employed very infrequently in dealing with the fifteen functional cost groups. One instance is the recommended allocation of credit cost to products. The cost of credit is obviously dependent primarily on the characteristics of customers rather than products. The average amount outstanding would appear to be a reasonable way of measuring this cost. The most directly traceable product contribution to amount outstanding would appear to be the dollar sales volume. Each dollar of product sales is assumed to contribute equally to the average amount outstanding.

If the reader should assume that a deliberate attempt was made to avoid allocation by dollar sales volume, he would be correct. This book supports the viewpoint that this basis should be used only after exhausting the alternative possibilities. The fallacy of any general use of dollar sales as an allocating factor should be abundantly clear. Yet there are instances in which large sums have been spent for so-called marketing cost analysis with nearly every functional cost allocated on the basis of sales.

Suppose the company has just two product lines. It has a gross profit of 40 percent on product line *A* and a gross profit of 20 percent on product line *B*. The analyst decides to allocate all costs as a percentage of dollar sales, which turns out to be 25 percent. On this basis he concludes that 40 percent less 25 percent gives him 15 percent net profit on product line *A*. If he subtracts 25 percent from the 20 percent gross profit on product line *B*, he ends up with a 5 percent net loss. But this is obviously circular reasoning. The only excuse for going to all the trouble to calculate net profits by products is the well-founded suspicion that gross profit and net profit do not always move in the same direction. If the analyst allocates on the basis of dollar sales volume, he knows the answer without making any calculation whatever. He will always get his highest net profit where he gets his highest gross profit.

To the reader this may seem to be belaboring the point. But there is a strange fixation among accountants that allocation by dollar sales volume is neutral and does not affect the result. It is anything but neutral, as pointed out above. Suppose that the analyst has labored hard to find appropriate allocating factors and then is confronted with some costs of a very general nature such as administrative overhead. Having little information as to how top management spends its time, he would like to find a neutral allocating factor. In other words, he would like to have the relative net profit on products and customers come out just the way they were before. Obviously the only factor which is neutral in this sense is the sum of all other costs.

FURTHER DETAILS OF PROCEDURE

After this digression on how not to allocate, the final stages of procedure will be summarized once more. The analyst will end up with ten to fifteen allocating sheets, one for each functional cost group. He will have filled in all sixteen cells in the case of the four by four table. That is to say, he will have allocated a portion of the cost to each group of transactions representing the sale of a class of products to a type of customer. He will now use a summary sheet and add through to get total costs for each cell. That is to say, he will list the ten or fifteen figures appearing in cell A-1 and add them up to get the total of all functional cost groups as applied to that cell. He will do the same thing for all the other cells from A-2 on to D-4. Finally he will add the columns vertically to give him totals by territories or customer groups, and he will add the rows across to give him totals for products.

To complete the calculation he will subtract operating costs from gross profit, product by product and territory by territory. Or to go back one more step, he will subtract cost of goods sold from dollar sales volume to get gross profit and, in turn, subtract operating cost from gross profit. It is a little shocking at times to find that a firm has rather poor information on gross profit, to say nothing of net profit. As a matter of fact, a major part of the task in marketing cost analysis is often that of establishing valid gross profit figures. The raw materials entering into the product may fluctuate rapidly in market price. The discount structure on the end-product may have been deliberately designed to conceal the facts rather than reveal them. Sometimes it is discovered that the cost of goods sold on a product is close to break-even before making any allowance for marketing costs.

APPLICATION OF MARKETING COST ANALYSIS

Marketing cost analysis is a primary tool for system planning but not the only one. After this presentation of the elements of cost analysis, attention can be directed to its application. The methods of application represent a considerable advance over what has been done in the past. By drawing a sharper distinction between types of variables and using the computer for cost projections, the analyst can employ marketing cost analysis most effectively for planning or replanning marketing systems.

First, however, it should be pointed out that there is a glaring fallacy in the criticism most commonly leveled against this technique. Marketing cost analysis is said by some to ignore marginal considerations and to rely solely on average costs. Actually the marginal cost principle is built into the methods which have been presented in a way that has been completely overlooked by these critics. This fact can be illustrated by a simple geographic example. Suppose a wholesaler wants to determine his natural area of operation within which he has an advantage over wholesalers located in other cities. Assume for a moment that the only variable cost is the cost of freight or delivery. A map of his territory broken down into counties or other geographic units might look something like that below.

WHOLESALER'S TERRITORY

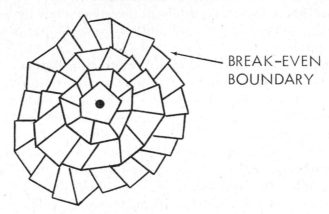

BREAK-EVEN
BOUNDARY

Headquarters City Shown in Center

All other costs being equal, the cost of delivery will increase as the wholesaler moves outward from his headquarters city. He will eventually reach a point at which the price received for his goods just equals his total costs, including delivery. Regardless of the direction in which he moves from the center, he will eventually reach this break-even boundary.

If he has made a marketing cost analysis, he will have a cost figure for each territory. His margin over costs will gradually decrease as he moves out toward the break-even boundary and finally disappear. As a matter of fact, if he goes on beyond this boundary, he will begin to accrue losses which increase the further out he goes. The analyst tells him that he should not go beyond this boundary and, if he does, he will be forfeiting some of the profits he made nearer to his home base. The application of marginal analysis in the example should be obvious. It is true that the analyst has used a rather coarse grid. He does not attempt to draw the break-even boundary in terms of the last dollar of sales which will just be absorbed by costs. He is content to deal with the last thousand dollars or the last five thousand dollars. His judgments are approximations which is all he can ever hope to make them in a practical world. He knows about where the break-even boundary lies without trying to identify the last retailer he should try to serve.

The marginal principle is at work in various directions and not only in the geographic dimension. If he analyzes the business in terms of size of order, he will find that there is a level below which he cannot afford to take an order. While additions of products to inventory may favor an increase in sales volume, there is a point at which inventory cost will absorb all the additional revenue. Sales can be increased by increasing the number of products stocked, but there is a break-even boundary which will eventually show up on this front. Now the virtue of marketing cost analysis is that the tabulations show all of these approaches to the margin operating at the same time. While the approach along each dimension is only an approximation, the sum of these approximations is generally conclusive. In most cases the business is better off if it will quit selling products it appears to be selling at a loss and quit selling customers it is selling at a loss. By refusing unprofitable business the firm retains the profit it makes on profitable products and customers. To transfer the sales effort expanded on unprofitable business to profitable customers and products is simple gumption once the figures are determined.

There is a major complication, of course, in the fact that marketing outlays indirectly affect production costs. Added marketing expenditure may cause production costs to fall enough to more than offset the rising costs of marketing. These effects on production costs should be taken into account in any projection of future cost estimates. The argument that a product should remain in the line if it merely contributes something to overhead overlooks the possibility of replacing it with a better product. The fact that it is losing money at the marketing level would appear to indicate that it is difficult to sell. The question may arise in a multidivision company as to who is entitled to use the argument about contribution to overhead. There is always the possibility that the reason a product fails to show a profit in marketing terms is that it is not being properly marketed. There are occasions when a product is sold at no better than break-even as a matter of well-understood marketing policy. It may be, for example, that a company engages in a further stage of manufacture to protect profits further back in the line. By and large it makes sense to require every product to stand on its own feet in making its way in the market place.

EFFORT VARIABLES AND RESPONSE VARIABLES

Optimal application of the results of marketing cost analysis requires that a distinction be drawn between effort variables and response variables. Effort variables might be called structural variables except for the possible confusion with the use of this term in another connection. These are the variables which are inherent in the structure of the situation as, for example, variations in cost by size of order. Relative effort increases as size of order decreases, and this is the inescapable penalty for accepting smaller orders. Effort variables are most clearly represented in such costs as delivery, billing, order handling, and purchasing. It is not that efficiencies are not available with respect to effort variables, but the route to these efficiencies is another story to be discussed later.

Most characteristic of the response variables are advertising and selling. The presumption is that the market responds or may respond as advertising and selling expenditures increase. It is important to know the shape of these response functions in making marketing plans. A response function may be in the region of increasing returns or decreasing returns. It may be at about the point where costs will equal returns or it may be some distance away. It is conceivable that the analyst might arrive at erroneous conclusions when a large amount of promotional expenditure was being made or was contemplated. A product might be barely breaking even with no advertising expenditure. Yet it is possible that a large advertising expenditure would greatly increase sales and have a very favorable effect both on production costs and on the percentage of total marketing costs to sales. At the other extreme is the product on which there appears to be a fair margin of profit but the point of market saturation is near at hand so that an increased advertising expenditure will bring only a disappointing response.

Actually most companies today have little knowledge of where their products stand on the response functions relating advertising expenditure to sales and profits. These curves can vary greatly in shape as indicated in Figure 20–1.

Figure 20–1

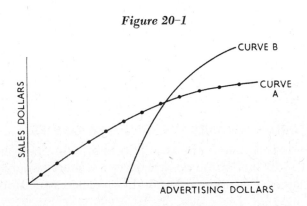

The two curves have different ceilings or saturation levels, curve *B* reaching the higher level. In addition, curve *B* has a threshold. That means that it does not start rising from the point of origin as does curve *A*, indicating some response to advertising from the start. Instead curve *B* cuts the horizontal axis which means that a substantial amount of money must be spent for advertising before there is any response at all. This might be the case with a new packaged food which might have to have powerful advertising support even to get on the grocer's shelves. If the response function for the product was curve *B* and the sponsor imagined that he was operating on something like curve *A*, he might reach decisions that were directly contrary to the facts. He might, for example, spend a moderate amount for advertising which would have no effect if he spent less than *X* dollars. If the situation were reversed and he based his policies on something like curve *B* while actually curve *A* was closer to the mark, he might waste advertising dollars at the higher end of the range. That is to say, he could be trying to push the product toward a higher saturation level when it was already leveling off in accordance with curve *A*. The lack of quantitative information about response functions for advertising means that mistakes of both kinds are bound to be occurring.

Progress for large business enterprise calls for steadily increasing knowledge of consumer response functions. The degree of uncertainty now faced is becoming intolerable for some managements. As one critic of advertising put it, nowhere in the American economy is so much money spent with so little knowledge of the results which can be expected. Some leading manufacturers and all the larger advertising agencies have set a goal of getting better answers to the question of optimal advertising expenditure, and steady progress is being made. Meanwhile a thorough marketing cost study must be supplemented by estimates concerning the shape of the advertising response function and the point on the curve where the business is now operating. These estimates are usually better than blind guesses even now. The saturation level can be approximated within broad limits. If there is a threshold of substantial proportions to be matched before advertising begins to pay off, the size of this threshold can be approximated too.

ADVERTISING AND OTHER RESPONSE FUNCTIONS

There are some very large advertisers with such massive budgets as to suggest that nothing really matters in their marketing expenditure except advertising. All other marketing costs are overshadowed by the advertising budget, and the one fundamental question is to determine where the company stands with respect to the response function. Even here something might be learned by a territorial analysis to find out where advertising is paying its way. This relationship is sometimes obscured by the tendency for manufacturers to distribute advertising expenditures on the basis of sales. Thus even though advertising was generally ineffective it could show a close correlation to sales because advertising is actually the dependent variable. That is to say, management takes last year's sales, territory by territory, and allocates advertising to each territory as a percentage of sales.

Figure 20-2

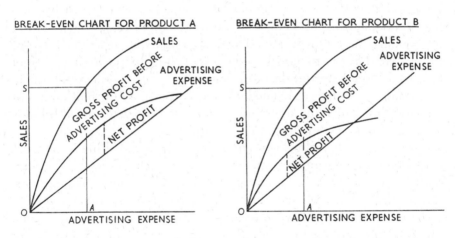

It could still be significant that total costs including advertising are in excess of gross profit even though the fact may not provide clear guidance for advertising policy. It may even mean that money is being wasted by inefficiency in other functions which should be used to increase the advertising budget. Market cost analysis simply undertakes to show whether segments of the business are currently making money or losing money when all costs are considered. By itself it will not show whether advertising expenditure should be increased or decreased or how much. In the break-even charts in Figure 20-2 for product *A* and product *B* the advertising expenditure is the same in each chart, and the dollar sales figure is the same. Yet advertising expenditure should be increased on product *A* and decreased on product *B*.

Advertising expenditure is plotted on the horizontal axis but it also is represented by the 45° angle through the point of origin.

The upper curved line shows how sales increase with advertising but gradually level off at some saturation point. The lower curved line shows gross profit after marketing costs other than advertising are higher for product *A* than for product *B*. The area between the diagonal line representing advertising expenditure and the lower curved line represents net profit. The dotted vertical line is the point of maximum profits in each chart. In the chart for product *A*, advertising should be increased because this vertical line is to the right of the point representing the present level of advertising. In the chart for product *B*, it should be decreased because it is to the left of the point representing the present level of advertising.

The advertising manager cannot tell whether to increase or decrease advertising expenditure, looking at current costs only. He must make some judgment as to the position of the curve showing the response of sales to advertising. He must also consider the costs other than advertising which must be deducted from sales to give gross profit before advertising.

Sometimes the planner will have some information available to him concerning the shape of the sales response function. At other times he will have to guess at its shape by estimating two values which must lie on the curve, namely the saturation level and the threshold, if any. The saturation level is the point where sales begin to level off despite the amounts spent for advertising. The threshold is the level below which there is no appreciable effect from advertising. Figure 20–3 illustrates how these judgments can be organized so as to make a decision as to whether advertising expenditure should be increased or decreased.

Figure 20–3

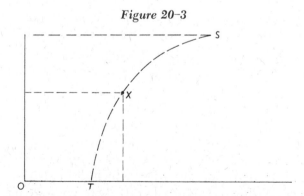

In this chart the horizontal dotted line is the saturation level. The threshold is indicated by *T* which should lie on the horizontal axis. The literal meaning is that there would be no response at all below this point but that the amount of advertising represented by the segment *OT* would have to be spent in order to get any results in sales. The point *X* represents the current relationship between advertising and sales. Under these assumptions the problem is to draw a curve passing through *X* and *T* and tangent to the horizontal line *S*. This would be the estimated function for the response of sales to advertising.

The next step is to guess at the curve showing gross profit before advertising and hence to derive the shape of the area in which net profits after advertising could be expected. This procedure will help to sharpen up this issue even if it cannot be carried out with great precision. Suppose, for example, that a product situation has the following characteristics relative to another product. The saturation level is well above the present level of sales. There is a high threshold before advertising begins to take hold. Costs other than advertising are high at the lower ranges of sales volume. All of these factors would argue in favor of a fairly intensive level of advertising expenditure. Or to put it another way, it would appear to call for a heavy expenditure or nothing since relatively modest expenditures would almost certainly be ineffective. The directly opposite situation would be a low level of saturation, no threshold, and moderate costs other than advertising. In this case the indications would be for a relatively modest advertising budget. In the first case, if current results showed a loss or break-even after advertising costs, there would be good grounds for increasing the budget in the hope of moving upward into the profit area. In the second case indications would be for reducing advertising expenditure in order to make a better showing.

The value of marketing cost analysis for planning marketing systems is still substantial despite the need for careful interpretation. Marketing cost analysis can sharpen the issues which require other data to assist in interpretation. Certainly the difficulty of interpreting cost data is not a valid argument against analyzing them in the first place. Often it may be desirable to consider costs other than advertising first and then take account of the cost of advertising. Suppose that the cost of personal selling alone shows that the salesman cannot pick up an order for less than $10. Then the company would lose money on all orders which did not produce at least $10 in gross profit before advertising. If there were reason to believe that the company was already covering most of the worthwhile customers and that an increase in advertising expenditure would result mainly in producing orders below the minimum level, then the verdict would obviously be unfavorable to advertising. Stated in a slightly different way, there must be a margin over the costs which vary with the volume of business handled on existing business. Only then can advertising contribute to profits by producing a greater volume of sales.

COST AND PROFIT PROJECTIONS

The full benefit of marketing cost analysis will not be achieved until there is a more general practice of making cost and profit projections based on past results. These projections would take the form of setting up a pro forma operating statement for the year ahead, using data from the year just completed. Projections of this type would require only a moderate extension of the budgeting process as it is carried on in some of the more advanced marketing organizations. In its most complete form this projection procedure would require a computer program covering all the major variables in the marketing system.

The suggestion has already been made that these variables can be divided into effort variables and response variables. Each effort variable tends to be a linear function of some measure of the flow of products in marketing. Billing cost, for example, is taken to be a linear function of the number of invoice lines, and shipping or delivery cost can often be regarded as a linear function of ton miles. These are the various activities which occur in responding to customer orders. It may actually be too costly to respond if the customer is located at too great a distance, if his average order is too small, or if he divides his business among many items requiring such extra services as special packaging.

The response variables such as that for advertising are likely to be governed by nonlinear functions. Advertising results, for example, are likely to show an increasing rate of returns at one point and decreasing returns at another. That is because the concept of market saturation is believed to have universal application. Response variables are found in the area which was previously called capacity costs. Cost of work depends on the amount of work performed, but cost of capacity depends on the response of the market. If the response is strong, the cost of capacity per unit of product is reduced. If still more money is spent to stimulate potential sales, the return may not be as large proportionately, and the cost per unit of product begins to increase again.

In creating a cost and profit model of the firm, each functional cost needs to be examined for possible nonlinearity. While advertising cost is generally of this character, selling cost may be a borderline case. Sometimes the selling job is merely order taking and can be expected to go up or down with the number of orders. In other situations the sales force is engaged in creative promotional selling, and hence the results achieved are subject to increasing and decreasing returns. The market may also respond to the breadth or depth of the product assortment. There can be an inventory assortment which is just right or, in other words, optimal for inducing this type of response. This means that the marketing organization is not selling individual items in isolation but that up to a certain point the items in the line tend to reinforce each other. Similarly there may be an optimal point with respect to the number of stores or distributors handling a product. Ideally it should be large enough to provide every consumer with an opportunity to buy it but not so large as to destroy the incentive of the individual to push the product. The rule of reason in this type of review is that the analyst can assume linear relationships to exist when the departures from linearity are in his judgment not too great.

A SIMPLE COST AND PROFIT MODEL

The construction of a projectable cost and profit model will be illustrated for a firm which has only three products and three sales territories. For each product the analyst will need to set up cost functions relating cost to some factor such as ton-miles for delivery cost or invoice lines for billing. This is an exercise in detailed forecasting by functional cost groups rather than total costs. The forecasts for the two functions mentioned might look like Figure 20-4.

Both of these are effort variables and a straight line should give a close enough approximation. In the first chart it is assumed that ton

Figure 20-4

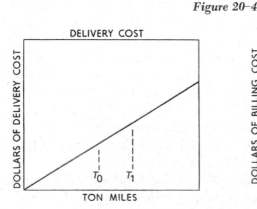
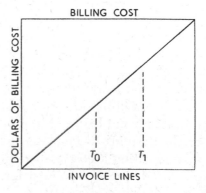

miles increase at the same rate as dollar sales. In the second chart it is assumed that invoices lines would have a steeper slope than dollar sales, since increased sales may come in larger degree from smaller customers. Dollar sales is shown as a dotted line on the chart but only to indicate that it might be useful in helping to determine the slope for invoice lines in relation to billing cost. In each chart T_0 indicates the total functional cost as determined by the latest marketing cost analyses, and T_1 is the projected cost for the period ahead. After two or more cost studies have been made the analyst would begin to have greater assurance that he knew the shape of the functional cost curves.

Methods for estimating the shape of the function for the response variables have already been presented. Product by product the firm may be enjoying increasing returns on some products and already running into decreasing returns on others. It is reasonable to assume that the products enjoying increasing returns would receive the largest share of any increase in promotional expenditures. In fact, a major purpose of the whole forecast is to show what might happen to costs and hence to profits with a change in the allocation of promotional dollars. The three-product case assumed in the next illustration would lead to a summary projection like the following:

Cost Projections for the Year 196X

	Products		
Functional Costs	A	B	C
Cost Group #1.............			
#2.............			
#3.............			
#4.............			
#5.............			
#6.............			
#7.............			
#8.............			
Totals.............			

There are three other projections to be made to complete the analysis. One is a projection of the sales which should result from the new level of promotional expenditures. A second is a projection of cost of goods sold, taking account of both fixed and variable costs. One reason for greater advertising expenditure on a product may be that substantial production economies are expected at the higher level of sales. The third projection would be made of gross profit directly rather than regarding it only as the difference between sales and cost of goods sold. There may be a downward drift in prices so that moving the same tonnage or the same number of cases will not result in as large a dollar volume.

The analysis of costs by territories is an essential supplement to the analysis by products. In the case which we have been considering, each of the products *A, B,* and *C* would be scrutinized more closely with respect to the results forecast for territories 1, 2, and 3. Suppose the firm is located in the West, which is territory 1. It is moderately strong in the midwestern states, or territory 2, and it is quite weak in the eastern states, territory 3. Suppose that the largest expansion of sales is expected on product *A.* But it is clear that this increase will come mainly from the East and secondarily from the Midwest. The company will be able to maintain its price level fairly well in the Midwest, but it will cut its prices considerably to penetrate the more competitive markets of the East. Thus there will be lower prices on eastern sales which may be partially offset by achieving lower production costs at the larger volume of sales which entry into the eastern market will make possible.

Costs will also be affected by moving into eastern markets. If the company absorbs freight, then delivery costs will increase on sales further away from headquarters. A number of orders in territory 3 during the first year may be trial orders so that clerical costs will also tend to increase. These effects on effort variables should be predictable with considerable assurance. Finally an estimate will have to be made concerning the response variables in territory 3. This estimate is subject to a greater range of error since the company has had relatively little experience in this territory. It would be good practice to run some test campaigns in territory 3 before making a full-scale entry. In other instances it might be possible that company experience in other territories would repeat itself so that some estimate could be made of the period over which the company would have to invest in advertising before the market began to respond in satisfactory fashion.

The model for projecting future costs and profits begins to be fairly complex even when there are only three products and three territories. It would contain the following elements, all essential to the preparation of the forecasts:

1. Cost functions by products for effort variables.
2. Cost functions by products for response variables (some of these functions are likely to be nonlinear in form).
3. Forecasts by products of sales to be expected on the basis of sales and advertising programs.

4. Cost functions for both fixed and variable costs in production.
5. Independent forecast of gross profits related to some measure of physical volume such as cases sold.
6. Cost functions for effort variables by territory.
7. Cost functions for response variables by territory.
8. Forecasts by territory of sales to be expected on the basis of sales and advertising programs.
9. Forecast of sales volume based on elasticity to price.

Once the various cost functions had been fed into the computer it would not require a very large computer program to produce the cost and profit projections for a year ahead. Suppose the company's business was to be divided up by 10 product lines and 10 territories. A single set of projections, related to a specified manipulation of the response variables, could be produced with not more than 2,500 calculations. Generally speaking, the calculations required would be proportional to the number of products multiplied by the number of territories. For the 10 by 10 matrix, calculations could be made very quickly for one alternative plan after another on an analog computer of moderate size.

THE LANGUAGE OF PROFIT CONTROL

The dollars of net profit or loss resulting from a marketing cost analysis or a cost and profit projection will need to be expressed in several ways to be meaningful. Several simple ratios have been used, including profit as a percentage of investment and profit as a percentage of sales. A third ratio, favored here, can be called marketing yield. The formula for this measure is as follows:

$$\text{Marketing Yield} = \frac{\text{Gross Profit} - \text{Total Marketing Cost}}{\text{Controllable Marketing Cost}}$$

The numerator of the expression on the right is actually net profit. It is stated in a particular way to call attention to the fact that only those costs controllable by the marketing department are included in the denominator. The marketing department is responsible indirectly for what happens even though some costs such as freight may be under the direct control of a traffic manager or director of physical distribution. However, the resulting net profit is divided by controllable costs only to reflect a marketing yield per dollar. In the three ratios mentioned above, net profit is divided respectively by investment, by sales, and by controllable marketing costs.

Each of these ratios has a primary area of usefulness. The investment ratio is obviously most useful in making investment decisions.

It is the appropriate guidepost in determining whether plant capacity should be expanded for a given product. It is less useful in marketing because the marketing executive has a smaller amount of investment under his control. Nevertheless the kind of cost analysis and cost projections which have been recommended will be useful in determining whether the outlook is favorable to new investment. For example, a product which otherwise looks favorable for plant expansion may be about to reach a point of market saturation and hence not be inviting for investment in new capacity.

Net profit as a ratio to sales has special merit in considering changes in price. Suppose, for example, that a product has a large net profit to sales ratio but has a low sales volume compared to competition. It is well to consider what might be accomplished by a price reduction. It will be easy to calculate the sales volume which would be required to produce the same net profit at the lower price. Suppose the product now carries a net profit of 20 percent and it is proposed to cut the price so as to yield a net profit to sales of only 10 percent. If costs, including production costs, remain the same, sales would have to be doubled to maintain the same dollars of net profit.

On most products demand is not nearly so elastic to price. A 10 percent cut in sales price would not result in a doubling of sales. A larger price cut might be justified if it led immediately to lower costs of production. In the example just cited it will be assumed that the cost structure is pictured in Figure 20–5. The two bars show net profit at the top, then distribution cost, and production cost at the bottom. The division of a dollar of gross revenue as shown in the first bar is production cost 60 percent, distribution cost 20 per-

Figure 20–5

COST STRUCTURE

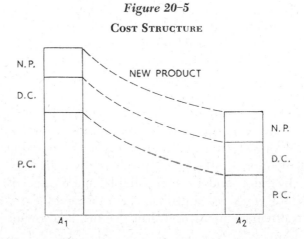

cent, and net profit 20 percent. We will assume that this is a new product where a cut in price will have a marked effect on production costs. Here it is assumed that cutting price by 40 percent will lead to a 100 percent increase in sales. The production cost curve is falling rapidly at this point and, in fact, results in cutting production costs in half as shown in the second bar. Distribution costs remain at the same dollar figure per unit. Net profit per unit is decreased in dollars per unit by one half. If sales are doubled, the firm will come out with the same dollars of profit after the price cut. It is this type of cut which expands the volume on new products rather than the more moderate type of cut designed only to meet competition.

If a product is losing money or barely breaking even, a price increase may be considered. Sometimes this means that many customers will buy this product from another supplier. The result would normally be to stop the losses on the product or even to make a little money on it. The seller may be deliberately pricing himself out of the market but still be better off than he was before.

Finally there is the measure of marketing yield which has already been described. If this ratio is high, meaning that there is a large return per dollar of controllable cost, there should be room to spend money for increased marketing cost. The most likely situation is that more money can profitably be spent on such response variables as advertising. If marketing yield is low, there are several things to look for in trying to improve it. There may be inefficiency with respect to such effort variables as order filling or billing. This might be taken as a signal for restudying the procedures in these areas. A second possibility may be that the advertising budget for the product is wasteful because the product has already reached the point of market saturation.

THE CRITICAL ASPECTS OF MARKETING SYSTEMS

It is now time to look at the vertical dimension of marketing systems. This chapter has been concerned up until now with the horizontal dimension in which one typically makes judgments among the products to be carried by the system or territories to be served. The vertical aspect deals with a sequence of events. This sequence is assumed to be repetitive in considering the design of a system. The system performs certain operations over and over and generally performs them in the same order. In this section a search will be made for design principles which can provide direction in establishing a sequence of repetitive operations.

One phase of the sequence has been subjected to intensive analysis. This is the part called the inventory system. The sequence consists of procuring the item from sources outside the system, carrying it in stock until demanded, and then filling customer orders. Sometimes back orders are entered with suppliers when the item is out of stock, but sometimes the customer order is lost if it cannot be filled immediately. Data must be gathered and analyzed to exercise control over the inventory system. The simplest formula, known as the square root formula, balances the cost of carrying inventory against the cost of reordering. This model is shown in Figure 20–6.

Figure 20-6

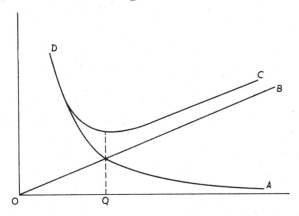

The diagonal line through the point of origin *OB* is the inventory carrying cost which rises steadily over time. The line *DA* is the cost of reordering. This cost comes down as the number of orders grows less and less frequent. The line *DC* represents the sum of these two costs. This cost curve is at its lowest point at the dotted line marked *Q*. The inventory in the system, under an optimal policy, will range between *O* and *Q* or an average amount of $\frac{Q}{2}$. The optimal value is as follows:

$$\frac{Q}{2} = \sqrt{\frac{A}{2\,I_c}}$$

The numerator of this fraction stands for reordering cost and the denominator for inventory carrying cost. The whole expression is under a square root sign which has some interesting implications. It means that as sales increase inventory should increase only as the square root and not in direct relation to sales.

This chapter will not go any further with this elementary discussion of the inventory problem since the basic problem in designing the vertical dimension of a system must be seen in a broader framework. A single firm stands at some point in a marketing channel and is only one of the firms in the system to hold an inventory. The analyst should look at the whole system as if it were controlled by a single firm. This will give him the basis for deciding what the relations among the several stages in the sequence should be. This type of inventory system is called a multiechelon system. Most of the problems of multiechelon systems are yet to be solved analytically.

The first question to be answered, looking at the vertical system as a whole, is how many steps or stages there should be in the system. The analyst in a large company often has such a choice to make in determining whether he will use wholesalers or sell directly to retailers and whether he will use brokers or sell directly to wholesalers. In any case, to create a system initially or to modify a system, it is a useful approach to consider what the system ought to look like from the standpoint of the total trade or industry and then to see what is required to move the system toward this ideal.

The economic process is said to create time, place, and form utility. The creation of time utility means having goods on sale at the time when people want to buy them. They buy fresh fruits according to season at various times of the year as they become available but buy most products according to their current needs. There are peak months for the purchase of clothing, for fuels for household heating in the winter, and air conditioners in the summer. The planner starts with careful statistical studies of the quantities required by consumers for his type of product and when the products must reach the retail stores in order to be on display and ready for selection by consumers.

Looking at the system as a whole, it is clear that the cost of carrying inventory should be kept to a moderate figure by starting just in time to prepare the inventory for the next season. Many considerations go into a definition of the phrase "just in time," but the longer goods are in process or in storage, the higher the carrying charges will be. Furthermore the rate at which carrying charges accumulate takes a jump at each stage along the way. It costs less to carry goods at wholesale than retail and still less at the manufacturer's warehouse. The difference in cost of carrying is related to the price of the goods. Higher prices, as we move down the channel, reflect the cost which has been added to the goods. Retail inventory is worth more than wholesale inventory because the goods have been shipped from the wholesaler to the retailer, and the lowest price is attached to the goods while they are still in the hands of the manufacturer. The principle of having the goods ready just in time at each stage minimizes the cost of creating time utility.

Creation of place utility and form utility operate on a different principle. The problem of economic lot size is involved in both instances. If time utility was all that mattered, a product might be shipped one item at a time in a continuous flow to reach each consumer "just in time." This is not done because of the problem of economic lots for transportation purposes. If there is great advantage in shipping the product in carload lots, this may be done even though it means some increase in the average size of inventory. A purchaser can readily determine whether to order in carload lots or some smaller quantity. He will favor the larger lot if $S_2 - S_1 \geq C_1 - C_2$. That is to say, the larger lot is justified if what he saves by accepting the more economical lot size for shipping is equal to or larger than what he loses in the difference in carrying cost.

The earlier discussion, leading up to the square root rule for inventory control, assumed that the economic lot size for shipment is a continuous variable. Actually there are usually only a few breaking points which need to be examined. Those include carloads, truckloads, and full cases. In some trades wholesale deliveries are made even for the smallest and most expensive unit, namely, the individual package. This is often true for the retail drug store which carries some items which are rarely called for. It is not unusual to see the quantity 1/12 of a dozen on the druggist's order to his wholesaler. If it should happen that a second customer should call for one of these rare items on the same day, the product would have to be back ordered. The customer, realizing that his demand is unusual, is likely to be more tolerant than if the store were out of an item sold by the hundreds every day.

To coordinate a sequence of independent steps in a channel requires a good information system just as it does for the single firm coping with its own internal inventory control problem. Advanced information systems have been developed for such marketing organizations as department stores and wholesale grocery warehousing. In these systems there is a reorder point determined by the extent to which the inventory has been depleted and the probable time delay in securing replacements. Where computer control has been installed, the fact that the reorder point has been reached is immediately brought to the buyer's attention. In fact, it would be theoretically possible on staple goods for the computer to be activated by the reorder point signal and print out orders in the right quantities to be mailed to the appropriate suppliers. For example, a chain warehouse buying Campbell's pork and beans in truckloads would simply buy with somewhat greater frequency as the peak season approached. This procedure would approximate the lowest combined cost of replenishing and carrying inventory.

PRODUCTION OF FORM UTILITY

In designing a total system, considerations concerned with form utility are somewhat more complex than those associated with place utility. Economic lot size is determined by setup costs which may require plant equipment to shut down for varying lengths of time during a change-over. There is also a problem affecting the overall costs of production of smoothing out the labor requirements to minimize either overtime or layoffs. While the contact of the market planner with production is largely through market forecasting and the question of economic lot size, he should be aware of any unusual demands on the production department which are generated by marketing. Preparation of deal merchandise properly marked and sometimes with special premiums inside the package is such a problem. In the ideal situation marketing would present its market forecast and also the schedule of priorities for the delivery of various finished products. In speculating about the design of a control system, the control information would necessarily originate with marketing.

In the simplest terms the plant is processing goods to go into an inventory just as the shipper is shipping goods to go into an inventory. The principle should still hold of getting there "just in time" with the needed products, taking account of economic lot size. The case is especially clear when the manufacturer maintains an inventory in his own warehouse. He is most likely to do so when the economic lot size is large so that he is forced to produce for stock instead of operating on the basis of individual orders from customers. The economic lot size for processing may be many times as large as the economic lot size for shipping. The manufacturer's warehouse is the first point for breaking bulk. Not only is the economic lot size smaller for shipping than for processing, but many carloads are mixed cars to which production runs on a number of different products have contributed.

Economic lot size is assumed to be a continuous variable in the processing case. That is to say, production can cease at the nth unit whatever the value of n. Somewhat more precise solutions can be obtained when a manufacturer is producing to stock and can set the economic lot size at just the right point to minimize total costs including carrying costs. Carrying cost is a continuous variable also. Actually there may be some discontinuities in economic lot size, but they can probably be ignored for this purpose. A plant may run on a given item for a certain number of days and turn out a quantity which approximates the economic lot size. Materials needed for one model may be exhausted before the full amount of the economic lot has been produced. But these variations would not enter into the broad design for a marketing system.

In some industries the marketing requirements for diversity of product have gone a long way toward dissipating the advantages of mass production. One place where technological advance is imperative is in finding compromises between the thrust toward heterogeneity in the end-product and preserving the advantages of mass production which depend in part on considerations surrounding economic lot size. A sharp contrast is found in the adjustment which has been made by the automobile industry and by the companies which supply upholstery for the interior of the automobile. At the Ford assembly plant it is said that they could run a million and a half variations in style and accessories through the assembly line without ever slowing it down. This is equivalent to saying that the problem of economic lot size has virtually disappeared at the level of automobile assembly.

The upholstery manufacturer is not in so fortunate a position. He once had three or four numbers to produce and a loom could run on leading item numbers for as much as six weeks at a time. Later he came to have as many as two hundred varieties in fabric, style, and color, so that change-over from one item to another became increasingly costly. This characteristic seems to be inherent in the textile industry but a partial answer may still be found. The switch of the carpet industry from weaving to tufting apparently represented such a partial solution. Steel rolling mills have also partially solved this problem. Hot steel billets come down the rollers in a continuous stream and may end up in as many as a hundred different end-products during a single day. Technicians stationed at various points along the way are able to make the adjustments required by one lot after another so rapidly there is scarcely a break.

The lower the threshold of economic lot size in production can be reduced, the less account needs to be taken of it in producing to stock. More and more the controlling principle is that of getting the inventory finished just in time to take care of demands originating further along in the channel. This principle was described in an earlier book as the principle of postponement. This terminology turned out to be confusing since many associated this principle with procrastination rather than recognizing it as a principle requiring close calculation in the interest of economizing the cost of carrying inventory. The application to economies in transportation cost would imply that the amount reordered would usually be matched with some unit such as a carload or truckload which offered economies in transportation. Several carloads or truckloads might be included in the same order if the rate of sale was very high. The clerical costs of reordering might not be significant, but the operator might want to have the stock in the house to serve various other purposes such as retail displays or back-up stocks.

The essential procedure for creating a total system starts by calculating the total time required in preparing to meet consumer demand for a given period. The shipments designed to generate place utility should not be made until there is just a reasonable time remaining to meet these requirements. Similarly, the processing which creates form utility should not take place until it is estimated that there is just time enough to meet the demands of the market. These delays will provide greater assurance that materials will be made up and combined in the products that are needed and that the finished products will be shipped to the places where they are most needed.

SORTS AND ACTIVITIES

Another approach to an understanding of the vertical dimensions of marketing processes is to regard it as a sequence alternating sorts and transformations or activities. Materials are sorted to prepare for manufacture. If the manufacturer has no warehouse, goods are sorted into the piles destined for various customers as they come off the production line. Shipment is an activity which changes the geographical location of goods just as production processing is an activity which changes their form. When the goods arrive at the wholesaler's place of business, they are added to the respective stocks of the goods on hand which is another form of sorting. The next activity is the rather passive one of storage in which time utility is being created. When the goods leave the warehouse, they are again sorted into the piles going to individual retailers. After another transit to the retailer locations, goods are sorted into the retailer's displays. When the customer has made his selections, the goods are wrapped or packed in forms in which he can carry them home. Thus the alternation is invariable throughout the series. There is always a sorting operation to prepare the product, materials, or components for the next transformation.

The total marketing process can be looked upon as a balance between the number of sorts and the number of transformations. This can best be seen by looking at an enclosed system in which the only transformation is a change of place through shipment. United Parcel will pick up packages anywhere in its territory destined for any other place in the territory. The pickup is made in a small truck which takes the packages into a collection point. Here the packages are transferred to a large truck and sent to a central hub. The cost per package per mile is substantially lower in the large truck than in the pickup truck. At the hub the packages are either shipped to another hub in an over-the-road truck or go directly to a distribution point. At the distribution point they are again transferred from the large truck to a small truck for door-to-door delivery.

The paradox of this system is that some packages are carried many more miles than the most direct route between origin and destination. The sender and the receiver could theoretically be only a block or two apart. But the system would obviously be far too expensive if it undertook to make direct connections between every origin and every destination. The offsetting factor is that the cost per package per mile is a very small fraction of that for direct origin to destination delivery. The key question in designing or redesigning such a system is whether additional sorts would increase or decrease the average cost per package per mile. Consider, for example, whether a super hub should be inserted between the hubs on long trips with piggyback trucks on railroad cars taking packages in and out of the super hub. This would open up the possibility of sorting by truck loads or other large containers rather than by packages at the super hubs. The labor cost of the additional sort would have to be more than offset by the saving in the average cost of movement from hub to hub. At present the volume of traffic is probably not enough to sustain one or more additional sorts. But even though the volume should expand to permit further sorting a limit would presently be reached on other grounds. One advantage of the system as it stands is that it can promise delivery within two days throughout its territory. Additional sorts take time and also make the process more roundabout with the average package traveling more miles. At the limit, one more additional sort would make the service unattractive even though it saved cost.

SYSTEM PLANNING AND INDIVIDUAL ADVANTAGE

The first part of this chapter dealt with the horizontal aspect of system planning from the viewpoint of the individual firm. Yet the decisions made by the individual help make the system as a whole work more smoothly. For example, the firm may decide to give up a territory in which it has been losing money. This means that someone else in the system may be able to pick up this business and do it at a profit. Looking at the horizontal aspect leads each firm in the direction of doing what it can do best. This is the same thing as saying that the firm should occupy its distinctive niche and that it is likely to lose money when it ventures beyond this niche. Perhaps it is more accurate to say that, while a firm may venture into new areas from time to time, it needs to make a careful evaluation of the cost of expanding its niche. The section on cost and profit projections points in that direction.

In looking at the vertical dimension of systems, the planner has been advised to look beyond the limits of his firm and plan for the whole system of which he is a part. He does this in his own interest because what is only an ideal today may become reality tomorrow. If a way of organizing or reorganizing the total system is in the public interest because it leads to lower costs, then someone is going to find a way of moving toward this ideal because it turns out to be in his individual interest as well. For the time being, the individual may be able to influence only that part of the process in which he operates. To make himself a more effective link between his suppliers and his customers is generally to move in the direction of making his own business more profitable. Following the total systems approach to marketing will also make him sensitive to the more drastic changes which occur from time to time and permit him to make an advantageous adjustment.

Selected References

ASHBY, ROSS. *Design for a Brain*. 2d ed. New York: John Wiley & Sons, 1960.
> The opening section on the nature of systems is one of the most lucid accounts to be found anywhere.

FORRESTER, JAY W. *Industrial Dynamics*. New York: John Wiley & Sons, 1961.
> A business system is pictured as containing feedback circuits for information and control. Written clearly and with a minimum of mathematics required.

LONGMAN, DONALD AND SCHIFF, MICHAEL. *Distribution Cost Analysis*. Homewood, Ill.: Richard D. Irwin, Inc., 1955
> A comprehensive treatment of costing methods, both for products and customers.

TAGGART, H. F. *Distribution Cost Analysis*. Washington, D.C.: Marketing Research Division, U.S. Department of Commerce, 1939.
> A summary of methods developed over a period of years in a series of studies undertaken by the Department of Commerce.

Problems

1. Discuss the difference between the grouping of expenditures for accounting purposes and for cost analysis purposes. Explain why accountants do not group expenditures according to function.

2. Discuss the reasons for not advocating the use of dollar sales as an allocating factor.

3. Evaluate the following statement: Marketing cost analysis ignores marginal considerations and relies solely on average costs.

4. Discuss the importance of response variables in marketing cost analysis.

5. Discuss the relationship between sorts and transformations.

Chapter 21

OPERATION UNDER A
DETAILED MARKETING PLAN

~~~~~~

Previous chapters have dealt with planning principles pertaining to the primary end products of planning. This chapter returns to the subject of marketing campaigns and deals with some issues involved in operating under a detailed marketing plan. A plan is reviewed and tested before it is adopted. Once a plan is adopted, there may be a time allowance for its installation before the organization begins to operate under the plan. Meanwhile, attention is usually given to the detailed procedures which must be developed to make the plan effective. The fully detailed version of a plan, with programs, procedures, schedules and budget may be designated as the administrative model. It verges on an operating manual describing all of the activities which must be carried out to insure the success of a campaign.

TESTING A PLAN

There are two primary possibilities for testing a marketing plan. One is a live test in the market place. The other is simulation of the planned activities on an electronic computer. Market testing has developed into a widespread practice employed by many consumer goods manufacturers. The usual procedure is to prevail on retailers to stock the new product in one or more test cities and then set up an auditing system for measuring the flow through these stores. Some firms have virtually designed their plans in the market, gradually correcting their initial errors as they expand across the country from market to market.

A major disadvantage of market tests is that they constitute complete disclosure of a plan to competitors. One of the merits of a good strategic plan is that it may take the competition by surprise and cost them considerable delay before they are able to come up with an effective counterattack. The only way to preserve the element of surprise is to launch a crash program for gaining national distribution immediately rather than taking two or three years to "go national," market by market. The costs of a crash program are so great that only a few large companies can afford it and an even smaller number are willing to take the large risks involved. The success of these crash programs in several notable instances suggests that their sponsors must have had some means of validating these programs in advance other than market tests. There are two main possibilities which may in fact be parts of a single testing procedure.

The first factor is to make doubly sure of the factual assumptions underlying the plan. Some of the companies who sponsor crash programs engage in massive marketing research. They have taken more than usual care in measuring potential demand. What is even more crucial is to determine the shape of the respond functions showing how consumers will react to marketing effort. It is also desirable, if a crash effort is to be used, to carry product research to the point where the new product has a definite edge in important characteristics over products already available.

In addition to having reliable data about the market and competition, there is a need for a simulation model to test the logic of the plan as well as its underlying assumptions. There was a brief discussion of simulation methods in an earlier chapter. The subject was also treated somewhat more fully in *Marketing and the Computer*, edited by Alderson and Shapiro.[1] A simulation model sets up some simple mathematical functions to show how the constituent variables of the real situation react on each other. A common form of simulation model uses difference equations to predict the values for the variables in a given period based on the values of the same variables in the previous period. Two simple graphic illustrations follow, presenting the type of flow diagrams from which simulation models could be developed. The first of these would be useful for testing the external impact of a campaign on the market. The second illustration is concerned with a marketing intelligence system consisting of flows of information inside the company. This diagram was used in a consulting situation involving a problem of reconciling marketing and production plans as part of a consistent total program.

---

[1] Wroe Alderson and Stanley J. Shapiro (eds.), *Marketing and the Computer* (Englewood Cliffs, N.J.: Prentice-Hall, Inc., 1963).

STATE DIAGRAMS AND CONSUMER TRANSITIONS

Marketing is concerned with customers as well as goods. The visible and outward sign that the two have been brought together through marketing is the physical movement of goods. But marketing effort is directed toward bringing about movement of consumers as well. Consumers move to points at which goods are to be consumed such as a restaurant or theatre. The seller is primarily concerned, however, with movement in a figurative sense. The consumer is brought "closer" to the product through a series of psychological states. A consumer moves into the state of being a potential user of a product perhaps without being aware of the product or an incipient need to buy it. This change may consist of coming of age, of getting married, of entering a specific type of employment, or of buying a house or an automobile.

From that point changes of psychological states may begin which can be influenced by the active efforts of the seller. First, the prospective user may need to be convinced that he has a problem or be made aware of a potential need. Motivating a consumer to do something about a problem involves convincing him that the problem is important and that it is possible to do something about it. Specifically he must be persuaded to believe that the sponsor's product can serve the purpose.

Figure 21–1 sets up these psychological states and consumer transitions for an important class of products, namely, automobile tires. Car owners are not likely to be in the market for replacement tires until the car owned is three years old. With the greater durability that is built into tires, the average car will probably need at most two sets of tires after the original set has worn out. The final set in many cases will be retreads. Certainly the primary market is for the first replacement set while the car is still presumably in the hands of an owner who places a high value on the quality and safety of his automotive equipment.

The car owner reaches this point in his progress toward being a prospect for tires by steps that can be influenced materially by advertising. Car owners might be induced to travel more miles and hence have greater need for tires, but this is the kind of goal which might be achieved through the combined efforts of car manufacturers, oil companies, and others interested in travel, and not of the tire manufacturer alone. For the producer of tires the first use of advertising is to get a proportion of car owners to prefer his brand to any other. If it does seem feasible to inculcate this degree of preference, then the minimum objective is to gain acceptance for the brand as one of the standard makes that is eligible for purchase, all other things being equal.

Figure 21–1

STATE DIAGRAM

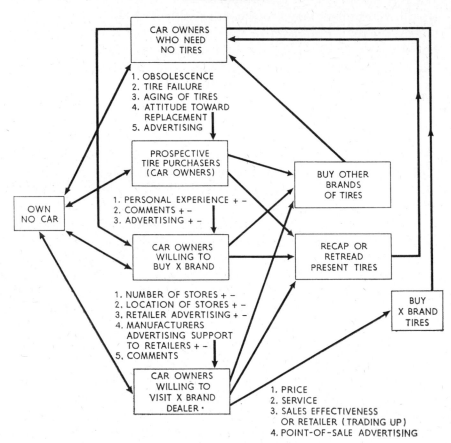

Replacement Purchases
(Passenger Tires only)

In the sale of tires many retailers tend to specialize on a single brand. Some of these stores are owned by the manufacturer, and others are exclusive agents. In order to buy a given brand of tires, the consumer will generally have to enter a retail store where these tires are sold. Plans and programs are conceived with this aim in mind as well as to influence brand preference.

There are further transitions in the sequence of states which influence the future purchases of the tire user. One is to complete the indicated replacement purchases whether of the given brand or a competitive brand. That carries the customers back to the beginning of the cycle and puts them in the class of people who may want tires at some future time but do not need them for the present. Some consumers meanwhile drop out of the population of potential users through death or by ceasing to drive a car. These losses are usually more than offset by new drivers who come of age and purchase automobiles. The replacement demand for tires can also be strengthened by a moderate drop in the level of consumer income. This can lead to people holding off on buying new cars and replacing their tires in order to drive the old car longer.

The market planner studies the sequence of transitions and the probabilities that individuals at a given state will move to the next one during the planning period. The purpose of advertising and promotion is to influence these transition probabilities in a favorable direction. Suppose that a preliminary judgment has selected two successive transitions as the one which the seller might attempt to influence. To use the tire example, let it be assumed that 50 percent of those in the market for tires accept the given brand as eligible for purchase. Suppose that 40 percent of these can be induced to enter a store carrying the brand and that 60 percent of those entering a store buy one or more tires of the given brand once they are in the store. On the rule of compound probabilities this would result in 12 percent of those needing new tires buying the given brand. The purpose of an active program of promotion is to increase this percentage.

It will be assumed that investigation has shown that the degree of success is mainly dependent on the skill of the salesman once the prospect is in the retail store. A plan is designed to improve on the compound probability of the first two steps. Suppose that the percentage accepting the brand as eligible for purchase could be raised from 50 percent to 60 percent and the percentage of these entering the stores which stocked the brand could be raised from 40 percent to 50 percent. That would be equivalent to increasing the compound probability of these two steps to 30 percent, or of all three steps to 18 percent, and would thereby result in a 50 percent increase in sales, the efficiency of the retail salesman remaining the same. The table below summarizes these calculations. The probability ratios in the first three columns are multiplied together to get the compound probabilities in the last column. The table reflects the hypothetical results of a promotional campaign designed to have an effect on the number of tire buyers accepting the brand and on

the number accepting who enter stores in which the accepted brand
is stocked.

	Probabilities			Expected Incidence of Purchase
	Brand Acceptance	Entering Store	Responding to Salesmen	
Before campaign...........	.50	.40	.60	.12
After campaign............	.60	.50	.60	.18

THE INTELLIGENCE SYSTEM

The intelligence system may be defined as the flow of information into decision centers and the flow of orders or instructions from the decision center to those held responsible for carrying out decisions. It is the instrument for the management of a marketing operation. Messages come in from key points in the transformation system to indicate whether it is in balance, on schedule, and proceeding according to plan. There should be a screen or filter in this information flow so that messages get through to the decision maker only when corrective action is needed. Orders are issued which are calculated to restore the normal pattern of operation. This power to take corrective action is the essential virtue of a feedback system.

A recent consulting assignment for a manufacturer of paper and paper products led to recommendations concerning the intelligence system for the company. The problems to be met included an extreme degree of tension between the production and marketing sides of the business. The economics of paper manufacturing places a high premium on running each papermaking machine to capacity, these machines costing upward of 25 million dollars apiece. They were being operated in this company at close to 95 percent of capacity calculated on a 24-hour basis. Even these levels are barely satisfactory in an industry which was on allocation for many years because of inability to meet demand completely.

There is an equally strong case for market orientation in this company considering the extremely diversified character of its line and the importance of customer service in maintaining its sales volume. It is no longer possible to drop customers whenever more profitable volume is temporarily available and then expect to get them back when their business is needed to fill up open time on the machine. The company has entered some phases of paper conversion on a major scale. Conversion facilities are tied to specific end-products and customers who desire a regular and dependable source of supply.

It does not appear feasible to organize production and marketing on identical lines with each mill matched by a corresponding sales organization. The sales divisions are each serving a particular class of customers, in most instances handling many grades of paper drawn from a number of the company's mills. Each side of the house makes decisions that are very distressing to the other. Production may shift a given product from one machine to another without notice to marketing, sometimes greatly increasing the costs which are charged against it. Thus, a sales division manager who has been pushing a product which appeared to have a good gross margin suddenly finds that these efforts have made his performance record look bad because the base has been changed. Marketing, on the other hand, makes sudden demands on production in connection with promotional campaigns which cannot be met in an orderly and economic fashion.

There are other problems related to inadequate forecasting procedures which fail to utilize significant data which are fully available. Trends in demand are stable and projectable. The supply situation a year ahead can be known reliably by taking account of mills now in operation or under construction. These are the working materials for predicting price and volume both in the short range and the moderately long range. There are important issues with respect to regional markets and the product lines which should spearhead entry into new territories. In some product fields it is difficult to tell from the company's standard reports whether profits on a product come primarily from paper manufacture or from conversion. The chart in Figure 21–2 embodies in simplified form the new intelligence system recommended for the purpose of meeting some of these difficulties.

The chart is designed to show schematically how the intelligence system takes off from company goals and short-range and long-range forecasts. From the short-range forecasts the marketing divisions are expected to come up with estimated requirements for the year or quarter ahead, broken down by paper grades. This statement of requirements is presented to the production department which schedules the production on the paper making machines for the greatest overall economy. The production schedule now becomes the basis for transfer prices at which each product is assumed to move from production to marketing.

Marketing plans are now developed, line by line, for moving the production which has been scheduled. Each division manager takes the transfer prices as the basis for calculating his gross profits. Marketing expense budgets and profit expectations are established accordingly. Transfer prices provide a common benchmark for measuring the performance of both marketing and production, and the benchmark is unchanged throughout the planning period. At the end of the period the separate and joint performance of production and marketing are evaluated in relation to stated company goals. An evaluation factor not shown on the chart is the analysis of marketing costs by lines and of manufacturing costs by machines.

Figure 21–2

ASPECTS OF AN INTELLIGENCE SYSTEM

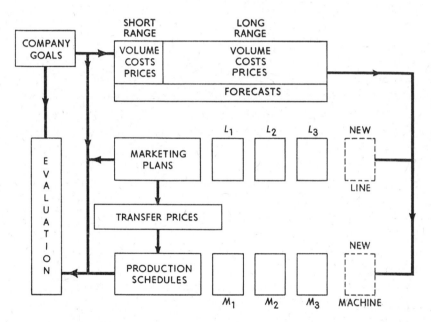

The long-range forecasts have both quantitative and qualitative aspects. On the one hand, the need for new capacity is determined, taking account of expanded demand for existing products and the possibility of adding new products to the line. Capacity increases are then translated into the need for a new machine as of the date that its output will be needed in order to fill demand.

The search for new products is continuous, the long-range forecasts being concerned with changing patterns of demand for paper. New products sometimes require new machines since they fall outside the range of products which can be made with present machines. However, the new product and the new machine do not necessarily correspond. Sometimes a machine might represent a big step forward in efficiency of production for standard grades of paper. The transfer of such production to the new and specialized equipment opens up machine time which might well be used to the best advantage on new products.

PROGRAM, SCHEDULE, AND BUDGET

A campaign consists of a program, a schedule, and a budget. A program is the sequence of activities designed to carry out the company's strategies and achieve its goals. A schedule names specific dates for beginning and ending the program and for accomplishing various intermediate steps. In the case of a very carefully planned campaign, the schedule becomes a manual of instructions with names of people and places and what they are expected to be doing on given dates. A budget is a set of detailed cost estimates for controlling expenditures, providing a framework for evaluating individual items of expenditure as they occur.

This full and precise description of a campaign, made up of these three components, might be described as the administrative model of a plan. It is contrasted with the operating model which has already been disscused and in which many details are stripped away to reveal the basic logical structure of the plan. The end-result which the line executive wants to see is the administrative model. In some instances he is responsible for the refinements of detail which are required by the administrative model. In other cases he may collaborate with the planner or provide the detailed information which will enable the planner to move from the operating model to the administrative model.

Little more needs to be said with respect to the program aspect of a campaign except that the program now needs to be developed into specific procedures. When dates are assigned to aspects of the program it becomes a manual of instructions. Scheduling and budgeting are treated in greater detail because they are introduced here for the first time. The development of a sequence of activities was described in an earlier chapter, but it is in dealing with concurrent sequences of activities that the planner is obliged to come to grips with the calendar. The development of the administrative plan from the operating model is a gray area in which the planner and the line executive share the responsibility. In any case, the installation of a plan cannot be considered as accomplished until the administrative plan has been completed.

SCHEDULING CONCURRENT SEQUENCES

The art of scheduling consists of the two steps of first allocating time to the successive components in each sequence and then relating the several sequences to each other. The obvious way to work with an individual sequence is to start with a final deadline date and work backward. When time has been allowed for the final step in the sequence, the date for beginning this step establishes the terminal date or deadline for the completion of the next preceding step. In the same fashion, the beginning date for the next to the last step establishes a deadline for completing the step just before that. Working on backward through one step after another, the planner comes to what might be called his initial deadline, namely, the latest feasible date for starting the first step. Having worked his way back to the starting point, he may find that several adjustments remained to be made. He is obviously in trouble if the indicated starting point is earlier than the proposed date for launching the program as a whole. He will then have to check through the time allocations for the successive steps to see whether the time can be reduced in any individual case. Whether or not he has run out of time in this first allocation to the steps in the sequence, the rechecking of the allocation should be a regular routine. He should look first at the steps to which the greatest allocation of time has been made and make explicit judgments as to the possible advantages of marginal shifts of time from one step to another. That is to say, he should consider the possibilities of improving the overall pattern by shifting a month or a week from the step with the largest time allocation to some of the minor steps. Similarly, he should consider the possibilities of picking up a day here or there from the smaller steps to give more adequate time for carrying out the largest step. There is another possible answer when the sequence appears to require more time than the total time available for the program. It may be possible to cut a sequence into two sequences which can run concurrently or at least overlap in part.

The problem of getting sequences to conform to each other involves a consideration of the manpower or other resources available by time periods and the adjustment of phases of the program in such a way as to avoid either idle time or bottlenecks. The beginning of some sequences may have to be delayed until others are completed and manpower is available to go to work on another aspect of the program. This shift from one activity to another can take place only within definite limitations because of the specialization of personnel on one marketing function or another.

Figure 21–3 is designed to illustrate the two stages in the scheduling of marketing activities. Five sequences of activity are shown in the upper half of the chart, ranging from one step to five steps in length.

The right-hand margin of the chart indicates the final deadline for the program as a whole. In the first half of the chart all the sequences are shown as if they terminated at this final deadline. Also, for convenience of illustration, the same amount of time is allocated to each of the fifteen steps making up the components of

Figure 21–3

Two Stages in Scheduling Concurrent Sequences

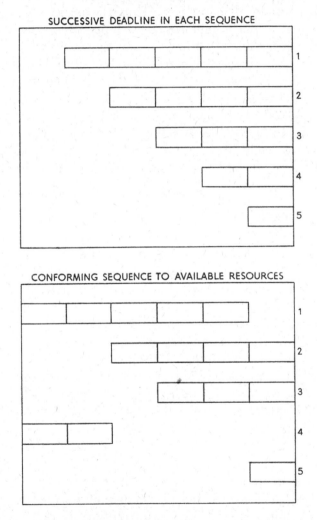

the five sequences. In practice, of course, the time allocation to various steps would be of different length, but the same principles of adjustment would still operate.

In the second half of the chart some adjustments have been made in the position of the sequences to conform to a restriction on the

resources available during the six periods which make up the total
time for carrying out the marketing program. The restriction, which
is assumed to be in effect, is that there is only enough manpower
to carry on two sequences during the first three intervals of time.
In the simple illustration which has been used, it was possible to
accommodate the schedule to this restriction simply by moving two
of the sequences over to the beginning of the time period. It will
be seen that the schedule might also accommodate itself to the differences in specialized manpower. Thus the personnel which carried out sequence one might be competent, after completing this
sequence, to turn their attention to sequence five and to complete
that sequence before the final deadline. The same kind of transfer
of specialized manpower might occur from sequence four to sequence two. That leaves sequence three, which evidently would
have to be carried out by manpower which was not occupied with
the program during the first half of the total program period.
Sequence three could also represent the activities of some outside
group, such as an advertising agency or a set of independent brokers
or agents who were to be engaged in the second half of the program.

BUDGETING PROCEDURES

The aim of the budgeting process is to match the total money
value of the available resources against all the detailed sequences
of activity and separate steps which make up a marketing program.
In preparing a budget it is possible to start from either one end or
the other. That is to say, budgeting consists either of breaking down
or of building up. The planner starts with a total and tries to stretch
it to cover all the steps. As an alternative he assigns costs to each of
the steps and builds up a total requirement. Actually both breaking
down and building up are likely to enter into any comprehensive
budgeting process. Some operating men may regard budget ceilings
as hampering restrictions on creative marketing. Actually, the necessity for working within budgetary limits generally serves to stimulate ingenuity and to result in a tighter and better-balanced program.

Short-range marketing budgets often contain some reserve for
contingencies. Deciding on the proper magnitude of reserves is an
important planning decision for any marketing situation. The larger
part of the budget should be committed and scheduled as part of
the initial plan in order to make the most effective use of marketing
dollars. In fact, the proper goal of planning would be to commit all
dollars in advance if it were not for competitive moves or unpredict-

able events of other kinds which might upset the program during the course of the operating period. While some reserves are, no doubt, desirable, too loose a budget could lead away from planning back toward the waste and frenzy of day-to-day operations. A practical standard toward which the planner might strive is that of advanced commitment and scheduling of 75 percent of the marketing dollars. Even with respect to the remaining 25 percent, it would usually be good practice to have a general commitment as to the nature of the anticipated expenditure with formal procedures for budget revisions under well-defined limitations.

An important tool for use in middle-range planning is the pro forma operating statement. Such a pro forma statement provides a breakdown of income and expense for some future year. In some actual planning assignments pro forma statements have been prepared for a series of three to five years ahead. There is no need to provide an illustration of such a pro forma statement since the structure is precisely the same as that for a past operating period. The only remarkable thing about it is that it bears a future date. Several of the items in the statement might be forecast separately or all might be related to a basic sales forecast. For example, given the sales forecast, the planner might allow for a minimum profit requirement in order to determine what was left for all production and marketing costs. A more detailed breakdown of both types of costs would then be made, taking either one or the other as the more fundamental. If marketing was regarded as paramount, it would then be put up to the production department to get costs down to provide the necessary marketing margin. The reverse procedure would be a heavy pressure on the marketing department for innovations in marketing if production costs were taken as fixed.

In summary, the coordination of activities to constitute a well-ordered plan is concerned with time in several of its aspects and with the allocation of resources among the time intervals making up the operating period. Time is no longer merely the relationship of before and after but is measurable in duration as a scarce element to be managed like other resources. To some extent time is interchangeable with other resources. That is to say, it is sometimes necessary to incur higher money costs in order to save time. Similarly, when there is less stringency as to time, it may be possible to economize man-hours by spreading an activity out over a longer period.

Calendar time is a means of relating activities to the specific phase of the history of a firm or of controlling events and conditions in its environment. External coordination must take account of the probable timing of market trends or competitive moves which may affect the outcome of a marketing program. Internal coordination may take as a basic reference one activity as the main flow to which other activities must be coordinated. Thus, the various steps in an introductory program might be dated provisionally from the first public announcement of the availability of the product.

Schedules and budgets are planning tools which must be used in conjunction, and devices are suggested for facilitating the allocation of manpower and money to the time intervals which make up the operating period. The same tools are employed in controlling an operation to keep it on target with respect to the objectives of the plan. More detailed discussions of these uses of schedules and budgets will appear in later chapters. It is these concepts which give a firm and ordered structure to the pattern of action and open the way for more formal quantitative analysis.

INSTALLATION OF A MARKETING PLAN

The installation of a plan or program means taking whatever steps are necessary so that the organization will begin to conform its actions to the plan. The executive who has the authority to approve a plan usually directs the line executives who will carry it out. Installation is the process of getting the execution of the plan under way. Sometimes this can be done in simple and effective fashion at a single conference. The salient features of the plan are taken up one after another, and the group discusses the action to be taken in activating that recommendation. The leader of the group fixes responsibility for action on each point as a result of the discussion. In some cases he has the initials of each of his subordinates opposite his portion of the program before the meeting is over. A slightly more formal procedure is for this conference group to have a secretary making note of the various decisions. After the meeting he writes up an executive order describing the assignments. This order becomes effective when signed by the executive directing the whole operation.

Installation is sometimes a more elaborate and time-consuming process and may extend over a number of days or weeks. In fact, the description in the last paragraph is likely to be an oversimplification because each of the executives in the conference which inaugurates the plan officially may have a number of things to do to carry out his part of the plan or program. Specifically he is, in effect, installing a part of the plan by having a similar understanding with his subordinates. The program may have to sift down through several stages in the executive hierarchy before it can be regarded as having become effective. The purpose of a plan is to induce concerted action from the entire organization so that it might ultimately be installed in the minds and attitudes of everyone whose efforts are to be coordinated.

Installing a marketing plan or program is not quite parallel to the issuance of a military field order. Under the emergency conditions of wartime and the military tradition of unquestioned obedience, conforming to a plan can be required by command rather than persuasion. In a marketing organization it is essential that subordinates react to the program with enthusiasm. Much of their effort will be expended at points remote from headquarters where close and continuous supervision is not practical. Often they must perform their tasks under the plan in the face of serious obstacles and discouragement. They must believe that the plan will work, which does not mean working without exception but working comparatively well. The obvious benchmarks for comparison are with unplanned activity, with last year's program, or perhaps with principal competitors. A plan is part of the constant effort to do better. It cannot eliminate misses, but it should increase the number of hits. The best program is not necessarily the one that is working for a competitor, but a salesman is entitled to know something about what led to the choice of one approach as more appropriate than another.

The requirement that a program must be "sold" means that it is desirable, where feasible, to allow for participation in the planning stage by those who are to be guided by the plan. While the opportunity to participate may be severely limited, it will help to keep the group informed to the extent that time and commercial security will permit. In particular, the first echelon or two of line executives should have some general idea of what is coming so that they can begin to anticipate what will be involved in the installation of a plan. If a staff planning group engages in short-range programming, it should be able to provide a synopsis of the program before the details are completed. The synopsis might indicate the nature of the improvements or gains to be obtained through the program and the main line of attack on this target.

Beyond persuasion, the installation of a plan or program may require other steps, such as explanation, instruction, training, or even recruitment of additional personnel. A clear exposition of the way the plan is to work may have to be prepared in case of a major modification in existing operations and presented to a number of headquarters and field units. The staff planner should be on hand to make the initial presentation, if requested, or at least to help answer questions if the actual presentation is made by an operating executive. Sometimes minor adjustments must be made in the best of plans as it goes into effect in one region after another. The staff man who participates in the presentations might well be the one to undertake the adjustments or to persuade the organization that the plan can go ahead without adjustments.

Explanation of a plan shades over into instruction, particularly at the lower levels of responsibility. To explain it effectively is to tell the individual just what he is to do and how it is to be done. A carefully worked out installation procedure sometimes demonstrates how a step is to be handled by means of a playlet, audience interest on behalf of the salesmen being heightened by role playing on the part of their superiors. Even more meticulous instructions may be presented in written form and each participant put through a dry run by answering a questionnaire to show that he comprehends the procedure.

Sometimes new personnel will have to be recruited to carry out the program, or existing personnel will have to receive new training to handle it. On-the-job training can be handled by having those responsible for the plan travel with each salesman in turn. Sometimes it is a crew operation to be carried out in one market after another. The planner who conceives the program or someone else who thoroughly understands it might be on hand in the first several cases to provide leadership or counsel. In other cases the field sales organization might be pulled out of the line for a week or longer for really intensive training. This might be required, for example, in an industrial marketing organization which was introducing a really radical innovation.

PERFORMANCE STANDARDS AND CONTROLS

One step in making a plan effective is to establish controls that will tend to keep performance in line with expectations. This is closely related to the installation steps which have been mentioned, but it is not quite the same thing. Installation is completed before the fact. Controls pertain to measures which should be in effect while the plan is in actual operation. A control is a feedback device which reports variation from the intended pattern of action and thereby initiates corrective action. Some controls operate so smoothly and rapidly that those who use them forget that they exist. An individual starts to lift a suitcase which he believes to be empty. If it turns out to be heavily loaded, sensory impressions travel back to the brain, and if the desire to lift the suitcase persists, motor impulses go out to the muscles to cause a greater effort.

In a system of action, such as that constituted by a marketing organization, the problems of control are of quite a different kind. The fact that the problem exists is evident, but often there is no effective mechanism for handling it. A control can break down at several crucial points in the feedback circuit. First there has to be an observation at the point of impact, and this observation must be made in a form that lends itself to action. Ideally the record should state the direction and amount of the departure from the standard established in advance. Comments in more general terms, such as that performance is good or poor are ordinarily not of much help. The reporter is applying some personal subjective standard, and these subjective factors would have to be known back at the control center in order to interpret his message. Even though a message with operational meaning is received at the control center, the means of correction may not be available. The control executive may be in a position similar to that of the general who receives the message that his left wing is caving in but has no reserves to throw into the battle. One of the limitations on the use of the reserves available to the marketing executive is the lack of sufficient versatility and mobility in the manpower that is not fully engaged.

There are many instances, fortunately, in which the means for correction are available to the control executive. He can send out supplementary or revised instructions for the use of resources already on the ground. It may be clear from reports that the failure to meet the performance standard reflects a failure to use resources according to plan. The salesman may have moved into a situation barehanded instead of using carefully prepared materials supplied to him to meet a given problem. The control executive may be able to suggest other approaches where the recommended approach is running into difficulties. A budget increase can be allowed where the estimated expenditure proves inadequate. A technical specialist may be dispatched from headquarters to assist the salesman in dealing with the problem on the spot.

In too many cases nothing happens as a result of the report from the field. Executives at the control center receive the information but take no corrective action. Sometimes this means that no thought has been given in advance to the types of correction possible, or to the response which might be called for if a given type of message was received from the field. In some cases the information from the field must be processed in some way before it becomes the basis for action. Perhaps any retailer who had not been called on for 60 days should go on a priority list for a call in the next week or two. Their names must be identified and sorted out of call reports before a list could be prepared of those dealers where calls were urgent. There is a tendency for information on what is going wrong in the field to be passed upward to the next level of responsibility rather than being disposed of at the first control center.

The readiness to take action is thus an essential component in the exercise of controls. Meaningful signals must be received from the field. A repertory of possible actions must have been identified for each type of signal that is anticipated. The control executive must be prompt in interpreting the signal and in selecting the corrective action that is to be initiated. The smooth operation of the plan requires not only that the program should specify the normal pattern of behavior for the individuals and groups to be controlled but also that it should include the corrective procedures to be followed by the control executives.

A central aspect of control is to keep activities on schedule and expenditures within the budget. A variety of charts and graphic devices are used in business for this type of control. The prototype of such charts was developed by the noted industrial engineer, H. L. Gantt. The term "Gantt charts" has come to be a generic name for a diversity of charts used to relate activity and expenditure to the passage of time. One type of chart widely applicable in marketing is illustrated in Figure 21-4. Pairs of bars are shown for three activities. The top bar in each represents the percentage of completion of the activity while the lower bar represents the percentage of budget which has been spent. The bars can be compared with each other or with the time elapsed so far.

The elapsed time as shown on the chart is now 2½ of the 6 periods to be covered. The program consists of several sequences which are scheduled to run concurrently. The sequence A is definitely behind schedule, but the budget is still in balance. For sequence B the activity has been kept almost up to date, but at the cost of running well ahead of the budgeted expenditures. The sequence C is in a very favorable position with progress on the activity running well ahead, but with expenditure falling behind the budgeted figures. In order to plot progress in this chart, the control officer must have an accompanying table which gives the budgeted figures for the percentage of activity to be completed and the amount to be spent by the end of each operating interval. The actual figures are then translated into relatives based on the budget, and it is these relatives which determine the length of each bar in the chart.

Figure 21-4

ELAPSED TIME
VERSUS
ACTIVITY AND EXPENDITURE RATES

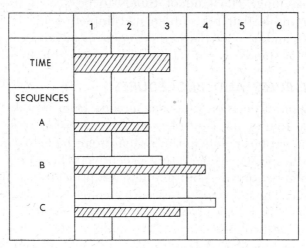

Remedial action is required with respect to sequences *A* and *B*. In the case of *A* those engaged in the activity should be shown how they can speed up their activities to get back on schedule. Preferably this should be done wihle maintaining the present balance between activity and budget. Sometimes a choice has to be made between gaining time and saving money. In the example those responsible for sequence *A* may merely need to be inspired with a greater sense of urgency in order to get on with the job. Sequence *B* is a case in which fundamental economies will probably have to be worked out. At the rate at which it is now going, the budget could be exhausted for this activity, with the activity still less than 80 percent complete. Possible actions would include finding a basically cheaper way of finishing this task, scaling down the amount of activity originally visualized in order to stay within the budget, or picking up the amount required to meet the deficit from other activities, such as *C*, which appear to be running a surplus. Decision as to the nature of the correction would depend in part on judgments as to whether internal or external factors had thrown the operation off schedule and the range within which the situation would respond to corrective action.

The three separate activities might represent the separate programs of three divisions or operating units with profit responsibility. The comparative showing could then be used as a means of stimulating the unit which was lagging behind to do better. More generally, the measures of performance would be limited and specific and might not even be directly comparable. Suppose, for example, that the three activities pertained to advertising, selling, and physical handling. The kind of things to be accomplished are so incommensurable that percentage of completion figures are again maintained, and a schedule, agreed upon in advance, is about the only basis for standards which would be applicable to all three.

DECISION RULES AND PROCEDURES

The notion of decision rules has already been introduced in discussing the role of the control executive. Decision rules might be operative at various points in the system from the field salesman upstream to the principal marketing executive. The word "policy" is used in a number of ways, but in one sense it means just this type of decision rule. The policy or decision rule comes into play when a situation arises which does not conform precisely to the expected patterns or prescribed procedures. The policy sets up some criteria for classifying the case at hand and rules for disposing of cases in each class. In applying a decision rule, the individual with the problem is expected to conclude that, all things considered, the case belongs in a specified class and that the prescribed procedure for that class or a variant of it can therefore be applied.

Usually there are some general instructions for the application of decision rules. If the amount involved is below some minimum figure, the person immediately responsible may be required to decide promptly, but perhaps he must report on the case and its problem aspects afterward. Other types of cases might be identified as peculiarly sensitive from a legal or trade relations standpoint, or as so important that the man in the field is not expected to make decisions if the issues are at all ambiguous. He may refer the case to his superiors, asking for instructions of one kind or another. He might simply be given an answer as to how he should deal with the given case on the assumption that it is unique. He might be given a new rule as to the way of handling all such cases in the future. He might be required to recommend a solution with reasons to support the action rather than another.

Good practice would suggest that reports be made on borderline cases regardless of the method used in deciding them. In a rapidly changing market a continuous analysis of borderline cases would appear to be indicated. The frequency and character of borderline cases arising under the program may lead to important changes in the next program to be activated. A rising trend in exceptional cases might well indicate that the pattern of consumer behavior was drifting in a given direction, thus rendering obsolete the practices considered standard in the past.

The discussion of controls and decision rules shades over into the consideration of procedures. The design of a procedure is something like the design of a program, although one tends to emphasize repetitive elements and the other nonrepetitive elements. Sometimes the planning group is responsible for detailed procedures as well. More commonly, the design of a program takes certain procedures for granted, but the planner needs to be well advised on what the procedures are. The planner is within his rights if he calls for a revision of established procedures on the ground that they are too cumbersome to serve the requirements of the plan. There is an analogy here to the function of a production manager in trying to find a way to make a new product on existing machines. He may conclude that a moderate volume of production is feasible pending the installation of new equipment.

Procedures characteristically evolve over a considerable period of time. They change through a series of small steps, each step reflecting a judgment that the process will still work and usually that it will work better. The structure and continuity of much of the daily activity of any large organization is procedural in nature. Stability and order require that individuals know just what to do and that they know what others will do in turn. A marketing organization usually has well-established formal procedures before it undertakes formal planning or programming.

A plan, as compared to a procedure, places more emphasis on strategy and function, while a procedure is concerned with the repetitive details of execution. Short-range programming, however, tends to lie somewhere between the two. In other words, an operating program usually should be expressed in concrete procedural terms and should be geared to the fixed procedures which are not modified by the program. In fact, the distinguishing feature of the administrative version of a plan or program is that it has been carried far enough to facilitate systematic and efficient administration.

Selected References

BRINK, EDWARD L. "Analog Computers in the Simulation of Marketing Systems," *Marketing and Computer* (WROE ALDERSON AND STANLEY SHAPIRO, eds.). Englewood Cliffs, N.J.: Prentice-Hall, Inc., 1963.

Describes the way in which an analog can provide instant "results" once the system model has been created.

KUEHN, ALFRED A. *Complex Interaction Models in Quantitative Analyses.* Homewood, Ill.: Richard D. Irwin, Inc., 1962.

Discusses models and simulation, with a final section on applications in marketing.

MASSEY, W. F., TALLMAN, GERALD B., AND AMSTUTZ, ARNOLD. "The Complex Marketing Game—Accomplishment and Opportunity," *Marketing and the Computer* (WROE ALDERSON AND STANLEY SHAPIRO, eds.). Englewood Cliffs, N.J.: Prentice-Hall, Inc., 1963.

Description of the M.I.T. marketing game and suggested implications for testing marketing plans.

NIELSON, A. C. "Where Marketing Plans Go Wrong," *Management Review,* February, 1957.

A leading market researcher presents a list of the eleven most common marketing areas which might be used in testing the concept of a marketing plan.

Problems

1. Contrast the live test of a marketing plan with the simulation of the plan on a computer.

2. Discuss the use and importance of the pro forma operating statement in middle-range planning.

3. Discuss the various methods for the proper installation of a marketing plan.

4. Explain why controls are important in the successful completion of a plan. Why are controls of a marketing plan especially difficult to enforce?

5. Discuss how decision rules can aid in the successful completion of a marketing plan.

Chapter 22

PERSPECTIVES ON THE PLANNING FUNCTION

In this final chapter an attempt will be made to put the planning function in perspective, looking at it from the various viewpoints of the planner, the top executive, and his subordinates at various levels in the organization. We should begin, however, by adopting the perspective of the business as a whole and considering what planning in marketing or planning in general can mean to the business as a whole.

These comments on the broad perspective will be followed by a more detailed consideration of the planning function and the positioning of planning in the organization. Finally there is the section called a paradigm of planning which undertakes to bring the whole subject into final form based on what has gone before. A paradigm is an analytical outline which exhibits a basic theme or subject matter in all of its diverse manifestations. The purpose is to present a summary view of what planning is, both in general and by the various type of planning tasks in marketing.

MATCHING MEANS AND ENDS

Planning in marketing is one approach to the matching of means and ends. To recognize the need for planning is to concede that there is considerable complexity on either side or both. The carpenter who reaches for his hammer when he wishes to drive a nail is matching means and ends but he is scarcely engaged in planning. He may have done some rudimentary planning before he left for work in the morning, anticipating the character of the day's work and deciding on the tools he should take along.

Planning generally contemplates a plurality of both means and ends. It does not match one tool against a single limited task but considers a tool kit in relation to a complete operation. More precisely, planning is the design of a pattern of activity to promote the achievement of a set of objectives. But there are some issues to be faced before the matching of ends and means begins. Problems arise as to the ways in which plural objectives may be related to each other, and parallel problems arise as to the classification and management of means.

The individuals making up any human organization always reflect in their behavior a diversity of objectives. Even if the organization came into existence to sell goods and make a profit, there are differences as to the statement of goals which could affect the program of marketing activities quite significantly.

Within a plurality of ends a pair of goals may be related in one of three primary ways. They may be neutral toward each other so that they are related chiefly through competitive claims on the available means. This might be true for a marketing organization selling both coffee and salad dressing or for a consumer buying these two products. A pair of goals may be in direct conflict so that success in one may increase the risk of failure in the other. A case in point would be a drug manufacturer who lost out in the prescription field because of his success with over-the-counter medical products.

Finally two goals may support and complement each other. The degree of complementarity between two goals may be moderate or so great as to make each an essential condition for the success of the other. The rapid rise of low-sudsing detergents was tied to the swing toward automatic washing machines. At the same time washing machine manufacturers and their distributors and dealers promoted the sale of low-sudsing detergents. The dealers made a direct profit on the sale of the packaged product, but they were concerned more fundamentally with the indirect influence on the sale of automatic washers.

Much more could be said about the problem of clarifying company objectives as a phase of planning. Here it will suffice to mention the characteristic methods of reconciling goals that exhibit the three primary relationships. If two goals are neutral, the planner has the relatively simple problem of allocating resources or effort to each. If two goals are complementary, a decision may still have to be made as to which is dominant. Even though a refinery makes money on both lubricating oil and gasoline, it will want to maximize the relative sales of one or the other at a given time, according to the prevailing market conditions. If a pair of goals exhibits conflict, one may have to be eliminated or separate organizations created to give concentrated attention to each. A surprising number of marketing organizations find it necessary to have two or more sales forces, not merely because different skills are required but because the attitude and approach which is appropriate in one field may be actually harmful in another.

The means employed in marketing can be classified in various ways, as, for example, by the functions of physical movement of goods, advertising to stimulate consumer demand, and selling to secure the cooperation of intermediary channels in reaching the consumer. For a first view of planning, it is more important to classify resources by factors affecting their manageability. Resources vary as to their degree of scarcity or abundance, the extent to which they can be divided into smaller units or remain indivisible, and their fitness for broad and general use or narrow specialized use.

The need for management in human affairs arises out of scarcity. The elementary response to scarcity is allocation. The simplest version of the economic problem is the allocation of scarce resources to objectives that are in neutral relation to each other. If only allocation were needed the matching of means and ends would hardly require anything so formal as an organized planning procedure.

In practice, management is faced with complications in the allocation of resources. It is often convenient to talk about labor as one of the primary factors of production, but there are actually many grades and kinds of labor, each to be assigned its appropriate task. Planning in marketing soon passes beyond such broad classifications as available retail outlets and considers the functional differences among types and the way each fits into a marketing program. Some types are scarcer than others either in absolute numbers and capacity or in relation to the marketing needs of the supplier.

There is a wide range of variation in the degree of specialization. Some salesmen are more versatile than others. Some advertising reaches masses of people, and some is directed to very limited segments of the market. Some schemes for securing trade support have general appeal while some are of special interest only to the drug store, the supermarket, or the department store. A resource or program with general application has the virtue of being relatively easy to apply and control. More specialized facilities are justified by their greater efficiency in the situations for which they were designed.

In the planned use of resources, specialized facilities tend to be assigned first to the tasks for which they are most efficient. More versatile facilities take up the slack wherever they are needed. Zipf has shown for a variety of fields that general laws tend to govern the balance between facilities of general and specialized use. Analytical techniques such as linear programming have been devised to deal with the complications introduced into the allocation problem by specialized facilities.

The marginal analysis of productivity assumes that management can always add a little bit more of any production factor until it is utilizing just enough. A serious limitation is that some resources are available in large and indivisible units. In a plant producing pig iron, the ore can be broken down by pounds or fractions of a pound. A blast furnace is an indivisible unit and either operates as a whole or must be shut down. Indivisibility is also a limiting factor in the management of marketing resources. A company decides to open a sales office in Denver or get along without it. If the decision is positive, some minimum level of cost is involved in opening the new office. Indivisibility presents critical problems in the management of advertising. The decision to use or not to use a given television program may affect the disposition of most of a company's advertising budget.

Planning is particularly concerned with the time dimension of the indivisibility of resources. The decision to build a plant or to make a major installation of equipment is equivalent to committing resources for a number of years ahead. Such commitments are often made with a full knowledge that it will be some time before this production capacity can be fully used. Similar considerations arise with respect to marketing inputs. Funds are allocated for product development or for promotion with an expectation of profits some years ahead. Decisions concerning distribution channels, such as to use a given type of wholesaler or broker, usually must stand for some time. The costs and difficulties of changing channels are considerable in reversing such a decision.

FORESIGHT AS ORGANIZED HINDSIGHT

A cynical story, circulated in various versions, attempts to challenge planning by calling attention to the limitations on foresight. One form of the anecdote pictures the driver of a car sitting behind the wheel blindfolded. He steers the car by listening to the reports of an associate who is facing backward and looking out the rear window. Ridiculous as this image appears, it has analogies in human affairs which work out quite successfully. Consider the instrument landing of a transatlantic plane in a fog. Or the driller sinking a well on the advice of a geologist who has obviously never seen the pool of oil which he thinks may be located at that point. Or the building which takes shape in the way indicated by the architect's drawings even though there has never been another building precisely like it.

The future by definition is that part of history which has not yet been revealed to us and which we can only know by inference. Most people accept the inference that the sun will rise tomorrow because a similar event has occurred every day of their lives. Some geographers infer that the polar ice cap will start to move south again because they detect trends in the recent past which, if projected, will cause such a movement. A retailer counts on advertising support in the sale of a product because he accepts the promise of a responsible supplier. In summary, inferences about what will happen in the future are based on recurrent events in the past, on trends observable in past events, or on commitments already made to bring about a future event.

The planner should accept the challenge of the cynic and concede that foresight can only rest on organized hindsight. In fact, this notion can be the source of another useful perspective on planning. The planner must determine how best to organize the available knowledge of the past to provide some guideposts for future action. From the viewpoint of planning, the present is not the passing moment but the slice of time required to create and install a plan. The relevant past is that for which information has been collected and analyzed as the basis for planning. The relevant future begins when the plan is activated and can be expected to have some impact on the marketing operation. If the planning gap between past and future grows too long, the inferences from one to the other become increasingly hazardous. These relationships between past, present, and future are pictured in Figure 22-1.

The block representing the future is heavily crosshatched to indicate darkness—not the darkness of gloom but the darkness of

Figure 22-1

PAST, PRESENT, AND FUTURE IN PLANNING

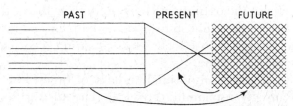

ignorance. The past is pictured in more open form, reflecting the fact that it is possible to peer into the past but with diminishing clarity as the period lengthens. The curving arrows at the bottom are intended to show that inference runs from the past to the future and then back into the planning present with respect to the nature of the plan required. The point of convergence in the space representing the present is the date of completion and approval of the plan and the beginning of plan installation.

There is probably an optimal relationship as to the length of the past and future periods which can be constructively related through planning. The past period should be long enough to provide a stable basis for projecting a trend for the stated future period. For most purposes one past year would be inadequate for predicting the pattern for a year ahead. The issue depends, of course, on the kind of variation which must be taken into account in planning. A month-by-month program for a year would require a forecast of seasonal variations in operations. Monthly figures for five previous years would be fairly satisfactory for determining what kind of a seasonal pattern should be expected.

For intermediate planning related to a future period of three to five years, trend figures for the past fifteen years might be adequate for most planning purposes. That would cover several upward and downward movements of the business cycle and provide a fairly stable base for judging secular trend or testing a forecasting formula. For some types of long-range forecasting which have been described, past and future periods of about equal length might be suitable. That is to say, broad speculations as to what may happen in the next quarter century could be grounded on what had happened in the last one. There are some related issues which are considered in somewhat greater detail in the chapter on forecasting.

OPTIMAL PLANNING AND THE PLANNING HORIZON

One way of appreciating the need for planning is to recall that time is in some sense the scarcest of all resources. With respect to any given operating period, planning operates to make the most of the time available. Suppose that the planning assignment is designed to increase the outputs of the system over the next five years. But some part of that time must be used up in creating the plan before it can be put into effect. Thus planning also makes use of the scarce resource of time.

In principle there is an optimal amount of time to be devoted to planning in any given planning problem. The answer lies in finding the point of balance between two opposing considerations. On the one hand there is need for time to complete an adequate plan. On the other hand the plan needs to be in effect for as much of the total period as possible in order to have maximum impact on the operation. There is a best division of the total time between planning and the improved operation under any given set of assumptions as to the effectiveness of planning. Figure 22–2 illustrates the determination of the point of balance under one simple set of assumptions.

Figure 22–2

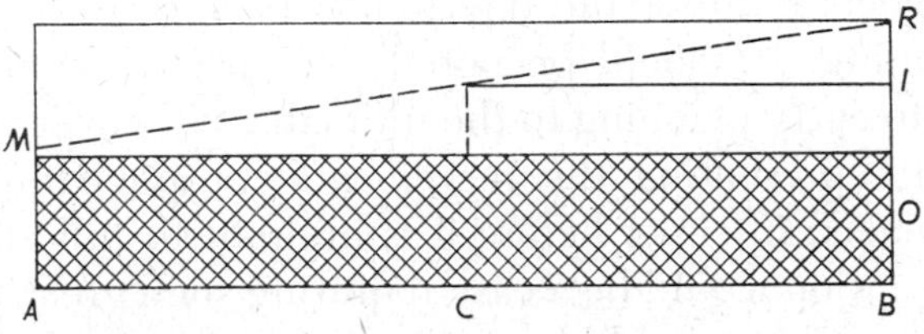

The distance from *A* to *B* represents the total time to be divided between planning and improved operation. The shaded rectangle *O* at the bottom represents the ordinary output of the system if it should go ahead without benefit of planning. The dotted line *MR* represents the incremental productivity of the system as a result of various amounts of time devoted to planning. Under the assumption as to a linear increment from planning, the point *C* is the one which optimizes the results of planning. Geometrically that means that the rectangle *I*, representing the incremental result, has its maximum area at this point.

The assumptions used in this illustration are highly arbitrary. Somewhat more realistic assumptions are embodied in Figure 22–3. A formal solution would not in general be practical but this brief consideration of the basic relationships should help to sharpen intuition in dealing with the problem.

In this chart the same total time period is considered. The dotted line *MR* is modified to reflect a more probable situation with

Figure 22–3

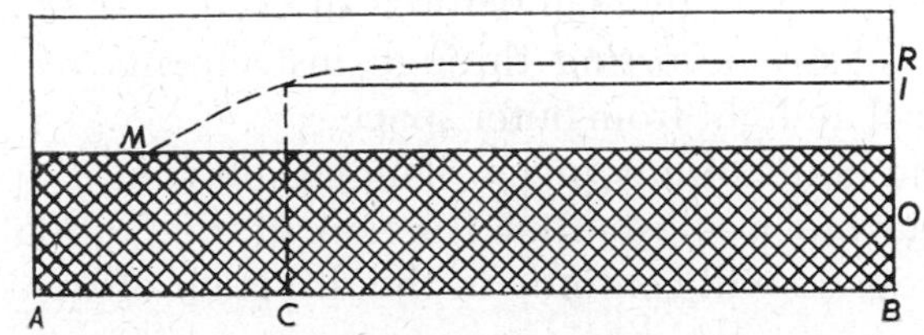

respect to the incremental output from planning. Instead of a linear function it is now assumed that this relationship is marked by both a threshold and a ceiling. That is to say, planning must be carried to a substantial point before it would influence the operation at all. Thereafter the value of planning arises rapidly but shortly levels off.

The point C, at which the rectangle representing the incremental output from planning is at is maximum value, now moves to the left. The time spent in planning no longer covers half the period but is less than one third. This is consistent with intuitive judgment about planning time derived from experience. A useful rule-of-thumb for research projects is to devote one fourth to one third of the total time to planning. It should be noted that in both charts it is not appropriate to carry planning to the ultimate. Whatever the shape of the function representing the incremental output from planning, the plan is placed in effect before it is brought to full effectiveness. The only exception would be a case requiring such great precision in planning that a plan would have either zero effectiveness or full effectiveness. This type of planning requirement is more suggestive of rocket launching than of marketing programs.

The concept of the planning horizon has had some currency among planners in relation to the issue of optimal planning efficiency. There is an intuitive appeal to the notion that planning should be limited to the future period for which foresight can be exercised with some certainty. Yet it is clear from the last section that the kind of certainty required varies with the type of planning assignment. An alternative way of stating the same thing is to distinguish among types of horizons. There is the action horizon which might be likened to how far one can jump as compared to how far he can see. Even in terms of vision there are differences in the horizon according to the amount of detail which must be seen and whether the viewer is using the naked eye or a telescope.

The telescope in this case is the formal forecasting technique used to peer into the future. While much remains to be done, forecasting techniques for specific purposes have undergone substantial improvement. Horizons are being pushed further away in planning as in astronomy. The first 200-inch telescope brought galaxies within the horizon never seen by man before. An even greater expansion of the horizon is now occurring through instruments receiving radio waves rather than light from outer space.

Within the limits of any given planning horizon it appears to be fruitful to devote a substantial fraction of the available time to planning. Progress will continue in the direction of speeding up the planning process. The development of electronic computers is contributing to accelerated planning in several ways. One is in making it possible to handle more rapidly the comprehensive background data. Another is through the simulation of a proposed operation as compared to more time-consuming forms of testing.

THE PLANNING FUNCTION

Perhaps the most difficult problem of organization planning is how to provide for the planning function itself. Where should the planning staff be located in the organization structure? What type of people should staff the planning activity? Who should set the objectives for the planning group or should give it its assignments? What standards of performance should be applied in determining whether its work has been effective? These are some of the questions which might perplex any top management which was about to establish formal planning as a regular function. Aside from these specific questions there is a fundamental problem of organization dynamics. Every new organization unit has a problem of making a place for itself within the behavior system constituted by the firm. The newest unit is likely to be the one that is most difficult to staff adequately and operate efficiently. Thus it is especially vulnerable to attack if it seems to threaten any of the units that are already established. Formal planning is likely to appear as such a threat when first adopted, since it expresses the concern of management with external market changes and the possible need for corresponding changes on the inside. In organizing for planning, an organization is preparing to transform itself and its program of activities but with the hope of avoiding disruption of current operations.

Unless the groundwork for systematic planning has been unusually well prepared, the planner finds himself in the vortex of change even while he is trying to cope with change as it affects the organization as a whole. In planning, as in marketing research, the staff man is often confronted with a chaotic situation and is expected to reduce it to some system and order. His job is to make life easier for the operating man so that the major resources of the company can be deployed in a more efficient manner. Because of the conditions under which he is forced to work, the planner of activities may appear relatively inefficient and disorganized. He often misses many of the satisfactions of a job well done because the credit for a successful operation is likely to be attributed to the vigor and competence of its execution rather than the excellence of the plan.

Before the detailed problems of organizing for planning are discussed, it may be useful to consider why business has lagged behind the military services in the adoption of staff planning. One may suppose that the size and critical importance of military operations have led to an earlier recognition of military staff planning. On the other hand, there are modern corporations which command greater resources than some of the victorious armies of the past, and success or failure of a business operation is always of vital interest to the people concerned. The growth of military planning may have arisen largely out of the alternating periods of peace and war. The German general staff in Bismarck's time spent years of peacetime preparation for its relatively brief wars with Austria and France. In peacetime an officer has no opportunity to win distinction on the battlefield and the principal road to recognition is through staff activities.

Business firms are never at war in the sense that they set out to destroy each other's plants and personnel, but neither are they at peace as armies are sometimes at peace. Action in business is current and continuous, and the exercise of line authority continues to be the principal route to recognition. The activities of a first rate executive are perhaps more similar to those of Hannibal than to twentieth century commanders. One of the master strategists of all time, Hannibal commanded an army in the field for most of his adult life. He gathered information, weighed alternatives, and created remarkable designs of grand strategy. IIe was, in effect, his own staff, keeping his own counsel, largely making his own investigations, and carrying out his own plans as he conceived them.

The opportunity for systematic planning and marketing grows out of aspects of modern business which are somewhat more parallel to twentieth century military activity. While a business is already engaged on one or more fronts, top management may still be considering new fields to conquer. The drive for continual expansion by nearly every major enterprise results in wide concern for new products, new markets, and new marketing methods. The invasion of new areas of competition poses hazards and promises rewards of a relative magnitude similiar to those faced by the Allies at the invasion of Normandy. To enter a new competitive field usually means going up against skilled and resourceful opponents who are already familiar with the market terrain. The elements of surprise and of close coordination of the attack can be just as important as in the military sphere. It is not surprising that one of the first areas in which planning is gaining some corporate stature is in the planning of new ventures.

Planning is favored in large marketing operations because of the scope and diversity of the marketing fronts on which the company is competing. Here the marketing executive's experience is more similar to that of Eisenhower than to that of Hannibal. The supreme commander does not lead an army in the field but deploys and coordinates vast resources which may be operating at a distance of perhaps hundreds or thousands of miles. Through the overall direction of what is happening in each sector or each segment of the market, he hopes to make each separate action contribute to the grand objectives. Systematic planning offers the chief hope of mediating between these objectives and the complex diffused pattern of action.

It turns out then that the civilian and military attitudes toward planning are not as different as they may appear at first glance. Attitudes toward planning converge as problems of planning and coordination become more similar. The great gift of a field commander or a field executive may be to extemporize on the spot once the battle is joined. However, in the contemporary scene both must deal with theaters of action which are beyond their personal reach and in the midst of battle must prepare for battles yet to come. The really crucial difference is the historic one that conditions requiring systematic planning have developed a little later in business. Planning in marketing is apparently still on trial, but nevertheless the challenge and the opportunity is there.

STAFFING FOR PLANNING

A basic practical problem in setting up for formal planning is finding the personnel which is equipped for the task. Planning as an activity differs from direct line responsibility and also from the more detached analytical view which is appropriate to technical or marketing research. The planner must be vitally concerned with action and able to think creatively in terms of operating systems and yet content to leave the actual execution of his ideas to others. He must be willing to work devotedly for the improvement of marketing operations without any authority to compel the adoption of his plans. He must rely on persuasion and on the power of ideas to sell themselves.

In setting up the initial staff the question inevitably arises as to whether to draw from other staff functions such as marketing research or from personnel with primarily line experience. Characteristic difficulties are encountered in either case. The market research director has generally been accustomed to report on the marketing environment in which action must take place. His recommendations for action programs are likely to be carefully hedged and qualified. Unless he has had actual sales experience or has conducted studies which required traveling with salesmen, he may make unrealistic assumptions as to the extent of control which can be exercised through a marketing plan. The line executive who is suddenly given responsibility for planning is sometimes completely at a loss as to where to start. He has been accustomed to respond to emergencies by throwing reserve resources against them or supporting the salesman who has a problem by his own skills and contacts. He simply lacks an alternative framework for organizing his own daily activities around the somewhat longer-range objectives of market planning. Sometimes he struggles to retain command of his line responsibilities to preserve a sense of day-to-day accomplishment. Any compromise by top management toward giving a line executive planning responsibility as a secondary function has little chance of working. The current emergencies on which the line executive has been accustomed to spend his time will continue to have first claim and little will be accomplished on the side of planning.

If formal planning is to have any serious impact, it must be the continuing full time responsibility of one or more competent individuals. If they are undertaking this type of activity for the first time, they will almost certainly need some preparation for the planning task. The various executive training programs now operated by the universities give an executive an opportunity to see his company in the perspective of what other companies are doing. If his experience has been largely with a single firm, it may come as a revelation to learn that there are other ways of performing the same function or of structuring similar operations. Perhaps the root idea of planning is that alternatives exist and that there may be a big payoff for the company in evaluating its present operations against these alternatives.

If top management has exercised sufficient foresight with respect to the need for formal planning, it may be able to grow its own planners on the inside. Since planning, as broadly defined, is always present in any organization that looks ahead as far as tomorrow, there are opportunities for executives to exhibit some talent for planning before they are given responsibility for heading a formal unit. The individual may sit as a member of an operating committee in which progress on current projects is reported and individuals are given assignments for the next step. He may be designated to head an *ad hoc* committee which is charged with carrying out some special project such as the introduction of a new product. In some companies there is a very high level committee concerned with the outlook for company growth and expansion. An individual who serves as secretary to such a committee has an opportunity to understand the long-run company objectives and to observe the generation of plans and strategies as it emerges from the discussions among major executives of his firm. It would be a natural progression for such an individual to be given staff assignments by the committee beginning with specific chores in preparation for the next committee session. If the chief executive is looking forward to the installation of formal planning, he might bring in a qualified individual and regard his service to the committee as preparation for his ultimate assignment.

Under one conception of the planning function, most of the staff so engaged would be only temporarily assigned to planning. Quite often a task force is drawn together by detaching individuals from their regular positions. This procedure has advantages, but it probably cannot function at its best if it is regarded as a substitute for a central planning staff. A better method would be to assign such individuals to the central planning staff for the period of a specified project. There needs to be a permanent nucleus of individuals familiar with the techniques of planning to insure the effective use of line executives temporarily separated from their duties. Here is one area in which the perspective on planning has evolved further in the military services. Generals and colonels are sent to the war colleges where they temporarily report to and are instructed by captains or lieutenants on permanent staff assignment. A procedure which approximated this military approach took place a few years ago at General Electric. Line executives were brought together from all the divisions concerned with electrical appliances to spend two years working out a future program for the distribution of major electrical appliances. While working with this task force, they were teamed with other individuals with backgrounds in marketing and operations research. One thing that should be better understood in the use of such task forces is the reversal of roles that should take place when operating executives are assigned to a research and planning operation. It is the research man who is most likely to be equipped to command the group if it is currently engaged in research activities. The line executives who participate should be schooled to accept subordinate roles for the period of their temporary assignment.

There are great advantages in the type of procedure described, especially when the project is one of great moment to the company.

The line executives go back to their regular positions with a full understanding of the plan they have helped to develop and are especially equipped to assist with its installation. They also become educated to a better understanding of the planning function and what the planning specialists have to offer. While this type of experience cannot be given to more than a small fraction of the executives in a large company, it should produce a leaven of opinion which will influence favorably all executive personnel. More and more leading firms are assuming an interchangeability of line and staff as compared with the traditional assumption of a sharp cleavage between types of people and corresponding careers. A combination of the two should help to give the individual both the breadth of perspective and the sure grasp of detail which are essential as he moves into positions of larger responsibility.

POSITIONING THE PLANNING FUNCTION

The last chapter discussed the alternative possibilities for positioning a staff function within an organization structure. Usually it is a safe principle to have a staff unit directly responsible to the line officer who is expected to take action on the basis of staff recommendations. This principle does not apply so clearly in the case of formal planning in marketing. It may be that several different line executives are supposed to act on the basis of the same recommendations and that the main virtue of a plan lies in the coordination of their efforts. It is not even clear that the chief of market planning should be subordinate to the chief line executive for marketing. There is an increasing tendency for these two executives to be expected to work together as coequals and for both to have reporting relationships to top management. In some companies top management is divided, in turn, between two executives, one giving most of his attention to current operations, and the other to the future outlook of the company with its planning implications for every business function. In this structure the two top marketing executives might each report to the appropriate top management executive. There are other cases in which the marketing executive in charge of current operations will report to a marketing executive who is primarily concerned with planning. The reporting relationships should reflect the judgment of top management as to whether current or future problems should be given equal weight or whether one side should be regarded as more serious than the other.

Wherever market planning is placed in the organization structure, it will have problems of relationships to other functions outside of marketing. Some of these vital connections are already recognized and reflected in the organization structure of leading firms. Sometimes production scheduling is placed under market planning on the ground that a marketing perspective is essential in setting the production priorities for successive units. Where there are important cost differentials related to economic production lots, there is need for continuous discussion and adjustment between marketing and production. Market planning in turn is placed under some constraints by considerations of supply and quality which are normally under the control of the production department.

Perhaps the most obvious relationship is between market planning and technical and marketing research. Both aspects of research are concerned with the development of new products and new markets which are also the essential concern for market planning. Goal coordination with marketing research, which will presumably report also to the principal staff executive in marketing, should generally prevail. Complications arise, however, if marketing research is going on at the divisional level while market planning takes place in a central staff unit. There has also been a multiplication of such staff units as operations research groups which might more readily be coordinated with market planning than with traditional marketing research. With respect to technical research and development there is no substitute for close and continuous communication with the market planning unit. In some cases an individual with some technical background is assigned to the market planning staff with the sole function of maintaining liaison with research and development. When such groups are first brought into contact, a common response is one of pleasant surprise over the extent to which they recognize common goals. The research chemist or engineer is not typically content with an ivory tower insulation from the commercial world of buying and selling. Most applied researchers in particular are interested in products as meeting a need in the market place and in shaping their efforts to meet this objective.

Market planning also has vital relationships with such service departments as personnel, law, and finance. Reference is made in Chapter 19 to the need for regarding a marketing organization as a flow of executive and sales personnel. The market planner who is looking as far as five years ahead is largely concerned with new markets and new products which in considerable measure will be sold by new personnel not yet associated with the company. With respect to law, the market planner needs to be aware of any special legal constraints under which his company is operating or any

changes in the legal environment which may be reasonably anticipated for the future. The importance of law as a planning consideration is strikingly illustrated by the position of the large meat
packers. These companies have operated since 1920 under the so-
called Packers' Consent Decree. This decree imposed some drastic
limitations on the commodities the packers could handle and the
marketing functions they could perform. With the present effort to
obtain relief from the consent decree, planning groups in these companies are obliged to make contingent plans, assuming either the
perpetuation of present conditions or the modification of the consent
decree along the lines requested.

Planning in marketing is inevitably involved with the policies
and programs of the finance department. Finance is perhaps the
only other business function which might challenge the right of
marketing to take the leadership in business planning. Marketing
plans for the firm as an operating entity whose primary objective is
service to the market. Finance, however, plans for the business as
a profit-making vehicle for its owners. Obviously neither marketing
nor finance can plan effectively without recognizing the interdependence of these objectives. A business continues to serve the market subject to the requirement of making an adequate profit showing. A business can increase the assets and earnings of the owners
subject to the requirement of adequate service to customers and
suppliers. From the perspective of this book, it seems proper that
marketing should exercise some leadership in overall business planning. Capital budgeting, a primary feature of financial planning,
certainly requires the guidance of market forecasts and must assume
some advance determination of marketing policies and programs.
Another major problem of financial planning is that of obtaining
adequate funds for expansion and modifying the financial structure
of the business to suit its evolving operations. Obtaining additional
capital through such means as marketing securities involves a number of executive skills. It seems incontestable, however, that in the
long run the demand for the assets or shares of stock in a company
rests on a demand for the products it supplies to the market.

The following table summarizes the organizational relationships
involved in the coordination of market planning with other activities. The table is divided into three sections by short-range planning, middle-range planning, and long-range planning.

In the short range, the planner is vitally concerned with other
units within the marketing department and primarily with production so far as other business functions are concerned. In the middle

Coordination of Market Planning with Other Activities

Short-Range Planning	Middle-Range Planning	Long-Range Planning
(Within marketing)	New product research and development	Capital budgeting
Selling		Cash flow for current
Advertising	Product improvement	expenditures
Sales Promotion		
	Price appeal through	New financing and
(Outside of marketing)	cost reduction	corporate structure
Production scheduling	Foreign markets	Legal constraints on
Supply priorities		marketing techniques
Quality control	Personnel procurement and training	and strategies

range, he is concerned with the expanding operations of the firm and corresponding changes in marketing personnel. In the long range, he is concerned with the financial objectives of the company and the legal constraints under which it operates. He, in turn, constitutes the principal authority on long-run changes which others must take into account, including technological and cultural changes which may influence the destiny of the firm years later. In long-range planning, the planner must have the vision to conceive of a new company operating in a new world and to translate these ultimate results into the transition stages which must be encountered along the way.

TOP MANAGEMENT AND MARKET PLANNING

This section will assume a situation in which the impetus for formal planning comes from top management and the chief executive is lending his support in getting the planning function established. If a planning unit exists and does not have a clear mandate from top management, then obviously it is in the first stages of bidding for top-management support. In this period planning faces all the uncertainties of any new activity which does not yet have official recognition. It must sell its services as broadly as it can within the company with the hope of getting favorable responses at some point and of eventually winning recognition at the top. The unit which is officially designated as a planning staff is likely to be in competition with others who are promoting their own conceptions of what the company's program should be. The planning staff will probably be politically weak in relation to some of these internal competitors, and its chances for success will depend on its technical strength as expressed in its ability to be more objective, more thorough, and more creative in the strategic concept which it proposes.

In the situation in which the chief executive wishes to support formal planning, there are some questions as to how he can make his support effective. In general, he will encourage the planning director to report to him but to sell his recommendations at each of the lower levels where decisions are to be made. It would usually be less effective to pursue the alternative course of adopting the plan himself and then ordering others to put it into effect. The chief executive should regard his basic objective to be that of getting commitments from his subordinates in order for them to carry out their respective responsibilities within some coordinated system of action. Meaningful commitments are easy to get if each man has had a chance to sell himself on the segment of the plan he is to execute so that only minor adjustments remain to be made for full coordination.

The planning director, with the backing of the chief executive, should regard himself as offering a service at various executive levels. The chief executive can encourage the use of such services by the requirements that he places upon the line executives. There are some major companies, for example, in which the approval of operating budgets for each sales division is contingent upon the presentation of a marketing plan showing how the funds allocated will be spent. When budget requests are turned down because they are inadequate, the sales manager may seek the help of the planning director voluntarily, or it might be suggested to the sales manager that that is a good place to go. Similarly, the chief executive who believes in market planning can put pressures on research and development and on finance. In each case when they submit their programs to him, he would question them to determine whether their proposals were built on a factual knowledge of market opportunity and of policies and programs for directing marketing effort in developing market opportunity.

With respect to middle-range plans of substantial importance, a formal action of acceptance and termination of the planning assignment should be followed. In the ideal situation, all of the principal executives who are expected to act in unison under the plan become familiar while planning proceeds with the portions of the plan that are pertinent to their own operations. Acceptance of the plan might well take the form of a meeting including these executives, the planning director, and the chief executive. At this meeting the chief executive gets a statement from each of his subordinates in turn as to any remaining reservations about the plan or the action that may have already been taken to put it into effect and as to the further steps which are contemplated to activate the program as a whole. If the ground has been properly prepared for such a meeting, it should result in the plan being that of the organization rather than that of the chief executive or the planning director.

A cardinal difficulty of managing a planning staff within an organization is that of placing some objective measure on its performance. A salesman very properly gets full personal credit for the sale he makes regardless of what staff services or facilities might have been available for his use. However, he could well deserve as much or more credit for his use of the staff facilities as for actually bringing off the sale singlehandedly. The planner, on the other hand, cannot be credited by any measurement of the results except insofar as there would be universal acclaim at all levels of the marketing organization for the success of a novel and comprehensive marketing program. The opportunities to create such plans and to gain recognition are not an everyday occurrence in the life of the planning staff.

The only feasible answer, as in other intangible business services, seems to lie in some combination of objective and subjective judgments. The objective criteria can be applied only to such fundamentals as diligence, speed of operation, and contribution to the creativity of the planning group as a whole. The subjective factors of evaluation will operate at various levels, from the salesman in the field to the chief marketing executive. At the various levels below the top, a valuation is likely to be very short range, based on what the planner was able to do for the individuals concerned last month, or, better still, on the day before yesterday. Thus responsibility comes back to the chief executive who favors formal planning to engage in continuous evaluation of what planning is doing for him from a somewhat longer viewpoint. Only he can fully appreciate the strains and tensions which formerly arose from the piecemeal handling of decision problems in planning. Only he can say how much help planning is giving him both in improving the accuracy of his own judgments in the allocation of resources and in obtaining meaningful commitments from his subordinates for using these plans effectively.

The chief executive is in a position to assess the value of planning not only in terms of the direct contributions of the planner but also in terms of the change in attitudes which he may be able to observe in his line executives. The chief executive should not adopt formal planning unless he intends to use it as a major tool of management and as self-education for himself and for his subordinates. Having

once made this choice, planning becomes the center of his method
of operation. From then on, it should be his view that planning cannot fail but an incompetent planner may. He is obliged therefore
to apply the most rigorous standards in selecting his planning staff
and to impose severe requirements on the planners for advancing
themselves professionally and for advancing the company's future.

THE COORDINATION OF PLANNING ACTIVITIES

Planning itself poses a problem of coordination as great as any
other activity. If two or more persons are responsible for several
segments of the same plan, there will be some difficulties in fitting
the pieces together. Planning remains in some measure an intuitive
art, and two planners working independently are not likely to have
identical conceptions of the plan as a whole.

Coordination of planning is an exceptionally difficult task when
there is a multiplicity of planning units, to say nothing of personnel.
This problem is illustrated in the various phases of defense planning
and has been analyzed in an enlightening way for the special case
of the Air Force. The two criteria for good planning were stated to
be consistency and timeliness. Both were essential, but they were
generally found to be in direct conflict. To make plans completely
consistent required so much checking back and forth that the plan
could never be ready in time. Since many other activities must wait
upon the termination of planning, the ideal of a completely consistent plan was highly impractical.

A working solution was found in what was designated as triangular planning. This amounted to limiting communication to a one-way
flow among units. Each unit would like to know the end-results of
every other unit before making its own results final. Some of these
needs for information were found to be more essential than others.
A schedule of termination dates was established, and as each unit
completed its work, its results were available to the other units.
This scheme was designated as triangular planning. It is illustrated
in the upper half of Figure 22-4. Team *A* completes its task first,
and the results are fed into the stream of information available to
team *B*. Similarly team *B* completes its task and provides some of
the groundwork for team *C*, and so on until the last team reports,
taking into account the results of all the others.

The lower half of the chart deals with the process of installation
of a plan. It is believed that the notion of triangular planning can
be helpful in installation as well as in planning. Here is a reverse
triangular matrix with the activities which are going to take longest

or which may be necessary antecedents to other aspects of installation getting under way first. Thus, while the subject matter of planning is the determination of the optimum sequence for a set of activities, the problem of sequencing is basic to planning itself, both in the development of the plan and in its subsequent installation.

Figure 22–4

COORDINATION OF PLANNING AND INSTALLATION

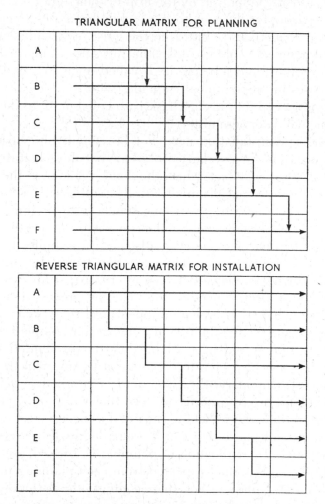

TRIANGULAR MATRIX FOR PLANNING

REVERSE TRIANGULAR MATRIX FOR INSTALLATION

With respect to the sequence of steps in installation, there are various considerations determining the choice of a place to start. A comprehensive change of marketing program and organization might involve both the appointment of a new director of marketing and the retraining of field salesmen. Conflicting considerations might be urged, one based on the time required for the retraining process and the other on the necessity of establishing the authority of the new director of marketing from the start. Both of these considerations might have to be examined critically in the particular case in order to find a solution. Perhaps the training job can be broken up into two parts, such as an understanding of what is to be done and the finer points on how to do it. Perhaps the new marketing director is already employed by the firm in some other capacity and can be preparing for his new position while his appointment is still confidential. Sometimes he enters in the guise of an outside marketing consultant and is able to take the measure of his prospective executive responsibilities before he is called upon to exercise them. In other cases his appointment coincides with the beginning of the planning project so that his first task is to collaborate in developing the plan he will later administer.

Planning and installation need not be completely separated in time. On occasion the overlap is so great that most features of the plan are already in effect when the final version of the plan is reported. Where formal planning is fully established, a number of planning projects may be at various stages from preliminary consideration to final installation. Similarly, various aspects of the same planning project may run concurrently, and this applies to installation as well as other phases. The exception would be the type of project in which the choice between alternative strategies was not to be made until near the end of the planning process. It may even be that the objectives of a plan are open until the very end or that a final judgment on feasibility must await the completion of the plan. Installation would have to be deferred or limited to those phases which were expected to be common to any plan that would be adopted. In summary, the criteria to be applied in scheduling installation tend to give priority to steps that will require the greatest amount of time, those that are regarded as necessary antecedents to other steps, and those that can be regarded as firm and final.

Another tool of coordination in planning is fairly detailed specification of the end-product expected from each planning unit. That means specifying form rather than content, the latter being the responsibility of the planner. Requiring a report of a given form should not constrain the creative efforts of the planner. Rather, the fact that he does not have to waste time inventing the form gives him more time to devote to content. Specifications will probably have to remain fairly broad for major planning assignments covering such matters as the essential component parts of a satisfactorily written plan.

A PARADIGM OF PLANNING

Definitions of Planning

1. Planning in marketing is the exercise of foresight to increase the effectiveness of marketing activities.
2. Planning undertakes to deal with a network of interdependent decision problems where it is not practical to separate them for individual solution.
3. Planning tries to balance means and ends, to weigh the desirability of objectives against their feasibility in terms of resources.
4. Planning becomes more precise and quantitative to the extent that means and ends can be expressed as the inputs and outputs of an operating system.
5. Planning from the viewpoint of the systems concept seeks an optimal relationship between inputs and outputs through the application of structural principles.
6. Planning is the design phase of problem solving when elements must be arranged in a pattern or sequence as a preliminary to making a choice among alternatives through evaluation.

End-Products of Planning

The end-products of planning are campaigns, facilities, organizations, and systems. To show the relationship among these four end-products, it is convenient to bring systems to the front of the sequence and use some connecting words as follows:

| Systems | mount | Campaigns | using | Facilities | and | Organizations |

Definitions of the End-Products of Planning

A *campaign* is the arrangement of activities in a time sequence.
A *facility* is the arrangement of components in a spatial pattern.
An *organization* is the arrangement of individuals in a hierarchical structure of authority and delegation.
A system is the integrated arrangement of facilities, organization, and procedures operating under plans and policies to optimize net outputs. It has been suggested that in one sense the primary output of a well-planned system is a set of campaigns.

Optimizing Principles

Principles of optimization can be stated for each of the end-products of planning as follows:

Campaigns optimize use of time.
    (*a*) Maximize outputs for specified period
    (*b*) Minimize elapsed time, subject to constraints on cost and risk

Facilities optimize use of space.
  (*a*) Minimize movement
  (*b*) Maximize exposure
Organizations optimize decision power.
  (*a*) Maximize expected values
  (*b*) Minimize policy exceptions
Systems optimize operational effectiveness.
  (*a*) Maximize competitive adjustment
  (*b*) Maximize channel cooperation

Planning Levels

Three planning levels can be identified for each of the end-products of planning as shown in the table.

End-Product		Planning Levels	
Campaigns	Sequence	Duration	Dates
Facilities	Proximity	Area	Site
Organizations	Hierarchy	Duties	Personnel
Systems	Objectives	Models	Operations

Structural Principles of Design

There are structural principles corresponding to each end-product at each of the planning levels. They may be summarized as follows:

Campaigns
  Sequence—principle of precession
      Start with the end-result and put in every step which appears to be a necessary antecedent for the following steps.
  Duration—sequence, manipulation
      Check each step as to instrumental or detrimental consequences for the steps which follow, adding instrumental steps and dropping or postponing detrimental steps.
  Dates—
      Relate the campaign to the calendar by balancing the competitive advantage of an early start against the market disadvantage of a premature start.
Facilities
  Proximity—principle of access
      Establish a control center, plot lines of traffic flow connecting it with all subspaces and select an appropriate optimizing principle for the ideal path or the average path.
  Area—functional balance
      Divide the available area between access areas and occupied areas.
  Site
      Balance current efficiency at the selected site against future flexibility.

Organizations
  Hierarchy—principle of accountability
      Design the power pyramid for complete accountability, varying
      such elements as span of control versus levels of control.
  Duties—communication principle
      Assign duties in such a way as to minimize ambiguities in com-
      munication.
  Personnel—morale principle
      Assign personnel in such a way as to preserve the pattern of mo-
      tivation and morale.
Systems
  Objectives—level of aspiration
      Balance desirability against feasibility to determine the level of
      costs and risks in relation to the level of aspiration.
  Model—level of aggregation
      Select a model which allows for the appropriate degree of detail
      and diversity and changes over time.
  Operation—level of control
      Adopt a general policy as to the degree of central control to be
      exercised over the scheduling and coordination of campaigns.

INPUTS AND OUTPUTS OF A MARKETING SYSTEM

In one sense the prime output of a marketing system is a set of
campaigns, but in another sense outputs can be labeled as operating,
financial, and systemic. In operating terms the business has such
inputs as labor skills and raw materials and such outputs as the
goods and services which it sells to its customers. This is the basic
economic function which the firm fulfills in the market, providing
an outlet for materials, components, and labor and constituting a
source for products demanded at the next level.

The financial inputs and outputs of a business operation are inputs and outputs as seen by owners and investors. The business
requires inputs of capital to get a foothold or to expand its place
in the market. If it is successful, it will have an output of profits to
be disbursed as dividends or reinvested in the business.

Systemic inputs and outputs are those that are related to the life
history of the system itself. Business firms and other organized behavior systems behave as if they had goals of survival and of evolving into something larger or with a changed character providing
greater satisfaction to all concerned, including those engaged in
active management. The major input from the standpoint of these
assumed systemic goals is an increase in executive capacity whether
in the form of new people or progress on the part of men already in
the system. Better people are needed to build a better company, and
a better company is needed to attract better people.

	Inputs	Outputs
Operating...............	Labor skills & raw materials	Goods & services
Financial...............	Capital	Profit
Systemic...............	Executive capacity	Organization improvements

INTERNAL AND EXTERNAL RELATIONS

A marketing system has a structure appropriate to the function it performs and to the types of inputs and outputs which it handles. The structure of the system, for planning purposes, can largely be described in terms of certain internal and external relationships. The relationships inside the company which are probably most important for market planning are those between the marketing function and the functions of production, finance, and technical research and development. The external relations to the market can be characterized as those between the marketing organization and its customers, its distributing trades, and its competitors.

These relations can be partially specified in terms of certain communications flowing to or from the marketing organization and other components in the total marketing system. An attempt is made to picture these elements of structure in the next table.

RELATIONSHIPS WITHIN A MARKETING SYSTEM

	Communications Flowing	
External Relations	*from Marketing*	*to Marketing*
Consumers	Advertising	Consumer reactions
Trade channels	Selling	Orders
Competition	Marketing strategy	Counterstrategy

	Communications Flowing	
Internal Relations	*from Marketing*	*to Marketing*
Production	Scheduling data	Product information
Finance	Market forecasts	Budget allocations
Research and	Information on	Information on product
Development	consumer needs	possibilities

The marketing department is at the vortex of these relationships. All of the major internal functions must base their actions in substantial degree on information about the market. The marketing department is the channel through which marketing information reaches them. It is also the agency through which ideas or developments in any other part of the company can have an impact on the market.

A STANDARD PLANNING OUTLINE

A list of fourteen planning steps will now be outlined in somewhat greater detail. This standard planning outline is not presented as an answer to all planning problems. Rather it is presented as a point of departure in determining planning method for any given assignment. Each major assignment is likely to require a pattern of procedure which is in some degree unique. The planner will endeavor to select the most appropriate tools for each case. He should also give careful attention to the optimizing principles and structural design summarized in an earlier stage of this paradigm.

1. *Defining the Planning Task*
    a. Type of planning assignment
    b. Responsibilities of the planner
    c. End-result expected: form and content
    d. Personnel and resources available
    e. Completion date
    f. Techniques to be utilized
2. *The Preplan Audit*
    a. Assessment of market position
    b. Factors of success or failure in recent years
    c. Differential advantages over competitors
    d. Unexploited opportunities: products and markets
    e. Operating assumptions of management
        i Feasibility assumptions
        ii General preference as to goals
3. *Forecasting: Demand and Competition*
    a. Expected growth rates: industry, firm, and product
    b. Relation to growth rates of population, economic activity, home construction, etc.
    c. Consumer response functions for price, promotion, and product improvement
    d. Forecast of costs including costs of promotion
    e. Probable timing of competitive entry or major moves by competitors
    f. Forecast of turning points: technological breakthroughs and cultural changes
4. *Generation of Strategies*
    a. Competition as race or game
    b. Strategy as best use of firm's resources without regard to competition
    c. Strategy as outguessing competition
    d. Strategy as redesign of action system to meet new conditions or requirements
    e. Dimensions of variation in possible strategies

    f. Sources of strategic ideas
    g. Screening and selection of strategies for further development
    h. Choice of strategy as the determinization of direction for program development
  5. *The Preliminary Program*
    a. First sketch of programs embodying one or more strategies
    b. Final estimate of cost and time required for completion
    c. Request for additional facilities if needed
    d. Possible recasting or broadening of project
    e. Request to terminate if project does not appear promising
  6. *Clarification of Objectives*[1]
    a. Require further development of the alternative programs which have been submitted
    b. Make a final selection of a given strategy and program
    c. Provide a more specific statement of objectives and of the resources available to achieve them
    d. Direct the planner to start over and to consider additional strategies
    e. Terminate the project
  7. *Determining Sequence of Activities*
    a. Check list of customary order
    b. Create new list by working back from end-result, putting in steps which appear to be antecedents for following steps
    c. Test doubtful steps for position by "principle of postponement": pushing forward and possibly eliminating
    d. Give special attention to steps which cause increased costs in subsequent steps, which have detrimental consequences rather than instrumental consequences
    e. Consider proportioning of successive activities to avoid bottlenecks
  8. *Providing for Coordination of Activities*
    a. Cordination of successive steps in a sequence
    b. Coordination of several sequences making up the program
    c. Coordination of program with external conditions and events such as competitive moves
    d. Work back from final termination of operating period to establish deadlines and check points
    e. Budget allocations among sequences and steps in each sequence
    f. Pick reference sequence where possible and relate other budgets and schedules to reference sequence

---

[1]The clarification of company objectives to be served by the proposed plan goes on throughout the course of a major planning project but might be given special attention at particular points. Clarification begins when management makes the original planning assignment. In setting a target for the planner, management necessarily makes some conscious assessment of its own goals. The next stage of clarification occurs when management has a preliminary program or programs before it for consideration. With this first test of feasibility at hand, it may then do one of the listed things.

      g. Relieve pressures in crowded sequences by cutting into sequences which can run concurrently

      h. Restudy traditional techniques to accelerate time-consuming steps

9. *Testing by Simulation and Other Methods*
    a. Test marketing in selected cities
    b. Confidential checks with trade sources as to acceptability and effectiveness of plan
    c. Develop mathematical model and simulate plan on electronic computer
    d. Simulate portions of plan through business games with company personnel as players
    e. Investigate operation of most similar plan used by competition or in other industry

10. *Administrative Detailing of Program*
    a. Manual of instructions stating individual responsibilities under plan
    b. Standards of performance to measure success of plan such as sales forecast and budget variances
    c. Rules of action for handling exceptions
    d. Situations to be referred to superiors for decision
    e. Bonus compensation or other incentive for performance under plan
    f. Specified reports for control while operation is in progress

11. *Consideration of Organization Changes*
    a. Additional manpower needs
    b. Training requirements
    c. Changes in organization structure
    d. Shifting of present executives to new responsibilities
    e. Special problems of absorbing personnel as a result of mergers

12. *Acceptance of Plan and Commitment of Resources*
    a. Formal step of official adoption
    b. Assigning major responsibilities under the plan
    c. Discharging planning group from its responsibilities
    d. Final look at objectives of plan as compared to alternative market opportunities
    e. Official approval of budgets required to carry out the plan

13. *Installation of Plan*[2]
    a. Recommendations as to installation procedure
    b. Preparing presentation of plan to be used at various levels in the organization
    c. Participation in the actual presentations
    d. Adjustment of difficulties or inconsistencies in the plan which show up in the course of installations

---

[2]The planning assignment should clearly indicate whether the planners are held responsible for any phase of its installation. Among the possibilities are those listed.

14. *Review of Planning Procedure and Performance*[3]

    a. Possible revisions in the overall approach to a similar assignment

    b. Unforeseen obstacles which were met in the course of planning

    c. Difficulties of coordination within the planning group itself

    d. Failure of communication in dealing with top management or line executives either in understanding what was wanted of the planner or in gaining acceptance of the plan by those expected to use it.

THE PLANNING YEAR FOR A LARGE ORGANIZATION

Once planning in marketing is established as a continuing procedure, the most critical exercise of foresight is the effort to foresee the planning tasks for the year. The most fundamental issue in planning for planning lies between external strategy and what has been called internal strategy or the state of readiness. External strategy is expressed through campaigns on either old products or new products. The state of readiness depends on facilities, organization, and the condition of the marketing system as a whole. At the beginning of the planning year a decision should be made on how much effort should go into overhauling facilities, organization, or the total marketing system and how much into specific marketing campaigns. If the system or some vital part of the system is on the verge of breaking down, the need for modification becomes paramount. It is of little avail to generate clever strategies incorporated in well-coordinated plans if the system is no longer capable of executing them.

In a large organization some component of the marketing system is likely to require attention each year. A new warehouse or a new territorial alignment is needed. A new organization structure is required to cope with new forms of competition emerging in the market. The marketing system is due for a new evaluation of the effectiveness of market adjustment, both horizontally and vertically. The first decision of the director of planning concerns the amount of time to be put against these planning tasks which might be grouped under the heading of system maintenance and improvement.

The next issue for both the planner and the top executive is the relative amount of effort, including planning effort, to be devoted to old products and new products. Often the old products are

---

[3] A staff planning unit, wishing to progress in professional competence and in service to its company, should make a post-audit of its own work at the end of each major assignment. The items to be considered include those listed.

called upon to generate the revenue which will be used to finance the new product ventures. A decision must be reached as to the number of new products which can be introduced in any one year and still have a satisfactory surplus for net earnings. The postponement or advancing of a product introduction will have an obvious effect on the load of the planning department for the year. Since the determination of basic market posture on a new product is so fundamental, it must be given very high priority, second only to efforts in system maintenance designed to maintain the state of readiness.

Finally the planning effort on existing products should be carried as far as the more pressing requirements of system maintenance and new product introduction will permit. In particular, contingency planning should be given adequate attention on both new and old products. An attempt should be made to foresee the major contingencies facing the firm and to prepare for them by developing at least preliminary plans. Suppose the principal competitor is free to choose among alternatives *A, B,* and *C*. If the chance that he will choose alternative *A* is not much better than the chance that he will choose one of the other alternatives, contingency planning might be urgently needed. It might be folly to work out a very detailed plan based on the assumption that the competitor will choose *A* and leave *B* and *C* completely uncovered.

The system-maintenance decisions and the new-product decisions tend to offset each other to a certain extent. If some part of the system is badly in need of overhauling, there may be a tendency to hold back on new products during the year. A more aggressive policy on new products may be appropriate if the system is in an excellent state of readiness. But the degree of specialization in planning will also affect the program which is carried out during the year. Thus, there is a growing tendency in companies employing the product-manager concept to assign some product managers to work on plans for old products only and to assign the more resourceful and experienced men to work on new product introductions.

In the system-maintenance area, the work of market planning is interconnected with planning efforts in other departments. For example, the marketing or operations-research group might determine the location pattern for warehouses, but a more specialized consulting group inside or outside the company might be concerned with the floor plan of the warehouse and its use of mechanical handling facilities. In many firms there is a special group dealing with organization planning which may or may not work closely with the market planner where a problem of marketing organization is to be considered. Organization planning is one of the primary fields for the use of outside consulting firms. One reason is their genuine skill in organization matters, and another is their greater objectivity because they stand outside the orbit of the firm's continuing activities. There is also the area of planning production facilities where the market planner may be responsible for a forecast of future demand for the outputs of a plant but others are clearly more qualified to design the plant.

With all these qualifications it still appears useful to suggest a pattern for the planning activities of a large organization during the planning year. The program will be broken up into quarters, but the planning year will not necessarily correspond to the calendar year. In a given case there might be good reason to have the planning year begin July 1 rather than January 1. The same general view with respect to priorities would hold in any case.

First Quarter
1. Determine planning policy for the year dealing with such basic issues as
    a. System maintenance versus campaigns
    b. New products versus old products
    c. Contingency planning versus fully committed plans
2. Initiate system overhaul or modification of components such as
    a. Facilities
    b. Organization
    c. Procedures

Second Quarter
1. Concentrate on planning for new product introduction or entry into new markets.
2. Give adequate attention to contingencies on both old products and new products.

Third Quarter
1. Complete forecasts for the three- to five-year period, including forecasts of demand, cost, and price.
2. Consider the possible emergence of structural changes over the period.
3. Reexamine strategies, competitive moves, and informational needs in relation to these structural changes.

Fourth Quarter
1. Complete the programming of special campaigns for the year ahead.
2. Review what has been learned about planning during the year.
3. Consider the long-run range outlook for the company, what kind of a company it is in process of becoming, and what kind of a world it will be operating in ten or twenty years hence.

In conclusion, it is clear that there are almost as many variations in the pattern for planning as there are companies. These differences relate both to the company stage's of development in the use of planning and to the nature of the company's planning problems. It is hoped that this book will contribute to some degree of standardization in a third direction—the more general recognition of the nature of planning in marketing and greater familiarity with the available techniques.

Selected References

BESSE, RALPH M. "Company Planning Must be Planned," *Dun's Review and Modern Industry*, April, 1957.
  Covers several essentials in planning perspective, including favorable climate, training for planners, and the assignment of responsibility.

BUELL, VICTOR P. "Organizing for Marketing Planning," *Journal of Marketing*, 1956.
  Planning is treated in the major functional areas, including advertising, distribution, and pricing.

KAST, FREMONT AND ROSENZWEIG, JAMES. "Minimizing the Planning Gap," *Advanced Management*, October, 1960.
  The authors address themselves to the problem of how much to plan in order to achieve expectations without an excessive cost for planning.

MANDELL, M. "Organized Dreaming: How Futuristic Models Pay Off," *Dun's Review and Modern Industry*, July, 1959.
  The three types of futuristic design considered are speculating projections with no present plans to act, pre-prototypes of products which may be produced in the near future, and end product designs based on a supplier's materials and components.

Problems

1. Explain how a pair of goals may be related and the problems encountered with each type of relationship.

2. Explain the following statement: "Foresight can only rest on organized hindsight." Do you agree with this statement? Why? or why not?

3. Discuss the proper position'ng of the planning function in the organizational structure.

4. Discuss a possible method for evaluating the performance of a planning staff.

5. Discuss the more important internal and external relationships that a planner should be concerned with. What is the marketing department's function in these relationships?

INDEX

INDEX

This book has been set on the Linotype in 11 point Caledonia, leaded 2 points, and 10 point Caledonia, leaded 1 point. Part and chapter numbers and titles are in Tempo Medium. The size of the type page is 27 by 46½ picas.